Life and Death under Stalin

Kalinin Province, 1945–1953

KEES BOTERBLOEM

McGill-Queen's University Press
Montreal & Kingston · London · Ithaca

Legal deposit third quarter 1999
Bibliothèque nationale du Québec

Printed in Canada on acid-free paper

This book has been published with the help of a
grant from the Humanities and Social Sciences
Federation of Canada, using funds provided by the
Social Sciences and Humanities Research Council of
Canada. Funding has also been received from the
Nipissing University Research Council.

McGill-Queen's University Press acknowledges the
financial support of the Government of Canada
through the Book Publishing Industry Development
Program for its activities. We also acknowledge the
support of the Canada Council for the Arts for our
publishing program.

Canadian Cataloguing in Publication Data

Boterbloem, Kees, 1962–
    Life and death under Stalin: Kalinin Province,
    1945–1953
    Originally presented as the author's thesis
    (Ph.D.-McGill, 1994) under title:
    Communists and the Russians.
    Includes bibliographical references and index.
    ISBN 0-7735-1811-8
    1. Kaliningradskaia oblast' (Russia)–History.   I.
    Title.
    DK511.KI54B68 1999   947'.240842   C98-901391-4

This book was typeset by True to Type in
10/12 Sabon

Contents

Tables

Acknowledgments

I would like, first of all, to express my profound gratitude to Dr V.J. Boss of McGill University, without whose constant support it would have been impossible to produce this book. In addition, the following people and organizations furnished invaluable aid and assistance at different stages of the research and writing of this work, for which I am indebted to them:

In Canada, I am indebted to my editor, Ron Curtis, without whose aid this work would have been much less readable; to the Social Sciences and Humanities Research Council and its Aid to Scholarly Publications Programme; the History Department of McGill University; Dr Helen Anderson and the staff of the Inter-Library Loans Department of McGill's McLennan Library; Dr Philip Cercone, Dr John Zucchi, and the late Dr Peter Blaney of McGill-Queen's University Press as well as its editorial staff, and the administrative staff and my colleagues at Nipissing University. In Russia, I was assisted by Professor A.N. Sakharov and L.P. Kolotdinova of the History Institute of the Russian Academy of Sciences; Professors V.G. Osipov and N.N. Lukovnikov of the State University of Tver'; I.A. Sakharov, V.A. Feoktistov, director of the Tver' Centre of Documentation on Modern History, A.A. Lukovkin, senior collaborator of the same centre; M.A. Il'in, director of the State Archive of Tver' province; and by two German scholars, Dr Jan Foitzik and Dr Carola Tischler, both currently in Berlin. The very early stages of this project can be traced to the Netherlands: I am grateful to Professors W.H. Roobol and M.C. Brands of the Universiteit van Amsterdam and Dr Martin van de Heuvel of Clingendael Institute, and to the late Nico Boterbloem, Johanna Boterbloem-van Bockhoven, Klaas-Jan Boterbloem, and Martin Pluis.

Jodi Sutherland of Nipissing University deserves special mention for her fine work on preparing the map for publication. Susan Mooney's support was instrumental for the execution of the project during all stages of its preparation; I am especially grateful for her editorial corrections and criticism of the different drafts. Finally, it must be noted that I alone am responsible for any errors or deficiencies in this study.

Note on Translation and Transcription

All translations of Russian secondary sources, archival documents, and answers of the survey respondents are my own. In translating direct quotations, I have tried to stay as closely as possible to the original Russian. Therefore, lower and upper cases are used in the same way as in the original Russian.

When the original Russian of certain quotations was grammatically incorrect or stylistically flawed, I have, for the most part, corrected grammatical errors, while leaving some stylistic ones untouched. Therefore, some of the quotations might come across as awkward to the reader, but I have decided to concede the stylistic errors in the following account, because they convey something of the education of most protagonists, as well as their particular manner of speaking and writing.

The transcription of Russian names and words generally follows that of the Library of Congress, unless a name or word is commonly known in another transcription (for example, Voznesensky is used instead of Voznesenskii). All translations of secondary German or French sources are mine as well.

Dates for events before 31 January 1918 (13 February 1918 in the West) usually correspond to the Julian calendar that traditionally prevailed in Imperial Russia (sometimes called "Old Style"). For events after January 1918, the Gregorian calendar is used ("New Style").

Occasionally, the references to archival documents have the abbreviation "ob." added to the numbers of the *listy*. This indicates that the verso side of the *list* (page) had no separate page numbering. Thus l.244ob. (Russian: obratnyi) means *list* 244, verso. References to the respondents' answers in the survey of 1992 in Tver' province are designated by the phrase "testimony of [initials and last name of respondent] in the survey."

Translations of the Russian terms and acronyms used throughout this book are provided in the glossary.

Introduction

Until recently, the archives of the Communist Party of the Soviet Union were closed to Western researchers. Since August 1991, however, researchers have been able to investigate many documental and oral sources without undue interference by the Russian authorities. The following account is based on these newly opened archives and on interviews with people who witnessed postwar developments in the Soviet Union in what was until 1935 Tver' province, a region in the northwest of European Russia that was reborn in 1935 as Kalinin oblast'. The purpose of this book is, first, to provide a detailed portrayal of Russian life in the Soviet Union during the last years of Stalin's life. The book focuses more on the experience of the people targeted by the policies introduced by the central leadership of the Communist Party and Soviet government than on the activities of the powerful policymakers in Moscow.

Second, the following pages attempt to portray the relationship between the "haves" and the "have-nots" in Soviet society. Leszek Kolakowski has given a perceptive appreciation of the mindset of the haves:

Later Stalinism (and Marxism) was a reasonably fair approximation [of the *Idealtypus* of totalitarianism]. Its triumph consisted not simply in that virtually everything was either falsified or suppressed – statistics, historical events, current events, names, maps, books (occasionally Lenin's texts) – but that the inhabitants of the country were trained to know what is politically "correct." In the functionaries' minds, the borderline between what is "correct" and what is "true," as we normally understand this, seems really to have become blurred; by repeating the same absurdities time and again, they began to believe or half-believe in them themselves. The massive and profound corruption of the language eventually produced people who were incapable of perceiving their own mendacity.[1]

The haves (the "functionaries") were provincial leaders who derived their social status not from having property but from wielding political power. Responsible for the implementation of the policies devised by the central leadership, they were the bosses of the Communist Party, the provincial secretaries and their staff, the members of the provincial party committee, and the secretaries and members of the district party organizations and some of the smaller party cells. Only party members were usually appointed to leadership positions in the provincial and district government. Many of the more important positions in party and government were held by officials directly appointed by the party's Central Committee apparatus. Of course, Leszek Kolakowski's opinion was strongly influenced by his own disagreeable experiences as an intellectual in postwar Poland. Kolakowski belonged to a stratum of society called the "intelligentsia," whose members were always under the suspicion of being "class alien." The society under construction in postwar Eastern and East-Central Europe was designed to be a paradise not for intellectuals but for industrial workers – the proletariat.

It remains to be seen whether sources support the thesis that political leaders in Russia during the immediate postwar period behaved according to Kolakowski's assessment. Local party leaders, to be sure, functioned as a transmission belt, conveying orders from above to the great majority of the Russian population, who were called upon to accept unconditionally the wisdom of these decisions and to behave according to the strict rules of the Stalinist order and the chimerical vision of the workers' state and its inhabitants. The following pages examine the veracity of two contrasting points of view: one, Kolakowski's position that Soviet society was built on massive, corruptive indoctrination imposed by an extraordinarily oppressive regime upon an unwilling populace; and two, the standpoint that (as a simplified *Idealtypus* in the Weberian sense) considers Soviet society to be one in which the authorities acted upon a broad consensus between citizens and government about policy.[2]

This book also aims at providing a picture of what are often called the "unknown years," the period between V-E Day and Stalin's death.[3] The majority of scholarly works on Stalin's Russia neglect the postwar period to a significant degree, with the exception of Fainsod's *How Russia is Ruled* and Conquest's *Power and Policy*.[4] This neglect is curious in that the enormity of the Soviet experiment is never more apparent than during the immediate postwar period. In 1945 it was possible to start on a new footing, to avoid or correct mistakes committed during the 1930s and earlier. Yet, it appears that the central leadership deliberately let this opportunity pass. The scanty attention paid by historians to the final years of Stalin's regime has partially been the outcome of the restricted access to primary sources prior to glasnost' and the dissolution of the USSR, and partially a consequence of Western historians' fickleness when it comes to this period.[5] Our understanding of the late Stalinist period has been broadened somewhat thanks to revelations following glasnost' and perestroika.

Few Western scholars writing about Khrushchev's, Brezhnev's, or Gorbachev's tenure as Soviet leaders could avoid discussing Stalin's legacy. The starting point for many a book has been the war and the so-called postwar reconstruction, yet without a very detailed investigation of these years. As is the case with 1929, 1941, and 1945, the death of Stalin marks a turning point after which many aspects of Soviet life changed fundamentally, mainly for the better. A study of the immediate postwar period seems therefore opportune.

Within the historiography of the Soviet Union, a rather acrimonious debate has been raging during the last twenty-five years between those who would like to blame Stalin, the Communist Party, and their evil ideology for creating this totalitarian state and those who have attempted to come to a more positive appreciation of the Communist era, stressing that not all was as bad or morally corrupt as the dystopian picture painted by Kolakowski. The latter group, sometimes called the revisionist school, admits that Stalin committed heinous crimes but points to the Soviet victory during World War II and the subsequent status of the USSR as the "other superpower" as evidence of the strength of the system forged since 1917.[6] The revisionists propose that a government built upon the threat and use of violence alone would not have been capable of these feats. According to them, Stalin's autocracy was an aberration and, even when he was the unchallenged leader, his control was not as all-encompassing as argued by most Western Sovietologists in the 1940s, 1950s, and 1960s. Common sense adds ammunition to the revisionist argument that the utopian society that was supposedly being constructed and the opportunities the transformation opened up for social advancement would have an appeal for the Russian population. Did not Stalin and his six or seven closest friends need positive support from the masses for their policies? Was it humanly possible for this inner circle to keep a close watch on a realm the size of the Soviet Union with a population nearing 200 million by 1950?

Western revisionists are not alone in challenging the notion that repression came strictly from one side. A.N. Sakharov has pointed out in a criticism of Western concepts of totalitarianism that it is false to pronounce only the authorities guilty of the startling cruelties under

Stalin – as has been done by some Westerners and, in recent years, by (former) Soviet specialists – for "Stalin, the stalinist bosses, and the administrative-command state-political apparatus are one thing, and the suffering narod is something completely different. We are dealing here with an artificial opposition: all horrible characteristics of totalitarianism emanated from the former part of society, while the latter part only plays a role as poor non-resisters, as lambs, ready to be slaughtered, for whom the only thing that was left was crying."[7]

The examples of Hitler's Germany, Pol Pot's Kampuchea, or the recent tragedy in Rwanda have made it clear that uncritical, active, and sometimes enthusiastic participation of large groups of people in morally despicable deeds against their fellow human beings on the instigation of the political leadership occurs regularly in certain ideologized societies in this supposedly civilized age. The ardent involvement of rank-and-file Communists in collectivizing the peasantry and the craze of denouncing "enemies of the people" elucidate the point.

Although revanchism must have played a part in the subconsciousness of certain zealous participants in the repressions, it seems esoteric to explain the terror of the 1930s as a grandiose retribution exacted upon the better-off by the formerly downtrodden masses for all the social injustice suffered by them and their ancestors.[8] Sakharov's hypothesis derives from a particular reading of long-term developments in Russian history. If we accepted his point of view, it would remain inexplicable why the victims of collectivization – and particularly the purges – often came from the same social background as their persecutors.

Whatever the case might have been, most of the suppositions of Russian and Western scholars used to be based on tentative historical evidence. Until the late 1980s (or perhaps even until August 1991), there was little chance to reconstruct on the basis of solid documentary evidence the life and thought of the two basic classes that in Soviet mythology made up the nascent socialist society after 1929 (or 1917?) – the working class and the peasantry. Archives were closed to both Soviet and Western researchers. Average Soviet citizens before the heyday of perestroika and glasnost' were too afraid to speak their minds openly.[9] Obviously, this reluctance formed one of the gravest objections to the thesis that there was considerable support for the regime: if people had so enthusiastically embraced the socialist dream, why did such a palpable fear exist among them to speak their minds? N.P. Poletika thus would appear to be closer to the truth than the revisionists or Sakharov when he suggests that the wholehearted collaboration of only a certain minority (20 percent of the population) was required to unleash the terror necessary to turn the large majority into mortally afraid and almost unconditionally obedient subjects of the Stalinist regime.[10]

One must recognize that politics played a significant role in the life of every Soviet citizen between 1929 and 1953. Of course, there were always stretches of time when personal affairs temporarily overshadowed politics. Nevertheless, no one was able to ignore, and all had to participate in, the tremendous changes begun in 1929. Everyone (if lucky enough not to become victims themselves) was expected to applaud the purges in the second half of the 1930s, and no one escaped the ravages of the war, in which virtually all lost a relative. After the war, the sociopolitical situation became more settled in the territories that had been part of the Union before 1939, except for the areas where indigenous ethnic groups were deported in retaliation for their alleged collaboration with the Nazis. Arrests for political reasons took place more selectively, but were not yet a thing of the past. The party tried to mobilize the population with a renewed ideological offensive, but many of the slogans had grown stale.[11]

In spite of this erosion of enthusiasm, the tremendous loss of human life, and the material damage in the war-ravaged western part of its territory, the USSR remained capable for more than forty years of maintaining its status as the "other" superpower. It gained this elevated postwar status mostly from the triumph of its armed forces in the war, as well as by default. Germany had been defeated, while Great Britain and France had either cleared the field or were in the process of doing so. The decolonization process ushered in after 1945 and the tremendous cost of the war relegated the Western European countries to secondary global status. Still, the important contribution of Stalin's eminently shrewd and crafty foreign policy to the enormous increase of Communist-controlled territory on a global level cannot be denied.[12]

Much of the rationale for Stalin's policies has been extensively discussed in Western publications and, more recently, in the historiography that has appeared in the former Soviet republics. The study of his personality and personal involvement in, or responsibility for, the many crimes against Russians and other nationalities within the USSR perpetrated by Soviet government officials, members of the Communist Party, and agents of the security organs has been rather overbearing. Even though the last word on Stalin has obviously not yet been written, this book will largely refrain from scrutinizing the actions and motives of the Soviet dictator. His imprint on the lives of the Russians, however, will always be discernible in the following account, and therefore a few words about the dominant influence of Stalin on postwar developments seem warranted here.

While Stalin could have resigned himself to the internal rebuilding of the devastated USSR in 1945, he chose to act otherwise, in keeping with his ideology and policies of the pre-1941 era. Although he advocated "Socialism in One Country" in the 1920s, the prospect of Communism's international triumph – in its Stalinist version – remained paramount in the mind of the Vozhd'. He therefore rejected the Marshall Plan (even if the American offer was designed in such a way that refusal became the sole option for the Soviet leadership).[13] Stalin's choice of action involved the simultaneous rebuilding and defence of the Soviet Union and the new empire won in Eastern Europe and East Asia with the limited means available within the Soviet bloc. Somehow Stalin's postwar empire presented the image of an economically and militarily competitive stronghold to Western eyes, and somehow the Soviet citizens helped support this edifice. In retrospect, much of the strength of this empire turned out to be only a facade, but at the time the facade was convincing enough not only to the West but perhaps also to Stalin. Toward the end of his life, he may have thought that the USSR was indeed just a few steps behind the impressive progress of the United States since 1941. To Stalin, his own and Westerners' perception of the might of the Communist empire legitimized the extreme material sacrifice imposed by his policies upon the Soviet population.

From 1988 onward, the Soviet public (and the Western reader, too, for much writing appeared quickly in translation) was treated to an avalanche of disclosures about the past in the "thick" journals, books, newspapers, films, and documentaries. Rapidly, one after the other, icons of the Soviet past were destroyed, beginning with Stalin and ending with Lenin (in 1991). Soviet historians finally began to write about the past unfettered by the ideological straightjacket of Marxism-Leninism; Western historians were allowed to inspect archives. During the height of this "Age of Discovery," I visited the disintegrating Soviet Union in the autumn of 1991, and then, soon after, a newly "democratic" Russia in 1992, to study declassified documents of the Stalinist period and conduct interviews with those who had had first-hand experience with the system, generally as children and teenagers during the 1920s and 1930s and as young adults after the war.

Despite some difficulties with the archival records of the Communist Party in Tver', it is possible to get a fairly clear and detailed overview of the manifold aspects of the activities of the party in the oblast', and, consequently, of the life of the inhabitants of Kalinin province. I was unable to inspect one essential archival source: the records of the local and central security organs. There is no doubt that these records would add some otherwise hard to obtain information about life under Stalin.[14] One suspects that it is deemed to be politically inconvenient and perhaps even dangerous to allow people to inspect these records without restriction. Quite likely, the devastating results of opening the Stasi records in Germany have reinforced the idea among the members of the Russian government that at this point free access to the KGB archives would be a grave political mistake. After all, not only in Moscow but also in Tver' today the political leadership is preponderantly made up of ex-Communists, who probably have all been involved at some stage of their careers in reprehensible acts of political harassment or oppression.[15]

Roy Medvedev, rather curiously, has claimed that NKVD documents, especially, falsify reality, although he has not offered any evidence to support this argument.[16] If this claim were true, which I doubt, there would be no need to lament researchers' inability to comb the archives of the security organs. Medvedev's point can be confirmed only when independent investigations in the archives of the former NKVD, MVD, MGB, and so on, are permitted – provided that nothing of these records has been or is being deliberately destroyed.

We can only hope that Russian and foreign researchers will eventually gain access to all archival collections, however incomplete, but for now we have to fill in the gaps by other means. In order to enhance the picture derived from archival materials and secondary works, I decided to turn to oral sources.[17] A large oral history project has been set up at the Russian State University for the Humanities in Moscow under the auspices of Dr Dar'ia Khubova. Iurii Afanas'ev, a radical of the early perestroika time and currently the rector of this university, explained that "this [type of research] is extremely important, because the archival resources in many ways reflect the freakish nature of the state's social organization imposed on Russia and the former Soviet Union: the living conditions, the thoughts and feelings of the majority of the Russians were of little interest to the state agencies that were supplying the archives."[18]

Oral history has a specific additional advantage for those who try to understand and analyse the mentality of individuals:

The first thing that makes oral history different, therefore, is that it tells us less about *events* than about their *meaning*. This does not imply that oral history has no factual validity. Interviews often reveal unknown events or unknown aspects of known events; they always cast new light on unexplored areas of the daily life of the nonhegemonic classes. From this point of view, the only problem posed by oral sources is that of verification ...

But the unique and precious element which oral sources force upon the historian and which no other sources possess in equal measure is the speaker's subjectivity. If the approach to research is broad and articulated enough, a cross section of the subjectivity of a group or a class may emerge. Oral sources tell us not just what people did, but what they wanted to do, what they believed they were doing, and what they now think they did. Oral sources may not add much to what we know, for instance, of the material cost of a strike to the workers involved; but they tell us a good deal about its psychological costs ... The organization of the narrative reveals a great deal of the speakers' relationships to their history.

Subjectivity is as much the business of history as are the more visible "facts." What informants believe is indeed a historical fact (that is, the fact that they believe it), as much as what really happened.[19]

In November 1991, I reached an initial agreement with two professors of Tver' University to conduct a series of two hundred interviews with inhabitants of Tver' oblast' who had lived through the postwar period. In the end, because of some communication problems and time constraints, only 109 interviews were conducted.[20] The answers of the respondents reveal the priorities in their lives under the Communist regime and, more specifically, at the time of Stalin. The elderly Russians discussed events that made a lasting impression on their memory, as well as some of their reactions to certain policies and measures of the time. Naturally, the answers varied greatly; although the survey was by no means representative, it supplies insights into the life of ordinary individuals in Stalin's time, perspectives that would be impossible to acquire by using only published and archival materials.[21]

Peter Rutland remarked recently that "[n]o doubt Sovietology will make great strides forward in the next few years, as more memoirs are published and documents slowly released. The last major surge in our knowledge of the Soviet system came in the mid-1950s, with the publications from the Harvard interview project. This time around, however, scholars will be able to interview not displaced persons and ex-POWs, but former members of the Politburo and Central Committee."[22] And, I might add, referring to my own research, scholars will be able to interview former citizens of the USSR, that is, those who were exposed to the consequences of the policies of the Central Committee and Politburo.[23]

Since 1992, under the impact of Russia's severe economic crisis, many retired Russian citizens have become overly nostalgic about the Stalinist past. As luck would have it, when the interviews for this book were being conducted (in the summer of 1992), the fear of stating one's opinion openly had finally disappeared, while most participants had not yet fully felt the consequences of the economic policies of the

Yeltsin governments. The account they gave of the consequences of the Stalinist regime for their personal lives was more frank than could be expected today. The current support among pensioners for the Communist Party of the Russian Federation (KPRF) would indicate that older people now have a renewed appreciation of the benefits and security of the Communist system. One would presume that the same group of respondents, when interviewed today, would be, on the whole, far less critical of the postwar period than they were in 1992.[24] The timing of the interviews was all the more felicitous because the average age of most Russians has fallen below sixty by now; since 1992, several of the interviewees have died. The longer the project had had to be postponed, the more unlikely it would have become to find a sufficient number of eyewitnesses of Stalin's time.

Since my visits during the last gasps of the Communist Party and the first months of post-Communist Russia, the atmosphere for research in Russia has unfortunately deteriorated too: the promise of free access to KGB and NKIu or military archives, as well as to the by now notorious "Presidential Archive," has not been fulfilled.[25] We cannot assess how many documents are under lock and key at the present moment and how many have simply been destroyed in the recent or more distant past. The absence of an archival law after the collapse of the Soviet Union in August 1991 made it possible for me, with the aid of some prodding, to inspect documents that may have now again become classified. By electing to go to Tver', I avoided some of the rapidly growing anti-Western sentiment that I experienced at the central archives in Moscow. In the archives of Tver', the assistance shown to me was, on the whole, extremely generous.

> Who, except hopeless bureaucrats, can rely on written documents alone? Who, except archive rats, does not understand that a party and its leaders must be tested primarily by their deeds and not merely by their declarations?
>
> Stalin[26]

Few outside the Soviet Union have tried to approach the history of Russia from a regional point of view. The value of such an approach was, nevertheless, recognized long ago by the Russian scholar Afanasii Prokofievich Shchapov, who in 1859 was appointed to the chair of Russian history at the University of Kazan. His arguments in his inaugural lecture about the pertinence of regional studies are still relevant today:

[H]ere is another principle which is not yet firmly established in our researches: the principle of regionalism. Until now the prevailing idea has been that of centralization; all the variegated strands of provincial history have been swallowed up in the general theory of the development of the State ... Yet the history of Russia is, more than anything, the history of differing local groups, of constant territorial change, of reciprocal action and reaction, of the various regions before and after centralization.[27]

One notable regional historian is Helmut Altrichter, who, despite his very limited access to Soviet sources, has written a remarkable account of the life of the Russian peasants in Tver' guberniia during the 1920s.[28] Thanks to the capture of the Smolensk Archive by American troops at the end of World War II, another seminal account of life in the Russian provinces could already be written in the 1950s by Merle Fainsod.[29] In addition, Stephen Kotkin has recently written an extremely comprehensive work on the transformation of Magnitogorsk during the first five-year plans, which may aid the reader in understanding an area that was much more dynamic in its industrial development than Kalinin province.[30]

Both the Soviet Union and Russia are far too large in terms of geography and demography to serve as subjects of a comprehensive yet concise socio-political history; moreover, the scope and depth of the research done in this field has until now been far too limited. To write such a history, researchers need to explore systematically the regional dimension of the history of the Russian and non-Russian areas. A considerably more detailed and deeper understanding of the history of the former Soviet Union and its people will emerge from this type of study.

The deficiency in studies of geographically more peripheral areas of the Soviet Union owes much to researchers' lack of access to primary sources for the post-1917 period, but also to our impression that everything of importance in the hypercentralized USSR was being decided in Moscow. Although the majority of the Soviet population lived in the countryside during Stalin's time, the prevailing presupposition has been that if Moscow's machinations became clear, a picture would automatically emerge of the historical development of the Soviet Union as a whole. In fact, according to one Soviet historian writing in 1989, the USSR became an industrial country only in the 1960s.[31] Soviet history therefore presents a deceivingly simple facade: after all, the rules were laid down in Moscow, and we assume everybody had to comply with them. For example, the wages for similar work in industry were the same everywhere; everyone had the right to the same amount of housing space. Nevertheless, decisions had to be executed by human beings, who were perhaps indoctrinated but remained human all the same, suffering from the usual human flaws, such as personal bias. Despite the Leninist utilitarian morality, many party officials preserved a pre-Communist set of norms and values; empathy often overcame allegiance to the cause and thus interfered with a mechanical execution of orders from above.

Although some of what follows may have only a regional relevance, the study of Tver'/Kalinin province often offers a "microcosmic" view of the historical development of the Russian Socialist Federal Soviet Republic (RSFSR) and the USSR in their entirety, for several reasons. The province was and is representative of the Russian "heartland" because of its economy and history. Around 1960, two Soviet ethnographers, L.A. Anokhina and M.N. Shmeleva, noted that it "appears to be in an economic and cultural sense in many ways typical of the central provinces of the RSFSR."[32]

Tver' province boasted a long industrial tradition by Russian standards. Industrialization began in the two major towns of Tver' guberniia, Tver' and Vyshnii Volochek, at the same time as in St Petersburg and Moscow.[33] The province's economic landscape is representative of European Russia, within which predominantly agricultural or industrial areas have evolved as a result of industrialization. Since the last century, Tver' province has consisted, similarly, of two distinct economic parts divided by the Nikolaevskii, or October, Railroad. The province's industry is concentrated along the railroad and in the southeast, while the western and north-eastern areas are predominantly agrarian.

During World War II, the west of the province endured Nazi occupation, but the eastern part remained in Soviet hands throughout. The German advance was halted in the province in December 1941, and the first serious Russian counteroffensive in December of that year succeeded in liberating the capital of Kalinin. After the middle of 1943, the last Germans left Kalinin province and retreated from all of the territory of the RSFSR.

In order to understand the setting of Tver' province in 1945, I first explore, in chapters 1 and 2, the epochal changes within the region from before the Bolshevik insurrection to the end of the Great Patriotic War. With the exception of prerevolutionary industrialization, those changes, as a result of the authoritarian nature of the regime of the tsars and their communist successors, were almost all instigated from above or imposed upon the Russians of the Tver' region from outside: the abolition of serfdom during the 1860s, the Stolypin reforms in agriculture, World War I, the 1917 revolution, the Civil War, the NEP, collectivization and Stalinist industrialization, the purges of 1936–38, and World War II. With Stalin's triumph over his adversaries in the Politburo in 1929, Tver' province embarked upon the most radical phase of change it has ever witnessed.

Modernization, introduced at a forced pace in 1929, was bound to lead to a demographic deficit in a region not noted for its heavy industry or vital resources. The demographic consequences of the upheaval of Stalin's Great Turn, nevertheless, remain astonishing. Chapter 2 endeavours to estimate the extent of the loss of so many inhabitants, whose disappearance contributed to the tortuous postwar recovery of Tver' province. The area showed signs of vitality before 1929, as expressed in its healthy birthrate; after 1929, the province saw a sustained long-term population decline, owing to the policy of the central leadership of party and government.

Chapters 1 and 2 (part 1) set the historical and demographic parameters for the discussion of postwar events. From chapter 3 onward (part 2), the postwar events themselves are the focus of discussion. The events of the 1930s and the war show that this was a society driven by coercion. Therefore, in chapters 3 to 5 the discussion of postwar developments begins with the organizations that enforced this oppression and their success in mastering the population. The Communist Party was a political party only in name. In practice, it was the organization that made and executed the policies that ruled the Soviet Union.

After May 1945, the Communist masters would again fetter personal freedom as much as possible. From 1944–45 onward, the regime employed the same prewar strategies to make Soviet citizens swallow the propaganda that they lived in the best of possible worlds. The war had annihilated an entire generation of devout believers in the communist dream. From before November 1917 until June 1941 religious worship had worn away, besieged by modernity and the intensive persecution of the church, but traditional religious customs proved harder to extirpate. Apart from the armed resistance in newly acquired western territories, organized struggle against the political and economic offensive of the "postwar reconstruction of socialism" hardly occurred in the Soviet Union, partially because of the suspected omnipresence of the security police, whose tentacles, it was thought, were wrapped around all of society; perhaps the fear of the "organs" was out of proportion, but it would appear that the strong arm of the penal system was tangible, its presence a constant reminder that deviance was dangerous.

Chapters 6 and 7 portray life in the towns and villages of Stalinist Russia. How did people survive this degrading regime? How did the standard of living in the towns compare to that of the villages? Chapter

8 tries to answer the question whether there is a connection between the poor living conditions and the reforms of Malenkov and Khrushchev in 1953. Some evidence about the credibility of Stalin's regime may be found in the reactions to Khrushchev's Secret Speech in 1956: Were the partial disclosures by Stalin's successors received as a total surprise (which would indicate loyalty and unwavering faith in the system), or did the speech open, albeit briefly, the floodgates? The reactions to the speech, as outlined in the final chapter, may underline some of the observations made on the basis of other archival and oral evidence concerning the history of Tver' province during the last years of Stalin's life.

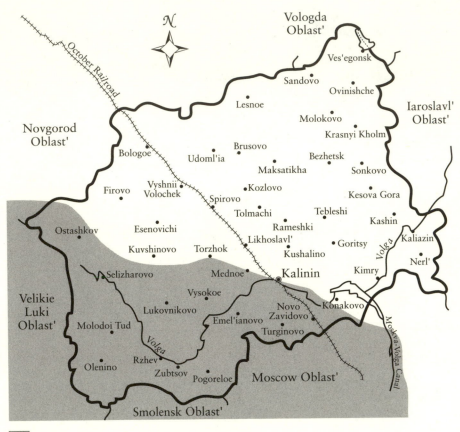

Furthest advance of the German Army, autumn 1941

Kalinin Oblast', 1944–57

PART ONE

The Background

CHAPTER ONE

Before 1941

Already by 1921 it could be doubted whether the abolition of "the repressive aspects of the social order" of the tsarist regime justified the revolutionary violence and the casualties resulting from the Civil War that had been provoked by the Bolshevik coup d'état of October 1917.[1] An unshakable faith in a schematic, mechanistic, nineteenth-century philosophy of history led, however, to a fatally naive understanding of the workings of Russian society among the Marxist believers ruling the country and their helmsman, the infallible interpreter of the canon. By 1929 their ill-conceived policies would result in a fall in the standard of living for the next quarter-century, while millions of people would be brutally persecuted and executed. In order to understand the setting of Tver' province in 1945, I will first explore the momentous changes within the region from the Bolshevik insurrection to the end of the "Great Patriotic War."

GEOGRAPHY, DEMOGRAPHY, AND ECONOMY

Although the borders of Tver' guberniia, or Kalinin oblast', have been redrawn many times, its geographic size remained roughly the same from the end of the eighteenth century until 1958.[2] Its approximate postwar area (1945–58) of 65,000 square kilometres was as large as the combined territory of the Netherlands, Belgium, and Luxemburg today. Tver' province, which is part of the so-called Central, or Central Industrial, Region, lies in the heartland of European Russia on the Russian Plain. From medieval times onward, the comparative proximity of Moscow and, later, St Petersburg exerted a significant influence on the economic, political, social, and cultural development of the Tver' lands. The proximity of these cities caused a steady exodus of natives from the province to the two capitals.[3]

Around 27 percent of the oblast' today consists of forest. Despite an abundance of rivers, lakes, canals, and smaller waters, as well as swamps, the soil is poorly suited for agriculture. The population density in 1959 was the lowest of all oblasts in the Central Region: twenty-one persons per square kilometre.[4]

January is the coldest month of the year: in Stalin's time, the temperature averaged −8°C in the western and −12°C in the eastern parts of the oblast'. The warmest month of the year is July, with an average temperature between 18.5°C and 19.5°C immediately after World War II. In these years, the vegetation period lasted 130 to 150 days annually, while precipitation varied between 52 and 63 centimetres annually.[5] When the land finally was free of frost, by mid-April, the peasantry or collective farmers could begin with their field work. Even in May work was sometimes interrupted because of a cold snap. In the late 1940s and early 1950s real summer weather commenced in the middle of May, lasting until mid-September, when the average temperature dropped below 10°C. Spring and autumn were short, subzero temperatures returning around the first of November. Apart from the unpredictable cold spells, pre- and postrevolutionary agriculture also suffered from excessive rainfall during grain harvesting and haying. Because of this excessive humidity, most traditional peasant villages used to be located on elevated land. Slopes of the hills were ploughed, while hay was grown on the very wet lower lands.[6] Circumstances of climate and the soil in the province were too poor for large-scale cultivation of wheat; most of the grains grown were rye, oats, and buckwheat.[7] The months of April and May brought the sowing of oats, summer rye, flax, summer wheat, barley, and buckwheat.[8] At the end of June meadows were mown, even after 1945 often with scythes. Before the introduction of combines, grain crops were harvested in July and August with sickles to avoid losing ripe ears. Grain was subsequently dried in a kiln or dryer, and in the fall after the conclusion of the fieldwork, threshed with a flail (although simple threshing machines were sometimes used in the north). Fields were ploughed for the coming spring sowing at this time of the year, and some were sown immediately with winter grains. The collectivization of agriculture would not overly interfere with these climatological, geological, and seasonal parameters, which would determine the rhythm of farm work before and after 1929. Greenhouses, soil improvement, and even mechanized equipment were introduced at such a slow pace that still in 1953 the yield of arable and pastoral farming was heavily contingent on forces beyond human control.

Before the collectivization of agriculture, the average household owned a horse, a couple of cows or calves, about three sheep, an iron

Table 1
Population of Tver' Guberniia and Kalinin (Tver') Oblast', 1926–91

	Total Population (in 1,000s)	Urban Population (in 1,000)	Rural Population (in 1,000s)	Urban Population (%)	Rural Population (%)
1926 (1967 borders)	2668.0	324.7	2343.3	12	88
1926 (1926 borders)[1]	2241.9	282.0	1959.9	13	87
1939[2]	2489.2	609.2	1879.4	24	76
1939[3]	2169.8	585.5	1584.3	27	73
3 January 1946	1611.3	488.8	1122.5	30	70
1959[4]	1806.8	787.4	1019.4	44	56
1 January 1991[5]	1676.2	1203.2	473.0	71.8	28.2

[1] The numbers for 1926 are from the census of 17 December 1826. The numbers given in *Kalininskaia oblast' za 50 let* do not correspond to the numbers of Vershinskii and Zolotarev, *Naselenie*, 12–13 or of *Kraevedcheskii atlas*, 4; we have to assume that the first numbers in the table are for the oblast' in its larger incarnation of 1967; see n2 below.

[2] The numbers for 1939 are supposedly from the census of 17 December 1939. These numbers are highly doubtful, as the result of this census for the whole of the USSR was secret when *Kalininskaia oblast' za 50 let*, in which these numbers are to be found, was published; again, we do not know which borders have been used. Furthermore, there was no census on 17 December 1939, but only one in early 1939 (see Conquest, *The Great Terror*, 487; Drobizhev and Poliakov, "Istoricheskaia demografiia," 470; Poliakov et al., "Polveka," II, 49).

[3] As given by I.P. Boitsov to Voznesensky and A.A. Kuznetsov in May 1946; these numbers differ from the first set of numbers for 1939 because the former included the contemporary population of the territories that were added in 1957 and 1958. Smirnov et al., *Ocherki*, 530–1, mention the same numbers.

[4] These numbers are from the census of 15 January 1959. The capital Kalinin had at this point 261,000 inhabitants (33% of all town dwellers); Vyshnii Volochek 66,400; Rzhev 49,000 or 42,000; Kimry 41,200; Torzhok 34,900; Bologoe 30,300; Bezhetsk 27,000; Ostashkov 19,500; Kashin 16,200; Konakovo – the successor to the inundated Kuznetsovo – 13,500; Kuvshinovo 13,500; Kaliazin 11,100; Likhoslavl' 9,500; Krasnomaiskii 8,000; Ves'egonsk 7,000 (see *Tsentral'nyi Raion*, 541, 550, 555, 558, 563–4, 567, 569, 571, 573, 577, 580, 583–4). These must be numbers for the oblast' territory as constituted after 1958. In the USSR in 1959, 48% of the population was urban and 52% rural (Ryan and Prentice, *Social Trends in the Soviet Union from 1950*, 17).

[5] The numbers are for the borders of 1991, encompassing the town of Tver', consisting of the urban raions of Zavolzh'e, Moskovskii, Proletarskii, and Tsentral'nyi and the workers settlement Sakharovo; the towns of Bezhetsk, Bologoe, Vyshnii Volochek, Kashin, Kimry, Konakovo, Nelidovo, Ostashkov, Rzhev, Torzhok, and Udomlia; and Andreapol', Bezhetsk, Belyi, Bologoe, Ves'egonsk, Vyshnii Volochek, Zharkovo, Zapadnodvina, Zubtsov, Kalinin, Kaliazin, Kashin, Kesovogora, Kimry, Konakovo, Krasnyi Kholm, Kuvshinovo, Lesnoe, Likhoslavl', Maksatikha, Molokovo, Nelidovo, Olenino, Ostashkov, Peno, Rameshki, Rzhev, Sandovo, Selizharovo, Sonkovo, Spirovo, Staritsa, Torzhok, Toropets, Udomlia, and Firovo raions.

The numbers are based on *Kalininskaia oblast' za 50 let*, 12; *Kraevedcheskii atlas*, 4; *Chislennost' naseleniia soiuznikh respublik*, 4, and 221–5; Smirnov et al., *Ocherki*, 530–1; Pako, 147/4/63, ll.132, 135.

or wooden plough, a wooden or iron harrow, and one or two scythes and sickles.[9] Peasants reserved livestock mainly for personal use.[10] In the summer cattle grazed together under supervision of a village herder. Already in the 1920s a shortage of fodder crops existed in the guberniia and continued to plague the authorities until long after World War II. Consequently, the average daily yield per dairy cow was a low six to eight litres of milk. The increasing sowing of clover and vetch on the fallow gave a little more flexibility to cattle husbandry during the New Economic Policy (NEP), roughly the period from March 1921 to the fall of 1929.[11] Increased potato cultivation had a similarly beneficial effect, for potatoes could be used as feed. Animal manure was used as fertilizer, while horses did the ploughing.

Russians engaged primarily in agriculture before the revolution of 1917, and the predominantly Russian inhabitants of Tver' province were no exception.[12] However, because of the rather unfavourable agricultural conditions in this northern and overpopulated area, many peasants were forced to take up other work on the side or adopt a permanent nonagricultural trade.[13] Around 1900, one quarter of the rural population was engaged in some form of handicraft, and every second family had its migratory workers.

After the revolution of 1917 most of the traditional rural artisanship that had existed disappeared because of a lack of demand and the prohibition of certain trades. Consequently, during the 1920s more intensive animal husbandry had to substitute this source of income, and peasant families acquired as many additional animals as their lands allowed.[14] The peasantry's habit of migratory and seasonal work reasserted itself somewhat before 1929, for its fundamental cause, the overpopulation of the countryside, remained in force.

1917 AND BEYOND

Tver' guberniia was far from "Bolshevized" on the eve of the October Revolution.[15] The towns, nevertheless, witnessed a relatively smooth transition bringing the Bolshevik party to power. Several factors allowed for such an easy take-over there: the prior existence of Bolshevik organizations; the presence of soldiers' garrisons, generally inclined to support the new government if promised peace and, perhaps, land; the proximity of the revolutionary centres of Moscow and Petrograd; and the comparatively superior communication systems (telegraph, telephone, and railroad systems) providing local Bolsheviks with news and information – and with armed forces from Tver' and the two capitals. Some rural residents were willing to oppose Bolshevik rule with violent means, but most people were not sufficiently politicized to consider armed resistance against the new rulers, about whom little was known. The countryside was therefore won with more difficulty, but the lack of organization among anti-Bolshevik groups, the general confusion caused by inadequate and obsolete information, the collaboration of the "Left" SR party with the new rulers, and the promises of peace and land generally made the initial establishment of Bolshevik rule relatively simple. In the 1917–20 period, peasants were able to supplement their holdings with the lands of former propertied groups in the countryside, fulfilling a long-standing desire. The negative impact of the October Revolution on their lives became clear to them only when, in 1918, forced grain requisitions began in the countryside, but they were discontinued toward the end of the Civil War.

The Civil War was a precarious period for the Communists of Tver' guberniia, in spite of the fact that the territory was never occupied by any White Army units. By the summer of 1919, because of the Communists' extensive mobilization for the Red Army, the guberniia party organization had decreased by two-thirds, and many party cells in the volosti had been liquidated.[16] This change, and probably the general dissatisfaction with the government's Civil War policies, led to the growth of the influence of anti-Communists in the local soviets.

At the fifth guberniia congress of soviets that opened on 15 June 1919, only 42 percent of the delegates supported the New Regime. A Soviet source tells us that enemies, "who appeared at the Congress disguised as partyless delegates, tried to persuade [the peasants] to follow them [the enemies], and used the fact that many peasant delegates understood politics poorly. On behalf of the faction of partyless, which they [the enemies] organized against the communists, and in which, as a matter of fact, left and right SRs, as well as anarchists and mensheviks apparently could be found, they insinuated counterrevolutionary resolutions on the question of supplies and the current moment."[17]

This "moment," however, probably represented the nadir of Bolshevik success. Though the situation appeared precarious, when all was said and done, all Bolshevik Party members who stood as candidates for the executive branch of the provincial government were elected at the conclusion of the meeting.[18] After the congress, agitprop groups were assigned to counter the desertion in the countryside, while aid to the families of Red Army soldiers was increased. Together with intimidation and threats used by the Chekists, these measures appear to have stopped desertion from the Red Army and to have deterred any large-scale uprising.[19]

When, in October 1919, at the height of Denikin's offensive, the Bolshevik (or Communist) Party organized a "party week" to enlarge its membership, 2,557 people in the province enrolled, 1,303 of whom were inhabitants of the town of Tver'. Although Red Army soldiers and workers together accounted for 80 percent of the new memberships, more than 16 percent were peasants. This was a very good showing in comparison to the rest of the Bolshevik territory in Russia, where, on average, peasants represented only 7 percent of the new members. Perhaps the increase in Bolshevik membership shows the burgeoning support for the New Regime, but the population in general continued to suffer: during the following winter, famine, cold, and epidemics plagued the guberniia.[20]

When the Communist victory in the Civil War came in sight, the number of party members in the guberniia surpassed 10,000; the provincial organization sent ten delegates to the Ninth Party Congress in March 1920, one of whom was A.A. Zhdanov, a future secretary of the Central Committee.[21] Political opposition outside the party was effectively repressed before 1921. But until the Tenth Party Congress of that year, political dissent was tolerated within the party. In 1920 and 1921 the adherents of the Workers' Opposition and the Democratic Centralists voiced their opposition to the Bolshevik leadership's policies.[22] In Tver' province, the support for these oppositional factions was low among Communist peasants, artisans, and employees, who together made up 63 percent of total party membership. Bolshevik factory workers, however, expressed a more critical attitude towards authoritarian industrial management and party leadership than other Communists. Vyshnii Volochek was one of the most industrialized towns of Tver' guberniia, with a long-established "proletariat"; textile factories had already appeared there around 1860. It was there that in February 1921 a tough battle was waged between a group (or groups) that defended "anarcho-syndicalist platforms" and those who apparently defended the "Leninist" line at a local party conference.[23] The "proletariat" and its "vanguard" had begun to drift apart.

The decree on party unity at the Tenth Party Congress made even inner-party opposition virtually impossible after March 1921. At the same congress, the New Economic Policy (NEP) was announced. The government was forced to abandon its oppressive policy towards the countryside because of growing peasant resistance. In Central Russia, the most outspoken example of such resistance was the celebrated Antonov rebellion in Tambov province. Peasant rebellions also erupted in Tver' guberniia; at least one such "green" revolt occurred in the uezd of Novotorzhok.[24]

THE NEP PERIOD

Between 1914 and 1922, perhaps twenty-five million people died as a result of World War I, the Civil War, and the subsequent famine in the former Russian Empire.[25] Tver' province was, to some extent, spared the worst effects because most of the fighting during the Civil War bypassed it; the catastrophic famine of 1921–22 did not rage as vehemently here as in other areas of Russia. The exact death toll between 1914 and 1922 is difficult to establish, but perhaps at least 10 percent of the provincial population perished. The Civil War left the guberniia economically prostrate: there were shortages of grain, salt, and matches. Bartering had become the preponderant way of trading.[26]

The introduction of the New Economic Policy in 1921 led to a gradual recovery. From the summer of 1921, terror perpetrated by Cheka detachments, Red Army soldiers, and Communists subsided as well, although, as Aleksandr Solzhenitsyn has pointed out, during the early 1920s, Orthodox priests were put on trial in Tver'.[27] From the moment of their coup d'état, in fact, the Bolsheviks relentlessly assaulted the Church. But although organized religion was never left in peace by the Bolshevik authorities in the 1920s, it would be wrong to conclude that the attacks on religion automatically further undermined the popularity of the regime. Before the revolution, peasants and workers often considered priests and monks as agents of the tsarist government who lived off the fruits of their labour. In the countryside particularly, many semi-pagan traits of popular religion and tradition were unfavourably judged by the Church hierarchy.

Apart from harassment of the prerevolutionary aristocracy and the assault on the Church, the state's interference in the life of its citizens generally lessened after 1921.[28] A certain tranquillity reigned in the guberniia during the 1920s. The struggle for Lenin's succession hardly made an impression on the great majority of the provincial population who were living in the countryside (90 percent in 1923); most were engaged in rebuilding a life they imagined to have existed before 1914, or even before 1905. This quiet interlude found expression in an enormous rise of the birthrate. In the years from 1926 to 1928, natality reached between eighteen and twenty-one births per thousand inhabitants, while in 1913 it had amounted to only eleven per thousand. Still, natality in Tver' province lagged far behind the overall Union birthrate, which was nearly forty-five in 1927.[29]

Only at the end of 1927 did the number of industrial workers surpass that of 1913, and in the same year industrial output was for the first time significantly higher than in 1913 (23 percent).[30] In early 1929, the ranks of industrial workers swelled to 58,000, indicating a further acceleration of industrialization in the second half of the 1920s. But the lot of the factory workers remained unenviable even after they had supposedly become Russia's dictators: wages remained low, diet deficient, and housing circumstances primitive; many workers fell victim to diseases as a result.[31]

In 1923, 26,000 unemployed resided in the guberniia, almost as many as were employed in industry. Towards the end of the 1920s, before the great changes of 1929 and 1930, the level of unemployment began to fall: 23,700 people were registered as unemployed on 1 October 1926, and 12,000 on 1 October 1928. Workdays were relatively short during most of the 1920s, because of a low demand for many of the industrial goods produced by the provincial factories. For example, in 1928 a working day in the glass industry amounted to six hours.[32] Economic devastation resulting from World War I, the Revolution, and the Civil War was only slowly overcome. In the middle of the 1920s the most important field of industry remained textiles, accounting for 80 percent of the total factory production in the province. In the cotton mills, most of the workers were women. The share of the "means of production" (the manufacturing of industrial machinery) amounted to a mere 1.1 percent of total output.[33]

In the NEP period, most of the internal wholesale and retail trade belonged to private individuals. The NEP created possibilities for private trading, but in the course of the 1920s the private merchant and shopkeeper had to compete more and more with consumers' cooperatives. At the same time, the private trader's freedom of action was being restricted towards 1929.[34] Handicrafts had undergone an enormous decline because of the prolonged period between 1917 and 1922 when work and bread were scarce in the towns and because the demand for artisans' products had declined as well. Former handicraft workers returned to agricultural work; only the few who produced for the villages' small demand remained in business.[35]

The habit of working on the side regained popularity during the NEP: at least 45,000 people resumed their trade in the villages, and toward 1926 more than 124,000 inhabitants in the guberniia were migratory workers (otkhodniki). In 1927, roughly one-third of all rural households added to their income with one or more members practising a non-agricultural occupation. Farming failed to provide an adequate livelihood for many rural dwellers.[36] Before 1914 peasants left not only for the towns within Tver' guberniia but also for towns outside it, for Moscow and St Petersburg in particular. The troubled times from 1914 to 1921 temporarily reversed this trend, but the nomadic urge returned in the 1920s, while several tens of thousands of migratory workers chose to settle down permanently in the towns.[37]

Country dwellers' migration to urban areas has persisted until our own time: while the oblast' had fewer inhabitants in 1991 than in the 1920s (1.67 million compared to 2.24 million in 1926), the capital Tver' had more than 450,000 inhabitants, four and a half times as many as in 1926.[38] Obviously, Soviet industrialization and the gruesome rural life resulting from collectivization were causes of some urbanization, but migration to the towns had started before 1917 or 1929. The process resembles migratory movements in other industrialized countries during the nineteenth and twentieth centuries, but war, collectivization, and the Ezhovshchina would cause a remarkably steep decline in the Tver' region.[39]

On the eve of collectivization, the party was more disturbed by the perception that, after the land distribution of 1917–18, almost all peasants, rich and poor, had become small "capitalists" while remaining indifferent to Communist ideas, than by actual "kulak" activity or by the procurement crisis that was taking shape. Almost all peasants were inimical to any state interference in their affairs.[40] Altrichter actually discerns a trend in the 1920s towards a levelling of the difference between rich and poor in the countryside. Certainly, no polarization was developing between "kulaks" and the rest of the peasantry. The peasants were wary of the danger of excelling, because prosperity was a ground for suspicion: one might be stigmatized as a kulak as a result, which led already before 1929 to a loss of the right to vote for the local soviets.[41]

What really worried the party brass was the awareness that the countryside was almost outside its control.[42] It was thought that the peasants' resistance to cooperating with the state and their adherence to a production level geared to satisfy their own households' limited needs prevented production of a sufficiently large surplus to finance the party's ambitious industrialization plans. Radical measures were needed to induce the peasants to change their minds, forcing them to collaborate – enthusiastically, it was hoped by the more naive party members – with the accelerated building of socialism. Stalin apparently perceived the violence of collectivization as the only possible way to change the antagonistic peasant mentality. He might have had the illusion that after collectivization the peasants would be magically reborn as model collective farmers who would go on to selflessly dedicate their lives to the fulfillment and overfulfillment of the state-ordained plan in expectation of the radiant future of socialism and communism.

The belief that the peasants would soon see the light, following their entry into kolkhozy, was certainly not Stalin's alone. Many of the rural activists who enforced collectivization seem to have thought along the same lines. But even if the peasants did not understand the purpose of the agricultural rationalization, it would at least be easier to extort the surplus necessary to finance the ambitious industrialization plans and recruit labour for the expanding industry from the collective farms than from the small private production units of the single-household farms. In many ways collectivization would break the peasants' will, even though for a long while old habits and some traits of independence survived among them.[43]

The quiet interlude came to a close in 1928: at the end of October, the first guberniia conference of poor peasants' (bedniaki) groups took place, "uncovering a perversion of the class line" and of the party's policies in the countryside. Those dubbed kulaks are said to have countered by threatening the activist members of these groups in several uezdy during the winter of 1928–29. Until autumn, affairs did not escalate any further.[44] By the end of 1928, the guberniia party organization began to feel the cold wind blowing from Moscow: the Central Committee issued a resolution condemning a party conference in Vyshnii Volochek uezd for infringements of internal party democracy. The uezd representative to the gubkom was dismissed. It seems that the party bosses of Vyshnii Volochek defended the continuation of NEP policy but were overruled by the Central Committee in favour of a less conciliatory line towards the peasantry as proposed by a minority among the uezd party leaders.[45] Already by October 1928, seventeen leading volost' workers in the guberniia were released from their duties for "distortion of the class line and the politics of the party in the countryside."[46] The real defeat of the so-called Right Opposition occurred during the following year; the victors celebrated by unleashing the collectivization of agriculture in a rash and extremely brutal manner.

The crucial outcome of the radical transformation that was imposed during the 1930s was a society driven by a permanent and universal fear of persecution.[47] Only briefly interrupted during World War II, until Stalin's death the regime of the Communist Party could always rely on the threat of arrest to coax the Russians into conformity. After Stalin's death the anxiety gradually abated, but the renewed brutality of Stalin's last years left within Soviet society a legacy strong enough to prevent any large-scale deviation from the norm imposed from above for more than a generation. I must therefore set out to trace the origins of this paranoid atmosphere that engulfed the Soviet Union during the 1930s.

COLLECTIVIZATION

Although the all-out drive for collectivization began only in the winter of 1929–30, the first steps were taken in the fall of 1927. Grain deliveries had fallen far short of expectations, and for the first time since the activities of grain-requisition units during the Civil War, detachments composed of soviet, party, and OGPU representatives were sent into the countryside to find grain.[48] During the next autumn, the procurement crisis recurred because of a bad harvest, and in early 1929 the state once more organized forced requisitions.

In 1928 and early 1929, altercations took place between peasants and the authorities, and there were peasant revolts against the confiscations.[49] By the late 1920s, as we have seen, the party began to purge local authorities who advocated a "conciliatory" line. As it had done in the earlier delivery campaigns, the state tried, through the mediation of the village soviets, to exert most of the pressure on the richer farmsteads when it ordained its initial procurement quotas for the winter of 1929–30. This strategy, however, would oblige the authorities to remain dependent on the peasantry's cooperation; to avoid this, the Communist leadership decided to make a radical switch. The solution comprised all-out collectivization of agriculture and "de-kulakization."[50]

In Tver' province, even some people possessing one cow were dispossessed of everything they owned. Loss of voting rights was often a prelude to further repression. The internally exiled kulaks (the "third category," that is, those liable to the mildest treatment for the crime of belonging to the wrong class) would sometimes be organized into forced labour battalions to log, build roads, and the like.[51] One such victim was Nikolai Mironovich Mironov, a rural dweller of the area around Udoml'ia, not far from Vyshnii Volochek. In his district, perhaps five hundred people were de-kulakized during the 1929–30 wave.[52] Mironov was de-kulakized by the so-called poor peasants (bednota, or bedniaki) of the commune Moldino in February 1930, when his property was confiscated on the initiative of local authorities. A communal house for the newly formed collective was built from the logs of Mironov's house.

Mironov's family was evicted from their home, all property confiscated, and he was forced to resettle elsewhere as a khutorianin.[53] When the first wave of collectivization had abated, Mironov tried to appeal to the rural soviet of his village in Udoml'ia district for the restitution of his voting rights. In May 1931, his request was rejected because he had owned a "kulak farm" (kulatskoe khoziastvo). He subsequently worked in Rybinsk, then returned home, and bombarded the authorities with requests that justice should be done. The end came in 1937, when he was convicted by a troika as an "anti-Soviet element" and "enemy of the people." His sentence entailed "no rights of correspondence," a euphemistic phrase at the time, indicating that the convict was to be executed. The authorities apparently became fed up with the bothersome Nikolai Mironovich and decided to get rid of him at a time when old scores could be settled. Mironov's daughter was finally informed that her father had been posthumously rehabilitated on 16 January 1989, during the second wave of rehabilitations of Stalin's victims.

Within the rural area around Tver', fifteen thousand people lost the right to vote, 3.8 percent of the total number of voters. In an account written during the Khrushchev era, it was admitted (along the lines of Stalin's *Pravda* article "Dizzy with Success") that "erroneously" some seredniaki (middle peasants) were de-kulakized. The arbitrariness of the process is obvious when one compares Mironov's fate to that of the father of M.M. Kozenkova-Pavlova, who owned two cows, two horses, and much land.[54] She remembered that, when in 1933 [the year is probably not accurate] a kolkhoz was organized in her father's village, he somehow avoided de-kulakization because two relatives were factory workers. Likewise the father of A.K. Sumugina-Shepeleva was saved because one of his sons was a party member. In a similar manner in every village, popular members of the community survived despite their wealth, while those who were envied for their wealth or were otherwise unpopular were persecuted. The worst treatment was meted out to those households that were deported outside the borders of their own province. During the early 1930s (probably in 1931), the household of the parents of A.E. Malysheva was de-kulakized when she was a baby. The family was deported to Siberia, where they had to camp in the open for twelve days. Her brother died of exposure there, and her father was subsequently executed in 1937.[55]

The state shirked the responsibility of supplying farms with machinery by proposing the liquidation of the richer (kulak) households and the transfer of their equipment to the kolkhozy. For example, in Likhoslavl' raion in February 1930, 270 kulaks were expropriated and lost their tools, equipment, and all their livestock, after which their property was transferred to the "indivisible funds" (communal ownership) of the kolkhozy.[56] The poor and middle peasants (bedniaki and seredniaki) were made to join the collectives with promises, threats, and force. Their property also became part of the indivisible funds of the kolkhoz, after which it was rendered difficult or impossible for the owners to retrieve their share from it. Rules laid down for the funds dealt with kolkhoz property, production, investment, and consumption, effectively taking any decisions about their former possessions out of the hands of the individual peasants.[57]

Soviet historians of the Brezhnev period portray "kulak-propaganda" as the ground for the widespread slaughter of cattle that occurred at this time, but a far more likely cause was the threat of cattle confiscation by the kolkhozy, combined with the regime's promise of machinery to substitute for the cattle. Thus the peasants of Likhoslavl' raion brought 62 percent more cattle to the slaughterhouse in November 1929 than in September of the same year, while in the Kalinin/Tver' rural raion, the number of cattle would continue to decrease until 1935. Realizing the danger of resisting by refusing to join the kolkhoz, some decided to join them in order to distract the authorities' attention from other illegal practices they were involved in. These "pseudocommunes" (of Baptists, for instance) were subsequently exposed.[58]

Since a number of men were working as itinerant artisans or seasonal workers, the authorities had to apply pressure specifically on those women who took care of the family farm. Women's significance in agriculture had increased since before 1914 and was sustained after collectivization; for instance, in the fall of 1932, among 5,886 kolkhoz shock-workers (exemplary collective farmers) in the raion of Bezhetsk, 3,976 were women.[59] Opposition by peasant women to collectivization was sometimes mixed with protests against the persecution of Orthodox priests and the closure of the village church. Women in the countryside began to turn away from religion only after the establishment of the collective-farm system. Even so, not all were opposed: M.K. Chesnokova maintained that she immediately joined the kolkhoz in 1929, when she was seventeen. She had lost her father and she and her mother were probably classified as bedniaks, or poor peasants. For Chesnokova and her mother, the collective guarantee of the socialized farm for the well-being of its members had great appeal: a surrogate was found for the father's income in the family budget. The fact that mother and daughter were both devout Orthodox believers did not prevent them from welcoming collectivization.

The small number of Communists and the weakness of the government in the countryside hindered the collectivization movement in Tver' province. In 1929 the number of collective farms rose from 210 on 1 January to 492 on 1 July, but still comprised a mere 2 percent of all peasant households.[60] The situation reflected the unpopularity of the Bolshevik Party and its policies: few peasants signed up for the collective farm of their own volition. In Tver' okrug, where the situation was probably more favourable than in the other three okrugs of the former guberniia, there were 103 rural party cells, with a total of only 1,242 Communists among several hundreds of thousands of nonparty village dwellers.

Presently, on the instigation of Moscow, the local party leadership introduced schemes to collectivize certain raions completely by 1933 and resorted to force to persuade the reluctant peasantry to join the collective farms. Rather utopian plans cropped up, one of which deemed it feasible to create a huge agro-industrial complex in Likhoslavl' raion.[61] Resistance to the collectivization drive increased: activists were threatened, beaten, and sometimes assassinated. In Bezhetsk okrug more than fifty "terrorist" acts were registered in the last months of 1929. In four months, during the autumn and winter of 1929–30, more than nine hundred people were brought to trial here in connection with "terrorism." "Counterrevolutionary groups" were formed. Arson and the slaughter of cattle proliferated.[62]

Despite, or perhaps because of, this popular resistance to collectivization, local authorities became "dizzy with success" by December 1929: three raions of the Tver' okrug promised each other, by way of "socialist competition," to have their territory fully collectivized before the 1930 spring sowing.[63] Industrial workers began to propagate the virtues of the collective farms around the beginning of 1930. Two hundred industrial workers from the town of Tver' were sent with some fanfare into the countryside of the surrounding okrug to lead the collective farm movement.[64] Activists from Moscow, Tula, Smolensk, Briansk, Iaroslavl', and Ivanovo also joined in the collectivization drive in the four okrugs. In Rzhev okrug, 187 Communists and Komsomols were sent into the countryside, 36 of whom were women.[65] The idealism of the urban activists stood in sharp contrast to the cynicism and antagonism of the peasantry. Mironov's case indicates that the offer of rewards and the avalanche of arrests of those dubbed kulaks made most villagers enter the collective farm in this initial wave of all-out collectivization.

In early 1930 workers' activists were involved in setting up the first machine tractor stations (MTS); workers donated part of their pay to equip them. In 1932, there were about twenty MTS in the area of the future Kalinin Oblast'. A Soviet source says, somewhat euphemistically, that the workers' involvement was conducive not only to the most effective use of the agricultural machinery but also to showing "models of a high organization of labour to the kolkhozniks."[66] The MTS was initially very poorly equipped with either harvest combines or tractors. In fact, the stations served the purpose of an enforcement agency of Communist rural policy. As Robert Conquest observes, the

MTS "was seen as a node of proletarian consciousness, headed by party officials and staffed by workers, and was given considerable powers over the kolkhozes it served."[67]

On 6 February 1930 the Tver' okruzhkom ordered collectivization to be completed in the spring of 1930, that is, three years earlier than the Central Committee required for Tver' okrug. In the middle of February 1930, already 70 percent of the households were collectivized in the okrug of Tver', and on 1 March, 78 percent. Thus Tver' okrug surpassed the level of collectivization of the whole country, which stood at 58 percent in March 1930.[68] It should be noted that collective farms were rather ill-defined: the basic criterion according to which the farms were categorized as such was the surrender of privately owned tools, land, and animals to the collective. Collective agricultural labour and the planning of collective sowing, haying, harvesting, or ploughing was likely to be in an embryonic state. The height of the wave of collectivization occurred during winter; the operation of the farms had not been tested in any meaningful sense by early March, for agricultural work stood almost at a standstill during the winter.

While ever more peasants were persuaded or forced to join the collectives, resistance increased concurrently. This resistance was portrayed by official Soviet sources at the time and later as the work of the class enemy. According to the Soviet myth of collectivization, "[i]n the Tver' countryside the kulaks conducted malicious anti-soviet agitation against the kolkhozy, killed kolkhoz activists, burned kolkhoz property, inflicted damage on the kolkhoz lands, privateered, and destroyed the kolkhoz cattle."[69]

The snowball was transforming into a veritable avalanche, and drastic action was needed to avoid a disaster. The chaotic situation is summed up by a Soviet source in the following manner:

Socialization of all small animals and domestic fowl took place against common sense in the Likhoslavl', Tolmachi, Emel'ianovo, and Novotorzhok raions. Efforts to create giant kolkhozy and communes were undertaken. In various places voices were heard which deemed it unnecessary to have rural soviets in the areas of all-out collectivization. The harmful line on the withering away of the rural soviets was most pronounced in the raion of Rameshki. A chairman of one of the rural soviets in that raion gave the executive of the rural artel' all records and printed matter after a kolkhoz had been organized.[70]

Official Soviet sources, obviously understating the degree of resistance, list unrest among peasants in a number of raions.[71] Even among party members, reluctance can be observed to participate wholeheartedly in the effort to herd as many peasants as possible into the collective farms before spring sowing.[72]

After Stalin had called off the drive for full-scale collectivization in early March 1930, peasants abandoned the kolkhozy. Leading party workers were released from their duties.[73] The authorities now fed the population the wisdom that many peasants, in particular the seredniaks, had not yet been "ripe" for the radical transformation that was attempted from December to March of 1929 and 1930. A few of those middle peasants who had been mistakenly held for kulaks received their property back after Stalin's cautioning.[74]

The collective farms had been ill-conceived, without much of a management plan, and enforced upon unwilling subjects. The peasants had slaughtered much of their livestock before joining the farms, while after the formation of a kolkhoz, they had little idea of how to start with "socialist" cultivation of the land. The collective farm thus proved very unpopular: according to one Soviet source, in early May of 1930 only 4.6 percent of the peasant households were still collectivized in Tver okrug.[75] The peasants voted with their feet for a return to traditional ways of farming.

This massive retreat from collective farming would prove temporary, with only a handful of individual farmers surviving by the late 1930s. After March 1930, farming could not be taken up again by individual peasant households in the same manner as before the winter of 1929: many of their draught animals had been slaughtered, and the return of collectivized tools and land was difficult to implement. The different methods applied from the autumn of 1930 onward to pressure peasants to abandon private farming were of even greater significance for the ultimate "triumph" of the collective farms: kolkhozy paid significantly fewer taxes to the state than the individual peasants, while delivery quotas were increased to a level that rendered private farming impossible.[76] Already in 1931 a renewed wave of collectivization swept most raions in the former guberniia of Tver': in Bezhetsk raion that year the proportion of collectivized households rose from 3.2 percent to 69.9 percent, and in Kalinin raion from 3 percent to 50 percent. At the end of the First Five Year Plan (December 1932), the number of collectivized households in each raion was 70 percent or more. Thus, two and a half years after the excessive first wave of collectivization had been criticized and discontinued in early March 1930, collectivization in Kalinin raion (part of the former Tver' okrug) was again at the same level. When, in July 1934, the taxes and delivery quotas for individual peasants were once more increased, collectivization of all peasants' households began to near completion rapidly.[77]

In this province before 1929, subsistence agriculture provided for the basic needs of the household; the peasants were not disposed to produce a large surplus that could be sold on the market. Crop cultivation and animal husbandry were traditional, and the resulting output low. Many families sent one of their members away to seasonal work in the towns to add some money to the family budget and purchase goods that the peasants could not, or did not, produce themselves.

The authorities' rationale for collectivization might have seemed sound. Theoretically, mechanization of the production process and efficient organization of labour create high agricultural yields and free work-hands for industry. In practice, however, economic rationalization of agriculture failed. For example, shefstvo, the factories' patronage over collective farms (involving technical assistance and help with sowing, weeding, and reaping) was already widespread in 1931, when more than a thousand workers and employees in Kimry raion were sent into the fields to pitch in with harvesting.[78]

Strict order was imposed when propaganda failed to convince peasants of the great advantage of the collective farms. In 1932 the leadership resorted to the threat of force to discipline the kolkhozniks, particularly by the Central Executive Committee and Sovnarkom decree on "the protection of the property of state enterprises, kolkhozy and cooperatives and the strengthening of public (socialist) ownership" of 7 August 1932.[79]

Figures concerning the number of arrests in the countryside given by the highest provincial party leader in early 1938 indicate that coercion was a key cause of the peasants' enrolment in the collectives. Free movement within the USSR was prohibited: the introduction of the passport regime in December 1932 was aimed particularly at keeping the peasantry in their villages and collective farms.[80] Several party workers responsible for agriculture were sacrificed as scapegoats in the the purges for the failure of collectivization. In the Ezhovshchina, scores of references were made to wrecking activities that had allegedly hindered agriculture from achieving satisfactory results.[81]

Collectivization had come close to completion by 1937 in the re-created Tver' province, now called Kalinin oblast'. At the beginning of the second Five Year Plan (1933) the share of kolkhoz and sovkhoz lands was 56.7 percent of the sown area; 40 percent was still in the hands of individual peasants.[82] In 1934, 23 percent of peasant households were not yet collectivized, but in 1937 the individual peasantry had dwindled to 5 percent of the total households active in agriculture.

This was partially due to the beneficial effect of the introduction of a model statute, the Ustav, in 1935.[83] It guaranteed Soviet peasants rights to the cultivation of a small plot of private land as well as to a few personally owned farm animals to complement their income or diet (crops from the private plot and from the animals were heavily taxed, nevertheless). This last spurt of collectivization was, however, again accompanied by further repression, judging from the rate of arrests in these years in the countryside.[84]

In early 1933 only 34 machine tractor stations existed on the territory of the future oblast'; halfway through 1937 there were already 119, close to the number deemed necessary. Still, tractors supplied hardly more than 20 percent of all draught power in the oblast'. Horses remained the preponderant source of power.[85]

In January 1938, an obkom plenum was convoked once more to address the disappointing agricultural performance. Finally the cause had been discovered: deliberate wrecking by enemies of the people.[86]

Things were apparently looking up, because of "the crushing defeat delivered by the Central Committee of the VKP(b), the obkom of the VKP(b), the organs of the NKVD, and the local party organizations of Kalinin oblast', to counterrevolutionary nests, trotskyite-bukharinite spies, wreckers and diversants, to kulak and other enemy groups through whose base wrecking a serious loss was inflicted on the cause of socialist construction in Kalinin oblast'."[87]

These "enemies of the people" were accused of sabotaging socialist agriculture by all kinds of means, such as wrecking the planning of sown areas, confusing matters with respect to crop seeds and crop rotation, neglecting agro-techniques, causing the breakdown of the machine-tractor parks in a number of tractor stations, undermining and opposing the party line in the procurement system, distorting the regulations of the Ustav of 1935, or exterminating cattle.[88] The plenum prohibited oblast' and raion party organizations from increasing on their own authority the plans made by higher-placed organs. As was the habit, most of the other suggested remedies would increase the party's control over agriculture.[89] Little changed for the better in almost all aspects of agriculture in the first half of 1938: ailing flax production and an anemic animal husbandry ranked as the two most important defective agricultural branches at the third party conference of the oblast'.[90]

Matters had still not improved half a year later. The situation by then was sufficiently serious to prompt the Central Committee to issue a resolution in early 1939 condemning the obkom's vast shortcomings in agricultural management and to recommend corrections. The central party leadership now announced that several raikoms distorted their district's agricultural performance by concentrating on the spotty achievement of record results – which smacks of the Stakhanov method of exaggerating – while generally neglecting the diffusion of improved agricultural methods among the collective farms. This practice of concealing the truth was condemned at the fourth provincial party conference in February 1939.[91]

In the party's perception, one of the most fundamental problems plaguing agriculture was the lack of Communists in the countryside. Existing rural party organizations failed to exert the control over the farms necessary to boost results. Detachments of more capable and experienced Communist activists were regularly sent around the rural party cells to impart the correct socialist agricultural methods in the later 1930s. But the roughly 10,000 rural Communists of March 1940 (less than a year earlier there had only been 6,670) were still far too few to have much impact on the almost 13,000 kolkhozy of the oblast'.[92]

Some aid undoubtedly was forthcoming from the Komsomol's primary organizations, of which there were more than 4,500 among the kolkhozy in March 1940.[93] A major ideological offensive had been launched in the countryside with the propaganda for the USSR Supreme Soviet elections of 12 December 1937. Komsomol members from the towns and larger settlements of the oblast' descended upon the villages in the countryside with agitfurgony (agitation carts). On the collective farms they held discussions with the peasants and gave concerts but this propaganda offensive had a very marginal influence on agricultural results, as we can see from the strong criticism of 1938; one imagines that at best a handful of kolkhozniks were deluded by the election promise of the foundation of a genuine democratic socialist state as laid down in the Constitution of 1936 and were swayed by it to dedicate themselves more intensively to the socialized sector of the collective farm. It may be doubted that even these zealous Komsomols made much of an impression.[94]

Meanwhile, Brandin, the provincial Komsomol leader, noticed once again in 1937 that not all Young Communists could be trusted as worthy examples for the peasants. This complaint would be repeated by numerous and diverse voices in the Kalinin party organization after the war; consequently, the value of the Komsomol's presence was less than its numbers suggest.[95]

In 1939, still more than 50,000 khutory (homesteads located outside the central kolkhoz village) were counted in the oblast', proving that the completion of collectivization had not yet been achieved, despite subsequent utterances to the contrary. If the average household size was 3.6 (a reasonable estimate), this would mean that, of those engaged in collective farming in that year, still at least 180,000 people (more than 10 percent of the rural population) lived outside the central villages of the kolkhozy. Thus, it was more difficult for the authorities to control them, and they tried to, and could, escape part of their duties on the collective farm. To bring them into the fold, most of the khutoriane were resettled in houses within the kolkhoz villages in the spring of 1940. Despite all this, even by 1940, 3.3 percent of the peasant households of the oblast' were not yet collectivized at all.[96]

On the whole, the promise of mechanized, rationalized agriculture as a result of collectivization remained unfulfilled by 1940. In that year still less than 50 percent of plowing and just 5 percent of spring sowing and 13 percent of sowing of winter crops was done with machinery. Flax production, particularly, relied on manual labour long after 1945.[97]

The war would render the Tver' countryside unrecognizable in many respects. In the western parts of the oblast', most of the kolkhoz property would be destroyed and agriculture ruined. The east escaped severe war damage, but there would be a huge labour shortage owing to the men's departure to the front. After their army service, few returned to settle permanently on the land.[98]

At the end of the war, when victory was assured, first party secretary Ivan Pavlovich Boitsov made clear that the later 1930s were to be remembered as a time of unprecedented agricultural success, halted only because the war wreaked havoc: "[a]fter improving their organizational, economical and political relations, the oblast' kolkhozy developed all branches of kolkhoz production and increased their income. Every year the value of the trudoden' [labour day] grew. In 1940, for every trudoden' in the oblast' two kilograms of grain and three kilos of potatoes were paid."[99]

This picture of prosperity does not agree with the facts: Why was Boitsov overstating the prosperity of the kolkhoz system before the war? First, he was attempting to remind his audience of the Communist dogma of the general superiority of collective farms. Second, he was trying to hold up to the leading party workers of the oblast' an imaginary target to rival and surpass in the postwar reconstruction. Third, Kolakowski's argument (discussed in the introduction, above) may provide part of the explanation: Boitsov and his comrades, euphoric from their defeat of the German invaders, may have been unable to remember a truthful image of the first decade of collective farming in the province.

THE EZHOVSHCHINA

"Kalinin oblast' occupies a rather convenient place for diversionist work, wrecking work, because it is located along the border, on the one hand, and, on the other hand, between the two capitals. Although we do not have a Donbass, we do have wreckers," stated M.E. Mikhailov, the provincial boss of Kalinin province at the February-March Plenum of the Central Committee in 1937.[100] The plenum signified the beginning of the most intensive period of the Great Purge, when N.I. Ezhov headed the People's Commissariat of Internal Affairs from September 1936 to December 1938. Despite his honest confession, Mikhailov, the first secretary of the Kalinin party organization since its inception, fell victim to the NKVD "meat grinder" within a year.

There cannot be a shadow of a doubt that the Communist regime could have spared the lives of millions who perished in the collectivization, the Great Purge, and World War II by chosing an alternative route to modernization. The absence of any benefit from the slaughter of the Great Purge makes it, especially, the perfect illustration of the gratuitous violence unleashed in Stalin's revolution.

Part of the reason for the extreme application of coercion towards the leading cadres during the Great Purge was undoubtedly a misguided effort to improve, by way of repression, the efficiency of the economy, the government, and the party machine.[101] The classic official rationale for the purges was given in 1948 by Politburo member Voznesensky in his book on the USSR's wartime economy.[102] He maintained that the purges had removed "the roots of parasitic classes and groups" from society. The "cleansing" had forged a unified entity of the people, supposedly strong enough to withstand any outside attack, which was proven subsequently by the victory over Nazi Germany in World War II. However, this was a justification a posteriori, because during the Ezhovshchina an imminent German attack did not seem to be anticipated, in spite of the spy mania expressed in the show trials.[103]

The terror of both the Great Purge and the repressions of the first half of the 1930s might have provided an additional advantage for the regime: the purge was so widespread (Conquest justifiably calls it a "social phenomenon") that no one failed to witness some of its manifestations.[104] The horrible memory of it would have made anyone think twice about voicing criticism of the regime. This "benefit," however, would not be openly applauded by Stalin or any of his cronies. It would seem that the purges served no positive purpose at all for the country; on the contrary, the killings threw both defence and economy into disarray. The chaos, confusion, and terror of these years is obvious from the example of Kalinin province; nevertheless, even here a complete picture eludes the researcher.[105]

The investigation of the scope and nature of the Stalinist repression is hindered by the disappearance of documents on the purges and other crimes of the era, while there is evidence that official judicial prosecution did not always take place: N.A. Kotov witnessed the rearrest of many of his fellow villagers at the time of the Great Purge.[106] Kotov maintains that no investigation or trial ever took place before they were, once more, shipped off to the camps. A.N. Lukovkin was sent to the camps without any form of judicial process. He stated in his testimony in the survey that the same happened with many soldiers who, like him, returned from Finnish captivity after March 1940. In the camps of Norilsk, Lukovkin and his fellow former prisoners of war were handed a ticket indicating whether they had been sentenced to five or eight years. There was nothing in these cases by way of "normal" judicial procedures.

Recently, P.A. Aptekar' corroborated Lukovkin's story when he wrote that "[w]e do not know anything about the further fate of the POWs, who returned home to the Motherland [after the Soviet-Finnish War], except that, in accordance with the directives of the General Staff, they were sent to army camps for political reeducation and a further distribution into units or in the reserves. We can only guess at this point, as long as no corresponding documents will be found of the GULAG and NKVD, how much these directives were followed."[107]

The statements of these eyewitnesses and the remarks of Aptekar' cast grave doubts on the accuracy of the documentation used for the recent, supposedly more precise, estimates on the total number of arrests and convictions under Stalin (the estimates keep on changing, meanwhile).[108] Regarding the various estimates of Stalinist victims, the extraordinary juggling with the numbers on Soviet losses during World War II needs to be mentioned. Nobody has yet explained why the number of Soviet citizens killed in the war was suddenly increased from roughly twenty million to twenty-seven million a few years ago. Did Soviet leaders deem it convenient to transfer a large number of purge victims to the category of war victims?[109] In 1992 Oleg Khlevniuk stated that "[as] of now we simply do not know what the total number of repressions is," and we may seriously doubt if we will ever know.[110]

Let us propose that it does not matter if the Great Purge was the period of the greatest frequency of arrests or convictions for political crime under Stalin.[111] The evidence remains inconclusive, for not all relevant documents have been found or inspected, some orders and decisions were probably never written down, and many papers were destroyed. What is glaring about the episode is the utter senselessness of it, even more so than the carnage of "de-kulakization" or the appalling sacrifice of Soviet soldiers on the battlefront during World War II.

The interviews conducted in Tver' for this study give some idea of the effect of the Great Terror on the Russians, but they provide only an impressionistic account of the Ezhovshchina, for no direct questions were asked about the respondents' experiences during the 1930s.[112] As well, a large proportion of (former) Communists participated in the survey – most of whom joined the party after 1937. At times their stubborn belief in the radiant Soviet past made them refrain from befouling the image of the party by mentioning the terror of the Ezhovshchina. Even for most Soviet Communists who survived, the terror unleashed from 1936 to 1938 was a grave error and lingered as a very bad memory. Further explanations for the absence in some of the respondents' answers of any mention of 1937 may be found in their unconscious suppression of the gruesome events, while memories of the Ezhovshchina may have blended with recollections about collectivization and other instances of political persecution. Lastly, few victims of the Great Terror have survived the numerous executions and the atrocious life in the prisons and camps. Thus only one person among the 109 respondents (A.S. Lukovkin) had been a convict, and he was dispatched to the camps only in 1940, long after Ezhov's dismissal as People's Commissar of Internal Affairs.

Nevertheless, in the interviews N.A. Kotov felt it imperative to mention his father's and uncle's arrest, both accused of being kulaks, in 1937. Kotov senior was sentenced to ten years. He was apparently denounced by his fellow villagers after raion authorities had demanded that the kulaks in the village be named. Kotov maintains that, before the war, villagers who had been released from the camps were arrested again, after a brief spell of freedom, around 1937 and transported back to the camps without any investigation or trial. Similarily, the father of A.N. Nikolaev, who was the chairman of a kolkhoz in the village of Iamskaia (Khvoininskii raion, Leningrad oblast'), was arrested in 1937 for anti-Soviet activities. N. Nikolaev was sentenced to ten years of labour camp and served his time in the camps of Karaganda. Half a year after his return home he died. Nikolaev senior had been a "convinced Communist," but it is not clear if he indeed was an actual party member.

What could be established is that several respondents deliberately denied having had any knowledge of the camp system. For some it was a matter of omerta (a code of silence), as in the case of the former oblast' party secretaries Tiaglov and Kondrashov, who at the same time did admit to the threat of imminent arrest during 1937. Arrest was in both cases narrowly avoided by a stroke of luck. Others are even today afraid of sanctions if they divulge too much of their knowledge. For most of their lives, after all, anything they said about these kinds of events could have been and was used against them by the authorities. Who was to say that their interviewers were what they purported to be and not government agents?[113]

The experiences of the entire decade of the 1930s, however, turned out to have been so crucial in the lives of many respondents that they felt it necessary to say something about it during the interviews without being asked directly. Even though about one-fifth of the respondents mentioned the years 1936–38 when noticing arrests of family, friends, acquaintances, or colleagues, the elderly Russians related many more cases of arrest and repression that took place either before or after Ezhov's tenure as head of the NKVD.[114] Quite a few people referred to collectivization when they were asked whether they themselves or their family members had been exposed to political repression. The arrest of his father-in-law during collectivization for refusing to enter the kolkhoz did not restrain A.M. Afanas'ev from becoming a loyal party member. The testimonies in the survey of T.A. Novikova, M.V. Kornetova (who maintains that a quarter of the households in her ancestral village were de-kulakized), V.P. Pimenova, T.I. Bol'shakova, M.K. Chesnokova, and M.A. Sysoeva (whose grand-father was de-kulakized) are evidence of the profound impression collectivization made on the rural population. Naturally, particularly those who saw a relative arrested during collectivization referred to it: the father of E.A. Golubev was arrested in the early 1930s, and Golubev grew up without ever having known him. P.A. Kashinov's uncle was de-kulakized. The father of N.N. Golubeva was arrested in 1933 or 1934, when Golubeva was twelve years old, and died, accord-ing to her, at the construction of the Volga-Baltic canal. His arrest stemmed from the fact that he had been a tsarist army officer (despite his command of a Red Army unit in the Civil War). We have seen how the parents of A.E. Malysheva, who was three years old at the time, were de-kulakized in 1931 and sent to Siberia. Her mother fled twice from exile, and her father once. He was caught in Rzhev and sentenced to six years of imprisonment in 1937. He probably died in the North-Eastern Labour Camps (SVITL) of the NKVD. Her mother lost a son – she had been pregnant when they were de-kulakized – because he froze to death in exile in Siberia.

Documents corroborate that numerous arrests happened in Kalinin oblast' previous to Ezhov's appointment as People's Commissar of Internal Affairs. In March 1938, I.P. Boitsov, newly appointed first secretary of the provincial party, inadvertently admitted to astonishing persecutions, when he spoke of "[a]n enemy attitude towards the soviet, [and] kolkhoz aktiv, and the kolkhoznik was expressed by the fact that, in 1935–37, 59,000 people of the rural aktiv and of the kolkhozniks were convicted. In 1937 the oblast' court reviewed decisions in order to correct wrecking in the judicial practice, and the cases against 2,060 people were discontinued."[115]

The above number of almost 60,000 is startling; considering that during this period probably around 2.6 million people lived in the countryside of the oblast', it would seem that in these few years, which are post-collectivization and partially pre-Ezhovshchina, more than 2 percent of the rural population in Kalinin oblast' was arrested.[116] The momentum of all-out collectivization had begun to abate in the Kalinin region in 1934, when party, soviet, and OGPU workers were instructed to bring the indiscriminate arrests in the countryside to a halt. Local authorities were not discouraged from arresting rural dwellers altogether, but merely warned to be more selective.[117] If Boitsov's numbers are correct, these directives did not lead to any significant changes with respect to arrests; the decrees of the Central Executive Committee immediately after the assassination of Kirov in December of 1934 and the final steps towards full collectivization did apparently lead to a renewed surge of arrests, including the arrest of the 59,000 people in the Tver' countryside mentioned by Boitsov.[118]

It could be argued that Boitsov padded the numbers in order to blacken the record of his predecessors even more. This seems extremely unlikely, for in a speech a few months later at the third oblast' party conference he *understated* the number of arrests within the party elite of the province between June 1937 and July 1938.[119] In the speech of March 1938, from which the previous revealing quotation has been extracted, Boitsov also stated that in 1937 numerous complaints from citizens had been received by the oblast' and raion procuracies about all kinds of illegal proceedings and that "122,000 of the citizens of our oblast' searched for a settlement, for justice, in our court and procuracy organs."[120]

To restore a semblance of order, in or just before March 1938, USSR Procurator-General Andrei Vyshinskii felt obliged to dispatch a special commission to check on the operation of the oblast' procuracy.[121] It appears that in Tver' province overly zealous NKVD and NKIu officials had created a witch hunt by the spring of 1938 that had spun out of control and they called for intervention by the central authorities in Moscow. During 1938 this type of chaos became common almost everywhere in the Soviet Union, ultimately leading to a decree by Stalin and Molotov to reduce the number of arrests drastically.

Popular memory, as recorded in the interviews in the summer of 1992, does not distinguish between the 1936–38 period and the rest of the 1930s. Peasants had been largely coaxed into submission before 1936, but their ultimate end sometimes came in the Ezhovshchina. The Ezhovshchina also involved a further antireligious offensive. According to the testimony of N.V. Kurganova in the survey, around 1937 or 1938 rural soviet workers, who were apparently not always NKVD employees, took away Bibles and icons from the people in her village in Udoml'ia raion.[122] Zealous believers who refused to part with these possessions were probably arrested.

The exact scope of the persecution of those outside the Communist leadership during the Great Purge cannot be conclusively established from extant local party records. Nevertheless, victims unexpectedly surface in the documents. The example of the postwar director of the Kalinin philharmonic orchestra, V.F. Afanas'ev, a party member, may serve as a typical case of the devastating impact of the terror. According to an MGB check in 1947, two of his brothers had been arrested in 1937 and further relatives and in-laws were arrested by the NKVD in Moscow around the same time.[123] Peasants and members of the Soviet intelligentsia were victims of the Ezhovshchina, but the "leading class of Soviet society," the proletariat, was affected by the terror as well, although is difficult to estimate to what degree. G.V. Lubov, who in general during his interview praised the Communist regime, noticed that in Konakovo "before the war workers of the factory, of urban institutions" were arrested by the NKVD. He added that "we were of the opinion, that they were arrested for a reason, as these were people who, through anecdotes, had expressed an anti-Soviet mood."[124]

Peasants and factory workers aside, post-Soviet sources indicate that the Great Purge was indeed very much an attack on the hitherto largely untouchable Communist elite of the oblast'. Within two years, local bosses would be liquidated, sent to camps, or scared into submission by their peers' arrests. The membership of the Communist Party hardly increased during the Great Terror: by July 1938, a three-year increase amounted to around 1,350 people in total, or 1.7 percent annually, which, together with that of the first two war years, represents the lowest period of growth until the 1980s. A pause in accepting new members was another reason for the low increase. It is remarkable that in February 1939 (less than one year later) the party boasted a growth of roughly 24 percent in eight months, while in March 1940 membership reached 52,000, a growth of around 50 percent in one year.[125]

The impact of the Great Terror on the party organization of Kalinin oblast' is somewhat better reflected in the documents than the assault on those outside the Communist Party. Unfortunately, the records are far from complete, consisting mainly of changes (smeny) in the transcription of the stenographic accounts of party obkom meetings, two party conferences, and the protocols for these sessions. It is likely that some of the records on this period were lost during the wartime evacuation of the oblast' party archive, while others could have been deliberately removed.[126] Nevertheless, there is enough in the surviving documents to reconstruct some of the events and hysteria engulfing the party during the Purge.

At the February-March Central Committee Plenum of 1937, Kalinin's party chief M.E. Mikhailov engaged in a public criticism of his fief, promising to follow Stalin's advice to improve matters.[127] Mikhailov's comments indicate that the scope of the persecutions intended was not yet clear to him: the tone of his words seems moderate compared to his extreme utterances of a few months later at the second provincial party conference. Here, in June 1937, Mikhailov's voice seems distinctly more shrill and has already changed to that of a zealous purger.[128] By June, Mikhailov and most of the others who addressed the second party conference had been overtaken by the hysterical mood incited by Moscow. Enemies were spotted everywhere in the province: one after another, speakers tried to outdo each other in denouncing the vile deeds of the vermin. Some tried to save their skin by admitting to a lack of vigilance and promising to step up their watchfulness. For most of those present at the second party conference, these tactics were to no avail. Within half a year, most were under arrest. The zeal of the first secretary of the Kalinin obkom also failed to protect him against the onslaught. Towards the end of 1937, Mikhailov was excluded in absentia as an enemy of the people.[129]

At the conference of June 1937 in Kalinin, the most important reports on the state of affairs in the oblast' were delivered by Mikhailov and NKVD head Dombrovskii. The party and secret police chiefs referred to a whole network of Trotskyite and Rightist groups in the town of Kalinin, headed by Lipshits, Guzenko, Gorov, and other enemies of the people. A thorough purge of the town's party committees was under way by this time, bringing to the fore many young party workers. As a consequence, many women became secretaries of factory party committees in Kalinin for the first time.[130] Many of the candidates for the new obkom to be elected at this 1937 conference, mainly veteran members standing for reelection, were severely attacked in the preelection discussions. The military contingent had to sustain particularly strong criticism, a sign of the beginning of the Red Army purges. The speakers at the conference occasionally mentioned the recent unmasking of Gamarnik, head of the political branch of the army, – although not yet that of Marshal Tukhachevsky. It seems likely that the army commissar Ziuz'-Iakovenko, who remained on the list of candidates for the obkom, was arrested right after the elections. Among other things, he was taken to task at the preelection discussions for having worked as a military attaché in Germany. Ziuz'-Iakovenko disappears without a trace in local archival records and was present neither immediately after the conference at the "organizational" plenum of the obkom nor at any of the following plenums.[131] He received a camp sentence in 1939 and probably did not survive his term.[132] Division commander Stepynin was removed from the list for his ties with the unmasked enemy of the people, Enov, and for his support for the resolution at the Tolmachevskii political-military academy in 1928. This resolution had demanded that the army's political commissars be maintained, an assessment dubbed "trotskyite" in 1937.[133]

Just before the elections of a new obkom at the second party conference, all candidates were obliged to state whether they had ever deviated from the party's general line. At least one individual declined to remain on the list of candidates, declaring himself to be already too busy with his other duties; it is not clear whether this move saved him from arrest.[134] The Komsomol membership, according to Brandin, its first secretary in June 1937, had been similarly infiltrated by "enemies":

Thus, for example, in the October raion at the timber factory a group of Komsomols was discovered, led by a Komsomol-Hitlerite, led by fascists, in effect an underground organization, which in the course of a considerable period engaged in diversionist work at the factory. At the pedagogical *tekhnikum* in Kimry raion, a group of three people was exposed, all three committee members, who waged counterrevolutionary propaganda among the students. In Kalinin, in the medical workers' faculty, a group of Komsomols under the leadership of Sergeev was found, which succeeded in demoralizing the organization. The enemy led the Komsomol organization of the medical workers' faculty to a state of organizational-political disintegration.[135]

Brandin disappeared from the records after the conference in June 1937 (he was "repressed," but survived the camps and died in 1960, according to one source) and was succeeded on recommendations from the Komsomol Central Committee by Karatiaev.[136] In contrast to the party, Komsomol grew substantially during the Great Purge: by mid-1935, it had 35,000 members; less than two years later, 54,000; and in July 1938, already 82,000.

In all, there is documentary evidence for the exclusion of at least 51 members of the oblast' committee between January 1937 and December 1938, most of them labeled "enemies of the people," "members of counterrevolutionary anti-soviet organizations," "trotskyites," "wreckers," saboteurs, or spies.[137] This certainly does not imply that no more than around 50 people, at one time or another obkom members during 1937 and 1938, fell victim to the Ezhovshchina. Former members of the party elite had already been removed from the higher echelons by June 1937; the records are far from complete, and many obkom members disappear without a trace in the documents during this two-year period. This could mean they were transferred to other work without any serious consequences, but it could also signify that they disappeared into the labyrinth of repressions.

The obkom elected at the third oblast' party conference under the auspices of a new first secretary of Kalinin oblast', I.P. Boitsov, included virtually no veterans of the obkom elected by the previous party conference, thirteen months earlier; the fate of many of these veterans remains unclear.[138] A similar cleansing, but on a somewhat smaller scale, probably took place at the second party conference in June 1937, judging from the number of members of the last two pre-conference plenums in 1937 who were not reelected.

Around July 1937 Ezhov ordered the creation of a special judicial board, a troika, to systematize repressions in the oblast': it was composed of Dombrovskii, Rabov, and Bobkov. These three, or another troika that replaced them, were directed by the Central Committee to repress an additional quota of 2,000 people within six weeks in February and the first half of March 1938.[139] Rabov, the successor of Mikhailov as first secretary, enthusiastically helped to fulfill this plan, but nevertheless proved insufficiently fanatical, for in the July 1938 version, as presented by Rabov's successor, Boitsov, to the third provincial party congress, the former oblast' leaders at the time of Ezhov's "additional order," Rabov, Ivanov, and Gusikhin, were accused of "[holding] back the process of unmasking and extirpation of partakers of counterrevolutionary trotskyite-bukharinite bands, placed at the head of the most important parts of party, soviet, cultural, and economic work."[140]

In the official version of the provincial party's past published in the early 1970s, the disgrace of the three, which was staged in March 1938 at an obkom plenum, was judged to have been erroneous.[141] In

March 1938, however, the trio's condemnation was directly supervised by the leadership in Moscow: precisely at this plenary meeting, Politburo member A.A. Andreev and G.M. Malenkov, the head of the Central Committee cadres (personnel) department, made an appearance in Kalinin; it was also the moment at which I.P. Boitsov was elected first secretary of the oblast'.[142] A few months after his appointment, Boitsov accused his immediate predecessor, Rabov, of having, together with Ivanov and Gusikhin, continued the enemy work of Mikhailov and his clique. Though possibly still at liberty in July, Rabov would not have escaped arrest in the end, for Boitsov remarked that "[all] people who most closely surrounded Rabov, with whom he worked for a long period, have been recently unmasked as enemies of the people."[143] In March 1938, Rabov's fellow leader, Ivanov, was attacked for being a "bourgeois-nationalist" in his support of the Karelian minority, an original twist added to the usual accusations of sabotage and spying. The rights of the Karelians were severely curbed during these years, and their autonomous okrug was dissolved in 1939. Perhaps the Soviet-Finnish War influenced this last decision.[144]

After his venomous attack on the disgraced "Rabov gang" at the third party conference in July 1938, Boitsov noted that five of eleven obkomburo members, who had been elected in June 1937, had subsequently been unveiled as enemies of the people: former secretary Mikhailov and former NKVD head Dombrovskii were among them.[145] Boitsov tried to cover up the enormous metamorphosis that the oblast' party leadership had undergone over the previous thirteen months by deflating the number of leaders purged, possibly in order not to shock his audience too much – although many of them must have had some idea of the scale of the repressions.[146] Boitsov's subsequent party career was unharmed by his involvement in these "mistaken" campaigns. He would stay in Kalinin until late 1946 and then be promoted to lead the more important Stavropol krai, where at different times M.A. Suslov and M.S. Gorbachev, too, were groomed.[147]

In conclusion, enough evidence is extant to prove that the majority of the leadership of the province perished in the Great Terror. There are a few exceptions: one example is V.F. Zazulina, who in 1947 worked as head of the organizational and instructor's otdel (department) of the Kushalino raikom. She was the otdel or vice-otdel head of the obkom in the autumn and winter of 1937–38 but was dismissed and assigned low-level work as a reprimand for her close connections with "trotskyites" Mikhailov and Kalygina, according to the 1947 MGB report on her. Indeed, Zazulina must have known both individuals quite well, as she had apparently started working in the obkom apparatus in 1935.[148]

Stalin and Molotov formally called off the purge on 17 November 1938. The troikas in the USSR were dissolved. The height of the terror also came to an end in the Kalinin oblast' with the arrest of the province's five leading NKVD workers in December 1938. Two of the five apparently came off with very benign sentences and were released within three years; we do not know what happened to the other three.[149] The reasons for the order to stop the purges were probably both demographic and economic. Because of the continuous arrests, by late 1938 the population was so depleted that more arrests would have seriously damaged the economy, inasmuch as there was a danger that soon too few people would be free to work, particularly in managerial positions. Moreover, the economy itself was, indeed, damaged by the permanent turnover of cadres in 1937 and 1938, and labour productivity shrank dramatically. Everywhere in the economy, to evade arrest people tried to avoid appointments to positions of responsibility and eschewed making any imaginative decisions that could be construed as a sign of unorthodox thinking.[150] In addition, it is obvious that after two years of indiscriminate arrests, Stalin had made his point. No further universal purge would be unleashed during the rest of Stalin's life. Despite that, significant numbers still landed in jail after Beria succeeded Ezhov in late 1938. The arrests merely became more selective, but they were still frequent enough to perpetuate the atmosphere of fear.

In early 1939, the obkom cadre department and the oblast' NKVD exchanged reports with the NKVD of (Novo)Torzhok raion on the prosecution of excessively zealous purgers in that raion. These reports illustrate the aftermath of the Ezhovshchina. On 21 December 1938, a closed party-Komsomol session of the NKVD directorate of the raion was held, with the following outcome:

The violations of procedural rules have still not been fully eliminated. Individual employees of the militsiia [regular police] raion committee [RKM] still cope poorly with investigative work and are insufficiently familiar with the operations of the militsiia service. The individual workers of the criminal investigation department, BELOUSOV, MATVEEV, and SMIRNOV, were disposed to panicking and defeatism in their work. This is underlined by the fact that criminal proceedings have been instituted against BELOUSOV, MATVEEV, and SMIRNOV; their case is in the hands of the Special Inspection of the raion militsiia committees of the Kalinin oblast'.

Having discussed the question of the prosecution of BELOUSOV, MATVEEV, and SMIRNOV, the general party-Komsomol meeting is of the opinion that:

–they are made answerable for the fact that, in the period of the conduct of the campaign for the elimination of wreckers in society in 1937, they created artificial investigative cases about individual citizens, and arrested them.

–this operation took place under the immediate leadership of the enemies of the people who had penetrated the Kalinin oblast' Direction of the RKM : the head of the NKVD Direction Dombrovskii and the head of the RKM Direction Slonimskii.

–the former head of the raion NKVD department, MIKHAILOV, and the head of the raion militsiia plenipotentiaries, BOGDANOV, supervised directly the elimination of [these anti-Soviet elements] from the raion of Novotorzhok.

–MIKHAILOV and BOGDANOV appear to be in particular guilty of the illegal arrest of citizens and the fabrication of artificial cases. It was these men, who gave the militsiia apparatus the directive to "put pressure to the hilt," and suggested detaining called-up witnesses in the corridor of the raion NKVD department for twenty-four-hour periods.[151]

The chaotic and hysterical situation within the NKVD created by the purges during 1937 is evident from this record. Local NKVD workers in Torzhok lost all sense of proportion and started to round up too many people (at least in the estimation of their successors a year later). The NKVD workers' opinion that their colleagues had misbehaved – although not enough to hold them responsible in a serious way, since they had been under pressure from others higher up – probably found its roots in the aforementioned return to a more routine "revolutionary legality" in late 1938.

The participants in the party-Komsomol meeting of the NKVD of Torzhok raion requested the release of their three misguided coworkers.[152] The case against them and others had already dragged on for a year. To sweeten the pill, apparently conscious that the security police let suspects go only with the greatest reluctance, steps against Mikhailov and Bogdanov were suggested instead. The final outcome of this case remains in shadows; Mikhailov apparently was employed somewhere in the oblast' direction of the NKVD, while Bogdanov had been transferred earlier to the Buriat-Mongol republic.

D.S. Tokarev, NKVD head from early 1939, retained his post (later he became NKGB/MGB chief, while he relinquished his position as NKVD head when the NKVD was split into two people's commissariats during the war) until December 1946, another sign of a return to some kind of routine. He left the Kalinin oblast' when I.P. Boitsov was transferred.[153] Tokarev will remain forever notorious for his role in the Katyn massacre, which once more shows that persecutions were far from discontinued after November 1938.[154]

In Stalin's lifetime, party and security organs, not admitting to any "mistakes" or "exaggerations," preserved a very positive image of the Ezhovshchina. In January 1945, oblast' NKVD boss Pavlov gave a positive appraisal of the events of the 1930s and the role of the NKVD, declaring that "[i]n the period of peacetime construction, our organs protected the productive work of industry, transport, agriculture, etc., from the intrigues of foreign spies and internal enemies. We protected our society from spies, saboteurs, bandits, swindlers, and crooks, [and] ensured social order."[155]

One of the results of the 1930s terror was the enormous expansion of the labour camps in the Soviet Union. Penal institutions for political prisoners were not new to the Tver' area.[156] However, in Soviet times, Kalinin oblast' also "benefitted" from the forced labour of the convicts. In the middle of the 1930s, convicts of Dmitrovskoi lager' (camp) were building the Moskva-Volga canal near Konakovo. In all, 196,000 zeki (camp inmates) helped to build the canal. It was finished by the middle of 1937, although additions or improvements to the waterway continued until at least the end of 1938.[157]

After the dissolution of the Nilova Hermitage on Stolbny Island in Lake Seliger, near Ostashkov, in the early years of Soviet power, its secularized buildings first had accommodated a workhouse, then a children's labour colony. In 1939 it was transformed into a camp for interned officers of the Polish army and placed in the care of a NKVD bataillion.[158] Polish detainees started to arrive in September and October of 1939, and around 6,000 officers and gendarmes were interned in the Ostashkov camp.[159] By June 1940, however, the camp was empty of Poles. A few survived by swearing allegiance to communism, but the great majority had been transported in April 1940 to the NKVD jail in Kalinin. Systematically they had been executed, 250 a night, near a village not far from Kalinin.[160] The famous Katyn massacre might be more appropriately called the Mednoe massacre, for most Poles butchered during the tragedy were killed at Mednoe – 6,311 in all.[161]

SOVIET INDUSTRIALIZATION

In addition to collectivization and the Great Terror, Tver'/Kalinin province was in the grip of industrialization during the 1930s. More inhabitants, however, would move away and partake in the frenzy of the crash industrialization ordained by the First and Second Five Year Plans outside the province than within it. The plans concentrated on the development of heavy industry, and the environs of Tver' and Vyshnii Volochek were not deemed suitable for large-scale growth of this economic sector. Even so, party and government leaders and economic planners tried to drastically enlarge the light industry sector in the region, but with little success, for the level of state investment in light industry did not allow for a program of grand expansion. Industrialization had fewer catastrophic consequences for Russians than the purges or collectivization. It was sometimes even enthusiastically embraced by them, but it did not prove to be an unambiguously positive experience for those involved either.

A few years ago, a native of Tver' province lamented that "the liquidation of the artisan and the small cooperative had the same consequences for industry as collectivization had for agriculture. The factory and plant turned into bureaucratic institutions for the production of goods. The lace-makers of Kaliazin, the fullers, the wooden and stonetile makers, the masters of ceramics, the cobblers of Kimry and Ostashkov, the concertina makers of Tver' disappeared."[162]

The decline of cottage industries was certainly aggravated by collectivization and industrialization during the 1930s. As in agriculture, the small private producer disappeared from handicrafts. However, even though the long-term consequences of industrialization for artisanship were similar to the consequences of collectivization for agriculture, the process cost far fewer people their lives.

In 1932, after an initial effort to eliminate artisanry in the early phase of the First Five Year Plan, the government was forced to acknowledge the vital role of craftsmen in the economy, and it allowed them substantial economic freedom. Thus even at the end of the 1930s, footwear manufacturing around Kimry – where 9,800 cobblers were united in an industrial cooperative – still existed, as did net-knitting in Ostashkov, cloth-fulling near Kaliazin and Nerl', and knitted-wear manufacturing in several locales.[163] Nostalgic regret over the disappearance of the traditional artisans is understandable, but in this case the Soviet regime cannot be held solely responsible. The decline of handicrafts had begun with the industrialization of late nineteenth-century Russia; at different times in other areas in Europe large-scale industry has led to a similar demise of small artisanship.

The poor results of the first years of industrialization were caused, as mentioned, by a low level of government expenditure on light industry and by overly ambitious planning and maladjustment of former peasants to factory life. They were new to the towns and factories and were not yet used to the work attitude required in industry.[164] A great shortage of specialists complicated the intended rapid expansion of old industrial establishments and new factories that began to operate during the First Five Year Plan (1928–32): around 45 percent of industrial specialists were practicians (see "praktik," in the glossary) without special education.[165] The party worried even more about the fact that only 20 percent of all specialists were Soviet-schooled and that a mere 8.5 percent were candidates for or full members of the Communist Party. "Old" specialists were held responsible for "wrecking" in the territory's largest factories. But their persecution was economically self-defeating, for no viable replacements had yet been trained.

In order to compensate for the lack of Soviet-trained specialists, workers' faculties, a workers' college, and tekhnikums (technical colleges) were promoted, study-circles organized, and excursions undertaken. All these educational activities were aimed at the formation of a trustworthy group of managers and engineers, of so-called cadres with the proper class background. The results of the experimental education methods of the 1920s were now criticized for yielding an inadequate number of skilled cadres. To make matters worse, many teachers at tekhnikums and the Pedagogical Institute of Kalinin were scions of the priesthood, former landowners, or the bourgeoisie; moreover, these teachers allegedly engaged in "right opportunism" or even "SR opposition."[166] Despite the replacement of these enemy elements, the skills of students graduating at the end of the 1929–30 school year remained – not surprisingly – far from satisfactory. The level of graduates from the workers' faculties did not improve markedly in the later 1930s; the class of 1936 apparently demonstrated an appalling level of knowledge and a limited command of the Russian language.[167]

Tver' okrug, which included the town of Vyshnii Volochek, appeared at the end of 1929 to have overfulfilled the industrial goals of the First Five Year Plan. Setting the tone for the frenzied idealism of the 1930s, during which nonmaterial rewards often had to replace real prizes, the Soviet Union's first agreement on "socialist competition" (or "socialist emulation") was concluded in the spring of 1929 between textile factories in Vyshnii Volochek, Tver', and plants located in Moscow and Ivanovo-Voznesensk provinces. The agreement was intended to increase production by promoting competition between plants. At the end of 1929, meetings of "shock-workers" (workers who had overfulfilled their quotas and were thus worthy of emulation) were held in the okrugs for the first time.[168] "Socialist emulation" was taken up by almost every larger enterprise around this time, and for many decades to come it would remain one of the standard methods of stimulating workers' productivity, both in industry and agriculture.[169] On 7 September 1929, the Central Committee reintroduced one-person management (edinonachal'e), decreeing that from then on directors would be single-handedly responsible for the operation of the industrial enterprises that they headed.

In the towns of Tver' region in the early 1930s, official economic statistics were showing impressive growth, but this success, even if it really occurred at times, was brought about not with meaningful material incentives but through force. Communist-inspired tension had been mounting in the towns since early 1928: in the course of that year, several people holding responsible positions in the guberniia were prosecuted by the courts as a result of letters of complaint from workers' correspondents (rabkory) in factories and institutions.[170] The first foundation seems to have been laid for the surge of denunciations in the 1930s.

Under orders from the Central Committee in September 1930, the Communist workers of Tver' and other towns in the country "increased the struggle for labour discipline," a quality that was apparently lacking among the numerous new arrivals from the countryside who had found employment in industry.[171] Fluctuation of the labour force was another problem, undoubtedly because of the peasant background of many of the workers who were not yet accustomed to the different rhythm of factory work.[172]

Crash industrialization met with difficulties, as was obvious when a plenum of Vyshnii Volochek's raion committee announced a month-long drive to prevent wasted goods and production losses in December 1931.[173] In the same year, apparently, workers went on strike in the town, and Politburo member Kaganovich had to descend from Moscow to settle matters. In the paranoid atmosphere of 1937, the strained mood among workers that previously existed in Vyshnii Volochek was retroactively explained as the result of the wrecking activities of an enemy of the people, one Krivos. Even at the time of the First Five Year Plan, however, conspiracies of wreckers and other anti-Soviet groups abounded in the eyes of the authorities.

Industrialization's problems should not, however, be attributed to the deliberate acts of sabotage that the authorities attempted to convince the Soviet public of by staging a series of show trials. Following this official canon, a Soviet historian still felt obliged, many years after, to write the following assessment of one particular episode occurring during the chaotic early years of the plans:

Capitulationary and enemy activities were disclosed and eradicated at enterprises and institutions of the town of Torzhok. In the factory Krasnyi Kozhevnik party work was neglected, criticism suppressed. This led to serious violations of labour discipline, to the flourishing of absenteeism and drunkenness, a situation used by enemy elements in the mechanical workshop of the plant. They fulfilled orders for private persons using materials available in the factory, and during worktime systematically wrecked the preparation of orders for the workshops of their own factory.

All these irregularities were disclosed at the leather factory during a party purge, when criticism and self-criticism were deployed.[174]

Between the lines one reads that the main problem at the factory consisted of the imperfect adjustment to the work habits required in industry. The country's leadership attempted to solve the persistent problem of insufficient labour discipline by stepping up coercion, as we have already seen. This process culminated with a decree of the Presidium of the Supreme Soviet of 26 June 1940 that called for draconian measures in cases of labour discipline violations, while introducing an eight-hour workday and a seven-day working week. The decree was immediately applied in Kalinin: four workers in the rubber-sole factory were punished for absenteeism.[175] The quotation reveals, additionally, the beginnings of the "second economy." The "official economy" of the plan, from the outset, could not meet the population's demands for essential consumer goods.

The official Soviet version obviously lies when it states that the First Five Year Plan in the territory of the future Kalinin oblast' was successfully fulfilled in four years. There is, at the same time, no reason to disbelieve the information that the industrial work force in the town of Kalinin grew by 36.4 percent from 1929 to 1933, because much of the construction work in industry and housing had to be done manually in the expanding town.[176] Owing to lack of mechanization, the factories' production process was often very labour-intensive. New factories were under construction, while others were modernized and expanded. Together with the increase of the labour force and of production, workers' clubs appeared, more urban libraries and cinemas opened, and factory papers started to multiply around this period. With the First Five Year Plan, urban unemployment in the former guberniia of Tver' came to an end. One source claims that unemployment was eradicated by 1931, as was officially the case for the entire Soviet Union.[177]

The number of urban dwellers grew at a dramatic pace in the 1930s: while Tver' had 108,400 inhabitants in 1926, Kalinin was the home of 216,100 in 1939. The population of Vyshnii Volochek, Kimry, and Torzhok also roughly doubled during the same period, and that of Rzhev grew from 32,800 to 54,100. The urban population for the province as a whole around 1939–40 is given as being more than 650,000.[178] By 1935, already 250,000 blue-collar workers lived within the provincial borders. Yet on 1 January 1935 only 115,000 people worked in large-scale industry and a mere 95,000 were actual factory workers.[179] The old tradition of migration to Moscow and St Petersburg-Leningrad gained unprecedented momentum during the 1930s. Between 1930 and 1960, the rural population of the oblast' decreased by approximately one million people, according to a Soviet source; this phenomenal drain occurred predominantly between 1930 and 1945. Many of these people left for the towns and settled there permanently, but it is hard to establish how many actually moved to urban surroundings and how many suffered "unnatural deaths."[180]

Comparatively few new factories arose during the five year plans. Industry produced primarily consumer goods, such as textiles or glass. Heavy industry remained a small sector and was responsible, for example, for a mere 0.5 percent of the total machine-building output in the USSR. Yet new small-machine factories had started to appear in the 1930s, and Kalinin's peat-digging machinery and railroad-car construction factories grew. In the machine-building and metal industries, 25,400 workers (18 percent of all factory workers) were employed in 1936. Chemical industry had appeared in Kalinin and Vyshnii Volochek in addition to Redkino. Around 1939, the industrial production of the oblast' accounted for 1.5 percent of the USSR's total industrial production. Larger plants were located, as before, along the October Railroad and along the Volga, from Kalinin eastwards to Kaliazin, that is, in the southeastern part. The capital of Kalinin remained the territory's industrial centre: 30.4 percent of all industrial workers worked there in 1937, and the town's industry accounted for 44.2 percent of the total industrial output.[181]

In the second half of the 1930s, 98.6 percent of Kalinin's population was literate. Most people were housed in doma (apartment buildings) – really, barracks made of stone or wood. How many had modern amenities such as electric or gas stoves and running water is unclear. Far from all apartment buildings and houses had these: even in the summer of 1992, I witnessed several inhabitants of Tver' pumping water; they were living in wooden houses, albeit with a charmingly rustic appearance, in the middle of town.[182] In the middle of the 1930s, both in Kalinin and in the rural raions, electricity was in short supply. So was housing: in 1937, 805,900 square metres of floor space were available for 207,000 inhabitants, an *average* of less than 3.9 square metres a person. In 1939 the average had risen to exactly four square metres.[183]

During the 1930s, socialist emulation and movements such as the Stakhanovites, which offered largely nonmonetary rewards, were increasingly propagated. Take, for example, K.A. Shevaleva, who became a shock-worker during the First Five Year Plan. In 1936 she met the appropriately high targets to become a Stakhanovite at the Proletarka textile kombinat (industrial complex) in Kalinin, aided probably by party leaders and managers eager to prove their zeal. In December 1936, at the Eighth Congress of Soviets, which discussed the new constitution, Shevaleva, functioning as the token worker, was even allowed to give a speech.[184] She was one of the few model workers during the 1930s, portrayed in the newspapers and on the radio as ideal Soviet women, selflessly giving their best to build the radiant future.

It would be a mistake to conclude that the situation was gloomy for everyone living in towns during this period. Even though the New Regime was perhaps only interested in political indoctrination and in heightening economic performance by improving basic skills, education levels generally improved. In 1992 many natives of Tver' province, when asked about the positive elements of the socialism that had so recently come to grief, considered the opportunity to go to school to be one of them.[185] For some, life in urban surroundings was a change for the better, considering the greater deprivations in the countryside. Others believed that they were building a new society. Even factory workers who already lived in the towns before the First Five Year Plan sometimes imagined that life was taking a positive turn, however mistaken that perception was. In early 1947, the provincial paper reported that several textile workers in Kalinin looked back upon the positive changes in their lives thanks to socialism. Among them was Aleksandra Baburina, who declared that she could not have dreamt in pre-Soviet days of having her children attend secondary and even post-secondary schools, which all three had successfully completed.[186] In the same article other retired industrial workers expressed the belief that "[i]f there had not been Soviet power and the Bolshevik Party, we would still live in the swamp [the area where their apartments were located used to be a swamp with poorly constructed workers' barracks on it], lead a dog's life, and not see light. Soviet power and the party of the Bolsheviks made us into human beings. Because of all that we are profoundly grateful to them and bow humbly to our compatriot Iosif Vissarionovich Stalin!"[187]

Surely part of this is propaganda, but some perceptions were genuinely felt: during the 1930s, industrial workers thought that they had witnessed improvements over earlier periods. They did not receive any truthful information on the fate of their counterparts in other countries, and therefore it appeared possible that life was better than in any other country. After 1945, it was even less conceivable that life abroad could be better, since the USSR had proved itself to be the world's strongest power by the victory in World War II. Reinforced by pride in their contribution to this triumph, quite a few workers must have felt a certain degree of satisfaction with their lives.[188]

Despite the presence of some heartfelt emotions, much of the enthusiasm of workers and collective farmers had to be artificially stimulated by the leaders of the provincial and raion party organizations, the more so the longer tangible results of the economic transformation remained a chimera. The paltry spontaneity of "workers' initiatives" to stimulate production, such as the Stakhanov movement, is obvious from the text of one of the secret resolutions of the party oblast' committee in January 1937 outlining the most urgent tasks facing the oblast' party organization and the obkom departments during the upcoming four months:

To develop socialist emulation and the stakhanov movement according to the [following] lines ... the dispatch of all-round brigades in the textile industry for the struggle with waste goods, and the further organization of all-round brigades in other branches of industry ... the organization of railroad workers for the support of the Leningrad workers' letter [presumably a call for socialist emulation] ... the further development in agriculture of the movement of the milkmaids and of that of kolkhozy, who have pledged themselves to the obligation of procuring from each hectare five hundred kilograms of flax fibre for every kolkhoz.[189]

Disillusion had set in: apparently, the Communist party had to rely on persuasion, propaganda, and coercion rather than on utopian enthusiasm. One might ask whether the explanation for the bloodshed of the purges can be partially found in an attempt to foster a new spirit among the toiling masses, with fear replacing idealism as the source of inspiration for Stalin's subjects.

CHAPTER TWO

Ruin and Recovery

Until now, the history of the Soviet Union in World War II, or the Great
Patriotic War, as Soviet politicians and historians preferred to call it,
has been buried inside "the mosaic of lies and truth that for decades
ha[s] made up the sustaining myth of the Great Patriotic War, a mosaic
that served both to evoke the past and to cover up selected portions of
it."[1] This chapter will try to arrive at a more truthful version of the
Soviet experience during World War II by combining the suppressed
parts of the Russian collective memory with those elements that were
trumpeted before August 1991 as examples of the heroic struggle of
the Russian people of Kalinin province against the Nazi-led invading
army.

Only an approximate estimate of the extent of the damage inflicted
by the war and the loss of human life can be given, because there was
no reliable census between 1926 and 1959 in the Soviet Union and
because of the steady flow of emigrants who left the province from
1929 onward. The damage to industry, agriculture, housing, infrastructure, and private property is even more difficult to assess. Estimates have often been exaggerated, and it is unclear anyway what the
value really was of the plants, farms, houses, railroads, roads, and
bridges that were destroyed. There is, however, an abundance of evidence to indicate that the damage was enormous (even today bullet-
holes dating from the war can be found in the city of Tver') and that
many villages and towns were reduced to rubble.

THE COURSE OF THE WAR
IN THE PROVINCE

Not long after the invasion of the Soviet Union in June 1941, the
German armies reached Kalinin oblast', at that time still bordering

Latvia. German troops reached the centre of the province by early October 1941, advancing as far as the Volga river and temporarily occupying the capital town, Kalinin. Towards November 1941, 60 percent of the provincial territory was occupied by the Germans.[2] They destroyed "a large number of industrial enterprises and cultural institutions, more than 1,000 kolkhozy, thirty-one MTS."[3]

The capital, Kalinin, was occupied from the middle of October until 16 December 1941.[4] The chaos created by the poor preparation of the Soviet defence and the unexpected speed at which the Germans advanced into Central Russia was manifest on the eve of the German thrust to occupy the town: a mere five hundred regular Soviet troops were stationed in Kalinin to defend it, along with a unit of the Soviet-style home-guard (opolchenie), some cadets and telegraphists in training, and an NKVD search-and-destroy batallion. The latter was evidently left behind to destroy compromising materials and demolish strategic points of communications and transport, such as telephone and telegraph lines and railway connections, but also was given the task of sabotaging the German war effort by acts of terrorism after occupation.[5] A large part of the population escaped German occupation, however, when these minimal Soviet forces succeeded in temporarily halting the German advance for two days.[6]

Beginning on 5 December 1941, the Soviets launched an unexpected counterattack along the front in the environs of Moscow and liberated the central part of the province in which the town of Kalinin was located. The Red Army was aided by the exceptionally cold weather, for which the German troops were insufficiently prepared.[7]

The oblast' capital had been razed, however: the Germans obliterated more than seventy industrial enterprises, including the railroad-car factory, a factory producing weaving machinery, the cotton-fibre kombinat, and the Vagzhanov and Volodarskii textile factories. Seventy-seven hundred apartment buildings and the bridges over the rivers T'maka and Volga were in ruins. The electricity network, the sewers, the hydro system, and the streetcar, telephone, and telegraph lines were all out of operation. In the western parts of the province the picture would later be much the same.[8]

Reconstruction began hampered by the lack of materials and machinery, but patriotic enthusiasm compensated: a new élan was perhaps found in the struggle against the Germans, while the mobilization to which the Russians had accustomed themselves in the previous decade now further aided a speedy initial reconstruction of some of the vital installations of the city. Already on 27 December 1941 the first of Kalinin's hydro-electrical stations resumed operation, and two more stations were functioning by February 1942. On 6 January 1942, the executive committee of the provincial soviets (oblispolkom) stressed the urgent need for the reconstruction of schools, kindergartens, and hospitals in the capital.[9] During these early months after liberation, the oblispolkom introduced a plan for the restoration of the smaller industries and actively organized the rebuilding of roads, bridges, and crossings in and around the town. During 1942 a part of the railroad-car construction factory of Kalinin was rebuilt and resumed operations, as did the porcelain factory in Konakovo and the peat-chemical kombinat of Redkino.[10] In the battles for the central raion of Konakovo, 2,031 Soviet soldiers had lost their lives. Perhaps more telling, however, is the number of soldiers from the raion who perished at the front: over 6,000 did not return home, out of more than 17,000 who had fought in the war. After the terrible bloodletting in men and materiel, in Konakovo and elsewhere, party and government spent most of the funds and energy that were available, however small, on the reviving of the towns. As usual, the countryside was short-changed.[11]

In the late winter of 1942, measures were taken to revive some of the ravaged sovkhozy (state farms) in the province. The further west one went, the worse the situation became in the countryside: in the recently liberated raion of Turginovo, only forty tractors and 426 horses were available for spring sowing.[12] Most of the ploughing had to be done manually. The majority of the kolkhozniks lived in threshing barns, sheds, and houses of neighbouring kolkhozes that had escaped destruction. Discipline was immediately enforced: the party, already dissatisfied with the work habits of some collective farmers whose workdays did not surpass ten hours, admonished the political departments of both raion tractor stations to make the farmers toil harder.

The Nazi regime in the occupied areas of Kalinin province behaved as ruthlessly as in the rest of Eastern Europe. At times, willing participants in atrocities against the Jewish population, especially, could be found among locals. In the autumn of 1945, the former *Bürgermeister* (mayor) of Rzhev was discovered among a group of repatriated Soviet citizens by the NKVD. NKVD head Pavlov reported his crimes to Boitsov in early 1946:

KUZ'MIN VLADIMIR IAKOVLEVICH, born in 1900, in the town of Ostrov in the Leningrad oblast', partyless, seredniak ancestry, no criminal record.

In October 1941, after having deserted from the Red Army and gone over to the side of the enemy, KUZ'MIN took up residence in the town of Rzhev, which was occupied by the German armies.

In January 1942, KUZ'MIN joined of his own free will the German-installed authorities in the function of burgomaster of the town of Rzhev and worked as such until May 1943, that is until the expulsion of the Germans by Red Army units.

Through his subordinate apparatus, the police, and the town elders (starosty), KUZ'MIN established the fascist order in the town of Rzhev.

In May 1942, on the orders of KUZ'MIN, fourteen Jewish families, thirty-one people in all, were exposed in the town of Rzhev, handed over to the SD [Sicherheitsdienst, a subdivision of the SS], and all executed.

Aided by the active personal participation of KUZ'MIN in the years 1942–1943 10,000 inhabitants of the town of Rzhev were sent off to German slavery in Germany. KUZ'MIN carried out these measures in the following way [apparently a document is quoted, found by the NKVD in Rzhev or elsewhere, addressing Russian functionaries working for the Germans]:

"Utmost urgency, to all elders of the town quarters. The German command has asked the municipal authorities to evacuate immediately 500 persons of both sexes without children to Germany.

"As the municipal government is giving this question high priority, it proposes to execute these measures smoothly, without any roughness ... In order not to have to turn to the gendarmerie for help, you are obliged, upon notification, to give [the evacuees] a full explanation of the importance of the assignment and of the prospects that are lying ahead of them, that we have sufficient evidence about flourishing life in Germany. People are obliged to appear without any delay on 14 November 1942, at seven in the morning, at Decembrists' Street No.77, from where they will be directed to the village of Sapino for transport in railroad cars to Germany."[13]

After the recapture of Rzhev, Kuz'min fled with the German troops to Germany, but failed to escape repatriation. For such serious crimes Kuz'min would have been given the death penalty (however no trace of his sentence was to be found in the archives). He was probably one of the relatively few inhabitants of the Kalinin oblast' who can be genuinely called a war criminal.

The reconquest of Rzhev by the Red Army after a protracted bloody battle signified the last stage of the fighting on provincial territory.[14] When Rzhev was finally liberated in the spring of 1943, it was a heap of rubble.[15] The repercussions of the war lingered long after the hostilities had ended in western parts: by 1943, all livestock and orchards had been destroyed, and the area suffered a huge depopulation through deaths and evacuations. Around 1960, neither the town of Rzhev nor its environs had fully recovered from wartime devastation.[16]

By the middle of 1943, German troops had been cleared out of Kalinin province, while air raids had been reduced to a minimum.[17] By

early 1944 the Nazis were no longer able to launch serious bombard-
ments that far behind Russian lines.[18] The reconstruction of the
economy in the oblast' centre had already commenced in the second
half of December 1941, but the war continued to affect the inhabitants, for fresh conscripts were called up until May 1945. According to
one source, 350,000 inhabitants of Kalinin province fought at the
front.[19] The Red Army soldiers were not all immediately demobilized,
and many returned only in 1947.

In March 1943, the newly liberated town of Rzhev had actually welcomed Stalin himself, who was making his only excursion close to the
front line during the war.[20] The house near Rzhev in which Stalin spent
the night was quickly turned into a tourist attraction after the war.

In January 1945, first secretary I.P. Boitsov commended the partisan
movement in Kalinin oblast'.[21] He noted how, from the moment of
Stalin's first wartime speech on 3 July 1941, party committees had
been organizing partisan units. From July 1941 until the year's end,
three obkom secretaries were supervising these activities; in order to
lead the partisans, most prominent party and soviet workers were
ordered to stay behind in their area after the Germans occupied it.
Others were sent into the occupied zone later to take their place or
intensify the combat in the German rear.

However, Boitsov exaggerated the efficacy and popularity of the partisans in an effort to create, even before the war had officially ended,
the myth of monolithic resistance by the Soviet population to the
fascist hordes. He told his audience of party officials that the damage
inflicted by the partisans on the Germans was significant: many thousands of German soldiers and officers were said to have been killed by
the partisans during the war. The veracity of this high rate of success is
dubious.[22] It will remain a moot point whether the conference delegates in January 1945 realized this, but one is led to infer that Boitsov's
version was designed to contribute to the fictional official postwar
account of the war as the litmus test proving the solidity and superiority of the Soviet political and economic system. In other words, the
heroic fictional account of the war, the defence of the Soviet Fatherland
unblemished by any wavering on the part of the Soviet citizens, was
already constructed during the last months of World War II. The myth
proved enduring and is still, even now, often believed in Russia.

A recent German publication on German-occupied territories in the
Soviet Union does not indicate the area of the smaller Kalinin oblast'
as harbouring a major concentration of partisans. If one accepts the
information of this latter source, significant partisan activities were to

be found only in the later province of Velikie Luki.[23] Because the partisans were necessarily free from involvement by superiors, it is certainly plausible that they were generally more efficient fighters than regular soldiers and inflicted more damage on the German armies. After all, the Red Army had to follow orders based on the wolfish strategies of Stalin and his commanders.[24] Estimates of tens of thousands of Germans killed as a result of partisan activity can, however, hardly be taken seriously, for by the time the partisan movement picked up steam and began to recruit significant numbers among people in the occupied territories, Kalinin oblast' had been liberated.

It remains difficult to assess the Kalinin party organization's appreciation of the partisans after the war. Boitsov gave full praise to the partisan movement while the war was still raging in January 1945. He apparently felt obliged to petition Stalin himself in the summer of 1946 for decorations for all the former partisans.[25] In the end, more than five thousand partisans were said to have been decorated in the province for their wartime achievements, but it is unclear whether this number refers to those partisans who lived on the oblast' territory of before August 1944 or only to those who lived on the smaller post-August 1944 territory.[26] Apart from that, many decorations were probably awarded only long after the war, for only slightly more than one thousand provincial residents had been decorated by the USSR Supreme Soviet with different medals and decorations by December 1946. Ultimately, almost anyone, either working in the rear or fighting at the front, seems to have been decorated for their efforts during the war.[27]

It seems that the partisan movement as such was singled out for praise, but that the individual underground fighter was often distrusted. Distrust of the resistance was common in Europe under German occupation. Double agents were dealt with harshly everywhere when exposed, while collaboration with the Nazis was common in many parts of Eastern Europe, including Russia. Suspicion of collaboration, nevertheless, was more extreme among Soviet authorities, who had been indoctrinated by a rather paranoid ideology and emulated the example of their morbidly suspicious leader. The case of N.M. Gaponenko illustrates the vagaries of war in this respect.[28] In 1942 or 1943, Gaponenko distributed partisan literature among Czechoslovak troops who were part of the Nazi occupation force in Belorussia. Then he was forced to join the German side as a member of the Polizei. Ten days after his forced enlistment, Gaponenko and a friend arrested the chief of the German police when their Polizei unit was attacked by partisans. The two delivered the German commander to the partisans, who eventually executed the German officer – but also his captors, on the orders of their legendary commander, Kovpak. For being the relative of a so-called collaborator, Gaponenko's mother paid double the amount of taxes after the war, even though her husband and another son fought in the Red Army. In the end the KGB rehabilitated him, but only long after Stalin's death.

DEVASTATION

Official Soviet publications note that of the inhabitants of Kalinin oblast' during the war, 40,876 civilians were killed, 17,055 became prisoners of war, and 23,755 were forced to work in Germany, excluding the soldiers killed in battle. The Nazis behaved brutally: for example, when they captured a provincial psychiatric hospital in the fall of 1941, they massacred most of the patients. They organized concentration camps in Olenino and Rzhev and carried out mass executions of civilians in Rzhev and Zubtsov. Some civilians starved to death in 1941 and 1942. More extensive civilian casualties were avoided only because the Germans never stretched their hold much farther east than the oblast' capital, from which they soon had to retreat.[29]

In two secondary Soviet sources the total number of war-related deaths (military and civilian) for the oblast' is 248,000.[30] Both texts do not mention sources for this number. At the time of their publication, the oblast' was substantially larger than between 1944 and 1957, so that the deaths resulting from acts of war on the territory of the size of the immediate postwar period might have been closer to 200,000; one can then propose that around 160,000 natives of the province as it was immediately after the war died in the military.[31] Although the much briefer occupation of Kalinin oblast's western parts saved many civilians from the much worse fate of the Belorussians, the number of military deaths in the province is, nevertheless, staggering: it may have amounted to 9 percent of the total provincial population.[32]

It is unclear whether deaths resulting from the natural drop in the population in 1941–45 were included in the total of 248,000. Table 2 shows this demographic drop. The surplus of deaths over births and the high infant mortality indicate the hardship suffered by those in the rear even after the provincial territory was recovered by the Red Army.

The countryside especially suffered from the privations.[33] The negative growth rate of the population, the civilian losses, and the deaths at the front made it imperative to raise the province's birthrate substantially. In July 1944, old-fashioned family values were highlighted by Ermolov, the head of the oblast' health-care department, at an obkom plenum. Instead of frankly admitting that the party and government had realized it was necessary to increase the birthrate to compensate

Table 2
Natural Population Movement in Kalinin Oblast', 1940–48

Year	Average Birth Rate (per 1,000)	Average Death Rate (per 1,000)	Average Infant Mortality (per 100 births)
1940	24.4	21.1	22.1
1942	16.5	35.2	28.4
1943	7.6	27.0	17.9
1944	10.1	21.0	12.8
1945	12.5	15.2	9.9
1946	20.2	14.5	8.8
1947	21.4	17.0	13.8
1948	19.4	13.1	9.0

Source: Based on Pako, 147/4/1549, l.67. Numbers for 1941 were not given in the account.
Note: Deaths as a consequence of acts of war are not taken into account in these numbers. In 1950, for the whole Soviet Union, the birth rate per 1,000 was 26.7, and the death rate 9.7; in 1953, these numbers were respectively 25.1 and 9.1 (Ryan and Prentice, Social Trends, table 4.1, 38).

for the immense bloodletting of the war, he explained a recent government decree, which made divorce almost impossible, as follows:

Comrades, the Ukaz [decree] of the Supreme Soviet of the USSR on motherhood and infancy, published on 8 June, is a most important historical document for the party of the bolsheviks and the Soviet government. In the terrible days of the patriotic war the government issued a new law full of love for mother and child. This document once more underlines the concern of the government for mother and child, for the strenghthening of the foundations of the family, the basis of Soviet morality. The Soviet country liberated woman from great oppression, lifting up to a new height the woman-mother, who rears the children. The rearing of children has become a case of valour and honour.[34]

The Soviet Union had come a long way since the days of the advocate of gender equality, Alexandra Kollontai! Now girls had to be inculcated with the feelings of motherhood; special attention was to be paid to this in youth education. Perhaps this is merely a florid testament to the simple proposition that "the Communist state is interested in increasing the population, and consequently increasing the birthrate."[35]

The Communist Party's membership changed drastically in the war years. At an obkom plenum of June 1942, Secretary P.S. Vorontsov portrayed an exceptional renewal of leading cadres: in the countryside, for example, most collective farm chairs left to serve in the Red Army.[36] After the high turnover rate of kolkhoz chairs of the early years of collectivization and the bloodletting of the Great Purge, which had removed another batch of kolkhoz chairs, this was the third wave of almost complete renewal of leading collective farm personnel. Partially as a result of this departure, in June 1942, out of 6,545 kolkhoz chairs a mere 660 carried a party card, with a further 163 being candidate members and 68 chairs belonging to the Komsomol. Vorontsov, who did not give the impression in his ensuing career as a proponent of gender equality, lamented the insufficient level of promotion of women to responsible positions.[37] The motive for his complaint was surely the fact that the trifling number of men remaining behind could not fill all positions anymore. Many of those few males who stayed behind on the collective farms lacked competence or were physically too feeble to acquit themselves adequately of the demanding task of leading the kolkhozy.

By the spring of 1944, the situation on the farms had scarcely improved in the eyes of the party: few Communists were counted among kolkhoz leaders.[38] The Communist Party itself suffered from the loss of experienced professional party workers: seventeen secretaries of raion committees perished in the war, in particular those from the districts in the German-occupied western part of the oblast'.

While the provincial party was struggling to maintain discipline and competence among the cadres, the mood of the population outside the party was also cause for concern during the war. In June 1942 oblispolkom chairman Starotorzhskii stated that not all of the wartime loss of cattle could be blamed on the Germans, for "at the moment of the evacuation of cattle, one year ago, when many of our raions were being occupied, self-seeking elements appeared among the cattle drivers, as a consequence of which we had exceptionally serious losses of cattle. Incidents of the squandering of communal cattle took place and take place among the majority of the kolkhozy of the raions."[39]

In contrast to their studious care for the personal cow or pigs, the kolkhozniks did not look after the communal or socialized animals with much zeal. In the hard times of war they were forced to make a choice: since the reward for the delivery of milk and meat procurements continued to be extremely low, they neglected the communal animals in favour of their private livestock. Wherever the Germans captured provincial territory, the extent of the loss of communal herds was extreme, as table 3 illustrates.

Table 3
Livestock Loss and Recovery in German-occupied Territories (on 1 January)

	1941	1942	1947	Numbers in 1947 compared to 1941 (%)
Horses	82,700	5,000	14,300	17.4
Strong-horned cattle	108,300	400	93,400	86.2
Cows[1]	40,100	300	20,100	50.0
Pigs	19,900	–	11,500	57.7
Sows[2]	3,600	–	4,200	117.0
Sheep	94,900	100	81,800	86.2
Ewes[3]	47,900	–	55,500	116.2

Source: Based on Pako, 147/4/921, l.88.
Note: The figures are for the socialist sector of the kolkozy of 15 raions.
[1]Included in the total numbers for strong-horned cattle.
[2]Included in the total numbers for pigs.
[3]Included in the total numbers for sheep.

The disorganization caused by the war and the relaxation of the party's control over the collective farm system are expressed in many documents. Not only the cavalier attitude towards the collectively owned cattle worried the party: five months after Starotorzhskii's criticism of the irresponsible squandering of cattle, one Zubynin declared before a party audience that many kolkhozniks had taken to sowing grain on their personal plots; for instance, 22 percent of all kolkhoz households in Goritsy raion were involved in this practice. Zubynin noted that the kolkhozniks tried above all to secure cereals for their personal household. Many kolkhozniks indeed abandoned the socialized sector of agriculture during the war to engage in private farming instead; or in Soviet terms, "[t]he deterioration of the material situation of the kolkhozniks during the war also gave rise to negative phenomena, such as the revival of a greedy mentality of private gain."[40]

In 1945, Karelinov, head of the provincial agricultural department, reported to first secretary Boitsov on the extent of the most heavily damaged rural area and submitted the statistics given in table 4, which also gives the figures for July 1946, in comparison. On average, in these raions just 10 to 15 percent of draught horses, 30 percent of all horses, and 60 percent of tractors of the total of 1941 survived the war. Clearly, the damage was enormous, and it should be remembered that for a short while, apart from the above twelve raions, other raions were partially occupied.[41]

A report from Boitsov to Malenkov of 1 March 1946 shows that the

Table 4
Agricultural Damage from German Occupation

	Number of Kolkhozy			Hearths			Able-Bodied Workers	
Raion	1940	1945	1946 (July)	1940	1945	1946 (July)	1940	1945
Molodoi Tud	271	175	186	7,715	3,838	4,323	12,125	3,604
Olenino	270	171	180	10,836	7,736	7,834	18,776	6,735
Pogorel'oe	165	129	129	7,502	4,949	4,797	12,723	5,203
Zubtsov	233	168	168	6,556	3,380	3,462	9,270	3,009
Rzhev rai	364	226	232	12,817	8,116	7,733	22,756	11,331
Vysoko	158	116	118	5,859	5,099	5,267	12,356	4,705
Emel'ianovo	153	121	121	4,873	4,108	3,680	7,545	3,900
Kirov	261	257	258	9,854	8,669	8,654	20,277	7,929
Lukovnikovo	201	171	171	7,203	6,431	6,352	12,942	6,345
Ostashkov	202	167	161	6,558	4,714	5,415	11,520	5,192
Staritsa	270	220	222	9,846	9,274	9,212	17,471	10,839
Turginovo	117	93	94	3,362	2,837	2,992	7,298	2,796
Total	2,665	2,014	2,040	92,981	69,718	69,721[1]	165,329[2]	71,588

Source: Based on Pako, 147/3/1966, l.61, table 1; Pako, 147/3/1966, ll.39–39ob.
[1] 75% of the figure for 1940.
[2] 43% of the figure for 1940.

recovery of agriculture was slow and painful.[42] Instead of 3,067, only 2,310 collective farms operated in the formerly occupied raions; instead of the prewar number of 186,974 kolkhozniks able to work, only 86,484 were counted in March 1946. Draught horses numbered less than 10,000, compared to 64,143 before June 1941, and tractors only 884, compared to 1,484. Within the socialized sector of the collective farm, the average kolkhoznik had more than twice as much land to take care of, and each horse had to work nineteen hectares of arable land instead of 6.1 hectares previously. The most severe destruction occurred in Olenino raion, where after the German retreat, only eleven draught horses and twenty-one cows survived. More than 6,000 inhabitants of this raion had been deported to Germany as forced labourers.[43]

THE EXPERIENCE OF THE WAR
IN THE PERCEPTION OF PARTY
AND PEOPLE

Wartime events and conditions played an important role in the official and unofficial collective memory after May 1945. We have already seen the beginnings of the process that made the war into a myth and began to blur the actual experience of the survivors. It is remarkable, therefore, how many older Russians have preserved a less than heroic image of events between June 1941 and May 1945. We can again turn to the the testimonies gathered in the survey of 1992 for evidence of a continued prevalence of unadorned wartime memories. No survivor ever forgot the Great Patriotic War: the male population was decimated in certain villages, and virtually everyone lost family members in the war, both in town and country. Mariia Vasil'evna Bakhtina, a kolkhoz worker who was interviewed in the survey, still considers herself fortunate that her husband returned from the front. For Mariia Mikhailovna Golovnova, however, the consequences of the war could hardly have been worse:

I worked in the rear, helped the front. Brought up the [seven] children, milked the cow. I did not engage in combat, but my three brothers and three brothers-in-law were killed at the front. My husband they took to work at the mines, although he was excused from the front. In the mines he, too, found his end

The German [forces] did not reach us, the swamp stopped them. It is large here. Their machines also got stuck. The battles were huge, the killed soldiers were buried in the village of Selikhovo. Here several times more Russians were killed than Germans.

In 1941, the Germans threw a bomb on the village – it fell on our house, the house was in splinters – father was killed.[44]

A.S. Efremov recalled that after the war in his native village in Emel'ianovo raion, men returned from the front to only five out of eighty households.[45] Other than him, no one of his birth year returned home. The conscripts of the birth year 1925 all fell near Rzhev, according to Efremov. Those who did return had often become invalids. This atrocious rate of attrition was not unique.

Obviously, most women did not serve in the army, even though, in 1948, 7 percent of demobilized Red Army troops were female, and others worked as nurses. It was far more usual for women to assist in building defensive trenches, with logging, and so on. In 1941, almost 140,000 people, largely female collective farmers, were engaged in building defensive works.[46] In the rear, women took over many of the jobs involving heavy physical labour that had been done exclusively by men before the war. Pensioners rejoined the work force. The population in the rear worked between twelve and eighteen hours a day in the autumn of 1941.[47]

Men fought at the front, and almost without exception all were wounded. Often they were injured more than once, as in the case of

V.G. Gavrilov, who was demobilized in 1943 after his second injury, and in the case of N.A. Arkhangel'skii, P.A. Kashinov, and A.F. Antonov, who were wounded three times. The traumatic impression the war made can be seen from the length of the answers given to questions dealing with it in the survey. An extreme position regarding the war was taken by Petr Arsen'evich Kashinov, a carpenter and sometime joiner. Kashinov fought from 1941 to 1945 in the Soviet army and was wounded three times. He levelled a devastating criticism on the army staff's and officers' conduct of the war, since, in his opinion, "[t]his was not a war, but an extermination of the narod. We went directly through open fields to smash a pillbox. Our cover was the one-front shield of the gun. In the beginning my hair stood on end. In the river Volkhov there was more soldiers' blood than water."

Many people lived for a while under German occupation. Some became partisans, while others collaborated with the Germans, which was not such an outlandish move: the average native of Kalinin province was not immediately sure what was black and what was white during the chaotic first months of the invasion. Soldiers deserted the Red Army in 1941, having given up on the possibility of a Soviet victory. The kolkhoznik M.I. Gantsev deserted in 1941, rejoined the army under another name in 1942, and became a candidate member of the party in 1943.[48] In 1946 he was exposed and ousted from the party. The MVD was investigating the case further at the time of his expulsion.[49] D.V. Bobrov, born in 1899, became a candidate party member in 1943; he appeared to be an honest, if poorly educated, kolkhoznik. On 18 July 1946, however, the raikomburo of Kirov moved to exclude him from the party; first secretary Boitsov, in his quality as highest arbitrator in these kinds of questions, subsequently ratified their decision. Whether criminal prosecution ensued is unclear in this case. Bobrov's misdeeds were listed as follows:

Bobrov maintained contacts with the Germans when he lived on German occupied territory in the Kirov raion, and had German officers living in his house. Bobrov worked for the Germans, made them a wooden sledge, slaughtered cattle seized from kolkhozniks by the Germans, and made sausages. Bobrov confiscated potatoes for the Germans from the kolkhozniks. In contrast to the other inhabitants, Bobrov was not forced to leave his village when people of areas close to the front were forced to settle elsewhere by the Germans. At the time that he entered the VKP(b) as a candidate member, Bobrov concealed from the party that he had worked for the Germans.[50]

It is impossible to establish how many people deliberately stayed behind to welcome the Germans instead of attempting to flee. The surprising pace of the German advance prevented many from retreating in time, even if they had wished to do so. Thus, while a great number of the inhabitants of Kalinin were evacuated, not everyone left the town, which explains the seemingly contradictory answers given by Evgeniia Stepanovna Shirochenkova. When asked about her war experience, she answered that she continued to work in her profession as factory weaver. But in reply to the next question, whether she lived on German occupied territory at some time during the war, she stated that she did not, "and in Tver' the German [army] was only for a short while." This statement possibly indicates that she was concealing her residence in Kalinin in the fall of 1941.

In appreciating Shirochenkova's evasive answer, one has to take into account that after the war it was unwise to admit to having lived under Nazi occupation. Not only was the government highly suspicious of those who had, but even their neighbours might ostracize or denounce them. In the Tver' of today the war is often a sacred cow. Even now it is considered unwise to declare that one has not always been on the right side of the front line. Nevertheless, Nikolai Dmitrievich Eliseev provided us with the honest testimony of someone who lived for a short while in Kalinin under German occupation in the autumn of 1941:

I lived as a student for two months on temporarily occupied territory, when the German [troops] took Kalinin. Our family did not manage to evacuate: the bridge over the Volga was already mined and they did not allow us, a family and a handcart with luggage, to cross to the other side of the river. We returned home. German tanks came in sight in the direction of Migalovo. We boys, who still had no fear for the occupiers, went out into the streets. The German tank personnel gave us chocolate. In the area where the Iuzhnyi raion is today was a civilian airfield. The Germans used it as an airfield for their planes. In our house a German officer was billeted – the pilot Hans. And through the whole two-month period of occupation we lived under his guardianship without fear and without brutalities. Once two soldiers, obviously Finns, tried to take food from us, but when they saw an officer's uniform in our room they quickly cleared out. In our area the Germans did not commit acts of violence. It is true that I heard that they hung the raikom secretary Sergeev. Soon our troops liberated Kalinin.

The case of I.G. Tsvetkov, who was excluded from the party by the raikomburo of Olenino in October 1946, is typical of the ambiguous attitude of many Russians toward the Germans.[51] In 1940, working as vice-brigadier of an MTS brigade, Tsvetkov had become a full party member. He was about thirty-one years old when the Germans occupied his native district and was apparently unable or unwilling to leave this locale at that time. After burning his party membership card when the Germans closed in on his village, he remained a passive bystander during the occupation, neither resisting nor aiding the Germans. When the Germans retreated, Tsvetkov managed to avoid being caught in the crossfire, staying where he was. Now again on Soviet territory, he was sent to a district further behind the front line and was called up for service in the Red Army. From November 1942 until March 1945, he fought in the army without ever mentioning his prewar party membership to the Party cell of the army unit in which he served. This omission, combined with his passivity during the occupation, was the pretext for his exclusion from the party.

For the party elite in the province following the Marxist-Leninist canon, the war was a manifest illustration of how life unfolds as as a dialectic (or Manicheist) battle between the forces of Soviet good and Nazi evil. For a great number of Soviet citizens, however, life remained a rather more complex process. A number of them appeared willing to give the new masters the benefit of the doubt and perform certain tasks or services for the Germans without having to be coerced into doing so. In any event, the Soviet regime had hardly proved to be an unequivocal embodiment of good to the Russians during the previous dozen years. Tsvetkov's ambivalence seems fairly typical of many Soviet citizens at the beginning of the war. It would have seemed as if Party and Soviet government were on the verge of collapse, resistance against the Germans futile, and adaptation to the new rulers wise.

To paraphrase one wartime Soviet description, however, the Nazis generally behaved as if Russians were nothing more than a higher form of cattle, although many individual Wehrmacht soldiers approached the Russians as fellow human beings, as we saw above.[52] The invaders' disdainful attitude and murderous behaviour contributed greatly to the ease with which Soviet power was reestablished. To the detriment of its cause, the Nazi leadership never seriously attempted to court the Russians. On the whole, any German effort in the direction of a reintroduction of private farming or a capitalist economy seems to have been very limited. At an obkom plenum in June 1942, oblispolkom chairman Starotorzhskii exclaimed, probably with some relief, that "the Hitlerite German fascists tried a year ago to disorganize our economy, to destroy our kolkhoz system, counting on the collapse of the kolkhoz, on the weakening of the rear. It was inconceivable for the German burgher and for the German bourgeois a year ago, and hardly do they even now suspect, that our kolkhoz life was so stable, so much of a powerful factor in the economy of our country that we can rely on it with the fullest right and justification, precisely as on cement. On this firm basis our agricultural production is created."[53]

The surprise among the party membership itself at the endurance and tenacity of the kolkhoz system and its relatively simple restoration after the German retreat is palpable in this quotation. It should be noted, however, that many of the kolkhozy, particularly those near the front and those that were restored on recovered territory, appear to have been collective farms more in name than in deed until 1945. Only after the war could a concerted effort be made by party and government to reestablish the kolkhoz in which private farming was distinctly secondary to work performed in the collective sector of the farm.

An "anti-Soviet mood" did surface sporadically in Russian territories actually occupied by the Nazi troops, such as the western part of Kalinin oblast'. Here, however, as in most of Russia, the majority of the population remained loyal to the Motherland as a consequence of the occupiers' brutal behaviour. In the words of Starotorzhskii, the Germans found no sympathy in the temporarily occupied districts, apart from that of a few renegades. The degree of collaboration was undoubtedly less than in the nearby Baltic republics.[54]

Lack of enthusiasm for the socialist cause was widespread after "liberation," however, when "[t]he plenum of the VKP(b) notices that, as a result of poor political-educational and cultural-educational work in many towns and raions of the oblast', in particular in the town of Kalinin and in the raions of Rameshki, Kushalino, and Toropets, hooliganism and other amoral phenomena are growing among the youth."[55]

This indifference worried the party's leadership tremendously during the war. A determined propaganda offensive was unleashed upon the heads of those who had lived under German occupation, while the judiciary kept busy with a speedy resurrection of the passport regime in the liberated areas and with bringing active Nazi collaborators to trial.[56] In July 1944 the successor of Starotorzhskii as chair of the oblast' oblispolkom, Simonov, warned against the pernicious influence of the Germans on the minds of the locals:

In the first place, we should not forget that the absolute majority of those Komsomols, other youth, and the rest of the population liberated from the German occupation – who lived on territory occupied by the enemy for a longer period – were cut off from the Motherland, and, naturally, did not find out about all that has been happening during this time. They have not been explained, for instance, how the "miracle" occurred that all of a sudden a turn around took place and the enemy has come to the edge of destruction in the course of a war so unfavourable for our country in the beginning.

Secondly, at the time of the occupation, the Hitlerite blackguards spread around the most shamelessly lying demagogy about the course of the war, about the situation in the Soviet rear and the international position of the USSR. They tried to poison our people with the venom of doubt and disbelief in the possibility of the return of Soviet power and the previous life. They distributed the most vile slander about the system in the Soviet Union, tried to discredit the kolkhoz system and, although the efforts of the fascist occupants and their stooges to intimidate the population were shipwrecked, still some backward people came close to accepting the bait, apart from those traitors who wittingly sold themselves. Among them the opinion arose that the Germans were not all that bloodthirsty, not those kind of robbers as we portrayed them.[57]

Another speech at the same plenum by the chief judge of the provincial military tribunal, Starilov, gives a concrete picture of the lack of order in war-torn Stalinist Central Russia:

Except for khuliganstvo [hooliganism], a particularly common sort of crime is carrying arms, including firearms; moreover, these weapons are actually used in violent robberies. I will mention a number of examples that are a colourful illustration of the shortcomings of our work [with the education of juveniles]. At the railroad-car construction factory the secretary of the Komsomol committee, Martynov, stood at the head of one group of hooligans; together with others he had organized a group of hooligans who were armed with knives and revolvers. They kicked up rows not only at their own factory, but also in other places; these hooligans went into the Voroshilov club and provoked fights and beatings. Once they were arrested, they attacked the militsionery [policemen], killed one, while the other one had to flee.[58]

Crime also grew because of the burgeoning number of orphaned children resulting from the enormous loss of life during the war. On 1 January 1946, 7,480 orphans were counted in the oblast'.[59] Some of them became petty criminals, even when housed in an orphanage.

Forced by the partial collapse of the distribution system, resulting in scarce provisions during the war, apparently provided a way for people with few scruples to profit from their needy compatriots: in December 1944 alone, the local NKVD arrested 264 people for theft, speculation, and similar offenses. Another 114 were arraigned strictly for fraud and theft of grain in the countryside. In the same month, 350 Red Army draft evaders and deserters were still on the run. Some of these had already deserted in 1942. Bandits were also terrorizing some areas.[60]

Nazi propaganda was hardly responsible for these disorders. The Soviet system's breakdown in 1941–42 and the innate shortcomings of planned distribution led some people to believe that it was worth taking risks and attempting to profit from the temporary chaos following the German invasion. Others simply increased the scope of their illegal activities: in spite of official propaganda, "professional criminality" existed both before and after the war in Stalinist Russia.[61]

DEMOBILIZATION

In June 1945, an obkom plenum discussed the imminent return of the first wave of Red Army soldiers to the oblast', mainly the most senior soldiers.[62] In July the obkomburo ordered lower party committees to provide work for the veterans in which they could use skills acquired in the army.[63] The calibre of the new jobs was, furthermore, to equal the veterans' work before their call to service. Kolkhoznik veterans were to be provided with a personal cow, if their family did not already possess one. Factory directors were to organize special courses for veterans who were willing to improve their expertise. Several of the veterans would find employment in the NKVD/MVD: in 1946 alone, 1,013 were recruited by the security ministry.

In September 1945 a second group of servicemen was demobilized. The obkom secretary for propaganda and agitation warned at the time that "as a result of the Patriotic war and our victory, the contacts of our state with capitalist society have significantly broadened. Today and in the future many of our people are and will be abroad, directly mixing with the capitalist world. In this respect the possibility [has] increased substantially for penetration in our Soviet midst of bourgeois ideology, ideas, and attitudes."[64]

Despite good intentions, the reintroduction of the veterans into civilian life encountered obstacles. In August 1945 the Central Committee reprimanded the obkom for failing to provide adequately for demobilized soldiers.[65] Thus, in Kalinin some returning veterans discovered that their former apartments had been appropriated by others. Some apartments had not been rebuilt, while others were in urgent need of repair more than three and a half years after the reconquest of the town. Families of soldiers, who were demobilized, disabled, serving, or dead, did not receive the legal ration of consumer goods or the fuel due to them. Moreover, of the almost 10,000 demobilized who had arrived in the province by 15 August 1945, only 3,276 had found employment.

The situation did gradually improve after August 1945, but the obkomburo continued to attend to the problem until late 1946. By 1 October 1945, 22,904 army veterans had arrived in the province, of whom only 53 percent had found work. Their housing remained inadequate, and some had not received pensions or reductions in taxes. Rzhev was singled out for its neglect of the "heroic defenders of the Motherland." In the severely damaged town, more than 300 soldiers'

families were housed in dugouts and hovels for lack of decent alternatives. The head of the town's welfare department, Miasnikov, was dismissed by the obkomburo for what was called a "criminally negligent
attitude towards his work."[66] By 1 October 1946, however, 74,756
demobilized servicemen had arrived in the oblast', and 95.5 percent
had found work.[67] The continued supervision by the buro had an
effect.

The Central Committee had underlined the crucial importance of
political work among veterans in a resolution on 27 May 1946.[68]
Boitsov reported around this time to Central Committee secretary
Zhdanov on the veterans' reentry into the labour force, in particular
singling out the political work conducted among them. This emphasis
on (re)education was based on two perceptions: on the one hand, party
leaders in Moscow, like those in the obkom, feared that the minds of
the servicemen had been contaminated by perfidious bourgeois phenomena during their sojourn beyond Soviet borders; at the same time
army men and women had enlisted by the thousands in the Communist Party and would therefore play an important role in the postwar
rebuilding of the Soviet Union. Among the almost 70,000 in the
province by July 1946, 19,661 full and candidate party members were
counted. The enrolment of Red Army veterans was almost solely
responsible for the party's exceptional growth in the years 1945 and
1946. These novices often lacked the proper political preparation as
candidate members, and many had never been members of the Communist Youth League. Special attention to their political orthodoxy by
party ideologists was therefore deemed imperative.

In the end, perhaps 93,000 to 94,000 war veterans returned to
Kalinin oblast' from the Red Army (see table 5).

Another group of natives was also tracing its way home to Kalinin
province after the war: people who had been forced to work in
Germany (few had departed willingly). In the last three months of
1945, 3,481 such individuals returned to Kalinin oblast'. They all,
apart perhaps from the 113 children among them, underwent fil'trat-
siia: an NKVD check on their behaviour and activities in Germany.
NKVD head Pavlov informed Boitsov that thirteen people had been discovered who had been collaborators.[69]

The suspicion towards those who had "surrendered" to the
Germans remained high after the war. On 4 August 1945, the Central
Committee criticized measures taken by republican, oblast', and krai
party committees to reeducate Soviet citizens who were being repatriated from Germany. The obkom felt obliged to warn party and soviet
workers against underestimating the pernicious influence of "fascist
and reactionary bourgeois propaganda" on those who had been in

Table 5
Return of Demobilized Soldiers to Kalinin Oblast'

Total demobilized by April 1947	93,000
Total demobilized in 1948 (birth year of 1925)	731
Total demobilized by the end of 1948	93,731
Demobilized soldiers who served in the ground forces	77,722
Demobilized soldiers who served in the navy	473
Soldiers demobilized because of illness	246
Demobilized soldiers born in 1896 or before	7,837
Demobilized soldiers unfit for service, but fit for physical work	303
Demobilized female soldiers	7,150
Demobilized soldiers sent to urban areas	32,915[1]
Demobilized soldiers sent to rural areas	61,536

Source: Based on a report given by oblast' army commissar Cherniak to P.S. Vorontsov on 17 March 1948; see Pako 147/4/1391, l.2.
[1]The total of these groups sent to urban and rural areas combined is 720 more than the total number of demobilized soldiers given above.

"German slavery." Serious political education should be undertaken to prove the USSR's superiority, so clearly expressed by the victory of 1945. Moreover, propaganda workers were to explain to the repatriated that the Soviet state "had been ceaselessly worried about the soviet citizens who had been dispatched into German bondage."[70]

This was all rather hypocritical, considering the party's general disdain for those who had been in German camps or who had been recruited to work for the Nazi regime in Germany. In the party's opinion the repatriates should now feel enormously indebted to the Motherland for their liberation.[71] They should be taught again the meaning of socialist discipline. Radio, films, slogans, portraits, posters, and so on were designed to regenerate the proper sense of respect for the boundless achievements of the Soviet Union. The oblast' newspaper was ordered to publish items about the constant concern of the Soviet government and the Communist Party for their compatriots who had been captive in Germany. Obviously, the paper would have to fabricate considerably in order to inveigle these former captives into believing such heartwarming concern.

Towards the end of 1946, 3,492 former Soviet prisoners of war were also counted in the oblast', 396 of whom had served as Red Army officers. However, this number did not include those who had been placed in the "first category" by the MGB and MVD.[72] Ostensibly those who fell under this first category ended up in Soviet camps or were executed outright.[73]

All in all, the veterans' adjustment to peacetime circumstances was

comparatively smooth in Kalinin province. The authorities were sometimes suspicious of the veterans, but they could not afford to worry
overly about the demobilized soldiers' ideological orthodoxy. Because
of the labour shortage there was plenty of work for them, and in all
branches of the economy they were often trusted with supervisory
work. This may have come at the expense of women who had been
promoted to positions of greater responsibility during the war in the
absence of men, as we will see.

The eformer soldiers themselves must have been glad to have survived it all, longing for a more quiet way of living after the hardships
at the front. They were often lauded for their part in the defence of the
Motherland, received special privileges (for example, special stores for
war veterans) and preferential treatment when seeking work, while
many had become party members during the war, which benefitted
them even more. The party was, in the first two postwar years, very
concerned with the fate of the veterans, who were apparently seen by
the central leadership as potentially useful raw material from which
steeled cadres could be forged. The soldiers had generally proven their
value and loyalty during the war, even though the Kalinin obkomburo
was cautioned by the Central Committee: the veterans could be an
unruly bunch if not properly monitored.

Once the victory was no longer in doubt, around the summer of
1944, the provincial party was mobilized to guide not merely the
rebuilding of the economy but to enforce the reconstruction of the
entire Stalinist edifice and to reduce the comparative liberty enjoyed by
the narod between December 1941 and early 1944. The crackdown
was conducted in stages; the first milestone was the sixth provincial
party conference of January 1945. Steeled during the atrocious fighting, veterans and partisans, many of whom had joined the Communist
Party during the war, were deemed to be prime candidates to be the
party's agents in this restoration, but they were to be kept under close
watch by their superiors in the party hierarchy, for their political orthodoxy was not always infallible. The authorities' distrust of former
POWs and forced labourers was much greater; several would merely
move from Nazi to Soviet camps in 1945. Not all, however, were sent
to the GULag, but former POWs, particularly, were closely monitored if
they stayed at liberty.

EXTENT AND CAUSES OF
DEMOGRAPHIC DECLINE

The war inflicted substantial material damage but did not devastate the
entire province. An unusually frank report, written on the eve of

Stalin's death, noted that the Germans occupied only fifteen out of a total of forty-seven districts of the post-August 1944 oblast'.[74] In other words, about 30 percent of the oblast' had actually been occupied, much less than the 60 percent given in the "official" history of the Kalinin provincial party organization published in the early 1970s. Even before the territorial reorganization of 1944, the largest proportion of the population lived near the October Railroad and in the southeast, areas spared (prolonged) German occupation.

By inflating the damage, however, local Communist leaders and subsequent Soviet historians attempted to create an image of an utterly devastated province, which could then be used for a while as a convenient excuse to explain, both to oblast' inhabitants and to the central party leadership and government, difficulties and delays in the subsequent rebuilding of the economy after the German retreat. Exaggerated numbers served at certain moments as an excuse for the poor performance of various sectors of the provincial economy from 1943 to 1953, and even later.[75] We must remember that the destruction was nevertheless considerable: during the war, 1,394 schools, 236 clubs and theatres, 14 museums, 23 libraries, 375 hospitals, polyclinics, and out-patient departments, and 122 children's institutions were wiped out in the oblast'.[76]

In human terms, the damage is even harder to estimate. The geographical boundaries of the oblast', and consequently the size of the population, varied widely over the years. Apart from that, there are, as mentioned, no detailed population statistics for the USSR for the period 1939–59, and the numbers for 1939 are very questionable. Therefore, it seems reasonable to estimate that 300,000 to 320,000 deaths were related to the war in the area the province occupied in 1944–56 (those who perished as a direct result of the war together with the 100,000 who died above the "normal" mortality between 1941 and 1945).[77]

A couple of reports written in 1946 by first secretary I.P. Boitsov exaggerate the population losses.[78] This macabre padding of the numbers should be understood as an appeal for some clemency from the central leadership towards his domain through adding to the wartime losses the deficit resulting from the Great Purge. Boitsov estimated a total population of 1.6 million for 1946, which, he argued, constituted a drop of more than half a million since 1939. The number of 1.6 million agrees with other postwar approximations of the population numbers given in a report some five years later. One can try, for example, to calculate the population by using some fairly reliable statistics from the local archives in Tver'. Between 1946 and 1948, around 92,000 children were born and survived childbirth in the province; roughly 400,000 children up to fourteen years old lived within its geographical borders in early 1949. The actual number of births from 1946 to 1948, including infants who died before reaching the age of one, was probably around 100,000. Consequently, the annual average number of births was roughly 33,000 during these three years, around 20 per 1,000 inhabitants (see also table 2). By dividing 33,000 by 20 and multiplying the result by 1,000, one calculates that the population of the oblast' would be around 1.65 million in early 1949.[79] This last number is actually mentioned in a letter of 21 June 1951 by first secretary Konovalov to Central Committee secretary Malenkov. Konovalov's intention was to request more funds from the Central Committee, at least for the party organization of Kalinin oblast' and perhaps for its government and economy too. As part of his argument, Konovalov stated that on 1 January 1951 the oblast' had more than 1.6 million inhabitants, of whom 551,000 were urban dwellers.[80]

The population of 2.1 million listed by Boitsov for 1939, however, is a much less believable number. The war, as we saw, may have caused a decline of some 300,000: rather less, therefore, than the 500,000 that Boitsov gave in his report to the Central Committee in 1946.[81]

Whether the decline was primarily due to the war alone or to collectivization, emigration, and the purges of the 1930s as well, the decline from the 1926 population level is stunning. When the census of 1926 was conducted, Tver' guberniia was 3 percent smaller than Kalinin oblast' of the later 1940s: twenty years later the oblast' had 650,000 inhabitants fewer. Population numbers dropped between 1926 and 1939, as well as during the war. In 1928, the number of peasants' households in Tver' guberniia in the countryside had been 429,579, and the average household had 5.1 members: thus, the peasant population was around 2,190,000.[82] Although many who were not members of a kolkhoz were counted as rural dwellers, the number of kolkhoz households by 1941 was only 275,900, with a total population of 999,000.[83] According to these numbers, in thirteen years the number of people who worked as agricultural producers and their dependents in the province had declined by more than one million! The fall in size of the average household is also remarkable for such a short timespan: from 5.1 in 1928 to 3.6 in 1941.

It is highly doubtful that almost all of the loss of 550,000 was sustained during the war, as Boitsov maintained in May 1946. The losses during the war were due to war-related deaths and the natural decline of the population (320,000), as well as to emigration because of the evacuation, army service, and so on. But losses ascribed to these last factors cannot have been close to 250,000: the inhabitants of the more densely populated area of the oblast' were not evacuated in great numbers, or they probably returned soon after the Nazi retreat. Almost all the soldiers flocked home after demobilization or are accounted for among the military deaths.[84]

For the prewar population decline, three main causes are discernible: industrialization and the migration of rural dwellers to the industrializing towns outside the oblast', collectivization (particularly "dekulakization"), and the Great Purge. The 1930s saw a dramatic plunge in the natural growth rate, exemplified, for instance, by the decrease of the average household size in the countryside. After the war, this growth was more or less lost to the yearly emigration to places outside the oblast': in 1956 or 1959 the population of Kalinin province was probably the same as in 1946 or 1951.[85]

Migration to areas outside the oblast' has caused the total population to remain virtually stagnant for the last fifty years. Between January 1946 and January 1949 the annual natural growth rate must have been roughly 10,000 per year (calculated from table 4), and it was probably higher after 1948, because the worst postwar deprivations (particularly strong in 1946 and 1947) were finally over. But in April 1956, if we are to accept the estimate of one statistical handbook, the same number of people lived in the oblast' as in 1946 (or in 1951). Thus, in a period when there was not much loss due to "unnatural deaths," the surplus resulting from natural growth disappeared through emigration, a process that has continued until our time, when the province (although of a larger size than in April 1956) still contains 1.6 million inhabitants.[86]

For lack of trustworthy statistics, it is impossible to reconstruct the exact population movement in the oblast' for the 1926–59 period. It is therefore also not practicable to assess the precise causes of the population losses. On the basis of available evidence we may at least conclude that from 1929 onwards, collectivization, purges, and war led to hundreds of thousands of "unnatural deaths" in Kalinin oblast'.[87]

In the postwar period in Tver' province, the rural population was at its peak around 1948–49 (table 6) – at which time all wartime soldiers had been demobilized. Even then the kolkhoz population fell short of the figure of 1 January 1941 by more than 150,000 souls (approximately 15 percent). One source estimates an approximate loss in the largest oblast' towns of 40,000 between 1939 and 1950 (a loss of less than 10 percent).[88] According to official numbers, on 1 January 1951, 230,000 fewer people lived on the kolkhozy than on 1 January 1941; within the same decade the population of able-bodied adult workers had declined by 160,000 and teenage workers by 27,500. The total labour force – apart perhaps from full-time party workers who have not been accounted for in the statistical sources – was about 940,000

Table 6
Households in the Kolkhozy of Kalinin Oblast', 1941–53 (in thousands, on 1 January)

	1941	1947	1949	1950	1951	1952	1953
Number of households	275.9	260.3	264.0	260.1	254.2	243.3	235.2
Population in the households	999.0	784.4	847.5	825.5	768.6	696.3	–
Able-bodied workers in the households	498.8	325.9	382.5	368.9	332.6	296.9	–
Male able-bodied workers	185.6	98.1	125.4	122.4	104.8	90.3	–
Female able-bodied workers	309.2	227.8	257.1	246.5	227.8	206.7	–
Able-bodied persons working elsewhere[1]	–	–	25.1	25.1	20.4	24.2	–
Adults not able to work[2]	–	–	137.9	138.4	138.0	138.3	–
Teenagers	90.9	69.4	67.8	66.1	63.4	63.2	–
Children 12 and under	–	–	259.3	252.1	234.6	197.9	–

Source: Based on Pako 147/5/906, ll.1, 2, 11.

Note: In 1940, within the 1944–57 borders, there were 9,016 collective farms (two of which were fish farms); in 1950, after the first amalgamation, there were 2,010; in 1953, 1,919; and in 1955, 1,978 (see Narodnoe Khoziaistvo, 57). By the end of 1955, the number of households in the collective farms had further dropped to 220,300 (ibid.). In 1940 there were 38 sovkhozy in the oblast (1944–57 borders) with a total of 5,300 workers and employees; in 1950, there were 49 sovkhozy, with a total of 8,500 workers and employees; in 1953, there were 44 sovkhozy with a total of 8,700 workers and employees (ibid., 54).

[1] This category includes persons living in kolkhozy but working in nonagricultural organizations and enterprises.

[2] This category includes aged persons.

in early 1941, but in early 1951 only about 744,000. The loss of labour had come almost exclusively at the expense of the collective farms.[89] After 1949 the number of people living in the countryside started to drop once more. The number of people employed outside agriculture in September 1950 was almost the same as in September 1940 (table 7).

A Soviet publication estimates 941,500 rural dwellers in April 1956.[90] On the surface, this number seems hard to reconcile with the fact that in 1952 less than 700,000 people were living on collective farms. It is rather surprising to find that some 300,000 people lived in the countryside in 1956 without living on collective farms – almost one-third of the people living in the countryside. Between 1945 and 1953 only a few of these rural dwellers worked on state farms (sovkhozy). Many more were employed as craftsmen and craftswomen. Others had full-time jobs in the lumber, brick, or peat industries, while still others were probably permanent MTS, transport,

Table 7
Nonagricultural Labour Force in Kalinin Oblast', 1944–57 Borders (in thousands, in September).

Economic Sector	1940	1945	1950	1955
Industrial production	135.0	103.3	142.1	173.7
Construction (construction and assembly work)	17.6	11.6	18.5	18.8
Sovkhozy and subsidiary agricultural enterprises	11.5	15.9	15.9	14.2
MTS and meadow improvement stations	6.4	2.6	4.5	33.1
Railroad transport	23.6	25.4	21.1	21.6
Water transport	1.4	1.4	1.7	1.4
Automobile transport, other transport, and cargo labour	11.8	7.2	9.6	14.2
Communications	7.0	5.4	5.8	5.9
Trade, procurements, material-technical provisioning and sales	25.6	15.3	24.1	22.4
Social catering	8.6	8.6	6.8	8.0
Education (schools, scientific and cultural-educational institutes, colleges)	35.5	27.4	31.5	33.6
Healthcare, fizkul'tura, and welfare	16.6	16.3	21.5	23.5
Credit and insurance institutions	3.2	2.2	2.6	2.5
Apparat of organs of state and economic directorates and social organizations	22.9	18.4	17.0	12.5
Other sectors (geology, forestry, capital goods repair, etc.)	24.5	18.6	25.4	26.8
Members of cooperative industrial artels	32.9	26.1	19.3	21.3
Total number of workers and employees	351.1	279.6	348.0	412.8

Source: Based on Narodnoe Khoziaistvo, 70.

services, government, or administrative workers. Their dependents – and here and there some pensioners – should be added to the total in order to comprehend fully the existence of such a large group of rural dwellers who were not on collective farms.

As usual, the demographic effects of the epochal events taking place between 1929 and 1953 were most pronounced in the countryside, but the population drop affected the province as a whole. Any society or economy would have trouble cope with such a tremendous population loss in such a short period, a loss that brings to mind the devastation of the Black Plague in Western Europe in the fourteenth century. The area showed signs of vitality before 1929, as expressed in its healthy birthrate; after 1929 the province became a wasteland thanks to the policy of the central leadership of party and government. In most years the population fell or remained stagnant. Even after the savagery of the 1930s and World War II, population growth was rare. Those with ambition who had been born in the provincial countryside left for the towns and the capital; those born in the urban areas often preferred to leave the province for the twin capitals of Leningrad and Moscow. Improved communications, access to institutions of higher and professional education, as well as army service, often enabled inhabitants to circumvent the strict terms of residence that applied to these cities.[91] Thus the drain continued after 1945.

POPULATION GROWTH AND HEALTH

In the nineteenth century, Tver' guberniia had a very high child mortality rate, even in comparison with neighbouring guberniias. During the years from 1887 through 1891, on average 344 of every 1,000 newborn children died annually as infants.[92] As is clear from the numbers in table 2 and table 8, during the immediate postwar years the rate was significantly lower.[93] Although statistics are incomplete, the average percentage of infant deaths constituted roughly 10 percent of the number of births in 1945–47, a drop of more than three times (from about 35 percent) in the span of a couple of generations.

The significance of this decrease depends on the yardstick by which it is measured. In the 1980s the mortality rate of children under one year of age would be approximately five times lower in the RSFSR and more than four times lower in the USSR than in the immediate postwar period in Kalinin oblast'.[94] Nevertheless, the drop is impressive; for still in 1940, 22 out of every 100 children had died before reaching the age of one. The numbers indicate a distinct improvement in health care in Kalinin oblast' during and after the war, probably because of advances in medicine such as penicillin and other remedies. Traditionally, the majority of the births in the countryside took place at home, but after the war most births were assisted by official midwives (akusherki), thanks to which the involvement of "ignorant old women" (nevezhestvennye babki) had been almost eliminated. In 1940, only 67.7 percent of the births in rural locations were assisted by official midwives, but already by 1945 the proportion had grown to 91.6 percent. By 1948, only 4.5 percent of home births went unsupervised.[95] Meanwhile, all births in urban areas were administered by official medical personnel. This practice did not always translate into a well-monitored birth: in his interview, I.A. Rulev blamed medical negligence for the death of his daughter in a maternity home (roddom) in the early 1950s.[96]

Abortion had been illegal in the USSR since 1936 (only to become legal once more in 1955). Nevertheless, health-department head Lapchenko reported in early 1949 to first secretary Vorontsov that in

Table 8
Monthly Births, Deaths, Marriage, and Divorce in Kalinin Oblast', 1944–48

Month	Births	Deaths	Infant Mortality[1]	Marriages	Divorces
11-1943	966	2,951	107	439	69
12-1943	1,014	3,420	115	476	88
01-1944	1,303	3,715	139	559	91
02-1944	1,132	3,619	269	625	111
03-1944	1,290	3,544	168	539	110
04-1944	1,098	3,236	140	540	94
05-1944	1,060	3,008	144	624	105
06-1944	1,238	2,255	108	494	87
07-1944	1,514	2,064	135	582	104
08-1944	1,640	2,198	173	510	–
09-1944	1,473	2,036	195	492	–
10-1944	1,386	2,146	116	436	–
11-1944	1,365[2]	2,033[3]	137	592	1
12-1944	1,398	2,507	130	604	1
01-1945	1,759	2,483	178	738	–
02-1945	1,565	2,605	175	640	1
03-1945	1,818	2,980	215	777	2
04-1945	1,519	2,378	194	444	3
05-1945	1,485	2,115	155	653	6
06-1945	1,574	1,818	115	709	3
07-1945	1,854	1,538	111	774	3
08-1945	1,783	1,456	136	958	8
09-1945	1,602	1,417	133	1,257	7
10-1945	1,746	1,591	109	1,315	5
11-1945	1,530	1,747	122	1,869	9
12-1945	1,649	2,034	162	1,868	13
01-1946	2,065	2,161	210	2,330	5
02-1946	1,891	2,288	204	2,315	3
03-1946	2,069	2,687	250	1,641	16
04-1946	1,950	2,043	192	1,494	16
05-1946	2,108	1,912	138	1,588	18
06-1946	2,287	1,453	139	1,645	11
07-1946	2,678	1,553	239	1,647	17
08-1946	3,811	1,705	305	1,861	20
09-1946	3,602	1,646	295	1,617	17
10-1946	3,740	1,872	274	1,659	9
11-1946	3,308	1,920	257	2,133	19
06-1947	2,928	2,142	366	1,301	14
07-1947	3,028	2,399	492	1,112	18
08-1947	2,928	2,354	532	1,269	29
09-1947	2,820	2,051	399	1,105	17
11-1947	2,354	1,890	274	1,958	15
05-1948	1,968	1,852	252	1,343	35
06-1948	2,260	1,501	165	1,313	36
07-1948	2,751	1,426	206	1,193	34
08-1948	3,058	1,497	214	1,319	25

Table 8 (continued)

Month	Births	Deaths	Infant Mortality[1]	Marriages	Divorces
09-1948	3,032	1,333	195	1,148	35
11-1948	2,980	1,465	166	1,852	59

Source: Based on Pako, 147/3/2748, l.15, 46–6ob., 57–7ob., 105ob., 222-2ob., 289-9ob.; Pako, 147/3/2749, ll.92–2ob., 136ob.–37, ll.230–1, ll.253–4; Pako, 147/4/66, ll. 2–3, 83–4, 94–5, 183–4, 198–200; Pako, 147/4/67, ll.1–2, 36–8, 49–51, 154–6, 157–9, 191–3, 219–21; Pako, 147/4/1132 ll.82–3, 126-7; Pako, 147/4/1133 11.5–7, 44–5, 53–5.
Note: Unfortunately, I was unable to locate the numbers for October 1947 and October 1948.
[1]Deaths of children up to 1 year of age.
[2]According to Pako, 147/3/2748, l.15, the number is 1,373.
[3]According to Pako, 147/3/2748, l.15, the number is 2,194.

1947, 3,681 abortions had been performed and that in 1948 the number had more than doubled, reaching 7,802.[97] The figure must have disturbed Lapchenko and Vorontsov, since the same report mentions a total number of newborns (up to one year old) of about 34,000 in the oblast'; thus, at least one in five pregnancies was illegally terminated in 1948. The actual number of abortions was presumably even higher, for it seems unlikely that all abortions would have been discovered by the health department. Lapchenko noted that the incidence of abortions was particularly high in the larger towns, but although he did not suggest this in his report, it is probable that many abortions performed in the countryside escaped the authorities' attention.

In order to combat the high level of abortions, the oblispolkom had instructed the lower soviets to organize special committees, composed of representatives of trade unions and social organizations. In 1947 a female doctor was put on trial for performing abortions.[98] Russians have often been prudish about their sex lives, however, and hardly any survey respondent brought up the subject of abortion. Once or twice someone noted that it had been prohibited at the time. However, many respondents, male and female, said they would have liked to have had more children. Some pointed to the difficult life at the time when asked why they did not have or want more children. Quite a few women and men mentioned unspecified "health reasons," probably infertility caused by bungled illegal abortions at this time.

In 1949 Lapchenko reported to Vorontsov that two of the goals of his department in the Fourth Five Year Plan were the "steady increase of the natural growth of the population, [and] the decrease of infant mortality."[99] The birthrate had in fact dropped dramatically during the war in all of the RSFSR, as is illustrated by the demographic numbers in table 8, which is proof again of the crucial importance given to the issue of demographics by the party leadership in the province. It comes as a surprise that the overall mortality in the winter of 1945–46 surpassed the natality once more, even though 1945 was supposedly a good agricultural year for the oblast'. The seasonal fluctuations in table 8 are logical, however: mortality was highest in March, when winter reached an end and the reserves in the countryside were becoming scant.

Although the mortality rate, both overall and for newborn children, was significantly higher in 1947 than in 1946 or 1948, the numbers are still in fact lower than the numbers for 1940. As mentioned, the quality of medical care improved during the war, so that fewer people died on average after 1944 than during the 1941–44 period, even in a year of deprivation such as 1947. The connection between the economic situation in 1947 and the flagging birthrate was made in Lapchenko's report of 1949, when he stated that "the fall in births began in the second half of 1947, in connection with the economic peculiarities of 1946," and reached a minimum in April–May 1948, and then the number of births rose, but the annual total did not reach the level of 1947.[100] Indeed, the peak of the birth rate in the early postwar period seems to have been reached in August 1946, when the birth rate was almost twice as high as in May 1948.[101]

The cause for the growth in absolute numbers of deaths in the months from July 1946 onwards, compared to the same period in the year before, can only be the devastation of the drought that struck the Soviet Union, even though it is unclear to what extent the climatic adversity afflicted Kalinin oblast'.[102] The mortality of 1947 was higher than that of 1948, which confirms the existence of economic hardship. From other evidence, one can deduce that deaths surpassed births for several consecutive months during the fall and winter of 1946–47.[103] It is, however, difficult to assess the exact impact of the drought of 1946 on population numbers in the Kalinin oblast'. Deprivation caused the postponed effect of a drop in the birthrates. Child mortality was high in July, August, and September 1947, a confirmation of difficult circumstances resulting from the adverse weather of 1946.[104] The total number of deaths for the months of June until September 1947 was always higher than 2,000, while in the summers of 1945, 1946, and 1948 considerably less than 2,000 died monthly.

In a telegram sent by the Leningrad party leadership to Central Committee secretary Zhdanov in Moscow in October 1946, traces of great difficulties in agriculture are noticeable.[105] The Leningrad party committee complained that vegetable and potato deliveries to the city fell far short of plan targets. Zhdanov forwarded copies of this

Table 9
Cases of Epidemic Disease in Kalinin Oblast', 1940, 1947, and 1948

	1940	1947	1948
Typhoid/enteric fever (briushnoi tif)	1,098	485	572
Dysentery	8,840	1,167	2,133
Spotted fever (typhus)	204	1,089	339
Measles	11,074	7,364	10,996
Scarlet fever	2,025	3,059	7,331
Diphtheria	2,884	354	552
Malaria	16,976	10,533	8,267

Source: Based on Pako, 147/4/1549, l.61.

telegram to the party bosses of Ukraine (N.S. Khrushchev, at the time), Gor'kii, Velikie Luki, Pskov, Vologda, and Iaroslavl' oblasts, as well as to Boitsov in Kalinin. The performance of Kalinin province was marginally better than that of the others, even though it had procured only 42.2 percent of the planned deliveries to Leningrad.

Directly after the war, D. Fedotov, then head of the health department, reported to Boitsov that "[t]hrough written and oral evidence from the raion of Olenino, it has been established that a substantial number of cases of venereal disease are found here, largely among the repatriated citizens."[106] In 1949 the health department also expressed its concern about the incidence of tuberculosis, infectious diseases, and illnesses of the metabolic and blood-circulation system.[107] Cases of typhoid and malaria were still regularly found in the oblast'. Malaria, nevertheless, was on the way to being eradicated. A widespread prophylactic program between 1948 and 1953 curbed the incidence of this disease from more than 8,000 cases in 1948 to 33 in 1953.[108] Brucellosis started to plague the farm animals of the oblast' around 1945 and sometimes infected humans. In 1948 nineteen cases were registered.[109]

In early 1949 the health department was aware of the utilitarian nature of its attempt to strengthen the population's health, for it professed to be trying to minimize job absenteeism. The utmost effort was also being made to reintroduce war invalids into the work force. Control was to be exerted over the observance of sanitary and hygienic rules in all sectors of the economy. Although the prewar network of hospitals and clinics had been fully restored by early 1949, health care institutions still fell short of the required norms, particularly in the formerly occupied areas. The veterinarian Nadezhda A. Smirnova, for example, said in the survey that she was forced to treat people as well as animals, for the nearest hospital was too far from the village where she was stationed.[110]

In July 1951 the province still lacked more than eight hundred of the doctors it needed.[111] In September 1951 the standard of medical care in certain raions was in urgent need of improvement, for doctors had to perform surgery by the light of kerosene lamps, as there was no electricity in their areas![112] In 1953 in Rzhev raion men, women, and children had to share the one available room in a hospital.

No statistics on the average life span of the inhabitants of Kalinin oblast' could be found for the period, but it is probably true that those who had survived the war lived on average longer than their prewar peers, particularly because, despite the deprivations, health care was slowly improving.[113]

The health statistics indicate that in the postwar period living conditions gradually improved. The improvement of the general state of health after 1944 is evident in the slow increase in the population of the province because of a surplus of births over deaths between January 1945 and November 1948 (even though for several months during this span death rates may have surpassed birth rates when the consequences of the drought of 1946 were felt in Kalinin oblast'). The province seems to have been spared the worst of the famine of 1946–47.

After 1948 improvements in the health of the residents of Tver' province were less marked: although the Russians were healthier in the last years of Stalin's life than in the 1890s, the authorities failed to eradicate small outbreaks of various epidemics of contagious diseases, which flared up at regular intervals. In most instances, they seem to have been related to a lack of clean drinking water and a failure to observe hygienic standards.

Party and state policy toward the birthrate was clearly ineffective: births surpassed deaths after the war, but not at a rate that would swiftly compensate for the bloodletting of the previous fifteen years. The virtual prohibition of divorce in 1944 did not start the hoped-for baby boom; the great number of illegal abortions leads one to conclude that many women and men looked upon Stalinist society as a not particularly promising environment to bring up children. Since, furthermore, migration out of the province continued after 1945, the authorities were continuously faced with a serious labour shortage in Kalinin province after the war.

PART TWO

The Postwar Years

CHAPTER THREE

The View from Above: The Communists

The postwar developments in Kalinin oblast' can only be understood against the historical background sketched in the previous pages. From here onward, an in-depth discussion will follow of life in the province during Stalin's last years. After the war the utopian goal, the triumph of Communism throughout the world or, at least, the defence of the Communist bastion against surrounding enemies (imaginary or not), continued to justify the means, which more often than not led to the ruthless exploitation of, and totalitarian control over, the Soviet people.[1] Soviet citizens had only duties – no rights. In 1986 Molotov, on the verge of death, wrote that "the fundamental principle of socialism (in distinction to communism) is the fulfillment of the labour norms as established by society."[2] Was Stalin ever seriously concerned about how these principles of barracks' socialism had made his people suffer? The ultimate Communist victory was the theoretical justification for the inhumane policies of Stalin and his close comrades; as long as Communism had not triumphed on a global scale, all Communists and all Soviet citizens were expected to sacrifice everything they had on the altar of the cause.[3] In return for their efforts, they were not supposed to expect anything until some unspecified point in the future, when the worldwide proletarian revolution would be victorious.

Because this was a society driven by coercion, we should first turn our attention to the organizations that enforced the oppression. The Communist Party was only in name a political party. In practice it made, executed, and controlled the policies that ruled the Soviet Union. Important decisions were made by the Central Committee, its Sekretariat, or the Politburo and Orgburo in Moscow; the provincial sekretariat, the first secretary, or the obkomburo were called upon to see through the local execution of these decisions in as smooth a manner as possible. Although essential decisions and policy changes originated in the higher party organs in Moscow (and, if they seemed crucial enough to him, were made by Stalin), the provincial party leadership not only ensured political conformity and oversaw the execution of economic plans but had to decide upon a number of smaller issues on its own. The rather primitive state of transport and communication in many sections of the oblast' alone made it impossible for the Central Committee apparatus to oversee all the minute details that affected the lives of 1.6 million people living in a province the size of the Benelux. Particularly with regard to decisions made about agricultural issues, the provincial and district party leaders had some room to manoeuvre. They had to tread with caution, however, for they were under the watchful eye of the employees and informers of the NKVD/NKGB and its successors. Any unorthodox activity was bound to end up on the desk either of a member of the Central Committee staff or of the secret police chief – or both – and would come back to haunt the person responsible for allowing the irregular practice.

The fate of the party leaders in the postwar period will be charted in this chapter; the interaction between those outside the party and those inside will be discussed in chapter 4. Since this relationship was so strongly based on (the threat of) political or criminal persecution, a separate chapter (chapter 5) will address this aspect of the lives of rulers and ruled. The two subsequent chapters (6 and 7) will attempt to concentrate more strictly on the question how the inhabitants of Kalinin province constituted their lives in urban and rural environments, attempting to survive while fulfilling the economic plans and the orders of the party. Chapter 8 will address some of the fundamental longer-term consequences of the Stalin years.

Although any important issue was decided by the higher party leadership, the Communist Party always preserved the pretence of being a democratically organized political party in which lower levels elected officials to lead them and in which the Communist footsoldiers decided on matters of policy or were at least entitled to criticize them. To keep up this democratic smoke-screen, once in a while a provincial party meeting gathered in Kalinin, as was the case in January 1945. Far from being elected by the primary party organizations (the lowest party cells in the hierarchy), representatives had been hand-picked by the provincial party leadership. In the last section of this chapter we will see how in reality the central and provincial leadership's instruments of power functioned in the province.

In 1945, at the outset, the mood of the sixth party conference might have been optimistic and self-congratulatory as a result of the victory over Nazi Germany that could be seen on the horizon, but the party secretaries made sure to put a damper on exaggerated expectations about postwar policies. It would be the last party conference presided over by first secretary Boitsov, for he was to be succeeded in the autumn of 1946 by his second-in-command, P.S. Vorontsov, another survivor who had been promoted during the Great Purge. Vorontsov would fall in late 1949 for reasons probably unrelated to the state of the provincial party or the economic health of the oblast'. His successor lasted for an even shorter while and was demoted but apparently resumed his career under Khrushchev. In the summer of 1951, therefore, the province was led by its fourth postwar leader. This Kiselev disappeared soon after Stalin's death, possibly because he and some other provincial leaders were part of the "Malenkov gang" which relinquished control within the party to the team of Khrushchev from March 1953 onward.

Let us now turn to January 1945, when the elite of the All-Union Communist Party (Bolsheviks) of Kalinin oblast' listened to their leadership's estimation of the current state of affairs in the province and the plans for its future after the imminent victory in the war.

THE REPORT OF BOITSOV

In 1945 it was feasible for the Soviet leadership and the Soviet citizens to start on a new footing, avoiding or correcting mistakes committed during the 1930s and earlier. Yet the central leadership deliberately let this opportunity pass. It can be asked, as well, how far the policy changes of the war's first years were inspired at all by any desire to abandon the methods of the 1930s; perhaps they had merely been introduced for reasons of expediency when survival of the Soviet Union and the rule of the Communist Party were in grave danger.

In January 1945 the sixth provincial party conference took stock and charted the course of future development in relation to both the ruin inflicted by the war and further "building of socialism." In 1946 the Fourth Five Year Plan would coordinate the development of the oblast' economy more extensively within that of the whole USSR, but while the war was still raging the provincial leadership was left to fend for itself to some degree.[4] Reconstruction was not yet the first priority for the Central Committee.

Second secretary Vorontsov opened the conference the evening of 13 January 1945, setting the proper tone when he announced that the participants were to critically appreciate "the great shortcomings in the labour of the party obkom and other oblast' organizations and to show the way to the elimination of these shortcomings."[5]

It is surprising to find this party chief so critical of the provincial organization. After all, victory was assured in January 1945. The party could have been portrayed solely as the successful organizer of the defeat of the Nazis. Instead, Vorontsov lashed out at "shortcomings." The key to understanding Vorontsov's unexpected criticism is the peculiar mentality forged within the party during the 1930s. Too many party leaders had been accused of complacency in the Ezhovshchina and purged as a result. Knowing that his fate and the fate of his colleagues depended on economic and political success, Vorontsov obviously tried to forestall such accusations. The powerful memory of the Great Terror had not lost much of its force.

In some ways, nevertheless, this conference was a moment of triumph for the first party secretary of the oblast', I.P. Boitsov. Ivan Pavlovich was a survivor: his appointment as provincial boss had come late enough in 1938 for him to avoid the fate of his predecessors. He had gone on to become a heralded defender of the malaia rodina against the invaders. Boitsov deserves pride of place as the most important party leader of Tver' province during the entire Stalinist period. In the 1930s and 1940s, Boitsov became a leading paragon for A.A. Kondrashov, a young and upcoming party leader, and he stood at the cradle of Kondrashov's career.[7] Without this initial support, Kondrashov would have never been able to rise as high in the hierarchy as he did in the time of Stalin, Khrushchev, and Brezhnev. Even though Kondrashov witnessed the immoral methods applied at times by the Stalinist party secretary in governing Tver' province, Boitsov remained a faultless godfather to him. Boitsov's style of leadership was a beacon for him: Kondrashov led the province with the same lack of scruples, though with less violence, in the 1950s and 1960s.

Boitsov's tenure of the first secretaryship of Kalinin oblast' was unusually long, from the spring of 1938 until the end of 1946. It is worthwhile to explore Boitsov's career in Tver' province, for he represents the epitome of the successful Stalinist apparatchik. When he introduced himself to the provincial party organization as the successor of P.G. Rabov in March 1938 he included a short political autobiography of his early career:

I was born in 1896 in the former Guberniia of Vladimir, in the Shuiskii district, in the village of Chasevo. I lived there until 1915 and worked at a factory. In 1915, I was in the old army – rank and file –; after I was demobilized from the old army, I worked at the railroads at the Fifth Division of the October Railroad, in the function of traindriver-helper. In October 1918, I was taken into the Red Army, served in the railroad armies – in the Fifteenth Railroad Company, later Batallion, later Division, thus its name changed. In 1925, I was, for reasons of age, demobilized, and I was in Leningrad at party work; at the time of the Zinovievite Opposition, I worked as secretary of the party committee of the Finland division of the October Railroad; in 1926, I was transferred to study in the courses for party workers in Moscow, after which I was sent to the disposal of the Leningrad party obkom and assigned to work as a raikom secretary not far from Leningrad.

After this I worked as partkom [party committee] secretary of the Engels' works: in 1930 I was sent to the Leningrad branch of the Institute of Red Professors. Until 1932 I studied, after which I was again taken into the Red Army. Following that, I was sent to the Academy as a teacher. By a decision of the Central Committee in 1934, I was assigned work as a party organizer. In 1937, I worked as a secretary of the committee of the Pskov okrug. I have been a party member since March 1919.

Voice: "Were there any party penalties?"

I never had any. I did not take part in the oppositions, [and] took part in the struggle with those people everywhere I happened to work; nor was I in anti-party groups.[8]

Boitsov's self-portrait gives an impression of a relatively flawless past, but elements in this (or any party leader's) biography could have provided a motive for his destruction if party and NKVD had elected to do so: service in the tsarist army and employment near Leningrad at the time of the "Zinovievite Opposition" would have been cause enough. But for whatever reason, Boitsov survived. More than anything else, he lacked the imagination even to consider joining the oppositions against the "general line," to which he referred in his presentation. Although portraying himself as a worker, it can be assumed that he actually came from a peasant background, a member of the first generation of Russians who resettled in towns and found employment as industrial workers. It is a sobering thought to speculate that, had he been born in another European country, he probably would have worked on the railroad for the rest of his life.

In late 1946 I.P. Boitsov was transferred to Stavropol krai; his appointment as first secretary constituted a promotion.[9] He was succeeded by second secretary P.S. Vorontsov, who fared less well as provincial chief. Boitsov's promotion was rather curious under the circumstances: 1946 was a year of hardship for Kalinin province, but the insufficient deliveries of agricultural produce by the province in October 1946 did not prevent his transfer to Stavropol krai just a few weeks later.[10] The Stavropol region was a far more important territory than Kalinin province; its economic significance depended almost entirely on its high agricultural returns. What could have been behind the promotion of a first secretary who recently had failed in acquitting himself satisfactorily of one of his most important jobs, the supervision of agriculture?[11] Boitsov escaped retribution because miserable results were achieved everywhere in the Soviet Union in this year. In the case of the Leningrad procurements (discussed in chapter 2), his province still outshone the others mentioned in the Zhdanov telegram. A further explanation should be sought in the appreciation by the Politburo of Boitsov's other talents. After all, he had proven himself a faithful executor of party orders in the 1930s, while leading the provincial organization adequately throughout the war. Similarly, Gorbachev's less than successful stint as party leader responsible for agriculture under Brezhnev did not prevent him from becoming general secretary of the Communist Party of the Soviet Union. Gorbachev and Boitsov apparently demonstrated other, compensating merits, while, of course, both had the good fortune of ingratiating themselves with the right patrons in Moscow.

During his residence in Kalinin, Boitsov's greatest moment to shine in the public limelight came at the sixth party conference. He read the political report, a task usually given to the primus inter pares at any level of the hierarchy. The reader may find the following discussion of the report at times hard to digest, but it may help to remember that when the speech was actually delivered in 1945, the audience listened to a much longer version lasting many hours. The rhetorical style is unimaginative and repetitive. Like his successors, Boitsov epitomized the colourless apparatchik. The attention of his audience must often have flagged during what seems to us a stunningly boring discourse, but the listeners at the time would have pricked up their ears whenever their particular domain was discussed. Boitsov indicated by praising or criticizing individuals' fiefs whether they were currently enjoying the favour of the higher party echelons or not. Negative mention could be the portent of worse things to come; how bad they could get was well remembered from the prewar era.

As was usual with this type of speech, each section, after some minimal praise for certain accomplishments of individuals and organizations, was filled with reprovals. Boitsov had also learned his lesson from the Ezhovshchina. Despite this, his account of the situation and prospects in January 1945 betrayed a sense of confidence about the development in the postwar years. His expectations of economic prosperity were to be proven wrong, but this gradually became clear only after he had left the province.[13]

Boitsov began his report with a criticism of construction labour, a sign of the priority it had in the provincial party's policy, still very much focussed on the revival of the areas destroyed during the war. The major building organizations had not fulfilled their plan in 1944, due to labour shortages and lack of mechanization.[14] Yet there had been room for improvement, for available workers were not efficiently deployed, owing to the absence of proper training, and they were poorly rewarded for their efforts. A fluctuation of manpower was the result. As was always the case at party conferences, obkom plenums, or sessions of the obkomburo, the first secretary accused the party gorkoms and raikoms (and in this case the obkom itself as well) of being responsible for poor supervision and flawed control. As a result of the oversights in construction work, the housing situation was singled out as particularly bad in the Proletarskii and Novopromyshlennyi districts of the town of Kalinin and in the town of Bezhetsk.

In 1944 industry had performed satisfactorily on the whole, inasmuch as it had fulfilled the state plan by 103.5 percent.[15] Despite this fine overall performance, some factories had not come up to scratch and were admonished. The railroad-carriage construction factory, one of the most renowned in the province, had met the production plan in 1944 by only 89.7 percent. Boitsov was not satisfied with the explanation of factory managers that it was all due to the lack of raw materials; after all, the factory had lost in ten months of 1944 a total value of 1.3 million rubles to wastage. Production stoppages had reached 23,000 man-hours at the factory during this period. Consumer goods were another branch of deficient production: ceramics for electrical stoves, soap, textiles, and furniture were among products mentioned that had been produced in insufficient numbers.

In general, the party blamed low labour productivity on an inefficient use of technology and an unintelligent distribution of the labour force within the production process. Boitsov did not discuss here two fundamental causes that plagued light industry particularly, of which his fief had a much greater share than of heavy industry: labour production here suffered more from obsolete machinery and poor remuneration for the workers than from managerial incompetence.

Boitsov stated that stoppages above planned norms happened in almost all branches of industry. Shortages of qualified people and problems resulting from the shoddy organization of labour were perceived by him to be additional causes for low labour productivity. After the war, Gosplan head Voznesensky would add an erratic supply of fuel, electricity, and raw materials to the explanation of the deficient results of light industry during the war.[16] What was allowed to a politburo member in hindsight (and some have suggested that his comparatively honest account of the Soviet economy during World War II was a factor in Voznesensky's demise) was not allowed to Boitsov during the war: he realized that significant investment in light industry would not be forthcoming soon from Moscow. The only way of improving results was to crack the whip over the human cattle employed in the factories, however imperfect a strategy this might be.

Part of the problem here, as in construction, stemmed from the unsteady work force. In 1944, for example, in the textile factory "Proletarka" 669 people were hired and 477 left; in the rubber-sole factory, 514 workers were taken on, while 351 left. Lack of housing and other primary necessities constituted a major cause of this rapid turnover of workers.[17]

Incentives offered to the labour force were largely immaterial. The most important stimulus was the socialist emulation movement, which had been joined by most factories: in textile and light industry, 92.3 percent of the workers participated. Trade unions were berated for not propagating and stimulating advanced methods of production frequently enough.[18]

In order to better performance, Boitsov concluded his discussion by recommending the emulation of the decisions of the Eighteenth All-Union Party Conference of 1941 and Stalin's wartime speeches. Boitsov's admonitions were all stick and no carrot. He had no significant increase in remuneration to offer, while his analysis was too broad to be of much use to factory managers present at the conference: the party secretary spent little time studying industrial production and factory operations in detail, partially because industry fell under the competence of others. The obkomburo and its chief were far from the only authorities responsible for the state of factory production in the province.[19] After the conclusion of the war, the state would remain reluctant to invest any significant monies in provincial industry, which was for the most part of little significance to the USSR. The party leaders and the industrial managers were thus continuously told to rely on their own strength to raise or maintain production levels.

Further on in the speech Boitsov expressed satisfaction with the failure of Nazi propaganda to undermine kolkhozniks' apparent faith in the superiority of the kolkhoz organization.[20] Immediately after liberation, he glowingly acknowledged, kolkhozniks, MTS workers, and sovkhoz workers, under the lead of the party, had begun to resurrect the destroyed farms. Although this might be attributed to loyalty to the Communist cause, one tends to doubt the extent of the enthusiasm involved. Private farming had been effectively suppressed during the 1930s by applying extreme coercion in the countryside. The spirit of private gain, however, had not disappeared: it had found an outlet within the collective farm structure in labour on the private plot. After a dozen years of collective farming, most kolkhozniks (or, more appropriately, kolkhoznitsy, for the majority of those working in the farms were women during the war) understood very well, nevertheless, that it was unwise to risk the wrath of the regime by attempting to insist on the preservation of the greater scope allowed to private farming during the darkest days of the war. Whenever such an urge did express itself, the party members involved in the reconstruction process made sure that it was suppressed. Furthermore, the expertise or the means necessary to run a farm on one's own were scarce by 1943. However low the enthusiasm of the population may have been, some progress had been made: but to what degree collective farms or MTSS were in fact operating satisfactorily was open to question.

Boitsov lauded the efforts of the collective farmers of the unoccupied eastern raions in giving support to their brethren in the west by sending construction workers and carters to help out: they had helped 139,000 people move from dug-outs (zemlianki) to new houses.[21] Some patriotic feeling certainly played a role, but one is inclined to ask whether the eastern kolkhozniks were given the option to refuse to help, while the dimensions of the effort are less spectacular than imagined. The term "house" (dom) can be misleading here: in July 1953 the raikom secretary of Rzhev raion, Fochenkov, described these constructions as built from old army dugouts, railroad sleepers, and decrepit farm houses. Such emergency structures could not be kept up between 1945 and 1953, inasmuch as Rzhev raion had no forests and therefore hardly any wood to repair houses.[22]

Boitsov notes that in briefly occupied raions, agriculture had made a remarkable recovery in terms of crop cultivation and animal husbandry; although the collective farms suffered from a lack of draught power and the slow pace of housing construction and communal-building construction in his opinion.[23] In the raions that had not been occupied, harvest results were supposedly extremely good in 1944. The average yield of grain crops in 1944 was said to be 12.2 tsentner per hectare, and of potatoes, 121 tsentner (a tsentner weighs 100 kilograms).

Boitsov's numbers are suspect, however. A report circulated among the provincial Party leaders in the early 1950s noted that in no year from 1947 to 1952 had harvest yields of cereal crops been higher than 9.4 tsentner per hectare, while for potatoes 108.1 tsentner per hectare had been the maximum achieved during the same period. The grain yield mentioned is also remarkably high if we compare it to the average grain yields for the whole USSR between 1933 and 1937, which was 7.1 tsentner per hectare. In 1949 to 1953 it reached 7.7 tsentner per hectare. What, then, could be the explanation for potato yields of 121 tsentner per hectare and grain yields of 12.2 tsentner?[24]

First, wartime agricultural production was higher because of a relatively flexible policy towards agriculture. The ideological orthodoxy of the production process took a backseat to the achievement of good yields: this contributed to better results. Second, Boitsov used the method of measuring the crop "standing in the field," as was common under Stalin; in contrast, the report of the 1950s only counted the actual collected harvest.[25] Third, the disappearance of patriotic zeal and lack of workfolk, combined with bad weather or soil exhaustion, made agriculture perform worse after the war than during it. Finally, Boitsov (or others) may have deliberately exaggerated the yield per hectare in his speech; the official wartime results were to be the yardstick by which agricultural output would be measured after the war. Delegates from rural regions were given the message that in future years at least similar yields would be expected. Many of the conference delegates were leaders of rural raions (for example, Party secretaries or raiispolkom chairs) and therefore responsible for their fief's agricultural results: Boitsov may have thought it wise to convince them that these exalted crop-yield levels had been reached even during the difficult years of 1943 and 1944. These kinds of tactics used by Boitsov resemble those wielded by the party and government in Moscow, who were in the habit of setting astronomical production targets based on false statistics for the five year plans for the whole of the USSR.[26]

The most consistent and best results in agriculture were attained in the eastern-most raions. Harvests were low in the majority of the sovkhozy, and in Firovo, Lesnoe, Novokarel', Spirovo, and Kozlovo raions. Boitsov saw the primary cause of mediocre yields in violations of the elementary rules of agro-technology, of which the failure to introduce the proper crop rotation was the most glaring. In the entire province, more than seven hundred kolkhozes remained "backward," around 10 percent of the total number. The average reaping of cereal crops at these collective farms did not surpass 600 to 700 kilograms per hectare. In light of the numbers for later harvest results given above, such a yield seems hardly worth criticizing.[27]

Boitsov went on to argue for the system of using small brigades or links (zven'ia) in field work, not only for flax cultivation (they had dealt with 81 percent of the flax production in 1944) but also for grain cultivation.[28] Zven'ia had cultivated 24 percent of the sown area for grain and 44 percent for potatoes. They were most adept in cases where intensive manual labour was needed. Especially during the war, with little agricultural machinery available, this system was apparently quite useful. Boitsov noted that many zven'ia, after their formation in springtime, dissolved during the agricultural season. The first obkom secretary did not explain what happened to the members of these links or who took care of agricultural production after their demise. The kolkhozniks probably gathered the harvest individually: if the harvest

Table 10
Livestock in Public Herds of the Kolkhozy in Kalinin Oblast' (thousands of animals, on 1 January).

	1941	1945	Percentage Change, 1941–45	Percentage of Plan Fulfillment for 1944
Strong horned cattle	352.3	350.0	102.1 (sic)	105.8
Cows[1]	137.2	88.9	64.7	101.2
Sheep and goats	276.9	353.1	127.6	106.8
Ewes[2]	126.9	191.9	150.1	108.7
Hogs	60.2	65.7	109.0	102.1
Sows[3]	11.9	21.0	176.6	112.3

Source: Based on Pako, 147/3/2679, l.10.
note: These are Boitsov's numbers for livestock not in personal ownership of the kolkhozniks.
[1] Included in the figures for strong-horned cattle.
[2] Included in the figures for sheep and goats.
[3] Included in the figures for hogs.

yields given by Boitsov earlier in his speech are to be believed, it was a task not done all that badly by them.[29]

Machine Tractor Stations, numbering ninety in January 1945, often failed to fulfill the entire range of duties ordained by the plans. Machine repairs were behind schedule, hindering a smooth execution of spring sowing, and cadres were inadequately trained. Meanwhile, labour suffered from inept organization, and flawed leadership by the party prevailed as much here as in other areas. The complaints about the tractor stations echoed those voiced before the war. Boitsov's remarks on the sovkhozes were very brief, a reflection of their insignificant role in the provincial economy. Their livestock production had prospered in 1944, but their grain harvests amounted to a pittance.[30]

Surprisingly, Boitsov stated that the province had more livestock in late 1944 than before the war. He proudly added that the oblast' took first place in animal husbandry among the centrally located provinces of the RSFSR: table 10 was added to the transcript of his speech to prove the point. One is led to wonder whether Boitsov actually read out the columns in the table: his audience may have been on the verge of already nodding off at this point, for he had been speaking for several hours.[31]

More uplifting results were reeled off about milk production from dairy cows. Already within eleven months of 1944, 98.2 percent of the annual plan had been met; the average yield per cow was 1,080 litres, while the plan had aimed at 1,100 litres for the full year. These results stand out brightly against the sombre background of continuous

Table 11
Total Number of Cattle in Tver' Guberniia and Kalinin Oblast' (in thousands, on 1 January)

	Strong-Horned Cattle	Cows[1]	Hogs	Sheep and Goats	Horses
1916	765.3	405.8	77.6	883.4	366.8
1928	990.8	529.7	187.4	1543.6	480.0
1941	582.9	342.5	198.3	744.7	249.0
1945	629.5	266.6	113.9	815.3	106.7
1950	767.4	356.7	338.0	997.2	140.7
1953	577.1	317.8	289.3	761.9	168.3

Source: Based on Pako, 147/5/663, l.17; the numbers for 1928 are corroborated by Altrichter; for 1916 they are higher than Altrichter's numbers (Die Bauern, table 10, 209).
Note: The borders here are those of the smaller oblast of approximately 63,000–65,500 square kilometers. The numbers for the 1940s and 1950s are suspect: the number of cattle seems inflated, even though some cattle were owned by people and organizations outside the collective farming system (such as urban residents or state farms).
[1] Included in the figures for strong-horned cattle.

grumblings about the performance of animal husbandry of subsequent years. In 1949 the highest level of milk yield per cow was reached for the years from 1945 to 1953, when the annual provincial average reached 1,140 litres. In 1947, 1950, and 1951 the average yield per cow would be less than 1,000 litres, and 1,100 litres was surpassed only in 1948 and 1949. One suspects that the key explanation here was the greater freedom enjoyed by the kolkhozniks during the war, for much of the milk originated from their private cattle. Nevertheless, the other reasons mentioned earlier for undermining our faith in the figures on crop yields may apply here too.[32]

Collective farmers owned more cows privately in January 1945 than before the war. Whereas before the war 21 percent of kolkhozniks did not personally own a cow, in 1945 only 9 percent of kolkhozniks survived without one. The improvement, however, was almost entirely due to the dramatic wartime population drop. If one calculates the relative distribution of personal cows among the kolkhozniks, Boitsov's numbers are correct, but on 1 January 1946, in absolute numbers fewer cows were found for personal use in the province than in January 1941.[33]

The combined number of pigs and sheep owned by kolkhozy and kolkhozniks had declined, while kolkhozniks' ownership of goats had risen in absolute numbers. Tables 11, 12, and 13 indicate how the latter trend continued until at least 1953. They also indicate the disastrous consequences of the slaughter mania in the early stages of collec-

Table 12
Cattle in Personal Use among the Kolkhozniks of Kalinin Oblast' (in thousands on 1 January)

	1941	1946[1]	1947	1950	1951	1952	1953
Total number of households	275.9	–	260.3	260.1	254.2	243.3	235.2
Strong-horned cattle	190.6	233.4	215.0	233.3	170.1	155.2	123.5
Cows[2]	174.6	167.2	175.4	169.6	140.1	137.0	108.8
Hogs	90.5	26.7	22.8	108.2	55.8	57.1	76.6
Sheep	406.1	302.3	234.1	300.2	132.6	115.1	97.6
Goats	14.3	42.6	–	88.6	82.6	97.6	115.0

Source: Based on Pako, 147/5/906, l.1, 11; Pako, 147/4/921, l.88ob.; *Narodnoe Khoziaistvo*, 44.
[1] According to *Narodnoe Khoziaistvo*, 44; Pako, 147/4/811 gives numbers that are slightly lower (0–5%) than these.
[2] Included in the figures for strong-horned cattle.

Table 13
Kolkhoz Livestock, 1941–47 (in thousands, on 1 January)

	1941	1942	1945	1946	1947
Horses	230.8	114.4	–	101.5	99.1
Foals	–	–	–	–	10.7
Strong-horned cattle	352.3	91.4	350.0	346.4	333.9
Cows	137.2	41.2	88.9	107.1	101.4
Oxen	–	–	–	45.4	47.1
Sheep and goats	276.9	89.4[1]	353.1	341.0	310.3
Ewes and female goats	126.9	49.0[2]	191.9	215.0	211.3
Hogs	60.2	16.1	65.7	64.9	62.7
Sows	11.9	5.9	21.0	23.3	24.3

Source: Based on Pako, 147/3/2679, l.10, 147/4/528, l.6ob., 147/4/921, l.88; *Narodnoe Khoziaistvo*, 44.
[1] The figures for 1941 and 1942 are probably for sheep only.
[2] The figures for 1941 and 1942 are probably for ewes only.

tivization: the total number in public and private herds combined of strong-horned cattle, sheep, and goats in 1941, 1946, or even 1956 fell far short of the numbers for these animals in 1928.[34]

Although one would expect Boitsov to celebrate the recovery of cattle herds to prewar levels, the death of a great percentage of sucklings disturbed him: 11.7 percent of calves, 24 percent of lambs, and 9.4 percent of piglets had perished in 1944. This would remain a problem in subsequent years.[35] Excessive deaths among young cattle and low milk production were allegedly caused by irresponsible tending of livestock, execrable organization, and faulty remuneration of labour at the animal farms. In the eyes of the party's leadership, therefore, human error lay at the basis of the problems; a more likely cause, such as scarcity of fodder in the dire war circumstances, was never even suggested.

The worst sector of animal husbandry was horse breeding. Annually the number of horses decreased, as too few foals were born and many horses perished. In 1944 the number of horses had fallen by 6 percent. Boitsov omitted any mention of the fact that from collectivization onwards the number of horses had never again reached the level of 1928.[36]

At this point of the speech, the turn to be chided came to a group of raions that were performing exceptionally poorly in breeding and caring for horses. Lack of personal responsibility (obezlichka) and barbarous attitudes towards the horses were cited as the main causes of the fall in their numbers. Raikoms and raiispolkoms were not taking measures to combat these shortcomings.[37]

Finally, somewhat surprisingly to his browbeaten audience, the first secretary noted that the province had been able to discharge completely its procurement obligations assigned by the state for all areas of crop and livestock production from 1941 to 1945.[38] In 1943 and 1944 even more than the required amount of cereals and potatoes had been delivered. One reason for the fulfillment of agricultural production quotas was undoubtedly the fact that the state procurements were assessed at a much lower level during the war than before or after it.

Concluding his discussion of the provincial economy, Boitsov reminded his audience that any successes recounted should not inspire smugness, for "Comrade Stalin continuously warns us against the danger of complacency, which unavoidably leads to showing off, to the enfeebling of our work, and to the coming apart of successfully started work."[39]

The political mood of provincial dwellers was next on the agenda: Boitsov began to elaborate on the extent of the citizen's loyalty. He noted that subscriptions to state loans were below expectations.[40] He could not deny, however, the provincial inhabitants' exceptional sacrifices in their previous "voluntary" contributions toward the war effort. In the form of loans, they had donated more than 900 million rubles for such items as the deployment of a full tank column in battle. Apart from this, 78 million rubles of obligations to the defence fund had been bought, and in four lotteries 143 million had been collected. These numbers were quite significant, considering the oblast's total budgetary income in 1942 (289.6 million rubles) and 1943 (304.1 million rubles).[41] Virtually every household in the oblast' held obligations for state loans after the war. State loans were resented: in hindsight, complaints were often uttered in the 1992 survey about these "voluntary" loans, which siphoned off the last little extra that people earned. Even G.V. Lubov, otherwise an unreconstructed Communist, noticed that he and his family, even though as urban dwellers they were more eager to contribute to these state loans than collective farmers, complained about the high level.[42] In fact, state loans functioned as a kind of surtax. In May 1945 a new state loan would be issued for the recovery and development of the USSR economy. Subscription went well in most urban areas, where the loan target was quickly reached, but the new loan received a less than enthusiastic welcome in certain rural areas.[43] By 6 May, 97.9 percent of the planned subscription by workers and employees was fulfilled, but only 74 percent of the planned subscription by kolkhozniks was fulfilled. In several raions, the level of the loan subscriptions planned exceeded the "available means" of the population. Peat diggers refused to subscribe, for example, as they had not been provided with work clothes, consumer goods, and decent nourishment.

The balance of the provincial budget and local public investment were discussed briefly by Boitsov.[44] The topic was of secondary importance to the provincial Communists, for the oblast' organization had little control over the allocation of funds. The obkom, the raikoms and gorkoms, and the soviet ispolkoms at the different levels of the government administration were at the mercy of the limits of the financial and economic plans set by Gosplan, the government, and, ultimately, the Politburo and Central Committee Sekretariat. Provincial authorities had authority only over decisions on distributing financial resources directed by the centre to the oblast' or over the limited revenue that the central authorities allowed the provincial government to retain. With this money, provincial and district party committees and soviet executive committees had to execute public works, build houses, bridges, and schools, or operate the educational and health care systems. The means allocated were always too limited, as the tediously difficult and drawn-out resurrection of Rzhev shows. The first economic priority centred on meeting economic production plans. The oblispolkom was left with very meagre funds to spend on areas such as public housing, health care, or culture. Records for the period reveal a continuous call to economize within these areas, to manage with the means available. One can only conclude that at no point in this period was enough money left to drastically improve things such as municipal services in any sustained manner. That, as we know, was indeed not something about which Stalin and his clique worried unduly. Most resources, even after the war, were dedicated to the maintenance and improvement of the country's defence, a result of the leadership's paranoid fear of foreign intervention.[45] Largely agrarian with mainly auxiliary industry producing consumer goods and no longer bordering a foreign country as it had before 1940, Kalinin oblast' did not play a major role in the leadership's plans for the development and maintenance of Soviet defence.

From this point onwards in his speech, Boitsov concerned himself with the Komsomol and party proper. Boitsov stated frankly what the first priority for the party organizations in the oblast' should be:

The decisive standard of measurement in all our work should be the ability to organize the blue-collar workers, the engineering-technological workers, the employees, and the kolkhozniks for the fulfillment of the plan. An appraisal of the work of a factory party cell must be done by establishing how much it is able to guarantee the deliveries for the front, how much the factory is fulfilling the productive obligations with respect to the assortment of goods, and, for a kolkhoz and territorial party cell, how much it is able to discharge its obligatory state procurements, to increase the total amount of agricultural produce, and so on.[46]

In other words, economic criteria were of key importance to the provincial leadership in their appraisal of party cells.

Boitsov stressed the importance of control over the execution of decisions made at higher levels of the Communist Party and over decisions made by regional organizations in the oblast'.[47] Leadership positions in the province had been infused with new blood because many prewar incumbents had left to join the Red Army or the partisans or had accompanied the evacuated enterprises. From 1 January 1942 through December 1944, 22,860 people (of whom 12,270 were women) were appointed to take on "leading work."[48]

The ample attention that Boitsov devoted to the situation with cadres here was probably a result of criticism of the obkom by the Central Committee in December 1943. A plenum in April 1944 had directed its undivided attention to the question of cadres.[49] Frequent changing of jobs by leading cadres had continued after this meeting. In 1944, 908 (27 percent) of the workers in the obkom nomenklatura were replaced. In 1943–44, the oblispolkom had replaced people in 830 out of 1,370 leading positions (60 percent).[50] The composition of the oblast's leading cadres underwent a considerable renewal after June

1941: 80 percent of the incumbents of higher office in party and state had been appointed during the war years. Most of these individuals were young and had joined the party only quite recently. Leading cadres in the countryside, particularly, had been renewed extensively in the war years: 79 percent of raion agricultural departmental heads, raion plenipotentiaries for the people's commissariat of procurements, and MTS directors were appointed after the German attack.[51] In agriculture, the lack of skilled cadres was most pronounced: in January 1945, the oblast' lacked fifty crop specialists (zemleustroiteli), 139 cattle technicians, and 168 veterinarians.[52]

Boitsov was disgruntled with the high number of cadres with merely primary schooling. This undereducated lot was hardly equipped to carry out the tasks required of someone in a position of authority. Certain measures had been taken to ameliorate the quality of the new local leaders, such as having them follow special courses or attend the annual oblast' party school. The yawning lack of necessary experience and education had been countered in 1943–44 through short-term courses in which 6,000 leading raion workers participated: among this group were, for example, the heads of raiispolkom departments, the above mentioned plenipotentiaries, and the judges of the People's Courts.[53] Notwithstanding the graduation of 500 young specialists from the oblast's twelve secondary technical institutions in the 1942–44 period, a shortage of 600 engineers and 1,200 technicians beleaguered industry. Many people in responsible positions were dismissed for not being able to cope with their duties.[54]

Agitprop and the printing press were the next items on Boitsov's agenda. The importance attributed to agitprop by the party leaders is evident from the fact that the obkom had discussed its state of affairs at two plenary meetings during the war.[55] In 1942 there were complaints that the party cells in the province, particularly in the areas near the front line and recently liberated raions, were not sufficiently or seriously enough engaged in the "liquidation of the consequences" of the German occupation. "Detrimental rumours and unhealthy moods" among certain sectors of the population immediately after liberation had been ignored. In January 1944 the Central Committee had apparently informed the obkom about its continued displeasure with the popular mood in the province. Again it had been noted that the people's attitude was insufficiently monitored by local party organizations. Reports of grievances were to be sent to the higher levels of the party hierarchy.[56]

As a result of these admonitions from above, agitprop had been intensified.[57] Immediately after liberation, special propaganda groups of party and agitprop workers had been sent into the formerly occupied raions. In January 1945, 1,100 agitational collectives formally existed in the province, comprising 12,000 agitators. This was an astonishing number if one keeps in mind that the total population was around 1.5 million at the time: one agitator was fielded for every 125 persons! Yet in several raions the raikoms had not actively supervised their agitators. As a result, agitation work among the people had been neglected. This was seen as a crucial cause of these raions' failure to comply with the obligations of the economic plans.[58]

The equation of languishing political propaganda with lack of economic output is common in party policy discussions for the period up until 1953. Agitprop had to serve as virtually the sole catalyst for higher labour productivity of workers and peasants, since material incentives were not made available. Many of the raikoms, however, probably shrugged off ideological missions because they were swamped by the great amount of time spent on organizing and supervizing the economy. In the final reckoning, raion leaders knew that the economic results of their territory constituted the yardstick by which the obkom measured their competence.

Finally Boitsov reached the conclusion of his report. In his opinion, the provincial party had indeed travelled a difficult road but could now begin to dedicate itself to rectifying all the shortcomings noted. The most pressing issues of the moment were the successful discharge of flax, timber, and other deliveries to the state, and the rapid execution of preparations for spring sowing in the countryside. The revival of industry and construction were of prime importance. Everyone should try to work even harder for the final victory in the war that was still being waged by the Motherland. The training of party members and candidates, the dissemination of Marxism-Leninism, and the education of cadres needed to improve. The political work among the population should be intensified.[59]

Boitsov's report has crucial significance: while it provides a picture of the bleak atmosphere in which the party was operating, it also marks the transition from wartime to peacetime. The audience was told in a straightforward way that the leadership demanded the resurrection of the prewar political and socio-economic system and that no drastic change was to be expected. The people who attended the sixth party conference went home with the clear message that any hopes of fundamental change would be futile: just as before, plans were to be fulfilled, orthodoxy instilled, vigilance observed, criticism suppressed. Boitsov's speech would certainly indicate that any wartime lessening of Communist control over society and economy had been no more than a temporary tactical move. The party was once more firmly in the saddle.

THE FAILURE OF
BOITSOV'S SUCCESSORS

Boitsov's longevity in office derived from lucky coincidences and the fact that he was probably a client of a more senior boss in Moscow who did not fall from favour between 1938 and 1946. Boitsov arrived too late in the purges to fall victim to them himself; during the war he led a province in which the German advance was halted for the first time. Then, within the first postwar years, the province's economic performance was passable. Of course, whoever supported Boitsov in Moscow undoubtedly contributed to his success. Unfortunately, we can only speculate who his sponsor was in the higher echelons of the party, for I could find no clear evidence of a particularly close relationship between Boitsov and one or more of the Politburo members of the time in the records.

In 1948, two years after Boitsov's transfer to Stavropol krai, the Central Committee summoned the provincial leadership to Moscow. The meeting took place in the Orgburo, which was now under the command of G.M. Malenkov, at the time second only to Stalin within the party.[60] Participating individuals included the new first provincial secretary, P.S. Vorontsov, who gave an account of the situation in Kalinin oblast', a Central Committee inspector named of Kiselev, who presented an accompanying report, and Central Committee candidate Storozhev.[61] Apart from Malenkov, the meeting was attended by several other bigwigs.

The Central Committee reprimanded Vorontsov for the state of affairs in his satrapy. In agriculture yields of grains, potatoes, and other crops were far below the norm. The socialized cattle herd was being squandered and was perishing. The results of dairy farming were poor: in 1947 only 878 litres of milk per cow had been produced. Labour discipline on kolkhozes was often lax, and quite a few kolkhoz members escaped punishment for avoiding any work in the socialized sector of their collective farm.[62] In industry in 1947 total production reached only 57 percent of the prewar level. Textile factories were especially disappointing: in 1948 only 24 percent of the prewar output was produced. (This, it was admitted by the Central Committee, resulted partly from lacklustre aid to the Kalinin textile industry by the Ministry of Textile Industry.) The obkom failed to take measures to ensure swift development of the construction-materials industry, leading to a stagnation of industrial building projects, and the like.[63]

The Orgburo noticed that insufficient attention was paid by Party, trade union, and economic organizations to the urban workers' housing conditions, some of them lived in poorly constructed apartment buildings and "communal" houses. Nor were workers' needs satisfied with respect to municipal services, in particular in Rzhev, Kalinin, and Torzhok. Schools and education, particularly in former German-occupied areas, were in tawdry condition.[64] The obkom was neglecting political work, resulting in the bad operation of many primary party cells, which were found wanting in influencing favourably the situation in kolkhozy and factories. For lack of supervision, many Communists did not attempt to enrich their political knowledge and education. Agitational work among the population was deficient because local party leaders failed to pay much attention to it. The root of the problem was perceived to lie in the ineffectual way the obkom was leading the provincial party, for obkom leaders did not themselves intervene to improve the situation at lower levels.[65]

The Central Committee appeared primarily interested in an increase in flax deliveries, for as a technical crop flax had more importance for the economy of the Soviet Union than most other provincial agricultural products. The emphasis on flax production, together with the meagre attention paid by the party forum to industry, reflects the fact that industry fell only partially within the obkom's competence, while other agricultural crops were produced in such small quantities that they were almost irrelevant to the Soviet Union's economy.[66] The obkom was obliged to report to Moscow on 1 January, 1 April, and 1 June 1949 on the mechanization of both flax cultivation and its primary processing. A few days later the Council of Ministers authorized the obkom to transfer more than 3,000 households from the east of the province to the western regions, in order to overcome the labour shortage in these formerly occupied territories. In the government's resolution the importance of flax cultivation was reiterated.[67] Vorontsov would be given little time to remedy the situation, which had apparently not improved sufficiently since Boitsov's memorable speech of January 1945. On the contrary, in certain areas things had deteriorated in the eyes of the Moscow leadership.

P.S. Vorontsov's career as a professional party worker had seemed in jeopardy previously, in 1937, when he had failed to get elected to the revision committee of the obkom.[68] When Boitsov arrived in Kalinin in the spring of 1938, however, he had to find party members with unblemished records to substitute for all those who had disappeared in the Great Purge. The fact that Vorontsov had been snubbed by the June 1937 obkom plenum probably worked to his advantage, for almost all participants of that meeting had been unmasked subsequently as enemies of the people. Vorontsov, who was a long-time resident of the province and had worked in a factory in his younger years, was appointed as Boitsov's successor within a decade. Then in November

1949 Vorontsov's stellar career came to an end: he was removed from his duties. The timing of Vorontsov's dismissal leads us to suspect that there is a connection with the fall of N.A. Voznesensky and A.A. Kuznetsov and the purge of the Moscow and Leningrad Party organizations that accompanied their demise in the same year.[69]

The provincial economy was not in a bad enough state to warrant the dismissal of its leader for incompetence. Vorontsov could have argued in his defence that in 1948 and 1949 the province had shown the best agricultural results since the war. Circumstantial evidence suggests that Vorontsov's downfall had, indeed, different origins. Within a few weeks after Zhdanov's death in 1948, the obkom secretary had been called to Moscow to give an account of the current situation in Kalinin province. Malenkov, who had previously seen some hard times, had returned from partial disgrace, and his star was now rising again.[70] Zhdanov's death gave Malenkov the opportunity to take revenge on those who had supported Zhdanov in the rivalry between them between 1946 and 1948. Upon his return to the highest echelons, Malenkov concocted the Leningrad Affair in which Voznesnesky, A.A. Kuznetsov, and other high-level officials were eliminated from the party's leadership. In April 1949, at a time when the Leningrad Affair was heating up, the noose around Vorontsov's neck tightened. Zhdanov had connections in Kalinin which went back to prerevolutionary times; Vorontsov had been appointed at a time when Zhdanov was at the peak of his career in Moscow. We can speculate that Vorontsov fell victim to Malenkov's revenge on those who had enjoyed close ties with Zhdanov after his former rival's death.[71] Again, crucial sources, however, were not accessible to me to verify this hypothesis.

Officially, however, Central Committee and obkom had lost patience with the lack of economic performance and accused Vorontsov of engaging in nepotism and promoting his friends:

The plenum of the obkom notices that, in the work of the party obkomburo and of the first obkom secretary, comrade Vorontsov, serious errors and shortcomings have crept in. The leadership of the party's obkom suppressed criticism and self-criticism in the party organization, while it failed to take necessary measures for the straightening out of discovered shortcomings in party and economic work. The obkomburo of the VKP(b) and [comrade] Vorontsov allowed for an unbolshevik approach in the selection of cadres, promoting to leading positions people who had been unproven, and those who had compromised themselves in their former work. In the practical work of the first obkom secretary [comrade] Vorontsov incidences of running affairs by decrees (administrirovanie) took place. The great shortcomings in the leadership over the economy of the oblast', noticed in the resolutions of the Central Committee of the VKP(b) of 4 October 1948 concerning the Kalinin obkom of the VKP(b), have not been righted until now; the organizational-party and party-political work remains as before on a low level. [Comrade] Vorontsov has shown himself to be unprepared for the leadership of the oblast' party organization.[72]

When Central Committee representative Dedov (a vice-head of the Central Committee Department, or Section, of party, trade union and Komsomol organizations) explained to a November 1949 obkom plenum the reasons for Vorontsov's dismissal, he elaborated on these points.[73] Vorontsov's second-in-command Zimin explained that the Central Committee had penalized Vorontsov and oblispolkom chair Sadovnikov for organizing two festive gatherings for the province's leadership. Zimin implied that these drinking bouts led to the strengthening of the sense of "familyness" (semeistvennost') among the leadership. Vorontsov himself pointed at a severe reprimand from the Central Committee of April 1949; in his "farewell speech," he claimed to have lost his self-confidence from that point onwards.

Another factor contributing to (or that was a pretext for) Vorontsov's downfall may have been a political case at the railroad-car construction factory, exposed in 1949 (discussed further in chapter 5, below). A number of politically "unreliable" individuals had been hired in previous years at this most prestigious factory. This practice was not uncommon in labour-short postwar Soviet factories, but it could now be conveniently used to seal the fate of the provincial boss.

The Central Committee tolerated Vorontsov's successor, N.S. Konovalov, for a mere thirty months. Konovalov showed, according to his critics, little competence in managing the provincial economy, and he lacked initiative, relying too much on the advice of his colleagues in Kalinin. Poor economic results, however, were the main reason for Konovalov's dismissal. Agricultural output was significantly lower than during the tenure of Vorontsov, who at least had been able to make the oblast' procure the required amount of grain for the state. It is likely that Konovalov's fall was caused by the search for a local scapegoat for the failure of rash reforms in agricultural policy. Stalin and those close to him reverted to tried-and-true tactics to preserve the image of an infallible Soviet leadership among the Russians: Konovalov served as the necessary sacrifice, but he came away from the episode without much harm. Konovalov had better political sponsors in Moscow than Vorontsov, however, since he was merely demoted to a position within the Central Committee apparatus.[74] His career was not wrecked by his supposedly poor performance as the leader of the Kalinin party organization. By 1956 he would work as second secretary of Kaliningrad oblast', subsequently becoming first secretary of this province and serving as a full Central Committee member during the early 1960s.

Konovalov's disgrace was staged in a similar manner to that of his predecessor. Storozhev, a Central Committee representative who had arrived in Kalinin to explain the practical consequences of a Central Committee resolution on mistakes and shortcomings of the provincial party leadership, took centre stage at an obkom plenum to condemn the province's poor economic record.[75] Despite a number of previous admonitions, the Central Committee felt called upon to interfere once more in the affairs of Kalinin province. An earlier resolution of August 1950 had apparently failed to wake up the recently installed Konovalov, even though this resolution was probably of a limited scope.[76]

The plenum of July 1951 would serve as Konovalov's swan-song in Kalinin; the first secretary was depicted as the main cause of everything that had been going sorely wrong in previous months. The decision to remove Konovalov had been made beforehand by the Central Committee, but, as in the case of Vorontsov, the pretence of form was kept up by having the first secretary dismissed by an obkom plenum. Storozhev, like Dedov a vice-head of the Central Committee Department of party, trade union, and Komsomol organs, strongly denounced Konovalov's leadership. He began by angrily pointing to the Central Committee's repeated intervention in provincial affairs during the previous two and a half years: in October 1948, November 1949, August 1950, and June and July 1951.[77] He proceeded to sketch what he considered to be the deplorable state of agriculture in the oblast'. Industry and transport were equally bad. Welfare and health care were deficient, while the distribution network continued to malfunction. Owing to the obkom's neglect, the party organization was in a sorrowful state: some of the leading party workers did not, in fact, subscribe to any newspaper. The sins of various other oblast' and raion party leaders were even worse: they neglected to subscribe to the collected works of Lenin and Stalin, which were being published in installments. Others had signed up for these essential tomes, but were not picking up their copies in the shops.

Compared to its prewar size in rural areas, the party had certainly grown there, but the competence of the rural Communists was deplorable, since "they do not take active part in party and community life, carry out poorly their vanguard role in production, abandon their labour in the kolkhozy, and on their own initiative depart to find more lucrative employment. In the last two years the number of communist kolkhozniks has fallen by almost 2,000 people. A most serious short-coming in the activities of the kolkhoz primary party organizations is the fact that they do not surround themselves with the kolkhoz aktiv, do not invite nonparty kolkhozniks for open party meetings, seldom communicate with them on matters of productive and economic importance for the kolkhozy, and poorly organize socialist emulation."[78]

For this type of error, 3,329 people had been excluded from the party between July 1948 and July 1951. Thirteen hundred Komsomol organizations operated on the kolkhozy, but their prowess was undermined because they were left to cope on their own without any supervision from above. As a result of party and Komsomol inadequacies, many religious customs were still being observed in the countryside. These exerted a negative influence on rural youth and, furthermore, distracted a significant number of kolkhozniks from work on the collective farms.[79]

At a recently held provincial party conference, Konovalov had shown himself for what he was, "a weak-willed, liberal leader," in Storozhev's opinion.[80] The spineless secretary had ignored the critical plight of agriculture, as had his colleagues in the leadership, Sadovnikov, Shatalin, and Borisov. Yet Storozhev had to admit here that the plight of agriculture was partially a consequence of the adverse weather conditions and the haphazardly conducted amalgamation of collective farms in 1950. In his concluding remarks, Storozhev nevertheless advised the plenum to replace the leadership. Thus Konovalov was made the scapegoat and dutifully axed.[81]

Kiselev, the last of Kalinin province's party leaders in Stalin's lifetime, witnessed as first secretary further economic hard times, but it remains in doubt why he was transferred, recalled, or dismissed after Stalin's death. It is not out of the question that he was dismissed because he was considered to belong to the circle of one of Khrushchev's rivals.[82]

It is true that the provincial bosses failed in the postwar period to create a vibrant economy, but it would be incorrect to level the blame squarely on individuals like Vorontsov or Konovalov. It was not primarily the local leadership's incompetence but rather policies introduced by the Central Committee of the Communist Party and the Soviet government and, more particularly, by Stalin that had created economic problems. The devastating effects of these policies during the 1930s have been noticed, but after the war, the party would still stubbornly cling to them. Local leaders were given little room to manoeuvre within the system and proved incapable of fulfilling the high expectations that Moscow had about the provincial economy: on the surface, it would seem that this alleged failure led to the rapid removal of Vorontsov and Konovalov, but other factors may have played a more significant role, such as the "wrong" political patronage. The Central Committee exchanged first secretaries of provinces at high speed; at district levels, meanwhile, the turnover often occurred at even higher speed.

THE INSTRUMENTS OF POWER

Ruling a province the size of Kalinin oblast' was a balancing act for the first secretaries, and only one, I.P. Boitsov, came through with flying colours in Stalin's lifetime. Personal talent played only a marginal role. Boitsov's limited education might have contributed to the failings of the provincial economy, but as we have seen, it was Boitsov who fared best among the six secretaries who ruled from 1935 to 1953. Boitsov's limited competence in the management of provincial industry or agriculture was apparently outweighed by other qualities, among which his loyalty to someone who had clout in the Politburo should be emphasized. In addition, a straightforward correlation did not exist between the economic success or failure of a province and the competence of its boss. Central party and state organs interfered directly in certain matters, as, for instance, Gosplan and the ministries responsible for heavy industry or defence did in the planning and organization of factories that produced machinery or arms. So, if party secretaries were removed on the pretext that they had failed to run the economy well, the accusation of mismanagement would have been hard to prove in an impartial court. Such courts, of course, did not exist in Stalin's Russia, and party leaders were replaced at high frequency before and after 1945. For this practice, one can find a number of explanations, including denunciations that were used by the MGB on orders from above, the typical Stalinist effort to combat any feeling of complacency among lower party levels by frequently removing (and often arresting) minions, Stalin's personal whim, or the rivalry between different factions that may have formed under the lead of the lieutenants Malenkov, Zhdanov, and Khrushchev.

The first secretary of Kalinin oblast' was an extremely powerful man, even though army and security organs in part lived a life of their own. The army detachment stationed in the province and the army's political section led an almost wholly separate existence from the provincial leadership of the Communist Party. It seems that more often the MVD and MGB controlled the party than the other way around, but the party chieftain received information from the security organs about the state of affairs in his satrapy. These reports can be found only sporadically in the party's archives: undoubtedly some were destroyed and others are even today under lock and key, while some reports were given orally only. Some MGB/MVD reports, however, were sent directly to higher levels without the first secretary ever setting eyes upon them. These reports certainly played their role when he was evaluated by the highest leadership of the country.

The first secretary's leadership over the Communist Party and the Communist Youth League of Kalinin oblast', in which a combined 10 percent of the population was enrolled by the early 1950s, was the basis of his position as the most powerful man in the province. Soviets and trade unions, officially independent, although not responsible for any significant policy decision at any level, were wholly subordinate to the party and its local boss in Kalinin.

In the war years 23,364 Communists, or 43 percent of the total number of party members and candidates, served in the Red Army, while 8,807 Communists left in connection with the evacuation, and 3,870 members and candidates transferred to the newly created Velikie Luki and Pskov oblasts.[83] Through all this, party membership dwindled from 50,277 members and candidates on 1 January 1940 to a mere 27,987 on 1 November 1944, or by 44 percent.

The party's feeble control over country folk and country ways persisted: in July 1945, among the 6,940 kolkhozy only 167 boasted party organizations, while 47 had candidate groups.[84] To a great extent, the party had to rely on the "territorial" party organizations, which were often based on a rural soviet and had to supervise a number of collective farms simultaneously. Apparently the party had difficulty after the German retreat in reestablishing itself in the liberated areas: no kolkhoz in the raions of Vysoko, Emel'ianovo, Zavidovo, Zubtsov, Molodoi Tud, and Pogoreloe had a party organization as of July 1945.

In January 1945 Boitsov noticed a slight increase in the Communists' schooling. However, the absolute number of members with more than merely primary education (which at this time still meant four years of school) was not very high during the war (11,391 in 1944; 13,072 in 1940).[85] The low education level within party ranks reflects the social situation in general: on average in the 1930s – and this seems a somewhat optimistic guess – a child on the collective farm received five to six years of schooling (which was still more than children received in the 1920s).[86] It is no surprise that the postwar party membership was so poorly educated.

Boitsov's speech of January 1945 indicates the metamorphosis of the party's membership during the war. At the end of the war only a minority of party members had been in the provincial organization since before the war. With the exception of the membership of the highest

Table 14
Communist Party Membership in Tver' Guberniia/
Kalinin Oblast' (on 1 January)

Year	Full Members	Candidates	Total
1917	150	–	150
1922	3,218	384	3,602
1928	8,236	3,637	11,873
1935	18,477	8,934	27,411
1936	17,013	7,470	24,483
1937	18,931	7,653	26,584
1938	18,236	7,314	25,550
1939	20,697	12,160	32,857
1941	34,205	19,811	54,016
1942	12,711	3,325	16,036
1943	14,972	4,311	19,283
1944	18,072	8,232	26,304
1945	20,747	7,920	28,667
1946	32,511	9,604	42,115
1947	45,977	10,183	56,610
1948	51,804	9,738	61,542
1949	53,629	7,323	60,952
1950	54,575	5,285	59,860
1951	55,150	5,577	60,727[1]
1952	55,337	6,146	61,483
1953	55,753	5,776	61,529
1956	60,670	2,714	63,384
1970	127,784	5,478	133,262

Source: Based on Ocherki, appendix 1, 690–1.
[1] According to first secretary Konovalov (at the eighth oblast'
party conference), 16,281 out of these were women (Pako,
147/5/2, l.7). Another report stated that of the full members,
42,216 (76.5%) entered the party during or after the war (Pako,
147/5/199, l.4).

body in the provincial party hierarchy, the obkom, most Communists
in senior positions within the party had little job experience. The party
swelled significantly between 1945 and 1948 (table 14); for a while,
ever greater numbers of inexperienced new members joined.[87] The correlation between loyal service in the Red Army and party membership
is clear. When demobilization was almost completed, the ranks were
closed, selection became more disciminatory, and any growth was
checked until 1953. Whether the veteran soldiers guaranteed a better
quality of Communist may be questioned.

Although party membership and candidacy on 1 January 1949 had
grown by 32,285 since 1 January 1945, more new members had been

Table 15
Exclusions of Communists by the Party Organization of Kalinin Oblast', 1949 and 1950

Cause of Exclusion	Number Excluded 1949–50	Percentage of Total Number Excluded	Number Excluded, 1949[1]	Number Excluded, 1950
Theft, embezzlement and abuses	948	33.0	488	466
Drunkenness, Hooliganism, unworthy way of life	337	11.8	180	157
Observance of religious rites	150	5.3	–	–
Losing party documents	112	4.0	–	–
Cessation of payment of party fees and violations of party discipline[2]	674	23.3	401	334
Unauthorized departure from the organization	272	9.5	–	–

Source: Based on Pako, 147/5/199, ll.12, 26.

Note: Of the total of 2,681 (1,865 full members and 996 candidates) excluded for both years, 484 (213 in 1950) were workers, 695 (302 in 1950) kolkhozniks, and 1,682 (708 in 1950) employees. In 1950, 71% of those excluded had joined the party during the war, and 18% in the postwar period, and thus only 11% had joined before June 1941.

[1] The numbers for 1949 and 1950 have been differentiated as far as possible.

[2] The numbers on this line are apparently the result of a miscalculation in the records.

admitted than that, because 5,749 Communists (roughly 10 percent of the membership) had been excluded during the years 1945–49. The growth during and after the war was so rapid that in late July 1946 the Central Committee felt forced to caution local party organizations not to accept everyone who had written a statement requesting to be admitted as a candidate (table 15 sets out the causes of exclusion in 1949 and 1950).[88]

Apart from outright exclusion, party members were disciplined for unsatisfactory behaviour by warnings, reprimands, and penalties, which could be noted on their party membership card. The effect was obviously watered down whenever too many Communists were reprimanded. In 1952, Kiselev observed that local party bosses had been guilty of this error when more than 22 percent of the party membership in seven raions had been penalized.[89]

It certainly was no unmitigated pleasure to be a Communist, for one was under much closer scrutiny than people outside the party.[90] In order to improve the sense of security within the party, during a discussion in local party cells of the new party statute that was to be prepared for the Nineteenth Party Congress (1952), one person proposed to make it a rule to exclude members who had slandered honest people! Nevertheless, party membership aided one's career: it was a necessity for those with ambitions.[91]

The number of 12 voting delegates for the Kalinin oblast' at the Nineteenth Party Congress more or less conformed to the ratio of 1 delegate for every 5,000 members; such a ratio seems to have been the rule.[92] If the provincial population at this time was about 1.6 million, the number of party members for every 1,000 people was low (34.69) in comparison to the robustness of the Moscow or Leningrad Party membership, but certainly on a par with many of the other RSFSR oblasts.

The postwar party leadership of Kalinin oblast' seemed to remain concerned with the size of the workers' contingent among the membership. Gender influenced the drop of the proportion of factory workers during the war: most of the males had been recruited into the Red Army, while hardly any of the women who took their place at the work benches were Communists. Women continued to make up a small proportion of the party's membership.

The party was led by the provincial committee (obkom), or rather by its buro, in which three obkom secretaries, the head of the security organs, the newspaper editor, the chairman of the executive committee of the provincial soviet (oblispolkom), one secretary of the town committee (gorkom) of Kalinin, and the head of the provincial Komsomol always had a seat after 1945. As Fainsod has noticed, the obkom secretariat was assigned two main tasks, the successful acquittal of which was imperative for the political (and sometimes physical) survival of the secretaries: to achieve economic results and to guarantee sufficient political loyalty towards the Communist regime among the population.[93] The intensive effort by the obkomburo to control the oblispolkom, gorkoms, gorispolkoms, raikoms, raiispolkoms, factories, institutions, party cells, raions, and collective farms, as well as individual inhabitants, is expressed in the tremendous number of documents now kept in the provincial archives of Tver'. The buro discussed everything from pig breeding to drinking bouts of local party brass.[94]

In postwar Kalinin oblast', the obkomburo and its secretariat were the real government that made policy decisions and guided their implementation and those made by higher-placed party and state organizations. There is no evidence to suggest that the "official" government of the oblast' (the executive elected by the provincial soviet) was able to make a decision in any critical matter without having received definitive instructions from the obkomburo or the first secretary.[95] The chairman of the executive committee of the provincial soviet was always a member of the buro, while lesser government administrators were members of the obkom. The latter never ranked very high in seniority within the party. The position of A.I. Sadovnikov, head of the oblispolkom from the end of 1948 onwards, was somewhat exceptional for a government official: he functioned virtually as second-in-command in the early 1950s. This was not so much the result of Sadovnikov's position as leader of the oblast' government, however, but more a result of his exceptionally long work-experience as a high-level administrator in the oblispolkom. Beginning his career in the Kalinin oblispolkom as one of the vice-chairs, Sadovnikov became caretaker chair for Simonov and finally was appointed chairman. Konovalov and Kiselev, as newcomers to the province unfamiliar with the specifics of the Kalinin oblast', were forced to rely on Sadovnikov to some extent, which resulted in the latter's comparatively strong position.[96]

In July 1951, at the meeting of the obkom plenum that ratified the removal of Konovalov, the party secretary of the Proletarka textile works, A.I. Voevodina, harshly reprimanded Sadovnikov.[97] Voevodina pointed out that Sadovnikov was just as responsible for the languishing state of the economy as Konovalov. Was Sadovnikov not head of the oblispolkom at the time of Vorontsov's ouster? Had he not, consequently, failed to draw the right conclusion from that episode, namely, that things had to change in a radical way if they were to improve? Konovalov was a newcomer to the province, while Sadovnikov had been part of its leadership since the war years. He had been one of the oblispolkom leaders since December 1946, so in a way Voevodina's criticism was right: why get rid of Konovalov while leaving Sadovnikov in place?

Voevodina tongue-lashed Sadovnikov for managing affairs through the party organization instead of through the oblispolkom and the soviet executive committees of the raions. She was courageous enough to say to her audience that "at an earlier plenum comrade Vorontsov was dismissed owing to a decision of the Central Committee. That, comrades, was unforgivable in our eyes, as we lost our own worker, who had been reared by our party organization."[98] Voevodina's attack was to no avail, however, for Sadovnikov was allowed to carry on in his function. Voevodina, in contrast, payed for her frank criticism: she was not reelected as a full member of the obkom at the next oblast' party conference in September 1952.[99]

In order to survive as long as he did in the leadership of the Kalinin party organization, Sadovnikov must have been either a very talented politician or, more likely, under the patronage of someone higher up in the party, for he was criticized severely at other times as well. In contrast to the disgraced Vorontsov, Konovalov, and Borisov, to mention a few of the more noteworthy obkom secretaries who were removed, Sadovnikov held on to his position. So did S.N. Shatalin, who became one of the obkom secretaries in 1947.[100] It is obvious that he survived because of the presence of his brother, N.N. Shatalin, in the cadres section of the Central Committee Secretariat and the Orgburo. Shatalin was little appreciated in the 1992 survey by the few former party members who remembered him. D.A. Dikushin portrayed him as an arrogant small-time dictator, conspicuous for his shouting and pressuring when he visited Konakovo raion; in 1950 Shatalin even went as far as openly threatening kolkhozniks who were unwilling to join the amalgamated kolkhozes with camp sentences. In 1952, at the ninth Party conference, Dubinin, the ispolkom chairman of Kamen raion, suggested explicitly that the presence of N.N. Shatalin in the Central Committee was the cause of his brother's longevity in the Kalinin leadership.

At least verbally, S.N. Shatalin endured as much criticism as, if not more than, some of his colleagues in the obkomburo, but somehow, unlike many of them, he never lost his job. In 1952, Kiselev came to Shatalin's defence and, after a brief discussion about Shatalin's candidature for the obkom, the latter was allowed to remain on the list of candidates and reelected.[101] Shatalin was concomitantly elected as a delegate to the Nineteenth Party Congress of the Communist Party by the ninth party conference.

In early 1953 the obkomburo generally convened once every two weeks, although in exceptional cases it met weekly. Power was concentrated in the obkomburo and obkom secretariat of Kalinin province, in the same way that the Politburo and Central Committee secretariat monopolized political power in the USSR as a whole. The relationship between the secretariat and buro at the provincial level was similar to their relationship at the all-union level. The provincial secretariat was organized along the lines of the Central Committee secretariat: in early 1945 it comprised six departments (otdely): one for cadres, headed by a full-fledged obkom secretary; a second for propaganda and agitation, also led by a full secretary; three more departments for organization-instruction, agriculture, and schools; and a department for military matters. These last four were led by otdel heads, who ranked lower than the secretaries.[102]

Stalin's personal secretariat under Poskrebyshev was mirrored in the obkom's "Special Sector."[103] How far this sector counted as a genuine department before the autumn of 1948 is unclear. The most varied information ended up, by way of the Special Sector, on the table of the first secretary of the Kalinin party organization and ranged from reports on crime and the MVD/MGB, to reports on agriculture, industry, construction, and welfare. The size of the archives today reflects the enormous amount of paperwork handled by the first secretary. Much moaning and groaning in July 1951 over Konovalov's tenure at the head of the party organization focused on the paperwork the obkom apparatus generated, something that Soviet critics in hindsight would call "cardinal failings born of the Stalin cult, red tape, inflated staffs."[104] However, considering the extremely centralized control that the first secretary was supposed to exert over affairs in the province, it is difficult to imagine how someone like Konovalov could have worked in a significantly less bureaucratic manner.

In 1945, seven obkom vice-secretaries dealt with economic matters, an arrangement imposed by the Eighteenth Party Conference of 1941. Each of them handled a specific branch of the economy: animal husbandry, heavy industry, textiles and light industry, lumbering, machine building, transport, and food. In 1948 the obkom's organization was altered: from then on, there were five full-fledged secretaries and eleven obkom departments, analogous to the concomitant reorganization of the Central Committee Secretariat.[105] In 1951, the obkom agreed to create a separate department of education, which was split off from the otdel for agitation and propaganda.

What is striking about the presence in archival documents of the postwar provincial party leaders is the almost complete absence of character traits to distinguish them: Vorontsov may have been drinking too much for his own good, but that was not uncommon among party leaders, while Konovalov seems almost to have lacked the hard edge typical of the Stalinist bureaucrat. Among the bosses these traits hardly mattered. None of the leaders did very well or very poorly during their tenure. One is inclined to agree with Walter Laqueur's estimation that the "practice of negative selection and the reign of self-perpetuating mediocrity" was the norm.[106]

One step below the obkom and its secretariat were the raion and town party committees (raikomy, gorkomy). A detailed description of them here is unnecessary: their organization and operation should be understood as a condensed version of those of the obkom. For the town as a whole, Kalinin had a gorkom, but the provincial capital was additionally divided into four raions, all with their own raikoms. The towns of the oblast' subordination (oblastnoe podchinenie) had their own gorkoms.[107]

Raikoms and gorkoms acted with limited independence. In Krasnyi

Kholm raion in 1944, for example, the raikom received more than three hundred telegrams on the most diverse subjects from the obkom, its departments, and the secretariat.[108]

In early 1945, Boitsov complained that primary cells in the town of Torzhok, as well as in several raions, were poorly led by their district party committees.[109] This complaint would be belaboured again and again in the following years. The underlying reason – then and later – for reprimanding the raikoms and gorkoms can be traced to the fear of the consequences of poor economic performance. In the immediate postwar period hardly any raikom or gorkom (or the obkom itself) escaped such criticism. Often a few were singled out as scapegoats for shortcomings existing within all local party organizations. When a few districts had apparently strengthened, other ones took their place, while the substance of the criticism often remained the same.

Conceivably, deficient performance in certain areas actually did improve after a wave of finger pointing. In the first place, some local party leaders who were thus pressured might remedy matters within their realm – or perhaps they only pretended that matters had improved. The appointment of a more capable local leadership that managed affairs more competently could sometimes better the situation, a measure to which the obkom turned in extreme cases. Finally, the obkom would become actively involved in improving the state of affairs at a local level, which could lead to praiseworthy results in some cases. An example of this attention, which could translate into measures of economic aid, was the increased agricultural mechanization introduced in the formerly occupied western parts of the oblast'. After it had dawned on the obkom, towards 1950, that it would be futile to wait for the arrival of sufficiently large numbers of settlers to augment the labour force in these areas, the lack of manual labour was partially compensated for by the use of farming machinery, although funding for this effort remained seriously inadequate.

The attrition rate among raikom secretaries was perhaps less severe than in Soviet Belorussia directly after World War II, but dismissals and transfers were a common phenomena among these functionaries.[110] In 1951, twenty-three incumbent first raikom secretaries of the forty-four rural raions changed their jobs, and eighteen second raikom secretaries did so. Similarly, twenty-five out of forty-seven heads of the agricultural raikom otdels were replaced in this year, as were forty-seven out of eighty-eight secretaries of raion Komsomol organizations in the countryside.

Lack of education was one reason for the poor leadership of some secretaries. As table 16 shows, in early 1952 only about one in seven party chiefs could boast a post-secondary degree. Indeed, the fact that

Table 16
Profile of Leading Cadres in the Kalinin Oblast', 1 January 1952

Time of Entry into the Communist Party of Full Party Members in Leading Positions (N=1,388)

Before 1917	0
1917–20	23
1921–25	29
1926–29	111
1930–34	165
1935–38	48
1939–40	277
1941–42	204
1943–45	338
1946 and after	193

Age of Leading Workers (N=1,467)

50+	129
46–50	229
41–45	242
36–40	301
31–35	257
< 30	309
Average age	38.6

Education of Leading Workers (N=1,467)

With completed higher education	212
Engineers	24
Agronomists	16
Other agricultural specialists	6
Economists	16
Lawyers	11
Medical doctors	49
Pedagogical Institute and university graduates	77
Graduates of other institutes of higher education	13
With incomplete higher education	252
With completed specialized secondary education	282
With completed general secondary education	235
With incomplete secondary education	325
With primary education	161

Education of Former Participants in Special Party Schools (N=224)

Complete higher party political education	12
Through higher party school under the Central Committee	11
Incomplete higher party political education	146
Through the two-year oblast', krai, and republic party schools	140

Table 16 (continued)

Secondary party political education	66
Through the higher school for party organizers under the Central Committee	4

Nationality of Leading Oblast' Workers

Russians	1,377
Karelians and Finns	48
Ukrainians	16
Jews	15
Belorussians	7
Latvians	1
Other	3

Work Experience in Present Function of Leading Cadres

> 10 years	100
5–10 years	328
2–5 years	442
1–2 years	249
< 1 year	348
Total	**1,467**

Source: Based on Pako, 147/5/201, l.1–1ob.

Note: A total of 1,507 functions were defined as "leading work," of which 1,467 were filled; 276 (18.8%) of these positions had been taken by women; 1,427 were filled by party candidates (39) or full members (1,388); 40 people who were nonparty members had leading positions, 11 of whom were Komsomols.

such data on the leadership's educational background was documented by the Communist Party reveals a concern for the low level of expertise. Because more than half the leading cadres had joined the party during or after the war, experience was also sorely lacking.

Despite the high attrition rate of personnel at upper levels, some survived and moved up in the ranks. We have already met A.A. Kondrashov at the beginning of this chapter. His education was typically unimpressive, for he had enjoyed only seven years of general education at a rural school between 1918 and 1925, and a few years of trade school, where he learned weaving. In 1928 he became assistant foreman in a weaving factory; at this time, aged seventeen, he joined the party. Kondrashov's long career as a party chief began during the Ezhovshchina, when he was appointed to his first important position as raion plenipotentiary for the People's Commissariat of Procurements in Torzhok. Subsequently, he was promoted to secretary and chair of the district executive committee of Torzhok raion. His career was interrupted by the war, but after he was wounded and demobilized in 1943, he became once again raiispolkom chair, this time in Sonkovo raion. In 1945 Kondrashov was promoted to chair of the gorispolkom of Kimry and served from 1947 to 1952 as first party secretary in the same town. After a brief spell in the obkom apparatus in 1952–53, he studied by correspondence at the Higher Party School under the Central Committee. He would end his career in the party in 1970 as obkom secretary of the Kalinin oblast'.

Primary party organizations (table 17) formed the basis of the party's hierarchical structure. They were theoretically supposed to enjoy some independence in political, social, and economic decision making; yet in practice upper party echelons bypassed these cells when deciding on even the most trivial matters.[111] The execution of decisions made higher up depended, nevertheless, on the actions of authorities at a lower level. No matter how much the obkomburo attempted to supervise everything that happened in its fief, simple logistics made it impossible to keep a close eye on each move made by lower levels of the party, government, or economic authorities.[112] M.A. Smirnov was a director of a brick factory in the countryside between 1946 and 1951, after which he served as head of the rural soviet of his area for the next two years, before returning in 1953 to manage the brick factory once again. He recalled, when interviewed, that "[t]he taxes, the tough, or sometimes cruel, laws came from above, but the realization of these laws ... could be done in different ways: either with arbitrariness and cruelty or with maximal understanding and the appreciation of people's psychology."[113] Smirnov admitted, though, that his factory was often visited by an MVD/MGB plenipotentiary who talked to the workers and gauged their mood, and wrote denunciatory reports on some of them as a result.

Table 18 indicates how paltry was the education of the provincial party elite. District leaders of lower rank had received even less education. In 1946 the nomenklatura of the raikom of Sonkovo, a rural area, consisted of 514 positions.[114] Three hundred and ninety-nine or 80 percent of the workers in these positions had primary or unfinished secondary education (that is, about five or six years of schooling). Many lacked, therefore, the sophistication to see through the propaganda and to establish what was actually meant by the double-talk emanating from higher up.

Local leaders were often caught in a conflict between satisfying the demands of their "handlers" in the party – who supposedly knew what was good for the people even though their decrees seemed detrimental – and their desire to represent the interests of those working under

Table 17
Primary Party Organizations in Kalinin Oblast', 1 January 1949 and 1 January 1951

Type of Organization	Number of Organizations		Membership	
	1949	1951	1949	1951
Industrial	395	392	12,095	13,103
Transportation and communications	224	246	5,206	5,195
Construction	30	34	582	691
Artels of industrial cooperation	137	140	1,425	1,409
Municipal	–	34	–	592
Trade, procurement, and public catering	89	160	1,379	2317
Education, science, culture	207	272	3,127	3,424
Healthcare	87	120	1,087	1,303
Institutions and organs of government, party, and the economy	782	673	12,338	11,150
Sovkhozy, MTS, MTM	139	151	2,193	2,205
Kolkhozy	1,011	1,481	5,266	13,536
Rural territorial party organizations	1,056	375	13,359	3,571

Source: Based on Pako, 147/5/199, l.23.

Table 18
Profile of Leading Raion and Urban Party Workers in Kalinin Oblast', Early 1945

	Number	Percentage of total
Total working in raikoms or gorkoms	369	100
Female party workers	96	26
Work experience in function		
Up to 1 year	107	28.9
1 to 3 years	212	57.4
3 years or more	50	13.5
Party membership		
Beginning between 1917 and 1925	21	5.7
Beginning between 1926 and 1934	142	38.4
Beginning between 1935 and 1940	144	39.0
Beginning between 1941 and 1944	62	16.8
Education		
Higher and unfinished higher	57	15.9
Secondary and unfinished secondary	192	52
Primary	120	32.5

Source: Based on Pako, 147/3/2679, l.18ob.
Note: These workers were part of the obkom nomenklatura. The total nomenklatura of the oblast' committee was much larger; in 1944 the obkom controlled the appointments of 3,813 people, according to obkom secretary Vorontsov (Moscow, 17/44/546, l.82ob.). In these positions, 955 women were employed (about 25%).

them in their institutions, factories, or collective farms. The loyalty of these rank-and-file party members did not immediately change when they entered the party.

On certain occasions determined by the Central Committee, the lesser gods within the party leadership were permitted to find fault with previously designated members of the obkomburo. In the wake of Storozhev, a long list of lower party bosses demolished the stature of Konovalov further. One of them was the secretary of the party committee of the railroad-car factory, Baranov, who was rewarded for his efforts with an appointment as secretary of the Kalinin gorkom and membership of the obkomburo soon after.[115]

Baranov's scathing attack probably originated from the Central Committee, because it was unthinkable that a relative underling like him would be allowed to criticize the contemporary obkom leadership in the following way:

All the comrades know that, when the decision of the Central Committee of the party came down on the dismissal ... of the first secretary of the obkom, comrade Vorontsov, many of the obkom members made, one after the other, an appearance and said that, you see, they had already noticed for a long while the great errors – suppression of criticism and so on – beating themselves on the chest with their fists, and promising to remedy the situation. But quite some time has gone by, and once more great errors are noticed in the work of the party obkomburo. We had two members of the obkomburo appearing here, comrades Cherkasov and Vakhmistrov, [who] said, too, that they noticed great errors made by comrade Konovalov, but they did not tell us what they tried to do to prevent them from being made.[116]

Baranov blamed the mistakes committed by the obkom secretaries on a lack of attention to criticism from below and the infrequent visits by obkom, gorkom, and raikom chiefs to primary party organizations. Since Lenin's last writings, party leaders at all levels had been regularly exhorted to listen to the voice of the regular member who was not a professional party worker, but this advice had been as regularly ignored, with impunity. Baranov's reproach served the pretence of the existence of inner-party democracy. V.G. Gavrilov remarked in the interviews that "[w]e were not permitted [to criticize] higher politics, but concerning local trifles all was possible, we both swore at the [local] leadership and silently fulfilled any kind of stupidity."[117]

The party leadership had such a plethora of business to deal with that more intimate involvement with the lower party organizations was practically out of the question. In the interviews Z.M. Vinogradova, who was the chair of a kolkhoz in Vyshnii Volochek raion during the last few years before the first amalgamation of 1950, summed up the ambiguous relationship with higher authorities as follows:

We had many authorities above us; whoever wanted ordered the kolkhozy around, but the most important was, of course, the raikom. But it would be sinful to complain about the raikom secretaries. Even if they happened to demand something stupid from us, they were mostly ordered to do this from above and we knew that. For example, once in 1949 or 1950 we had already sown potatoes; they called me in and gave me the task of sowing another thirty hectares. But we did not have any more seedlings, nor did we have land [to sow with potatoes] left. However, in order not to let them down, we gave them some kind of written statement [on the presumed extra sowing]. After all, who of the oblast' [committee] would come to measure our land?"

While in reality the party controlled the state, the provincial government was officially formed by the oblispolkom.[118] Similar executive committees comprised the official government at raion and town levels. The lowest governmental level was found in the soviet executives of the rural and urban districts. In some ways the postrevolutionary executive committees of the soviets at the provincial and raion level were similar to, and politically as powerless as, the prerevolutionary zemstva. The village soviet had taken over many administrative tasks of the skhod, which had possessed major discretionary powers in the local affairs of the village until collectivization.[119]

The fact that 312 of 596 delegates at the ninth oblast' party conference were deputies of the oblast', town, raion, and rural soviets makes it clear how many party leaders doubled as government functionaries.[120] In early 1951, there were in all 15,896 deputies of local soviets in Kalinin oblast'. The provincial soviet had 142 deputies.

Although the net of party cells and soviets was closely knit and allencompassing in principle, it did not result in an efficient governmental system. Oblast' departments of the party and oblispolkom, as well as lower levels of party and government, needed to be constantly supervised in order to guarantee some degree of efficacy. Kiselev complained in September 1952 that the obkom had been neglecting control over the execution by the state and economic apparatus of decisions of the party and USSR government.[121] People engaged excessively in paperpushing, and a vast number of superficial decisions were made by provincial authorities.

The first and traditional duty of Soviet security organs was to investigate alleged "anti-Soviet" elements, spies, saboteurs, wreckers, and so

on. This original task had become, more or less, the terrain of the
NKGB/MGB after the split of the security organs during the war. As the
provincial NKVD head, Pavlov, pointed out to the sixth provincial party
conference in January 1945, the NKVD/MVD engaged in a plethora of
activities, such as anti-aircraft defence, fire prevention, construction,
the fight against the neglect and homelessness of children, the maintenance and security of prisoners' camps, the labour of convicts and prisoners of war, and, together with the party and the soviets, ensuring and
assisting in the execution of political and economic measures.[122] Pavlov
was hard put to find any area of the economy or of social and political activity in which the NKVD organs did not play a "positive" role.

The material in state and party archives dealing with the "organs" is
far from complete. It is impossible to establish which documents
exactly are missing, let alone assess why, specifically, these documents
have disappeared. Particularly for the last four years of Stalin's life, evidence of the activity of the MVD/MGB is very slight in archival documents. The relationship between the local branches of the MVD and
MGB and the provincial party is difficult to assess using the Communist
Party or government records. It is fairly obvious, nevertheless, that
M.A. Smirnov rightly points out that "[a]t that time the leaders
[locally, in the towns, raions and villages, of the factories, and rural
soviets], as a matter of fact, as part of their function, were freelance
(vneshtatnye) collaborators with the [security] organs and were obliged
to give any kind of information."[123]

There was at least one occasion when the provincial MVD head,
Pavlov, appealed to his superior to make the obkomburo withdraw a
reprimand.[124] In May 1946, MVD minister S. Kruglov supported Pavlov
in his decision to remove nine hundred prisoners of war from work on
different industrial projects in the province and assign them to the construction of a highway under the auspices of the USSR MVD. At first
Pavlov was reprimanded by the obkomburo for this, but Kruglov
demanded that the obkomburo remove the reprimand from Pavlov's
record. This the buro apparently did, considering the fact that the reprimand was not mentioned by the obkom secretary who wrote Pavlov's
biography for internal purposes a few years later.

In early 1948 the obkom complained to V.D. Nikitin (a functionary
of the Central Committee Directorate of Cadres) that the MVD paid no
heed to the established order of changing and appointing cadres that
officially fell under the authority of the obkom's nomenklatura.[125]
Without the obkom's agreement, MVD workers were often called away
and appointed to positions in other provinces, while others were
appointed who had compromised themselves in their former functions.
For all intents and purposes, therefore, MVD and MGB functioned
almost wholly independently from the local party and were directly

controlled by the All-Union leadership of the Communist Party. The "organs" were assisted by informers, some of whom, out of a sense of duty and loyalty to the system, helped the organs voluntarily, while others were "recruited."[126]

Chapter 5 will address some of the more sinister tasks assigned to the organs, such as the operation of the labour camp system, the custody of prisoners of war, and the enforcement of political conformity.[127] The same chapter will also briefly discuss the operation of the judicial courts.

The authority of the army was distinctly separate from that of party, government, MGB, and MVD. During and after the war, a provincial military commissariat (Oblvoenkom) existed, while at the raion level raion military commissariats (raivoenkomy) functioned. Formally, these were partially subject to the obkom's authority; thus in 1947 first secretary Vorontsov had the MGB carry out a background check on all functionaries of the provincial military commissariats.[128]

All young males had to undergo medical tests for conscription. After the war, the usual army service for recruits amounted to three years. The army was an important and convenient means for creating conformity among young Soviet males. Before joining the army, a boy could escape most indoctrination by avoiding politics. However, military service would make an obedient and acquiescent Soviet citizen out of him.[129] This is, of course, not specific to the Soviet Union under Stalin, but the level of political indoctrination in Stalin's army was incomparably higher than in most other countries at the time. The fondness for recruiting into the party of those who served or had served in the army, particularly during the war, might have been a consequence of the authorities' extraordinary appreciation of military culture, which had been the Russian tradition long before Bolshevik times. A preference for recruits from the military could also help to explain why far fewer women entered the party.

The army's presence in the town of Kalinin must have been conspicuous: in 1948, units of infantry, two army schools, the Fifty-Sixth Air Force division, a communication unit, and more, were stationed in the town.[130] Even today, most military matters remain under lock and key in Russian archives, a reflection of the autonomy established and preserved by the Soviet Army and its Russian successor.

In April 1942 the provincial Komsomol came under the attack of the Central Committee of the VLKSM.[131] The provincial leadership was criticized for the flawed reorganization of the Komsomol in recently liberated areas. Komsomol obkom secretary Ivanov complained two years later about the small proportion of Komsomol membership among the oblast' youth. Of the more than 300,000 youngsters who were of Komsomol age, only 60,000 had chosen to join.

Komsomol membership fell from 138,135 in 1941 to 51,928 in October 1944, 63 percent of whom were young women.[132] Most of this loss came as the result of the Red Army mobilizations and the evacuation of sections of the population before the German occupation, while the loss of territory to the Velikie Luki oblast' (created in 1944) contributed as well to the shrinkage. Party members and candidates were extremely scarce in the Komsomol: only 1,297 in all were counted in the early fall of 1944. By then, 3,372 Komsomols were employed in functions of authority, of whom roughly 1,500 were deployed in rural areas.

During the war, Komsomols had filled the places left open in industry by their comrades who had departed for the front. Political education had been conducted at an insufficiently serious level before the war; I.P. Boitsov remarked that "[this] explains to a great extent why a significant part of the Komsomols remained behind on territory occupied by the Germans. Eight hundred and forty-six Komsomols have been excluded from the league for direct relations with the enemy."[133]

Many Komsomols reluctantly pursued the required political education. In Kimry raion, not occupied during the war, more than two hundred kolkhozes were bereft of a Komsomol organization, and two members of the raion Komsomol leadership were not even members of the Komsomol.[134] A similar situation prevailed in several other raions in early 1945. The feeble presence of the youth league in some areas of the province was by no means exceptional, for on 1 January 1945 the Komsomol in all liberated areas of the USSR had but 40 percent of its prewar membership. The depletion of the ranks had been extremely severe in the areas of the province that had undergone occupation, since at the moment of the liberation of the last of them in thirty-eight formerly occupied raions of Kalinin oblast' as it was constituted before August 1944, only 9,213 Komsomols were counted, where there had been more than 47,000 in 1941.[135]

Until 1947, the Komsomol barely survived in certain areas. In Brusovo raion, merely 16 Komsomols engaged in a form of political study out of a total membership of 1,000 in 1946. Meanwhile the entire organization was thought to be in danger of collapse because of the members' high rate of departure. In 1947, Komsomol organizations existed on 108 of the 303 kolkhozes of the Kalinin rural raion. At the end of 1947 there were no Komsomol organizations on almost

half the farms of the Kalinin oblast'.[136] In the same year, of the conscripts of the birth year 1929 who were tested for military service, 12.2
percent in the oblast' boasted Komsomol membership. In many rural
raions, however, membership did not surpass 10 percent among the
conscripts.

The Komsomol membership increased from 66,000 in 1946 to
128,000 in 1954.[137] In August 1951 the oblast' Komsomol newspaper
began to be published for the first time since its discontinuation at the
beginning of the war. In the years 1949 and 1950, the membership
increase was particularly sharp: more than 100,000 members were
counted in 1950. The Komsomol had become "an all-embracing mass
organization of Soviet youth rather than an elite category second only
to the Party."[138]

The growth of the Komsomol in the Kalinin province kept pace with
the growth in the USSR as a whole; total USSR membership rose from
9.3 million in March 1949 to more than 16 million in August 1952.[139]
On the collective farms, however, Komsomol popularity remained less
than desired after 1947, for, as Komsomol secretary Beliakova
lamented in July 1951, "[i]n a majority of the cases [of Komsomol cells
at collective farms] a minority of kolkhoz youth is a Komsomol
member. Every month the number of kolkhozniks who enter the Komsomol decreases; every month the number of kolkhoz organizations
that have not accepted more youth to their ranks increases. When compared to the numbers of entry of young kolkhozniks into the Komsomol in 1949, then those numbers in this year have decreased in several
different months roughly by two to three times."[140]

Beliakova apparently was unaware of the negative effect on membership levels of the exodus of rural youth, to which more attention
will be given in Chapter 8 (numbers for 1953 are given in table 19). In
1952 the kolkhozniks' Komsomol membership fell by another three
thousand. Members were sometimes less than enthusiastic about the
Komsomol as well, since about 12 percent of them failed to pay membership fees on a regular basis in 1951. In 1949 even leading Komsomol members had their children christened, visited churches, and
observed other Orthodox customs.[141]

The Komsomol's postwar transformation from elite to mass organization for Soviet youth did not happen without difficulty. Party organizations at all levels were unable to provide the necessary supervision,
and consequently some Komsomol organizations were left to fend for
themselves. As a result, some of the provincial youth fell under the
influence of "backward elements," violated labour discipline, and
behaved in other unworthy ways.[142]

Apart from setting the example on the collective farm or on the

Table 19
Komsomol Membership and Professions of Komsomols on the Collective Farms,
1 May 1953

Profession	Number
Kolkhoz chairs	13
Heads of tovarnye fermy	153
Brigadiers of field-crop brigades	668
Team leaders of zven'ia	666
Komsomols engaged in animal husbandry	3,325
Komsomols engaged in crop tillage	16,233
Tractor brigadiers, tractor drivers, and MTS mechanics	1,539

Source: Based on Pako, 147/5/769, l.96.
Note: In 1,774 kolkhozy – out of the total of 1,905 collective farms – Komsomol organizations with a total membership of 22,776, 21,058 of whom worked on the collective farms. There were 221 Komsomol organizations with 5 members or less; 434 with 6–10 members; 1,027 with 10–25 members; and 97 with 26–50 members.

shopfloor, the teenagers and young adult members of Komsomols were obliged to supervise the activities of the "Young Pioneers" organization, created for children below the age of fourteen and somewhat similar to our Boy Scouts and Girl Scouts and Cubs and Brownies. In 1948, 100,060 children belonged to a Pioneer group in the province.[143]

Even where sufficient supervision existed, the party and Komsomol leaders responsible were ruefully deficient in their political education. In 1948 the provincial first Komsomol secretary met with the second Komsomol raikom secretary of the Ovinishche district.[144] He found that she was "illiterate" in matters of party theory and history; she was of the opinion that Churchill (who at this point was a major villain in the eyes of the party, since he had shown himself a "warmonger" in his Iron Curtain speech in 1946) had died long ago. Even more telling about the heterodoxy of the Komsomol is the apparent existence from 1947 until 1953 of the "Union of the Eastern Branch," a group of Komsomol district secretaries of raions located east of the October Railroad in the province.[145] During these years, some of the "presidents" of this informal organization had unwittingly been promoted to the party apparatus. The group met in Kalinin and new members paid a fee that financed restaurant dinners, with subsequent drinking bouts. In Kiselev's report on the group to an obkom plenum it was hinted that young female Komsomol secretaries had been taken sexual advantage of. Kiselev cited the example of this "Union" to warn against gruppovshchina (group forming) and the formation of "cliques" or "families."

In the capital of Kalinin of 1953, 21,000 young people belonged to the Komsomol, but their political and general education was often mediocre.[146] Only 3,500 of them had completed secondary school or more. Party leaders expressed the opinion that inadequate education translated into "amoral deeds," such as violations of labour and state discipline, as well as the observation of religious ceremonies. The oblast' prosecutor, Gerasimenko, complained about the large number of youths among suspects in criminal court cases. Most crimes, according to Gerasimenko, were committed under the influence of copious amounts of alcohol, often consumed on religious holidays. In Kalinin a group of secondary school students had beaten up a teacher.

On the surface, the Komsomol promised to be a monolithic organization of aspiring Communists, of the most promising youth in society. In practice, however, the organization had to deal with a continuous stream of impediments to its efforts to educate and discipline young people to become obedient, vigilant, and enthusiastic subjects of the Soviet state. Because of the Komsomol's exceptional postwar growth, it became even less possible to control the ideological orthodoxy of all members. Provincial youth engaged in the usual pursuits of young people in a modern society, some of which trespassed into the realm of crime. What the authorities saw as misbehaviour of the young was perpetrated by those both inside and outside the Komsomol of Kalinin oblast'.

CHAPTER FOUR

Party and People

"A double life?" I asked. "A double life of course," said Criminale, "Over there in those days we lived in a time when the only rule was to lie. By the wrong emotion, the wrong gesture, you betrayed yourself. But if you knew how to lie, if you supported the regime in public, you were allowed your thoughts in private. If you allowed them to use your reputation, you were not called to the police station. If you stood up for their history, they permitted you your irony. We were a culture of cynics, we were corrupt and base, but it was the agreed reality. Those people loved great political thoughts, they loved Utopia, totality. The revolution of the proletariat, a madhouse."[1]

After the war the regime renewed its attempt to make its subjects believe they lived in the best of possible worlds. The propaganda of utopian ideals had had some effect before the German invasion, but although after the war the policy of inculcating loyalty and obedience was probably less haphazardly organized than in the stormy thirties, the receptiveness of the population seems to have declined markedly after 1945. Cynicism began to show among many who were exposed to the constant barrage of agitprop. Russians learned to lie about their innermost thoughts, and many became bold enough to try to profit from the scarcities that resulted from the poor state of socialized agri-culture, the insufficient production of consumer goods, and the flawed operation of the distribution system. The question remains why there seems to have been so much more enthusiasm during the 1930s. Perhaps people were intoxicated by the promise of the ultimate horn of plenty and the imminent just society; perhaps they only seemed enthu-siastic out of fear of arrest. Probably the ardour that has been recorded was the result of a combination of these motives. It is certainly true that the war had decimated an entire generation of young men – and to some degree, women – who could have become the next generation of enthusiastic builders of socialism. At the same time the reduced risk of arrest, about which more will be said in the next chapter, removed some of the threat of the stick that had been so brutally used together with the utopian carrot during the 1930s. It is difficult to live one's life without believing in some higher purpose, however. Although religious belief had eroded as a result of the combined onslaught of modernity and the intensive persecution of organized religion between November 1917 and 1941, religious habits proved harder to eradicate. In many cases, the void left by the disappearance of rule of the God of Heaven was filled by the God on earth, who ruled like the Devil.

THE POLITICAL CONSCIOUSNESS OF THE POPULATION: TOOLS OF INDOCTRINATION

After 1945 the United States and, to a lesser extent, the West as a whole – to which Yugoslavia was added in 1948 – replaced Nazi Germany as the USSR's new mortal enemy. During and after the war, the most successful element of political propaganda was Soviet patriotism.[2] Older Russians are tremendously proud of the victory over Hitler's Germany and the achievement of superpower status by the Soviet Union. Many of the pre-1930 generation also believe that full employment, free health care, and free education were unrivalled achievements, unique to the Soviet Union.[3] The harsh labour conditions, the questionable quality of health care, and the fees for secondary education reintroduced by Stalin are conveniently forgotten. For many respondents to the survey there was no crime under Stalin, although, in fact, the remembered order did not exist, as statistics on crime indicate.[4]

These "positive aspects" of postwar society forged a certain amount of loyalty among Soviet citizens and perhaps made people accept other less pleasant features of their lives that resulted from Communist policy as well. Yet most of the survey respondents were a long way from being zealous, politically conscious – in the Marxian sense – adherents of the ideology of the Communist party under Stalin. In fact most of the respondents' praise was for the social benefits introduced by the party and government. Ironically, their approval supports the argument that the working class was able to develop only a "trade-union consciousness," as Lenin had already maintained in 1902.[5] In this chapter, the propaganda machine and its efficacy will be explored: Which elements of the Soviet myth propagated by the regime found a resonance in the minds of the people? Why were there so few zealous communists despite the seemingly lavish expenditure on political education?

After it was twice berated for the poor state of agitation and propaganda, from early 1944 onwards pains were taken by the obkom to improve the political consciousness of the provincial inhabitants. Party educational rooms and libraries began to receive the necessary literature and supplies. Since 1943 evening universities in Kalinin, Kimry, and Torzhok had been operating to educate leading Communists in the province; forty leading oblast' workers studied by correspondence with the Higher Party School under the Central Committee. The year 1943 also saw the creation of raion party schools in towns and raion centres. In 1944 the obkom ordered the creation of general educational studies for leading cadres. In January 1945 ninety-five leading oblast' and raion workers studied by correspondence in the Kalinin Pedagogical Institute. Others were students of the provincial correspondence school for secondary education, and more attended district schools for general education.[6]

The method of independently studying Marxism-Leninism was revived in the oblast' during the war years. Yet, many of the students of the canon neglected their studies. Permanent and temporary lecturers of the obkom and of the raikoms and gorkoms had been giving talks in 1944, but they were often considered deficient in quality and content. Lecturers seldom discussed the history of the party – as laid out by the *History of the Communist Party of the Soviet Union* (the *Short Course*) – and questions concerning the Soviet economy.[7]

At the end of 1946 an obkom plenum discussed the ideological state of affairs in the province. The discussion was called forth by Zhdanov's attack on "unprincipled and apolitical" attitudes toward ideological work within the Communist Party.[8] The opening report at the plenum was given by A.K. Kalachev, at the time obkom secretary responsible for agitation and propaganda. He harshly criticized the general lack of vigilance and political ignorance that was rampant in Kalinin province. His lambasting was a personal last stand, inasmuch as he was ordered to go back to school himself to study Marxism-Leninism only a few months later.[9] This undoubtedly was a banishment for Kalachev, who was until March 1947 a full member of the obkomburo. The fact that Kalachev, the most senior authority in these matters in the province, was sent back to school to study Marxism-Leninism illustrates the low level of political education in the province. Kalachev had been steeped in the canon, and even his understanding was apparently questionable. What to think, then, of the ideological sophistication of the many new members, who were taught in the most amateurish manner about the party's history:

What, for example, can come out of the sessions of the evening party school of the gorkom of Torzhok? At one of these sessions our workers [of the obkom otdel of agitation and propaganda] were present. The session was conducted by comrade Afanas'eva. The theme of the session was the seventh chapter of the *Short Course* of the history of the VKP(b). The session was conducted by the following method: the teacher phrased questions – "What did the workers want?" The students answered as a choir: "Freedom." "What did the peasants need? The students shouted: "Freedom." "Could the tsarist government satisfy the workers and peasants?" – The students answered: "No."[10]

Elections were soon to be held for the RSFSR Supreme Soviet.[11] To make the population willingly go to the urns and vote for the one candidate in their district, propagandists were ordered to diffuse an image of a government and party continuously concerned about the well-being of Soviet citizens. Many of the agitators were not up to this rather daunting task, in a year in which another famine plagued the country, and were often apprehensive about confronting the voters and answering their questions. Considering the low level of education of the majority of the population, and even of some of the party propagandists, it does not come as a surprise that some questions posed to the party agitprop activists revealed a high degree of ignorance.[12]

Examples abound of the lack of what was considered proper political knowledge: thus in 1948 two rural schoolteachers could not tell which position Stalin occupied in the government.[13] One of them erroneously thought that he was chairman of the RSFSR Supreme Soviet and had heard nothing at all about Zhdanov! This stands in rather stark contrast to the supposed adoration of Zhdanov in the toilers' collective memory professed by the obkomburo in a telegram after his death sent to Moscow on 1 September 1948. It seems likely that before Zhdanov died hardly anyone outside the obkom membership in the 1940s even realized that he had begun his career as a Bolshevik in Tver'.

Certain questions posed to agitprop workers and party lecturers, however, show a high degree of (improper) political insight among voters for the Supreme Soviet:

Can one elect a priest to the RSFSR Supreme Soviet?
Will the course of the foreign policy of the USA change in connection with the victory of the Republicans in the senatorial elections?
Do we receive at the moment, and if so, then from which countries, grain?
Do we receive at the moment goods from the Western zone of Germany?
How could it happen that in France the socialists at the election got less votes than the communists, but that the former lead the government?[14]

To a certain extent, the party succeeded with its propaganda about the evil machinations of the capitalist West. Part of the explanation for Soviet citizens' acceptance of hardships rendered by the regime's poli-

cies can be found in the successfully created image of mortally dangerous foreign enemies, which struck a chord in the minds of the people.
The experience of the real horrors of World War II made many want
to avoid a recurrence of war at any price.[15]

These pre-electoral meetings provided one of the rare occasions
when the population could openly voice their grievances. In 1946
many urban dwellers asked for improvement of public works.[16] In
Kalinin people wanted to know why public bathhouses operated irregularly and why there was frequently no hot water there. Others
demanded to know what measures were being taken to combat hooliganism, speculation, and theft. Complaints were uttered about the
irregular availability of goods in the shops. In rural eastern raions
people wanted to know if localities would be better provided with
bread in 1947. At the meetings government representatives promised
to improve matters, and that was that – at least formally. That the situation actually ameliorated is doubtful. In the case of individual complaints, some people turned to writing letters to the party, or, in the
case of the nonparty members, to their district delegates at the different levels of soviets.[17] Improvements were ephemeral in most cases,
and this incompetence helped to erode the trust in the propagated
concern for the workers. Pre-electoral gatherings were at the same time
a means for the party to gauge the mood among the populace.

The toilers had a further opportunity to express grievances at lectures given by propagandists.[18] In 1948 some listeners asked if a party
congress would be held soon: it had been nine years since the last one,
a violation of party rules that was ignored by the party leadership in
Moscow. Others asked when another price reduction for foodstuffs
would be implemented or wondered about increases in the price of
train tickets and electricity. Questions about the reason for the high
taxation of the peasantry must have been considered as outrightly subversive by the provincial party leadership.

Uncritical obedience was impossible to enforce; the narod and even
the party membership preserved a measure of critical thinking and was
sometimes courageous enough, or perhaps naive enough, to ask rather
embarassing questions publicly. In 1949 in Udoml'ia raion, somewhat
of a rural backwater at this time, village dwellers wondered why one
could not buy any ploughs or harrows if industrial production had surpassed the 1940 level by 18 percent.[19] Others wondered whether the
dictatorship of the proletariat would still be necessary in the transition
of socialism to Communism or whether the Eastern European peoples'
democracies were also governed by a dictatorship of the proletariat.
Another person even wanted to find out how the Palestinian problems
could be solved. It is no wonder that reports on these perceptive
queries ended up on the desk of the obkom secretaries.

In May 1951 Communists at lower levels in the raions were acquainted with two secret letters, one emanating from the Central Committee alone, the other one from the Central Committee and the Council of Ministers combined.[20] In closed sessions, party members discussed the letters' contents. Provocative questions were asked by the rank-and-file Communists of Bezhetsk raion; for example, "How can one make all private plots of equal size for all kolkhozniks?" "Why did several kolkhozy become weaker after the amalgamation?" "Why did the Central Committee of the VKP(b) not correct comrade Khrushchev immediately for the errors that he committed in his article [in *Pravda*] on the questions of the amalgamation of the kolkhozy?"[21]

A kind of impatience is expressed with the actions of the party's leadership and the leaders themselves. The first two questions indicate a sense that some of the Party's recent measures had been unrealistic, made without sufficient consultation with lower levels of the hierarchy. In the question about the Khrushchev article, which concerned the creation of "agrotowns," a feeling of perplexity can be discerned.[22] The party leadership had shown for years nothing but an appearance of monolithic unity. The fact that a difference of opinion had risen between the leaders, played out partially in the forum of the national newspaper, must have shocked Communists. After all, what would the population's reaction be to this exposure of fallibility of a Politburo member? Why was Khrushchev not cautioned earlier, even before his article was published?

In 1952 political meetings took place to discuss the directives for the Nineteenth Party Congress, the Fifth Five Year Plan, and the new party statute. The toilers of the province again came forward with sometimes ingenuous questions: "Which new machines will be assigned to agriculture?" "How much will be designated for the defensive needs of the country?" "How can one understand the increase of wages when at the same time retail prices are to be lowered no less than 35 percent?"[23]

More critical utterances were also heard. The kolkhoznik Popov (not a party member) stated at a political meeting on the projects that were to be dealt with by the Nineteenth Party Congress that he was taxed for 1,150 rubles but that his plot was barely large enough to take care of his and his wife's needs.[24] He could not derive enough income from his plot to pay these taxes and he was receiving virtually nothing for his workdays on the collective farm (trudodni). How was he then to understand the promise of increased affluence for kolkhozniks in the blueprint for the five-year plan? Others wondered why kolkhozniks were not entitled to trips to sanatoria. Was one to pay for secondary education, when it became obligatory in the country?

The party leadership aimed in principle for total control, for "a system [demanding] that each individual participate in fulfilling the ruler's aims and [suppressing and stultifying] all the people, including oneself," but in practice these aims were impossible to achieve as a consequence of the primitive state of transport and communications and of the ignorance about current political orthodoxy among the population and the lower levels of the party hierarchy.[25]

Most refrained from openly criticizing the state of affairs. Even overtly nonpolitical questions could have unpleasant consequences: N.S. Kokorin criticized the teaching at the military academy where he studied; he was forced to leave the army. Often people blamed local leaders, but hardly anyone directly attacked policies of the party leaders and central government in Moscow. People were arrested after the war for telling sarcastic anecdotes about the powers that be or for cursing the leadership in a moment of carelessness – so-called anti-Soviet agitation. The mother of M.M. Kozenkova-Pavlova barely escaped arrest after she spoke out against Stalin after the war. A young Komsomol member wanted to denounce her to the authorities and told her so openly. Pavlova senior was spared the denunciation after the village's elderly people talked the "vigilant" Komsomol member out of the plan.[26]

One might easily conclude from the records that no stone was left unturned to inculcate political orthodoxy in the average citizen. In late 1950 and early 1951, for the second time after the war, elections were held for local soviets. The number of agitators involved in agitprop work for this event was staggering: 54,612.[27] In the countryside, agitators were distributed by allocating one agitator for every ten households, while in the towns the agitators were assigned separate floors or full apartment buildings, depending on their size. Konovalov reported to the Central Committee that 1,098,500 people attended lectures and reports on the significance of the elections. It was hard to escape some form of political propaganda. Not just this propaganda but fear of reprisals led to a voter turnout that was almost universal.

What did the regime attempt to impress on the populace as its achievements? After his election to the Supreme Soviet in 1946, Simonov, head of the oblispolkom, boasted in the provincial newspaper of literacy, the increase in harvest yields, industrialization, the constant care for Soviet mothers and children, child benefits, health care, pensions for the elderly, pensions for invalids and those who had lost a bread-winning relative in the war, and credits for housing construction as achievements of Communist rule.[28] In its stress on all real and imagined improvements brought by Soviet power, Simonov's message is typical of the election propaganda in other years.

The elections themselves offered a holiday. Many voters lined up in front of election bureaus even before they had opened.[29] Older people were transported by automobiles and carts to polling stations. At these stations (located either in buildings of the local soviet or in clubs of the kolkhoz, factory, or town quarters) concerts were held, groups of amateur artists performed, and films were shown in rooms adjacent to those in which the voters' booths were placed. Election reports to Moscow paint a happy picture that is not entirely false. It was left unsaid how much the mood improved because of the overabundant intake of alcohol.[30]

Voters were possibly stimulated as well in their enthusiasm by the money they received for their participation. Nadezhda A. Smirnova remembered in testimony for the survey how "[E]aster and the elections for the soviets were especially celebrated. These [the parties for soviet elections] were aided by the means for their celebration given to kolkhozy and enterprises."[31]

In 1949 there were about 90,000 radios in Kalinin province, distributed among apartments of workers, clubs, reading corners (krasnye ugolki), and in village reading rooms (izbi-chital'nye).[32] This more modern means of communication did not reach every person; again, the situation in the countryside was probably the least satisfactory. M.M. Kozenkova-Pavlova reported in the survey that her village had neither radio nor electricity. By 1961 in the village of A.K. Sumugina in Rameshki raion electricity and radios had not made an appearance. In June 1949, in only slightly more than 400 kolkhozy (out of more than 7,000!), in 360 rural soviets, in 19 sovkhozy, and in 38 MTSs, radios transmitted Muscovite and local broadcasts.[33] It is doubtful that the newspaper press filled the gap, since so many of the oblast' inhabitants were still partially unlettered. Furthermore, the radio did present the dangerous possibility of picking up foreign broadcasts. In April 1951 the oblast' committee of the trade union of workers and employees at MTSs and agricultural organizations complained about the widespread practice of people on kolkhozy and at technical institutes listening to the "slander" of foreign radio stations.[34]

In March 1951, fifty-six newspapers with a total circulation of 256,000 copies were published in Kalinin province. Concomitantly, several of the All-Union papers published in Moscow were distributed in the oblast'. The figures are certainly impressive, but no paper appeared daily, and even the largest one, *Proletarskaia Pravda*, was only four to six pages long.[35] A study of the editorial plan of *Proletarskaia Pravda* for November and December 1946 indicates that this most important province-wide paper had the almost exclusive purpose of serving as a propagandistic instrument.[36] Before publication, the obkomburo discussed and ratified the editorial plans for the coming two months. Editor Iuzhakov was present at these discussions as a candidate member of the obkom which shows the party's conviction that the newspaper could greatly help it achieve its aims. The editorial plan was discussed by the obkom on 30 October 1946.[37] Articles were to appear illustrating the exemplary role that the party and individual Communists or Komsomols played in Soviet society and the economy. The obkom wanted much space dedicated to the classic works of Lenin and Stalin and the significance of their actions and writings. In every issue reports on the progress of agriculture, industry, and transport would be found, with suggestions and advice on how to improve their results by emulating shining examples of economic efficency. Efforts at improving health care and cultural provisons were to be highlighted, and some local literary efforts as well as works from nationally acclaimed authors were to be published. Room was additionally allocated for international news and speeches by important All-Union personalities.

Hardly any room was left for news in the sense of reporting on new occurrences. News was what the obkomburo had determined a priori to be news, not some unpredictable event that might happen in the future. This preconceived program for the paper sometimes led to embarrassing mistakes. In 1949 a *Proletarskaia Pravda* correspondent reported on the exemplary labour of the kolkhoznitsa Ol'ga Zheleznova. Yet Zheleznova was not working at her kolkhoz anymore at the time of publication, for she had been sentenced, three years earlier, to eight years of imprisonment.[38]

Apart from their propagandistic value, newspapers also served the security organs and judiciary. In 1952 *Kalininskaia Pravda* regularly published compromising material on people accused of various abuses.[39] According to its proud editor, scores of people had been prosecuted within the party or by the courts on the basis of the paper's materials; because of *Kalininskaia Pravda*'s exemplary vigilance, more than 100 people had lost their jobs and 4,000 had been punished in other ways.

In 1951, one library was supposed to serve, on average, the territory of more than three rural soviets in the countryside. Consequently, in many villages people were unable to enjoy the use of a library. Few books were sold, few newspapers read in the countryside. Films were shown irregularly, and their quality was poor: they often broke, there was no sound, and so on. One wonders whether the kolkhozniks really minded the poor projection of films such as *The Battle of Stalingrad*, *The Young Guard*, or *The Fall of Berlin*, which were universally distributed.[40] Perhaps anything was better than nothing at all. In some rural clubs people watched the same film over and over again. The selection for a kolkhoz "film festival" in 1946 seems hardly appealing: the features offered included the classics *Socialist Animal Husbandry, Fertilization and Harvest, For a High Harvest of Potatoes,* and *The Vitamin.* Fictional films were also announced, but their titles were not mentioned in the paper. Even in October 1953 almost one third of the villages and hamlets in the province hardly ever saw a film.

Heads of village reading rooms and rural clubs were often not erudite enough to impress peasants. In 1951, for example, 135 had enjoyed only four to five grades of school and more than 400 others were inexperienced, having been on the job for less than a year.[41] It is impossible that someone with so little expertise would have been able to explain coherently the intricacies of Stalinist dialectical materialism as laid down in the *Short Course.*[42] The environment for study and reading, furthermore, possessed little appeal: many clubs were in a shambles, and they were often unheated in winter.

In February 1953 the obkom once more condemned the high incidence of varied religious practices among Communist Party members.[43] Some owned icons; others had their children christened. Whereas the level of indoctrination of Communists was impressive on the surface, it proved extremely difficult to eradicate, root and branch, old customs and ways of thinking and to forge a genuinely atheistic Communist mentality. Popular culture proved resilient against the ideological attacks by the party, both in the countryside and in the city. In the countryside, the inadequate means allocated to the effort were part of the reason for this tenacity, but the Russians in the towns, too, often proved immune to the sustained brainwashing attempted by the authorities.

In early 1948 an obkom plenum rededicated itself to the "improvement" of ideological work in the party organization, as a further consequence of the stepped-up ideological offensive.[44] A secondary school teacher was criticized for maintaining that the poet Mayakovsky's weltanschauung had been influenced by Cervantes.[45] Lecturers at the Pedagogical Institute of Kalinin had perpetrated mistakes in their teaching of the Soviet Union's history. Others at the same institute had kowtowed to the West in articles on Merimée's appreciation of Pushkin and on Gorky and Western European literature. An actor of the oblast' drama theatre, Veitsler, had even had the gall to declare that political literacy would not improve his acting.

The heavy hand of socialist-realist literary criticism came down on local literati in 1948 as well. In 1947 a provincial literary magazine published its first issue and was exposed to strong criticism by the obkom, basing itself on Zhdanov's attack on the journals *Zvezda* and *Leningrad* of August 1946.[46] In an editorial in 1948 in the second issue

of *Rodnoi Krai*, A. Parfenov, obkom secretary for agitation and propaganda, panned the contents of the first issue:

The obkom further noticed that a number of the contributions, printed in the
first issue of the almanac, were of a low ideological-political and creative level,
did not conform to the demands of the Central Committee of the vkp(b) on
Soviet literature. One is required to serve the education of the people, to serve
the strengthening of their moral and political unity. These contributions were
severely criticized. The poor supervision of the editors of the almanac over the
authors was pointed out, as well as the low artistic quality of the literary material printed in the almanac ... any reflection of the fundamental theme of today,
the example of the selfless labour of Soviet people fighting for the fulfillment
of the postwar Stalinist Five Year Plan, could not be found; the life of the
oblast' in light of the current tasks was not represented.[47]

Despite this criticism, obkom secretary Siriapin noticed in March
1948 that the second issue contained many mistakes similar to those
littering the first one.[48]

The party itself had undergone a transformation during the war years.
In January 1948, 80 percent of its membership had become Communist during or after the war. The political reliability of some of these
new recruits was suspect, while, on the other hand, older cadres
behaved overzealously in attempts to discipline them:

In a number of town and raion party organizations, the opinion has been diffused that anti-party behaviour and party exclusions apply to that part of the
communists, who have arrived from the Soviet Army, in which they have
entered the party, and on whom no demands were made [when they became
members]; thus, we, so to say, now have to sort them out, and "put things in
order." Above all, this is an injurious anti-bolshevik theory, which does not
conform to reality. With the help of this "theory" several comrades try to hide
their own shortcomings with respect to recruitment by the party and education
of young communists.[49]

In late 1946, still around one fifth of the roughly 55,000 Communists did not partake in any form of political education.[50] This worried
the obkom all the more, because the Central Committee had not long
before issued a decree on the necessity of the inclusion of all Communists in the system of political education. Apart from this large number
of Communists who did not even formally study, many participated
merely formally in some form of political study (for this offence,

several oblispolkom and obkom workers had even been thrown out of the correspondence department of the provincial Higher Party School). In late 1946, many Communists were forced to study on their own, since there were not enough study circles and schools. The supervision of these political autodidacts was sorely inadequate, if one believes the words of the propaganda secretary of the obkom, Kalachev. In 1946 the Central Committee made it obligatory to organize twice a year ten-day (or longer) seminars in political education for raikom and gorkom secretaries.[51]

By 1948 ideological education of Communists had formally become better organized: it began with a stint at a political school (polit-shkola), followed by a study of the *History of the All-Russian Communist Party (Bolsheviks): Short Course* (mentioned earlier in this section).[52] The next step comprised a study of the *Short Course* combined with selected works of the classics of Marxism-Leninism, succeeded by courses at the evening party school. Finally, full political education was completed by study at the university of Marxism-Leninism. Again, this signifies the intensified ideological offensive that had commenced in 1946 and would not let up until 1953.[53] By 1951 the system of party education had become even more elaborate. Seen from the top down, Communist orthodoxy was instilled by 3 evening universities for the study of Marxism-Leninism, 69 town and raion evening party schools, 432 circles for the advanced study of the *Short Course*, 1,566 for the basic study of the same book, 576 circles engaged in the study of the biographies of Lenin and Stalin, and 1,350 political schools.[54] More than ten thousand Communists independently studied Marxist-Leninist theory. Ninety-five percent of the roughly 60,000 Communists were engaged in some form of party education, together with 6,750 Komsomols and 16,270 nonparty aktiv.

In 1951, 9 full-time and 25 part-time lecturers were at the disposal of the obkom.[55] The raikoms and gorkoms had an additional 756 part-time lecturers at their service. Despite this increased effort, the limited education of the great majority of the people and of a large amount of the Communists, prevented propagandists from successfully explaining the theoretical basis of Soviet society to the narod.[56]

THE POLITICAL CONSCIOUSNESS OF THE POPULATION: THE SUCCESS OF INDOCTRINATION

The avalanche of indoctrination had some effect. The set of beliefs and values of the Russians often became an idiosyncratic mixture of Communist slogans, adherence to a concept of social justice, traditional trust in the infallible leader, meshchanin (Philistine) culture, loyalty to family, and non-utilitarian morality.[57] The postwar conformism of the narod was mainly the result of exhaustion from the war, the security organs' control over the population, and a common human wish to believe in utopia in this life or hereafter. Soon after 1945, however, the belief in the reality of the radiant future of Communist society came into conflict with the harsh postwar life.

Fear of political persecution also determined individuals' actions, but even the brutality of collectivization and the Great Terror had not always been successful in inculcating slavish obedience. The audacity or naïveté of A.M. Afanas'ev, a participant in the survey who had joined the party as a twenty-year-old conscript in 1940, is surprising. About two years after his demobilization in 1944 he began to work in the raikom of Udoml'ia. He asked the head of the local MVD how he could find out about the fate of his father-in-law, who had been arrested during collectivization. Afanas'ev was told to forget about the issue and not to speak anymore to the MVD chief about it. The next day a raikom secretary admonished Afanas'ev for conducting "unhealthy conversations" and warned him that one could not work in the raikom with such an attitude. Afanas'ev repented and promised to better himself.

N.D. Eliseev maintained that he never believed in Communism, but had joined the Party nevertheless in 1956, after thirteen years in the Komsomol. He did believe, however, in Stalin. Today Eliseev appreciates the abundant food he was able to buy under the Communist system (he was part of the "workers' aristocracy" as a locomotive engineer) but criticizes the many injustices of the past. Furthermore, people had confidence, in his opinion, in what the future would bring, which he believes has been lost today. It seems that Eliseev believed in the possibility of a better life for the country by following socialist policies but was realistic enough to consider the creation of a communist paradise a millenarian idea.

A most curious former Communist Party member was the cobbler V.F. Nepriaev. He welcomed the death of Stalin, whom he felt to be a cannibal.[58] Nepriaev had seen the early results of collectivization and the destruction of the peasantry's life, for which he would never forgive the Communists and Stalin. He stated that all the crying about Stalin's death was done on command. Nepriaev was one of the most bitter survivors of Stalin's rule who was interviewed, probably because he seemed to be one of the more perceptive.

We have seen that the obkomburo attempted to scrutinize all activity in Kalinin province in an impossible effort to achieve total control and prevent any unwelcome surprises. The prevalence of criticism, warnings, admonishments, and the like is proof of the buro's perception of a lack of cooperation among the population. One can deduce that the highest leadership did not deem the lower levels in the party organization and government fit to take care of matters on their own. And indeed, it seemed to the buro members that as soon as their attention temporarily slackened, the Russians took the opportunity to misbehave: they became inebriated, committed fraud with ration cards, and slaughtered pigs without permission, while lower ranks abused their authority.[59] As Djilas wrote, "[t]he state is not merely an instrument of tyranny; society as well as the executive bodies of the state machine are in a continuous and lively opposition to the oligarchy, which aspires to reduce this opposition by naked force."[60]

The examples of bad faith towards the regime and deviant behaviour are legion in the archives of the former Communist Party: here we find one kolkhoz chairman (a Communist even) who stated, in 1946, that he would rather spend time in jail than give grain to the state, for he did not want to leave his kolkhozniks without any.[61] There we have a certain forester, Boikov, who was fired after the oblast' newspapers had received letters complaining about his abusive behaviour on the job. His offences ran from being systematically drunk at work to felling trees and selling them off for vodka, letting cattle graze in the forest area that he supervised, and illegally cultivating hayfields in the woods.

It seems that an ongoing battle was waged between life (the people) trying to reassert itself whenever and wherever possible and stultifying discipline (maintained by the party and more particularly, its obkomburo). We already saw in chapter 3 how at all levels the party's functionaries attempted to find the optimal equilibrium between the often unrealistic orders from above and the constraints imposed upon them by the willingness of the people to cooperate and by the limitations of nature. But the party membership was always inclined to pressure the population to the hilt to fulfill the orders, for informers were omnipresent and overt support for the labourer's wishes to lower targets could be, in the final analysis, interpreted as criticism of the party's infallible plans.[62]

Party leaders at obkomburo, All-Russian, or All-Union levels often willfully ignored information from the localities about impediments to plan targets because, in the eyes of the leadership, any area could always deliver more, given adequate input. Planning became somewhat more realistic after the First Five Year Plan but remained to a large extent based on rather esoteric and abstract ideas about the production potential of industry and agriculture. This is evidenced by the continuous disappointment of the central and provincial leadership about agricultural and industrial production. For the mind reared by the science of Marxism-Leninism, the possibility that life was more complicated than conceived by the plan could not be an explanation of failure. Both in industry and farming, people lied about the fulfillment of production plans, as was noticed, for example, in September 1951.[63]

During the 1940s obligatory state loans amounted to extra taxation for the people, leading to a further slice off their income. As a result, particularly in the countryside, the population remained precariously close to subsistence levels. M.V. Kornetova, a rural soviet secretary, had to agitate for the subscription to these loans as part of her work. She noted in her testimony in the survey that widows with children gave their last for the resurrection of the country, whether out of fear or out of conviction. N.V. Kurganova said that she was not impressed by the demeanour of employees of the security organs when she encountered them at the subscription to the loans, and declared that she "didn't like them: fat mugs, holding onto their pistols; we were probably frightened. We subscribed, granted, although not out of fear, but because it was necessary."[64]

Some of the party's lack of trust toward the peasantry was a consequence of the belief in the essential petty bourgeois quality of the peasants; such a view was a tenet of Marxist theory and was part and parcel of Lenin's political philosophy. In spite of the legal equality of workers and peasants proclaimed by the Constitution of 1936, distrust of the peasantry permeated the Communist Party and was one of the causes of the repeated threat of force against undisciplined peasants after 1945, as expressed, for example, in the resolutions of September 1946 and February 1947 and subsequent measures emanating from the Supreme Soviet, the Central Committee, the USSR Council of Ministers, and from lower party and government organs, such as the obkomburo of Kalinin province. Even today the intelligentsia has difficulties coming to terms with the perceived "uncultured" ways of the narod.[65]

The fundamental opposition between party and people should not be exaggerated, however: the population itself denounced to the authorities those among them who were guilty of abuse, while a measure of genuine enthusiasm among the population for rebuilding the fatherland after the war or even for building socialism was present. Nevertheless, this enthusiasm would rapidly decline after 1945, when any genuine improvements in the quality of life of most citizens failed to occur.[66]

Vasily Grossman has aptly described the peculiar lethargic state of mind of the Soviet population that Stalin's repressions had forged, a population for whom "[t]he divinity, the faultlessness, of the immortal state, it now turned out, had not only crushed the individual human being, but had also defended him, comforted him in his weakness, shielded him, and provided justification for his insignificance. The state had taken on its own iron shoulders the entire weight of responsibility; it had freed individual human beings from any qualms of conscience."[67] As a novelist, however, Grossman overstates the point; enough evidence exists to suggest that the human desire to pursue one's own interests instead of those of the collective never seems to have disappeared in the Soviet Union during its entire history. Immediately after the war, popular interests were more than ever of an economic nature. The trials and troubles of the 1930s and the war induced the large majority to crave, initially, nothing more than an existence in which they could feed themselves and their families adequately and in peace.[68]

Some sparkle of compassion was not entirely lacking in the obkomburo and lower party committees. Sometimes they did come to the defence of those who were unable to fend for themselves or lived in squalor. But compassion was often mixed with a callous desire for better economic results. In May 1945 the obkomburo discussed the insufferable situation within Soviet convict and POW camps, which meant that inmates acquitted themselves poorly of assigned tasks. Some concern was expressed about the inmates' well-being, but this solicitude stemmed almost solely from an irritation with withering economic results:

The obkomburo has established that leaders of a number of industrial enterprises, construction organizations, heads of camp directorates, and of camp sectors of the NKVD act with an intolerable indifference towards the deployment of workers of the special contingents and POWs. A review found out that the [authorities at several camps] organize the labour of special contingents and POWs very poorly; [inmates] working at industrial enterprises and construction objects are not always given daily roster tasks, while workers in a number of cases work en masse, not organized in workers' brigades and links, and no one within the brigades is assigned responsibility for the necessary fulfillment of work. There is neither a strict order of the workday, nor obligatory labour discipline, nor do workers know their output norms, because of which they do not work with intensity and have a very low labour productivity; the average productivity of labour in the month of April 1945 being 82.8 percent in the POW camps, and labour productivity fluctuated within the range of 60–75 percent in some enterprises ...

The low labour productivity of the POWs and special contingents is also caused by the fact that the heads of camp sectors tolerate a frequent change and transfer of workers from one workshop to another, failing to offer them an opportunity to study the production process.

The heads of the camp branches and the directors of the enterprises analyze their contingent poorly with regard to its specializations and, as a result, specialists are not always used in the right way (lathe operators, metal workers, carpenters, etc.). Lack of fulfillment by camp sectors of the agreed norm for the supply of industrial enterprises and building objects with work hands is a great shortcoming in the use of special contingents and of POWs; a number of occasions were discovered by the review when camp branches used a significant part of the contingent to do supplementary work for the upkeep of the camps ...

Until now a business relationship to organize the deployment of labour forces has not been established between heads of camp sectors and leaders of industrial enterprises and construction objects; after concluding an agreement, economic managers have little concern for the creation of normal sanitary living conditions for the labour contingent, badly provide them with special clothes, necessary bed linen, living space, and fuel.

The oblast' NKVD directorate loosened the control over the camp operations [which was necessary] to use POWs and special contingents within the economy of the oblast' to the utmost.[69]

The document continues with resolutions to improve the situation: the first resolution obliges NKVD head Pavlov and the camp heads to maximize the labour capacity of POWs and the special contingents. Part of the third resolution reads,

To oblige leaders of economic organizations, in whose enterprises camp labour is being used, to guarantee the execution of agreements with camp sectors; to create for the labour[ers] of special contingents and the POWs minimally required living and sanitary conditions (special dress, bed linen, living space and extra food for the overfulfillment of output norms).[70]

Other resolutions also ordered

[that] the heads of camp directorates and of camp sectors, and ... managers of economic organizations ... guarantee the preparation of camps for the winter period, to pay special attention to the procurement of fuel and building materials for the winter.

... [that] c. Pavlov ... organize in June 1945 a separate sanitary camp for the weakened contingent of POWs ... and use fully the contingents of light work for the tasks of preparing consumer goods, of shoe repairing, and of repairing clothing.

... [that] the heads of the camp directorates and camp sectors ... cease to allow special contingents and POWs not to go to work in case of insufficiency or absence of guards ... [that] c. Pavlov ... examine the question about the possibility of assigning the guards' units of the NKVD to heads of camp sectors.[71]

Another resolution obliged Pavlov to continue to maximize the amount of labour he could extract from the inmates.[72]

The rural folk's unwillingness to cooperate with authorities partially caused the failure of the attempt to repopulate the depleted countryside of the western raions with inhabitants from the eastern raions. In all, in 1948 and 1949, 1,016 households (4,147 people) were transferred to the west of the province.[73] Yet five raions sent less than 10 percent of their quota of households westward. Some of those who did move returned to the east, because in some raions new settlers were placed in unfinished houses or even – in Rzhev – in apartments.

Many party members at lower levels identified more with their own family or community than with the party itself.[74] Typical of the flawed zeal among party members may be the behaviour of "[t]he head of the raion [Sonkovo] office of flax procurements, comrade Tsvetkov, [who] was dispatched in March 1946 to the kolkhoz 'March 8' of the Sheldomezhskii rural soviet to report on the speech of comrade Stalin of 9 February 1946. After his arrival, he was told that the report had already been given there. Tsvetkov did not give the report and instead asked at a kolkhoz meeting if they could sell him a cow, and a cow was sold to him for 750 rubles."[75]

The behaviour of Tsvetkov and the kolkhozniks reveals a startling indifference to Stalin's speech of 1946.[76] Tsvetkov was bothered by a more pressing matter at the time. This defiance and irresponsibility must have infuriated the loftier party cadres.

In June 1948, an obkom plenum met to discuss the widespread habit of "private farming." Many peasants had almost completely withdrawn from the socialist sector of agriculture. According to Zobnin, plenipotentiary of the Ministry of Procurements for the province, almost 50,000 households grew grain on their extremely small private plots.[77] In Lukovnikovo, Molokoe, and Rzhev districts, half or more of kolkhoz households cultivated grain in such a manner. Of a total of about 260,000 kolkhoz households in 1947, apparently 20 percent preferred working for themselves, no matter how grim the odds were. These almost 50,000 kolkhoznik households were not edinolichniki (individual peasants, not belonging formally to a collective farm).[78] Some of them were excluded from the collective farm and would be classified in Sovietese as okolokolkhoznoe naselenie ([members of] the semi-kolkhoz population). These semi-kolkhozniks had been excluded from the collective farm for a variety of reasons, most frequently for not having worked the required minimum at some point or for simply refusing in general to work for the socialized sector. In 1950, 1.9

percent of the membership of the USSR kolkhozy did not take part at all in kolkhoz production, while a much larger percentage participated only infrequently.[79]

The measures taken by authorities or kolkhozes against those who neglected work for the kolkhoz and attempted to survive on the production of private plots and cattle varied.[80] Many raion or collective farm authorities could ill afford a severe punishment of these "shirkers." The shirkers might contribute to the production of necessary crops and livestock products (on their private plots, or even as a result of their limited involvement in the socialized sector), which could help fulfill procurement plans. Kolkhoz authorities could hope to lure them into more intensive involvement in kolkhoz work or to persuade them to return to the kolkhoz altogether. Because they would be definitively lost as potential work hands when sentenced to a camp or jail, it was self-defeating to have more than a few scapegoats juridically persecuted. This explains the limited amount of people exiled on the basis of the Supreme Soviet decree of 2 June 1948 (discussed in chapter 7 below), another effort to restore discipline in the countryside.[81] As a result of extreme labour scarcity in the countryside, the threat of sanctions remained mostly without effect; kolkhozniks knew very well that the chair of a collective farm could ill afford to mete out harsh penalties. When Stalin was alive, nonetheless, some kolkhozniks were persecuted by raion courts for a poor work attitude, to set an example. Therefore many kolkhozniks endeavoured to avoid labour within the socialized sector without provoking hazardous interest from the authorities.

In Udoml'ia raion in early 1949, twenty-six khutory were counted, some of which consisted of more than one household.[82] A total of 106 households lived in khutory, compared to more than 6,000 households living at the more than two hundred kolkhozy in the raion. Khutor households had not been involved in collective farming. Some of them had recently resettled in kolkhoz villages under pressure from the authorities. These households should be considered as part of the "semi-kolkhoz" population that had failed to comply with the legal minimum demanded from collective farmers. Even after the war, a few genuine edinolichniki survived.[83]

The proliferation of individual farming after the war in Kalinin oblast' was substantial. Even by 1949 agriculture in the province was only imperfectly collectivized: monolithic uniformity was the aim in the countryside, but the Russian peasant proved resilient. Even though the peasants who dodged collective farming were in a minority, their numbers do surprise: twenty years after the party ordered collectivization, thousands of people persisted in resisting the kolkhoz system.

Russians not only avoided working on collective farms by returning to a form of private farming. They could appear conspicuous in doing so, and could therefore be easily found out by the authorities. They also left farming altogether: the exodus from the countryside, to which we will return at a later stage, was another sign of the population's efforts to avoid the crushing state-imposed burdens.[84] Because of the enormous shortage of work hands in all branches of the economy after 1945, one could find work outside agriculture without much difficulty.[85] Employers in need of labour were often willing to turn a blind eye to job applicants lacking officially necessary working papers. In early 1948, for instance, three Communists, two kolkhozniks and a tractor driver, quit their jobs without permission from their collective farm and party cell and sought employment in Rzhev.[86] When their activities were brought to the obkom's attention, it transpired that they had been hired by the MVD and were working at the camp point No. 104 in Rzhev, even though none of the three had the required papers. Labour shortage caused even the GULag administration to bend the rules.

In 1950 the party decided to amalgamate the kolkhozy to increase the efficiency of the collective-farm system; amalgamation across the Soviet Union began in the early months of 1950.[87] The Central Committee felt obliged to interfere in the process when it seemed to progress haphazardly and without preparation or organization. It issued a resolution on 30 May 1950 that gave guidelines for the process. After this, amalgamation was massive. The impact was particularly profound in the provinces of the Central Region of Russia, where before the kolkhozy had been quite small. It seems that the timing of amalgamation – in the middle of the agricultural year – was poorly chosen. In comparison with collectivization, amalgamation took place at a more inopportune moment in the year.

In Kalinin oblast' three hundred people were sent into the countryside to fortify the agricultural cadres.[88] These were selected from the party and soviet workers and agricultural specialists: one-third had received specific training in agronomic technique, while the rest consisted of people with practical expertise. The amalgamation led to a sharp increase in party membership among kolkhoz directors: on 1 January 1951, 64.2 percent (1,172) of all chairs were party members or candidates. The education and work experience of collective-farm management improved somewhat, thanks to the mergers, but chairs, vice-directors, brigadiers, and those responsible for farm animals were already replaced at a high frequency during the first half year after the initiation of the process. The most striking change brought about by the amalgamation was the relative increase in Communist party and Komsomol membership among the cadres.[89] Most collective farm leaders running the enlarged farms had enjoyed no more than the four to seven years of primary school. A mere 67 of all the approximately 1,900 chairs were women, a remarkably low percentage considering the overwhelming majority of women working on the farms.[90]

The following remarks of Kalinin's first obkom secretary Konovalov would have us believe that collective-farm amalgamation proceeded like clockwork:

[The] unification of the small kolkhozy was conducted on the basis of strict voluntariness, through the organization of widespread explanatory labour among the kolkhozniks, with the utmost support for the initiative by the kolkhozniks themselves. Leading party and soviet workers and agricultural specialists were sent into the countryside to carry out the organizational work for the amalgamation; they explained to kolkhozniks everywhere the superiority of large collective farms over small ones, and aided with the unification of the kolkhozy.[91]

The scenario strongly resembled that of collectivization. But the reorganization of the farms provoked far less resistance than in the 1929–34 period, inasmuch as kolkhozniks did not stand to lose from this transformation of agriculture in the same way. The worst part of the process was the threat of having to abandon the ancestral village for a central kolkhoz centre.[92] After the criticism of Khrushchev's proposals for the creation of "agrotowns," however, this plan for relocation was shelved. The mergers received the most hostile reception in economically more prosperous kolkhozy, which stood to gain little from unification with weaker counterparts.[93] How much force, or the threat of it, played a role here remains hard to assess, but the peasants' wish to preserve their old kolkhoz did not translate into the kind of resistance of the collectivization period: one is hard-pressed to find any sign of real resistance in the records, partly because of the constant oppression of the peasantry since 1929. In the end, what was called "mass-political work" led to unanimous endorsements of the unification in most collective farms.

The party's prime motive for collective-farm consolidation was to attain more efficient control over agriculture, to combat "harmful manifestations" of semiprivate farming and abandonment of collective farms.[94] Despite the Communists' increased presence on the farms, results did not improve after 1950. On the contrary, many of the enlarged kolkhozy and their chairs were in a state of confusion after the amalgamation. In theory, perhaps, the consolidation "was a highly effective measure"; in practice, it was not, at least not in the Kalinin oblast'. Initially, output decreased on many of the unified kolkhozy.[95] Many raion authorities, kolkhoz chairs, and kolkhozniks were baffled by the standardization of private plots, while others mismanaged the resettlement of the kolkhoz livestock of several former kolkhoz villages into one or two kolkhoz centres. Indiscriminate relocation led to a large congestion of cattle in sheltered places in these centres and to the cattle's death.

On the bright side, a few of the newly appointed kolkhoz chairs were agricultural specialists who had previously worked in raion centres or towns. Now they could finally apply their special expertise. But this benefit did not measure up to the costs. Soon it became obvious that, even though almost every farm had a party cell, the efficacy of Communist guidance remained low. Belov, chairman of the successful kolkhoz Krasnyi Putilovets of the Kashin raion, explained in September 1952 that it was impossible for the secretary of the party organization of an amalgamated kolkhoz to ensure adequate political education for all collective farmers.[96] In the first place his kolkhoz now consisted of 180 households distributed over seven villages. Second, on Belov's own kolkhoz political work was poorly organized, because the secretary was mainly occupied with agricultural work and had to care for her old mother and her two children as well. Belov urged the delegates of the ninth party conference to release party secretaries on collective farms from kolkhoz labour and to have them concentrate solely on political work. In other words, few collective farmers worked harder because they were persuaded by Communist doctrine.[97]

In July 1951, party secretary Baranov of the railroad-car works remarked on kolkhozniks' deliberate undermining of collectivized agriculture.[98] He claimed that while townspeople went in one direction in order to aid kolkhozniks with harvesting, kolkhozniks literally went the opposite way and carried baskets and bags full of goods to the kolkhoz market of Kalinin. At the same meeting of July 1951 the provincial prosecutor, Gerasimenko, opined that criminal inclinations lay at the basis of the poor resonance of Communist ideals among the peasants:

We have on many kolkhozy in a number of raions of the oblast' the most crude violations of the Statute of agricultural artels; particularly widespread are the following violations of the agricultural artel' Statute: the embezzlement of money in the kolkhozy, the removal and squandering of kolkhoz property, the seizure of kolkhoz lands, the wrong expenditure of trudodni, the violation of the democratic principle in the management of the kolkhozy, the large indebtedness of the kolkhozy, the criminal treatment of draught animals and of the labour force in the kolkhozy, and the failure to fulfill the minimum of trudodni by the kolkhozniks. For these violations in 1950, criminal proceedings against 1,694 kolkhozniks were instituted, and in the first half-year of this year against another 414, in all against 2,008 people.[99]

Apparently 160 chairpersons of the collective farms in those eighteen months had fallen under criminal investigation.[100]

When one takes into account that the peasantry nearly starved to death at various points during Soviet rule, one cannot but understand these "anti-Soviet" attitudes. The condemnation of the peasants' "criminal attitude" by the likes of Baranov or Gerasimenko provides us with the essence of perverse Communist morality: something is good only if it is for the good of the party.[101]

When ideological persuasion failed, as it almost always did, the authorities tried to improve work disposition by the threat of sanctions. How difficult it was to coerce kolkhozniks to work harder in socialist farming can be gathered from the description of a visit to a collective farm by a vice-chair of the oblispolkom who in 1951 toured the countryside of the province, together with a Central Committee representative and said afterwards to a party forum:

What especially appalled me was the fact that work began one and a half hours after the obligatory time, and, moreover, that it was not those milkmaids who appeared who had been officially assigned to the cows, but two old women who replaced their granddaughters; the latter had enjoyed themselves at a party the night before and slept in.

Furthermore, what startled us at this livestock farm was the fact that the cattle stood in a place where the filth was so bad that, one could say without exaggeration, when the cows lay down, only their horns and heads were visible, since all the rest was submerged in the dirt.[102]

GOD AND DEVIL

The prewar effort to stamp out religion had had some effect. Before 1941 the party's policy had been implacable toward the Orthodox Church to which the great majority of Russians in Tver' province still belonged in 1917. To fill the religious void, the regime offered, with varying results, the promise of Communist Utopia on earth instead of the ascension to Heaven in the afterlife, while it substituted Stalin for God and Tsar. After the war, oddly enough perhaps, the belief in Stalin, perhaps closer to the Devil incarnate than most human beings in history, was more resilient than the belief in an earthly paradise. Yet the Orthodox religion proved persistent as well. By juxtaposing the comments made by the interviewees in the survey of 1992 and the evidence from the Tver' archives, we can gain insight into the peculiar state of religion in this province during the last years of the dictator.

The destruction of churches, as the milker N.V. Kurganova and the tractor operator and kolkhoznitsa M.A. Sysoeva remarked in the survey, made it difficult to preserve one's beliefs. Without a priest's guidance and communal participation in religious rites in a church and without icons, it was necessary to rely on one's own devices and imagination based on memory or the authority of an older relative. The claim of K.R. Fedorova in the survey that many "lost" their religion partly because of the absence of any physical manifestation of the church rings true. M.S. Kul'menina described her renunciation of Orthodox religion as follows:

My parents were religious; in their life religion had a very significant meaning. Even when the churches were destroyed and faith was not encouraged (at work, socially) they still observed fasting and prayed and read religious books. I am only today returning to religion, for school and the Komsomol not only tore me away from God, but also because unpleasant things threatened [if one was religious within the school or Komsomol]. We received regularly in the Komsomol committee information from the raikom about people who baptized, who married in the church, and we had to penalize them to the extent of excluding them from the Komsomol.

N.N. Panova testified that she was baptized, but somehow lost her religion when she moved from the countryside to Kalinin. On the other hand, M.V. Bakhtina was so strongly influenced by her mother's strict piety that she never lost her faith.

Propaganda for atheism resumed in 1944, but barely reached the countryside; some raions ignored it altogether.[103] The renewed propaganda is a sign, however, that the wartime relaxation of the policy towards religion was already on the wane by January 1945, when victory was certain. Archival documents testify to a sharp decline of the authorities' tolerance for religion at the time when the ideological offensive of the Zhdanovshchina of late 1946 and 1947 was picking up steam. In only one year, 1947, ninety-four requests were made to inaugurate a church.[104] A mere four groups of petitioners were granted permission. Meanwhile, 1947 would be the last year that any places of religious worship were reopened in Kalinin province during Stalin's lifetime. In 1947, ninety-seven churches were still active in the province, but their number declined to seventy-two by 1951. Concomitantly, petitions for opening new churches dwindled from ninety-four in 1947 to eleven in the first half of 1951. Nevertheless, in 1947 hundreds of signatures could be found on many petitions for permission to start a church.

Continued allegiance to the Church among a substantial part of the population can be inferred form these facts. Most believers understood that further petitioning was useless – and perhaps dangerous – after 1947 and resigned themselves to some surrogate for church services. The party did not like even this recourse, but the believers were tenacious as the provincial records show. A few typical examples reflect the survival of religion against all odds. During the early 1950s, with the aid of a nurse who had been brought up in a convent, religious rites were illegally performed by Orthodox priests in the provincial hospital for tuberculosis patients.[105] Sects such as the Baptist-Evangelists, hardly present in Kalinin before the war, surfaced in the late 1940s. In 1951 complaints reached the provincial secretariat about a Baptist Church in Kalinin in which Young Pioneers attended services because their own organization did not offer sufficient activities.

In the 1950s the True Orthodox Church appeared in Kalinin province. At a certain point, around 1952, this religious organization was active in eight raions, had followers in forty-seven settlements, and operated eleven illegal churches. Dekushenko, head of the MGB, described the scene in 1952:

Even the leaders of this organization themselves said that large-scale anti-soviet work went on behind its religious cover. At secret meetings, the participants called on all kinds of resistance to the measures of Soviet power, such as declining to work in the kolkhozy or only working to keep up the private plot, not subscribing to state loans, not paying taxes, crossing out on the ballots for the candidates of the bloc of communists and partyless at the time of elections for the soviets, and spreading diverse slander against leaders of our party and the Soviet state.[106]

Presumably, the organization had been exposed before September 1952 and, at that time, had been at least temporarily suppressed.[107]

In the 1950s, the Kalinin party organization was particularly dismayed that observance of religious holidays in the countryside led to economic losses:

It has been established that, in the raions of the Kalinin oblast', a majority of the kolkhoz peasantry celebrates several religious holidays in the course of the year. The celebration of religious holidays is accompanied by large-scale absence of kolkhozniks from their labour in the course of two to three days. Because of the religious holidays, every kolkhoz by the most sober calculation loses three to three and a half thousand man-days on average. Many holidays take place at the height of the agricultural labour season; because of this they incur a huge material loss to agriculture, lower the pace of work, and lead to a significant loss of the harvest. The celebration of the holidays by the kolkhozniks cannot be considered a result of their religiosity, inasmuch as the influence of the church and the clergymen has markedly decreased lately.[108]

Indeed, the presumed watchdog of political vigilance in the country-side, the vice-director of the MTS for political affairs, indulged in the celebration of these holidays in 1952.[109] Part of the authorities' concern about religious holidays was provoked by the high incidence of crime accompanying the feasts. The widespread celebration of traditional holidays, meanwhile, cannot be seen automatically as a sign of great piety.[110]

The observance of these holidays was not a custom surviving exclusively among rural folk but remained popular even with industrial employees. In 1952 at a raion party conference a kolkhoz chairman in Zavidovo raion warned the directors of industrial enterprises of the district to stop attending celebrations of religious holidays on kolkhozes, for this disrupted farming even more.[111] In 1952 and 1953 young workers of the Vagzhanov factory of Kalinin visited their ancestral village to celebrate religious holidays under the pretense – and with the help of a telegram to make matters look genuine – of having to bury a relative or to take care of a sick family member.[112]

Some people took a very practical view of these matters. T.A. Novikova considered herself to be devout and baptized her first children, but when her husband became a party member, she declined to baptize her last two children because this was not allowed of party members. As a Komsomol and subsequently as a party member, Z.M. Vinogradova said in the survey that she was not permitted to believe in God. But she feared sometimes that God might exist and that he would punish her for her sins. Thus she did not attend church, but, during the war, she prayed furtively at home for the safety of her husband (who eventually died at the front) and for the health of her only child. L.V. Egorova, on the other hand, never believed in God for, in her opinion, if he had existed, he would not have allowed the injustice of the life she had led.

Instead of God in Heaven, the Communists offered God on Earth: the Lenin of Today, I.V. Stalin. The evidence for Kalinin province indicates that Stalin's cult reached its apogee around the time of the Nineteenth Party Congress of 1952. Some voters scribbled delirious devotions to the infallible leader on their ballots during local soviet elections in February 1953. The wish of one person for "our father" to live on for many years did not come true, however.[113] Another, one

Drozdov, unconcerned about secrecy, wrote a poem on his ballot and signed his name underneath:

On February 22, I vote for you, for the beloved maker, friend and father Stalin. For friend and father Stalin, the first fighter for peace, helmsman of communism, loved by all the world. Loved by all the world, no other happiness for us, [than] STALIN in our town's soviet, more happiness does not exist! More happiness does not exist, children sing about Stalin too, songs are sung everywhere on earth, Stalin hears all in the Kremlin. In the Kremlin Stalin hears all, he goes to all the lands, the people with Stalinist labour, build the house of communism. They build the house of communism, it is seen by all the world, for the beloved leader, our people will always go! On the Sunday in February, all come to the election, that will be on a radiant day, and for our dearest Stalin we will put in the ballot.[114]

Even though Stalin's personal prestige may have reached an all-time high in Kalinin oblast', many of its inhabitants still deplored their poor standard of living.[115] It did take courage and a certain independence of mind to write something critical on the ballot. Courage, because, for instance, one ballot in the Proletarskii raion that was deemed to contain anti-Soviet remarks, had been sent on to the MGB. In Novopromyshlennyi raion 366 voters had written something on their ballots. In 352 cases the writing was positive; only fourteen voters had dared to write a complaint or criticism. One voter complained about the presence of a mere three public baths in the whole of Kalinin, with its population of 250,000! Others demanded that the tax on childless women be abolished. Still another was bold enough to point out that thousands were living in "insufferable circumstances," which a different voter graphically illustrated by writing that she, a widow, lived with her seven-year-old son and five others in a room of fourteen square metres and had to sleep on the floor. Someone requested the construction of a water pump, while many more lambasted the absence of goods in shops. One town dweller addressed candidate Kiselev directly, asking him to pay attention to the poor condition of the province's kolkhozy. On one ticket, a voter had supported the abolition of serfdom on the collective farms!

Here and there people jotted down anti-Semitic remarks, but these few ballots do not conclusively prove that, instigated by the discovery of the "Doctors' Plot," a wave of anti-Semitism had taken hold of the province.[116] In the Zavolzhe raion, for example, four persons had entered an anti-Semitic remark on their sheets. The worst of these was the request to banish all Jews to Kolyma, where particular hardships were suffered at the time.

Many Russians recall their grief upon the news of Stalin's death in March 1953.[117] Most cried, while many feared the future without their beloved helmsman. Why did they mourn for the creator of such a murderous regime? D.A. Volkogonov provides us with a rather plausible four-pronged explanation of Stalin's popularity, referring to Stalin's skills as a politician, the successful portrayal of him as a faultless leader, the religious-political tradition of the Russian people (who had believed in a superhuman Tsar, the representative of God on earth), as well as the general level of ignorance among the Soviet people, who accepted the propaganda uncritically.[118] N.V. Kurganova recalled in the survey that under Stalin old people were respected. One presumes that she meants respected by their fellow citizens, for the much-beloved helmsman did not find it necessary to provide a pension for the elderly in the countryside, where Kurganova lived. The frustration with the confused situation today induces many to long for the days of certainty under Stalin. A.V. Zelentsev, a metal worker and sometimes welder of Vyshnii Volochek, compared the radiant past with the difficult present, decidedly preferring the past, for "after the war I had to be treated in hospital on several occasions ... all was free. And now even to receive a certificate [probably for a prescription] in the polyclinic, you have to pay money. They need to shoot them all!" Zelentsev was never a party member, but A. Portelli's remarks about the allegiance of Communist Party members to their leadership and to the popularity of Stalin among the CPSU membership and the Soviet population suggest another key:

The leadership plays ... a role similar to that of mediators in Claude Lévi-Strauss's structural interpretation of myths: two-faced creatures that hold together conflicting but equally necessary presuppositions. In this case, the contradiction – we, the makers of history, must be right, and yet history is wrong – is explained through the agency of individuals who are *with* us and stand *for* us (in the party, which they represent) but are not *of* us (not members of the working class in terms of status, power, education, language, life-style, and sometimes income: as Androsciani says, *we* rent, *they* own). The ambivalent, internal/external position of the leadership keeps it all in the family, and yet saves the family from guilt and blame. Allegiance to the party was not based (as outside critics often claimed) on a mythic faith in its infallibility, but rather on the ability to shift its failures to the sphere of myth.[119]

One dissenting voice in this respect was that of Ninel' Sergeevna Smirnova, who hoped that the death of Stalin would lead to fundamental change. Smirnova had seen both her parents arrested in 1937 in Leningrad and had been reared in an orphanage for children of "enemies of the people." Her lack of enthusiasm for Stalin is, to put it mildly, understandable. Similarly, A.N. Nikolaev began to hate Stalin after his father returned from the camps after completing a ten-year term. He hoped for a renewal of life in Russia when Stalin died.[120]

In the countryside the reaction to Stalin's death was different. Stalin seemed more remote to most kolkhozniks. Propaganda had made less of an impression on kolkhozniks than on town dwellers. In the villages the bombardment of Communist slogans was impaired by the absence of radios and newspapers, the lower level of literacy, the rareness of visits by agitprop activists, and the scarcity of rank-and-file zealots. In addition, Stalin's name was equated by many with the system that so ruthlessly exploited peasant labour. P.N. Bashilova scolded Stalin and held him responsible for the terrible life she was living, even though she maintained she had voluntarily joined the kolkhoz in 1929. A.E. Malysheva hoped that his death would bring the extraordinarily high taxes to an end. She remembered how she sang at the time, "Thank you Stalin, you made me a lady, and I am a horse, and a bull, a peasant woman and a muzhik, too."[121]

The memory of the brutal policies of the 1930s and the revulsion provoked by the atrocities experienced during the war made the Russians crave peace and tranquillity and fulfill to the best of their abilities the authorities' extreme demands after 1945.[122] The examples of severe criticism of the regime described above are so rare in the records that one can propose without hesitation that the narod generally refrained from publicly voicing any. The narod had no safe opportunity to do so; the paucity of the comments on the election ballots reveal this lack. The Russians might have hoped for less party and state interference in their lives, but they almost always restrained themselves from expressing this desire, even in a most tentative way. Every conversation partner could be an informer.

Apart from the armed resistance in the Baltics and western Ukraine, opposition to the renewed political and economic offensive of the postwar reconstruction of socialism hardly emerged in the Soviet Union. After May 1945 the authorities would again limit personal freedom as much as possible. For some individuals what remained was hope for a better future (socialist, communist, or something else), but the more sceptical ones did not expect any swift improvement in their fate. They adapted their lives as well as possible to the circumstances, trying to exploit scarcities resulting from the imperfect distribution system. Most people, after trying to fulfill their daily work norms, retreated to the relative privacy of their homes to enjoy the little they had, which at least included peace after 1945.

Some people had joined the Communist Party during the war, or would join after it, perhaps in the hope of grabbing as many privileges as possible from membership. A minority of genuine Communist zealots remained, while rather more truly believed in Stalin. Their number was reinforced by those swayed by wartime propaganda about the inevitable Soviet Russian victory over the Nazis, largely achieved because of the wise leadership with which the Russian people had been blessed. On the opposite side of the scale were those who had lost their faith in the system or who had never adhered to it in the first place, of whom a significant number was held in confinement. To those victims I will turn now.

CHAPTER FIVE

Victims: The Penal System

The Russians of Tver' province had been exposed to an unprecedented degree of brutality by the Communists during the 1930s. Exactly how many people perished in Tver' province in the 1930s and how many during World War II will have to remain a moot point, but there is sufficient evidence to suggest that 500,000 deaths altogether is a cautious estimate. In other words, out of every five persons, one died as a result of the violence between 1929 and 1945. Even though this was a bloodletting of chilling proportions, the CPSU did not relent in its efforts to establish unconditional obedience after May 1945. In the postwar Stalinist years in Tver' province arrests, executions, and camp sentences were not as frequent as before the war, but the penal system was always handling new customers in sufficiently high numbers to ensure conformity outside the prison fences.

POSTWAR POLITICAL CRIME

In Kalinin province the greatest share of Communist Party membership consisted of urban dwellers. But even in the towns enthusiasm for the regime was often less than desired. In September 1952 a head of a factory workshop in Kashin tried to analyze the tenacity of "capitalist survivals":

It is well known to many of the comrade delegates here present that the town of Kashin in the past was a town of merchants, a town of churches, of priests, of speculators, of whoever you want, and the remnants of capitalism in the minds of the people manifest themselves here more clearly. The struggle with these relics demands a tremendous show of strength from all party organizations of our raion. The struggle with the survivals of capitalism would be made significantly easier through the development of industry in the town of Kashin, but until now industry has very poorly developed in Kashin. The present enterprises in the town cannot absorb the quantity of work hands, while rather high numbers of this idle labour force are not involved in socially useful work, and often lead a parasitic way of life.[1]

The discovery of actual "enemies" of the Soviet state was rare after the war. Whenever someone was labelled as such, however, prosecution was hard to evade, and verdicts were seldom reversed. At the end of 1945, first secretary Boitsov received a report from the substitute prokuror (state prosecutor), Nazarov, about the revision of certain cases of "counterrevolutionary crime."[2] Eight of the accused had been convicted as traitors of the Motherland, four had been involved in aiding and abetting the enemy, and nine people were sentenced for counterrevolutionary agitation. None of the twenty-one people was judged to deserve a retrial. The few cases explicitly described in the report were all concerning individuals who had collaborated with the Germans.

The respondents to the 1992 survey conducted in Tver' province recalled few arrests during the postwar period. V.P. Pimenova knew of one drunken blacksmith who in 1950 shouted something anti-Communist in Udoml'ia.[3] The blacksmith disappeared and was never seen again. N.A. Kotov agreed with Pimenova that the postwar scale of arrest was only a faint echo of the deluge of the 1930s, particularly of the "de-kulakization" period. A.M. Afanas'ev remembered only one case of what was construed as subversive behaviour: a schoolteacher had been arrested for accidentally breaking the glass in front of a portrait of Stalin and received a sentence of approximately three years for her unintentional offence.

Evidence for Kalinin oblast' confirms Fainsod's impression of selective, as opposed to mass-scale, arrests after the war: such tactics kept the people in a sufficient state of fear of misbehaving and falling into the hands of the security organs.[4] "Political vigilance" became quite lax at times, leading to a terse admonition from the MGB head at the eighth provincial party conference in March 1951.[5] The provincial security chief warned his audience of flippant people in Kalinin and the rest of the province, whose talk could reach the ears of the American or British military attachés. The oblast' was, after all, accessible to foreigners.

Did the concern expressed by the MGB head help increase "vigilance"? It did not cause a recurrence of the spy mania that had been part of the Great Purge. For purely economic reasons, Kalinin province could not sustain another wave of massive arrests after the war: the observation of many survey respondents about the absence of large-scale arrests is reflected by most other evidence.

Some people had apparently been so traumatized by the events of 1937 and 1938 that they lost all perspective. In Kalinin in 1947, a school director accused unruly and often absent pupils of counterrevolution and told them that they deserved to be shot.[6] After all, in the director's opinion workers were shot when they were absent without permission from their jobs in the factories. To this he added that the security organs needed to take care of matters.

Within party ranks someone was sporadically discovered who had hidden his or her prohibitive kulak, bourgeois, or clerical ancestry or who was a relative of an enemy of the people.[7] Some army deserters were arrested, as well as a few outright Nazi collaborators. In 1950 political allegiance of employees at one of Kalinin's electro-stations was considered doubtful. Close to half had lived on German-occupied territory, while a few had actively collaborated.[8]

Occasionally, sanctions were taken against someone who had spoken out against certain sacred cows of the regime. The biology teacher Tret'iakov was thrown out of the party and lost his job at the Pedagogical Institute of Kalinin in 1952 for accusing the renowned Russian-Soviet psychologist I.P. Pavlov of having been unprincipled – and a Bukharinite to boot.[9] Tret'iakov deemed Pavlov's theories of minor importance. He was also denounced for having completely ignored in his course on zoology the significance of Michurinite biology. On another occasion two teenagers damaged with some kind of slingshot – apparently deliberately – a portrait of Stalin hanging in the building of their industrial school.[10] Sanctions were undoubtedly taken against them.

The obkom fretted about former convicts' activities.[11] In 1950, to its horror, the provincial party's leadership found out that the engineer Kruzhkov, a consultant for a study group on foreign policy, had been earlier convicted of political crimes. Another former convict was an outright enemy of the Soviet state: even though twice sentenced to labour camps, in 1931 and in 1933, and receiving a further additional term in 1935, V.E. Komissarov had worked from 1942 through 1946 as the chair of the rural soviet of Tolmachi. Komissarov, surprisingly, managed afterwards to be appointed to the position of soviet chair (that is, head of the local administration for several villages). Despite, or more precisely owing to, the eight years he served in the camp system, he advised kolkhozniks repeatedly to leave the collective farms, while undermining labour discipline on the kolkhozes with his negative opinions about the Soviet state and collective farming.

A political case forged against the management of the most important provincial factory, the railroad-car works, creates the impression that still in 1949 political vigilance was at a dangerously low ebb in the estimation of the authorities. By then, the Zhdanovshchina and succeeding ideological offensives had already led to an atmosphere resembling the Great Purge in other places in the Soviet Union.[12]

An investigation was conducted within the Communist Party organization of the railroad-car works, in which party inspectors attempted to establish why the gorkom of Kalinin was forced to exclude from the party such an exceptionally high proportion of the factory's workers and employees.[13] The investigation blamed the situation on the cavalier attitude of the factory's party committee toward selecting and controlling party membership at the plant. The committee had failed to scrutinize factory employees recommended for promotion. Managers and party organizers hired in senior positions quite a few former political convicts who had almost all been previously sentenced for political crimes as defined in the infamous Article 58 of the Criminal Code of the RSFSR.

The roots of the affair are shady to some degree: one can exclude, as usual in these trumped-up cases, the existence of any real conspiracy of former convicts.[14] In general, the fanfare that, behind the closed doors of the seventh provincial party conference, surrounded the investigation probably served the purpose of inculcating among party chiefs a sense that renewed vigilance was the order of the day. More specifically, the victims of the railroad-car case had possibly been connected (or accused of having been connected) with some of the main accused in the Leningrad Affair, which was discovered at the same time. The invention of the case may have been intended to undermine the embattled Vorontsov even further (on Vorontsov, see Chapter 3). Obviously, the railroad-car employees could have fallen victim to the fertile imagination of MGB investigators, who were trying to prove to their superiors that their vigilance had far from dulled. The Leningrad Affair may have signified to local MGB departments all over the Union that it was opportune to prove their raison d'être.

The party investigation unearthed sufficient suspicious leads to hand over the case to the MGB, who found an extraordinarily high number of workers and employees, 406 in all, possessing criminal records, while another 6 had been convicted of political crimes.[15] A further 220 had been repatriated to the USSR after the war, and 15 of them occupied leading posts. One Redel'man had been promoted to head the factory's labour and wages department, even though his past conviction should have disqualified him for this position. Upon his release from the camps in 1946, Redel'man had approached factory director M.I. Rumiantsev.[16] Even though Redel'man told Rumiantsev about his camp sentence, the director did not see any problems in hiring a former political convict. On the contrary, Redel'man and Rumiantsev became good friends. Thus Redel'man was allowed to use some of the factory's trucks to transport construction materials to his dacha near Moscow, and he frequently visited Rumiantsev at home. The director invited Redel'man and other factory employees to celebrate Soviet holidays in his apartment, where people consumed unlimited amounts of alcohol that had actually been designated for technical use in the factory. Redel'man, with the help of Rumiantsev and party committee secretary Ionov, also received the necessary papers to reside in Kalinin, even though possession of such papers should have been prohibited to Redel'man. To the amazement of the MGB employees who wrote the report resulting from their investigations, Ionov and Rumiantsev even attempted to have Redel'man's conviction overturned.

During its investigation the MGB found several other politically compromised individuals employed in prominent positions at the factory. Their sins ran from living on German territory to serving time in Soviet camps, having been born as kulak children, drinking excessively, and having languished in German captivity.[17]

Rumiantsev was also accused by the MGB of embezzlement and fraud. He had used factory money for private purposes, such as to buy furniture for his own office. Motorcycles, bought on behalf of the factory, had been distributed among prominent employees. Rumiantsev himself had appropriated the launch purchased for the plant's benefit and had kept an airplane at the factory for years, which, while expensive to maintain, was not used. These abuses were convenient to bring up, but in reality rather trivial. They would never been held against him if he had not lost the party's trust because of his liberal hiring policy.

The railroad-car factory case was convenient to trump up, as it involved a few Jews, former convicts, and descendants of (or even actual members of) "former" classes among the suspicious elements. How many were convicted out of the twelve people investigated is unclear, even though the crimes of some may even have been too trivial for the rigorous Soviet standards of the time. When one reads, however, that, afterwards, the former convicts among the accused were still labelled as enemies who had "elbowed their way up at the factory to head some of the factory's departments," one fears that few escaped unharmed.[18]

For their political and economic shortcomings, the factory's director Rumiantsev, the secretary of the party's factory committee, Ionov, and the chairman of the factory committee, Osipov, were ordered, by a decision of the obkom, to leave their jobs.[19] The three were not considered part of the core of the conspiracy but were held responsible for offering the "enemies" the opportunity to organize the plot.

The MVD and MGB actively tried to force people to denounce colleagues at work after the war. Fear of their own arrest and of that of their relatives was common among the Russians of Tver'. Especially those who had spent some time outside their native surroundings and those not born in Tver' province admitted to knowledge of the existence of the camp system when they were interviewed in 1992. M.V. Kurganova reported in the survey that she was confronted with the Kolyma camp system when her husband served in Magadan with the MVD troops between 1951 and 1954. At the time she gave little thought to the life of the countless convicts around her, even though she had some female convicts working for her as housekeepers. The faithful party man N.S. Kokorin, who even today has not lost his faith in socialism, nevertheless said in the survey that he was appalled when he was confronted with the camps' existence during his wartime military service in the Far East. He recalled how he "encountered by accident a large cemetery in a forest where they had buried 'campers'; on several of the graves there was not even an inscription or cross. It seemed then ominous to remember the words of Kaganovich on the radio, that we had mobilized three people per square metre for the construction of the Baikal-Amur railroad."[20] In this way it became clear to Kokorin that the NKVD and NKGB were organs not for the defence of the people but for their oppression.

CRIME AND PUNISHMENT

Already in August 1944, the obkomburo felt it imperative to order the militsiia to organize a campaign against the growing incidence of crime, particularly in the towns.[21] Conscripts and juveniles were the main culprits. Daily, the militsiia intensively patrolled afflicted urban areas, and in Kalinin the town market was under close surveillance. Frequent checks of identification papers took place in the provincial capital. Because of the militsiia's offensive, the crime rate dropped in the oblast' from 2,757 registered cases in the third quarter of 1944 to 1,876 cases in the first quarter of 1945.

Criminality was not eliminated, however, which moved the NKVD to organize a special ten-day operation against banditry, the third within a year, in June 1945.[22] Soldiers and citizens were checked in settlements and towns within a radius of five to six kilometres from railroads and paved roads. Certain more remote settlements and forests in which bandits, deserters, and other "criminal elements" were rumoured to lurk were combed. The operation led to the apprehension of 2,458 people: bandits, deserters from the army and defense industries, draft dodgers, "criminal elements," escapees from POW camps, "special" camps, and prisons (including prisoners' transports), speculators, and homeless and neglected children. In all 368 firearms, 357 grenades, and 37 knives and daggers were confiscated. After the war, the NKVD hunted down deserters and those who evaded army service. In the last three months of 1945, thirty-seven operations took place to trace deserters in the oblast'.[23] Forty-four were found, while another 87 remained on the loose. Many of these were roaming armed around the province and committed burglaries and robberies to survive.

Although during these three special operations seven thousand suspected criminals in total had been taken into custody, Soviet law continued to be violated: in the months of September, October, and November of 1945, "economic" crime was singled out.[24] Sixty-four local people were arrested in the town of Kalinin for "speculation": selling rye that 4 people had illegally procured from a kolkhoz chairman in Molokovo raion was one example of this type of offence. The rye was sold for "speculative" prices on the bazar (public market) of Kalinin. Another 79 were arrested who were not provincial residents. Some of the latter had bought spare parts, tools, and electrical appliances in Moscow, Leningrad, Kiev, or Kharkov and had tried to sell them on the Kalinin market. Several of the "speculators" had been offering soap for inflated prices. The militsiia had to admit that arrests did not result in a cessation of speculation. The opportunity for this type of crime was extremely favourable until at least the summer of 1947, when the worst shortages connected with the war and postwar drought gradually began to disappear.

In November 1945 the local NKVD had to report to Boitsov that, in spite of all the efforts since August 1944, the crime rate in the first nine months of 1945 remained disturbingly high.[25] The incidence of khuliganstvo (hooliganism, vandalism, assault, drunkenness, involvement in brawls) and theft had actually grown in comparison with the first nine months of 1944. According to the report, even war invalids engaged in crime when unable to find work. Security chief Pavlov listed the activities of the NKVD in organizing crime-prevention measures such as increased patrols, regular checks of documents and passports, and stronger discipline within the militsiia. The judicial practices of the 1920s and 1930s had not been forgotten by the NKVD chief, for Pavlov advised Boitsov to oblige the provincial courts and procuracy to speed up their examination of cases, to end their "liberal" attitude towards criminals, and to systematically conduct show trials (pokazatel'nye protsessy) at enterprises and army units. Newspapers and radio broadcasts were to report on the criminals' sentences handed out by courts and tribunals. More security guards for storage depots, warehouses, and other public buildings were suggested as well, and janitors were to be ordered to lock the doors of apartment buildings at night.

One could argue that the high crime levels of 1944 and 1945 were connected with wartime disorganization; indeed, the crime rate abated in 1946 compared to 1945, but still in the first three months of 1946 1,358 crimes were registered by the MVD. In the first quarter of 1948, 1,096 cases of all manner of crime combined were listed by the MVD in a report to the obkom; in the second quarter there were 1,036 cases, and in the third quarter, 943.[26] In 1948 the authorities decided to bolster the size of the militsiia by creating auxiliary police in the countryside. The size of the auxiliary militsionery brigades indicates that the authorities believed crime to be rampant: 11,000 members of this auxiliary force, organized in brigades, were to combat samogon (moonshine vodka) distillation and hooliganism and to protect the harvest in the fields as well as gathered crops.[27] This veritable army looks impressive on paper, but its effectiveness must have been extremely limited, as no trace of it can be found in records after June 1948. The recruits were probably villagers who were not particularly keen on having their peers prosecuted by the state for such offences. Conceivably, this auxiliary militsiia quietly disbanded soon after its inception.

Before late 1947, when rationing was abolished, many instances of fraud were uncovered with the ration-card system. Ration cards were supposed to be destroyed immediately after receipt, but in 1944 some shop employees had recirculated them.[28] In October 1946, 52 people were under investigation for this type of offence. In November of the same year in the larger provincial towns, an all-out examination of the passports and house-books of the urban population was conducted to combat ration-coupon fraud.

Drunken brawls remained a fact of life. In 1948 the head of the provincial militsiia expressed his disapproval of the celebration of religious holidays and the ensuing fights in the countryside, which were mostly provoked by the copious consumption of alcohol at holidays, weddings, or birthday celebrations. The state monopoly on vodka distillation was an old Russian tradition; the peasants' custom (now on the collective farms) of distilling their own hard liquor – at a profit – was less ancient but very tenacious. The custom survived into the 1940s, at least. In June 1948 the head of the provincial militsiia, Krylov, fulminated that much grain was being squandered, in his opinion, by the illegal distillation of alcohol among kolkhozniks.[29] (Some kolkhoz chairs personally supervised these practices.) Incomplete figures for the months of March, April, and May 1948 show that the militsiia had instituted criminal proceedings against 267 illegal distillers.

One of the many tasks of the MVD was to maintain order during spring sowing and harvesting. In the spring of 1946 MVD raion departments reported to the obkom on the institution of criminal proceedings against fifty-four individuals for theft of grain or kerosene and "irresponsible agricultural labour management," which usually referred to the drunkenness of a particular kolkhoz chair or brigadier.[30] At the same time MVD employees were engaged in "prophylactic" work. The focus in the spring of 1946 was on the condition of storage buildings on collective farms and machine tractor stations.[31] After a thorough inspection the MVD concluded that the guards of these buildings were generally too old for their task. MVD vigilance caused sixty-five of them to be dismissed by raion party and soviet organs. Twelve more kolkhoz guards were under criminal investigation. The labour of the MVD required for this checkup was nothing short of prolific: 4,576 kolkhozes were visited and 75 tractor stations!

All this activity may create the impression of a staggering amount of control, but in reality the population often evaded the heavy-handed legal organs of socialism. Many laws provided stiff penalties for violating discipline in the workplace or theft of state property, but their application was not indiscriminately rigid. The law of 4 June 1947 against the theft of state and public property did not lead to a marked increase in prosecutions.[32] Around 1950, the obkom expressed its displeasure with the high level of criminal proceedings against violators of labour discipline and the overly harsh treatment of those convicted of avoiding helping with harvesting.[33] The obkom's complaints may have reduced the number put on trial. One may infer, again, that economic motives forced the obkom to water down the disciplinary sanctions: further thinning of the labour force would imperil the productive potential of the factories. The legacy of the bloodletting of the 1930s and the war lingered on.

The labour shortage may have been the ground for a modification of the "absentee laws" in July 1951, when special "comrades' courts" (tovarishcheskie sudy) were fashioned.[34] The officials presiding over these courts were elected by and from among workers and employees of institutions and enterprises. Court members were supposed to judge their peers' infringements. Trials were intended to have an educational value, something of which Soviet legal practice was rather fond. Whether this meant in fact a waning in severity in dealing with absenteeism is uncertain. By early 1952, at certain factories comrades' courts were said not to gather at all. Because of this, labour discipline seemed to falter.

Despite this kind of imperfect (or hesitant) enforcement of the law, numbers show that the authorities had their hands full. More than 1 percent of the citizens of the province were sentenced by a court during 1949, and the figures for 1950 do not indicate a real drop in those convicted.[35]

The provincial MGB chief declared at a party gathering that 80 percent of those prosecuted for crimes were young people, of whom 94 percent were first-time offenders.[36] In 1953 provincial prosecutor Gerasimenko tried to analyze crime among provincial youth.[37] He argued that violence occurred mostly under the influence of alcohol, particularly enjoyed on religious holidays, while theft and burglaries were mainly committed by those who did not have a regular job. One of the most graphic incidents he reported was a case of a gang rape of an underaged teenager committed by six secondary school pupils in a rural area. To underline the seriousness of the problem, Gerasimenko related how, over the course of eleven months in 1952 in the town of Bezhetsk, 276 neglected (beznadzornye) children had been detained, some of whom were the children of party and soviet workers. Often homeless (besprizornye) or neglected children were perpetrators of crimes. In 1951 and the first three months of 1952 more than 2,100 of them were detained by the provincial MVD and ended up in orphanages.[38]

Stalin's rule had not been able to eradicate crime. The point cannot be illustrated more eloquently than by the frequency of crimes perpetrated by Communist Party members. In the records a number of crimes committed by Communists came to light when their exclusion from the party was confirmed by Boitsov in October 1946.[39] They were forced to hand back their party cards when sentenced by the courts for criminal activities. Among the delinquents were a rural baker of Krasnyi Kholm raion who was sentenced to two years of imprisonment for the theft of ten loaves of bread and a kolkhoznik who was convicted of manslaughter in a brawl and was sentenced to eight years. If one was caught committing an illegal act when employed by the railroads, the sentence could be very severe, for the railroads were part of the domain of the MVD/MGB. Thus in May 1946 the Communist Lavrov was sentenced to three years of imprisonment for stealing 2.5 litres of wine and being intoxicated at work. Apart from providing evidence of the surprisingly high number of Communists violating the law, these cases also indicate how jail or camp terms were meted out in unusual proportions around this time when compared to what is customary in the Western world today.[40]

Regularly, party members were excluded for criminal activities such as theft, fraud, squandering of goods, khuliganstvo, repeated loss of their membership cards, and simply not being involved in the party organization.[41] For the last two offenses no criminal prosecution usually followed; for the other offences hardly anyone escaped being brought to trial. It must have been unsettling for the raion party leaders – and for Boitsov or Kiselev – to find out that so many of their Communists were not the role models they were intended to be. Party membership may have inspired a sense of invulnerability in some of them, inciting them to abuse their privileged status. Whatever the causes, illegal activities of party members provide further evidence of the high incidence of what was labelled crime by the regime.

Regular party members, employees of the state procuracy, the MVD, and the militsiia – which was part of the MVD – were involved in corruption as well. In Moscow, Malenkov received an anonymous letter in 1946 from "a group of toilers of the town of Kalinin" and sent it on to Boitsov, ordering him to investigate and take appropriate measures if necessary.[42] In the letter even the assistant state prosecutor of the oblast', Grigor'ev, was accused of accepting bribes from speculators and criminals.

Cases of corruption, abuse of power, theft, and drunkenness among MVD functionaries were legion in a report to the obkom secretariat on the state of affairs within the MVD in 1946.[43] Thirty MVD employees were excluded from the Communist Party between January 1946 and February 1947: eleven for hooliganism and morally reprehensible behaviour, thirteen for drunkenness and the violation of labour discipline, and five for abuses of power, taking bribes, and misappropriation of funds.

In 1949 and 1950 Motorin, an investigator of the procuracy of Udoml'ia raion, was reported to the obkom by a raikom secretary. Motorin's behaviour perhaps best demonstrates how abuse of power remained a constant:

I deem it necessary to bring to your attention the unparty-like behaviour and the deeds of a criminal character of the investigator of the procuracy of the Udoml'ia raion c. [comrade] MOTORIN F.S.

At a priestly holiday (Christmas) in the village of Glinovka this person was a guest at the place of citizen Arkhipov. First, he began to drink, praising the good quality of the samogon; continuing to drink, he began to break the tableware and to bother the wife of Arkhipov, because of which Arkhipov gave him several slaps on the face and, with a black eye, he was thrown out.

Having become intoxicated, MOTORIN galloped on a horse through a closed bar and broke it, but using his position, he proposed to c. Kalugin, a railroad foreman, to annul the report that had been drawn up and to let the case, so to say, die down.

When MOTORIN was in Kotlovan, on an assignment, he made the acquaintance of the citizen SKVORTSOVA (who was an acquaintance of the former prosecutor Baranov), began to visit her often, engaged in drinking bouts, slept with her; then he lost his horse when he was drunk and started a ruckus, for which he was thrown out of the house.

In the rural soviet of Mushino, MOTORIN engaged in quality control of samogon, welcomed the good samogon, polished off the bad one; he became drunk and went up to the apartment of a female teacher, where he created a scandal.

In the village Kurovo of the rural soviet of Bykovskii he drank for two consecutive days at a religious holiday (Egor's day), visited the homes and extorted fare, went drunk to Ivanova Valentina, slept there and bothered the mother, while Ivanova worked as a bookkeeper of the lumber office of the lumber enterprise Oblmesttop; she embezzled 5,000 rubles ... and MOTORIN did not institute proceedings against her.[44]

The state procuracy had more than two hundred employees within the province in 1947; its main office was in Kalinin, where thirty-seven people worked in the procuracy apparat. In the towns and raions, fifty-four raion and town prokurory were found, most of whom were assisted by one of the forty-six assistant prosecutors and by the seventy-two people's investigators (narsledovately).[45] Most criminal cases in court were handled in the province by the so-called people's courts, headed by a people's judge (narsud), assisted by people's assessors (narodnye zasedateli). These were "elected" at regular intervals. Electoral choice was typically limited: the group of eighty-two judges elected in December 1951 had all enjoyed a certain measure of legal education and were without exception Communists or Komsomols.[46] There were more than 6,000 assessors, 44.5 percent of whom were Communists. The elections of these functionaries were accompanied by a holiday, similar to those for soviet elections.

In January 1951 Shiklomanov, the secretary of the Novokarel' raion, noted that the judiciary worked so ploddingly that investigations were neglected.[47] As a consequence, all purloiners of kolkhoz property remained unharmed. In 1950, on every single kolkhoz of his fief embezzlement and theft of socialist property took place, but no one had been held responsible by the judiciary. One is tempted to deduce that the judiciary often was rather more discriminating and cautious in its interpretation of the law than the party, MVD, or MGB were willing to tolerate.

V.E. Tsvetkov was a member of the Kalinin provincial court from 1947 to 1949, then deputy chairman of this court from 1949 to 1951, and, from 1951 to 1956, head of the oblispolkom directorate of the

RSFSR ministry of justice. In his interview in 1992 he described the relationship between security organs and procuracy:

I knew the penal system and its politics first hand. I participated in open and closed meetings in the NKVD and MVD. I was acquainted with the directives of those organs. The direct practice of judge and prosecutor gave food for thought.

The Stalinist period of punitive policy of our state could not but call forth internal protests against its unjustified cruelty, its fight with the so-called enemies of the people.

A rather large faith in the force of coercion ruled at the time. Two decrees of 1947 – "The strengthening of the protection of the personal property of the citizens", and the decree of 4 June 1947 "On the strengthening of the criminal responsibility for the theft of state and public property" – established the most severe penalty: up to twenty-five years of camp.[48]

Tsvetkov added that the provincial courts handled about twenty to thirty "political" cases a year after the war. He remembered how the court gathered once in Bezhetsk to judge the case of an eighteen-year-old invalid who had defamed Stalin at a beer stall. The court returned the case for further investigation, not convinced that the suspect was an actual counterrevolutionary. But the provincial MVD chief, Grebchenko, resolved to have the matter dealt with by the Special Board (OSO: osobye soveshchanie) under the MVD: which gave the teenager five years in the camps.[49]

Tsvetkov's testimony leads one to conclude that the incidence of political crime was comparatively low, but the exact number of those prosecuted for political offences is impossible to establish, since a wide array of courts could potentially deal with this type of crime. Likewise, many cases of nonpolitical crime, one could propose, resulted from the poorly designed or executed policies imposed by the regime. For cases of what was strictly defined as political crime, apart from the special boards, the notorious military tribunal of the MVD troops continued to function after the war. This court dealt with high treason but also with more pedestrian cases such as theft of socialist property. In addition, it was involved in inspections of labour discipline at enterprises of the defence industry, where its activities around 1945 and 1946 succeeded in reducing the desertion of workers from the factories.[50]

A myriad of legal organs stretched out their tentacles in Kalinin province after the war: (auxiliary) militsiia, MVD, MGB, the procuracy, the regular courts, and the comrades' courts. It is impossible to assess precisely their efficacy in preventing and solving crime. Undoubtedly, as Judge Tsvetkov's testimony underlines, these organs meddled in each others' territory. Numbers unearthed indicate great activity among the officials of the judiciary after the war. The more than 26,000 convictions in 1949 and in the first months of 1950 by the people's courts testify both to a high level of popular defiance of the authorities and a merciless practice of the law. OSO and military tribunals sentenced people as well during those fifteen months.[51] At least 1 percent of the provincial population was convicted annually by the courts after 1945. If we forget about repeat offenders for a moment, this translates into 125,000 people convicted by the courts until 1953, an astoundingly high number, even if not all of them received jail or camp terms.

THE ISLES OF KALININ
IN THE GULAG ARCHIPELAGO

In 1943, after an abortive attempt to split the People's Commissariat in two in 1941, the NKVD was divided into the NKGB and the NKVD. The former dedicated itself to activities that in the West are usually associated with the operation of a security organ.[52] OSO and the military tribunals fell from that point onwards under the authority of the NKGB/MGB, while the MVD supervised the operation of the camp system.

When, around 1955, just after Stalin's death, the first Western attempts were made to establish the extent of the Stalinist forced labour camp system in the USSR, only two or three camps were thought to have operated in Kalinin province: one in Kashin (no. 240) and another near Ostashkov around Lake Seliger (no. 41), both engaging in wood procurements. Furthermore, information existed about a top-secret camp: "[on] one of the islands of Lake Seliger is located a camp for specialists, directly under the wing of Moscow; here earlier an experimental station for missiles was located."[53] The camps at Lake Seliger were those in which Polish officers had been interned in 1939 and 1940.

Earlier Western estimates for the number of labour camps on provincial territory, however, have been far too conservative: many more islands of Solzhenitsyn's proverbial GULag Archipelago were located in Kalinin province[54]. At the end of the Soviet era, a permanent exhibition on the Stalinist terror of 1929–53 opened in the Tver' museum of local history.[55] Documentary evidence is not always wholly conclusive for the existence of every penal institution presented there, but there is sufficient proof of the existence of a great number of them after 1945. Prisons were found in the towns and raion capitals, and there were corrective labour colonies in twenty-two locations at one point or another in Stalin's time. More than ten operated between 1945 and 1948. There were, as well, two detention centres for juvenile delinquents and five orphanages primarily intended for children of enemies of the people.[56]

In early 1947 the provincial MVD had under its auspices fifteen corrective labour camps and camp sectors for prisoners of war and interned people; camp personnel numbered *at least* 1,299: this is the sum of officers, administrators, technicians, and guards studying the canon of Marxism-Leninism at the time.[57] A cautious estimate would propose a population of about 20,000 inmates in the corrective labour colonies of Kalinin oblast' in 1946.[58] On 1 March 1948 eleven corrective labour colonies, four separate camp points, one children's labour colony, and one transfer prison existed. The combined population of these amounted to 10,037: 7,083 men and 2,954 women. Almost half (4,750) served less than three years, one-fifth (2,046) three to five years, about one-third (3,071) five to ten years, and only 99 inmates served sentences of more than ten years. Allegedly, corrective labour colonies were populated by convicts with sentences of no more than two years, but the records for 1947 undermine this presumption.[59] At least some of these camps contained convicts serving longer terms. One of them was Lev Kopelev, who served time in a camp located close to the Volga near Kimry. Many of the inmates described by Kopelev were criminal rather than political convicts. This emphasizes another problem of interpretation of the above list of camps: were all colonies intended for political convicts? Which camps were strictly for criminals? How should one categorize those inmates convicted of offences that at any other time and place would be considered either too trivial to prosecute or of a political nature? These questions are important, inasmuch as many sentenced criminals in Russia serve their time in work camps even today.[60]

From 1944 onwards the provincial leadership heartily welcomed the addition to the camp population of German and Eastern European prisoners of war, who provided some relief from the enormous labour shortage within the province.[61] Inmates were used for a variety of projects during the postwar revival. Just after the war around 18,000 POWs engaged in mostly unskilled labour, such as peat digging, farming, logging, factory work, or construction.[62] Conditions were harsh, for at least 20 percent of them were treated in special convalescence units in February 1946.

Many of the interned foreigners and prisoners of war returned home towards the end of the 1940s. At least some of them, however, were to stay for much longer, because they had been found guilty of crimes committed in the POW camps and sentenced to camp or jail terms. In

1947, ninety-two POWs were convicted, and almost half of them received sentences of more than ten years in camps or jails.[63]

Data on penal institutions for Soviet citizens are scarcer within party records than data on POW camps, but sometimes the Soviet citizens' fate appears in documents alongside that of POWs. The demographic reports from the head of the militsiia to the first obkom secretary for the period do not furnish the death rate among prisoners, except one report of June 1945, which noticed that at least 10 convicts had perished in Vyshnii Volochek.[64] Considering that these camps usually had between 1,000 and 2,000 inmates, this report indicates that conditions in the camps were harsh even in summer. Starvation was not uncommon outside the camps until the summer of 1947, but inside the situation was worse. In March 1946 Fedosenko (head of the provincial corrective labour camps of the NKVD) reported to Boitsov that the food supply of both camp guards and convicts had been deficient since the beginning of the year.[65] The absence of fish and vegetable oil in the older colonies and the additional shortage of vegetables in the recently created camps had led to a serious deterioration of the health of the zakliuchennye.

Fedosenko warned that "[w]ith the onset of spring it is not impossible that a wave of epidemic diseases and an increase in the mortality of the convicts will occur. Apart from the absence of ... products, at this time, with the poor condition of the roads, there are no possibilities for their delivery to the children's colony of Ostashkov, to the Kesova Gora colony, to the glass factory of Borisovo, and to a number of other colonies."[66]

Fedosenko petitioned Boitsov to help avoid these impending disasters, but it is unlikely that the first secretary was capable of bringing much relief, at least in the short term.

Life in the camps in early 1948 was as dreadful as it had been two years previously:

the circumstances of confinement of the convicts have a strong impact on production work. In a number of colonies convicts are badly provided with clothing [and] ... footwear, which in general consists of patched-up summer shoes; as a result, instances of frostbitten feet occur ... [Often] convicts do not have a change of underwear and after a bath dress again in their dirty underwear, because of which a number of convicts have lice ... colony No. 5 of the town of Vyshnii Volochek has a maternity home, in which women who have newborn infants are held in confinement; serious shortcomings occur here, which lead to a large mortality among the babies.

In the course of 1947, of the 360 children in [one] colony, 105 died [from various diseases].[67]

From 1946 onwards, convicts were gradually transferred to camps outside the province on the order of the MVD leadership of the USSR. In August 1948, 5,000 people remained in the colonies, of whom at least 1,000 were employed by the local MVD for their own particular purposes of consumer-goods production and agricultural labour. This decrease was lamented by Vorontsov in a letter of August 1948 to Central Committee secretary A.A. Kuznetsov, for it had delayed completion of several construction projects within the province.[68]

The evidence is mostly sketchy for the existence of the camps in the archives that were accessible. We may conclude that many documents have been removed on the orders of the security organs, but sufficient proof could still be found that the GULag operated uninterruptedly in Kalinin province until Stalin's death. Still by June 1951, convicts confined in local corrective labour colonies continued to help rebuild the economy of Kalinin province. Soviet convicts were deployed both in Vyshnii Volochek at the Proletarskii Avangard textile factory and in Kalinin at Proletarka.[69] To the dismay of Konovalov, the directorate of the MVD GULag of the USSR had once again commanded the local MVD to transfer convicts to areas outside the province. Both MVD minister S.N. Kruglov and A.N. Kosygin, Soviet Minister of Light Industry at the time, were asked by Konovalov to leave at least 1,300 convicts working at the textile factories.

In April 1952 security in camp sector no. 1 was reported to be deficient at the construction site of a wood-working factory. The fences, watchtowers, and warning zone of the camp itself were in a neglected condition, while convicts readily mixed at work with the free labourers at the project.[70] Indeed, management of the camp system was often as poor as in other branches of party and state. The usual vices of drunkenness, weak labour discipline, and slipshod camp utilities reduced the efficiency of convict labour. Sometimes this led to massive escapes, as apparently happened in 1946 at colony no. 12.[71]

We have seen how the NKVD/MVD supervised the provincial orphanages as well. In January 1945 the NKVD directly administered six "child reception and distribution" centres and one colony for juvenile delinquents.[72] In that month 330 children were detained in those seven institutions. But this number is deceptively low, for 6,302 children had spent some time in one of them in 1944 alone. Since the beginning of the war, more than 13,000 neglected and homeless children had been processed through these institutions. Many parents of these orphans had perished during the war, but some "orphans" were in fact children of parents serving camp sentences. Directly after the war orphanages were frequently left to languish. Around 1 September 1945 the situation in some of these institutions was brought to the obkomburo's attention, which voiced its displeasure.[73] The fuel stock for the coming winter was not being amassed, food was inadequate, supervision poor, and medical care lacking. In the Il'in orphanage of Kimry, cases of typhoid had occurred, while first-aid items such as bandages and iodine were unavailable. The children were neither taught elementary knowledge about hygiene nor about prevention of illness. Children of orphanage no. 2 of Ostashkov were roaming in the neighbouring countryside, stealing potatoes and vegetables from kolkhoz lands. Other Ostashkov orphans manufactured baskets to sell to local consumers. To correct all this, the obkomburo proposed heightened involvement of the Komsomol, which was obliged to exert stronger control over the orphans, partially by reinvigorating the orphanages' moribund Pioneers organizations.

In 1946 Boitsov confirmed the exclusion from the party, proposed by the raikom of Ostashkov, of the director of orphanage no. 2, who had in fact disappeared by the time he was excluded, following his dismissal or voluntary departure in 1945. The motive for the director's disgrace is obvious from the documents on his case in the party archive, which tell us that "Buchnev used to be drunk and started fights in front of the children at the time of his work as head of orphanage no. 2; he squandered and appropriated products intended for the nourishment of the children. As a consequence of his neglect of the condition of the obshchezhitie, the children fell ill and fled the orphanage."[74]

In April 1952 the USSR Council of Ministers felt obliged to issue a decree to attempt to bring the proliferation of homeless children in the RSFSR to a halt. Commissions were to be set up under the authority of town and raion soviets to accommodate orphans. By early 1953 few committees actually functioned in Kalinin province; some raions had not even bothered to create them in the first place.[75] Instead, the militsiia, without much zeal, was trying to supervise these children. In the orphanage of Kamen' hooliganism was a frequent occurrence, schoolwork neglected, attempts to escape common.

In the early 1990s, hardly anyone interviewed in the Tver' survey recalled the existence of labour camps within their own province. Only a few, most of whom had travelled outside Kalinin oblast' at the time or had seen a relative arrested, admitted to knowing more about the camps.[76] N.D. Eliseev did not know of the camp system as such, but at the railroad depot where he worked, he and his colleagues sent on letters that were thrown out of trains transporting prisoners. A.N. Nikolaev saw his father return from ten years in a camp. Several respondents from Konakovo raion remembered the convicts working at the construction of the Moskva-Volga canal in the 1930s. M.V. Kornetova lived in Magadan, where her husband served in the MVD troops, who guarded the local concentration camps. When P.A. Kashinov worked for some time in the Far East, helping to build Komsomolsk on the Amur, he encountered many political prisoners and exiles. Kh.I. Leibovich, an army officer, served for a while in the Far East, where "there was not one large town without camps in the neighbourhood."

Local party chiefs Tiaglov and Kondrashov showed their selective memory when they maintained that they had no knowledge of labour camps when serving as raikom or gorkom secretaries in the 1940s and early 1950s. In contrast to them, veteran Communist A.V. Kruglova, a party member since 1939, did admit to having known about camps for "enemies of the people," even though she otherwise spoke with extreme caution. She added that in Stalin's time every day she felt unsure whether she would be allowed to go home from work in the evening.[77]

One of the interviewees, who chose to remain anonymous, worked after the war as a camp employee for one month, which was all he could take. He did not want to describe what went on there, because "now we know everything already [about them]." What he witnessed in the camp was worse than anything he saw in the war, even though he had fought at Stalingrad. He still finds it hard today to believe that Stalin himself signed documents ordering executions.

Ignorance about the camps may be explained by faulty memory or subconscious repression of unpleasant facts. Nevertheless, it is hard to believe that only one person in ten was aware of the GULag: in July 1945, for example, the NKVD OITK advertised for an economic specialist in the provincial newspaper.[78] Granted, the labour camp administration was represented only by its abbreviation, but most readers must have realized that the advertisement offered employment in the camps.

N.A. Zabelin, more knowledgeable than most because of his age and his activities with the local society of kraevedy (students of local history, geography, and folklore), said in the survey that he knew of a camp on the territory of the kombinat Proletarka in Kalinin and remembered the hamlet Peremerki near Kalinin as having been one big camp in Stalin's time.[79] Zabelin went on to say that the town of Kalinin was reconstructed not only by its inhabitants but also by convicts and POWs. His observations are indeed corroborated by archival evidence.

CHAPTER SIX

The Towns:
Economy and Society

As Laqueur remarks, in "Soviet society ... like most others ... a majority [was] wholly preoccupied with the challenges of daily life, lacking the initiative and energy" to be involved and interested in politics.[1] Politics, economics, and society were, however, always intricately intertwined. A dichotomy between public and private life did not really exist, for the regime attempted to control both. The inhabitants of Kalinin province were constantly forced to adapt to the rules laid down by the party, government, and security organs; no one could afford to forget about the ever-watchful authorities.

Despite its zealous efforts, the Communist regime was more successful in creating a public image of a monolithically uniform Soviet citizenry than in fully manipulating people's private lives: we have seen already how many stubbornly worked to achieve their individual goals in life and only reluctantly strove for the achievement of the collective goals of socialist society as prescribed by the regime. Total conformity was too difficult to achieve or maintain: the Communists' means were often too primitive, the Communists who implemented policies were fallible, and the subjects of these policies dissembled successfully.[2]

As before the war, in the last years of Stalin's life the presence of the party and the security organs was felt more strongly in the towns than in the countryside, for the membership of the Communist Party was much higher in relative terms among urban inhabitants than among rural inhabitants, while informers were more easily spotted by the villagers in the countryside than by the urban workers and employees in the office, on the shopfloor, in the apartment building, in the obshchezhitie, or in the workers' barracks.

Besides living under this watchful eye, in the postwar years in the towns people found their lives were fraught with other difficulties. Industry recovered only slowly, and the quality of goods produced by the factories was frequently deficient, while wages were minimal and social benefits meagre. The shops often were empty. The housing shortage that had existed before the war had worsened as a result of wartime destruction, and the housing space accorded to most town dwellers remained extremely limited. Not all suffered, but a better life was enjoyed only by those few who were part of the "New Class." Men usually fared better than women in material terms, although there were many more women than men in the labour force of the province. People placed their hopes in their children; urban inhabitants seemed to have been convinced that, although they themselves would never be able to escape their bleak life, perhaps education could offer their offspring a way out.

THE CHECKERED RECOVERY OF INDUSTRY

The preponderance of swamps and forests rendered farmland comparatively infertile and scarce in the provincial northwest. The south and southeast were more thickly peopled traditionally, particularly in the areas where flax was grown.[3] Besides an adverse natural environment, there were historical grounds for the industrial underdevelopment and low population density of the western half of the province. Since the beginning of the eighteenth century, places like Vyshnii Volochek, Tver', and Torzhok had been postal and waterway stations along the route from Moscow to St Petersburg. The opening of Russia's first railroad reinforced their prominence in the guberniia. Since the second half of the nineteenth century, population density further increased in the more industrialized regions along the October Railroad and in the southeastern area of the province. Wartime circumstances reinforced this distribution by thinning the population of the western part through army service and through the evacuation and killing and deportation of civilians.

Thus, in the 1950s more than half the urban dwellers and industrial workers resided along the October Railroad. Along this route the entire cotton-fibre industry of the oblast' could be found. Around it were located the provincial chemical, rubber-asbestos, and polygraphic industries, as well as almost all peat production, glass factories, and a large share of the machine building, construction-material, knitted-wear, and garment industries. The railroad passed through the factory towns of Bologoe, Vyshnii Volochek, Likhoslavl', and Kalinin, and through a number of so-called urban-type settlements, such as Spirovo, Izoplit, Novo-Zavidovo, Redkino, and Kalashnikovo. Only the factories for the primary processing of flax were distributed throughout the territory of the oblast'.[4]

Table 20
Oblast' Production in 1955, in Proportion to Total USSR production

Product	Share
Passenger wagons	large share
Excavators	10.0%
Cotton weavings	6.0%[1]
Window glass	3.6%
Leather footwear	2.5%
Felt footwear	3.6%
Paper	1.8%
Peat	5.7%
Primary processing of flax	20.0%
Oblast' size	0.3%[2]
Population	0.8%[3]

Source: Based on *Tsentralnyi Raion*, 532
[1] Sixth in the USSR.
[2] Percentage of total territory of the USSR.
[3] Percentage of total population of the USSR.

By 1960 the population density in rural areas (9.4 persons per square kilometre) had plummeted by more than three times since 1914.[5] The provincial economy, taken as a whole in 1960, was linked to the planned economy of the entire Soviet Union: coal was imported from Moscow oblast', chemical fertilizers from Moscow and Leningrad provinces, salt from the Donetsk area, sugar from Ukraine, cotton fibre from Central Asia, and rye and other grain from Ukraine, the Trans-Ural region, the lower and middle Volga areas, and the Altai region. Wood was exported to Moscow and Moscow province; potatoes, vegetables, butter, and strong-horned cattle were shipped to Leningrad and Murmansk oblasts, milk to Moscow. Flax was transported to factories around the Central Region. Industrial products ended up everywhere in the Soviet Union, although the bulk of the production – such as footwear, clothing, and underwear – was destined for Moscow (further details are provided in table 20).

In Stalin's time and after, the greatest obstacle to satisfactory industrial performance was the dearth of investment.[6] The industrially manufactured consumer goods of Kalinin province were not of crucial importance to the Soviet Union. Only the railroad-car factory and the machine-building industry – including the defence industry, which fell outside the competence of the obkomburo – were of great significance to Moscow.

The predominantly light industry of the province also suffered from competition within the Union. Provincial textile factories had to compete with those of Ivanovo-Voznesensk and the Moscow oblast', while processing of leather and production of footwear was common in many parts of the Soviet Union. To compensate for the meagre investments, other means had to be applied to induce industry to operate more profitably, such as maximizing the use of confiscated German equipment, saving on expenditure of raw materials, fuel, and electricity (a strategy called ekonomika), or reducing waste output.[7]

These methods led only to marginal improvements, at best. Provincial industry received a small share of the confiscated German and Eastern European industrial machinery and equipment after the war. Yet the value of these goods for the revival of the economy was negligible. Confiscated capital goods were not used very efficiently. In October 1946 the secretary of the party committee of the town of Bologoe complained that although all factories in the town could use "trophy goods," only three had received some of this equipment. A report of the gorkom of Vyshnii Volochek illustrates the quandaries with the confiscated machinery – in this case for a new wood-processing plant – for "[o]n the day of the inspection, the majority of the equipment was standing under the open sky. The complexity of the equipment remains completely unintelligible, for no one knows the technology involved in the new production process. The only thing that has been established is that it does not operate on steam power. The question where the factory is going to be built has not been decided either."[8]

In January 1946 textile manufacturing was responsible for about 13 percent, footwear for 7 percent, passenger cars for 6 percent, machine building for at least 5 percent, confectionery for 4 percent, other food processing for 7.5 percent, and paper, wood, glass, and construction materials for about 10 percent of the monthly value of provincial industrial production.[9] Twenty percent of industrial production was accounted for by manufacturing cooperatives, which tenaciously survived. Plan fulfillments in factories and cooperatives in this month indicate that heavy industry (machine-building and passenger cars) and manufacturing cooperatives met production goals, but in other factories the record was patchy. The two larger factories of heavy industry in Kalinin (the railroad-car works and 1 May, which was involved in machine-building and, possibly, armaments during the war) managed to meet plan targets because of the Soviet state's constant higher investment in heavy industry. The glass factories and the confectionery factory surpassed their plans significantly, but bread factories fell far short of the targets, as did most textile factories.

Until Stalin's death, textile manufacturing, the greatest industrial employer centred in Kalinin and Vyshnii Volochek, failed to recover from wartime destruction and to reach planned production levels. Vyshnii Volochek had escaped occupation, but had been the target of German bombing during the first couple of years of the war. In October 1945 the obkomburo expressed its disapproval of the situation in both towns. The Proletarka factory in Kalinin, a source of pride for the prewar provincial party organization, was suffering from shoddily operated food canteens in which not enough cooking gear, sewerage, and water were available. Lavatories and corridors were extremely dirty and doors and windows broken, while the whole factory was in dire need of whitewashing. In 1945 the stock of wood and peat for the coming winter was far from sufficient in all textile enterprises of Vyshnii Volochek and Kalinin. Workers, housed in boarding houses and barracks near the factories, were living in an unhygienic environment. The party had little more to offer than the organization of a socialist competition movement among the residents "for a more sanitary keeping of their rooms."[10]

The production of large-scale industry was not very impressive after the war, when only the railroad-car and confectionery factories were conspicuous for the value of their output as single economic units. The performance of most other factories was rather insignificant and did not prove the supposed superiority of rationalized large factory production over the small-scale production of the industrial cooperative. The manufacturing cooperatives taken together boasted the highest output value within the province, indicating the persistent economic importance of small craftsmanship after the war. Raikom secretary Fochenkov of Nerl' raion noted in 1947 that members of the local population were still predominantly employed as artisans producing footwear.[11] Although they were supposed to concentrate on agricultural labour as well, inhabitants of the raion neglected animal husbandry and crop tilling, since returns from farm work were low. Income was primarily derived from the sale of boots and shoes, production of which was done on the side. The thriving performance of the more independent cooperatives may serve as an argument for the economic importance of personal initiative and responsibility.[12]

Overall industrial gains brightened soon after, and the industrial plans for the oblast' in 1946, 1947, and 1948 were fulfilled.[13] By early 1949 the level of output in industry approached the 1940 level. Light industry continued to lag behind, however, for in early 1949 its production reached only 64.7 percent of the level of 1940.

Production suffered not only from poor labour conditions and low investment but also from the complicated bureaucratic structure of industry. Some industries operated under the authority of the Central Union administration, others under that of the RSFSR, the provincial government, or raion soviets.[14] Formally, industrial cooperatives enjoyed the most independence but were still held to fulfilling a plan.

Some small factories, such as the Ostashkov leather plant, were apparently under the direct authority of the USSR government, while a similarly sized enterprise within the same branch of industry, the Krasnaia Zvezda footwear factory of Kimry, fell under the authority of the RSFSR government. To complicate matters further, at all these levels a distinction was made between manufacturing enterprises of the industrial People's Commissariats and those of nonindustrial People's Commissariats.[15] All People's Commissariats had to comply with instructions issued by Gosplan, the state planning committee, which developed production plans according to the economic guidelines set by the Central Committee, its Sekretariat, and the Politburo – or by a few members of the latter. It is impossible to establish which unit within these overlapping, disparate administrative levels was more important for the performance of the separate factories. Bureaucratic chaos seems to have been forged through overzealous and uncoordinated organization. Already at this time the average factory director must have been swimming in an overwhelming sea of red tape, a phenomenon which was better known in the last twenty-five-odd years of the existence of the Soviet Union. The necessity for middlemen, "fixers" who try in semilegal fashion to overcome supply shortages (tolkachi), seems perfectly understandable.[16]

The war had destroyed most of the industrial plant. Initially, the recovery of production levels was therefore slow and patchy but steady nevertheless, reaching the prewar level by 1949. The industrial labour force did not increase as much as in other regions of the Union during the Fourth Five Year Plan (1946–50). The resulting shortage of factory workers played its part in the halting recovery of certain industrial sectors. From 1944 to 1949 the work force in oblast' industry increased only from 104,000 to 122,000, far fewer still than the 160,000 workers who had been employed in 1940.[17] Workers were in high demand and the labour shortage in industry contributed to the depletion of the ranks of the collective farmers, as we will see in the next chapters. Nevertheless, hidden unemployment apparently existed in the smaller town of Kashin in 1952.[18] Even after the worst consequences of the war had been overcome, toward 1950, several branches of industry continued to show spotty results. A dearth of investment, bureaucratic chaos, and a shortage of workhands partially explain the unimpressive overall performance, but the problems were complicated by other factors.

Industry suffered after the war from the absence of qualified cadres, that is, workers, foremen, and managers with specialized education and long-term experience. Most with genuine expertise had either been exterminated in the 1930s or did not return from the war. This resulted in a high proportion of "practitioners" (practical workers) in many senior functions within the factories. Although the level of education of industrial specialists slowly improved after the war as a consequence of the influx of young graduates from vocational and professional schools, even by 1951 almost a third of engineers and technicians in Kalinin had no specialized education.[19] The enthusiasm of the practicioners compensated at times for their lack of schooling, but enthusiasm alone was not sufficient to drastically increase output levels and improve the quality of production. Likewise, a high proportion of party membership (and therefore a higher degree of ideological loyalty) among workers was not sufficient on its own to compensate for other flaws: at the bigger plants in the oblast' the party was well represented among the labour force.[20] Absence of enthusiasm for fulfilling the production norm was evidently therefore a minor cause for the weak performance of certain industrial sectors, even though we have seen in previous pages that not every Communist was a zealous and diligent worker.

In June 1951 the obkom reported to the Central Committee paltry progress in the restoration or construction of a number of enterprises.[21] These included some of the largest industrial employers, such as factories for cotton-fibre textiles, primary flax treatment, construction materials, and agricultural machinery. All textile factories were lagging behind output levels of 1941, their thwarted revival was exemplified by the cotton-spinning and weaving factory Proletarka of Kalinin.[22] Here, the spinning shop's turnout was at only 25.8 percent of the prewar level, and the weaving shop's was at only 15.8 percent. Even the usually well-operating railroad-car factory did not meet plan targets during the first months of 1951, a problem that was attributed by the obkom to the recent introduction of railroad passenger cars into the production line, which had impaired output. It stands to reason that the purge at the plant played its part here, since it had forced out a number of senior managers, but the obkom report omitted any mention of this possible cause.[23] In 1949 and 1950 both the peat-digging and lumber industries failed to fulfill the plans.[24] In the lumber industry most work was done manually until 1947–48, at which time some aspects of production had been mechanized, but not to the extent that workers managed to fulfill the production plan for any of the years from 1949 to 1952. Meanwhile forests had been consistently thinning out in recent decades, for planned tree planting had not been taking place. Much of the work in the forest industry was done by seasonally hired kolkhozniks, who were therefore sometimes absent from spring sowing, which suffered as a result.

In July 1951, Central Committee representative Storozhev, although primarily concentrating on the lamentable state of agriculture, depicted industrial development in harsh terms.[25] More than 200 enterprises had not satisfied their plans in 1950: industrial production had again taken a turn for the worse. In the summer of 1951, 328 enterprises were not achieving planning targets. The quality of many wares did not meet the required standards, nor was the required assortment of goods produced. Machinery breakdowns occurred frequently, and lengthy factory stoppages were common. Following Stalin's famous adage about cadres deciding everything, Storozhev explained most problems as a consequence of a lack of care for cadres. This deficiency led to an enormous turnover of the labour force and to many violations of labour discipline. The shortage of stable cadres especially troubled the lumber industry, Storozhev explained to his audience.

Production results in industry were on the whole more gladdening to the party's provincial leadership and Central Committee by September 1952, when larger enterprises were meeting their plan targets, although smaller industry particularly, which was the responsibility of the oblast' government, showed continuously disappointing results.[26] But even the successfully operating branches may have laboured with less flourish than was reported at this time, for the industrial statistics preserved in the formerly secret party records are likely to be unreliable. Party cadres, industrial managers, or foremen of workshops exaggerated plan fulfillment by their enterprises. For example, on behalf of their workers some foremen routinely entered labour never performed in the books. In August 1946 the obkom was forced to condemn this practice, after which the abuse briefly subsided.[27] Nevertheless, this habit continued to plague the prestigious railroad-car factory in the months thereafter.

Quality of production presents a further impediment in estimating the exact value of industrial output. Some effort was made to produce better goods, but the emphasis was on quantity rather than quality.[28] Because of the mania for fulfilling economic plans in the factories, a peculiar rhythm of labour had been forged, so that "at the factory for automobile garage equipment in Bezhetsk, work is organized according to the principle – if one can describe it as such – [by which] the first ten days of the month are lethargy, the second ten are loosening up, and the third ten are storming [shturm]. As a rule, at the end of every month at this factory the workers of the assembly workshop work overtime, and at the beginning of the month they rest for lack of work."[29] Especially at the end of the month, every effort was made to meet planning targets in industrial enterprises, whether goods were defective or not (this was called to "storm the targets," or shturmovshchina).

Bleak industrial results were also the consequence of poor remuneration and general neglect of workers' living conditions.[30] In 1951 communal housing hovered at 75 percent of prewar levels. Apart from that, the prewar network of children's institutions, public baths, and cultural and sports facilities had yet to be restored. Repair shops were lacking: in urban areas their number had dropped dramatically from 720 to 589 in the previous two years. Because trade unions were unable to alleviate the workers' plight, wages were being paid late, the incidence of injuries and illnesses was high, and workdays were too long. Food and tea canteens were unkempt.

Participants in the survey testified in 1992 that quantity and quality were undermined by often appalling labour conditions in industry. N.A. Kotov began to work as a metal worker in the cotton-fibre kombinat Proletarka in 1951. At the plant "affairs were badly organized: all work was done by hand, without specific machinery. It happened that one had to drag iron oneself." P.A. Samarova, a weaver at Proletarka, remembered how one had to carry cast iron and bricks by hand for the reconstruction of the plant after the war. One of the worst occupations must have been that of a peat labourer. In the middle of 1947 the provincial MGB reported that in one of the enterprises, workers were quitting every day to escape from the harsh labour.[31]

Working conditions in textile factories were equally intolerable at times.[32] Temperatures on the shop floor reached more than 30°C, with the humidity at 85 percent. Some older women, officially disabled because of tuberculosis or arthritis but still deemed fit enough to work, were assigned chores in the decrepit and damp factory basements. Occasionally they had to work with their feet immersed in water. Despite the legislation prohibiting workers from leaving their jobs without authorization from their superiors, the fluctuation of the labour force continued to afflict all industry in 1952.[33]

Trade unions were unimportant after the war: the head of the provincial trade unions complained in 1951 that since 1948 the obkom had not bothered to heed the opinion of the oblast' trade union council about any question even once.[34] The unions focussed strictly on the administration of social insurance for their membership and on increasing labour productivity. They were not supposed to attempt to improve working or living conditions. Nor did they negotiate wage levels, benefits, or insurance. These matters were contingent on plans by the party and government, after which the unions rubber-stamped the governmental measures. Probably because the first party secretary of the obkom was being dismissed, the head of the oblast' trade union council was courageous enough at the end of 1949 to protest that wages within the province were paid in general with a delay of ten to fifteen days and in some small enterprises sometimes not for months. This is almost the only example found in the records of a trade union representative more or less directly criticizing a shortcoming of the workers' employer, the state.[35]

The state social insurance system had compensated workers and employees since the 1930s for "loss of pay during temporary inability to work because of illness, accident, pregnancy, and childbirth; for pensions in case of prolonged or permanent disability and in old age; funeral benefits; pensions to the dependent survivors of deceased workers."[36] It is hard to believe, but the meagre benefits to which factory workers were thus entitled often provided enough incentive for collective farmers to attempt to join the urban labour force. Mothers of large families had received child benefits since 1936. The level of these benefits varied, since the law in this respect, introduced in 1936, was changed in 1944 and 1947.[37]

Outside agriculture, the working week had been, on average, forty-eight hours since 1940 – six eight-hour working days – although during the war, because of the extensive labour shortages, people worked longer[38]. N.N. Panova said in the survey that she started to work as a weaver in Kalinin in 1946 or 1947; she often worked on her days off, in particular at the end of the quarter and year, when it was necessary to fulfill the plan and the management of the factory had to report on the fulfillment. Panova said that the workload was never the same, for, in addition to overtime work when planned production was due, stoppages resulted from interruptions in the supply of cotton fibre or from breakdowns of the looms. The fuel and electricity supply was regularly interrupted as well.

Stringent but misguided efforts by the provincial leadership after the war had little effect. The same refrain was heard time and again: in July 1953 it appeared that more than one-third of the enterprises in the light, food, and fuel industries and in cooperative industries systematically failed to fulfill state plans.[39] The rhythm of production in many enterprises was uneven, while labour productivity, the quality of goods, and the savings on production costs remained below the established norms. Poor labour discipline, wastage of fuel and electricity, and stoppages continued to plague industry. In Vyshnii Volochek, the textile industry was irregularly supplied with fuel and electricity, and wages were paid only after long delays. Construction and the repair of housing and public buildings failed to meet targets. These myriad shortcomings in industry led to a continuation after the war of the much smaller per capita industrial production in the Soviet Union compared to that in Western Europe and North America.[40]

LIFE IN THE TOWNS

In 1951 the square footage of available housing space within the city of Kalinin was 12.3 percent higher than in 1940.[41] It is difficult to assess whether this actually translated into more disposable living space per person, as the exact size of the town's population at this time is unknown. Tentative evidence would indicate that the number of inhabitants was close to that of 1939, so that, indeed, slightly more housing space per person had become available. It is impossible, however, that more than 5 square metres per inhabitant would have been procurable.[42] Kiselev and Sadovnikov reported in November 1951 to Malenkov that [the] "pace of the construction of housing seriously lags behind the growing demands of the population of the towns."[43]

The lack of sufficient housing had been one of the criticisms levelled at Vorontsov by the Central Committee in October 1948; in 1949, the worst situation was reported in Torzhok, Rzhev, and Bologoe.[44] In 1953 the party secretary of the Vagzhanov factory in Kalinin complained about the inadequate housing conditions of many young female workers at her factory who were renting living space in private homes, where they often had to live in a corner of a room. They were unable to do homework for the workers' youth school, because the landlord demanded that the light be turned off too soon.

Many industrial workers lived (with several people in a room) in barracks nearby their factory. N.S. Loshkarev said in the survey that after he was demobilized from the army, he and his mother first lived in an apartment together with people to whom they were not related. In 1948 his mother received her own room of 10 square metres, whither Loshkarev moved with his bride as well. Only in 1957 did they receive an apartment of 17 square metres for themselves. A.S. Lukovkin lived with his mother, wife, and daughter in a room of 11 square metres after his return from the camps.[45]

In the early years of crash industrialization, general deprivation probably led to the fact that children in the town of Kalinin were smaller and weighed less than their Muscovite counterparts.[46] Specific data on the physical characteristics of children during or after the war are scarce; but, on the basis of other information about the standard of living, one assumes that children of the years 1945–53 were only slightly, if at all, better nourished and healthier than their counterparts of the early 1930s.

Living conditions in other towns were frequently worse than in the provincial capital in 1951, when the amount of living space and the municipal services in Rzhev and Torzhok had yet to attain prewar levels.[47] In 1949 each inhabitant of the town of Rzhev had on average 3 square metres of living space. In the same year many of its schools had to work in three shifts due to the lack of buildings. In 1951 Rzhev had only half the supply of housing, schools, hospitals, clinics, and day-cares that it had had in 1940. At one factory in Kimry in 1952, 250 square meters of factory housing space was available for 700 workers, and at another, 40 square meters for 400 workers! There was no kindergarten for either factory, both of which employed mainly women. It was noted that the labour force was very unstable as a result.

In Bologoe in 1952 more than 270 families of railroad workers were in dire need of housing.[48] In spite of repeated pleas in 1951 and 1952 to come to their aid, these families lived in kitchens and hallways. Since the end of the war no new apartment buildings had been built in this town, which had sustained severe damage from shelling and bombard-ments. Most of the urban housing in table 21 would be the result of the crash building program initiated under Khrushchev.

Municipal governments had to work with grossly inadequate budgets after the war and therefore often could not commence public works or took an inordinate amount of time to complete them. Sanitary condi-tions suffered as a result. The incidence of intestinal diseases such as typhoid fever, intestinal infections, and dysentery was higher in urban environments than in the countryside. Sixty percent of these cases occurred in the larger cities, especially in Kalinin, Vyshnii Volochek, and Bezhetsk.[49] In the latter two towns good drinking water was not available. A general lack of sewerage added to the problems, and urban sanitation was poorly organized. Measures were taken from 1947 onward to remedy the bad state of sanitary conditions in the towns and in the smaller raion centres as much as was possible within budgetary limits. Public baths and washhouses were repaired and reopened, and the hygiene of several communal apartments (obshchezhitie) was improving because of renovations. In the spring of 1948 urban dwellers took part in a campaign to clean their towns. Despite these efforts, the lack of potable water led to an outbreak of typhoid fever in Bezhetsk and Vyshnii Volochek in 1948. Typhoid fever and dysentery remained common in larger towns: in 1949, every ten days saw a

Table 21
Housing Space in the Towns of Kalinin Oblast' in 1940 and 1960, in comparison with 1917 (post-1957 borders)

	1940 Compared to 1917 (%)	1960 Compared to 1917 (%)
Total space in towns and workers' settlements	148	290
In towns	142	260
Kalinin	137	260
Bezhetsk	106	180
Bologoe	128	350
Vyshnii Volochek	168	240
Kimry	147	220
Rzhev	560†	680
Torzhok	134	190
Kashin	73[2]	120
Konakovo	340	530
Ostashkov	109	160
Total for urban type settlements	370	1400

Source: Based on *Kalininskaia oblast' za 50 let*, 115.

[1] This number seems rather doubtful.

[2] This number is astonishing.

minimum of a dozen cases of dysentery and always some cases of typhoid fever in the town of Kalinin.[50] Dysentery in the capital spread increasingly during the summer and was at its peak in September, when more than forty cases were registered during every ten-day period. While spotted and typhoid fever infections were restricted to single cases in every ten-day period, dysentery presented a more serious dilemma. From July to September 1949, Torzhok was visited by a non-lethal form of dysentery, and 915 people fell ill, of whom 515 had to be hospitalized.

In 1951 in the formerly occupied raions, medical offices and clinics were sometimes housed in private dwellings, usually with less than adequate sanitary standards.[51] Several hospitals had not yet been rebuilt by that year, notably the provincial hospital in Kalinin and the urban hospitals of Rzhev and Staritsa. The health of urban dwellers was further jeopardized by the shortage of medical doctors that was noted in chapter 2.

Heating in the larger towns was provided by wood or peat: in 1948, wood still heated more than half the households and office.[52] In 1951 every urban dweller was serviced by the urban electricity network. By the same year the tramlines, as well as Kalinin's sewage system and waterworks, had been completely restored to their pre-1941 state. But public utilities must have been far from adequate, since Kiselev and Sadovnikov petitioned Malenkov in November 1951 for significantly more funds to improve the telephone network and the housing and streetcar system, and to build a sports stadium.[53]

In Soviet times the best cities to live in within the whole country were Moscow and Leningrad, where services and supplies were better. Similarly, within the microcosm of Kalinin province living conditions in the provincial capital always appeared better than in the smaller provincial towns: housing was marginally better, and so was the state of municipal public utilities. In 1952 no municipal waterworks or sewage system existed in Kashin, while for most household purposes people in Kimry had to use either the polluted water of the Volga or water from primitive wells.[54] The bridges over the river were dilapidated, and the cobblestone roads were falling apart. Kimry's public works department lacked the means for any new projects and even for the maintenance of existing municipal utilities. Still smaller settlements in the immediate surroundings of a number of towns had neither electricity nor sufficient water pumps. In these "workers' settlements" (rabochie poselki), the assortment of goods in the shops was often small, with shortages of essential products occurring regularly.[55] Public utilities in the raion centre of Maksatikha were in a desolate state in 1952: the public bath had crumbled, there were no electric lights, and the primary school building had burned down, forcing the school to close altogether.[56]

The eternal Soviet problem of a scanty supply and variety of goods in shops also plagued Kalinin province.[57] Although retail prices were regularly lowered after 1945, the purchasing power of wages remained lower than in the second half of the 1920s. Curiously, contemporaries applauded the regular announcement of lower prices without any effort to calculate whether this translated into an increase in purchasing power.

In early 1945, I.P. Boitsov lamented the flawed provincial retail network: many necessities were not offered to consumers.[58] He mentioned, among other things, an absence of pots and iron hardware and complained that these shortages were unnecessary, inasmuch as the raw materials for such products were to be found in the oblast'. Local industrial enterprises were being blamed for these scarcities, but it was actually the decline of the cottage industries that was making itself felt. Boitsov, however, was obviously not prepared to criticize the central government's decrees at the end of the 1930s that had prohibited kolkhoznik employment in nonagricultural trades. He demanded that the quality and quantity of consumer goods improve and urged the opening of more repair shops for the toilers.

The efficiency of internal distribution failed to improve during 1945.[59] At the end of 1945 in Vyshnii Volochek, Bezhetsk, Kaliazin, Kimry, Likhoslavl', and Bologoe, bread would often not be available for six to eight days, because of the absence of fuel for bread factories and bakeries. In several rural raions, most of which had suffered occupation, flour mills languished, and grain was sold directly to customers. In the winter and spring of 1946–47, bread rations were extremely low as a result of the drought.[60]

At the end of 1947 ration cards were abolished, but, except for a brief period of an abundance of goods, the usual shortages quickly recurred.[61] Survey respondent N.A. Arkhangel'skii was probably correct when he stated that the most important aspect of the abolition of rationing was its political effect. His opinion was underlined by that of N.N. Panova, a weaver, who believed that abolition was a means to pretend to the outside world that everything was going well in the USSR.

Privations of sugar, flour, meat, lard and butter, tinned food, and other staples often cropped up in both town and country in 1951. Just as much as in later times, the rudeness of customer services was deplored – in 1951 even by the first obkom secretary.[62] Many goods were stolen and squandered in the provincial retail trade network. Such theft was a risky but lucrative and common business. In 1952, during an inspection of sixty-five retail stores, it was found that in forty-three, customers were cheated by being given short weights or short measures or by mistakes in tallying up the bill.

The nostalgia today for the security and plentiful supplies of Stalin's times may seem to us rather absurd when we note, for example, that the first secretary of the gorkom of Vyshnii Volochek, the second provincial town, complained in 1951 about the regular formation of bread queues in front of shops and the absence of kul'ttovary (cultural supplies, that is, office equipment, musical instruments, and so on) and of motorbikes.[63] In his opinion the operation of the internal retail trade system in the oblast' needed dramatic improvement.

The causes of the shortage of consumer goods were manifold: low investment in light industry by the state; bureaucratic red tape; mediocre harvest yields and the poor state of animal husbandry inside and outside the province; the frequently enormous distances over which goods had to be shipped to reach Kalinin province; and the backward state of transportation within the internal trade network. For example, in 1951 the directorate for local trade used of 120 motor vehicles and 162 horses, whereas before the war it had used 204 motor vehicles and 297 horses.[64] In 1951 consumers' cooperatives had fewer cars, trucks, and horses than in 1941. Goods such as bicycles and radios were distributed very unevenly: at some point in 1950 or 1951, for example, a single shop received 720 radios, while the directorate of local trade received merely 380.

A delegate at the ninth provincial party conference summed up the results of the failing distribution network. Since he was not working in a nomenklatura job, the frustration he expressed may have been typical among many factory workers:

A little about trade. Try to obtain yeast, or bay leaf, when you dare. Nothing of the kind you will find, while speculators are selling them at every corner. Is it possible that the trade organizations cannot organize the sale of bay leaves? Or do you think that it's not convenient for your financial plan? It is, however, useful for the working class and the toiling intelligentsia [to buy these things for the official price,] because they overpay the speculators for these things; and one fails to understand how the organs of the arm of the law can overlook this in such a slipshod manner, as if they do not know what the speculators demand for a bay leaf.

There, comrade Kiselev, you reported that the organs of the militsiia and justice operate poorly. Let's grab these hucksters, these permanent residents of the market, and send them there, to the kolkhozy (Applause).[65]

Many town dwellers tried to make up for the shortages by cultivating a private plot on the outskirts of the towns, which probably perpetuated certain rural habits among these workers. G.V. Lubov said in the survey that he, his wife, and his parents, although all employed in the small town of Konakovo in factories or urban offices, continuously kept up a private plot. Lubov was and is a staunch supporter of the Communist regime, but he admits that the double income he and his wife had in these years was insufficient to provide adequately for their family of three. The private plot satisfied the family's demand for potatoes, cabbage, cucumbers, tomatoes, and carrots. They also kept chickens and pigs. Even a well-paid worker such as N.D. Eliseev, who worked at the railroads repairing locomotives, said that he continued to cultivate a private plot and raise some piglets. He sold the meat in Moscow, because the prices were much higher there. In Kalinin in 1951, 14,656 households owned a private plot but, due to stricter enforcement of the taxation on the produce of these plots, the number had fallen to approximately 10,000 by 1953.[66]

The annual salary in 1952 of an employee of a raion economic planning buro was 8,280 rubles per year, which was about the same as the average salary for wage earners and salaried employees outside agriculture for the same year (8,250 rubles).[67] In 1948 the average monthly wage of a factory worker was 700 rubles per month, which was five to ten times more than the cash income of kolkhozniks. For a book, journal, and newspaper vendor in a raion centre in the countryside, the annual wage was 4,920 rubles, far below the average, but not unexpected for this kind of job, which demanded little physical effort or skill.

Workers in small local industries earned on average 2,227 rubles annually in 1945; 2,806 rubles in 1946; 3,715 rubles in 1947; and 4,101 rubles in 1948.[68] Members of producers' cooperatives saw their average annual wage increase from 2,118 rubles in 1945 to 3,156 rubles in 1948. At the upper end of the scale, the railroad worker N.D. Eliseev said in the survey that he received about 15,000 rubles per year around 1950, while his colleague A.N. Nikolaev received between 1,500 and 1,700 rubles per month as a locomotive engineer in the early 1950s. Both men were part of the labour aristocracy at the time.

A metal worker with the tram depot of Kalinin, N.S. Loshkarev, said he received only around 600 rubles per month during the same period. The textile workers O.M. Korobova and T.A. Poliakova said they received 700 rubles monthly. E.V. Baranova, a textile worker, supplemented the income of her family by selling her knitted wear. T.A. Poliakova and F.K. Romashova, both textile workers, toiled in the factory on their days off in order to augment their income. Poliakova did the laundry and ironing for the management of her factory. A.I. Ryzhakova received a pension for her daughter because her husband was killed in the army; yet, as a nurse she still needed to work one and a half shifts to make ends meet, and to work on holidays and call upon relatives to help her out. According to N.A. Zabelin the monthly wage of a secondary schoolteacher in the 1945–53 period was 800 rubles, adding up to a gross annual income of 9,600 rubles, slightly above average. Primary schoolteachers earned less: in the countryside many cultivated a private plot to supplement their incomes.[69]

Exactly what could be bought for these sums of money varied and is impossible to assess, but it is obvious that most single incomes were far too meagre to support a half-decent existence. Only in the early 1950s did the real wages of workers and employees generally start to surpass the level of 1937, and only after Stalin's death did they reach the level of the later 1920s. By far the largest share of a family's income had to be spent on foodstuffs. In comparison to most industrialized countries at the time, in the 1950s "the position of the Soviet worker ... was still worse than it was in 1928."[70]

By the 1950s both adults of an urban household were obliged to work in order to guarantee a sufficient income for their family. And even then the double income did not suffice, as in the case of L.V. Vedernikova, a bookkeeper, and her husband, who worked for DOSAAF and its predecessors.[71] She stated in the survey that she had to supplement their income by doing odd jobs on her days off, and he, an inveterate fisher, added his catch to their meals. She did not even take her holidays, because she would be paid cash compensation instead, another welcome addition to their income.

Today quite a few Russians decry the appearance of beggars on the streets in recent years, which supposedly was unheard of when the Soviet Union still existed. Perhaps there were few indigents in Brezhnev's time. Nevertheless, beggars did appear in the streets of Kalinin during Stalin's years. In 1951 Mishchenko, of the Molotov military academy located in the centre of Kalinin, remarked:

If the secretaries of the raikom, gorkom, and obkom would take a walk along the streets of the oblast' centre, then they would notice that almost on every street corner some kind of beggar is sitting. It gives the impression that the centre of the town of Kalinin is beggarly. Citizens of the countries of the people's democracies study at the Molotov Academy. There is one indigent near the post office, who without fail seeks them out and begs. They will go home and relate that the town of Kalinin is full of beggars.[72]

In principle, the leisure time of factory workers and employees was distributed evenly throughout the year. In practice, however, urban inhabitants were obliged to work overtime at their enterprises, either because they were forced to do so or because they could thereby enhance their income. Some spent much of their spare time on their plots. Much time was wasted by having to queue up at the stores as well; women were understood to discharge most household tasks.[73]

The pace of work was different in agriculture: peasants followed more closely the traditional rhythm of life. Although less so than before collectivization, the winter was still a comparatively tranquil time. After the harvest the kolkhozniks were often recruited for work in wood procurements and had to treat flax at home. The peasants also stubbornly continued to observe religious holidays, and these often amounted to their time at play.[74] In their case, the modern concept of leisure became diffused only in the time of the reforms after Stalin's death, when, for example, actual paid holidays were introduced. Before 1953 the attitude towards work in the countryside remained predominantly preindustrial: a clear division between leisure and work time was not made, the rhythm of activities being determined by the religious calendar and the seasons.[75]

In urban areas spare time was spent participating in amateur music and drama groups, reading library books, visiting the theatre and cinema, attending concerts, and being involved in sports. Free moments were also sometimes enjoyed, as they were in the villages, at elaborate dinners at which plenty of food and drink was consumed with family and friends (zastol'e), or people strolled around the town. Older people preserved the rural habit of sitting around outside on benches in the evenings, savouring gossip about all and sundry.[76] Of course political meetings, as well as exercises within DOSAAF and its predecessors, occupied some spare time (one wonders how much the Russians of Tver' really enjoyed these gatherings). In contrast, many urban dwellers were in the habit of visiting the countryside to join the celebration of religious holidays; a good number of people, too, attended religious services.

Urban inhabitants earned a real annual vacation of varying length, depending on their job, but only a few – and they were all part of the party's elite – managed to make a holiday trip outside provincial borders. More urban residents (especially those who had joined the party) than rural dwellers seemed content with the activities available during leisure and holiday time.[77]

Life in the towns under Stalin was probably only marginally more endurable than life in the countryside. The queues in front of the shops, the lack of a diverse assortment of goods, the inadequate diet, the poorly insulated apartments or rooms, the low income, the long workday for both men and women, and the forced cohabitation with others in communal apartments led to an exceptionally high level of stress: some turned to the bottle as a result, a traditionally common habit in Russia in any circumstance.[78]

SOCIAL HIERARCHY
AND GENDER RELATIONS

The most powerful members within the social hierarchy resided almost without exception in the towns. Society's elite was formed by a group called the "New Class" by Djilas, or the "Nomenklatura" by Voslensky.[79] The members of this elite were Communists who held positions of leadership within the party, the government, and the economy. Boitsov, Vorontsov, Baranov, Gerasimenko, Sadovnikov, Kiselev, Kondrashov, and Tiaglov are some of the more conspicuous representatives in previous pages.

One cannot equate this elite group with the Soviet intelligentsia, although several members of the New Class could also be considered part of this stratum. Many people who were classified as belonging to the intelligentsia because of their professions, such as teachers or doctors, were not part of the elite. They did not enjoy any of the privileges of the Communist elite, while their wages were sometimes below

Table 22
The "Intelligentsiia" of the Town of Kalinin on 1 February 1951

	Communists	Komsomol	Partyless	Total
Leading party and soviet cadres	2,251			2,251
Communist workers in lower responsible positions[1]	3,491			3,491
Teachers	266	162	803	1,231
Scientific workers	84		86	170
Engineers/technicians with specialized professional education	1,254	425	1,173	2,852
Engineers/technicians without specialized education	368		943	1,311
Artists	45	5	111	161
Total				12,886

Source: Based on Pako, 147/5/214a, l.35.

[1] Other than in fine arts, science, teaching, engineering and medicine.

those of average factory workers. They stood in lower esteem than the workers, at least until Stalin's death.[80]

Intelligentsia is rather a grand term to describe some of the technical workers in the town of Kalinin (see table 22), of whom, in February 1951, 27.2 percent did not have any special professional education and were "practical workers" (praktiki).[81] This latter group was becoming extinct, for none of them was a Komsomol member, which indicates that they were from an older age group. More than 4,100 inhabitants were considered by the Party to belong to the professional group of engineers and technical workers: roughly one-third of them was Communist, and an additional 10 percent members of the Komsomol. Medical workers and teachers, numbering each about 1,400 persons, also formed part of the intelligentsia; the contingent of Communists and Komsomols was smaller among the teachers (respectively 24 percent and 11 percent) and even smaller among medical workers (respectively 11 percent and 5 percent).[82] Life was arduous for teachers. They did not share the same prestige and privileges of those leading party and government workers who comprised the Central Committee's nomenklatura. One school director lived in 1951 inside the school building in one noisy and smelly room .[83] Six of the school's teachers did not have housing at all and shared a room with their landlords.

The New Class was the Communist elite who enjoyed privileges and perquisites as a consequence of its investiture in leading positions. At each step down the ladder of the party hierarchy the benefits became smaller; rank-and-file members hardly enjoyed more privileges than their nonparty peers. The elite can be equated with the nomenklatura of the obkom, numbering between 3,000 and 3,500 people in all.[84] The elite within this elite was formed by the incumbents of positions within Kalinin province belonging to the nomenklatura of the Central Committee. Among them could be found the members of the obkomburo, the heads of the obkom otdely, the executive board of the provincial party school, gorkom and raikom secretaries, the executive of the oblispolkom and the chairs of gorispolkoms and raiispolkoms, the Komsomol obkomburo, the head of the provincial trade unions, the head of the provincial office of Glavlit (the bureau for censorship), the local correspondents of the press agency TASS, and the newspapers *Pravda* and *Izvestiia*, the head of the provincial radio, higher functionaries of the provincial MVD, MGB, and procuracy, directors of the larger factories (sometimes along with their main engineers), and the director and departmental heads of the Pedagogical Institute of Kalinin.[85] They were all appointed by the Central Committee.

Women were proportionally underrepresented among elite ranks, though the Soviet Union professed legal equality between the sexes.[86] But women's equality on paper had not translated into positions of power and influence in anything like the manner in which men had conquered (or defended?) the commanding heights in the days of Stalin. Even so, the provincial economy, like that of the Soviet Union in its entirety, depended on the labour of women after the war. After the upheavals of the 1930s and 1940s this was a society with an extraordinarily small number of able-bodied, trained, or skilled men.

In late 1950 women formed 57.7 percent of the non-kolkhoz work force (see also tables 6 and 23), while by 1 January 1951, women represented 68.5 percent of the work force of able-bodied adults on the collective farms.[87] We have already noted how, on the whole, health-care workers (including medical doctors) and teachers, though falling within the stratum of Soviet intelligentsiia, seldom belonged to the party and were remunerated comparatively poorly. The correlation between the high percentage of women in precisely these two fields and the low status of these professions seems evident. Women were of vital importance to the postwar provincial economy; yet, why did so few women acquire leading positions within the highest provincial party and government levels during or after the war? The answer to that question is complicated: the traditions of East-Slav societies, the universal prejudice against female equality or domination, and the Victorian male-chauvinist outlook of Communist Party chiefs (from Politburo down to raion committee) of Stalin's time all played their role. We will see how after the war women themselves had internalized many of the tacit premises on which this gender-bias was based.

Table 23
Non-kolkhoz Female Work Force in 1950 and 1955, on 1 October

	Number (in thousands)		Percentage of Total Work Force	
	1950	1955	1950	1955
Industry	82.1	98.3	57.8	56.6
Construction	6.4	6.3	34.9	33.5
MTS, etc.	1.2	5.0	27.3	15.1
Sovkhozy, etc.	9.6	8.2	60.2	57.5
Transport and communications	15.2	17.7	39.8	41.1
Trade, procurements, etc.	15.2	15.9	62.9	71.2
Public catering	5.9	7.4	86.7	93.3
Education	24.0	26.0	76.1	77.5
Health care	18.9	20.8	87.9	88.3
Apparat and financial institutions	10.9	8.6	55.8	57.5
Total	200.8	224.6	57.7	54.4

Source: Based on Narodnoe Khoziaistvo, 70–1.
Note: On 1 January 1945, the proportion of women in the total number of workers and employees in the oblast' was 68.3% (Kalininskaia oblast' za 50 let, 121).

Before the war hardly any women had been involved in the heavy labour of logging and timber rafting, but during the war they took on 90 percent of these tasks.[88] From 1945 onwards some men did return to this industry, but women still carried out a substantial part of the work. In 1949 the Presidium of the Soviet Trade Unions called upon lumber enterprises to release women from felling trees, manually transporting timber, and other similarly heavy tasks in the forest industry, but despite these guidelines, women continued to load timber. Labour conditions were so poor that in the winter of 1948–49 (which constituted the lumbering season) seven women were killed by falling trees. In the peat industry 17,000 women were engaged part- or full-time in 1949.[89] Apparently, roughly 30 percent of them performed heavy labour intermittently. Managers condoned this situation because the postwar dearth of men provided no alternative. Labour conditions in both branches of industry would start to ameliorate only after Stalin's death, thanks to the introduction of machinery.

Especially in textile production, where they had been traditionally numerous, women formed the great majority of factory workers. In the cotton-fibre kombinat of Vyshnii Volochek in 1949, of the 6,764 workers, 4,683 were women.[90] Among these cotton-mill workers after the war, one woman, Valentina Gaganova, stood out particularly. Her career may serve as the perfect specimen of the Soviet proletarian cliché. Her story, though an exception to the rule, was held up as the ideal. She would become, under Khrushchev, a paragon for women all over the Communist world.[91]

Valentina Gaganova was born in 1930 in Vladimir province.[92] When her father was killed at the battle of Rzhev during the war, Valentina, along with her siblings and mother, moved in with her aunt, in Vyshnii Volochek in the Kalinin oblast'. There she completed the four-year primary-school curriculum and continued her studies at a vocational school, where she learned the trade of lathe operator. After the war, she attended an evening secondary school and studied by correspondence at the Textile Institute. Even though her mother was Orthodox, Gaganova was not religious, for "[one] has to build one's life oneself, and shouldn't wait for someone from the clouds to build it." As a Komsomol member, furthermore, who was supposed to actively combat religion, Gaganova conducted atheist propaganda with zeal. Communism became for the daughter what the Orthodox Church was for the mother.

Gaganova made her career as a textile worker. She began on the shop floor as a weaver but, still during Stalin's lifetime, was promoted to brigadier. Under Khrushchev, she became an engineer, rose to vice-manager of her workshop, and ended up as the factory's vice-director. Gaganova thrived in the atmosphere of the factory and got along well with almost all her colleagues and even better with her superiors. The party secretary of her workshop was particularly fond of Gaganova. One suspects that this woman was instrumental in Gaganova's meteoric rise.

Gaganova incongruously remembered that in the postwar period, when she was still living at home, wages had been adequate, even though she did not earn enough to be able to dress herself up. Her satisfaction with her income was a result of the nostalgia with which many older people in Russia today view their past; the fact that she lived with a number of relatives probably meant that the combined family income was comparatively high. Her memories of those times as a golden age were so strong that she was convinced that in Stalin's time food was more plentiful and of greater variety than today in Russia. Even so, she remembered 1946 as a particularly poor year, when few goods were available in the shops. From 1947, however, the situation gradually improved. In her rather scarce leisure time after the war, she enjoyed the traditional Russian festive occasions, such as elaborate meals or dances, as well as the new entertainment modern Soviet culture had brought, such as concerts or films.

Gaganova lived until 1958 with several relatives in a small apartment. This was typical for the times, and she probably did not miss better housing, for everyone around her lived in the same overcrowded tenements. In 1958 she became a Soviet hero when she received her first major decoration. The delegation that came to honour her ordered the factory directorate to provide her with a decent apartment. Around this time, Gaganova married a truck driver, so her new housing was all the more welcome. (One may speculate whether the timing of the wedding was connected with the move). In 1959 she became a member of the Communist Party; the next year she gave birth to her only child, a boy. Private and public events are juxtaposed in her memory as milestones in her life, and are of equal importance.

Her career began to acquire stellar proportions and decoration followed decoration: Hero of Socialist Labour, the Lenin Order, and the Order of the October Revolution were among them. Gaganova was invited to rest at spas in the Crimea on several occasions and was often invited to be guest of honour at official occasions in Moscow. During the 1960s she began to accompany Soviet leaders, such as President Podgorny, on their visits to Turkey, Vietnam, or Bulgaria. Gaganova remained in retirement a true believer in the possibility of a socialist future for humanity and in the image of the infallible helmsman, Stalin. She had no reason to complain about her fate and continued to believe that her life showed how "a simple and hardworking person had great opportunities with us [in the Soviet period]."

Gaganova's career was an exceptional success, even in Soviet terms. It was based on a combination of luck, hard work, ambition, the right connections, unfaltering loyalty to Communist ideology, and a solid belief in the wisdom of the party's leadership. She seemed unaware that good fortune had such an influence on her career. If she had not caught the eye of the party secretary, she would never have risen above the level of a common shop-floor worker. When, during the 1950s, the leadership realized the prominent role of women in the cotton mills, Gaganova was discovered as the ideal example of a woman whose selfless efforts, grounded in a purist faith in the good of the cause of Communism, were to be emulated.

Her success is remarkable, not because it showed how much opportunity the Soviet Union offered its citizens but because it is so exceptional. For one Gaganova there were thousands of women stuck in a quagmire of menial jobs in Kalinin province, prevented by traditions of gender inequality and structural impediments of a poorly operating economy from receiving anything that can be remotely called a just reward for their back-breaking contributions to the postwar recovery of the Soviet Union and the preservation of its status as the other superpower after 1945.

Gaganova herself was certainly taken in by the Soviet myth. She seems to have been incapable of looking beyond the ideological hogwash. Her exaltation as a latter-day Stakhanovite, however, had much less effect under Khrushchev than did the half-mythical example of her counterparts in the 1930s. The language was similar, but the belief in working-class heroes had eroded by the later 1950s. Communists paid tribute to her achievements, but most Russians could no longer be inspired by such examples.

In another sense, too, Gaganova proved incapable of understanding the shallowness of her success. She had a brilliant career, but her various rewards were void of meaningful content. Gaganova's exertions were never translated into real political power: she served as a token woman for the leadership, paraded to the outside world as another representative of the equal opportunities available to women in this "most progressive country of the world," and celebated as another Valentina Tereshkova, the cosmonaut, or Ekaterina Furtseva, the only woman ever to serve on the Politburo (Presidium).

During the war the proportion of female party members more than doubled: from 22.2 percent of the total to 45.2 percent by 1944.[93] This proved to be a temporary anomaly: in 1927, 16.8 percent of party members had been female; in 1937, 23.8 percent; in 1947 the relative share of women had fallen again to 28.1 percent; in 1957 it was about the same (28.3 percent); only in the 1960s did the number of women in the party surpass the 30 percent mark again. The wartime entry of women into the party was a consequence, according to first secretary Boitsov in 1945, of the important role they assumed in all economic and government activities. Yet a simple calculation indicates that the absolute number of women in the party was hardly higher in 1944 than in 1940.[94] As in the case of Gaganova, simplistic deception was emloyed to have the Communists believe that progress had been made in fulfilling this part of the Communist promise. Few cared to wonder aloud whether they were duped by their chief. Owing to the enormous losses among the male population, the economic significance of women's work hardly diminished after the war. It was not, however, deemed imperative to have women represented in the party in proportion to their membership in the labour force.[95]

Contrary to what Fainsod thought in 1955, the role of women within the government and party seems, at least in Kalinin province, to have diminished after a brief period of relative prominence before and during the war. Before the war some women were quickly promoted as a result of the decimation of party ranks in the purges. In June 1937, eleven out of eighty-six obkom members had been women, and in July

1938, twelve out of fifty-eight.[96] In 1945, only three out of seventy-three obkom members were women, and by September 1952, a mere ten out of ninety-three were females. In July 1951, the first raikom secretary of Orshinskii raion, Belikova, pointed out that she was appointed to her leading position only after the Central Committee had started to exert pressure to appoint more women in higher positions in the party. It is evident, once more, that lofty principles did not translate into practical changes.

A telling example of the male view of the proper relationship between the sexes is embedded in remarks made by an obkom member in 1949 about the behaviour of party leaders' wives. He grieved over the fact that these women were not involved in any kind of useful occupation, their idleness rendering them philistines, compromising their husbands. He accused them of having become petty bourgeois, solely interested in the material perks and privileges of their husbands' posts. He hoped that "our responsible workers [will] put their spouses in [their] place in such a way that they will not compromise them and that they will be good helpers; that they will behave themselves in the way that a communist's and important worker's wife should."[97] These words show how the idea of gender equality, already advocated by Marx and Engels, was superseded by more traditional bias. Women had to avoid being petty bourgeois, but they were also told how to comport themselves fittingly so as to complement their spouses. Among many married couples, it was a mark of prestige when the husband earned enough to keep his wife at home. Even today – understandably, considering labour conditions and remuneration – many Russian women would rather be homemakers than sweep streets, work at the conveyor belt, or even teach children.[98] The opposite alternative of men attending to the household and women providing income was alien to the Russians.

The above complaint elucidates, meanwhile, the fact that wives of leading obkom members were able to stay at home, achieving the desired status so contrary to the original Communist ideal. This "idle" contingent was lamented after the war for the more specific economic reason of labour shortage: the number of housewives (domokhoziaiki) in the towns was tongue-lashed more than once. In October 1953 a kolkhoz chairman stated that it was unfair that country women had to perform heavy physical labour even if they had a number of children or were quite old, inasmuch as many women, sometimes educated as agricultural specialists – for which the state had paid – preferred to be homemakers, in some cases even without having to rear children.[99]

The abrupt influence of the law that rendered divorces more difficult in 1944 is reflected in table 8 (chapter 2).[100] The effect of the postwar euphoria and of the return of the Red Army soldiers can be seen in the rise of marriages from May 1945 onwards. The marriage rate was the highest in the *winter* of 1945–46, which indicates the continued popularity of the traditional time for weddings in the countryside – and perhaps even in the towns, inasmuch as many townspeople had grown up partially in the countryside. As well, after Stalin's collectivization the wintertime saw fewer economic activities in the village. Because of the economic benefits that a double income would provide, it seems that most women outside the elite continued to pine for the security of marriage: indeed, single mothers could hardly make ends meet. The shortage of men, however, prevented many young women from realizing this ideal after 1945.

In early 1949, at the seventh party conference, a brief effort was undertaken to pay more attention to the plight of women in the oblast'.[101] Astashina, the raion secretary of the Zavolzh'e raion of Kalinin, revealed a certain awareness among women of the injustice of the meagre representation of women in positions of power. The tradition of female revolutionaries such as Perovskaia, Zasulich, Figner, Krupskaia, and Kollontai had not been entirely forgotten.[102] Apparently, in early 1949 only three women were first raikom secretaries in the oblast'; none were chairs of a raiispolkom; no obkom department was headed by a woman; and there was no female secretary of the gorkom of Kalinin. This situation led Astashina to make the following comments:

I will mention three figures for our raion. In our schools work 237 teachers, 200 of whom are women. 49 people work as doctors, 36 of them are women. Of secondary-educated medical personnel there are 151, 128 of whom are women. At the railroad passenger-car works, 40.6 percent of the work force is female. Of the 146 women who are part of the engineering and technical staff, 24 work in leading positions. This indicates that women are seldom promoted to leading work.

The party's oblast' committee does not instruct the party's raikoms to improve the work with women and to promote women to leading work.

The report of comrade Vorontsov [who had given the report on the province's situation and its Party organization earlier at the same meeting] is an example of the fact that the oblast' committee pays poor attention to this problem, since he said literally two words about women. But in my opinion women in our Kalinin oblast' are not the last spoke in the wheel. Women are remembered on 8 March [International Women's Day, a holiday in the USSR], and then forgotten again. On 8 March, they are elected to a presidium, a few women are mentioned who have been promoted to leading party work and are the best production workers; after this, they are again forgotten for the remainder of the year ...

We have them [women who are capable of fulfilling senior positions], but no effort is undertaken for their benefit. They try to get rid of a woman who has been promoted ...

We also have other occasions of women who are kept at one and the same position in the party organization for ten to twelve years and are never promoted further ...

Thus at the party conference of the town of Kalinin, women were entered on the list of those who wanted to speak; only one did. At the beginning of this oblast' party conference, we have elected the leading committees of the conference. Women were not in the mandate commission, nor in the secretariat, nor in the editorial committee.[103]

Astashina then explained that the party should pay attention to the peculiar problems of women in higher positions.[104] All female raion secretaries shared the additional responsibility of rearing several children. Because of this extra burden, their lives were much more complicated than the lives of men in similar posts.

In 1949 some of the more perceptive provincial leaders realized that more than lip service had to be paid to women or that, at least, the party needed to do a better job at pretending to cater to women's plight. Blatant discrimination might lead to sullen resentment, which would harm an economy so desperately dependent on women's labour. Astashina's remarks signified the beginning of an abortive attempt to improve matters: in the course of 1949 the situation of women was discussed at several levels in Kalinin province. On 17 July 1949 a group of at least sixteen leading female party workers of the town of Kalinin met to exchange views on the problem; Astashina was among them.[105] The complaints heard here echoed those voiced by Astashina at the party conference. Thus one Lebedeva lamented the early hour (five o'clock in the afternoon) that day-care facilities were closing.[106] Apparently unable to imagine that men could also do some of these chores, she found it unfair that no one seemed to allow time for women to complete "female household tasks." Voevodina presented a more radical perspective: why was it that, after the war, so many women were banished to make way for men? Had not women proven themselves to be equal to the task? Indeed, had they not actually served better than many men in the same positions? Astashina elaborated on her earlier criticisms. She noticed that pregnant women were sometimes forced to work at night or made to carry loads of forty or fifty kilograms; as a result many had to abandon their work. She also grieved the fact that women were coming to her to seek help because their boyfriends had left them upon discovering that they had become prospective fathers. Bobrova had read in the paper that a special department for work among women had been created in the Ukraine. This she thought was a very good idea, apparently unaware of the previously ubiquitous existence of departments for women's affairs in the USSR.[107]

War widows and women who had lost their homes in Kalinin in 1941 often experienced difficulties in securing a decent apartment.[108] Newly completed apartments were not given as quickly to single women with children as they were to families composed of men, women, and children. Thus Ginsburg, present at the discussion in July 1949, had already been living for four years in one room with another woman who was not related to her, and Ginsburg was said to be suffering in silence. Another woman apparently lived with eight people in an apartment of sixteen square metres. In Vyshnii Volochek this kind of acute housing shortage was said to be rather common.

Many women could not afford to send their children to the expensive day care centres.[109] Despite the fact that the large majority of young mothers worked, day-care facilities in the seven largest provincial towns were few, having room only for between 7 percent and 20 percent of all children in each town. Incongruously, even in the larger towns many day-care facilities were not fully occupied in 1948.[110] An increase in fees had caused some women to take their children out of the day-care centres. In addition, some children transferred to kindergartens, while other children were reared at home because their mothers had stopped working. In rural areas very few day-care centres were available. Here, relatives took care of the children, although the rural elite might have had a nanny. The survey revealed that many women preferred their children to be brought up by a relative, in most cases by a grandmother.[111]

When someone lacked relatives, the situation could become extraordinarily difficult. In 1949 the sickly villager Zhukova could not take care of her three children, who went around hungry, barefoot, and so badly dressed that the oldest two did not attend school.[112] Malnutrition had given the youngest one rickets. Zhukova's private belongings consisted of one goat, a house without windows in which the floor had caved in at some spots, and a decrepit stove; she possessed neither enough beds nor adequate bedding. The executive of the collective farm of which Zhukova was a member had completely neglected her living circumstances.

Zhukova's experience shows the kind of abject poverty that existed sporadically in Kalinin province after the war. The careless attitude of the kolkhoz leadership and the kolkhozniks themselves towards one of their own is proof not only of the plight of widows from the war, collectivization, and the purges, but also of the dissolution of the social fabric that existed in the village before collectivization. In the past the villagers would have tried to support the needy people like Zhukova and her family. Their indifference may have been the result of their heavy personal burdens. Perhaps the kolkhozniks had decided out of sheer necessity to ignore her. Someone who did not work on the kolkhoz did not contribute to meeting the extremely high delivery quotas on which kolkhoz income depended. The obligatory labour for the trudodni and the cultivation of private plots – as well as the care for personal cattle – might have been so time-consuming that no one was able to worry about the unfortunate Zhukova.

On 22 July 1949 the obkom issued a resolution on the situation of women and established some measures to improve their fate within Kalinin province, including measures to improve their conditions of work.[113] Some shops in the larger towns were to remain open in the evenings. The number of consultation points for women was increased, to give them more opportunity to visit a doctor for specifically female concerns. It transpired soon after that several rural raikoms ignored the obkom resolution entirely.[114] In fact, nowhere in the province did authorities undertake a genuine effort to ensure the promotion of more women to leading work. A female obkom instructor who reported in January 1950 to the obkom on the effect of the resolution concluded that it should be executed more vigorously. Judging from women's weak presence in the obkom in the autumn of 1952, however, their position in practice did not improve.

During 1950, more detailed reports on the working situation of women were filed by urban and raion party committees.[115] Most measures designed to alleviate women's working conditions and status were restricted by the productive exigencies of industry and agriculture. Here and there, women with young children were relieved from night shifts, while more facilities for personal hygiene were created at industrial enterprises, and more medical checkups were conducted. Female workers were also attending lectures on menstruation, abortion (always cast in a negative light), cancer, and children's diseases. The reports often tried to stress the successful fulfillment of tasks set by socialist emulation, betraying the main reason for the sudden concern for women on behalf of the party.

The party's records leave the distinct impression that the postwar status of women did not improve in rural areas either. Even in 1943, less than 30 percent of kolkhoz chairs had been women.[116] This compared favourably to the 9 percent before June 1941, but the rise of women to managerial positions in the countryside was remarkably restricted; in 1943, 1,042 of the 7,942 kolkhoz chairs were war invalids, who seem to have been preferred over women. After the war, the gains of women proved temporary. In September 1951 the male chair of the raiispolkom of Zubtsov bemoaned the disappearance of all-female tractor brigades after the war.[117] He deemed this development counterproductive, since so few men were left on the collective farms and since women had proven themselves to be equal to the task during and directly after the war.

Public discussion of sexual relations was taboo after the war; within the classified documents of the party's archives in Tver' one can find little of it. A rather strange incident demonstrates the prudish official mentality prevailing in Stalin's Russia.[118] In 1949 a male employee of the raion procuracy of Udoml'ia accused a schoolteacher of having a lesbian relationship with her school's director.[119] He claimed to have compelling evidence proving that the director was a "hermaphrodite." According to him, she had become the talk of the town and her behaviour had a pernicious influence on the school's pupils. After the state attorney had called in the schoolteacher for questioning, the first raion secretary, the veteran party worker Glazunova, interfered. She summoned the lawyer to her office and, according to him, called him a scoundrel and a spineless creature and gave him a severe reprimand. The prosecutor asked for a transfer after this episode. Glazunova's seniority may have saved the schoolteacher and the director: seemingly, the case was not taken over by the secret police.

The documents on the affair reveal the authorities' tremendous sense of embarassment with the case. The obkom, ultimately, upheld Glazunova's reprimand to the attorney. The provincial secretariat preferred not to interfere in as delicate an affair as this. Lesbianism was not a topic, apparently, with which the obkom secretaries wanted to be confronted. Glazunova was a purge survivor and one of very few women who had a long career as raion chief in Kalinin province. Even though the story shows that she wielded sufficient authority before the obkom to thwart the efforts of the junior prosecutor, somehow she was never promoted to a higher position than first raion secretary. Prevented from becoming part of the all-male obkom buro, she seems to have been another victim, like many of the other women previously encountered, of the tacit antifemale bias prevalent in the postwar Communist Party.

Although it is probably true that the quality of education deteriorated after the October Revolution, the number of students taught certainly increased, albeit only after 1929. From this year onward, hardly any children did not receive at least the basic four years of general school-ing.[120] Even in 1992, however, two women were interviewed in Tver' who had remained illiterates all their lives, while another two were encountered who had enjoyed merely two years of education as adults.[121] Even in the heart of Russia the Communist education offen-sive was not all-encompassing after 1917.

During the war many children in the countryside enjoyed even less schooling than their counterparts of the 1930s, who often completed a mere five or six years of grade school.[122] The difficult situation of the war prevented them from attending more than three or four grades in which the level of teaching was often mediocre. Only in September 1949 did the seven-year curriculum became obligatory. Thus incum-bents of senior positions in the 1940s, such as kolkhoz chairs, had usually benefited from no more than six years of schooling. Most of the provincial elite, composed almost exclusively of party members, could not boast of a superior education.[123]

The paltry educational level of the Russians in Stalin's time is further underlined by a report of 1948 by the local military authorities to the oblast' sekretariat. In the previous year 16,555 young males born in 1929 had undergone medical and aptitude tests in order to establish whether they were fit for army service.[124] Forty-three had turned out to be illiterate, while 1,094 had been classified as semiliterate, for they had attended school for three years or less. The war only partially interfered with the education of this levy: most of the boys of the 1929 levy should already have been close to the completion of the fourth grade by June 1941. The military commissar of Kalinin province, Cherniak, concluded that the lack of literacy among conscripts was caused predominantly by inadequate control and supervision of school attendance and of schoolwork. Indeed, quite a few semiliterates came from the east of the province, which had never been occupied by the Germans. The incidence of illiteracy and semiliteracy was higher in the countryside than in the towns. If the literacy numbers for male conscripts are added to the traditional lower attendance of girls at schools in rural areas, the proportion of semiliterates and illiterates must have hovered around 10 percent among provincial youth in the 1940s.[125]

The value of learning is certainly recognized by almost all older Rus-sians today, even if they have not enjoyed much education themselves. Their appreciation of education might have increased since Stalinist times, but there is sufficient evidence to suggest that as young adults in the 1940s and early 1950s they held quite different views than their parents about its value.[126] Already before the introduction of the oblig-atory seven-year curriculum, many children were completing at least seven years of school, especially in urban areas. The Russians had begun to recognize that education was becoming a sine qua non for moving up the social ladder. If they were incapable of improving their own education, they could at least attempt to have their children educated. A swift drop of truancy after the war resulted from this more modern perception of the value of education by parents: in the school year 1946–47, 3,548 children of school age did not attend grades one to four; in 1947–48, 1,717.[127] In certain cases, however, destitution was the ground for children's absence in the classroom: schools had to aid children by giving them meals, shoes, and clothes. Although the provincial education network worked reasonably smoothly by 1951, some school-age children still did not attend classes.[128]

The quality of tutelage varied, but it is clear that children were inculcated with strong feelings of patriotism. One secondary-school pupil in the remote district of Lesnoe wrote in an essay:

We survived many scarcities and difficulties, many bitter losses and serious sacrifices. And we know our future is not a smooth road, but a prickly and difficult path, but at the same time we – the Soviet people – do not fear any scarcities and difficulties, and they do not stop us. All my strength and knowledge I will give to you, my Motherland! And when it is necessary, I will find the strength in myself to give you my life as well! To give one's life to the Motherland, to the people: that is the greatest happiness.[129]

Schools and teachers were better in the towns than in the country, where the quality of education was often hampered by shoddy maintenance of school buildings, scarcity of educational tools, and the like.[130] V.P. Krylov attended four grades of primary school in the war years in Udoml'ia raion. He found learning difficult because of his chronically empty stomach, while his school lacked notebooks, so that pupils sometimes wrote on newspapers, between the printed lines. After the war, these impediments disappeared only gradually. By 1948 it was still too cold in many schools in remote localities, while school furniture remained insufficient. Occasionally, glass shielded but a small part of school windows, blackboards were broken in classrooms, or lighting (by electricity or the far more prevalent kerosene lamps) was poor. Not only were educational results modest as a result, but children's physical development was thus endangered, too, according to school inspection reports.

Teachers in the countryside functioned as the "transmission belt" of the culture of the outside world to the village children. Nevertheless, still by 1959 and 1960 rural teachers' qualifications were noticeably lower than those of their urban colleagues.[131] The isolation of many rural areas and the time spent taking care of personal plots hindered educators from updating their skills.

Within the province, the most renowned seat of higher learning was the Pedagogical Institute of Kalinin. The life of its faculty was not easy after the war. According to the director of the institute, Polianskii, about sixty lecturers were living in students' dormitories in communal apartments (obshchezhitie).[132] This housing was apparently so appalling that many of the best teachers left the institute in 1950 and 1951, saying that they had never seen "such a poor attitude towards scientific cadres": in Kursk and Voronezh the teaching staff had received apartments long before. In 1946 and 1947, six apartments had been promised to the Pedagogical Institute, but five years later only three had been provided.

The provincial government had to deal with a dearth of means here as elsewhere. The housing situation of lecturers was simply not a priority. It is indicative of the situation that in 1992 a professor of the State University of Tver' (the successor to the Pedagogical Institute) was living with his wife, a music teacher in Tver', and two children in a two-room apartment of perhaps twenty-five square metres. The walls and doors on the inside seemed to have been made from a kind of cardboard. Not much improvement had been made in the forty-odd years after Polianskii's complaints.

Education at all levels was in poor shape in the province. Even at the treasured factory schools, the results fell far below expectations, as the following account indicates: "the labour production discipline of young workers, who have entered the FZO [factory] schools of the town of Kalinin, is characterized by the following facts: in 1951 alone, at No.7 of the light-industry system, in the Proletarskii raion of the town of Kalinin, fifty graduates quit their jobs without authorization, and in the first quarter of 1952, another thirteen out of the 116 that were in the program. These sixty-three people were convicted by a people's judge. Unauthorized departure of FZO schools' graduates out of the light industry training system was 54.3%."[133]

Life in the towns of Kalinin was fraught with extreme difficulties during the last years of Stalin's life. The Russians had to forego "Western comforts" in housing, clothing, and nutrition.[134] For most urban workers and employees remuneration for their legal employment allowed only a Spartan existence. Few fully accepted living exclusively on this bare minimum, and many used semilegal or illegal means to obtain some luxuries. Some attempted to add something to their meagre incomes by domestic craft (sweater knitting, shoe repairing, carpentry, and the like), exploiting the constant scarcity of consumers' goods. This strategy was risky, however, for it exposed them to the constant danger of either denunciation by an envious or politically zealous neighbour or a sudden decision of authorities to dress down those who worked on the side. Others spent their leisure hours on the market garden they had been allowed. Communist Party members at lower levels tried to exploit their privileges, which increased with promotion in the ranks. Many worked overtime, though the eight-hour workday was the official norm. It goes without saying that, regardless of gender, every adult had to work to keep afloat. Women were in a more disadvantageous position than men; if they had lost their husbands, it was hardly possible to make ends meet on their anemic wages. Married or single, mothers were stooping under the double burden of holding a full-time job and running a household. Most urban parents saw a vicarious way out of hardships by having their offspring complete at least seven years of general education and, preferably, more than that. While education was not as good a key to high social status as the possession of a party card, it nonetheless gave access to more opportunities in life.

To sum up, the picture of urban life in the immediate postwar period in Kalinin province is bleak. The sacrifices made before 1945 had been extreme, and the deprivations continued after the war. Only a few zealots seem to have been able to recognize in the general squalor that prevailed the contours of the proletarian paradise promised by the Communist gospel. The majority of urban dwellers ceased to believe that this dream could be realized. As a result of a quarter century of destitution and of promises broken by the regime, popular enthusiasm had dissipated too much to restore the belief in the imminent arrival of the classless society of plenty, despite some efforts made in this direction during Khrushchev's tenure as party leader.

CHAPTER SEVEN

The Countryside: Economy and Society

Life in the towns was hard after the war, but living conditions in the countryside under Stalin were worse. We have already seen some signs of the collapse of the social fabric in the villages as a result of collectivization, as well as the appalling state of education in some rural areas. The Marxist creed held that "the building of communism [would] eliminate the essential distinctions between town and countryside," but the difference between life in town and countryside remained palpable, and may have sharpened, under Stalin.[1] The amalgamation of the smaller collective farms in 1950 into bigger units did not make urban and rural existence more alike. Most Russians with some ability and ambition declined to reside in the villages. Rural dwellers abandoned farming in droves. The drop in the number of agricultural workers caused by the war was therefore never overcome. Instead, every year at harvest time, and sometimes during other periods when agricultural activity was at its height, collective farms had to rely on the temporary assistance of outsiders.

THE COLLECTIVE FARMS

Proletarskaia Pravda ran a leading article in July 1945 on the kolkhoz Krasnoe Trosukhino, where agricultural labour at harvest time was organized in an exemplary, rational, and efficient way.[2] The obkom-buro and newspaper editor habitually used the provincial newspaper as a tool to ameliorate farm operations by bombarding the readership with his type of educative reading material, highlighting the importance of the proper organization of agricultural endeavours and an accompanying positive attitude on the part of the collective farmers. These pieces were partially fictional, but not as far removed from daily reality in the collective farms that kolkhoz executives could not identify with their substance (and conclude that, following this recipe, the party demanded the same kind of flawless organization from them, too).

The reader of the article was informed how Krasnoe Trosukhino had overcome a shortage of workhands at harvest time.[3] Two zven'ia, each made up of twelve women, had been formed, after which fifteen kolkhoz members whose daily routines usually did not include fieldwork (the bookkeeper, the chair, the storage keeper, some livestock herders, and some milkers) were enlisted to help, as well as an additional thirty-six people found in the environs of the farm: twenty-three school children and thirteen elderly kolkhoz members, seventy-five people altogether. The work force was still considered too small, however, so the kolkhoz requested a nearby orphanage to lend another twenty teenagers. When daily tasks were distributed, twenty-eight people were assigned to harvest with sickles, and thirty-eight received lighter tasks, such as pulling seed vessels from flax stalks. Twenty draught horses were available, while carts were deployed to transport harvested crops. Two MTS tractors were hired, one to pull a threshing machine, the other to aid in sowing winter grains and ploughing the land for the following spring sowing.

This inventive use of scarce resources had made the harvest a success, if one believed the news item. Indeed, if all collective farms had been able to acquit themselves as well of their assigned tasks as Krasnoe Trosukhino in 1945, postwar crop cultivation and animal husbandry in Kalinin province would have been an outstanding example, fit for emulation throughout the Soviet Union. Somehow this was not the case during the later years of Stalin's life, however.

Rather more typical than the flawless collective farm paraded in *Proletarskaia Pravda* was information about developments in the same month in Kozlovo raion, east of Vyshnii Volochek, a district that had been spared German occupation.[4] This information did not make headlines in the newspaper; it was intended only for some of the higher party potentates, including the obkomburo membership. It transpired that on a number of kolkhozes the kolkhozniks started their workday late, while enjoying long breaks for lunch. The result was that in 1944, out of 217 organized production links (zven'ia), only 130 survived until the end of the agricultural season. Only five links received additional payment for deliveries of state procurements above the obligatory norms. The kolkhozniks neglected the horses and other livestock that were the property of their collectives, causing many animals to perish; meanwhile, some farmers had acquired an illegal pair of cows for personal use, and others had stopped doing kolkhoz work altogether and had taken up private farming. In Kozlovo raion 195 private farms that used kolkhoz land and kolkhoz pastures for their cattle somehow avoided taxation! The obkomburo urged the raion authorities to use severe measures to bring these practices to a halt. These instances of "civil disobedience" were not unique for Kozlovo raion. The large number of private farms shows that, more than ten years after collectivization, a defiant spirit was still alive among many peasants.[5]

· Besides the severe bloodletting of the war, the shortage of work hands was caused by the sustained departure of rural dwellers for the towns and cities, a phenomenon that will be discussed in greater depth in the next chapter.[6] The preponderant need for manual labour on the kolkhozy worsened the consequences of this scarcity. Moreover, far from all rural residents participated in socialist agriculture as members of a collective or state farm, although Soviet statistical handbooks falsely claimed that all agriculture had been collectivized in 1945.[7] As I noted, some individuals purposely withdrew from the collectives, while every year other artel' members were excluded from collective farms for failing to meet their obligations. These former members of the cooperative then tried to survive on their own little plots of land, which were heavily taxed by the state. It might be true that by 1945 all the peasantry of Kalinin province had belonged to a collective farm at some point in time, but many peasants survived outside the collective and state farming system and concentrated exclusively on the private plot to which they were entitled.[8] In formerly occupied raions, the plot was just large enough to allow for a precarious survival by way of cultivating cereals and technical crops (primarily flax) and by tending to private livestock. Furthermore, in spite of all manner of legislation against employment in nonagricultural occupations in the countryside, many rural inhabitants shunned the collective farms by working, for example, in small rural factories, industrial cooperatives, or for the government.

In August 1945 a joint resolution of oblispolkom and obkom reiterated Boitsov's criticism of a few months before concerning the insufficient progress that had been made in reviving farming in several of the formerly occupied raions.[9] People were still sometimes housed in dugouts (zeml'ianki) or in buildings adapted for temporary housing, or they shared a house with more than one family. Kolkhoz livestock lacked adequate shelter, since the building of stables and the like in the unoccupied areas was deficient, and farm animals, in particular young cattle, were lost as a result. The collective farms suffered from a plethora of problems with (re)building: a failure to organize permanent construction brigades, a lack of local building materials such as bricks, and a shortage of labour to assist the kolkhozy with construction.

Perhaps one way in which the countryside compared favourably to the towns was that the housing shortage in the countryside was less severe. Many of the former inhabitants of the German-occupied area never returned home after the war, while a constant stream of rural dwellers departed for the towns. This exodus increased particularly after 1949, which further lessened the strain on rural housing. *Proletarskaia Pravda* announced in November 1947 that every kolkhoznik had left the dug-outs and lived, once again, in a real house.[10] It should be pointed out, however, that several young adults (including married couples) lived in their parents' houses in the villages.

Comprehensive execution of construction plans on the collective farms, meanwhile, remained the exception. The authorities, in effect, had little to do with the resurrection of peasant domiciles: most rural dwellers built their houses themselves, with or without aid of relatives, neighbours, or even hired hands. A.E. Vakhmistrov said in the survey that he found enough trees in his neighbourhood in Udoml'ia raion for him and his brother, both sufficiently skilled carpenters, to build a house. Rural houses looked much as they did in the 1920s; V.K. Stepanov lived in the 1940s in his parental home, which he described as "a hut with three windows, a Russian stove, an inner porch, a farm-yard and a toilet – in the yard [that is, an outhouse]."

In order to restore delapidated or destroyed farm buildings and houses, kolkhozy were forced to hire so-called shabashniki, illegal itinerant artisans.[11] It seemed impossible to eradicate shabashniki, and they certainly filled a niche in this period. S.V. Kudriashov, who lost a limb during the war in 1941 and was thus officially an invalid, went back to work at a furniture factory after his return from the front. He said in the survey that even with his severe handicap he managed to do some carpentry, for which he frequently was paid with vodka, samogon, or food instead of money. He noted that one worked from early in the morning until late at night on these jobs. When he was hired by the state, he worked no more than the legal norm – often eight hours. The folly of planning mania made the authorities resign themselves to this type of concession and other improvisations within the agricultural sector. During the war, organizations, enterprises, and factories had been allowed to have their own subsidiary state and collective farms (the obkom itself had one in Avvakumovo, just northeast of Kalinin), some of which were maintained after the war.[12] Regular supply of essential foodstuffs for the labour force of the enterprise or organization was more or less guaranteed through a combination of produce from the subsidiary farm and goods provided by the distribution system.

In October 1946 Boitsov explained to Central Committee secretary

Patolichev why grain procurements did not proceed satisfactorily: inclement weather and the simultaneous task of potato picking were to blame.[13] Potato picking had begun earlier than the year before, in order to avoid the loss incurred by the late potato harvesting. On 1 October 1946 only 1,213 kolkhozy out of a total of 7,032 had effectuated the plan for grain procurements, and by this date 3,023 had not even met 65 percent of total deliveries, as required by the plan. The authorities, true to form, suspected foul play, but "wrecking" was not involved, for only at 174 collective farms had cases of grain squandering been uncovered. The harvest could be saved only by overcoming the labour shortage in a radical way: in order to ensure sufficient assistance for the harvesting and procurements, 62,000 town dwellers had been sent into the countryside in the preceding weeks, while trucks had been mobilized in the towns to aid with the agricultural work; this support for the anemic farms proved ultimately successful and saved most of the grain harvest.[14] Deployment of town dwellers at harvest time became the rule after the war, because kolkhozniks could not cope with the exceptional amount of work in that period. In 1947, between 42,000 and 54,000 inhabitants of towns, workers' settlements, and raion centres were helping daily with gathering crops. However, industrial performance suffered from town dwellers' prolonged absence from home.

In 1950 the obkom even ordered what were considered to be too many people into the countryside in certain areas: on one day in October the town of Vyshnii Volochek was obliged to transport 10,000 people into rural regions by car, about one-sixth of its population.[15] Factories had to interrupt the operation of certain workshops. This extremely high mobilization was one of the consequences of the disorganization within the collective farms after amalgamation. Meanwhile, Matveev, gorkom secretary of Vyshnii Volochek, argued in 1951 that this outside help had a negative effect on the kolkhozniks. Townspeople, he said, were already beginning to assist with sowing and weeding. On the same occasion, however, the raikom secretary of Zubtsov, Tychinin, claimed that aid from town dwellers was essential for successful agricultural operations: Zubtsov raion had to plant a larger area than before the war, while its labour force had been drastically diminished by the havoc created by German occupation. Matveev criticized Konovalov in 1951 for failing to maintain a proper balance between agriculture and industry. This criticism was another part of the operation to make Konovalov the scapegoat for the many difficulties beleaguering Kalinin province during the early 1950s. Konovalov left, but his departure did not solve the problem of labour shortage in the province.

Towns and factories had offered help (shefstvo) to collective farms and tractor stations in the countryside since the 1930s. They had furnished spare parts, repairs, new equipment and tools – as well as help at harvest time. The value of this latter practice was rather limited, however, as gorkom secretary Baranov of Kalinin admitted in 1953, for it had not led to any fundamental improvement of kolkhoz operations.[16]

Labour shortage was only one of several problems marring the development of postwar agriculture. After 1953 Soviet publications did not even try to deny that the situation of Soviet agriculture in the immediate postwar period was close to desperate.[17] In Kalinin province grain growing, flax cultivation, and animal husbandry did not present satisfactory results for more than two consecutive years between 1945 and 1953. The following discussion of the problems in these areas will attempt to indicate the plethora of reasons behind the poor results. First we should turn our attention to the regime's typical efforts to improve the operation of the socialized sector of pastoral and arable farming.

In August 1945 obkom and oblispolkom issued a resolution to condemn the practice of squandering cattle on the side. It was evident that this habit had become extensive, because in July of the same year the number of strong-horned cattle in the province fell by 11,863 head, of which only 3,000 were delivered to the state as part of meat procurements. The rest were squandered.[18] In some raions people went as far as to sell off, or slaughter for their own consumption, oxen that were supposed to substitute for the scarce workhorses and tractors. The slaughtering occurred more particularly in areas that had suffered damage in the war and were thus more in need of oxen. In September 1945 part of the problem was attributed to disorganization prevailing within the provincial and raion offices of the cattle procurement organization (zagotskot).[19]

In 1946 pastoral farming proved to be deficient in all respects: very few milkmaids or herdsmen received extra payment for overfulfilling the plan for milking or breeding cattle in the early part of the year. Apart from that, herds of all sorts of livestock and poultry in the socialist sector of the collective farms dwindled in the drought year 1946.[20] Plans thereafter, too, consistently called for high levels of milk production by the socialized herds (levels that were to surpass by far the production of kolkhozniks' privately owned animals). These plans were never met in Stalin's lifetime. Instead, the greatest share of milk production came from individual kolkhozniks' cows.[21]

In early 1947 the successful acquittal of the obligations of cereal deliveries to the state led to a diminished share of grain for the kolkhozniks as pay for their labour.[22] At one in twenty kolkhozy in the province no grain at all was given out to the farm labourers. At other farms only minimal amounts were parcelled out. Therefore, even in Kalinin oblast', although the drought failed to reach the damaging levels that other areas experienced, malnutrition and even starvation may have ensued. In chapter 8, the poor remuneration after 1947 will be further explained; for now, suffice it to say that members of agricultural cooperatives continuously received minimal pay in money and in kind for labour performed in the socialized sector of the farms.

Instead of trying to improve agricultural performance by offering better remuneration for kolkhozniks' labour, the Central Committee and the USSR Council of Ministers decided to issue a resolution in September 1946 which aimed at reallocation of means available within the kolkhozy.[23] In the Central Committee's opinion, many trudodni were awarded to individuals who were not directly engaged in farming: orders were given to cut them off from these additional sources of income.[24] The use of kolkhoz lands by kolkhozniks or members of the kolkhoz executive for private purposes above the legally allowed norms (or by local authorities and others who were not entitled to these lands at all) was additionally condemned. As a supplement to this resolution, the obkom and oblispolkom in Kalinin reiterated its contents in a joint resolution of 19 September 1946.[25]

The resolution of the Central Committee and Sovmin (Council of Ministers) was a sign to start a serious crackdown on the moderate amount of freedom that agriculture had been allowed during and since the war. For example, in the autumn of 1946, at meetings of the party aktiv of several raions, provincial and raion courts and the procuracy were criticized for being too lenient towards violations of the kolkhoz Ustav.[26] Firefighters, mail carriers, and others lost the additional remuneration of a few trudodni. The trudodni of others were whittled down. A concrete example illustrates the abuse that irked the Central Committee and Sovmin:

At the meeting of the party aktiv in Nerl' raion, the director of the food kombinat, comrade Kuznetsov, spoke about the fact that many leading workers of the raion had been involved in extorting the kolkhozy; thus the Upolminzag[raion plenipotentiary of the Ministry of Procurements], comrade Petushkov, took 3,000 tons of potatoes of the kolkhoz Krasnyi Pakhar without paying; the head of the MGB, comrade Rozanov, bought a cow for 1,080 rubles. The former raikom secretary comrade Martynov and the head of the raion agricultural department Bashinov each took a suckling pig without paying. The prosecutor Dmitriev placed his horse on the lands of the kolkhoz Niva to have it graze there.

Upolminzag comrade Petushkov pointed out that last year prosecutor Dmitriev mowed hay, which he sold in the spring for market prices. The head of the ispolkom department for mobilization, comrade Baranov, took without paying a sheep from the kolkhoz Michurin in 1945.[27]

Recriminations began to ricochet everywhere. Local party organizations were once more engaged in a frenzy of denunciations, reminiscent of the years 1937 and 1938. The Central Committee had wanted to reestablish strict adherence to prewar rules in the countryside with the resolution. It certainly succeeded in making clear that certain practices allowed during the war would no longer be tolerated. Thus, in Lukovnikovo raion the discussions of the resolution showed that two factions existed within the raikomburo.[28] The MGB chief, Severov, was pitted against the chair of the raiispolkom, Iamshchikov. Severov accused the latter of allowing people guilty of criminal negligence to come off scot-free and of trumping up the books. Iamshchikov admitted that Severov's criticism was justified, but wanted to bring the criticism before the upcoming party conference of the raion. This Iamshchikov had attended the second oblast' party conference in June 1937, when he failed to get elected as candidate obkom member.[29] He must have become rather nervous about Severov's accusations, for he had witnessed the avalanche of arrests perpetrated by the NKVD among party leaders in the purges.

At the end of October 1946 Boitsov was able to notify Central Committee secretary Zhdanov that 4,397 hectares of land, previously misappropriated, had been returned to the collective farms.[30] More than a thousand people not involved in agricultural production had been taken off the payroll of the kolkhozy. Furthermore, the remuneration of kolkhoz administrative and executive staff had been pared down. By March 1947, 59,230 cases of utilization of kolkhoz land for purposes other than collective farming proper in 4,095 kolkhozy (out of a total of 7,003 that had been inspected) had been registered.[31] Payment of trudodni had been halted to incumbents of 1,892 superfluous staff positions at the kolkhozy and to 5,224 people on kolkhoz payrolls who did not work on the collective farms. Furthermore, trudodni had been saved that used to be paid to administrative and service staff above the rate to which they were entitled. As a result 1,645,800 fewer payments of trudodni were made in 1946 than in 1945. Additional hardships descended upon those rural dwellers who were not members of the collective farms, for almost all of them lost their rights to ration cards in the autumn of 1946. Following the usual custom, many of the kolkhoz chairs were held responsible for the various troubles: in 1946, 2,287 (32.4 percent of a total of 7,059) were replaced, and at the annual general meetings of early 1947 another 1,483 negligent chairs were officially deposed (23.3 percent of the total of 6,364).[32]

Thus the resolutions of September 1946 had some success in punishing those abusing the system, but they did not solve the continuing problem of paltry results in the province. The effect of the resolutions proved temporary at best. In March 1952 an inspection was carried out in the province during which widespread violations of the September 1946 resolutions were discovered again: 5,772 hectares of kolkhoz land were used for aims other than collective farming; money had been embezzled everywhere, while 1,334 head of cattle, 554,200 kilograms of grain, 554,000 kilograms of potatoes, and 417,500 litres of milk had been squandered.[33]

On 4 June 1947 the harsh law on criminal responsibility for the theft of state and public property was issued by the Supreme Soviet of the USSR.[34] Penalties for this type of offence increased substantially. As a result, offenders in the dairy industry were slammed with extremely harsh sentences in 1948. The case of the foreman Stepanov and his wife is typical.[35] In exchange for 24,391 rubles they had allegedly embezzled 1,139 kilograms of milk products. Husband and wife were sentenced to ten and seven years of imprisonment, respectively. In the same year other workers in milk factories and procurement organizations were brought to trial as well.

Following Marx, the authorities remained subject to their belief that peasants on the collective farms were conditioned to deceive and shortchange them.[36] The only resulting action was to (threaten to) penalize the peasants ever more harshly for alleged abuses. Undoubtedly kolkhozniks quite often were involved in fraudulent practices, sometimes cheating out of dire necessity or, at other times, trying to improve their Spartan standard of living by outsmarting the authorities. This behaviour, however, was not a consequence of some sort of inherent antagonistic class attitude of peasants towards the proletarian regime. The Russians' latent (or sometimes overt) resentment was provoked by the agricultural policy of party and Soviet government. Party and state bore the responsibility for the continued failure of farming.

The only official postwar Central Committee Plenum before the convocation of the Nineteenth Party Congress (1952) took place in February 1947 and seems to have dealt predominantly with agriculture.[37] The famine that ravaged some areas of the USSR could no longer be ignored. Echoing the September 1946 resolution, the Central Committee called once more upon the provinces to bring the disorganization and illegalities within the collective farms to an end. As soon as the Central Committee Plenum had concluded its deliberations, a plenum of the Kalinin obkom convened to discuss their results. The Central Committee Plenum's resolutions strove to reestablish the (perhaps imaginary) well-controlled and well-organized prewar state of agriculture in a more orderly manner than the resolution of September 1946. The contents differed little in essence. Once again, kolkhoz directors were replaced at a rapid pace in 1947 and 1948, in the hope that this would lead to superior farming yields. Among their successors, quite a few demobilized soldiers were to be found.[38]

Despite the attention given by the highest party ranks to agriculture, the results of 1947 would not be much brighter than those of the previous year in Kalinin province. Problems prevailed from the very start of the agricultural year: when spring sowing began, extra seeds from state reserves could not be provided to kolkhozy experiencing a shortage after fulfilling the extremely high procurement levels of 1946 (for much of the grain stock was used to mitigate the effects of famine in other areas of the Union).[39] First secretary Vorontsov was clearly seething when he told the March 1947 obkom plenum that some better-provided kolkhozy had been using spring-sowing seeds for purposes other than sowing, including the distillation of alcohol for private consumption.

Considering the previous practices of the Communist Party, it is not surprising that on numerous occasions party and state reverted to the threat of force by introducing more severe disciplinary measures for those not meeting their production standards or cheating the authorities in other ways. But even these steps had a barely perceptible effect. By a decree of 2 June 1948 some kolkhozniks were exiled by kolkhoz meetings for their refusal to work honestly in socialist production.[40] As with previous and successive decrees, force was threatened to muster labour discipline for improving performance of collective farms. But only a few individuals were actually punished with exile for shirking socialist responsibilities as a result of the resolution. Most of those culpable pretended to become fully involved in the socialized branch of agriculture. When, at the end of 1948, the head of the agricultural department of the obkom reported on the measures taken on the basis of the decree of 2 June 1948, merely fifty-eight people were reported to have been exiled, while 1,369 households had joined a kolkhoz as a result of the decree.[41]

All these measures contributed little to an increase of labour productivity and better agricultural results. Relations between farmers and authorities were further strained through the glaring flaws of the distribution system, while inadequate means of transport and the poor state of the roads further affected production results negatively. In the areas located further away from the industrial artery along the October

Railroad and in the southeast, enthusiasm for the socialist sector was impaired because these parts hardly ever received their fair share of consumer goods. In 1945, the remoter areas suffered from a paucity of engines (of particular importance for their machine tractor stations), glass, salt, kerosene (for lamps), soap, matches, and sugar and other staples.[42] Supplies remained deficient: in 1951, essential products, such as kerosene and salt, were unavailable in many raions.[43] In the raions of Vyshnii Volochek and Esenovichi in the summer of 1951, collective farmers went without bread.[44]

Often the bases of the sel'khoznabzhenie were accused of theft and squandering of goods and of mismanagement, but there is overwhelming evidence in archival sources that the failure resulted from the organization of the distribution system in general. In one case at least, a kolkhoz in Turginovo raion discontinued its milk deliveries to the state owing to the constant absence of kerosene in the sel'po store.[45] Indeed, Storozhev lamented the flaws in the distribution system as a whole in July 1951.[46]

Another problem gnawing at agricultural output was the lack of adequate transport for procurements, particularly in the more remote areas. In Esenovichi raion in the second half of 1952, the plenipotentiary for the Ministry of Procurements asked the obkom for additional horses to transport state deliveries; the raion's office for milk deliveries possessed the only two motorized vehicles.[47] The slipshod state of roads in most rural areas likewise complicated agricultural transportation. Many kolkhozes were completely isolated from the outside world for long periods in spring and autumn. A late arrival of harvested crops at the delivery points ensued. Combined with the frequent unavailibility of machinery for sowing or reaping, this led to substantial losses of produce.

Perhaps the most embarassing agricultural sector to the leaders, both those in Moscow and those in Kalinin, was that of animal husbandry. In March 1948 the head of the obkom department for livestock, Zhuravlev, was daring enough to set the provincial livestock situation in historical perspective before an obkom plenum.[48] He compared contemporary livestock numbers to those of Tver' guberniia before collectivization. In 1947, he noted, the province had a mere 33 percent of the horses of 1916 and only 24 percent of their number in 1928. In 1916, 741,000 head of strong-horned cattle were counted in the province; in 1928, 890,000; but personal and kolkhoz cattle together amounted only to 602,000 in 1947. Zhuravlev detected a similarly drastic decrease in sheep and hog herds. Whether the obkomburo members were grateful for his candour is unclear, but it cannot have been a secret to most obkom members that animal husbandry lagged behind the level of the 1920s. There is, however, a difference between knowing some inconvenient reality and stating it openly. The minutes of the meeting would be sent to the Central Committee Secretariat in Moscow. They could be welcome ammunition in case the Central Committee decided to criticize the provincial leadership in Kalinin, which included Zhuravlev himself. Zhuravlev probably thought rightly that he was not disclosing any secrets to Moscow: the Central Committee was undoubtedly aware of this unpleasant truth about the live-stock.[49] Despite this embarassing confession, animal husbandry continued to disappoint during 1948, for only the development plan for sheep was met.

Even though the herds did not increase, 1948 was nevertheless the first buoyant postwar year in agriculture: all obligatory state deliveries were apparently met, even for flax.[50] Grain, milk, meat, and flax procurements surpassed those of 1940. Kalinin province's party head, Vorontsov, noticed proudly at the seventh party conference in February 1949 that, for the first time in twelve years, the collective farms had fulfilled the flax procurement plan. Some kolkhozniks were paid extremely well for their trudodni. Despite this, on the whole remarkable, success in 1948, more than eight hundred kolkhozy (that is, more than 10 percent) within the province remained "backward."[51] Nevertheless, for a brief moment it seemed that agriculture might have finally turned the corner. The good performance, so it appeared to the party brass, could only be enhanced by developments in agricultural science: 1948 was the year in which the Soviet leadership believed that it had found an easy panacea for its agricultural ills in the "defeat" of the genetic theory of Weismann-Morgan in biology, which was inspired by T.E. Lysenko. The party informed its agitators of the "triumph" of the biological theories of Michurin in early 1949 in *Bloknot Agitatora*, (which had been published since 1947 to help local propagandists spread the gospel of Communism) announcing that "[i]n 1948 the knockout blow was delivered to the idealist Weismanist-Morganist direction in biology; rejecting the teaching of Michurin on the transfer of acquired properties to succeeding generations of crops and animals, it was a huge hindrance for the development of the theory and practice of socialist crop tillage and animal husbandry. The victory of the Michurinist science was a victory of Marxism-Leninism and its materialistic dialectics."[52]

Could this announcement be comprehensible to the average propagandist? Would he or she be able to explain it to kolkhozniks? Enough has already been said about their education: most did not understand this victory for Soviet science, nor did it lead to any tangible improvements in the field of agriculture. After 1948 farming results in Kalinin province initially levelled out again and then deteriorated sharply. Favourable weather helped to produce yields in 1949 that were almost as good as in the previous year, but the winters of 1950 and 1951 were harsh, while 1952 and 1953 saw excessive rainfall.[53]

The consequences of inclement weather were made much worse by the radical enlargement of the kolkhoz. Before the amalgamation, the size of the collective farms had been small: around 85 percent (6,700) of all kolkhozy possessed less than one hundred head of strong-horned cattle, while 70 percent had less than twenty horses.[54] In early 1950 there were 7,500 kolkhozy in Kalinin province, with an average on each of 35 hearths, 49 able-bodied workers, 62 head of bovines, 17 horses, 22 pigs, 70 sheep, and 410 fowl. In theory, the idea of merging such small kolkhozy in Kalinin province was not without potential.[55] In practice, however, a repetition of some of the crucial mistakes committed during collectivization took place. Peasants once again were basically forced to join the amalgamated kolkhoz. The average kolkhoznik did not exert any influence on the organization of the mergers, which had serious consequences for the subsequent operation of the consolidated farms.

At the beginning of 1951 party and kolkhoz executives admitted that the harvest had been disorganized in 1950, which had caused many crops and much wild grass to be left unreaped.[56] Machine tractor stations were able to fulfill only one assigned task in 1950: the small portion of grain harvesting in which combines were used.[57] In 1950 no kolkhoz complied with the harvest plan for grains, while less than 1 percent did so for flax or milk production. Although it was left unsaid by the flustered authorities, the careless timing and preparation of the consolidation had been responsible. Kolkhoz chairs had already been frequently replaced: a flurry of confusion about the mergers reigned for a long time. In January 1951 Konovalov reported to Malenkov that "[i]n a majority of the collective farms after their merger the crop-tillage brigades have retained their former size, the number of them, as a consequence of the amalgamation, only shrank by 8 percent; the inequality in the distribution of land, work hands, draught power, and equipment among brigades has continued. Because of this, in several amalgamated kolkhozy, agricultural labour is unorganized, and the fulfillment of state plans and tasks is delayed."[58]

Konovalov's reference to the lack of growth of crop brigades hints at another futile farming reform: in 1950 in most forms of crop tillage the larger brigade was supposed to replace the previously popular smaller link (zveno).[59] This measure did not have the desired effect of increasing the size of the brigades in the province, apparently. A notable exception to the reform was the organisation of flax production, where the zven'ia were retained as the most efficient organization of preponderantly manual labour.

Instead of having bumper crops, thanks to the supposed rationalization ensuing from amalgamation, the consolidated collective farms in the Kalinin oblast' lagged behind the plan targets for the three central production sectors. The party's Central Committee believed that this disaster could have been avoided by a more judicious selection of kolkhoz chairs for the enlarged kolkhozy by the obkom and raikoms. Within one year 26 percent (509) of the chosen directors had been dismissed.[60]

The rash reorganization caused an increase in the number of "backward" (otstaiushchie) kolkhozy. On these farms, kolkhozniks were said to survive almost solely thanks to the produce from their private plots, while they derived hardly any income from the socialized sector.[61] By July 1951 this kind of backward collective farm comprised one-quarter of the total number of kolkhozy. By 1952 many kolkhozy had amassed an enormous debt of loans and deferred payments of obligations to the state. Indivisible funds in more than one-third of all kolkhozy had shrunk in 1951 by an average of 40,000 rubles for each kolkhoz. In 1951 more than 9,000 able-bodied adult kolkhozniks failed to work the legal minimum of trudodni, and more than 2,500 did not even work one trudoden'.[62] Every day at one notorious kolkhoz, out of the 270 individuals who should have been on the job, only between 100 and 115 chose to work in the socialized sector. On some collective farms kolkhozniks were paid irrespective of the number of trudodni they had worked. In numerous kolkhozy in September 1952, communal shelter for animals and equipment-storage room fell short and horses, carts, ploughs, or harnesses were kept in the kolkhozniks' private stables and storage sheds.[63] As a result, many kolkhozniks used animals and equipment for their own designs. In 1952 numerous collective farms hired herders, carpenters, or other labourers.[64] Outsiders were hired to do regular agricultural work. In 1952, out of a total of 13,600 who were tending the kolkhoz livestock, 4,500 herders had been hired on the side. Since the amalgamation of two years before, 45 percent of the kolkhoz chairs had already been replaced. Private farming continued in 1952, as Kiselev pointed out to the delegates of the ninth provincial party conference:

In a number of raions of our oblast', as a result of party raikoms fully inadequately conducting political work in the collective farms, a trend towards private property has begun to gain force among the kolkhozniks; this is harmful for the collective-farm system, and this incurs great loss to the socialist farming of the kolkhozy. The trend expresses itself in an extraordinary, exaggerated preference for the private plot to the detriment of socialist farming, as well as in the government-condemned, anti-kolkhoz practice of distribution of monetary income and income in kind by the kolkhozy, in which a significant part of the means is divided among the kolkhozniks for the trudodni, while at the same time little is assigned to the development of the socialist farming of the kolkhozy.[65]

The situation caused the central government to issue once more a resolution in November 1952 condemning the violations in Kalinin province of the collective-farm statute.[66] Notwithstanding the uninterrupted stream of orders emanating from the centre, 1952 was an extremely wretched year for the province's agriculture. Only three of 1,900 kolkhozy were honoured by the obkomburo for the full discharge of all obligations. Even the otherwise exemplary Bezhetsk raion was unable to fulfill all preconditions and obligations to be eligible for praise from the obkom and oblispolkom, and missed out on the Order of the Red Banner with which it had been regularly awarded previously.

Central and provincial party chiefs designated flax cultivation and animal husbandry as the mainstay of provincial agriculture, but during the early 1950s flax yields remained disappointing, while, despite a grandiose three-year development plan for animal husbandry, the number of livestock in the province actually decreased.[67] Deliveries to the state of meat, milk, wool, and eggs lay far below targets set by this plan. The collective farms of Kalinin province received very little cash income in the early 1950s because of low yields in arable farming and poor productivity of animal husbandry. Even horticulture and bee-keeping operated at a rate far below expectations. In July 1951 the Central Committee was particularly grieved by the drop in livestock production during the previous two years: in 1949 Soviet agriculture had embarked on a special three-year plan for its development, but the results of the enterprise had been appalling in Kalinin province. Different causes for the poor results were brought to bear by the local authorities, now stressing one problem, then emphasizing another. The obkom often harped on the theme of insufficient feed. In 1951 animal husbandry was seen to suffer from a lack of fodder crops and stables, while the quality of planted and wild grasses had deteriorated in comparison to 1950.[68] In a report to Central Committee secretary Malenkov in June 1951, prohibitive natural obstacles for cultivation and harvesting of hay and the use of land as meadows were singled out as causes for the province's inadequate fodder supply, for "many of these [hayfields and meadow lands] have turned into swamps, and shrubbery and woods have grown on them. Their productivity is extremely low. This situation of the natural fodder-crop lands is a fundamental cause for the large diffusion of the worm infections among the livestock, especially among sheep."[69]

A massive intestinal-worm infection was discovered among cattle in 1950, and 364,000 head of strong-horned cattle and more than 400,000 sheep were treated for this affliction in the province. In all, livestock losses amounted to 7.4 percent of strong-horned cattle, 12.4 percent of pigs, and 20.1 percent of sheep in 1950. By comparison, in the dismal agricultural year of 1946, 10 percent of horses, 6 percent of strong-horned cattle, 8 percent of hogs, and 16 percent of sheep of the socialized herds perished. Insufficient construction, again, compounded the problem. Brigades were formed to build adequate shelter for the livestock, but these kolkhozniks could not take care of this during harvesting. Additional difficulties were brought about by the usual lack of construction materials: in Torzhok raion there were none to be had in 1951.[71]

In 1952 feed shortages wreaked further havoc.[73] In this year, chickens, particularly, succumbed. During the first eight months of 1952 the number of fowl had fallen by 37 percent in the province. The main reasons for the dwindling livestock, according to agricultural specialists investigating the situation, were an incomplete fodder diet and inadequate shelter and care.

Once more, poor results were ascribed to the anti-Soviet attitude of many kolkhozniks. Again, however, although neglect and deliberate unauthorized slaughter and selling off of kolkhoz animals certainly played their role, the principal cause for the deterioration of livestock quality and quantity lay elsewhere.[73] The central authorities did not accept the decline in livestock as a consequence of natural causes in any case: thus, a telegram, signed by Stalin personally, arrived in the Special Sector of the Kalinin obkom around 1 July 1951.[74] In it Stalin voiced his displeasure with the progress in Kalinin province of the three-year development plan for livestock. Could this be another example of Stalin's fondness for holding other people responsible for the failures of his regime? Stalin's wrath, incurred by this poor showing of the Kalinin oblast', decisively undermined Konovalov's position as provincial secretary. He was dismissed only a few weeks later.

The Soviet leaders' opinion of the loss of cattle was reiterated by oblispolkom vice-chair Shcheplikov in 1951, when he argued that "the cattle does not die as the result of some kind of illness, but almost exclusively because of mismanagement, because at many kolkhoz cattle farms not even the most elementary arrangement of herding, protecting, and feeding of cattle exists. The preservation of manure is impossibly filthy; the congestion and draughts in the animal shelters, the absence of feeding troughs and of permanent cadres – those are the scourges of public animal husbandry."[75]

Far too few of the 11,900 kolkhoz Communists were seen to be working on kolkhoz livestock farms.[76] In September 1951 the USSR government and Central Committee issued a resolution that ordered an end to the squandering of animals.[77] As usual, Moscow (or Stalin in this case) had come to the conclusion that the "enemies" of the kolkhozy must have been responsible for the lack of success in farming.

The decline in livestock continued, however, in 1951 and 1952. According to Kiselev in September 1952, the number of horses, strong-horned cattle, pigs, sheep, and fowl had gone into an uninterrupted descent since early 1950.[78] To Moscow, the provincial leadership attempted to blame hostile natural circumstances for deficient results, but the obkomburo emulated the central leadership in its consistent refusal to accept adverse weather or soil conditions as a valid excuse from below for substandard production.

"[I]n general, in the area of animal husbandry everything proceeds well and no threatening phenomena can be discerned," wrote the agronomist Bol'shakov about Tver' guberniia in 1924.[79] One agrees with the conclusion of local and Moscow party chiefs that infections, privations of shelter and fodder, neglect, and the like cannot explain why in the 1940s and 1950s, the peasantry was incapable of keeping on the collective farms and in personal use at least as many livestock as had been tended on the small and relatively primitive farms in the 1920s. Instead of laying the blame on Konovalov or on the kolkhozniks, however, the Communists, in fact, could only have thanked themselves for wreaking the havoc.

After amalgamation, flax production never reached plan targets, not the least because the first treatment of flax after harvesting was predominantly performed by hand in many raions: in Sandovo raion 90 percent was done manually in 1951.[80] Biologically the capacity for growing flax in the province was vast, according to the director of the All-Union Institute of Flax in the summer of 1951, making yields of 400 kilograms and more per hectare possible. Yet on the whole, Kalinin province's actual deliveries to the state did not surpass 200 kilograms per hectare. Since collective farms were poorly mechanized, flax was not harvested when it should have been, causing rotting. The problem was compounded by the coincidence of the sowing of winter grains, the delivery of grains to the state, and the harvest time of grains and flax. Flax was often planted too late in spring, because autumn ploughing had not been extensive enough.

Provincial agricultural production continued to sink after Kiselev succeeded Konovalov. At the end of 1952 the obkom formed a com-

Table 24
Harvest and Livestock Production Results in Kalinin Oblast', 1947–51

	Average Yield per Hectare (in hundreds of kilograms)				
	1947	1948	1949	1950	1951
Cereals (approximate)	7.90	9.40	8.80	6.60	6.50
Flax fibres	1.61	2.46	2.55	1.98	1.61
Flax seeds	2.12	2.61	2.26	1.31	1.62
Potatoes	74.40	108.10	71.30	65.60	64.60
	Annual Production of Socialized Livestock				
Milk production per foddered cow (litres)	875	1,124	1,140	956	851
Wool per sheep, in the beginning of each year (kilograms)	1,440	1,700	1,640	1,145	1,070
Eggs, per hen	34	48	46	37	27

Source: Based on Pako, 147/5/906, l.9.

mission to find causes for the dwindling number of households and able-bodied workers in the collective farms in the oblast'. The commission's report provides a telling description of the low pay and constant scarcity that beleaguered the kolkhozniks.[81] The report admitted that the downward trend in the production of cereals, flax, potatoes, and in animal husbandry had continued in 1951, so that the results of that year were the worst annual results of the period 1947–51 (table 24).[82]

During the immediate postwar period, no attempts at either intensive or extensive cereal cultivation led to significant harvests. After Stalin's death, the poor results were admitted but were strictly attributed to faulty agrotechnology, by suggesting that "[a]long with a shortage of fertilizers (above all of manure), the causes of [of small grain harvests] need to be sought in the poor supply of quality seeds (the seed-growing labour in the oblast' has diminished in recent years), in a mistaken system of farming, [and] badly timed sowing, [and] harvesting."[83]

This analysis was partially true but incomplete: the lack of incentives, the misguided agricultural reforms, and the failure to reward initiative were all of greater importance. More remote raions in Kalinin province saw little or no improvement in the quality of life in the countryside. In 1952 the raion of Lesnoe lacked any paved road.[84] The district was without a pharmacy or a bus connection with the railroad (which was more than seventy kilometres away). In most villages of Kalinin province, even by the 1960s, water came from wells, hauled by traditional winches or sometimes a sweep. Only in the course of the 1950s had water fountains begun to appear. Most villages had artificial ponds originally created for fire prevention, which were used as drinking water for the livestock. Kolkhozniks swam and washed their clothes in these ponds; in the 1940s and early 1950s, the ponds were even a source of potable water. In 1951 the raion centre of Kozlovo still had no electricity: local authorities were using kerosene lamps.[85] Kozlovo was one of the districts that continued to miss out on the distribution of equipment that was intended to ameliorate agriculture. MTS representatives of the raion often arrived in Kalinin when all new machinery had already been sold to raions nearer to the provincial capital. Kolkhozniks from Kozlovo missed out on their share of concentrated fodder or farm equipment at the nearest railroad station because these products had already been sold to peasants of farms closer by who had arrived earlier.

In the entire province the results of planned organization were further marred by insufficient machinery and expertise in cultivation and livestock farming. Neither man nor machine was treated with proper consideration. During his part in the condemnation of Konovalov, Karelinov, head of the provincial agricultural department, offered telling examples of the authorities' lack of concern for agricultural specialists. The head of the provincial office for fodder crops, Stepanskii, lived with his family in a room of ten square metres, while the head of the office for Russian dandelions, the roots of which were used in the production of latex, lived in an apartment twelve kilometres from the town of Kalinin.[86] A young specialist just graduated from the Leningrad Veterinary Institute was severely hindered in his work at the veterinarian laboratory that had opened in Bezhetsk because a family that had nothing to do with laboratory work was housed in the laboratory. Other specialists were often not being paid.

In early 1945 there was a shortage of MTS cadres such as mechanics, tractor brigadiers, and combine and tractor drivers.[87] It was usual for many of these jobs to be temporarily filled by people who formally remained kolkhozniks. During the war up to 50 percent of tractor operators were new to the job every year. To make matters worse, a majority of MTS workers needed retraining. After the war ended, an effort was made to have returning demobilized soldiers take up these occupations, but the quality of the MTS work would still be deemed mediocre by 1953.

When MTS workers helped collective farms with ploughing, sowing, or harvesting, kolkhozniks were supposed to provide them with room and board.[88] Some of the collective farms, however, were less than accommodating, probably because they lacked the necessary means. In 1949, for example, in Bologoe raion tractor drivers had to spend the night in barns, sheds, and similar shelters, and received meals irregularly. On their own bases, to which they retired at the end of the agricultural year, full-time MTS employees were shabbily housed. Full-time employment at an MTS presented many deprivations: repair and maintenance of machinery was often done in unheated garages; employees' apartments were frequently far from their workplaces; as a rule, payment by the collective farms was late.

The existence of overlapping authorities, as in industry, created havoc for the MTS. In 1947 the director of the Pervomaiskii MTS of the raion of Molodoi Tud was to be fired because of theft, drunkenness, and absence from work.[89] It took, however, years of haggling between the raikom and the ministry of agriculture, before the ministry gave its final permission in 1951 to dismiss him (he was subsequently arrested). The lack of competent technical workers in agriculture often forced the obkom to transfer misbehaving MTS workers, instead of firing them. In 1951 in Molodoi Tud raion no senior livestock technician had been employed for two and a half years, while the raion was further suffering from a long-term absence of veterinarians as well.

Machinery was introduced at a snail's pace after the war. The grand propaganda about the superiority of Soviet agriculture – thanks to efficient labour organization on collective farms and the ingenious use of machinery and staff at strategically distributed tractor stations – was sheer window dressing. Beneath the surface scores of problems were encountered.[90] At the end of 1947 most tractors in use within the province were still pre-1935 models.[91] Thirty-one of the tractor stations at that time owned, altogether, 124 decrepit trucks for the transport of agricultural produce. Shortages of ploughs, harrows, cultivators, and threshers were common at tractor stations.

In 1950, 73 percent of spring ploughing and 88 percent of autumn ploughing was mechanized.[92] Sowing of summer and winter crops, however, remained a predominantly manual effort in this year, when only 13 percent of summer crops and 23 percent of winter crops were planted by machine. Harvesting, especially, was carried out by hand. Harvest combines played a negligible role in the gathering of flax, potatoes, and cereals: less than 10 percent of each category was harvested mechanically in 1950. Overall, the level of mechanized farming hardly exceeded that of 1940: only 23.5 percent of total ploughing, sowing, harvesting, threshing (of flax), haying, and siloing was done by the MTS.[93] A distinct increase occurred in 1951 and 1952 when the level of mechanization rose to 35.9 percent and 43.2 percent respectively. In most of the western raions, where the paucity of labour was most pronounced, the level was higher than the provincial average.[94] Hardly anywhere, however, did this stepped-up use of machinery lead to better yields.

The causes for the low level of mechanization were varied, according to a report submitted to the Central Committee in June 1951.[95] In the first place, farm workers continued to work manually, owing to a general absence of equipment and machinery, always insufficiently provided by the state during Stalin's lifetime. Second, there was a chronic deficit of spare parts for available machinery.[96] Often plans for repairing tractors and combines (repair work mainly taking place during winter) were badly fulfilled, owing to this absence of spare parts at the MTSs. Much MTS machinery was old and needed frequent repair. Fewer than one-third of the stations had electricity on their premises, preventing full-scale repairs during the dark days of winter and rendering repairs more cumbersome in general. Finally, adequate garages were insufficient, mechanics' housing was commonly poor, and there were few clubs for MTS workers to alleviate their spirits after work. Thus the tractor stations continued to struggle to keep their tractor operators: in the early 1950s more than 6,000 of them abandoned the stations, and many found employment in industry and construction.[97] An ambitious three-year plan was announced in October 1953 for the construction of garages, repair shops, storage areas, public baths (no of the MTS had public baths in 1953!), and houses on the MTS. This plan was to be, as with most Soviet plans, far from fulfilled.[98] Many of the 101 stations had a staff that was only minimally qualified: twenty-seven directors had less than seven years of general education; fifty-eight of the main engineers had been trained only by way of special courses; a slim 37 percent of the head agronomists had profited from higher education.

Fainsod notes that the tractor stations served the additional purpose of political control over the rural population by way of their political departments.[99] The February Plenum of the Central Committee of 1947 introduced a vice-director for political affairs with the tractor stations. But even here the MTS failed in its task, for the political dimension of the MTS was unable to influence or change the peasantry's attitude toward socialized farming.

Before 1960, at least, Soviet power had not been able to improve the soil in the less fertile lands of the provincial countryside. It shows how limited possibilities were for the Communists with respect to the planned improvement of agriculture before the 1960s. One wonders whether large stretches of farmland in Kalinin province would have been abandoned if market forces had been allowed to play their role in the way they had during the modernization and industrialization of Western Europe in an earlier time. The yields, due to the adverse conditions of climate and soil, would have been too low to rationalize arable farming in these areas. Unable to compete against domestic and foreign competitors, peasants residing in areas of excessive humidity and poor soil would have left the countryside and moved to the cities, while the few viable agricultural areas – such as the Bezhetsk region – might have prospered from the cultivation of flax. Even so, developments in the countryside in the 1920s seem to indicate that such an outcome was unlikely. Many peasants seemed quite satisfied with their moderate existence during the NEP; they seemed to worry little about their farm being less than viable in economic terms and appeared often uninterested in more attractive livelihoods earned outside their village.[100]

This type of speculation apart, one would tend to agree with Klaus Mehnert who noticed in the 1950s that if the regime had tried to return to the pre-1929 situation in the countryside, it would probably have done so in vain:

Most of the rural population no longer have any clear recollection of an independent peasantry. I have talked to many peasants, and I have no doubt whatever that what they long for is less compulsion in the kolkhozes, more land of their own, higher prices for their produce, and an easing of the pressure of plans and quotas. But whether they would really like to see the whole of the agricultural land divided again into small holdings among the individual kolkhozniki seems doubtful. There are, of course, some peasants with initiative who dream of land and a farm of their own. But the younger ones, who have acquired technical knowledge as tractor drivers, threshers, zoologists, and mechanics are not moved by any such urge. If they were given land of their own, they would probably want to cultivate it with collectively owned mechanics. In the villages there is no solidarity of ideas and purpose which, if Bolshevism collapsed, could put forward a clear-cut alternative.[101]

The last lines seem prophetic in light of the current lack of success in privatizing land and splitting up of collective and state farms, to which the farmers themselves are often opposed. Mehnert's remarks prove that Stalinist collectivization had been successful in one way: even the memory of traditional farming had become virtually extinct by the 1950s.

The best farming area before the revolution, in Stalin's time, and after 1953, remained the eastern area of the province: Bezhetsk raion and the raions surrounding it. A Soviet source remarks that at the end of the eighteenth century, the size of the ploughed area there was hardly smaller than in 1960.[102] One of the reasons for the intensive tillage stemmed from the congenial soil conditions in this area. In the swampy areas of the west and northwest, tractor labour, for example, would be hindered by hillocks, a moist soil consistency, and stones in the deeper layers of the soil. The preeminence of Bezhetsk raion proves the futility of collectivization with respect to improving agricultural results. Thirty years after collectivization the basic geographical pattern of agricultural success of Kalinin province was essentially the same as before 1929. Agriculture continued to thrive best in areas where, because of advantageous natural circumstances, it had already been doing well before 1917.[103]

Socialist agriculture in Stalin's time was a miserable failure. In their limited spare time, kolkhozniks had to make up for the socialized sector's shortcomings as well as possible. At least until the middle of the 1950s the production of personal plots in Central Russia was the main source of peasants' income and food supply.[104] Until 1953, as a result of the dire agricultural circumstances, the basic diet of the kolkhozniks remained similar to that of the pre-Revolutionary peasant, and it stayed below the level of peasants' consumption in the later 1920s. After collectivization the peasants ate fewer cereals and more potatoes. Before 1917 they produced on average roughly 78 percent of their personal foodstuffs; even by the 1960s not much had changed: 20 percent to 22 percent of food consumed was purchased on the market. At least until 1953 the private plot was cultivated essentially for personal consumption and not for the market.[105] The state taxed produce from a private plot heavily, particularly through obligatory procurements, so that little remained for most households to sell on the market. Only if anything was left after taxes was some of the plot's produce sold on urban (kolkhoz) markets, and some went to consumers' cooperatives.[106]

In Stalin's time some families continued to make ends meet with the help of the income of at least one member working as an itinerant artisan or employee in the towns. Urban inhabitants tried to aid their rural relatives as well as they could by bringing them foodstuffs, manufactured goods, or money. A measure of relief was found in regular forays into the woods to collect berries and mushrooms. A few were lucky enough to receive a pension for a husband who had been killed in the war; however, in the case of L.P. Felkova, who participated in the survey, the pension was a mere 68 rubles a month for three people, far from enough to survive in a decent way. According to several participants in the survey, even many of the rural "elite," such as teachers, government employees, MTS workers, and professional party workers, were forced to cultivate a private plot in order to get by. For example, raion party secretary Tiaglov's family had a garden and a pig.[107] M.A. Smirnov, who became the father of three children between 1947 and 1953, regretted that life had been too difficult to have fathered more, for, in his opinion, in the countryside large families lived the best kind of life. More children meant more hands to aid with the farmwork and, therefore, a superior income.

Only a few considered collectivization to have been a blessing that had improved their existence. Among former collective farmers interviewed in Tver' and its environs in 1992, only one person, A.K. Sumugina-Shepeleva, expressed a high degree of satisfaction with the collective-farm system despite the near "de-kulakization" of her father (a fate diverted because his son was a party member). After the war, in which she lost her husband, she worked in a field-crop shock brigade that always surpassed obligatory work norms. Her kolkhoz, Moriak, located in the raion of Rameshki, was a "millionaire" (an extremely prosperous collective farm), which paid well for the trudodni. She shared a house with her mother-in-law after the war, and there were times when, in the fall, they harvested on their private plot 9,000 rubles worth of crops and livestock products to sell on the market.

The failure of Soviet agriculture in Kalinin province (and no doubt in other areas of the USSR) is highlighted by the incredible amount of time and energy spent, or rather wasted, by local authorities – from the first secretary of the obkom to the simple rural activist – to improve farming, without ever being able to achieve any noticeable progress. The provincial party archives are packed with material witnessing the party's concern with agriculture. Communists proved, however, unable to introduce any structural improvement after collectivization.

At the time of Stalin's death, more than half the inhabitants of Kalinin province lived in the countryside. After thirty-five years, the Soviet experience had failed to change rural attitudes: religion had lost some terrain but was far from dead, while private gain remained a potent force in people's lives, and ecstatic parties were sometimes as often and as intensively celebrated as in the past. The Soviet surrogates of constant hard work, modern science, Marxist-Leninist ideology, and ardent "Soviet patriotism" had failed to undermine such "relics of the past."

Russian historians, too, have recently begun to question the idea that Russia was transformed overnight into a modern industrial society in the 1930s.[108] Russia was no longer a strictly agrarian country during the 1920s: its society was in flux, many of its characteristics were already distinctly modern before the First Five Year Plan. Economically, however, agriculture remained an important sector, as well as a sizeable source of employment, until the 1950s. Rural culture, albeit deeply affected by the "Revolution from Above," continued to be resilient. In the countryside of Stalin's time and in the towns populated by the many rural emigrants, premodern customs were only gradually superseded by more up-to-date ways.

In a technological sense, too, modernization in the countryside occurred more slowly than had been projected when the regime embarked on collectivization. Improvement of living standards notwithstanding, agriculture under Khrushchev operated unsatisfactorily. Among other things, mechanization – and electrification in particular – was deemed to be still insufficient in 1960, while the labour shortage in the countryside continued, and too little attention was paid to specific local circumstances in planning. On 1 January 1959 only 29 percent of all kolkhozy in Kalinin province had electricity. Large tracts of kolkhoz lands were often half under water; in 1961 it was estimated that perhaps 25 percent of all arable lands had turned into swamps.[109] The level of mechanization in 1960 was almost 90 percent for grain harvesting, and 100 percent for ploughing in autumn and spring; it was 72.5 percent for flax sowing, but for pulling flax only 30.5 percent, and for potato planting and gathering only 13.4 percent and 8.4 percent respectively.[100] Several other farming tasks were still carried out manually: for instance, the raking together of flax. In flax cultivation, the harvest results remained markedly better in the traditional flax-growing areas of the east (in 1960, around 400 kilograms per hectare on average) than those of the western part of the province (from 200 to 250 kilograms per hectare).

Despite all the clamour about an astonishingly fast process of modernization, some of the changes merely scratched the surface of Russian habits, values, and norms, which were the sum of centuries of slow historical evolution. Much of the grandiose Soviet transformation went almost unnoticed in the more remote parts of the countryside. The family everywhere remained a stronghold of private life on which the Soviet regime had encroached but little. It continued to provide the most significant formative element in the socialization of the rural, as well as the urban, child (although less so in the latter case, owing to more diverse influences outside the realm of the family in the towns). According to Kerblay, the survival of the family had been the sole cause of the persistence of a redeeming morality in Soviet society, without which people would have turned into amoral creatures.[111]

Perhaps the infrequency of cases such as that of Pavlik Morozov (in the early 1930s he supposedly denounced his parents to the authorities for hoarding grain and was subsequently murdered by his parents or by the whole village) proves Kerblay right: indeed, when the authorities had tried to destroy even the sanctuary of the family, as they attempted to do in the 1930s, some children turned into unscrupulous monsters.[112] It may be argued that Soviet collective farmers remained quintessential Russian peasants even by the 1960s: the family household remained the central focus of their life; their culture was decidedly distinct from Soviet urban culture; they enjoyed little prestige or status within Soviet society; and the bulk of their output was procured by the authorities.[113] Like the life of the Russian peasant before collectivization, the kolkhoznik's life was fundamentally determined by an unrelenting preoccupation with farming. More than thirty years after the onset of collectivization, Soviet Communism had not changed the essential quality of the peasants' reality.

After Stalin's demise, the party brass finally admitted that taxation and the work load were so enormous for kolkhozniks that they even lacked the time and incentive to care for their private livestock.[114] Many restricted themselves to keeping merely one goat, for which the taxation was lower. One can infer that the average working day from early spring to late autumn was close to sixteen hours, of which half was spent on the private plot and in coping with daily chores such as cleaning, cooking, or chopping wood.[115] A grueling life it was, bereft of leisure time, except for some intervals during winter and a few traditional or Soviet holidays (although the proverbial milkmaids could hardly ever rest for any length of time). Under Stalin, kolkhozniks did not enjoy many of the social rights of the Soviet citizen that had been constitutionally proclaimed in 1936. They did not have annual vacations, were not paid when ill, did not benefit from maternity leaves, and received no pensions.[116] Realization of plans for the socialized part of agriculture was important to them, in that they wanted to avoid sanctions for failing to meet ordained obligations. Besides threats, the authorities attempted to stimulate the kolkhozniks' work ethic with abstract incentives, but these attempts were unimaginative and unconvincing after the brutality of collectivization; and they were flawed to boot. In the more remote areas, the population was not even treated to films, lectures, reports, pamphlets, slogans, or newspaper windows.[117] Individual ownership of a telephone or radio was uncommon, as was the use of electricity.[118] The effects of the rather inefficient methods for inciting collective farmers to break their backs for the good of the cause diminished rapidly after the war. Were they ever very effective? If one considers the abundant evidence of the general apathy that reigned in the countryside immediately after collectivization, the answer must be a resounding no.

CHAPTER EIGHT

Exodus: Migration and Urbanization

A steady drip, not a cloudburst, wears down the stone.[1]

It was apparent soon after May 1945 that life on the kolkhoz offered few, if any, attractions to Soviet citizens: the experience of the Russians of Tver' province in this respect may again serve as an illustration. The amalgamation of 1950 was an attempt to solve the problem of insufficient work hands and inadequate supervision as well as to reallocate scarce means, but it did not stem the exodus of collective farmers. In late 1952, in a more profound manner than ever before, the oblast' leadership endeavoured to find out how the depletion of the membership of the collective farms could be halted. The obkomburo received a report in February 1953 that indicated the extent of, and the reasons behind, the desire, particularly among rural youth, to abandon farming. At the time perhaps nothing could be done on the basis of the findings of the report, but Stalin's death in March 1953 allowed for a change of policy by the central leadership toward the collective farms that was of great consequence.

In 1953 the new collective leadership introduced better remuneration for work on the kolkhoz and entitled kolkhozniks to benefits that had been enjoyed exclusively by urban workers until that fateful year. However, the migration from the countryside to the towns was not brought to a halt by these measures. Urbanization antedated the revolution of 1917, and the draw of the half-mythical modern city in the twentieth-century Soviet Union was not very different from its attraction to peasants in other modernizing or industrializing societies. Perhaps wholesale abolition of the collective farms would have diminished the exodus. But to make such a change, would, of course, have been to admit, implicitly, the failure of the regimented collective farming that had been introduced from 1929 onward. Collectivization was such a sacred cow for the regime that after 1953 Stalin's ultimate successor, Khrushchev, stopped short, in his criticism of his predecessor, at finding fault with collectivization. Condemnation of the process in official discourse remained beyond the realm of possibilities in the Soviet Union until the time of Mikhail Gorbachev.

Khrushchev's criticism of 1956 was, nevertheless, remarkable, not just because of its condemnation of the inhumanity of Stalin's regime but more particularly because most Soviet citizens were acquainted with at least part of the contents of Krushchev's "Secret Speech." The result in Kalinin province is telling: documents indicate that in 1956, for many Soviet citizens, the political leadership lost a great measure of credibility by admitting it had condoned unpardonable crimes against its subjects. For the time being, however, speaking out about the injustices suffered was discouraged. Too many members of the Soviet elite during the Khrushchev and Brezhnev eras had been implicated in these crimes to allow a frank discussion of what had occurred under Stalin. Public debate became feasible only when, in the middle of the 1980s, the reins of power in the Soviet Union were taken over by a generation that had only vicariously experienced Stalin's time.

THE COLLECTIVE FARM IN 1953

Between 1941 and 1947 the provincial collective farms lost 15,600 households and 214,200 people.[2] The depletion of able-bodied males was particularly pronounced, as their participation in kolkhoz labour fell by 47 percent. In a letter written in May 1946, I.P. Boitsov asked Central Committee secretary A.A. Kuznetsov and Gosplan head N. Voznesensky to exempt the province from further draining of its labour force. The tremendous difficulties that ensued from the population decrease are palpable in the letter:

The labour force in the oblast' has sharply decreased, because of the departure of more than 30,000 youth of the age of fourteen to fifteen from the raions through which the front line ran to eastern areas of the country in 1942, and the succeeding annual departure of youth from the oblast' as a consequence of the recruitment for FZO schools [factory schools].

As a result of this [including the wartime population loss] a strained situation with respect to the labour force has occurred in agriculture.

According to calculations of the planning organizations of the oblast' for this year's period of harvest work in the oblast' agriculture, there will be an average shortage of 15 percent of workers, while in certain raions these shortages will reach 50 percent, and this in a situation when the sown area of the collective farms in the oblast' has only reached 88.7 percent of the prewar level.

The oblast' still faces huge restoration and construction labour as part of the Fourth Five Year Plan ...

Despite the enormous shortage of work hands in agriculture and the great demand for workers by provincial industrial enterprises and construction organizations, the depletion of the labour force of the oblast' continues.

This all aggravates the shortage of work hands even more.

Because of the difficulties that have arisen in respect to the labour force, which will increase with the further development of the restoration and construction labour, the obkom of the vkp(b) asks to free the oblast' further from the removal of work hands, including that of youth on the basis of recruitment in fzo schools outside the oblast'.[3]

The appeal indicates how the egress from the countryside to the city would continue after the war and increase from the end of the 1940s onwards, when the number of kolkhoz households quickly began to drop. Kolkhozniks left to work in state enterprises and organizations.[4]

In the early 1950s, the situation was so somber that some of the party's observers noticed a surplus of labour available in the towns, while hardly any young, able-bodied people could be found on the collective farms. In January 1952 there were 20,700 (7.8 percent) fewer kolkhoz households than at the end of 1948; worse still, the number of people fit to work had fallen by 85,600, or by 22.4 percent in three years![5] Although in absolute numbers more women departed (50,400 or 19.6 percent) than men, relatively more males flocked to the towns (35,100 or 28.1 percent). After the number of kolkhozniks in the Torzhok rural raion had fallen by 1,500 in 1951, gorkom secretary Volkonskii of the town of Torzhok warned in September 1952 that soon no kolkhozniks would be left of the 7,000 still working on the collective farms of Novotorzhok raion.[6] In Likhoslavl' raion the kolkhoz population had decreased from 7,338 in 1947 to 4,048 in 1952, according to its first secretary in September 1952.

The direction taken by migrants depended on the location of their kolkhoz: in the north of the province, most departed for Leningrad and its surrounding oblast'; in the southern part, people chose to go to Kalinin and other industrially developed southern centres of the province.[7]

In late 1952 the obkom entrusted a commission with the task of finding an explanation for the massive exodus. The commission's in-depth investigation of the Likhoslavl' and Kirov raions took place in November–December 1952, just after the Nineteenth Party Congress, when Malenkov had announced that the grain problem in the ussr had been solved and agriculture was said to be thriving in the Soviet Union. The investigation established that in Likhoslavl' raion, which stretched along the October Railroad, the number of kolkhoz households dropped by 8.9 percent between 1 January 1950 and 1 November 1952. Even more telling was the plunge in population numbers, 25.1 percent, and of able-bodied workers, 30.6 percent.[8] Kirov raion, in the west, was located farther away from the industrial artery along the October Railroad but had experienced a similar reduction, for 15.2 percent of the households of the raion had left, 30.3 percent of the population, and 29.2 percent of the able-bodied workers.[9] Over the same period in both raions, the number of members of kolkhoz artels who worked in organizations and enterprises instead of on farms had doubled. Among adult able-bodied workers, their share had tripled!

The commission noted that, of physically fit adults and teenagers who left the collective farms, around a third left without the proper permission of the kolkhoz general meeting and the raion militsiia, which issued the necessary certificates of leave and passports.[10] Many kolkhozniks received their papers illegally from the executives of their farms, since their applications had not been discussed at a general meeting of kolkhoz members. Furthermore, quite a few enterprises and organizations engaged in the practice of hiring kolkhozniks who did not have the required papers. Illegal hiring by industrial managers was commonly criticized by the authorities.[11] In 1951 and 1952 at one peat-digging enterprise in Likhoslavl' raion, more than 10 percent of the hired kolkhozniks lacked the obligatory certificate from their kolkhoz that permitted them to work outside the collective farm. Some of the work-hands came from as far away as the villages of Olenino and Kashin raions. The direction of the peat works was apparently plagued by the common evil of labour shortage.

Kolkhozniks with acquaintances or family in Kalinin managed to escape the farms: relatives or friends helped them to receive permission to build a house upon a plot of land in the town. At one point, at the kolkhoz Pobeda, six trucks arrived in the middle of the night: they were briskly loaded with one kolkhoznik's possessions and swiftly departed into the darkness.[12] When the brigadier wanted to deliver the work roster to that kolkhoznik the following morning, both he and his property had vanished. Other routes were explored as well:

Members of a kolkhoz, who have been called up for the Soviet army or have left with the purpose of study, as a rule, do not return to their kolkhozy after demobilization or the completion of their studies. A great number of kolkhozniks have moved to the raion centres or settlements in recent years and have brought their houses to these places. Many of them do not have permanent employment, [and they] engage in private farming, and artisanship, and take refuge in seasonal and temporary jobs.[13]

Those who remained on their collective farms often failed to comply with the required duties of a kolkhoznik, for "they work in local cooperative enterprises and do not take part in the socialized farming of the kolkhozy."[14] Many of the roughly 10,000 kolkhozniks selected annually through the recruiting system for seasonal work in the forest and peat industries failed to return to their farms. With the help of the passports they received at their temporary workplaces, they tried to survive on their own and made their families join them.

What were the grounds for this sustained departure, which depleted the kolkhoz population to an extent that it imperilled the existence of many collective farms?

The rural squalor and the depressing atmosphere of the countryside has been depicted in the previous chapter; what is remarkable about the report, or, more appropriately, the mandate given to the commissioners by the obkom, is its candour: the commissioners tried to give a truthful and comprehensive account. The report remains, nevertheless, limited by ideology. The writers could not condemn collectivized agriculture as such, which would have amounted to sacrilege. Living the lie of Kolakowski, so to say, the commissioners seemed incapable of suggesting that collectivization in its entirety had proven to be a disaster. All the same, the report remains remarkable, for it does counsel a number of cardinal changes within the parameters of Soviet agricultural policy.

The commission's inquiry established various causes for illegal and legal departures since the war. In the first place, some migrants had found employment in raion or oblast' organizations or enterprises, had been called up by the army, had disappeared to unknown destinations, commenced study outside the province, or married. Others had been working as hired labourers, such as cattle herders, carpenters, and nannies (apparently, one could escape the kolkhoz sometimes as a nanny, since employment in that case was deemed more essential to socialist reconstruction than work on the understaffed collective farm). A few had been arrested or had died prematurely.[15]

The report (submitted by the commission in early 1953 to the obkomburo) had to admit, grudgingly, that one reason for the flight from the kolkhozy was the extremely low remuneration for work performed within the socialist sector of the collective farms. But neither the commissioners nor the leadership for whom the report was intended could admit to this error too easily. It was clear to all that the highest party chiefs in Moscow, specifically Stalin himself, had shown no inclination to entice the peasantry to work harder by offering them decent pay.

Poor pay was thus played down as a ground for the exodus, but, in fact, it was much more fundamental a cause than the party brass in Kalinin was willing to allow. Kolkhozniks were paid according to the amount of trudodni, or workdays, they had contributed to the production of the socialist sector. There was no exact remunerative standard for this trudoden'.[16] Its value depended on the income paid to each kolkhoz for procured produce, the extremely stingy price paid by the state for it, and tasks performed by a kolkhoznik on the kolkhoz (a brigadier earned more than an ordinary brigade member, for example). Little of the total income of the kolkhozy was given as remuneration to the kolkhozniks, either in money or in kind (table 25).[17] Ideally, the annual accounts were made up around February of each year at a time when the payments for the produce delivered to the state had been received; when the loan installments had been paid off; the tractor stations had been paid for their assistance; the necessary seeds for the upcoming spring sowing had been set aside; part of the grain and flax stock, in addition to the spring seeds, stored in reserve as insurance against calamities; crops for fodder had been subtracted; hired hands (some of those helped with harvesting or cattle herds) had been paid; and money had been deposited in the "indivisible fund" of the collective farm, which had to provide funds for the purchase of new equipment, tools, and cattle. After allowing for all this, produce in kind and some money was supposed to be available for settling the accounts with individual kolkhozniks for the trudodni they had worked in the preceding year.

As table 25 shows, this practice meant that in 1949 and 1951, on average, less than a quarter of a collective farm's cash income was distributed among its members; in 1950 it was almost one-third. In 1949 on average, kolkhozniks received in kind almost one-third of the total grain harvest, while in the subsequent two years they were apportioned less than a quarter of grain production.

Per capita income clearly illustrates how skimpy this remuneration was: in 1951, on average, each household member living on a kolkhoz received for work in the socialized sector of the farm 141.7 rubles, 127.5 kilograms of grain, 117.3 kilograms of potatoes and vegetables, 129.5 kilograms of hay and straw, and 37.5 kilograms of wheat.[18] This translates into a daily wage of 39 kopecks, 349 grams of assorted grain, 321 grams of potatoes and vegetables, 355 grams of hay and straw, and 103 grams of wheat. During the 1940s convicts in Soviet labour camps received 600 grams of bread if they fulfilled their work norms, which was, together with the broth of some cabbage leaves or beets, one or two teaspoons of butter or vegetable oil, and a bit of kasha, hardly enough to survive on. The kolkhozniks, therefore, obtained barely more than this almost starvation ration of the zeks.[19]

Table 25
Distribution of Kolkhoz Income, 1949–51

Distribution of Kolkhoz Revenue in Kind (%)

	Grain			Potatoes			Hay		
	1949	*1950*	*1951*	*1949*	*1950*	*1951*	*1949*	*1950*	*1951*
Obligatory state deliveries	11.5	12.6	9.0	16.3	17.7	19.2	5.2	5.3	5.3
Payment in kind for work done by MTS	13.9	13.1	16.1	0.1	0.2	0.2	–	–	–
Return of loans in kind	0.1	0.6	1.8	0.1	–	–	–	–	–
Seed insurance reserves	26.9	32.2	33.4	29.5	35.7	34.7	–	–	–
Fodder stock	9.9	10.0	10.2	26.3	25.2	27.8	86.4	90.8	87.5
Other reserves	1.6	1.2	1.3	0.3	0.3	0.3	–	–	–
Expenses for productive and other aims	4.7	5.6	4.6	2.6	4.0	2.5	0.2	0.2	0.3
Designated for pay of trudodni	31.4	24.7	22.7	24.8	17.0	15.4	8.2	3.7	6.9
Total	100	100	100	100	100	100	100	100	100

Distribution of Cash Income in the Kolkhozy (%)

	1949	*1950*	*1951*
Taxes, insurance payments and dues	20.6	18.9	22.1
Clearing off of long-term loans for capital investment	1.4	1.5	2.3
Expenses for productive purposes	28.1	24.0	27.9
Administrative-economic expenses	0.9	0.7	0.9
Additional payments to chairs/vice-chairs and accountants/bookkeepers	3.4	2.9	3.0
Pay transferred into reserves	20.1	19.1	18.8
Expenses for various needs	0.6	0.9	0.4
Designated for payment of trudodni	24.9	32.0	24.6
Total	100	100	100

Source: Based on Pako, 147/5/906, l.10.

It should be remembered here that quite a large portion of the grain – mainly oats and barley – was fed to the kolkhoznik's private cattle.

Such a comparison was out of the question for the commission at the time. Although refraining from spelling out the starvation-level per capita income, the commission felt compelled, all the same, to admit that the remuneration of the trudoden' was insufficient.[20] Certainly, the calculation made above merely represents a general average: the commission pointed out that in 1950 kolkhozniks received less than 500 grams of grain per trudoden' in 36 percent of all provincial kolkhozy; in 1951, this was the case in 17.6 percent of all kolkhozy. In 1950, 44 percent of all kolkhozes paid less than 60 kopecks per trudoden', and in 1951, 62.4 percent (1,186 of a total of 1,900). It is clear that an enormous number of kolkhozniks received less than the already extremely base level of pay calculated above. On top of that, it appears that in 1950 no wheat was paid in kind. The next year witnessed the addition of wheat to the remuneration in 82 percent of all kolkhozy. In both years, in less than half of all kolkhozy potatoes were part of wages; vegetables supplemented the pay in 1950 on only 13 percent of the farms, and in 1951 on only 8 percent. Neither hay nor (particularly) straw was paid everywhere.[21] Even though the commission did not engage in a similarly detailed calculation, the provincial leadership was given sufficient data to conclude that rural poverty had acquired significant proportions.

If collective farmers had had to rely on these earnings for their basic diet and for feeding their livestock, serious malnutrition would certainly have ensued and the cattle would probably have perished. As M.M. Golovnova astutely remarked in the survey, if they had been forced to live only from the trudodni, everybody would have died from starvation within a year. Her fellow milkmaid, A.E. Malysheva, described the payment for the trudodni as a "glass of water."

Of course, kolkhozniks were not supposed to bank only on the wages paid to them in return for their work in the collective sector. The straw and hay payment was provided to help them feed their personal cattle, while the kolkhozniks kept most of the potatoes.[22] At any time during this period the private plots had to provide both kolkhoznik and non-kolkhoznik with the main bulk of their vegetables, as well as with meat, milk, and eggs. Kolkhozniks tried to sell off part of this produce on the market, but this additional real income diminished after tax increases in August 1948.[23] A.E. Malysheva remembered in the survey that she paid an annual tax in kind of 320 litres of milk, 40 kilograms of meat, 240 kilograms of potatoes, and 40 eggs per year.

Given these circumstances, one could have expected the authorities to embark on a strategy of offering a superior basic remuneration for each trudoden' through better prices for the obligatory state deliveries. According to the logic of Stalin's Central Committee, however, the value of the trudoden' could be raised only through high production levels on each collective farm.[24] The more a kolkhoz produced, the better off its members would be, as there would be more left for the collective farmers.

The private plot and livestock were the kolkhoznik's lifeline. Unfortunately, even these yielded less in the early 1950s than before amalgamation. Compared to 1949, collective-farm workers received less hay and straw for their private cattle, because the production of fodder crops decreased markedly in 1950 and 1951, while the socialized cattle herds of the kolkhozy grew.[25]

Even the allocation of hayfields among kolkhozniks for feeding their own cattle was discontinued in 1950 and 1951.[26] According to M.V. Bakhtina, who participated in the survey, this was a reaction to kolkhoznik attempts to mow hay near swamps and in clearings in the forests. Lack of fodder led to a significant decrease in private livestock. As is pointed out by the commission's ominous report of early 1953, the number of kolkhoznik households without a private cow increased from 34.8 percent in 1949 to 44.8 percent in 1950, fell in 1951 to 43.4 percent, but increased once more during 1952 to 47.5 percent. Table 12 shows an ancillary drop in hogs and sheep, although a few more privately owned goats were probably to be found on the average collective farm at the beginning of 1953.

Besides the low value of the trudoden' and the fall in the number of personal livestock, the third reason noted in early 1953 for the kolkhozniks' departure was the denial of credit to them for the construction and renovation of buildings such as stables and sheds, as well as for repairs of their homes.[27] Houses and shelters for cattle and their feed fell into decay.

The fourth element of the official explanation was the attitude of rural youth who left to avoid the poorly paid work in the logging enterprises; the young kolkhozniks were carelessly trained for this heavy kind of work, particularly the girls.[28] As a consequence, their productivity was low, while the pay was so picayune that it was not even enough to cover the cost of food and clothing. Another source of dissatisfaction among the young was that there were few cultural amenities (radios, libraries, newspapers) in the villages, especially in more remote areas. Many young people sought an education in a field unrelated to work on the collective farm and, as the report reiterated, in a field with better pay than the remuneration for trudodni.[29] Young girls attempted to leave collective farms because most of their male peers were leaving for service in the army or to continue their studies.

As stunning proof of the disintegration of the villages' social fabric and the alienation caused by collectivization and the amalgamation of 1950, the report admitted that the collective farms were not habitually providing sustained aid for kolkhozniks in cases of illness, disability, and in old age.[30] The only needy people who were regularly supported by the kolkhozy were pregnant and nursing women. Nowhere did the special social-aid foundation (whose funds were limited to the equivalent of 2 percent of the total annual kolkhoz production) possess sufficient assets.

The sixth and last reason the report gave for the abandonment of the collective farms was the differential taxation of private plots. Workers and employees who lived either in rural localities or, especially, in workers' settlements and towns, paid lower taxes than kolkhozniks. Even though the plots of workers and employees were usually smaller, they retained more produce after taxes than a kolkhoznik. When the value of the trudoden' was as low as it often was on many collective farms, private plots and animals were not enough to make ends meet.[31] As a result, "[m]any kolkhoz households, composed of aging members and one or two able-bodied ones, try to send off further able-bodied members of their families, in order to attain a lowering of their agricultural taxes and of the tax on bachelors, and are thus contributing to the departure from the kolkhozy."[32]

Though it never trespassed ideological boundaries, the commission's report of early 1953 should startle us by its honest depiction of the plight of the collective farmers; in none of the other party records of the postwar Stalinist period can such a blunt account of the plight of the countryside be found. Quite a few of the problems cited were taken on by Malenkov and Khrushchev in 1953. The report is also surprising in that it predates Stalin's death: the hand-written date of completion is 10 February 1953. Remedial action to right the wrongs listed in the report, however, was undertaken only after 5 March 1953. First secretary V.I. Kiselev, to whom the report is addressed (as well as to oblispolkom chairman A.I. Sadovnikov), penned a note on the first page of the report on 10 March 1953 in which he asked S.N. Shatalin and G.A. Demirskii, both senior obkom members, to work out proposals for reforms on the basis of the report that could be introduced at an obkomburo session.[33]

The commission itself had suggested a number of changes in agricultural policy to bridle the countryside's labour depletion. With Stalin still alive, the cautious commissioners harked back to the strategy of heightened control over agriculture by local party and government, such as intensifying control by the raiispolkoms over the actions of the kolkhoz executive and the raion militsiia. Several proposals thus echoed suggestions made during previous party gatherings in the immediate postwar period. Careful observation of the rules on departure of individuals and families from the kolkhozy should prevail.[34] Passports were not to be handed out to those leaving their collective farms for temporary employment elsewhere or for study purposes. The raiispolkoms should check organizations and enterprises within their fief on the hiring of kolkhozniks. The release of kolkhozniks from obligations to work in the lumber and peat industries was advocated. Handicraft cooperatives should move from villages to urban locales when they did not use local raw materials: some kolkhozniks would be forced in this way to return to their ordained occupation. Family members of workers and employees in urban areas (some of whom were apparently unemployed) could then take over the labour in the cooperatives from kolkhozniks. On the consolidated kolkhozes, the same standard was to be used for the size of private plots for, within many collective farms, kolkhozniks of one village often possessed plots of a different size from those of the next village.

Apart from these restrictive measures, the commission emphasized the importance of an enhanced operation of the MTS.[35] This could be achieved through introducing better pay and more comprehensive benefits or more agricultural schools in the countryside to prepare rural youth for work in the MTS. It was not very realistic to expect the party to increase wages substantially, but, nevertheless, the more positive suggestion of an increase in remuneration of the trudoden' was fielded somewhere down the list. Other positive recommendations were added to this, such as increasing prices for livestock products and crops within the procurement system; trading bread, sugar, and vegetable oil for kolkhoz dairy products at the same, higher exchange rate that was being applied to the trade of these three basic staples for kolkhoz flax; paying kolkhozy in advance in money and in kind for the procurement of flax in the first half of the year; and ordering kolkhozy to pay their kolkhozniks, on a monthly or quarterly basis, an advance proportionate to trudodni worked – out of the income received for flax procurements and dairy deliveries.

On the eve of Stalin's death, for the first time since collectivization, plans were therefore suggested to establish a guaranteed income, immune to wide seasonal fluctuations, for collective-farm workers. Until then most kolkhozniks had been paid only once a year for their labour – that is, if there were any remaining funds to pay them. The value of the trudoden' had always remained a mystery until the annual accounts were calculated. This remunerative method had been designed to force kolkhozniks to work their utmost throughout the year. According to this logic, they would attempt to collect the highest amount of trudodni as possible. The commissioners tried to point out the connection between this kind of insecurity and the swelling exodus.

The commission also suggested an increase in the variety of products that kolkhozy received in exchange for their deliveries.[36] Petrol and lubricating oil for trucks and engines were mentioned in this respect, as were building materials, bags, rope, and harnesses for draught animals. Taxes on private plots, another recommendation argued, should be brought in line, so that kolkhozniks would not have to pay more than others.[37] The commissioners also proposed to lower the kolkhozniks' taxes on personal cows and potatoes.

Long-term credit should be offered by the state and more aid given by kolkhozes to kolkhozniks who wanted to renovate their houses or other buildings for personal use. Collective farmers should be paid with 10 to 15 percent of the total kolkhoz harvest of hay and straw (from 1949 to 1951, always less than 10 percent had been set aside for this purpose), distributed according to the trudodni each had earned.[38] More mechanization, an enhanced supply of goods, better cultural facilities, and so on, were added to the list of recommendations, items that had come up time and again before in the party's discussions of agriculture.

The investigation was commissioned on the verge of Stalin's demise. But Kiselev, probably encouraged by Stalin's successors, saw fit to act upon the report only after Stalin had died. It leads one to surmise that this report, together perhaps with similar ones in other territories of the USSR, might have been a guideline for some of the reforms in agricultural policy introduced in 1953.[39]

One can suggest that the investigation was commissioned by the Kalinin obkom alone. After all, farming continued to spiral downwards after Konovalov's removal. Kiselev was undoubtedly concerned that he would be punished for its failure in the same way as his predecessors had been. The provincial party leadership in Kalinin was aware earlier that an inordinate number of kolkhozniks had abandoned their collective farms. In 1946 Boitsov could hide behind the excuse that mediocre economic yields in agriculture were caused by the scarcity of labour and serious devastation resulting from the war. By 1953, however, the continued exodus was cause for much greater anxiety for the local potentates, for blaming problems on the effects of the war was no longer acceptable to the central leadership in Moscow. Obviously, if the exodus was prolonged, agriculture would continue to disappoint, for much production still demanded intensive manual labour. For Kiselev it must have seemed a matter of life and death to bring the exodus to a halt; experience told him that his competence would be judged by the Central Committee predominantly on the basis of his province's agricultural results.[40] It remains a mystery, however, what Kiselev and the obkomburo could have done on their own authority to upgrade the remuneration of trudoden' or to abate taxes. These matters were decided in Moscow, not in Kalinin. Kiselev could have tried to make his case in Moscow, but in Stalin's lifetime the party had never considered better pay for the kolkhozniks. Naturally, Kiselev, who had worked before in the Central Committee apparatus, was aware of its inexorable stance on that issue. On the basis of these considerations, one is ultimately led to conclude that the idea that the local leadership acted alone in commissioning the investigation has to be rejected.

Thus it is likely that during or after the Nineteenth Party Congress someone in the Presidium had decided to reconsider the Party's agricultural policy seriously. Similar investigations may have been conducted in other provinces, for the quandary was not limited to Kalinin oblast' alone.[41] Stalin, according to some sources, may have been incapacitated during the last months of his life.[42] If that was the case, one or more of his colleagues might have risked taking the initiative to find out what was truly amiss with farming in the Soviet Union. The reports from the regions would then have provided the basis for the reforms introduced after Stalin's death.

Stalin's death brought relief: the trudoden' in Torzhok raion was valued at 5.0 rubles in 1954 and 7.54 rubles in 1955, although by then cash remuneration had begun to substitute for some of the payment in kind (which disappeared).[43] The subsequent enactment of some of the reforms recommended by the report, however, proved to be futile in halting the exodus. The villages continued to empty during the next decades.[44] Some of this migration had historical roots that dated from long before the forced creation of the collective farms. The Russian peasant had been attracted to the city since the beginnings of modernization in the middle of the nineteenth century. Urban life beckoned. The contraction of the rural population had begun in the nineteenth century in Tver' guberniia with the migration of country folk (sometimes via a stint of seasonal work) to the guberniia's industrializing towns and to Moscow and St Petersburg. But incomparably more than in Western modernizing societies the trek to the towns was accelerated by Soviet agricultural policy. Collectivization disrupted old ties to the land and stamped out the incentive to work hard on one's own farm and prosper as a result: it became unattractive to remain "behind." The traditional rural economy was destroyed in the 1930s, and the most successful farmers had been carried off in "de-kulakization": the image of the successful farmer after collectivization was that of the tirelessly labouring, selfless kolkhoznik reaping rich rewards. Because this image bore little resemblance to the existence of a real collective farmer on a real collective farm, few people felt inspired by it. Their frame of reference widened, meanwhile, through education. They were inculcated with the image of a far superior urban society, and the young started to scorn the lives of their parents. Male wartime army service and the employment of many rural women in the rear, on the tractor or in the armament factory, brought many into direct contact with the world outside the village. After the war, few returned to their ancestral villages to stay. Every year a fresh group of young men left the village for the army; many never returned home to the arduous life consisting of hardly anything more (and sometimes even less) than the very basics of survival. V.K. Stepanov, for example, said in the survey that he worked as a MTS tractorist in his native raion of Maksatikha after his demobilization from the army. After he heard that one could receive clothes, food, and a stipend as a student at the professional school for machinists in Leningrad, he enrolled and departed for the far preferable life in the big city. He recalled that there had been no prospects whatsoever for a normal existence in the countryside. Indeed, many young people went to study in a more largely populated centre and decided to stay on after comparing their village experience with their current living conditions.

Soviet Marxists despised peasants and, as a result of their policies, it seems that they succeeded in bequeathing this disdainful attitude to their subjects, including the peasants themselves. In the eyes of a majority of children growing up in the countryside from the 1930s onwards, dignified labour and lives could be obtained only in urban surroundings. A.E. Vakhmistrov said in the survey that he hoped for an improvement in his life after the war, but the countryside continued to be "strangled" by the authorities: all who could left, therefore.[45] In Kalinin province, geography undoubtedly also played a part. The soil was less fertile than in the lands towards the south of Moscow, in the Ukraine, and in the Central Black Earth region. Too much precipitation and inordinately long winters impeded good results. Before 1929, many country dwellers were already compelled to find an additional source of income to augment the inadequate returns from farming.

It is rather facile, however, to blame the disappointing yields solely on the weather – as critics of Konovalov pointed out at the time of his removal.[46] The geography of Kalinin province encouraged the exodus in another sense, too. At least since the foundation of St Petersburg, the two largest Russian cities attracted people from Tver'. The advent of the railroad provided an easy link with these cities and a fairly simple escape route. An almost uninterrupted stream of immigrants has flowed from the territories of Tver' to Moscow and St Petersburg in the last century and a half.

Aleksandr Solzhenitsyn's hope that Russians would return to edifying country life in north-eastern Russia seems impossible today. Russians have grown far too accustomed to the urban conveniences (even though they are rather slight compared to those in some Western countries) – such as televisions, running water, paved roads, electricity, telephones, and a choice of shops – to long for the drudgery of arable and pastoral farming. Urban Russians remember the kolkhoz instead of yeoman farms: few desire, therefore, to return to the land and take up full-time farming.

In the 1960s, when country life became more hospitable, migration to urban areas became, perhaps unexpectedly, stronger (in absolute numbers) than ever before. Movement to the towns probably increased, as well, after the 1932 passport law was abolished in 1976–78 and rural inhabitants finally received passports.[47] The quality of life of the average kolkhoznik was far from that of the Soviet urban dweller in the early 1960s: the gap between town and countryside had hardly narrowed, thus belying the predictions of the Marxist-Leninist canon. The continued migration from the countryside even after 1960, albeit perhaps partially caused by increased mechanization of farm work, indicates that, at least in the minds of many kolkhozniks, their lot was inferior to life in the towns, despite claims that "the press, radio, cinema, mail, telegraph, and telephone [were] connect[ing] any faraway village with the whole country, bringing daily the latest news."[48]

During the 1960s, the rural localities of Tver' province continued to be depleted by the lure of urban life. Around 1970 widespread dissatisfaction with both work and life in general was expressed by those of the countryside of Kalinin oblast': more than half the unskilled manual labourers preferred to do other work.[49] The number of field labourers, livestock workers, skilled manual workers, mechanics, machinery operators, and white-collar workers in the Kalinin countryside who desired to move to the towns was almost twice as large as in Krasnodar krai, where agriculture was flourishing in comparison. Only among the rural intelligentsia was the proportion of those longing to settle in towns roughly equal for both territories. This does not mean that this more educated group was satisfied with life in the countryside: between one in four and one in three wanted to relocate to the towns.

STRUGGLING WITH THE LEGACY

Nineteen fifty-three, the year in which Stalin died, provided a clear break in the fortunes of the collective farms and of Russians in general. Soon after March 1953 the new leaders, Malenkov and Khrushchev, attempted to improve the welfare of the kolkhozniks for the first time since collectivization. Their measures stand in stark contrast to the ruinous strategy that for a full twenty-five years had been pursued under Stalin.

The local leadership of Kalinin province was not capable of changing its manner of thinking overnight in 1953. Stalin's death was an event that no one had dared to anticipate. Even a week before his death, the obkom had faithfully reiterated the old formulas when it met in full session to discuss the decisions of the Nineteenth Party Congress, Stalin's speech at the Congress, Stalin's recently published "Economic Problems of Socialism in the USSR," and the improvement of the party's supervision over the Komsomol.[50] The prominent careerist Baranov was given the honour of opening the plenum. His vigilance would have pleased Stalin:

We are obliged to make sure that ideological work will not be conducted absentmindedly and passively, but with principle, and that it will be directed at the merciless struggle with bourgeois ideology and its penetration into our sciences, literature, art, at the overcoming of remnants of capitalism in the consciousness of the people, against loafers, lazybones, squanderers of public property, bureaucrats, violators of state discipline and against other sick phenomena in our life, against persons fawning upon the corrupted, reactionary bourgeois culture, the capitalist way of life, against nationalist and cosmopolitan perversions, against "apoliticality" and lack of ideas in literature, art, and the sciences. To attain this, all ideological work will be dedicated to the education of the Soviet people and, in particular, to that of the youth, [so that it] will become cultured and broadly educated, bright and firm, and will not shirk its responsibilities in the spirit of the communist attitude to labour and public property, of proletarian internationalism, and of dedication to the cause of communism.[51]

The confusion about the significance of Stalin's death and the unclear road ahead continued during the first months of the post-Stalin era when his successors in Moscow were jockeying for position.[52] In April 1953, at the next obkom plenum, little could be perceived of the recent changing of the guard in Moscow. The party organization of the militsiia of Bezhetsk was criticized in the opening speech for accepting a man into its ranks who had been excluded in 1937 for his ties with counterrevolutionary elements and had spent the entire war in German POW camps.[53] The obkomburo, meanwhile, was trying to rename Novopromyshlennyi raion of Kalinin as "Stalin raion," a proposal that soon would be quietly shelved.[54]

In July 1953 the obkom convened to discuss the recent fall of Beria and again revealed the long-established paranoia in the party about enemy infiltration into its ranks.[55] Baranov compared Beria to Trotsky and Zinoviev, while noticing that the party's history was rather full of "adventurist" attempts of enemies on the party and the Soviet people.[56] For the first time, however, mild criticism was heard about exaggerated attention to the role of "heroes" in history teaching and in the dissemination of Marxism-Leninism; a "cult of the personality" was condemned.[57] Beria, the meeting was told, had been a foreign agent from the time he started his political career in Baku. According to the version disclosed to the Kalinin elite, Beria had used the MVD for anti-Soviet activities against the party and the government, and had destroyed the intimate friendship of Molotov and Voroshilov with Stalin. Kiselev introduced his audience to a creative version of the most recent past in which Stalin's wish to augment the kolkhozniks' material incentives, by way of increasing procurement prices of potatoes and vegetables, had been repeatedly sabotaged by Beria. In addition, the archfiend Beria had surreptitiously maintained contacts with the Yugoslav bandits Tito and Rankovic.

Transmitting faithfully, in tried Leninist fashion, the new course decided upon by the Presidium, Kiselev underlined Malenkov's demand for the genuine observance of a collective leadership within the party at all levels of its hierarchy.[58] The party, according to Kiselev, had lost control over the security organs' activities: at local levels, it did not know what they were involved in. The MVD operated in certain areas almost fully independently from the party: for example, in Kesova Gora raion, secret police employees had started to shadow the raikom secretaries and had organized a campaign of anonymous letters that slandered local party workers. MVD employees were accused of the standard abuse of engaging in drinking bouts. The first Party secretary blamed the raikoms for allowing the abuses of the MVD, but he must have realized that this accusation was rather disingenuous, particularly after his description of the situation in Kesova Gora raion.

Subsequent reactions to Kiselev's introductory speech at the plenum indicate that many speakers did not want to dwell too much on the MVD's past abuses.[59] Instead they described a few cases of laxity of the security organs with respect to crime after Stalin's death. This perhaps could then be attributed to the perfidious influence of Beria, the power-hungry imperialist agent at the head of the organs in Moscow. For the time being, attention was conveniently diverted from the question of who had been Beria's promoter in the past. The desire to maintain things as they were can also be discerned in the attempts to put Beria in the category of other enemies of the people, such as Trotsky, Bukharin, and Zinoviev.

The political criticism of Beria, and ultimately of Stalin, had to wait until 1956 before it was placed in a somewhat coherent framework, but implicit censure of previous economic policy was expressed in a rather significant overhaul of economic guidelines in the late summer of 1953 by Malenkov and Khrushchev.[60] In October 1953 the Kalinin obkom sat down to discuss the results of the recently held Central Committee plenum on agriculture.[61] After quoting Stalin in his opening report, Kiselev went on to dissect the sorrowful state of agriculture in the postwar Kalinin province. He refrained from making the connection explicitly, but he shared with his audience an awareness that the problems had been largely caused by the agricultural policies of the Moscow leadership under Stalin. His successors seemed finally prepared tacitly (or sometimes even openly) to admit previous errors. For the first time an attempt was made to improve agricultural performance by offering material stimuli, especially by increasing prices for farm produce and lowering taxation of private plots.

Kiselev began with a sketch of the outstanding dilemmas in farming:

If in 1946 the kolkhozniks owned 175,700 cows of their own, then on 1 January 1953 they possessed a mere 108,800 head, that is 38 percent less, while the number of kolkhoz households without cows increased from 84,800 to 136,300, which translates into 53.4 percent of their total number. In the same period the number of hogs personally owned by the kolkhozniks fell almost twice, and of sheep almost three times.

These violations of the principle of the just balance between kolkhozniks' socialist and personal interests have become a primary cause of the fall in number of kolkhoz households and of able-bodied kolkhozniks in many collective farms. Of course, if a kolkhoznik does not receive sufficient income for the trudodni and his personal interest in the private plot is also decreased, he will find the easy way out – he leaves for the towns and finds work in [industrial] production. This is especially common in our oblast', in which in the last four years the quantity of kolkhoz households fell by 10.7 percent, and the kolkhoz population by 23.4 percent, with the number of able-bodied kolkhozniks dropping by 29.5 percent.

One of the basic causes of the serious backwardness of a number of vitally important sectors of agriculture is the fully inadequate use of the powerful technology that we have in agriculture. That does very much apply to us. In a majority of the MTS of our oblast' the performance of tractors and combines per shift is still very low; large stoppages of machinery occur; during the important periods of the agricultural year the time necessary to acquit of agricultural tasks [thus] increases. This leads to losses in the end, and an incomplete harvest of crops.[62]

In order to rectify matters, the prices paid in the procurement system for cattle and fowl had been increased by 5.5 times, for potatoes 2.5

times, for milk and meat twice, and for vegetables by 25 to 40 percent.[63] Obligatory deliveries of livestock produce to the state by kolkhozniks, workers, and employees with a plot had been "significantly" decreased, as well as norms for the delivery of potatoes and vegetables by collective farms. In other words, kolkhozy in their entirety and individual kolkhozniks had been given the opportunity to keep more of their production. They could vend this surplus at higher prices to the state, to consumers' organizations, or at the kolkhoz markets.

The recent three-year decline of livestock numbers, dairy produce, and wool yields was attributed by Kiselev, furthermore, to a lack of supervision by responsible authorities, poor work by agricultural specialists, and a lack of interest by kolkhoz chairs.[64] These shortcomings had brought about an extremely high level of infertility among cows, ewes, and sows, as well as a steep mortality of sucklings. Whoever was guilty, nature or man, there was a chronic shortage of fodder for the animals. Kiselev proposed, in October 1953, intensified campaigns for drainage and cleaning of potential meadows and hayfields; maize, with which Khrushchev's name is still associated by many older Russian farmers, had already been brought to his attention as a possible fodder crop. Other causes of the decrease of the herds, Kiselev noted, included a paucity of cattle barns and stables, habitually mentioned in the postwar period, and the vending of cattle for internal kolkhoz needs (in other words to feed kolkhozniks or to let them earn a little by the sale).[65] Meanwhile, the sovkhozy had managed slightly better, but their profitability had been hindered by the high production costs of meat and wool.[66]

Procurement prices for flax had already been upgraded before Stalin's death. This had led to better results in 1952 than in 1951, but flax yields were still smaller than in 1948 and 1949. In October 1953 Kiselev noticed a plethora of impediments to flax cultivation, which remained inadequate until 1954 when procurement prices for the crop went up by 70 percent.[67] Some of the problems stemmed from the carelessness of kolkhoz chairs and kolkhozniks, others from a lack of expertise, the fact that the labour of flax cultivation and harvesting coincided with other agricultural tasks, and a dearth of farm hands for this labour-intensive crop.[68]

As with cereals and flax, yields of potatoes and vegetables had waned in the early 1950s. Potato and vegetable harvests were significantly lower in 1950, 1951, and 1952 than in 1940.[69] In 1952 the potato yield per hectare reached only 66 percent of the 1940 level. In October 1953 low procurement prices, the demanding level of deliveries assigned to the kolkhozy in raions surrounding towns, and the higher delivery norms for advanced collective farms were blamed for the loss of interest among kolkhozy in increasing production of these crops. The subsequent increase of procurement prices, the lowering of delivery norms, and certain other benefits that had been awarded to kolkhozy especially involved in growing these crops were all designed to provide a stimulus for increased cultivation of potatoes and vegetables. The earlier lack of incentive was thought to have been the primary cause of the prolonged period of potato harvesting and resultant substantial loss.[70]

The reforms of September and October 1953 lifted the spirits of collective farmers, as was directly noticeable in some productive sectors. Yet farming failed to meet the ambitious expectations of the Khrushchev era, even though the kolkhozniks' remuneration was steadily raised over the years.[71] Meanwhile, more restrictions were imposed on the private plot for certain categories of rural and urban dwellers.[72] In 1956 kolkhozniks who worked the legal minimum of trudodni became eligible for a two-week vacation paid according to their average pay in trudodni. Pregnant women were entitled to a two-month leave in the same year. By 1956, despite the better remuneration, kolkhoz livestock in Kalinin province was still in a pitiful state. According to the first secretary of the obkom, Goriachev, the number of sheep in the oblast' had fallen by almost 50 percent between 1951 and 1956. Bovines and pigs were also not as plentiful as desired.[73] Attitudes changed little: in 1956 many kolkhozy were suspected of engaging in unauthorized slaughtering of animals for their own fêtes. The solution to the problems in animal husbandry was sought mainly, as usual, in a more intensive and competent supervision over the sector by the party's representatives in the raions and on the collective farms.[74]

The first real attempt to expose Stalin's orchestration of some of the many crimes committed against the Soviet population took place in 1956, when Khrushchev took the stage at the Twentieth Party Congress to deliver his famous speech on "the cult of the personality."[75] Several analysts have pointed out the dangerous consequences for the regime that were inherent in this speech. Khrushchev tried to convince his audience that Stalin's errant ways began only with the murder of Kirov in December 1934 and that he had been unable to shake the firm socialist basis of the Soviet state. Although Khrushchev perhaps managed to persuade himself and some of his listeners that this had been the case, it is obvious from the immediate reactions in Kalinin province that the faith of several dedicated Communists and party sympathizers was shaken to its foundations. On 8 April 1956 in Bologoe "hooligans" foreshadowed the events in the USSR after August

1991 by damaging the sculpture of Stalin in one of the town's public gardens.[76] Khrushchev's speech was read in full or in part to a fairly large audience: in Bologoe, for instance, on 11 April 1956, 159 of the 166 primary party organizations listened to a reading of the speech, with a combined audience of 2,337 of the 3,108 party members and candidates.[77] Another 5,500 nonparty members in the town and surrounding raion were also treated to a reading.

The questions that arose after local readings of the speech in Kalinin oblast' show both the perplexity of some of the listeners, and the perception of others that Khrushchev's position that Stalin's crimes began with the murder of Kirov was untenable. Some wondered why Khrushchev and his colleagues had allowed the crimes to happen, while others uttered the usual complaints about inadequate housing, high prices, and the absence of goods in the shops.[78] Other questions were raised by the audience about the causes of the "cult" and its manifestation:

What was the aim of the investigations, of the execution of the old Bolsheviks and even of regular partyless people in 1937, because after all at the time the NKVD organs were led by Ezhov, and not by Beria?

How do matters stand with the names of towns, enterprises, institutions, and kolkhozy which have been named after Stalin?

Why didn't the members of the Presidium of the Central Committee of the Communist Party of the Soviet Union stand up and talk about Stalin's mistakes at the Nineteenth Party Congress?

What happened to Ezhov?

Why did only Postyshev have the courage to stand up openly?

Why does comrade Malenkov remain in the leadership?

How are the documents preserved about comrades Kedrov, Eikhe, and others?

Will Stalin remain in the Mausoleum?

Was Stalin really near Rzhev [in the war]?

How many wives did Stalin have and who were they?

Why did comrade Khrushchev state, in his conversation with Tito, that "we will not allow the debunking of Stalin," and a short while later he comes out with a report which debunks Stalin? Where is the logic here?

Why expose this all to the people, for it is better to have only Central Committee members know it, as now they will say abroad that we do not have unity in the party, no collectivity; what is all this supposed to show?

Why did Molotov, knowing the true "face" of Stalin, cry at his funeral?

Why was it difficult for the members of the Politburo to speak out against the cult of the personality of Stalin before Stalin's death? After all, a communist should not be afraid.

Will it be justified to consider Stalin an enemy of the people?

Did Stalin exaggerate with respect to the collective-farm system?
What was Stalin's attitude towards Jews?
Who turned Stalin into a superman?[79]

These questions were still rather timid in comparison with some of
the conclusions others made after listening to the speech.[80] In Kalinin,
during discussions after the reading of the speech, some Communists
and non-Communists drew the "wrongful" conclusion by accusing the
complete Central Committee of involvement in the "cult." One teacher
told his colleagues that one should not believe in Soviet power. Another
person came to the defence of Stalin by accusing Stalin's comrades-in-
arms of participation in, and responsibility for, the mistakes made
during the cult. He added to this, rather perceptively, that Khrushchev
and Bulganin were also engaging in a cult of their own, judging by the
newsreel of their trips to India, Burma, and Afghanistan to which vis-
itors to the cinema were treated.

It would still be a long while before the Russians were allowed to
become acquainted with the real extent of Stalin's crimes, the involvement of his cronies, and the political blunders committed between
1929 and 1953. When finally a genuine effort was made in the Soviet
Union to come to terms with its history, the system created under Lenin
and Stalin, and the party that had been its guiding light, the edifice collapsed almost immediately. Perhaps the remarks in the survey of
ninety-six-year-old P.A. Samarova, a former weaver of the kombinat
Proletarka, who had begun her work at this factory in 1908 when it
was still known as the Morozov factory, provide a fitting illustration
of the fatalistic attitude towards the powers-that-be acquired by many
Russians as a result of all the upheavals:

I began my life still under the tsar-little father. They say, that life was better
then. But I say: for a working person it was also hard to live then. When my
husband died [in 1932], good people fed us as if we were orphans. There were
more good people then.

I saw the tsar, he came to Tver': reddish, in a soldiers' gray coat, silent.
Under the tsar, life for a working person was bad. I remember our factory
owners: Ivan Abramovich Morozov and his strict mother Varvara Alekseevna:
she was an almsgiver and built a workers' club.

I had to work both under this and under the other system. Now they start
to build some sort of third kind of life.[81]

Society became consistently more corrupt after Stalin's death.
Khrushchev would be the last party leader until perestroika and glasnost' to try to reinvigorate revolutionary enthusiasm. Brezhnev, for all

intents and purposes, accepted Soviet reality and let the "second economy" have almost free reign in the country. In his years the train had come to a full stop against the buffer at the end of the track. The term Zastoi (period of stagnation) aptly describes the Brezhnev years. Sporadically, the leadership attempted to revive the attitude of selfless sacrifices and strict discipline of the 1930s and early 1940s. Occasionally some scapegoats – the party leadership of Georgia, the dissidents – were persecuted in those years.[82] Dissidents ran against a wall of complacency and conformism erected by their fellow citizens, who were glad to be finally left alone and who did not want to be bothered by having to imagine new changes, let alone experience them. They were all too happy to have the right to be smug. This right (witness the behaviour of Boitsov and Vorontsov described earlier) was obtained only after Stalin's death.

After 1953 most Russians had witnessed too many upheavals during their lifetime and were unwilling to jeopardize the low, but adequate, standard of living that greatly exceeded that of Stalin's days. Only with the coming of age of a new generation that had hardly experienced the deprivations and fear of the Stalin years could the success and initial popularity of Gorbachev's policies become possible. The nostalgia of some people for the time of Stalin is, therefore, baffling. The enduring success of that era's propaganda are exemplified by the remarks in the survey of E.V. Baranova, who had never been a Communist Party member. In the summer of 1992 she mechanically repeated what used to be written in the paper and announced on the radio or in meetings under Stalin, saying that "[w]hen remembering my life, especially in the period from 1945 to 1953, I am of the opinion that, then, the socialist system was beneficial and satisfactory, while life improved with every day."

The renewed repression of the postwar years, the failure of collective farming and the Spartan living conditions and minimal pay in the towns, and the revelations by Khrushchev in 1956 provided a fatal blow to the zeal for constructing a better society and the optimism about the future rekindled by the victory in war. The regime survived for twenty-five years after Khrushchev's ouster, but neither the rulers nor the ruled seemed to have been very enthusiastic about life in the Soviet Union and its prospects during this time. When the leadership under Gorbachev allowed for a new round of discussion about the mistakes of the (Stalinist) past, the Communist-controlled facade would be thoroughly discredited within less than five years.

Conclusion

More research into postwar developments in the USSR will be necessary before one can defend the thesis that events in Tver' province were emblematic of Soviet or Russian history in this period. Yet demographic, economic, and military criteria, as well as the similar structure of the Soviet government and Communist Party everywhere in the USSR, have suggested that this chronicle may serve in several respects as typical of the history of many Russian provinces in this period.

The first part of this book has indicated how traditional Russian life endured enormous changes in this century. Some of these changes resulted from developments that had commenced long before 1917. When industrialization first began in the Tver' guberniia during the 1850s and the abolition of serfdom allowed the peasantry a degree of free movement, its traditional Russian society started to change at an accelerated pace. The province's environment was not conducive to burgeoning crop yields because of its geographical location, poor soil conditions, and frequently overabundant rainfall. The countryside was, nevertheless, home to the vast majority of the provincial population, even though the land was overpopulated before collectivization. Many peasants were thus forced to take up employment on the side, some of them gradually abandoning farm work altogether. Despite these adverse conditions, most of the Russians continued to till the soil until 1929. Peasant attitudes remained predominantly "pre-modern": peasants did not elect to farm for profit but rather were interested in safeguarding a level of production sufficient to answer their basic needs. The idea of producing a surplus for the market seemed largely alien to them.

The people's initial enthusiasm for the New Regime that the Decree on Land had generated in November 1917 quickly evaporated. Grain confiscations led finally to peasants' revolts and the assassination of the authorities' representatives (as in Vyshnii Volochek uezd), forcing the Bolshevik regime to reverse its policy and enabling the peasants to resume momentarily the routines of pre-1914 life. In the towns, industrial production decreased during the Civil War. The industrial labour force dwindled as a consequence of factory workers' service in the Red Army or of their return to the ancestral village, while the spread of fatal epidemics diminished the urban population even further. Although textile factories had been founded early in Tver' guberniia, the region preserved its primarily agricultural character even after the NEP was introduced.

To a great extent, the advent of NEP meant a return to the pre–World War I situation. An uneasy symbiosis developed in the 1920s between traditional life in the countryside (where 85 percent of the population lived) and the ideologized culture of the New Regime, mainly concentrated in the towns. Because of the cautious policy of the regime under the NEP, a certain level of prosperity in the countryside was achieved, and gradually even industry began to surpass the pre-1914 level. As before 1914, some peasants joined the work force in the towns because a decent livelihood in the countryside was denied to them as a result of rural overpopulation.

In 1929 and 1930 the Bolsheviks launched a full-scale attack on the peasants' culture and spirit, as well as on what remained of factory workers' independence. Peasants and workers were mobilized in the Velikii Perelom in a manner that harked back to the period of War Communism.[1] At the same time, the authorities' patience had run out with the virtually non-Bolshevized way of life led by most people in 1929. The assault on traditional society appealed to certain people, some of whom saw a chance for a grandiose revenge for past wrongs inflicted by former exploiters. The latter, however, had become figments of myth rather than social reality. Because they did not exist, many people sufferered as scapegoats. Urban zealots participated in the offensive, believing in the possible creation of a better world of socialism or communism through the application of ruthless methods. But the richer peasants, for example, were generally innocent of exploitation of the poor and landless peasants, as is exemplified by the fate of Mironov.

In Tver' guberniia, collectivization and industrialization provoked a precipitous drop in agricultural productivity and an ancillary stagnation of the level of industrial output. The peasantry struggled desperately to escape the countryside. This exodus was partially checked by the introduction of the passport regime in late 1932. Five years later, the local agricultural boss admitted to the abominable agricultural situation during the Great Purge. His intention probably was to preempt accusations of covering up the real situation, but this did not save him from arrest.

In 1934 Stalin decided, *cum suis*, that success had been crippled owing to a failure to discipline people properly during the initial assault of the early 1930s. As a result, from early 1935 onwards the central leadership ordered a renewed offensive to force the population to obey the authorities' orders unconditionally. Boitsov's numbers of 1938 on arrests made in rural areas from 1935 to 1937 offer telling proof of the scope of this new onslaught. The climax came in 1937 and 1938, when it was made clear that everyone was liable to arrest if suspected of disloyalty or tainted by a disreputable background or connections. The attrition rate within the party was astounding during 1937 and 1938. As a result of the Great Purge, in the Kalinin obkom in December 1938 virtually no one remained from the elected group of leaders of June 1937. The NKVD had repeatedly hauled off throngs of obkom members who served briefly in the provincial leadership during the eighteen months following June 1937.

Arrests were a standard feature of life throughout the 1930s, judging by the evidence on Kalinin province. The apprehension of victims during 1937 and 1938 stood out, because society's more vocal portion, the Communist elite, was among the prime targets. Psychologically, the Ezhovshchina was a triumph for the regime. After the war, those years served as a grim reminder to anyone who thought critically of the leadership and its watchdogs, the MGB/MVD. The threat of arrest was always present in the collective consciousness.[2] Before the war, it is likely that the vast number of victims (those imprisoned, exiled, sent to labour camps, or executed outright) in Tver' province resulted primarily the from collectivization in the 1929–33 period and the Great Terror of the years 1937 and 1938, but even in the period between 1934 and 1937 thousands were arrested.

A possibly even greater number of provincial residents (around three hundred thousand out of a population of approximately two million) was killed during World War II.[3] Although the destruction wreaked was enormous in Kalinin province, it was deliberately exaggerated after the war in order to explain the province's plodding recovery. During the war the regime managed to invoke a brand of nationalism that was dubbed Soviet patriotism. The Nazi attack led to a temporary rapprochement between vlast' and narod. It was probably the regime's most glorious moment in all those years in which it had incessantly exploited the ghoulish image of "enemies" preying on the USSR. Indeed, in 1941 actual, deadly foes had materialized. World War II may have been the time in which the planned economy worked at its best. In the eyes of Communist leaders, the wisdom of their policies was vindicated by the victory over the Nazis. The prewar liquidation of the alleged "potential fifth column" in 1937 and 1938 was now presented as a far-sighted policy. It was not explained, however, why considerable numbers of Soviet citizens had passively observed the arrival of Nazi troops and why even some Communists had actively collaborated with the "Hitlerites."

Part 2 of this book began by sketching the theoretical possibility that existed in 1945 to begin with a clean slate, to make amends for the mistakes of the 1930s, and start afresh. Policies that would have addressed the needs and demands of workers, intellectuals, and peasants would certainly have been welcomed by most Russians. It is indicative of the nature of the regime, its ideology, and its hallowed leader that such a turnaround was not allowed to happen, as Boitsov already indicated at the sixth party conference of Kalinin oblast' in January 1945. While Stalin's Regime could have resigned itself to the internal rebuilding of the devastated USSR and a more adequate provisioning of its inhabitants, it resumed totalitarian policies at home, forced Soviet-style regimes upon the East-Central European countries, and spent most surplus funds generated in the Soviet economy on the further expansion of heavy industry, particularly of armaments.

Four months before the fall of Berlin, first secretary Ivan Pavlovich Boitsov delivered the political report at the sixth provincial party conference. Boitsov noted a plethora of problems but spoke nevertheless with a tone of cautious optimism: following the official positive discourse about the radiant future, he saw no reason to suspect that Kalinin province's problems were almost insurmountable. In 1951 Storozhev's list of shortcomings echoed that of Boitsov in 1945, for little had apparently changed for the better more than six years after the war. Towards the end of Stalin's life, matters only deteriorated further.

On the eve of Stalin's death, V.I. Kiselev, already the third leader of the provincial party organization after Boitsov's transfer to Stavropol in 1946, received the disturbing report on the province's agricultural development discussed in chapter 8. Peasants were leaving the collective farms in droves. The kolkhozy were apparently unable to offer any attraction to make their members stay. A few days after Stalin's death in March of 1953 Kiselev ordered the members of the obkomburo, S.N. Shatalin and G.A. Demirskii, to propose agricultural reforms on the basis of the report; these reforms would eventually improve peasant life, but they came too late to stop further depopulation of the villages. Agricultural production, meanwhile, has continued to languish to this day.

The provincial leadership had been forced to attempt to remedy the postwar state of ruin within the limitations of "Marxism-Leninism," for the thought of economic or political alternatives was strictly prohibited. No truly creative solutions to problems beleaguering Kalinin province during the postwar reconstruction period could have been proposed. Because of that peculiar, blindly obedient mentality that had been forged within the Bolshevik Party since the October Revolution itself, Boitsov and his successors were not able even to *imagine* an alternative to the rigid structure of Stalin's organization of state and society. The only methods applied to generate successes were coercion, threats, propaganda, and agitation, which frightened not only the average Soviet citizen but the local leadership as well. Boitsov's "victory speech" of January 1945 reveals a personal fear of appearing complacent.

Even though the province was close to Moscow, the decrees and initiatives from the centre often could be only imperfectly executed, owing to their adaptation to local circumstances by the local authorities or by the people themselves. Such tinkering was not the result of the periphery forcing the centre to cater to its interests, as some scholars argue today. It was almost always a reaction to the imprecise central policy that allowed a large degree of interpretation, to the horror of the local leaders. They knew that too liberal an interpretation of central policies would translate into insubordination and that the resulting penalty was usually severe. Many of Moscow's decisions applied uniformly to large stretches, or even the whole, of the Soviet territory. As a result, local authorities rarely carried the orders out to the letter and had to fear the consequences of this "disobedience." The oral accounts of the inhabitants of Tver' province have shown emphatically that the Russians were not the interchangeable cogs in the machine that Stalin would have preferred. All dealt with the same kind of difficulties, but every individual found a different way to cope.

The limited tolerance of local initiative allowed since the beginning of the war dwindled between 1945 and 1950. At the end of the 1940s, factory manager Rumiantsev and local-boy-made-good Vorontsov and his clan were removed for what would seem too liberal an attitude. The tightening of the screws only contributed further to the abysmally flagging economic performance of the early 1950s in industry, particularly of the textile factories, and in agriculture. First secretary Konovalov was quickly removed, making room for Kiselev, who started out as more of a hard-liner than his predecessor, owing to his "education" in the Central Committee apparatus. Soon, however, perhaps on instigation from above, Kiselev discovered that matters could not continue as before, specifically in agriculture.

The resources allocated to the Kalinin party organization by Moscow were extremely limited, for few vital industries were located in the province. This lack of funds, combined with the poor state of roads, the telephone, telegraph, and radio networks, and the low level of education of party and government personnel, making it difficult for the provincial leadership in Kalinin to organize and guide a province of this size in an efficient manner and to monitor the execution of Party and government decisions. Hence the continued economic failure, becoming sharply manifest after 1949. The largest share of responsibility for this failure, however, should be assigned to the strategy followed by the leadership of the Communist Party in Moscow and by Stalin himself.

In early 1946 agriculture, and in particular socialized farming, had to start virtually anew on the road to rationalization and mechanization that began with collectivization. The parallel is all the more striking if one takes into account the famine in 1946 and 1947, which appears to have been a repetition of the famine of 1932–33. The kolkhozniks relied mainly on their efforts on the private plot for their income and sustenance and tried to do as little as they could get away with in the socialized sector. The trudodni were so little appreciated – undoubtedly because of their pitiful remuneration – that they were handed out to all kinds of individuals who were legally not entitled to them, such as construction workers, employees of rural soviets, and mail carriers.

Collectivization had failed miserably, and the amalgamation of 1950 further aggravated the poverty and resentment of the peasantry. The authorities' interference by ordering the merger of the small collective farms was probably the main cause of the abysmal agricultural performance from 1950 to 1953. The adverse consequences of amalgamation are obvious when the comparatively positive results of 1948 and 1949 are contrasted with those of the subsequent years. In September 1946, February 1947, June 1947, and June 1948, the Central Committee and Soviet government decreed a slew of predominantly coercive measures to improve Soviet agriculture, but they did not succeed in Kalinin province. From 1948 to 1952 the upper echelons in Moscow reacted by issuing a series of specific resolutions for Kalinin oblast' that also failed to ameliorate farming. Two first secretaries of the provincial party organization were sacrificed within two years, but matters only worsened.[4]

Private farming survived against all odds: kolkhozniks excluded by the collective farms struggled on their own minimal plots; more emphatically, the kolkhozniks reaped an enormous share of total agricultural production from their private plots and livestock. Collective farming languished because the authorities imposed an alien organiza-tional system upon the tillers of the soil and deliberately neglected the welfare of the kolkhozniks. The much heralded mechanization of agri-culture failed to materialize: land was predominantly cultivated with the help of manual equipment, horses, and oxen. Specialization in the two agricultural sectors best suited for the lands of the province – flax and dairy farming – did not occur. Against all odds, every kolkhoz cul-tivated cereals on a large scale.

The kolkhozniks were obliged to deliver exorbitant quotas of crops grown within the socialized sector of their farms, for which they were allotted a picayune remuneration, mainly in kind (less than 500 grams a day for each person in 1951!). In addition, substantial amounts of produce from their personal plots and few private animals, which they had been allowed to retain under the Ustav of 1935, were paid as "taxes." As if this were not enough, the forced purchase of obligations for state loans further sliced the kolkhozniks' income. As a result of poor communications and a primitive infrastructure the authorities became resigned to a measure of control over the peasants' quotidian life that was weaker than their control over urban inhabitants. The level of literacy was lower in the countryside, fewer newspapers were read, and radio and electricity were often not available, even by 1953. When the collective farm managed to fulfill the obligations of procurement plans, its kolkhozniks were left alone to a large extent. The private plots were cultivated with intensity, leaving the Russians with hardly any time to try to keep abreast of events in the world outside the village.

The reader might have been struck by a seemingly excessive atten-tion to the fate of the peasantry in previous pages. After all, the Soviet Union claimed to be a workers' state, where the party of the industrial proletariat, the Communist Party, held political power. Yet demo-graphic statistics indicate that country-dwellers formed the majority of the population of Kalinin province even in 1953. The life of the factory workers, particularly after the war, deserves more study, but it would probably be more revealing to focus on an industrially developed area that shouldered a more substantial share of heavy industry than Kalinin province did.[5]

The nostalgia for these former "orderly" times among many older people today is rather curious. It is not true that crime did not exist in the Stalinist years, as many maintained in the survey. Although it might be correct that the incidence of theft perpetrated by fellow citizens was lower, one could argue that, for the countryside at least, the state's offi-cially sanctioned daylight robbery of the peasants' agricultural pro-duction was far worse under Stalin than the "crime" of today. Few people, however, came to this conclusion in Stalin's time, and yet the despair and squalor of kolkhoz life incited a massive flight from the collective farms during the early 1950s.

The centralized distribution system proved to be unmanageable in practice, and regular widespread privations ensued. The second town of the province, Vyshnii Volochek, experienced a relentless series of shortages of goods, and may serve as an example. In late 1945 there was often no bread in the town; in the early 1950s, bread queues were ubiquitous and other goods were scarce; even by 1955 the average resident consumed only 500 grams of meat per month! Life in the towns knew many other hardships: people were housed in abominable quarters, with no more than five square metres of space per person on the average. Roads and bridges were dilapidated, water supply deficient, sewers decrepit.

One of the crucial elements of the Russians' acceptance of the indiscriminate ruthlessness of Stalinist policies may be linked to their inability to compare their life with life in other societies.[6] Apart from that, some urban residents appreciated what seemed to be the improvements – in their thoroughly blunted memory – of the socialist state: guaranteed employment, universal education, official gender equality, paid holidays, free medical care, and pensions for some.

The position of women after the war was far from enviable. In practice, it did not reflect the socioeconomic equality with men that had been intended by the legal liberation of women from male dominance in 1918. It may be that, disproportionately, women had escaped the annihilation and suffering of the male population between 1929 and 1945. After the war, however, women were worse off than most men (except those who lingered in the GULag). Women performed most of the unskilled and semi-skilled labour of the most plebeian jobs, working as milkmaids, loggers, rank-and-file collective farmers, weavers, and spinners. Additionally, they had to rear their children and manage the household, sometimes because there was no man in the household (killed during or before the war); but realistically a man's presence did little to alleviate her double or triple burden.

The sobering industrial results, similar to those of agriculture, were precipitated by a dearth of investment: machinery had become obsolete, skilled workers were rare, and management was rarely competent, thanks to insufficient education, paltry remuneration, and the throttling of creative thinking. Wages were so anemic that the families of many factory workers could not survive even on the double income earned by husband and wife. Some were lucky enough to have a private plot at their disposal, while others worked on their days off or tried to augment their income by selling domestic crafts. The boldest ones resorted to theft and embezzlement.

The labour force, drastically reduced in the war, was far too small to execute a successful economic revival after the war. The leadership attempted to deploy prisoners of war and Soviet convicts, but forced labour was hardly efficient. Despite Vorontsov's or Konovalov's complaints, the contingents were gradually decreased by the MVD so that the limited contribution of coercive labour was cut down even further. Even so, the mind boggles when confronted with the pervasion of the GULag Archipelago in Stalin's Soviet Union. Kalinin province has never before been seen as a centre of convict labour, but it has been amply proven in Chapter Six that the Party and government of Kalinin province had tens of thousands of POWs and zeks at their disposal immediately after the war. The convicts worked in all sectors of the economy, from construction projects to factories, and even agriculture. In March 1948, fifteen camps, in which ten thousand Soviet convicts languished, operated on provincial territory.

The terrible repressions of the 1930s were a vivid memory for everyone, whether they were first secretary of the province, such as Boitsov, chair of the raion executive committee of the soviet, such as Iamshchikov, or simple toilers, such as many of our Tver' 1992 survey participants. Even if someone had always been toeing the line, never straying from correct political, social, and economic behaviour, there was the possibility of being called in for questioning by the organs. Arrests were arbitrary at times. Some were invited to show their loyalty by working as informers for the organs, an offer that could not easily be refused. Sometimes one was selected by the organs, sometimes one was denounced (even by one's relatives). At times one could be made culpable for acts (or the absence thereof) that one was either unaware of or unable to affect.[7]

Rather than a genuine political enthusiasm for the creation of socialism, it was a combination of fear and a desire to live a life without undue harassment by the authorities that made people carry out the duties with which everyone was burdened after the war. The economically extreme postwar deprivations endured by a great majority made a profound impression on their memories. For many elderly people, the anxiety, uncertainty, and economic hardships that have been concomitant with the dissolution of the Soviet empire seem to resemble the difficulties they coped with in Stalin's last years.[8]

Until 1953 agriculture would continue to stagnate or even deteriorate, despite all the Central Committee's warnings and threats and some measures taken to improve it. Only the substantial increase of procurement prices in that year would ameliorate performance and, temporarily, curb the exodus to the towns. In industry also, matters ostensibly improved after Stalin's death, although some factories (mainly in heavy industry) were meeting their plans even before 1953, probably because the remuneration and living conditions of their personnel were superior to those of others. Textile factories would fully recuperate only in Khrushchev's time: although heavy industry would certainly still be a priority (as Khrushchev's criticism of Malenkov in 1955 showed), the investment level in light industry (consumer goods) would increase. Consequently, by way of higher wages and technological innovation, the incentive became greater to enhance and increase in factory production.[9]

Industrialization and modernization are a traumatic experience for any community.[10] It is likely that the further industrialization of Russia would have been a painful and cumbersome process even without the Bolshevik coup of October 1917. But Stalin's merciless policies made the Soviet road to modernization an immeasurably worse experience than was necessary or desirable. A society was created that was almost the exact opposite of one "in which the free development of each is the condition for the free development of all."[11]

Under the guise of the benefactor who would create a Communist paradise on earth, Stalin took a slew of measures that profoundly shook the lives of his subjects. Yet his kolkhoznik remained essentially a Russian peasant, while the fate of the Russian factory workers under Stalin did not improve over that of their forebears under the tsars. Sickle and hammer, collective farmer and worker, waited in vain for the radiant future predicted by the dictator and his henchmen to be always around the corner: that future was nowhere to be found in Stalin's domain. With the possible exception of armaments production, Communist achievements were negligible in an economic sense, while the Soviet curtailment of social, economic, and political freedom dwarfed the comparatively superficial control of the narod by tsarist bureaucracy.

The example of Kalinin oblast' makes clear that the system gradually lost its ability to entice people to produce more after the war. Poverty after 1945 was as vast as in the 1930s; an indication of this lasting poverty was the very small natural growth rate of the population after the war. The Germans could be paraded as the culprits of the hardships after 1945, but for many of those who could remember the NEP, the sacrifices of the 1930s must have seemed incomprehensible. Indeed, by March 1953, twenty-five years after the announcement of the First Five Year Plan and ten years after the Nazi retreat from the province, little progress had been made in comparison to the 1920s. Lack of investment and the absence of any meaningful material incentives for the workers began to tell on economic performance. Initial revolutionary enthusiasm had led to herculean efforts, in particular among industrial workers, and contributed to much of the growth of heavy industry in the 1930s. The subsequent sense of patriotic duty during the war, combined with the limited room for personal profit, was not replaced with similar abstract or material incentives afterwards.[12] After the Soviet victory, the population at large was overwhelmed with apathy towards party propaganda promising a "radiant future." Perhaps for a few years after March 1943 people in Kalinin province were stirred by some of the slogans. But they tried to rebuild the economy as well as they could mainly for themselves, and not for the greater good of the Communist cause. Towards 1950 they ran out of steam, and almost everyone began to cheat the authorities in order to improve their personal existence.[13] The chimerical threat from the outside perhaps provided the strongest stimulus for some to sacrifice their health and well-being for the defence of the Motherland.

Youth began to grow restless towards the end of Stalin's life, a mood that was expressed by their inordinate presence in the judicial courts. Some of this rebelliousness was provoked by the flaws in the Soviet system itself, particularly by the failure of the economy to provide adequately for the people. The remuneration for factory workers, employees, and peasants was so dismally low that people engaged in "illegal" economic activities in order to avoid starvation. Shabashniki or kolkhoz markets made up for the system's inability to provide the required goods and services. Private enterprise had to be tolerated for the same reason. The scarcities created a situation from which less scrupulous (or more daring) individuals attempted to make a profit, not only through the sale of domestically produced goods (by using a sewing machine or carefully tending an apple tree) but also by outright crime. It was almost fatal to be found guilty of engaging in this type of activity, because penalties were severe until Stalin's death. But people covered for each other, so that many escaped retaliation. The higher provincial authorities were sometimes powerless to combat these activities; they eluded their view, which was impeded by a large and cumbersome bureaucracy. Moreover, some individuals within the elite tacitly allowed such activities or even became involved in them; this was perhaps the case with the director of the railroad-car plant, Rumiantsev, and his intimate set of collaborators, or with those in the legal system who received bribes from "criminals and speculators." Yet, sometimes the authorities expressed their displeasure with these activities by arresting the participants. The number of postwar arrests did not surpass those during the 1930s, but possibly one in every twenty inhabitants of Kalinin oblast' stood trial between 1945 and 1953.

It is impossible to prove conclusively, but, as this study suggests, the roots of the corruption at all levels of society, particularly during and after Brezhnev's time, can already be unearthed in Stalin's last years (1945–53). At this time, despite the heavy penalties, many people found more-or-less illegal methods to augment their pitiful wages. Some individuals were apprehended, but the narod must have felt intuitively that the authorities could ill afford a new Great Purge because of the tremendous population losses of the 1930s and the war. Therefore, many ran the risk of arrest – a dangerous gamble, however, as the high number of arrests in 1949 and 1950 indicates.[14]

Inevitably, economic performance improved markedly people were offered material benefits and some of the hard-line ideology emanating from Moscow or Kalinin was relaxed. Propaganda utterly failed to mould the inhabitants of Kalinin province into rational, atheistic, and modern Communist people during Stalin's lifetime. The regime lacked the technological means for genuine total control of society, even during the grim latter half of the 1930s. Therefore, "remnants of capitalism" clung tenaciously: religious practices were observed, and, in certain instances, the traditional solidarity of the villagers held out against the authorities, even though the village had by then become a collective farm. Religion had been under attack since October 1917, but the regime proved incapable of extinguishing piety and venerable customs altogether. Hallowed tradition outshone coercion and propaganda in many respects, although God and Tsar may have been replaced by Stalin in the minds of some. The Communists attempted to destroy traditional Russian culture but were unable to eradicate the Russian attitude towards property and family: the peasantry dedicated itself to cultivating private plots; the workers were interested in higher wages, enhanced benefits, and decent housing. Parents encouraged their children to abandon the squalor of life on the collective farm or in the factory by having them educated. The workers and peasants, in the name of whom the Communists ruled, tried in this way to vicariously escape their supposedly superior existence as manual labourers. After the failed Velikii Perelom of the First Five Year Plan, Communists resigned themselves to tolerating some ingrained Russian traditions. Owing to a threatening economic chaos, the authorities were forced to acknowledge that it was impossible to eradicate private property and the instinct for personal gain: hence the survival of private plots, hence the enticement offered to the Stakhanovites.

The evidence on the continued application of coercion in Kalinin province until 1953 gives little credence to the hypothesis of the "Big Deal" between the authorities and a vaguely defined middle class reached in Stalin's last years, as proposed by Vera Dunham.[15] Proportionately, the intelligentsia ostensibly suffered the most after the war from the renewed political repression. Due to the Zhdanovshchina, intellectuals were under intense scrutiny after the middle of 1946. Furthermore, the regime did not care about the material situation of those who remained outside the party. Many members of the intelligentsia were paid as little as, or less than, factory workers and lived in sordid circumstances; such was the case in the Kalinin province with the teaching staff of the Pedagogical Institute, agricultural specialists, and rural teachers. "Intelligentsia" was a grand label for many of those who were supposed to belong to the intellectual elite, but no more than a few dozen Kalinin residents enjoyed an education approximating contemporary North American university undergraduate standards. The general level of schooling was extremely basic: the reader should perhaps try to imagine how his or her outlook on life would be as an adult after a mere four years of grade school. The majority of Russians muddled through with such scant tutelage, and the alleged intellectual elite often fared with only a little more.

The nomenklaturnye were the only ones who could savour a degree of prosperity after the war. Nevertheless, their activities were examined just as minutely as those of the rest of the intelligentsia; many of the party elite were victimized if they did not meet the high ideological standards demanded of a Communist. The dismissal of members of the elite from positions of power was, however, more often a consequence of other flaws. For instance, a local leader's removal could be prompted by inferior economic performance in his territory. Rather arbitrary grounds for dismissal were often invoked: for example, one could fall victim to the system's need for an occasional scapegoat; membership in the wrong "clan" resulted in ostracism; and if disliked by too many people in influential positions, someone might be harrassed for no specific reason at all. In these cases, ideological motives played a minor role.

The dismissal of Vorontsov and Konovalov, the purge at the railroad-car plant, and the staggering turnover of Party functionaries at all levels contradict the idea of the Big Deal in Stalin's last years. Whether or not the regime attempted to copy the atmosphere of the Ezhovshchina from 1948 onwards is a moot point, but Elena Zubkova's argument to this effect, judging from evidence for the Kalinin province, seems more convincing than Dunham's suggestion of a truce between a certain section of society and the regime.[16] The Communist Party membership was certainly privileged as an abstract entity, but, on an individual level, the situation of each Communist was more insecure than that of nonmembers. The Communists, particularly, could expect at any moment the proverbial knock on the door.

It is better to speak of a rigid dichotomy between vlast' and narod in postwar Kalinin province, than of an integration between the two as a result of the opportunities for social climbing. Kolakowski's quotation at the beginning of this book applies rather to the elite than to the factory workers and peasants, for the lies about glorious Soviet life and its ever-increasing prosperity were hard to believe for the narod, who lived in squalor. Only a few million dedicated Communist believers, however, were necessary to rule Russia under Stalin. The party was considerably more numerous than the quarter million Bolsheviks who reigned over Russia in the early days under Lenin.[17] Prewar society was reconstructed after the war, and the chasm separating vlast' and narod was reimposed. Any independent mood, which had sometimes been fostered by the disorganization during the war, was suppressed after 1945 by means of ideological offensives and sporadic political arrests that kept the memory of the horrors of the 1930s alive. All were expected to do their duty and to forsake their human rights in expectation of the millennium.[18] Beneath the "happy few" (the higher party authorities), society was composed of individuals who more or less shared an equal status. In this light, the egalitarianism of Soviet society under Stalin might have appealed to some. Social justice reigned, since no one in fact possessed legal rights; all were poor, and everyone had to work to the point of utter physical exhaustion. At least there were few to envy, moreover, because the loftier party members managed skillfully to conceal most of their privileges.

It was clear by 1953 that zealous observance of ideological conformity and severe discipline had not yielded brighter economic results. The alternative to a loosening of the reins – a renewed avalanche of arrests similar to that of 1936–38 (perhaps considered by Stalin during the last year of his life) – was impossible for Kalinin province, for the population losses sustained during the 1930s and the war had not been compensated for by 1953. Far from it, in fact, because the population had remained roughly the same size in the eight years since the war. The deprivations of the war and postwar period, as well as the extreme tribute exacted from the population, afflicted the health of many and caused a very low natality. Health care in general was only very gradually improving.

By 1953 the resilience of human individuality and the imperfect means enforcing solid uniformity made the Soviet leadership tacitly accept its failure to create a "Homo Sovieticus." Khrushchev's or Gorbachev's efforts to rekindle the Communist dream seem limp in retrospect, for they lacked the ruthless determination and disregard for human life that Stalin had had. Even Stalin's methods, however, had been incapable of creating the dystopia of a perfect totalitarian society, in which human beings were controlled, body and soul, by the political leadership. Stalin's death was timely if it is true that he had decided once more on a renewed round of purges of the magnitude of the Ezhovshchina. His death opened the door for the introduction of moderately positive reforms. The beneficial effect of the reforms of Malenkov and Khrushchev was expressed in renewed economic growth in Kalinin province, while the standard of living of its population sharply improved.

A Note on Sources

Upon my first arrival in Russia in September 1991, during the chaotic aftermath of the failed coup by the Communist hardliners, the central archive of the former Communist Party appeared to be closed, or at least inaccessible to me. Later on, in the summer of 1992, it was possible to visit at least one section of the archive, which was kept on Sovetskaia Ploshchad' in Moscow, but the location of many of the documents concerning the party's policies towards Kalinin province in the postwar years remained unclear.

One part of the Central Committee archives appeared to be located in the buildings of the former Central Committee of the Communist Party of the Soviet Union on Staraia Ploshchad' in Moscow; another part was probably preserved within the Kremlin. Access to many of the records in these three collections is still restricted to Russians and other nationals of the former USSR and cannot be investigated freely by foreigners. The same applies to the archives of the former secret police and, for instance, to the military archives that are kept in Podolsk.

Apart from my research in Moscow, I spent most of November 1991 in the former Kalinin, which was given back its pre-1931 name of Tver' in 1989. Here I worked both in the State Archive of Tver' oblast' and in the former Party Archive, renamed at this time Tverskoi tsentr dokumentatsii noveishei istorii. In Tver' it proved much easier than in Moscow to locate important information on the province during the postwar period. For example, in contrast to extremely difficult – often humanly impossible – and time-consuming efforts to find material on Kalinin oblast' in the former Central State Archive of the October Revolution (TSGAOR), in Tver' the data were easy to locate and were handed over to me for inspection without cumbersome formalities. Only twice was I not allowed to look at a certain record in the State Archive of Tver' oblast' during this first visit, something that would be remedied in the summer of 1992.

The number of records in the oblast' archives in Tver' is staggering: in 1986 in the State Archive alone, according to its reklamnyi prospekt (advertising prospectus), more than 600,000 records could be found on the Soviet period. The former party archive possesses a similar number of records. Their length varies: some of them consist of a mere ten pages of text, others of several hundred. The State Archive harbours a large number of handwritten texts, much more so than the former party archive, where manuscripts form only a fraction of the total.[1]

The records of the Soviet period in the State Archive cover an enormous range of institutions and organizations, almost all part of the oblast' (guberniia, okrug) government, ranging from records "of the local organs of state power, state government, and state control, of the institutions of the judiciary, the courts, and the procuracy, of the organs of social order, planning, statistics, financing, credit, and state insurance, of institutions, organizations and enterprises of the economy, of communications, of the people's education, of culture, of science, of health care, of labour and social insurance and welfare, of fizkul'tur and sport, of social organizations."[2]

Although at first sight this collection seems like a veritable goldmine for anyone trying to study the life of the Russian people under Communism, on the whole most of these records are not very useful. Since they are official documents and were even to some extent open to the public in Soviet times, they recount, with some exceptions, only the official view of matters, the bureaucratic side of affairs, especially for the post-1945 period. If one were to base one's research merely on these documents, it would probably result in a tedious and rather positive account of life under Stalin. One interesting exception can be noted in the letters of constituents at the end of the 1940s and during the first half of the 1950s with complaints and requests to the RSFSR Supreme Soviet deputy, I.F. Gagurin. Here some idea can be gained of the real state of affairs in the countryside in particular, for Gagurin, a model tractor operator, represented a rural riding in the Supreme Soviet.[3]

It turned out to be far more interesting and worthwhile to concentrate on the records in the former party archive. In Kalinin oblast', too, these archives confirm Merle Fainsod's truism that "it was the Party which played the dominant role" in Soviet society.[4] Although the government was formally separate from the party, its sphere overlapped with that of the party, and the party made the decisions. Fainsod describes the omnipresence of the Communist Party in the postwar period. The party's ubiquity also applies to Kalinin province in the later 1940s and early 1950s. Among themselves, the members of the higher echelons of the Party in the provinces were relatively frank about the real state of affairs. The oblast' first secretary and the obkom secretariat received a continuous stream of information on all aspects of life in their fief; meanwhile, the Central Committee in Moscow considered the first secretary to be responsible for the successes and failures in the oblast'.[5]

As a result, there are several thousand dela (files) of various sizes for the period, now ensconced in the archive of the former Communist Party in Tver'. The party tried to be informed of every aspect of life in order to avoid unpleasant surprises in the field of ideological matters, the economy, and so on, for which the obkom members could be held responsible by Moscow. Obviously, the party obkom was aware that it was not possible to hide the sometimes unpleasant truth from the centre: the oblast' was at all levels under the surveillance of employees and stool-pigeons of the NKVD/MVD, NKGB/MGB, the representatives of the party Control Commission, of the central and RSFSR ministries, of Gosplan, and so forth. It appears that no detail could be left to the initiative of outside agencies, perhaps apart from some minor innovations in industry; any initiative for change came necessarily from the government and the party, and mainly from the central party and government organs at that. As Anatolii Rybakov writes:

HE [Stalin] created a party of a completely new type; a party, distinct from parties of all times; a party, that was not only a symbol of the state, but also the only social force in the state; a party, for whose members it was not only the main virtue to belong to it, but was also the substance and thought of their lives. HE created the idea of the party as such, as something absolute, substituting for everything: god, morals, home, family, morality, the laws of social development.

Such a party had not yet existed in the history of humanity. Such a party was a guarantee of the indestructable state, HIS state.[6]

Thus, by concentrating on the recorded concerns of the obkom secretariat, its departments, and its first secretary, one derives an impression not only of party life under Stalin but also of the existence of the great majority of the population, of that 95 percent or more who remained outside the party in Kalinin oblast'. The party records have been maintained far more methodically than the State Archive records: in the case of the latter, some collections were randomly transferred to the archive if a certain governmental (soviet) institution or enterprise no longer needed to keep the records on hand. Other records fell into the care of the archive when reorganizations took place, certain departments were dissolved, or the internal borders of the oblast' were redrawn, as in the case of certain raions that disappeared from the map in the 1950s.

While at first the material on the kolkhoz financial accounts of some raions appeared interesting, on the whole it proved disappointing: it might be of use only to researchers trying to offer a detailed account of the financial and economic viability of the different collective farms. Only with great difficulty can any impression of life on the kolkhoz be gleaned from these accounts.

Owing to the frequent reorganizations of the obkom apparatus, important leads were sometimes lost. Other leads disappeared because no standard method for the collection of the records prevailed throughout the various obkom departments. It is possible to gain a fair amount of data on the activities in the first postwar years of certain organizations that were part of the NKVD/MVD, such as those of the militsiia. These could not be found for later years, for the method of collection was altered and records on the security organs disappear from the inventories. It is impossible through scrutiny of the opis' (catalogue) to determine where these records might have ended up. One imagines that internal security was tightened and the records on the security organs were to be kept by the MVD/MGB themselves. After all, during his trial in 1953 Beria was accused of trying to place those organs above the party.[7] This accusation may have been part of an effort to make the security organs a scapegoat for the excesses of the Stalin era, while in fact Beria himself may have lost control over these organs in Stalin's later years. The accusations against Beria were not wholly a flight of Khrushchev's or Malenkov's imagination. For example, no transcript of the MGB representative's speech was entered into the stenogramma at an oblast' party conference in 1949; previously such a speech would not have been repressed. Based on circumstantial evidence, one infers that the representative spoke about a politically sensitive case at Kalinin's largest factory. V.A. Feoktistov, the head of the Tverskoi tsentr dokumentatsii noveishei istorii, suggested to me that this repression of the transcript was done on the request of the security organs.[8] By the late 1940s the security organs enjoyed the prerogative of prohibiting the obkom from recording the contents of the speech made by one of its employees, for reasons of secrecy.[9] Nevertheless, the security organs in Kalinin oblast' could not act in complete independence from the party. Meanwhile, the party itself was just as unscrupulously eager to avail itself of forced labour by Soviet convicts and prisoners of war.

I visited five major archival collections:

1 Tverskoi tsentr dokumentatsii noveishei istorii (Tver'), in which the archive of the provincial organization of the former Communist

Party of the Soviet Union is preserved. In the notes, references to this archive are indicated by the acronym "Pako" (Partiinyi arkhiv kalininskoi oblasti).

2 Gosudarstvennyi arkhiv tverskoi oblasti (Tver'), in which records are kept of the provincial Soviet government, as well as of economic, social, cultural, and related organizations. References to this archive are indicated in the notes by the acronym "Gako" (Gosudarstvennyi arkhiv kalininskoi oblasti).

Both archives in Tver' correspond to Patricia Grimsted's description of their operation: the collections first divide into fondy (archive group), which in turn branch into opisi (inventories).[10] Within an opis', the content of the dela (numbered file units) is listed briefly – sometimes, however, the opis' description of a certain delo is incomplete or inadequate. One can find out what a delo contains only by perusing it oneself. The delo contains actual documents. Often, and in the former Communist Party's archive even without exception, the materials are grouped together within the delo because they were the responsibility of the same department, or of the same person, as in the case of Gagurin's letters in the State Archive. Thus, the Party Archive categorizes the dela according to the different party obkom departments (otdely): there are dela of the special sector, the agricultural otdel, the industry and transport otdel, the administrative otdel, and so forth. The location of the delo was thus contingent on the administrative organization of the obkom departments at a certain time as well, since the Central Committee frequently reorganized the obkom administration after the war.

3 Tsentral'nyi gosudarstvennyi arkhiv Oktiabr'skoi Revoliutsii, vysshikh organov gosudarstvennoi vlasti i organov gosudarstvennogo upravleniia SSSR (Moscow), references to which would be indicated as "TsGAOR," but no material from this source has found a place in the text. Today it is called Gosudarstvennyi arkhiv rossiiskoi federatsii (GARF).

4 Rossiiskii tsentr khraneniia i izuchenie dokumentov noveishei istorii (Moscow), in which part of the archives of the former CPSU are kept, although the collection is far from complete and many records still are held (sorted out?) in the buildings of the former Central Committee on Staraia Ploshchad' in Moscow and possibly in the Kremlin itself. References to this archive are indicated in the notes as "Moscow."

5 The Newspaper Department, located in the Moscovite suburb of Khimki, of the (what was then known as) Gosudarstvennaia Ordena Lenina biblioteka SSSR imeni V.I. Lenina, where I perused the provincial newspaper Proletarskaia Pravda/Kalininskaia Pravda.

Notes

1 Kolakowski, "Totalitarianism," 129.
2 Some of the rank-and-file party members and district soviet officials belong to what I call the "people" (narod) here rather than to the category of the "authorities." I define as local authorities the oblast' (provincial) and raion (district) committees and their administrative apparatus, the security organs, and the officials of the raion and oblast' soviets. There is no clear-cut division to be made between the narod and the authorities (vlast'); at lower levels some people had to act at times as authorities, but at other times preferred to identify themselves as part of the narod. (For Russian and Soviet terms, please consult the glossary as well.)
3 Cf. Zubkova's recent monograph, which states that "[t]he period from 1945 to 1953 appeared to be one of these gaps, still not genuinely interpreted by either native or foreign historians." (Zubkova, *Obshchestvo*, 5). See as well the afterword in the same book by Academician P.V. Volobuev, esp. 189 ("Posleslovie," 189–98).
4 For example, Conquest, *Harvest* and *The Great Terror*; Volkogonov, *Triumf i Tragediia*; R. Medvedev, *Let History Judge*; Tucker, *Stalin in Power*; and Heller and Nekrich, *Utopia in Power* are thorough in their account of the 1930s and, sometimes, World War II, but they have comparatively little to say about the immediate postwar period.
5 The wave of social, political, and economic transformations, changing society irrevocably after 1914, seems to peter out after World War II. The focus of Western historiography with respect to Stalin's later years has been mainly on foreign policy and the different aspects of repression by the regime, such as Zhdanov's activities in the field of culture, the rise of Lysenko and its consequences for the sciences, the Leningrad Case, the

Doctor's Plot, state-sponsored anti-Semitism, the deportation of the nationalities, and the terror in the Baltics, Western Ukraine, Western Belorussia, and Moldavia. For the 1929–41 period, primary evidence can be found in the Smolensk archive, which is preserved in the United States, and sometimes in the testimonies of those who had managed to escape during the confusion of the war.

6 Sheila Fitzpatrick characterizes the "revisionists" as "the so-called revisionist movement in American Sovietology, which was associated both with repudiation of Cold War scholarship, particularly the totalitarian model, and with a challenge from social historians to the dominance of political scientists" (*The Cultural Front*, x). For an impression of some of the revisionists' works, see, e.g., Fitzpatrick, "Cultural Revolution as Class War," and Lewin, "Society, State and Ideology," or Rittersporn, *Stalinist Simplifications*. Their adversaries do not deny that a mere discussion of higher politics and the pivotal role played by politicial persecution is insufficient, however. As Richard Pipes has written, any historian should address "[t]he relationship between political, intellectual, and social factors [which] is by its very nature a complicated subject, with sometimes one factor, sometimes another serving as the prime mover. The historian never confronts a stark choice: for him, the problem is always one of emphasis." ("1917 and the Revisionists," 70–1). The revisionist application of "political science criteria" to Soviet history, according to Robert Conquest, has led, however, to an astonishing underestimation or even denial of the "sheer nastiness of the system and its paragons, or the blinkered triviality of their [i.e., those paragons'] ways of thinking." (Conquest, "Red for Go," 4). Peter Reddaway agrees with Conquest's criticism of the inappropriate application of social science methods ("The Role of Popular Discontent," 58).

7 Sakharov, "Revolutsionnyi totalitarizm," 61.

8 Ibid., 63–9; see, as well, another article by Sakharov, in which he tries to explain the historical roots of the events of the twentieth century in the USSR: "Demokratiia i volia," 42–53.

9 Cf., for example, Hochschild, *The Unquiet Ghost*, xxii–xxiii.

10 Poletika, *Vidennoe i perezhitoe*, 406–7.

11 In the 1950s Klaus Mehnert noticed a decline of interest in politics in comparison to the 1930s in the USSR (*The Anatomy*, 224–5).

12 Cf. Zubok and Pleshakov, *Inside the Kremlin's Cold War*, for a fine appreciation of postwar Soviet foreign policy.

13 Bullock, *Hitler and Stalin*, 919–20.

14 An indication of the kind of material that has been preserved in the archives of the former KGB is in the transcripts of the postwar telephone and domestic conversations between Colonel-General Gordov, his wife, Major-General Kulik, and Major-General Rybal'chenko. The criticism

they uttered in these conversations about the regime's policies and Stalin personally proved to be fatal to all four involved. Ella Maksimova wrote, rightfully, in the introduction to the article that "[t]his kind of thing we have probably not read yet, although papers of a similar kind are preserved more than sufficiently in secret archives, above all those of the KGB." ("Podslushali i rasstreliali," 7).

15 To give but one example: the dissidents Krasin and Iakir spent part of their banishment as employees of the Kalinin' typographical kombinat in the early 1970s. Undoubtedly some of today's local authorities must have gone along or been involved with the execution of the sentence against the two. At the moment, it could harm their political careers if they were confronted with participation in this type of case. The difficulties encountered by researchers, both Russian and foreign, who try to gain access to the former KGB archives are well illustrated in a recent article by Vladimir Abarinov in the English-language digest of *Nezavisimaia Gazeta* ("More Troubled Waters"). Further, there are organizational problems involved in making formerly secret archives available to the public that have recently been described by the vice-chair of the Committee for Archival Affairs under the Government of the Russian Federation, V.P. Kozlov, ("Ob ispol'zovanii dokumentov," 77–82). It cannot be denied that the lack of accessibility to certain records is partly due to the enormous amount of work involved in this reorganization and cannot be blamed solely on the ill-will of Russian archivists or authorities.

16 Cf. *Let History Judge*, 468n14. A.N. Mertsalov claims that many of the documents of the security organs have indeed been destroyed ("Stalinizm," 445–6). A.P. Fedoseev even predicted that other archival documents and the accounts of eyewitnesses would be highly questionable, for "[o]ne can almost be convinced that, even after the ruin of dictatorship in the USSR, one cannot succeed in revealing objective information through these documents. In documents, it seems that Soviet power is as clean as a baby. Of course, the evidence of the obvious will sharply contradict that, but the witnesses (as sources of objective, unfavourable, and dangerous information for the leadership) are under supervision as well, and the leadership takes any measure to keep trustworthy information out of their hands. That's why even this source will turn out to be incomplete. Essentially, in the history of a great people, a gaping lacuna will remain, and the ill-informed will perceive this time as an almost heavenly epoch" (*Zapadnia*, 340).

17 Oral history is certainly not an entirely new phenomenon in Soviet historiography; James Hoopes points out that "[one] of the greatest writers in the world today, Alexander Solzhenitsyn, might fairly be called an oral historian, because *The Gulag Archipelago*, his trilogy on the Soviet Union's forced labor camps, is based on the spoken accounts of his fellow

prisoners, who could not safely have written their stories." (*Oral History*, 11).

18 "The Case of the Russian Archives," 344–5.

19 Portelli, *The Death of Luigi Trastulli*, 50. Indeed, despite the rather large number of respondents in the survey conducted in Kalinin province who had become members of the Communist Party at some point during their adult lives, almost all show their individuality in their recollections, at times freely interpreting the party line in retrospect.

20 Although I intended to conduct a "sociologically representative" survey on the basis of socioeconomic statistics of Kalinin province in the postwar period, using geographical, occupational, gender, political, and other criteria, little came of this. Thus, the results of the survey are in some ways limited, but by no means irrelevant: they still illustrate many of the concerns and difficulties with which inhabitants of Kalinin oblast' had to deal in the 1945–53 period. For a full overview of the survey, please consult Boterbloem, "Communists and the Russians", appendix 1.

21 Of course, the survey resembles to a certain degree the Harvard Interview Project of Russian refugees in the 1940s and 1950s; nevertheless, due to the fact that those respondents managed and *wanted* to leave the Soviet Union in the war and postwar confusion, that project could not claim to be representative of the mentality of average Soviet citizens. In addition, the Harvard Project dealt chronologically with the period until approximately 1945. The survey in Tver' province focussed on the subsequent period. The results of the interviews in Tver' province can form somewhat of a counterbalance to the results of those surveys. For an example of the findings of the Harvard Project, cf. Inkeles and Bauer, *The Soviet Citizen*.

22 Rutland, "Sovietology," 122.

23 For a rather cynical, but quite humoristic, view of the limitations of sociological surveys, see Aleksandr Zinoviev's parody of the questionnaire of the Sociologist in *The Yawning Heights* (518). I must admit that some of the questions in it closely resemble the ones I conceived; even so, I do believe the Tver' survey yields some fascinating and startling evidence I could not have gathered otherwise.

24 For the resentment towards the recent changes, cf. Specter, "In 'Real' Russia," (1, 7), in which the author describes the dying village of Kushalino in Tver' province.

25 Cf. S.M. Miner, "Revelations, Secrets, Gossip and Lies," 19. No Russian or Western scholar has been allowed to publicize which historical documents are preserved within the Presidential Archive, but it is known that many sensitive papers are held there, to which only a select few have gained access since August 1991. See, for example, Miniuk, "Sovremennaia arkhivnaia politika," 16. KGB: stands for Committee for State Secu-

rity, the name for the secret police of the USSR between 1953 and 1991. It was previously called the MGB/MVD, and, before 1946, the NKVD. The NKIu was the People's Commissariat of Justice, redubbed the Ministry of Justice (MIu) in 1946. A new archival law was decreed on 7 July 1993 by President Yeltsin; for its terms, see "Osnovy zakonodatel'stva," 3–12.

26 Stalin, *Works*, 99.

27 Shchapov, quoted by Venturi, *Roots of Revolution*, 199. Peter Rutland also noticed this lack when he examined the contents of eighty-seven PHD dissertations written on Soviet domestic politics in the United States between 1976 and 1987 ("Sovietology," 115).

28 Altrichter, *Die Bauern von Tver*.

29 Fainsod, *Smolensk under Soviet Rule*.

30 Kotkin, *Magnetic Mountain*, 1995.

31 Cf. Lel'chuk, "Industrializatsiia," 354.

32 Anokhina and Shmeleva, *Kul'tura i byt'*, 5. See also Il'in, "Raskrytie," 11.

33 V.P. Danilov states that "[i]n Russia the process of industrialization on a capitalist basis began later than in economically advanced countries. At the beginning of the century, it disposed of a developed light industry, especially of textiles" (Danilov et al., "NEP i ego sud'ba," 175–6).

CHAPTER ONE

1 Cf. the argument of Barrington Moore about the small scale of the Terror of the French Revolution as compared to the "tragic toll of unnecessary death" of the Ancien Régime (Moore, *Social Origins*, 103–4). Richard Pipes would certainly deny this argument is applicable to the Russian Revolution: he has good grounds (Cf. Pipes, *Russia under the Bolshevik Regime*, 508–12).

2 It changed, however, between 1929 and 1935, when the area was split up roughly between the Western oblast' and Moscow oblast', and from 1935–44, when it was significantly larger (106,000 km²) than it had been since the eighteenth century, or would be after 1944. In 1957 the oblast' received most of its western territory of today – the raions of Belyi, Zharkovo, Il'inskoe, Lenino, Nelidovo, Oktiabr', Peno, Serezhinskii and Toropets – an expansion of almost 20,000 km². The town of Tver' was called Kalinin from 1931 to 1989, and the province was known during most of the Soviet era as Kalinin oblast' (Smirnov et al., eds., *Ocherki*, 337, 364; *Kalininskaia oblast' za 50 let*, 11. In the nineteenth century, the guberniia was 80 percent of the size of the enlarged oblast after 1960 (Akademiia Nauk SSSR, *Tsentral'nyi Raion*, 526). "Guberniia" and "oblast'" are used as synonyms of "province" in the text.

3 Cf., for example, *Tsentral'nyi Raion*, 527. In recent times, Politburo

members, such as Suslov and Brezhnev, enjoyed hunting in the Zavidovo raion south of Kalinin-Tver'. Even the current president invites his foreign guests to participate in the same activity there.

4 *Tsentral'nyi Raion*, 32–4, 42, 120, 525; the population density measured was of the area that included territory added to the oblast' in 1957; this sparsely populated western addition to the contemporary oblast' decreased the density. The population of the oblast' was larger before the war, and consequently, the density was higher (see table 1).

5 *Bol'shaia Sovetskaia entsiklopediia*, 431.

6 *Tsentral'nyi Raion*, 27–30, 206, 525. The same climatic problems still plagued agriculture in 1959, and, no doubt, still do today.

7 See Altrichter, *Die Bauern*, 289n8; see as well Kerblay, *Du mir aux agrovilles*, 30, for a description of the similarly inimical natural environment for agriculture in neighbouring Smolensk province.

8 Altrichter, *Die Bauern*, 68–72.

9 Altrichter, *Die Bauern*, 51–72, 92–5.

10 The term "peasant" is used in this book to denote a person who cultivates the land (cf. Jackson, "Peasant Political Movements," 273). "Peasant" corresponds to "kolkhoznik" (collective farm member or worker) for the post-1929 era. "[P]easants differ chiefly from farmers in that they have their own distinctive 'part culture' or sub-culture and regard agriculture as a way of life rather than a business" (ibid.). In George Jackson's opinion, in further distinction to farmers, peasants are allotted a low socio-economic status; they live in a family household closely connected with their neighbours in the village; they comprise the most numerous social group ("class"); and others dispossess them of the bulk of their produce. The last distinction, however, does not apply to the Tver' peasantry during the New Economic Policy: in the 1920s, the peasants consumed most of their agricultural output themselves. Only after collectivization would the largest share of the peasantry's produce be appropriated by the state. In Jackson's terms, until Stalin's death and even after, the cultivators of the soil undoubtedly remained peasants.

11 Altrichter, *Die Bauern*, 71–95.

12 In 1926, about 93 percent of the population was ethnically Russian, 6% Karelian (migrants who had moved to the environs of Tver' in the seventeenth century), while less than 1 percent was of other ethnicity (Vershinskii, *Kraevedcheskii atlas*, 3–4; *Tsentral'nyi Raion*, 72–3). The Karelians, as well, were mainly peasants.

13 Altrichter, *Die Bauern*, 13; Kerblay, *Du mir aux agrovilles*, 30–1. After the Emancipation of 1861, the average yield of grain that was fit for human consumption in neighbouring Smolensk oblast' hovered around 220 kilograms per capita, far below the average of the more southern areas of the Russian Empire.

14 Altrichter, *Die Bauern*, 71–95.

15 Il'ina, "Ustanovlenie sovetskoi vlasti," 33, 35, 36; Keep, *The Russian Revolution*, 455–6.

16 Smirnov et al., *Ocherki*, 228–9. For "volosti," and other Russian terms used in this book, see the glossary. The writers of *Ocherki*, following standard Soviet practice, give the anti-Communist peasants noted here the pejorative name "kulak" (which means literally "fist," but is used as an equivalent for "rich peasant," particularly in Communist terminology).

17 The Bolshevik support was furnished by 143 Communists and 54 sympathizers (sochustvuiushchie) of a total of 465 delegates at the congress (Smirnov et al., *Ocherki*, 230–1).

18 Ibid., 231.

19 According to Bol'shakov, in July 1919, there were on average six deserters per village in Goritsy volost' (Bol'shakov, *Sovetskaia Derevnia*, 76–7). A revolt broke out when some of them were arrested by the military commissar. Thirty-five Red Army soldiers were dispatched to the district to suppress the revolt and two of the leaders of the deserters were executed.

20 Typhoid fever, in particular, was a problem; Smirnov et al., *Ocherki*, 232, 243.

21 Smirnov et al., *Ocherki*, 234.

22 For the Workers' Opposition, and Democratic Centralists, see, for example, Fitzpatrick, *The Cultural Front*, 26–30.

23 Smirnov et al., *Ocherki*, 251, 253; Pipes, *Russia under the Bolshevik Regime*, 448–54. One of the few "genuine" workers in the All-Union Party leadership, Shliapnikov, was at this time also subscribing to an opposition platform.

24 See Heller and Nekrich, *Utopia in Power*, 105–6 and 114; Smirnov et al., *Ocherki*, 250–1; the former Party Archive of the Communist Party of Kalinin oblast' in the Tverskoi tsentr dokumentatsii noveishei istorii, fond 147, opis' 1, delo 527, list 129 (henceforth Pako, 147/1/527, l.129; for a discussion of the archival collections used in this study, and their divisions, see the appendix); Lewin, *Lenin's Last Struggle*, 12–13, 32; Pipes, *Russia under the Bolshevik Regime*, 454–5; see as well as ibid., 374–8, 386–8 on the Antonov Rebellion. A. Suslov and A. Fomin note that in the village of Kuvshinovo a "kulak" revolt took place in July 1919, which might be another revolt or the same one (*Torzhok*, 71). According to N.A. Akhov, who participated in the survey, in 1923 or 1924 a revolt erupted in the town of Korcheva, when de-kulakization was taking place. It is likely that he meant 1933–34, because no de-kulakization, according to all evidence, was conducted in 1923–24.

25 Drobizhev and Poliakov, "Istoricheskaia demografiia," 468–9. Cf. Wheatcroft and Davies, "Population," 62–4.

26 Smirnov et al., *Ocherki*, 250; Bol'shakov, *Sovetskaia Derevnia*, 41n2, indicates that the famine bypassed Tver' guberniia. Richard Pipes notes the areas that were worst stricken with famine (*Russia under the Bolshevik Regime*, 411).

27 Solzhenitsyn, *The Gulag Archipelago*, pts. 1–2, 325; pts. 3–4, 74; Abarinov, *Katynskii Labirint*, 45; for the "Assault on Religion," see Pipes, *Russia under the Bolshevik Regime*, 337–68.

28 Altrichter, *Die Bauern*, 41; Zhuravleva, "Konfiskatsiia pomeshchich'ikh imenii," 58–9.

29 Medvedev, *Soviet Agriculture*, 127; Smirnov et al., *Ocherki*, 263; Korzun, *Pervye shagi*, 94; Wheatcroft and Davies, "Population," 66; for population numbers see table 1.

30 Smirnov et al., *Ocherki*, 305, 317.

31 Ward, *Russia's Cotton-Workers*, 43.

32 Smirnov et al., *Ocherki*, 271; Korzun, *Pervye shagi*, 92–3.

33 Smirnov et al., *Ocherki*, 289 and 318; Ward, *Russia's Cotton-Workers*, 24.

34 Smirnov et al., *Ocherki*, 276–7; Altrichter, *Die Bauern*, 164–5.

35 Altrichter, *Die Bauern*, 79.

36 Ibid., 81, but cf. Sergeev, "Sel'skoe khoziaistvo," 265. This source is less reliable than Altrichter's solid work. Sergeev maintains that before collectivization all peasant households were dependent on work outside agriculture.

37 Altrichter, *Die Bauern*, 81.

38 See Vershinskii and Zolotarev, *Naselenie*, 8–9; *Goskomstat SSSR*, 22–3.

39 *Tsentral'nyi Raion*, 119; between 1926 and 1939 the population declined by 6.7 percent according to Soviet statistical handbooks (see table 1 and cf. the fifth section of chap. 2). During these years the urban population almost doubled.

40 Fitzpatrick, *Stalin's Peasants*, 38.

41 Altrichter, *Die Bauern*, 85–6; as is admitted by Alekseeva and Chernyshov, *Kalininskaia oblastnaia*, 215.

42 See for a similar opinion Altrichter, *Die Bauern*, 186.

43 Cf. Fitzpatrick, *Stalin's Peasants*, 313–20.

44 Altrichter, *Die Bauern*, 74; Smirnov et al., *Ocherki*, 312.

45 Ibid., 310–11; Korzun, *Pervye shagi*, 47.

46 Smirnov et al., *Ocherki*, 315; Korzun, *Pervye shagi*, 48.

47 "The foundation of the Soviet Imperium is terror and its inseparable, gnawing offshoot – fear. Because the Kremlin abandons the politics of mass terror with the deaths of Stalin and Beria, one can say that their departure is the beginning of the end of the Imperium. The thaw under Khrushchev and then the years of stagnation alleviate somewhat the

frightful nightmare of Stalin's epoch, but nevertheless do not radically eliminate it." (Kapus'cin'ski, *Imperium*, 314–15).

48 Altrichter, *Die Bauern*, 182–3. Cf. as well an interesting recent article on the Stalinists' attack in 1928 on the leadership of neighbouring Smolensk guberniia (Afanas'ev, "'Smolenskoe delo' 1928 g."). Afanas'ev argues with some justification that, in comparison with the well-known Shakhty case, the Smolensk case was far more important. In the Shakhty case accusations were forged against a comparatively small group of engineer-specialists of wrecking and connections with foreign intelligence services; in the Smolensk case a whole Party organization was accused of degradation and of "a political bloc with the kulaks," and the entire peasantry of the guberniia was accused of a transition to the capitalist way of development (58). It is likely that in Tver' guberniia an extensive purge of the leading party positions took place in 1929 as well, as the attack on the Vyshnii Volochek leadership mentioned earlier indicates, but that it was less severe than in Smolensk guberniia, where in 1929 "practically a new Party organization was created." (69; see the previous section).

49 Altrichter, *Die Bauern*, 183–5; cf. Fitzpatrick, *Stalin's Peasants*, 42; on the de-kulakization, see V. Danilov, "Kollektivizatsiia," 388–91; Bugai, "20-40-e gody," 41); and, for an understanding of the motives behind the assault and the consequences of de-kulakization, and the like, cf. Volkogonov, *Lenin*, 2, 163–4, 168–9.

50 There has been no shortage of Western publications discussing collectivization in recent years. See, for example, Fitzpatrick, *Stalin's Peasants*.

51 Il'in, "Raskrytie arkhivov," 11–12.

52 Today the nuclear power station of Tver' oblast' is located in Udoml'ia raion and has fundamentally transformed this formerly strictly rural raion. Ironically, in the 1960s the operation of the kolkhoz Moldino would be described in glowing terms in a series of articles by Leonid Ivanov in *Novyi Mir* ("V rodnykh," "Snova," and "Litsom."). For the persecution of troublemakers within the de-kulakization, see Fitzpatrick, *Stalin's Peasants*, 54–5. A similar case for the later Kalinin Oblast', near Rzhev, is noted ibid., 55–6.

53 Asinkritov, "Raskulachennyi," 4–5; see Altrichter, *Die Bauern*, 22, for a description of khutory.

54 Korzun, *Pervye shagi*, 83, 85; testimonies of M.M. Kozenkova-Pavlova and A.K. Sumugina-Shepeleva in the survey. For "Dizzy with Success," see Stalin's article of the same name. The original appeared in *Pravda* on 2 March 1930 (ibid., 205). Cf., as well, Conquest, *Harvest*, 160.

55 Testimony of A.E. Malysheva in the survey.

56 Smirnov et al., *Ocherki*, 346. Cf. Fitzpatrick, *Stalin's Peasants*, 56.

57 Altrichter, *Die Bauern*, 185; Afanas'ev, "'Smolenskoe delo' 1928 g.," 70;

for the evolution of Soviet legislation on agriculture and collective
farming, see Fitzpatrick, *Stalin's Peasants*, xvii–xx.

58 Smirnov et al., *Ocherki*, 338; Ledovskikh, "Kalininskii raion," 41;
Korzun, *Pervye shagi*, 82–3. Cf., too, Fitzpatrick, *Stalin's Peasants*, 40.

59 Anokhina and Shmeleva, *Kul'tura i byt'*, 268; Smirnov et al., *Ocherki*,
374; testimony of M.V. Chesnokova in the survey. A report of 15 August
1929 described the situation with religion and anti-religious propaganda
in the guberniia to the Tver' gubkom; still almost 1,000 churches and
monasteries functioned in the province, and 1,058 priests and monks had
survived up to that point (see *Tverskoi tsentr*, 11). Around 5,000 people
belonged to non-Orthodox denominations. The Old Believers were the
largest among these: they numbered approximately 2,800. For an account
of the results of the anti-religious offensive of the 1930s and further
examples of the marked antagonism of women towards collectivization,
see, e.g., Conquest, *Harvest*, 157; Fitzpatrick, *Stalin's Peasants*, 45, 65.

60 Altrichter, *Die Bauern*, 187–9. In the wake of the Sixteenth All-Union
Party Congress of June–July 1930, after a brief period in which the
province had been split up administratively into okruga, the okrugs were
dissolved and split up into raions, residing under the administration of
the Western and Moscow oblasti (or provinces; sometimes translated as
regions)(Smirnov et al., *Ocherki*, 361–2).

61 Smirnov et al., *Ocherki*, 337; Volkogonov, *Lenin*, 2: 167–8.

62 Altrichter, *Die Bauern*, 190; Smirnov et al., *Ocherki*, 338–9; Heller and
Nekrich, *Utopia in Power*, 237; Fitzpatrick, *Stalin's Peasants*, 42.

63 Korzun, *Pervye shagi*, 84; Altrichter, *Die Bauern*, 190.

64 Smirnov et al., *Ocherki*, 341. Altrichter (188–90) mentions December,
but the actual dispatch of these activists occurred later.

65 Ibid., 343–4.

66 Ibid., 344–5,d 373.

67 Conquest, *Harvest*, 181–2. Far from all city dwellers applauded the collectivization drive. See Kotliarskaia and Freidenberg, *Iz istorii*, 83.

68 Altrichter, *Die Bauern*, 191; Korzun, *Pervye shagi*, 84–5; Heller and
Nekrich, *Utopia in Power*, 234.

69 Korzun, *Pervye shagi*, 84.

70 Ibid., 85.

71 Ibid., 86; Smirnov et al., *Ocherki*, 349. Revolts against collective farming
and the forced closure of churches were taking place at this time as well.

72 Pako, 147/1/527, ll. 105–8.

73 Altrichter, *Die Bauern*, 192; Heller and Nekrich, *Utopia in Power*,
239–40; Korzun, *Pervye shagi*, 87; Smirnov et al., *Ocherki*, 351.

74 Smirnov et al., *Ocherki*, 347, 350. See Stalin, "Dizzy with Success."

75 Korzun, *Pervye shagi*, 87; Altrichter, *Die Bauern*, 192. According to
Danilov, from 1929 until 1932 half of the cattle in the country were

slaughtered (Danilov et al., "NEP," 181). In the areas that were designated in late 1929 for all-out collectivization all draught cattle and cows, 80 percent of hogs, and 60 percent of sheep and goats were to be socialized; as a consequence almost one-quarter of the stock of strong-horned cattle was lost in the USSR in just two months in the winter of 1930 (Borisov et al., "Politicheskaia sistema," 274–5).

76 The authorities resorted to confiscation of property in case the edinolichniki could not pay the high taxes (see Zelenin, "Krest'ianstvo," 22).

77 Smirnov et al., *Ocherki*, 352, 372, 376; Heller and Nekrich, *Utopia in Power*, 240; Danilov, "Kollektivizatsiia," 397.

78 Smirnov et al., *Ocherki*, 368–9.

79 Ibid., 373–4; Volkogonov, *Lenin*, 2: 171; Borisov et al., "Politicheskaia sistema," 275–6. Russian: "Ob okhrane imushchestva gosudarstvennykh predpriiatii, kolkhozov i kooperatsii i ukreplenii obshchestvennoi (sotsialisticheskoi) sobstvennosti". Sovnarkom: Council of People's Commissars.

80 Pako, 147/1/554, l.95; see the discussion of the Ezhovshchina later in this chapter for Boitsov's numbers; the exact date was 27 December 1932 (Conquest, *The Great Terror*, 21). The decree was connected with the famine that was gaining momentum in Ukraine, Kazakhstan, and in other places. "Passports were given to the inhabitants of towns, workers' settlements, raion centres, construction projects, sovkhozy, MTS, and introduced as well in a 100-kilometre-wide zone along the European borders of the USSR and in several suburban zones. In all other rural localities the population (the kolkhozniks) did not receive passports and were taken stock of by lists, that were kept by the rural soviets" (Borisov, "Stalin," 478). The introduction of the passports also led to a purge of "alien elements" among the urban population in 1933. The plan for this purge in Kharkov in the Ukraine called for the banishment of 50,000 people from the town (Khlevniuk, "30-e gody," 82). Some of the features of the passport regime, particularly the restrictions on settlement in certain towns for nonresidents, survive to this day (Borisov et al., "Politicheskaia sistema," 278). Only in 1974 was the right to a passport for all rural dwellers legally acknowledged in the USSR (ibid.); Kerblay claims that this was only the case in 1979 (*Du mir aux agrovilles*, 19).

81 E.g., Pako, 147/1/526, ll.66–74; see e.g., Conquest, *Harvest*, 340. Rittersporn gives a very convincing argument for the failure of collectivization and the tacit resentment it created among the peasantry in neighbouring Smolensk oblast'(Rittersporn, *Stalinist Simplifications*, 36–7).

82 Smirnov et al., *Ocherki*, 403–4. After the war *Proletarskaia Pravda*, the provincial newspaper, maintained that all peasants in the oblast' were collectivized by 1936 (*Proletarskaia Pravda* [from here PP] 8390, 18 October 1947, 2).

83   Cf. Zelenin, "Krest'ianstvo," 23–6.

84   For the rate of arrest, see in the statement of Boitsov at the third
      oblast' party conference of 1938, given in the discussion of the
      Ezhovshchina later in this chapter.

85   Smirnov et al., *Ocherki*, 404; *Zare navstrechu*, 189; cf. Klatt, "Review
      of Schinke," 676.

86   Smirnov et al., *Ocherki*, 445–7; Pako, 147/1/529, ll.7–8. This plenum
      was concerning itself with the local ramifications of the "first attempt
      at a national plan for agriculture," of 1938 (cf. Rittersporn, *Stalinist
      Simplifications*, 37).

87   Pako, 147/1/529, l.7.

88   Ibid., l.7.

89   Ibid., l.8.

90   Pako, 147/1/554, l.4.

91   Smirnov et al., *Ocherki*, 447 and 451.

92   Ibid., 443–6.

93   Ibid. After the purges, the party and Komsomol underwent a remark-
      able growth; less than two years earlier there had been only 1,926
      Komsomol organizations!

94   Smirnov et al., *Ocherki*, 445; *Zare navstrechu*, 209.

95   Pako, 147/1/526, ll.82–92.

96   Smirnov et al., *Ocherki*, 447; Korytkov, *Kalininskoe selo*, 31–2; cf. Fitz-
      patrick, *Stalin's Peasants*, 163–4. The average size of the household is
      based on the calculation for the kolkhoz' household size in 1941; cf.
      Smirnov et al., *Ocherki*, 443.

97   Smirnov et al., *Ocherki*, 452; *Narodnoe Khoziaistvo*, 57.

98   See Pako, 147/3/2679, l.80b (for an explanation of "ob." see the note
      on translation and transcription).

99   Pako, 147/3/2679, l.70b. On the trudoden', see chap. 7. In 1940, in the
      territory of the post-1944 oblast', there were 9,016 kolkhozy, composed
      of 282,600 households (*Narodnoe Khoziaistvo*, 57; Pako, 147/5/906,
      ll.1, 2, 12 indicates 275,900 households in the kolkhozy on 1 January
      1941. The number in *Narodnoe Khoziaistvo*, 57, might be for early
      1940). There were 999,000 people living in these 275,900 households
      (Pako, 147/5/906, ll. 1, 2, 12). Thus the average size of a kolkhoz
      household was 3.6 in 1941. The kolkhoz household received on average
      551 trudodni in 1940 (cf. *Narodnoe Khoziaistvo*, 57). The average cash
      income per kolkhoz was 24,368 rubles annually (ibid.), but this infor-
      mation is virtually useless, as it is difficult to assess how much of this
      income was distributed among the kolkhozniks as their wage.

100 "Materialy," (II), 17.

101 "[T]he mass repressions were not an accident, but an essential element
      not only of the political system of Stalin, but above all of the socialism

of Stalin: in a society where the stimuli for work had been undermined, precisely the fear for punishment, which was buttressed by the massive repressions, along with the still present enthusiasm of the masses, who believed in sacrifices in the name of socialism, were most important elements of the successful functioning of the political system" (Butenko, "O sotsial'no-klassovoi prirode," 76).

102 Voznesenskii, *Voennaia Ekonomika SSSR*, 4. Molotov, too, thought afterwards that the terror had been intended to liquidate a (potential) fifth column in case of war (*Sto sorok besed*, 338, 390, 417). An unintentional consequence of the Ezhovshchina was the rise to positions of power of certain former peasants and workers, but it should be stressed that this was *unintentional*. Djilas's perception seems true in this respect: "The social origin of the new class lies in the proletariat just as the aristocracy arose in a peasant society, and the bourgeoisie in a commercial and artisans' society"(*The New Class*, 41). Stalin and some of his cronies masterminded the onslaught which, perhaps even in their eyes, by the the second half of 1938 had begun to get out of hand.

103 Stalin explained his motives for the purge, which he shared only with the higher party echelons, at the 1937 February-March Plenum of the Central Committee ("Materialy," (I), 3–15). The sharpening of the class struggle and the efforts at destroying the USSR by foreign powers combined with a lack of vigilance, were among the main reasons for the sudden universal appearance of wreckers, Trotskyites, spies, foreign agents, murderers and other vermin, according to Stalin (ibid., 3–5, 10–11). Germany was not portrayed as being particularly threatening in Stalin's speech. Stalin's real motives can only be approximated, for the speech of 3 March 1937 seems as much a deception as Voznesensky's justification.

104 Conquest, "Academe and the Soviet Myth," 94.

105 For infant mortality and related issues, cf. Wheatcroft and Davies, "Population", 59, 65.

106 Testimony of N.A. Kotov and A.S. Lukovkin in the survey; cf. also Fainsod, *How Russia is Ruled*, 317.

107 Aptekar', "Opravdanu li zhertvu?," 44.

108 Cf., for example, Thurston, *Life and Terror*, 63.

109 For the twenty-seven million, see, e.g., Krivosheev (ed.), *Grif sekretnosti sniat*, 128. This publication maintains that the demographic loss sustained by all armed forces of the Soviet Union amounted to 8,668,400 (129). In other words, almost 19 million Soviet civilians were killed in the war, which seems to be an unlikely high number. For the negative natural population growth during the war, which should be taken into account when attempting to assess the number of war deaths, cf. Volkov, *Sovetskaia derevnia*, 263. Several sources agree on 194.1

million as the population of the USSR on 1 January 1940 (Eliseev and
Mikhailov, "Tak skol'ko zhe liudei," 31; cf. Heller and Nekrich, *Utopia
in Power*, 462). Volkov estimates 166 million inhabitants for 1945, but
it is not clear how much one can trust this number (*Sovetskaia
derevnia*, 263). In this respect Aleksandr Zinoviev's remark seems still
to be appropriate: "Who's going to be convinced by all these graphs
and tables. Everyone knows that any figures they see in our country are
pure fabrications, and there's no chance of anyone believing that they
are accurate. And the conclusions that can be derived from this sea of
figures are self-evident without any analysis" (*The Yawning Heights*,
517).

110 Khlevniuk, "Prinuditel'nyi trud," 74. Andrei Sakharov and Dmitrii
Volkogonov present the case for the destruction of vital documents, cf.,
for example, Sakharov, *Memoirs*, 531, or Volkogonov, *Triumf i
tragediia*, 1:2, 43.

111 The reader may want to ask: what was, in fact, a "political" crime?

112 After careful reflection, I deemed it unwise to confront interviewees
directly with what undoubtedly was often the blackest page in their
past, mainly for two reasons: first, the interviewees might have experienced grave emotional problems as a result (most of the interviewees
were children or teenagers in the 1930s). Second, direct questioning
about collectivization and the Ezhovshchina might have led some interviewees to refuse to continue the interview. Last, the focus of the survey
was the same one as that of this book, that is, the postwar years.

113 The testimony in the survey of M.I. Veselova was a case in point.

114 Ezhov was appointed People's Commissar of Internal Affairs in late
September 1936 and replaced by Beria in December 1938 (Conquest,
The Great Terror, 138–9).

115 Pako, 147/1/554, l.95. He mentioned this partly, it would seem, to
justify his own appointment and the removal of his irresponsible predecessors. It is surprising that Boitsov, apparently, was not reprimanded
for his frankness, for the regime was not very tolerant of those who
divulged its secrets, even to such a small forum of party faithful.

116 In early 1937 the oblast' population of the province of the larger size
of 1935–44, stood at 3.2 million (Poliakov et al., "Polveka", (I), 16).
Of them, roughly 20 percent must have been urban dwellers (see table
1), and the population must have been around 2.6 million in the
countryside.

117 Il'in, "Raskrytie," 12–13.

118 These decrees are described ibid. G.T. Rittersporn gives a description of
the methods of coercion used in the countryside to make the kolkhozy
meet the targets of the state procurement plans, based on the materials
of the Smolensk Archive. His description can serve as an additional

explanation of the staggering number of arrests in the countryside of neighbouring Kalinin oblast' (*Stalinist Simplifications*, 38–41). Further arrests could have been a consequence of difficulties experienced by the authorities with tax collection.

119 See below, in this chapter.

120 Pako, 147/1/554, l.96.

121 Pako, 147/1/554, l.96.

122 Another example of the pre-1936 repressions can be found at a permanent exhibition on Stalinist repressions in the Tver' museum of kraevedenie that provides evidence of a case against church functionaries in 1933.

123 Pako, 147/4/519, l.230.

124 A recently published guide to the local archives tells how a group of young workers was prosecuted for alleged political opposition during the early 1930s. Ultimately, most of them, as well as their relatives, perished in the purges of 1936–8 (*Tverskoi tsentr*, 13). Some of the atmosphere in Kalinin in 1937 is portrayed in the work of Anatolii Rybakov (e.g., *Fear*, 451, 469–502, 530–40, 552–61, 666–86). Rybakov mentions the – fictional? – arrest of workers at the Proletarka textile factory in 1937 (*Fear*, 489; Proletarka existed, in fact). During the summer of 1937 Kalinin became one of the towns that had passport regimentation, according to this novel, but a recent article on migration seems to deny the restriction on settlement in the provincial capital before 1956 (ibid., 680; cf. Buckley, "Myth of Managed Migration," 905, 906, table 1).

125 Smirnov et al., *Ocherki*, 424, 426–7, 444; Pako, 147/1/554, l.109.

126 Because the evidence is incomplete, the fifty-two exclusions of obkom members during 1937 and 1938 from party and obkom that could be definitively established represent an absolute minimum (cf. Boterbloem, "Communists and Russians," appendix 3, 823–51).

127 "Materialy," (II), 17–19.

128 Pako, 147/1/527, shows how Mikhailov supervises the screening of the proposed membership for the new provincial party committee.

129 At exactly the same moment, a party conference was staged in Smolensk oblast' (Fainsod, *Smolensk under Soviet Rule*, 59). Fainsod's description of Rumyantsev's behaviour as a Bolshevik provincial party leader could probably be applied to Mikhailov, although Mikhailov was more of a newcomer than Rumyantsev (59–60). Fainsod's description of Rumyantsev's zeal can be found, for example, ibid., 237. Mikhailov's behaviour was emulated at the same conference in Kalinin by other leaders. Time and again in 1937 and 1938, vigilance was supposed to increase and new nests of enemies were uncovered. A good example is the resolution of the obkom plenum of January 1938, which makes a fervently paranoid impression (Pako, 147/1/529, ll.7–8). Nevertheless,

following this resolution vigilance was apparently still not sufficient, because Andreev and Malenkov attacked the obkom leadership for its lack of vigilance in March 1938. Later, in July 1938, Boitsov still discerned everywhere in the oblast' remnants of anti-Soviet elements, and "the liquidation of the consequences of wrecking was only beginning" (Pako, 147/1/554, 11.4, 9). Mikhailov had worked in the Central Committe apparat in the late 1920s and was a student of the Agricultural Institute of the Red Professoriat in the early 1930s, and then, until 1935, head of the organizational department and secretary of the Moscow Party committee. He died in 1938, "illegally repressed," and was posthumously rehabilitated (see Alekseeva and Chernyshov, *Kalininskaia oblastnaia*, 451); Mikhailov's trial after he was "unmasked" as an enemy as First Secretary of the Voronezh obkom took twenty minutes (Conquest, *The Great Terror*, 339); see also *Literaturnaia Gazeta*, 1 June 1988, 12, on the Mikhailov case. Mikhailov was apparently accused of trying to organize a "feudal revolution" in the Soviet Union; his trial took place on 1 August 1938).

130 Pako, 147/1/526, ll.211, 213, 216–7.

131 Pako, 147/1/526, l.229; Pako 147/1/527, ll.7–8. Gamarnik committed suicide on 31 May 1937 and was for the first time publicly attacked on 6 June 1937 (Conquest, *The Great Terror*, 201). From 1 June to 4 June, the Military Revolutionary Soviet met at the People's Commissariat of Defense. Stalin himself attended and discussed the discovery of a "counter-revolutionary fascist organization" within the military.

132   Cf. Suvenirov, "Voennaia kollegiia Verkhovnogo suda," 144.

133 Pako, 147/1/527, ll.10–19. For the opposition at the Tolmachevskii academy, see Medvedev, *Let History Judge*, 423, and Petrov, *Stroitel'stvo*, 214–19, and, in particular, 217. For its role in the Great Purge, see Conquest, *The Great Terror*, 207. Strangely enough the "trotskyite" dual command was reintroduced on 8 May 1937 (194), making the accusation even more hypocritical.

134 Pako, 147/1/527, ll.3–130; the particular refusal can be found in Pako, 147/1/527, l.103.

135 Pako, 147/1/526, ll.81–2.

136 *Tverskoi tsentr*, 20; Pako, 147/1/527, l.70; Smirnov et al., *Ocherki*, 425.

137 Cf. note 126, above, for the sources on which this argument is based. Naturally, some might have fallen ill or died; others might have left on their own request, although that was probably not a healthy move to make at this time. Cf. Conquest's observation: "This was in accordance with a common practice of Stalin's. Arrest was decided on; the dismissal occurred; and then for months the victim was left in some minor post, never knowing when the blow would fall" (*The Great Terror*, 241).

A.S. Kalygina, former second-in-command in Kalinin, was arrested sometime between the February–March Plenum of 1937 and another Central Committee meeting in October 1937, when Stalin noted that this Central Committee candidate member was under arrest (Khlevniuk et al., *Stalinskoe Politbiuro*, 157).

138 Cf. Boterbloem, "Communists and the Russians," appendix 3, 823–51. In Pako, 147/1/526 it is noticed at the beginning of the record that at the second party conference the speech of Dombrovskii, who was the head of the oblast' NKVD at the time, is to be found in a separate file; this speech could not be unearthed in the archive of the former party in Tver' by the present author. Dombrovskii's speech probably gave an account of the sins of recently "unmasked" local leaders.

139 Gevorkian, "Vstrechnye plany," 18–19; the USSR NKVD was assigned 75 million rubles to execute the arrests that resulted from this order and spent more than 100 million between July and the end of 1937 for this purpose (Bugai, "20e–40e gody," 42). Rabov had succeeded Mikhailov as first secretary after the latter's transfer to Voronezh; Dombrovskii headed the oblast' NKVD; Bobkov was the oblast' state prosecutor, which confirms Gevorkian's idea of the composition of these special courts ("Vstrechnye plany," 19). Pako, 147/1/528, l.89, notes that Mikhailov had been appointed first secretary of Voronezh oblast' on 8 July 1937 by the Central Committee and that Rabov had been appointed his successor. Bobkov was criticized in July 1938 by Boitsov for insufficiently fighting the wreckers' activities within the oblast's procuracy (Pako, 147/1/554, l.95). Dombrovskii was arrested at some point between July 1937 and July 1938 (Pako, 147/1/554, l.120; Medvedev, *Let History Judge*, 426; Pako, 147/1/594, l.2).

140 Pako, 147/1/554, l.3.

141 Smirnov et al., *Ocherki*, 424

142 Pako, 147/1/554, l.30b., l.90b., ll.240–1.

143 Pako, 147/1/554, l.121; see below for Rabov's possible fate.

144 Pako, 147/1/554, l.122; Kotliarskaia and Freidenberg, *Iz istorii*, 117.

145 Pako, 147/1/554, ll.120–1. The obkomburo was the bureau of the provincial party committee, in which most matters of policy were decided and of which the most important oblast' leaders were members (it thus resembled the position of the Central Committee's Politburo for the entire USSR). Soviet sources seem to deliberately misrepresent the fate of the individual provincial leaders: Mikhailov was "illegally repressed" and died in 1938, but all indications are that the end came for him already in 1937 (Alekseeva and Chernyshov, *Kalininskaia oblastnaia*, 451). I.F. Gusikhin was either executed outright or died in a camp, according to Roy Medvedev (*Let History Judge*, 410), but according to Smirnov et al. (*Ocherki*, 703), he survived and worked in

a much lower position after the war (in 1937–38 he headed the oblispolkom and in 1946–53 the raiispolkom of Kalinin's Tsentral'nyi raion, according to this source, in support of which there is no evidence in the documents). Gusikhin and Rabov had been shunned at the end of June 1938 (Pako, 147/1/529, l.31). V.F. Ivanov, until June 1937 oblispolkom chair, died in 1938 at age 44, which probably means that he was killed in the purges (Smirnov et al., *Ocherki*, 703). P.G. Rabov died at age 39 in 1943, apparently not at the front – otherwise it would have been mentioned by the source – which probably indicates that he was another victim of the purges (Smirnov et al., *Ocherki*, 705). M.V. Slonimskii, head of the provincial militsiia (regular police) was excluded from the obkom and party on 1 September 1937 for being a Trotskyite and maintaining contacts with enemies of the people. He was killed in the purges (Pako, 147/1/528, l.122; Medvedev, *Let History Judge*, 426).

146 This kind of downplaying of the scale of the arrests continues today, although perhaps more out of oversight than for political reasons: a similar faulty calculation is made in the recent brochure of the former party archive (*Tverskoi tsentr*, 13). The archivists appear to have used Boitsov's statements of July 1938 as the source for their calculation.

147 Cf. Alekseeva and Chernyshov, *Kalininskaia oblastnaia*, 447–8; Boitsov would lead the kraikom of Stavropol' until 1956, after which he was transferred to the Party Control Commission in Moscow (see the first section of chapter 3 for more on I.P. Boitsov). Andreev was notorious as a ruthless purger within the higher party ranks by then (cf. Khlevniuk, *1937-i*, 110).

148 Pako, 147/4/519, ll.303–4; 147/1/528, l.124, l.129; 147/1/529, l.3. As we saw previously, perhaps I.F. Gusikhin survived as well, working in a lower position in the provincial government after his demotion (and possible arrest and camp or jail term) of 1938.

149 Gevorkian, "Vstrechnye plany," 19.

150 See Lorenz, *Sozialgeschichte*, 232–3.

151 Pako, 147/1/594, l.2; for the Torzhok case as a whole, see Pako, 147/1/594, ll.2–12. The document is also the first sign of P.S. Vorontsov after the purge. Vorontsov had now been promoted to head the cadre department of the obkom. The NKVD was led by Tokarev, who would occupy this position until shortly after the war.

152 Pako, 147/1/594, ll.2–12.

153 See, e.g., *PP* 8132, 29 December 1946.

154 See Remnick, *Lenin's Tomb*, 5–6.

155 Pako, 147/3/2679, l.880b.–89.

156 The source is the testimony of I.A. Yukhotsky in a recent work on Russian emigrés (Stone and Glenny, *The Other Russia*, 80, 82). For an account of the history of the camps from 1929–41 and the variety of

types of camps, colonies, places of exile, and so on, see Khlevniuk, "Prinuditel'nyi." See also Sysoev, "'Praktik marksizma,'" 84–7, which describes the career of Matvei Berman, one of the heads of the GULag in the 1930s.

157 Testimony of G.V. Lubov and others in the survey; Khlevniuk, "Prinuditel'nyi," 78; Sysoev, "'Praktik marksizma,'" 86. See the third section of chapter 5 for more on the camp system in Kalinin oblast' and the construction of this canal by convicts.

158 On the Polish officers in the Hermitage, see ibid., 44–54; Heller and Nekrich erroneously call Ostashkov Ostashkovo, but their account is similar to Abarinov's (*Utopia in Power*, 404–6). Conquest mentions the camp and calls the location Ostachkov (*The Great Terror*, 447). Remnick has reconstructed, to some degree, the actual executions, with the help of the testimony of the very old Tokarev (*Lenin's Tomb*, 3–6).

159 Abarinov, *Katynskii Labirint*, 46–7.

160 Remnick, *Lenin's Tomb*, 5; Zoria, "Rezhisser," 175–80; Abarinov, *Katynskii Labirint*, 47, 51–3..

161 *Jamestown Monitor*, vol. 1, no.25, 5 June 1995. Executions took place as well at Starodub and Katyn.

162 Petrov, "Kul'tura v provintsii," 265.

163 Korzun, *Pervye shagi*, 53; Khlevniuk, "30-e gody," 79; Alampiev, "Promyshlennost'," 15; Pervozvanskii, "Kozhevenno-Obuvnaia promyshlennost'," 77; see also Lorenz, *Sozialgeschichte*, 228.

164 Cf. Moshe Lewin's description ("Society," 52–6, 61–2). Also Borisov et al., "Politicheskaia," 277: "The industrialization of the country led to a rapid growth of the urban population, on the whole as a result of the massive migration of the rural population into the towns. [Because of an] acute housing crisis, a shortage of foodstuffs, of industrial products ... those who were until recently peasants [experienced] difficulties with adapting to the circumstances of urban life."

165 Korzun, *Pervye shagi*, 58, 72–3. One such case was discovered by the OGPU at the railroad car factory in the early 1930s (Badeev, "Neozhidannyi povorot," 41–3). The frequent interruptions of the production process, although probably due to the delirious frenzy of the first years of crash industrialization, could, in the mind of the party, only be due to the activities of "masked enemies." As Danilov noted: "The back-breaking speed of the development of industry immediately resulted in violations of technological demands, a sharp fall in the quality of labour and production, accidents in the mines, electro-stations, and construction projects, nonfulfillment of planned targets, deterioration and interruptions in the provision of consumers' goods, a sharp lowering of the living standard in the country. For all this, engineers, planners, distributors, 'economic workers' in general were made to answer.

One after the other, trials were conducted against 'wreckers' in the mines, at the electro stations, in the provisioning network" (Danilov et al., "NEP," 185).

166   Korzun, *Pervye shagi*, 59–62. This pattern is illustrated by Kotliarskaia and Freidenberg: an old employee of the oblast' library stated that when she started working at the library in 1931, all former employees with higher education had to resign from their jobs because they were priests' children. Because his father was a priest, the subject of this biography, Vershinskii, also lived in fear in the early 1930s but remained unharmed (*Iz istorii*, 53, 104).

167   Korzun, *Pervye shagi*, 63; Kotliarskaia and Freidenberg, *Iz istorii*, 107.

168   Smirnov et al., *Ocherki*, 320–1, 359; Alekseeva and Chernyshov, *Kalininskaia oblastnaia*, 226. The emulation between the factories was called the "Agreement of the Thousands." The First Five Year Plan was officially accepted by the Sixteenth Party Conference of the Bolshevik Party in April-May 1929 (Danilov, "NEP," 179).

169   Smirnov et al., *Ocherki*, 360; Korzun, *Pervye shagi*, 89. Rittersporn, *Stalinist Simplifications*, 34–6 argues that the Stakhanov campaigns, which first began at the end of 1935, can be seen as a similar effort to improve labour productivity. In his opinion they were a political and economic failure. Undoubtedly the enthusiasm for this kind of movement grew rather stale after a few years, particularly because the workers derived little material benefit (some premiums mainly) from it.

170   Smirnov et al., *Ocherki*, 310; Borisov et al., "Politicheskaia ," 275; Gordon and Klopov, *Chto eto bylo?*, 98; see also Kotliarskaia and Freidenberg, *Iz istorii*, 84.

171   Smirnov et al., *Ocherki*, 363; Heller and Nekrich, *Utopia in Power*, 226.

172   Smirnov et al., *Ocherki*, 363; Garmonov, "Bor'ba partiinykh organizatsii," 65; see also Rittersporn, *Stalinist Simplifications*, 33–4. Causes for the "weakness" of the Russian workers and their low productivity in comparison to the factory workers of more advanced industrial countries at the time are suggested by Gordon and Klopov (*Chto eto bylo?*, 63, 65).

173   Smirnov et al., *Ocherki*, 363; Pako, 147/1/526, l.49. The strike in Vyshnii Volochek was not unique, if one believes a recent article by O. Khlevniuk ("30-e gody," 77–8). Khlevniuk describes a whole wave of protest in the spring of 1932 that was provoked by a reduction of the ration-card norms for bread in the towns. In the frenzy of the purges, the cause of this strike was flatly explained as the result of wrecking, but the lack of adequate housing, the unhealthy labour surroundings, the low wages, the price rises of the 1930s, and the lack of goods in the shops were more likely causes for it, judging from the postwar situation

in the town's industry (see also, e.g., Gordon and Klopov, *Chto eto bylo?*, 98). In 1931–32 the workers had apparently not lost the courage to stage a strike, but Kaganovich, with the possible help of the OGPU (the Unified State Political Directorate, the predecessor of the NKVD), might have made them understand that strikes were a thing of the past.

174 Korzun, *Pervye shagi*, 50.

175 Garmonov, "Bor'ba partiinykh organizatsii," 68; Smirnov et al., *Ocherki*, 436. In the 1930s five-day weeks had been in force: four days of work in shifts of six to seven hours followed by one day of rest (see Lel'chuk, "Industrializatsiia," 349). However, most industrial workers also worked on these days of rest, and on workdays many worked overtime.

176 Smirnov et al., *Ocherki*, 366–7; see Heller and Nekrich, *Utopia in Power*, 230. If one looks at the 1967 statistical handbook on the development of the oblast' during fifty years of Soviet rule, one is struck by the fact that hardly any numbers are listed for the production of industrial goods in 1928 and 1932, so that it is impossible to get a clear idea of industrial development in the First Five Year Plan (see *Kalininskaia Oblast' za 50 let*, 42–3). It is perhaps telling that the production of woollen cloth actually decreased between these years. The numbers cited on pages 23–5 of the same book are even less reliable, as only percentages are listed. Cf. Depretto, "Construction Workers," 189–92.

177 Smirnov et al., *Ocherki*, 377; Korzun, *Pervye shagi*, 93, 98. Cf. Heller and Nekrich, *Utopia in Power*, 226.

178 *Kalininskaia Oblast' za 50 let*, 13; Smirnov et al., *Ocherki*, 442; the 650,000 included the later-separated area in the west.

179 Smirnov et al., *Ocherki*, 384. The terms "workers" and "factory workers" are not clearly distinguished in the Soviet literature on the oblast'.

180 Anuchin, "Novozavidovskii raion," 45; *Tsentral'nyi Raion*, 525. The term "unnatural deaths" was used by a dissident who, as a resident of Kalinin in the 1970s, tried to establish the extent of the demographic consequences of Stalin's policies for the USSR (Dyadkin, *Unnatural Deaths in the USSR*).

181 Alampiev, "Promyshlennost'," 5–17; Pashkevich, "Khlopchatobumazhnaia promyshlennost'," 52; Garmonov, "Bor'ba partiinykh organizatsii," 66–7; Smirnov et al., *Ocherki*, 434–5; *Tsentral'nyi Raion*, 120, 127; Morozov, "L'naia promyshlennost'," 67; "Osnovye proizvodstva," 87; "Pishchevaia promyshlennost'," 94; Pervozvanskii, "Kozhevenno-Obuvnaia promyshlennost'," 74, 77, 79; Pigulevskii and Novik, "Lesnoe khoziaistvo," 109, 115; Braude, "Mashinostroitel'naia," 38.

182 Leshchinskii, "Gorod Kalinin," 28. Baths were taken in public bathhouses.

183 Smirnov et al., *Ocherki*, 396, 435. In the second half of the 1980s, the

average living space per person hovered, in general, around 15–16 square metres in the USSR and RSFSR, according to Soviet sources; in urban areas this average was somewhat less: between 14.3 and 15.5 square metres for the USSR and 14.4 and 15.7 square metres in the RSFSR. It should be noticed that the average for people living in a family was much lower in 1989: 10 square metres for the whole USSR and 9 square metres for the RSFSR (see *Soiuznye respubliki*, 98–100). Cf., as well, Rittersporn, *Stalinist Simplifications*, 40.

184 Smirnov et al., *Ocherki*, 411, 413, 419; Garmonov, "Bor'ba partiinykh organizatsii," 65.

185 See some of the answers to the survey discussed in the third section of chapter 6. In 1930 the four-year curriculum of primary education became obligatory in the USSR (Lel'chuk, "Industrializatsiia," 346).

186 See *PP* 8197, 19 January 1947, 3; cf. Barber and Davies, "Employment and Industrial Labour," 104.

187 *PP*, 8197, 19 January 1947, 3.

188 Before the war the population, particularly the many peasants who had joined the urban work force and the peasantry at large, possibly compared their standard of living with that of the 1920s, which had been generally higher, although more particularly so in the countryside. The fall of the standard of living was expressed in a declining birth rate in the USSR in the First Five Year Plan (Lel'chuk, "Industrializatsiia," 346; Lewin, "Society," 53). The (former) peasants would not forget the "Golden Age" of the 1920s as easily.

189 Pako, 147/1/528, l.29; for the full text of the proceedings of the plenum see Pako, 147/1/528, ll.27–34.

CHAPTER TWO

1 Tumarkin, *The Living and the Dead*, 45.

2 Smirnov et al., *Ocherki*, 464; Karpenko, *Pod fashistskim igom*, 34.

3 *Bol'shaia Sovetskaia entsiklopediia*, 432. According to obkom secretary Boitsov, the Germans eliminated 80 MTSs and MTMs, 20 sovkhozy, more than 5,000 kolkhozy, more than 115,000 communal buildings, and 67,000 kolkhozniks' houses, and they stole and slaughtered 543,000 head of cattle. The total value of the damage amounted to more than five billion rubles (Pako, 147/3/2679, l.8). When Boitsov, however, mentioned these numbers in January 1945, he exaggerated. He conveniently included the damage done to the raions that had become part of the Velikie Luki and Pskov oblasts in 1944. See also Smirnov et al., *Ocherki*, 486, or Strizhkov, "Deiatel'nost' SNK SSSR," 57, who gives a lower number for the cattle that were lost. For the area of the German advance, see the map.

4 Vershinskii, *Boi za gorod Kalinin,* 25-36.
5 These istrebitel'nye units are mentioned in Smirnov et al., *Ocherki,* 461-2. The units were apparently engaged in the combat against criminality and banditry as well. They were subordinate to the NKVD, and many members of the party and employees of the militsiia joined them (Konev, "Vospominaniia," 62; Panov, "Etapy bol'shogo puti," 12).
6 Vershinskii, *Boi,* 7-8; *Na pravom flange,* 157.
7 Boshniak et al., "Kalininskoe operatsionnoe napravlenie," 51; also Konev, "Vospominaniia." Konev, later commander-in-chief of the Warsaw Pact armies, was the commander of the Kalinin front. The severity of his command is obvious from an order of 12 October 1941 by which his subordinate Khomenko was enjoined to immediately execute deserters, cowards, and those who panicked (Boshniak et al., "Kalininskoe operatsionnoe napravlenie," 17). Konev also demanded a conviction by a military tribunal of one Colonel Rotmistrov for unauthorized retreat (19-20). Zhukov, however, felt that Konev himself was responsible for many of the mistakes on the Western Front and that Konev put the blame for his own failures on others (14).
8 Smirnov et al., *Ocherki,* 484-5; Strizhkov, "Deiatel'nost' SNK SSSR," 54.
9 Ibid., 40, 53; Smirnov et al., *Ocherki,* 484-5; Rossiiskii tsentr khraneniia i izucheniia dokumentov noveishei istorii (Moscow), fond17, opis'43, delo741, listy1-3. Records from this archive will be indicated henceforth in the following manner: Moscow, 17/43/741, ll.1-3.
10 Strizhkov, "Deiatel'nost' SNK SSSR," 43, 45, 55. The railroad-car factory also made mines and grenades for the front during the war; see *Obelisk pobedy*; Lubov, *Material,* 9-10.
11 Lubov, *Material,* 9.
12 Moscow, 17/43/741, ll.14, 28-9.
13 Pako, 147/4/66, ll.17/170b.
14 Tumarkin, *The Living and the Dead,* 20-1
15 Smirnov et al., *Ocherki,* 484-5. Part of the destruction was apparently due to the "scorched earth" strategy of the retreating German troops (Müller, "Überblick," 84-5). On certain aspects of the Battle for Rzhev, see Samsonov, *Znat' i pomnit',* 94; Konev, "Vospominaniia."
16 *Tsentral'nyi Raion,* 571-4.
17 That is, if one limits oneself to the geographical territory of the oblast' of the immediate postwar period. On 23 August 1944 the Velikie Luki and Pskov oblasts were formed, to which the western-most part of Kalinin oblast' was given: see *Gosudarstvennyi arkhiv Kalininskoi oblasti,* 116; Smirnov et al., *Ocherki,* 507; the province lost twenty-three raions to Velikolukskaia oblast' and three to Pskov oblast'; see *Kalininskaia oblast' za 50 let,* 11.
18 Smirnov et al., *Ocherki,* 485.

19 Korytkov, *Kalininskoe selo*, 37; cf. the second section of chapter 4, below.

20 Smirnov et al., *Ocherki*, 486; Pako, 147/3/2701, l.1900b.

21 Pako, 147/3/2679, ll.20-1. It is still a matter of debate how far partisans were entrusted with political responsibilities immediately after liberation. Soviet sources argue that they were, while Western specialists have indicated that the Soviet regime did not trust the partisans. Official publications after 1953 on the war period never fail to dedicate a large passage to the partisans during the war. See, for instance, Kirichek, "Vozrozhdenie," 80; Smirnov et al., *Ocherki*, 473-83; Alekseeva and Chernyshov, *Kalininskaia Oblastnaia*, 268-83.

22 Pako, 147/3/2679, ll.20-1. Since the Germans already had retreated by March 1943 from the territory of the oblast' of post-August 1944, Boitsov's account of the partisans' feats for this period (from the spring of 1943 to the spring of 1944) was rather superfluous.

23 See the map of Müller, *Die faschistische Okkupationspolitik*, 628-9; Smirnov et al., *Ocherki*, 482-3. This latter, Soviet publication cannot be accused of outright lying about the heroic resistance, because by 1971 Kalinin oblast' had regained a large slice of the oblast' of Velikie Luki, dissolved in 1957. Cf. as well Laqueur, *The Dream That Failed*, 16: "there was little partisan activity during the first eighteen months of the war, when the Red Army would have needed it most; it became a factor of some military and political importance only after the winter of 1942-43, when the tide of the war had turned."

24 This is denied by a very recent publication on the war casualties (Krivosheev, *Grif sekretnosti sniat*, 129, 391). This publication maintains that the USSR sustained roughly the same number of military deaths as Germany and its allies during the war, but its information is suspect (see the section on the Ezhovshchina in chapter 1). An even more recent article challenges the number of twenty-seven million victims (Sokolov, "Tsena poter'," 5). Sokolov arrived at the startling number of forty million deaths during the war, of which twenty-six million were military deaths. He added that the losses on the Eastern Front translated into nine and a half Russian deaths for each German or German-allied death. The number of people who served in the Red Army during the war was forty-three to forty-four million, more than one person in five of the total Soviet population. Sokolov's numbers are supported by V.I. Kozlov ("Dinamika," 17n2).

25 Pako, 147/4/63, ll.175-6.

26 Alekseeva and Chernyshov, *Kalininskaia oblastnaia*, 274, 283. This source indicates that about 10 percent of the growth of the party between 1941 and 1944 consisted of partisans. See the third section of chapter 3.

27 *Bloknot agitatora*, 1948, 1, 23-6.

28 The account is based on the testimony of his brother, L.M. Gaponenko, in the survey.

29 Pako, 147/3/1966, l.88; see the map in Müller, *Die faschistische Okkupationspolitik*, 632; cf. the publication *Kalininskaia oblast' v gody*, and Karpenko, *Pod fashistskim igom*, 4, 27. Some of the German atrocities against Communists, Komsomols, nonparty members and Jews are described in the publication *Ne zabudem! Ne prostim*, 3-5. The atrocities against Jews described during the war in Soviet accounts were omitted in postwar publications (*Ne zabudem! Ne prostim*, 17-18; Karpenko, *Pod fashistskim igom*, 19). For the RSFSR the total number of civilian victims may have been around 1.8 million; 400,000 inhabitants of the RSFSR were forced to work in Germany (see the table and text of the essay of N. Müller, "Überblick," 96).

30 *Kalininskaia oblast' v gody*; Osipov and Kosarev, *Obelisk pobedy*. Both publications were commemorative and therefore not written on the basis of extensive archival research. V.G. Osipov, the co-author of one of the publications (Osipov and Kosarev, *Obelisk pobedy*), had never seen the inside of the party or army archive before the autumn of 1991. If one calculates on the basis of the 350,000 soldiers serving in the Red Army in the province of the greater size of 1967, roughly 273,000 inhabitants of the territory of the oblast' in its 1944-56-size may have served. Since only 93,000 to 94,000 returned after demobilization, one may estimate that about 180,000 soldiers were killed during the war; this is rather more than the 165,000 estimated here. If one adds 40,000 civilian deaths attributed to the war, then the total number of victims would amount to 220,000 for the province in its 1944-56-size (cf. table 5 below). The number of Soviet army troops and partisans killed on provincial territory as it was in 1967, meanwhile, may be higher than 200,000, but the chaos created by the initial German attack prevents us from arriving at any precise estimate for this. See Krivosheev, *Grif sekretnosti sniat*, 4 and 252; *Kalininskaia oblast' v gody*; Osipov and Kosarev, *Obelisk pobedy*.

31 Smirnov et al., *Ocherki*, 472; see table 1. If one extrapolates Lubov's numbers for Konakovo raion (6,000 deaths out of 17,000 soldiers), then around 110,000 soldiers (roughly 35 percent of 320,000) would have been killed in the war, substantially fewer than in this estimate.

32 The figure of 9 percent is based on an estimate of 165,000 Red Army and partisan deaths during the war (78 percent of the 200,000 military and partisan deaths for the oblast' in its size of 1967; the oblast' in 1945 – see table 1 – was approximately 78 percent of the size of the oblast' in 1967-70).

33 See tables 3 and 4; cf. Zelenin, review of *Ural'skaia derevniia*, 170.

34 Moscow, 17/44/546, l.1660b. In 1936 abortion had become illegal once more, which led to a rise in "back-alley abortions" and to the use of

contraconceptive home remedies that were dangerous to health (Engel, "Engendering Russia's History," 319). See also the final section of chapter 2, on the extent of illegal abortions after the war.

35 Kurganoff, *Women in the USSR*, 147; Moscow, 17/44/546, l.1660b.

36 Moscow, 17/43/741, l.79. The number of communists after the German retreat in the liberated areas of the RSFSR stood at 38 percent of the prewar level; see Kondakova, "Partiia," 26.

37 Moscow, 17/43/741, ll.81-810b. However, the percentage of party members among kolkhoz chairs was also not high before 1941.

38 Cf. Moscow, 17/44/546, l.730b.

39 Moscow, 17/43/741, l.390b. See table 3 for the extent of the extermination of cattle in 1942.

40 Anokhina and Shmeleva, *Kul'tura i byt'*, 286; Moscow, 17/43/741, l.141.

41 Pako,147/3/1966, l.62. Cf., for example, Pako, 147/3/1966, l.76; 147/3/2701, l.86.

42 Pako, 147/4/63, ll.67–670b.

43 Cf. Pako, 147/3/2679, l.8; see table 4. Boitsov also added in the abovementioned report to Malenkov of 1 March 1946 the raions of Ostashkov and Staritsa (see Pako, 147/4/63, ll.67–670b.); Korytkov, *Kalininskoe selo*, 42.

44 It is noteworthy that many of the survey respondents used the singular Nemets for the Germans (Nazis) instead of the plural Nemtsy. The use of the singular transforms the enemy into something not altogether human, something quintessentially evil. As Laqueur writes rightfully, "[t]he 'Great Fatherland War' has been the central event in Soviet postwar consciousness." (*Stalin: The Glasnost Revelations*, 213). Cf. Zubkova, "Obshchestvennaia atmosfera (1945–1946)," 5.

45 In the sixty households of the village of Korostelevo only three of the men returned home after the war (testimony of A.K. Sumugina-Shepeleva in the survey).

46 Korytkov, *Kalininskoe selo*, 38.

47 Korzun, "Kalininskie vagonostroiteli," 276, 279; Korytkov, *Kalininskoe selo*, 38.

48 Pako, 147/4/57, l.659.

49 Not all collaborators automatically received capital punishment, but the penalties given to those exposed after the return of the Soviet army were severe. For example, T.V. Karavashkin was sentenced to ten years of labour camp in late 1942 for having worked as a village elder under the Germans (Pako, 147/4/519, l.80).

50 Pako, 147/4/57, l.535.

51 Pako, 147/4/57, l.597.

52 Karpenko, *Pod fashistskim igom*, 36–41. The Nazi behaviour was part

and parcel of their racist theories that had declared the Slavs to be *Unter-menschen*. Karpenko indicates that the Germans tried to create "communal farms" (obshchinnye khoziaistva), led by German functionaries and, in areas further away from the front, reintroduced large land ownership (Karpenko, *Pod fashistskim igom*, 28-9).

53 Moscow, 17/43/741, l.39. The vacillations and "anti-Soviet mood" among the population of Moscow in the autumn of 1941 can be found in "Moskva voennaia," 101–22.

54 Moscow, 17/43/741, l.39. And the German attitude was, of course, by comparison more benevolent to the Baltic peoples than to the Russians.

55 Moscow, 17/44/546, l.113.

56 Bilenko et al., "Vozrozhdenie," 115; Kondakova ("Partiia-organizator ideino-politicheskoi raboty," 25) names two general resolutions, one of 1943 ("On measures for Strengthening Cultural-Educational Work in Raions Liberated from German Occupation") and one of 1945 ("On the Organization of Political-Educational Work with Repatriated Soviet Citizens"), although there were many more, in particular resolutions confined to one specific republic or oblast'.

57 Moscow, 17/44/546, l.1490b. According to A.A. Kondrashov (testimony in the survey), Starotorzhskii had made way for Simonov, because of the promotion of the former to the Council of People's Commissars of the RSFSR.

58 Moscow, 17/44/546, l.154.

59 Pako, 147/4/63, l.1360b.; Bilenko et al., "Vozrozhdenie," 114–15; see the second and third sections of chapter 5.

60 Pako, 147/3/2748, ll.18–22, 23–5, 28–31.

61 See chapter 5, below, in particular. The hardened criminal convicts in the labour camps, who are to be encountered in almost any description of camp life under Stalin, provide other testimony of flourishing crime in the USSR.

62 Moscow, 17/45/732, ll.3400b–98. This discussion was provoked by a Supreme Soviet decree of 23 June 1945 that called for the demobilization from the Soviet army and navy of the oldest veterans among the conscripts: those that belonged to the thirteen oldest years of birth (Volkov, *Sovetskaia derevnia*, 43).

63 Pako, 147/4/811, l.129; Pako, 147/3/2701, ll.178–9.

64 Moscow, 17/45/732, l.74.

65 Pako, 147/3/2702, l.56.

66 Pako, 147/3/2702, ll.241–3.

67 Pako, 147/4/63, l.214; out of the 10,554 of the most recently demobilized contingent, 95 percent had found work.

68 Pako, 147/4/63, ll.179–800b. The title of the resolution was "On Political Work among the Demobilized Members of the USSR Armed Forces in

Connection with the Demobilization of the Third Group of Personnel of the USSR Armed Forces" (Pako, 147/4/63, l.179).

69 Pako, 147/4/66, ll.17–22.

70 Pako, 147/3/2702, l.640b.; Pako, 147/3/2702, l.630b.–65. The resolution was called "On the Organization of Political-Educational Work with Repatriated Soviet Citizens."

71 Pako, 147/3/2702, l.640b.

72 Pako, 147/4/67, ll.226-260b.; the report is of 31 December 1946.

73 Fainsod's sober appreciation of the treatment of repatriates and the demobilized is probably close to the truth (*How Russia is Ruled*, 257). It is hard to assess how many of the repatriates were former émigrés, and how many had been either prisoners of war or forced labourers, although it seems obvious that the first group must have been very small in Kalinin oblast'.

74 Pako, 147/5/906, l.1. Cf. Smirnov et al., *Ocherki*, 485. See also the *Bol'shaia Sovetskaia Entsiklopediia*, 19:432, in which it is stated that the oblast' was liberated by March 1943.

75 Witness as well the pre-August 1944 numbers on the razing of MTS, MTM, and kolkhozy in the first section of chapter 2, above. The houses and public buildings of Rzhev were still not completely rebuilt in 1961, eighteen years after liberation. Elena Zubkova notes that these tactics were common among all local party leaders after the war (Zubkova, *Obshchestvo*, 43)

76 Smirnov et al., *Ocherki*, 485; Pako, 147/5/906, l.1.

77 See the section of chapter 1 on the Ezhovshchina.

78 Pako, 147/4/63, l.132,d 135. These numbers are also mentioned in Smirnov et al., *Ocherki*, 530–1, which probably used the same source as I did (their source is impossible to establish, however, since the party archive's records have been reorganized and renumbered since *Ocherki* was written). Cf. the numbers for the USSR as given by I.M. Volkov, "Zasukha," 4. One report was addressed to A.A. Kuznetsov, the other to N. Voznesensky and A.A. Kuznetsov. Voznesensky and Kuznetsov were prominent Central Committee members.

79 Pako, 147/4/1549, l.57. The mortality of newborns is taken as 10 percent, which conforms to the numbers given in the same report – 8.8 per 100 newborn babies died in 1946; in 1947, 13.8 percent; and in 1948, 9.0 percent (see table 2). Table 2 indicates that for 1946 the birthrate was 20.2 per thousand, for 1947 21.4 per thousand, and for 1948 19.4 per thousand inhabitants. In 1948, according to the report, 32,000 children were born that survived (Pako, 147/4/1549, l.57); an additional 3,000 might have been born who died at or soon after birth – although, of course, some of the newly born would still succumb to a fatal illness before their first birthday. Thus the total births were around

35,000 in 1948, when the average natality was 19.4 per 1,000. This would produce a total population in 1949 of 1,800,000. This number seems rather high, since the kolkhoz population in January 1950 was 825,500 (Pako, 147/5/906, l.2) and the population of the larger towns was estimated to be around 435,000. More than 500,000 people would have had to be living in smaller towns, raion centres, and urban type settlements, or they would not be kolkhoz members but still living in villages. It will be argued below that the latter group probably numbered closer to 300,000.

80   Pako, 147/5/36, ll. 135–6. The way the number is written in the letter means that the oblast' had more than 1.6 million but less than 1.7 million inhabitants. When these numbers are compared to Boitsov's numbers for "1939,", it is clear that by then the urban population was back to its prewar and pre-purge size. If we follow Konovalov's numbers and combine them with the numbers for the kolkhoz households in table 6, then the total population of roughly 1.6 million would have consisted of 550,000 who lived in urban communities and almost 770,000 who were members of collective farms or were their dependents. That would leave about 300,000 unaccounted for, the same 300,000 who seem hard to place in 1946 or 1956. Kerblay has noticed the increase in the proportion of rural dwellers that were not employed in agriculture: "In 1923, the non-agricultural population living in the countryside surpassed by about 6 percent the total urban population of the USSR at the time; in 1955 one may estimate that more than 30 percent which is classified today as rural has no ties to agriculture" (*Du mir aux agrovilles*, 329n1). Konovalov was, of course, aided or hindered in this by the fact that there had not been an All-Union census since 1939 and most of the data of that census had been suppressed. One might suspect that perhaps fewer people lived in the oblast' than the local party chief actually thought in June 1951 or that he even deliberately added dead souls in order to extract more means from Moscow. It is unclear how people like Boitsov or Konovalov arrived at their population numbers. Guesswork no doubt played its part.

81   On population losses in the war, see the previous section. If one estimated, reasonably, that the demographic drop amounted to 320,000 and the total population (of the smaller oblast') had been around 1.9 million in 1941, one-sixth of the inhabitants of Kalinin oblast' would have been killed in the war. Some of the population losses during the war were due to the evacuation of inhabitants to the East. Boitsov mentions in the letter of May 1946 cited above the evacuation of 30,000 young people in 1942, for example (Pako, 147/4/63, l.132).

82   Altrichter, *Die Bauern*, table 6, 205; cf. tables 1 and 6 of this book.

83   In 1941, perhaps 250,000 of the people who lived in the countryside did

not belong to an agricultural collective. It is impossible to estimate how much of this drop was caused by migration and how much by "unnatural deaths"; the natural growth in the 1930s probably was not very high if in 1940 the natality per 1,000 inhabitants was only 3.3 higher than the mortality (see table 2); in 1940 the birthrate was 24.4 per 1,000 and the deathrate 21.1 per 1,000, while 22.1 children died of every 100 born. The mortality for 1940 was so high – as high as it would be in the war year 1944! – that I thought there might be a confusion in the document of 1941 with 1940, but since the year 1940 is repeated twice in the document, while no numbers for 1941 are given, the numbers are most likely right. It was probably impossible to give any numbers on birth and death rates for 1941, when the oblast' was in a state of utter chaos in the second half of the year. If the growth per 1,000 inhabitants was 3.3 in 1940, then the absolute population growth in the oblast' in that year – if for the sake of convenience Boitsov's numbers for 1939 are applied in the calculation – was slightly more than 7,000. In contrast to the 1930s, the natural population growth in the period 1926–29 was probably quite high (see Altrichter, *Die Bauern*, 68).

84 Cf. Lorenz, *Sozialgeschichte*, 287, for a discussion of the re-evacuation.

85 A statistical handbook gives an estimate for April 1956 of 1.6 million for the total oblast' population (*Narodnoe Khoziaistvo*, 6). In 1959, according to the census, Kalinin oblast', which had grown about 25 percent in size with the addition of a number of sparsely populated raions in 1957, had 1.8 million inhabitants (see table 1, and see the second section of chapter 3 for Boitsov's letter of May 1946 on the emigration).

86 Pako, 147/4/1549, l.57.

87 For reasons of convenience, 1.6 million – which was probably not too far from the actual number of the oblast' population – is considered to be the population between 1945 and 1953.

88 Pako, 147/5/906, ll.1–2; *Kalininskaia oblast' za 50 let*, 13. In the USSR as a whole, the kolkhoz population had fallen by 18 percent in late 1944 in comparison with 1940, and the able-bodied workers on the collective farms even by 38 percent (Volkov, *Sovetskaia derevnia*, 42). The number of male kolkhoz workers had decreased from 14.6 million in 1940 to 5.1 million at the end of 1945, i.e., by 2.9 times. By late 1945 in the USSR the number of adult and underaged (teenagers between twelve and sixteen in this case) kolkozniks who actually worked on the collective farms was still 18.7 percent less than in 1940, in spite of the arrival of the first two waves of demobilized soldiers (Volkov, *Sovetskaia derevnia*, 44). Cf., too, Zubkova, *Obshchestvo*, 38. Nelidovo was not a part of the province between 1944 and 1957. The towns of Kalinin, Bezhetsk, Bologoe, Vyshnii Volochek, Kashin, Kimry, Konakovo, Ostashkov, Rzhev, and Torzhok had, according to a census of December 1939, 476,500 inhabi-

tants; according to the estimate made in *Kalininskaia oblast' za 50 let*
(13), in 1950 they had a total of 435,300 inhabitants; this number confirms more or less Boitsov's number of 1946. The share of urban inhabitants in the province rose from 27 percent in 1939 to 30 percent in 1946
and 44 percent in 1959; in the USSR as a whole, it rose from 33 percent
in January 1940, to 40 percent in 1951 (Volkov, *Sovetskaia derevnia*,
106).

89 This conclusion is based on the assumption that the labour population on
1 January 1941 was composed of 351,000 workers and employees and
590,000 teenage and adult kolkhozniks, and on 1 January 1951 of
348,000 workers and employees and 396,000 kolkhozniks (see tables 6
and 7).

90 Cf. *Narodnoe Khoziaistvo*, 6, with table 6. *Narodnoe Khoziaistvo* 25,
indicates 216,949 kolkhoz households on 1 January 1957 – that is, in
excess of 26,000 less than on 1 January 1952. If each household was
comprised on average of three persons – as was shown above – then
about 650,000 people were living on kolkhozy in early 1957. Only 8,500
people worked in 1956 on the oblast' sovkhozy (*Narodnoe Khoziaistvo*,
54). The number of 941,500 for April 1956 was an estimate that was
probably somewhat off because the statistician(s) may have looked only
at the results of the last census of 1939, held eighteen years earlier and
probably false! The number might have been partially extrapolated from
the results of that census or, perhaps, from the 1926 census. A substantial
increase occurred in 1957, when nine raions were added to the oblast', so
that it increased by 17,100 square kilometres. Thus in 1959 it was about
25 percent larger than in 1956, but the census of January 1959 counted
only 200,000 people more than the estimate for April 1956 (cf. *Kalininskaia oblast' za 50 let*, 11–12). See as well Kerblay, *Du mir aux
agrovilles*, 329n1 and Abramov, *The New Life*, 69, 70–2). The brick
factory in Diagilovo near Udoml'ia was an example of one of the rurally
based factories (testimony of V.P. Krylov and M.A. Smirnov in the
survey).

91 Cf. Buckley, "The Myth of Managed Migration," 905, 908, for ways to
acquire a propiska (giving permission to reside in a certain locale).

92 See Mazanov and Frolova, "Zdravookhranenie," 6. In Novgorod
guberniia the child mortality in this period was 326 per 1,000 annually;
in Pskov guberniia 287 per 1,000; in Russia as a whole 269 per 1,000.

93 Table 8 is based on reports of the head of the militsiia of the oblast' to
the first obkom secretary on the monthly population movement.

94 *Soiuznye respubliki*, 50, gives the mortality of children under the age of
one, from 1985 to 1990 inclusive, as between 17 and 20 per 1,000 newborns in the Russian Republic and as between 21 and 26 for the Soviet
Union in its entirety.

95 Pako, 147/4/1549, l.56. These numbers refer only to the first half of the years 1940, 1945, and 1948; the ameliorated medical supervision was probably another cause of the decrease in infant mortality.

96 Pako, 147/4/1549, l.67. MGB chief Dekushenko noticed in 1951 that in 1950 the mortality of children up to one year old had fallen by 3.8 times in comparison to 1940 (Pako, 147/5/2, l.146). Already in 1943 the death rate of newborns had fallen to 17.9 per 100 and reached 9.9 per 100 in 1945 (see table 2). The infant death rate in 1942 was exceptional: it was higher than the annual rate for the whole of Russia in the five-year period from 1887–1891!

97 Pako, 147/4/1549, ll.56–7. In all likelihood, Lapchenko did not want to give Vorontsov the idea that his department was incompetent in these matters. In 1948 there were 400,000 children younger than fourteen in the oblast', and 23 percent were younger than three years old. Therefore around 8.5 percent of the 400,000 – or 34,000 were younger than one. For the legislation concerning abortion, see, e.g., Kurganoff, *Women in the USSR*, 140, or Mazanov and Frolova, "Zdravookhranenie," 12. The decree on the prohibition of abortion was issued by the Central Executive Committee and the Sovnarkom of the USSR on 27 June 1936. In 1955 a decree of the Supreme Soviet was issued by which abortions were allowed once more (Lagutiaeva, "Razvitie rodovspomozheniia," 71).

98 Pako, 147/4/1413, l.83ob. More general explanations for the fall in birthrate after the war are given by V.I. Kozlov ("Dinamika," 9).

99 Pako, 147/4/1549: the report on population can be found on ll.42–70; the quote is on l.42. See table 2.

100 Pako, 147/4/1549, l.67; cf. Table 2.

101 See table 8. Nevertheless, in the first postwar years the birthrate for the oblast' was less than half that of the USSR as a whole in 1928 (44.3 per 1,000), and also far less than in the 1930s in the Soviet Union in general (e.g., in 1930 it was 41.2 per 1,000; in 1935, 31.6 per 1,000; in 1938, 38.7 per 1,000) (Gordon and Klopov, *Chto eto bylo?*, 162n1). In Kalinin province, the birthrate for 1946 was 20.2 per thousand; for 1947, 21.4 per thousand; and for 1948, 19.4 per thousand inhabitants (see table 2).

102 Lapchenko, as noted, referred to "economic peculiarities of 1946" that affected the birthrate in the second half of 1947 and early 1948 (Pako, 147/4/1549, l.67). The mortality was also higher in 1947 than in 1946 or 1948 (see table 2). However, there is no indication of large-scale starvation in 1947 in the records. In March 1947 Vorontsov spoke of a drought that had touched large parts of the European part of the USSR in 1946, but he did not seem to imply that Kalinin oblast' had been exposed to it (Pako, 147/4/528, l.13).

103 See table 8. Although the effects of the drought probably were less
      severe in the Tver' region than in more southern areas, the overall situa-
      tion in the Soviet Union caused hardships here as well (see Volkov,
      "Zasukha," 4, 7; cf. Zima, "Golod v Rossii 1946–1947 godov," 41).
      Zima confirms that the rural population in Kalinin oblast' declined as a
      consequence of the high mortality in 1947 (Ibid., 42). It is telling that
      no population statistics for the months from November 1946 to June
      1947 could be unearthed. Someone, somewhere along the line, in the
      obkom apparat or in the former party archive, might have tried to
      discard them for "reasons of state" (this drought and the resulting
      famine were never really admitted to the Soviet public or the outside
      world) or might have entered them in some file that dealt specifically
      with the consequences of the serious economic situation. I was also
      unable to find further demographical numbers for the period after
      November 1948. I.M. Volkov experienced similar problems with regard
      to the sources about the drought when he prepared for an article on its
      precise extent a few years ago (Volkov, "Zasukha," 3): "In the docu-
      ments of these times, such as materials of local Soviets, party organiza-
      tions, among which different calculation materials are sent to central
      organs, the difficulties that were experienced by the kolkhoz, the raion,
      the oblast', the republic, as a rule, were played down. With respect to
      the very poor situation of the population, malnutrition, famine and ill-
      nesses connected with it, data, being especially secret, are not men-
      tioned in the documents ... Little can the researcher find in materials of
      medicine and health-care statistics. They are not complete; in them the
      only facts given are about doctors' and hospital institutes, which did
      not envelop a large part of the rural population, who on top of that
      seldom turned to these institutes for aid. Apart from that, not without
      grounds it was noticed at the plenum of the scientific-medical and sani-
      tary-statistical commission of the Ministry of Healthcare of the USSR
      (December 1946) that considerable smoothing over was perpetrated in
      accounts of medical institutions with respect to the severity of the situa-
      tion, and with regards to downplaying of the extent of illness." Appar-
      ently, the authorities in Moscow declined the suggestion to investigate
      the exact extent of sickness among the population in 1947, because of
      which precise data about the famine remained unknown there. V.F.
      Zima confirms Volkov's opinion that some of the statistics sent to
      Moscow are rather suspect ("Golod v Rossii 1946–1947 godov," 44).

104 See tables 2 and 8; inadequate nutrition of mothers during pregnancy
      and the scarcities of the pre-harvest period, for example, could have
      caused this phenomenon. In the USSR as a whole infant mortality
      increased by 81 percent, which was more than in Kalinin oblast' (Zima,
      "Golod v Rossii 1946–1947 godov," 42; cf. table 2).

105 Pako, 147/4/63, ll.232/233. See I.M. Volkov, "Zasukha," 7. In the documents one rarely encounters anything that could be proof of the existence of a real famine. The circumstantial evidence of the demographical numbers (see tables 2 and 8) lead one to conclude that considerable scarcity existed but that mass starvation was avoided. The scarcity was probably caused by intense pressure by central authorities to have Kalinin province fulfill the procurement plan, which succeeded in the area of grain deliveries (Volkov, *Sovetskaia derevnia*, 273–4; on the famine see Volkogonov, *Triumf i tragediia*, 2:2, 31). As a result, not much grain remained behind at the kolkhozy to be distributed among the kolkhozniks. It all depends on one's perception, of course. Some of the survey respondents refered to the consumption of grasses and goosefoot immediately after the war in order to avoid starvation; a few of them pointed explicitly to the last months of 1946, and first months of 1947. Even in the towns, shortages were sharply felt in 1947. The testimony of the survey respondents is supported by information given in the article of I.M. Volkov of 1991 ("Zasukha," 14).

106 Pako, 147/3/2759, l.172.

107 Pako, 147/4/1549, ll.61–2; V.S. Smirnov, "Bor'ba s infektsiiami v Kalininskoi oblasti," 36; cf. table 9. For a more detailed discussion of the exact incidence of specific diseases, cf. Boterbloem, "Communists and the Russians," 513–28.

108 Pako, 147/4/1549, l.42; Korzhenevskaia et al., "Likvidatsiia zabolevaemosti maliariei," 116. Their numbers were confirmed by those of Lapchenko in the report on which the table of cases of epidemic diseases in Kalinin oblast' is based (see Table 9).

109 Pako, 147/4/1549, l.64.

110 Ibid., ll.42, 44. "Deliveries happened in maternity hospitals, but [the incidence of] child mortality, in fact, did not change in comparison with the 1920s: in 1940 it was even higher than in 1926. A definitive step forward happened only at the turn of the 1940s and 1950s thanks to the appearance of antibiotics" (Gordon and Klopov, *Chto eto bylo?*, 96). See also the second section of chapter 6, below.

111 Pako, 147/5/10, l.20.

112 Pako, 147/5/105, l.24; 147/5/662, l.69.

113 See Gordon and Klopov, *Chto eto bylo?*, 113–14. There is a considerable gap between the average life span of men and women of the war generation (eighteen or older in 1945) in the USSR, who reached the age of sixty by 1987 at the latest (Kozlov, "Dinamika," 4). The average age of death of men in 1989 was sixty-five, of women almost seventy-four, and these averages have dropped sharply since in the Commonwealth of Independent States. The average life span of both men and women in the USSR at the end of the 1980s was at least five years shorter than in Western Europe.

CHAPTER THREE

1   "Totalitarianism involves a systematic effort to control every aspect of social and intellectual life. Thus the Nazi *Gleichschaltung*, the top-down coordination of economy, politics, education, religion, culture, and family. Radical control, control in detail: perhaps earlier rulers dreamed of such a thing, but it became technically feasible – this is one of the central themes of *1984* – only in the twentieth century" (Walzer, "On Failed Totalitarianism," 106). Totalitarian control became indeed technically feasible but was certainly far from the Soviet reality of the 1940s and 1950s because of the underdeveloped state of Soviet technology in many aspects; despite that, *the attempt was undertaken* to control every aspect of social, intellectual, political, and economic life.

2   *Sto sorok besed*, 553.

3   This attitude differed only to a certain degree from the other "Old Bolsheviks." As Conquest remarks: "Non-Party people were hardly taken more into account, even by the better Old Bolsheviks, than slaves were by Plato." (*The Great Terror*, 27). Cf. Molotov: "As long as imperialism exists, this all will repeat itself again – rightists, leftists. As long as imperialism exists, we will not get rid of it." (*Sto sorok besed*, 406). Molotov also explained the continuous shortages of consumer goods in Stalin's time and under Brezhnev as a consequence of the continued existence of "imperialism," which should be attacked by the Communists, instead of trying to live with it in "peaceful coexistence" (383, 388).

4   The official introduction of the Fourth Five Year Plan by Gosplan chief Voznesensky in the highest legislative assembly of the USSR, the Supreme Soviet, occurred in March 1946 (cf. Hahn, *Postwar Soviet Politics*, 23).

5   Pako, 147/3/2679, l.1.

6   Almost fifty years later Boitsov was fondly remembered in the survey by Kondrashov; PP 7669, 1 January 1945, 1.

7   He stood in a similar relationship to I.I. Tiaglov, whose career mirrors that of Kondrashov (see below).

8   Pako, 147/1/555, l.244-5. The Academy mentioned by Boitsov was army-political (see *Kalininskaia oblastnaia organizatsiia*, 447).

9   Smirnov et al., *Ocherki*, 465; ibid., appendix 2, 701, *Kalininskaia oblastnaia organizatsiia*, 285; *Biographic Directory of the USSR*, 91. Boitsov replaced A.L. Orlov, who had been fired by the Central Committee for his failure to press for the "fulfillment of grain procurement quotas" (Hahn, *Postwar Soviet Politics*, 60n115). He led the Stavropol krai until 1956, after which he was appointed deputy chairman of the Party Control Commission of the CPSU.

10   Cf. the second section of chapter 2.

11   The oblast' was not performing particularly well in the field of procure-

ments in comparison with 1945. The level of fulfillment of the procurement plan for many agricultural products was similar to or even below that of 1945; it is doubtful that the plan was met for many kinds of production, although it was apparently met for grain (see above). The report was dated 23 October 1946; Boitsov left somewhere in November for Stavropol (*Kalininskaia oblastnaia organizatsiia*, 447–8).

12 This was undoubtedly partially due to the emulation of the "seminary" style of Stalin, while originality was not a quality much appreciated by the higher leadership of the USSR.

13 In July 1951 the head of the obkom department for agitation and propaganda, Moiseev, lamented the fact that during the war the economic plans were fulfilled, in contrast to those of recent years (Pako, 147/5/10, ll.104–5).

14 Pako, 147/3/2679, l.5. The primitive operation of the building industry comes as no surprise, because it had not been mechanized to any great extent in the 1930s either (Depretto, "Construction workers," 192–4).

15 Pako, 147/3/2679, ll.5–6.

16 Voznesenskii, *Voennaia Ekonomika SSSR*, 114.

17 Pako, 147/3/2679, l.6. For a description of this problem in the 1930s, see Rittersporn, *Stalinist Simplifications*, 33–4. It is rather surprising to encounter this problem, since in 1940 labour laws had been introduced that made it much more difficult to change jobs (Heller and Nekrich, *Utopia in Power*, 321). It seems that, in practice, it was not all that difficult for industrial workers to change employers.

18 Pako, 147/3/2679, ll.60ob.–7.

19 Kaplan, *The Party*, 146–7. Heavy industry, for example, was directly supervised by central ministries in Moscow. The relationship between gorkoms, obkoms, and Gosplan and ministry personnel was complicated and uneasy.

20 Pako, 147/3/2679, ll.70ob.–8.

21 Pako, 147/3/2679, l.8.

22 Pako, 147/5/662, l.69.

23 Pako, 147/3/2679, ll.8–9.

24 Pako, 147/5/906, l.9; Heller and Nekrich, *Utopia in Power*, 472. The numbers for 1943 for cereals, flax, and potatoes were even better; Boitsov added that in 1940 the average yield of grain per hectare had been 11.8 tsentner in the oblast', of flax 3.1 tsentner, and of potatoes 160 tsentner (Pako, 147/3/2679, l.80ob.).

25 For the inflated way of measuring the harvest crop, see Volkov, *Sovetskaia derevnia*, 232–6. Still most of the potato production came from the personal plot of the kolkhoznik! (see, e.g., Volkov, *Sovetskaia derevnia*, 51) In 1940, 65 percent of the potatoes were grown on the private plots, in 1945 even 75 percent.

26 "Agriculture under Stalin was an arena of constant attack, campaigning, and uncertainty" (Kaplan, *The Party*, 21).

27 Pako, 147/3/2679, ll.80b.–9.

28 Ibid.; Volkov, *Sovetskaia derevnia*, 171.

29 Pako, 147/3/2679, l.9.

30 Pako, 147/3/2679, l.90b.

31 Pako, 147/3/2679, ll.90b.–10.

32 Pako, 147/3/2679, l.10; Pako, 147/1/906, l.9.

33 Pako, 147/3/2679, l.10. A comparison between tables 11 and 12 indicates that there is a remote possibility that Boitsov's statement is true that more cows were owned by kolkhozniks in absolute numbers in 1945 than in 1941. On 1 January 1941 the total number of cows possessed by collective farms and kolkhozniks in the oblast' was 311,800, and the number of cows that were part of the socialized herds of the kolkhozy amounted to 137,200. The kolkhozniks possessed for personal use 174,600 cows (table 12). On 1 January 1945 the total number for the oblast' was 266,600 cows and the kolkhozy had 88,900 of these. Therefore, in January 1945 the kolkhozniks had a maximum of 177,700 cows, but the unknown number of cows possessed by those outside the collective farming system should probably be subtracted (cf. table 11).

34 Cf. Altrichter, *Die Bauern*, table 10, 209 and *Narodnoe Khoziaistvo*, 44. For 1916 Altrichter gives a total of 714,700 head of strong-horned cattle, i.e., still more than in either 1941, 1946, or 1956. In January 1950, except for horses, 1916 levels were within reach: the disastrous amalgamation of collective farms, begun in this year, would lead to a dramatic decrease in the number of farm animals, with the exception of horses (cf. table 11).

35 Pako, 147/3/2679, l.10.

36 Ibid.; cf. tables 11, 13; *Narodnoe Khoziastvo*, 44. Even in the war year of 1916, when many horses had been requisitioned by the tsarist army, Altrichter indicates that more horses (347,100) were counted in the province than in Soviet times (Altrichter, *Die Bauern*, table 10, 209).

37 Pako, 147/3/2679, l.100b.

38 Ibid.

39 Ibid.

40 Pako, 147/3/2679, l.11.

41 *Bloknot Agitatora*, 1948, 4, 5, 65: in 1945 there were 508,000 obligation holders; in 1947 more than 570,000. Janet G. Chapman argues convincingly that this compulsory purchasing of government bonds in fact functioned as an additional tax (Chapman, *Real Wages*, 116). They added around 50 percent to the total amount of taxes paid by Soviet households in 1944, 1948, and 1952 (119). Every year after the war, the state "borrowed" money in this way from the Soviet citizens (see Zelenin, *Obshch-*

estvenno, tables 14, 15, 220–1). Only in 1958 was the practice discontinued (ibid., 222).

42 Pako, 147/3/2679, ll.11–110b.

43 Pako, 147/4/63, ll.133–4; testimony of G.V. Lubov in the survey. In the second section of chapter 4, more will be said about the "voluntary" state loans.

44 Pako, 147/3/2679, l.11.

45 Some observers are convinced that Stalin was actually preparing for a new offensive war towards the end of his life that would bring the blessings of Soviet Communism to the rest of the world (e.g., Heller and Nekrich, *Utopia in Power*, 504–6).

46 Pako, 147/3/2679, l.170b.

47 Pako, 147/3/2679, l.18.

48 Ibid. The function of kolkhoz chair was about the lowest rung on the ladder of "leading work," in the way it was understood here.

49 Pako, 147/3/2679, l.190b; cf. the third section of chapter 2 and Kaplan, *The Party*, 86, 91–2.

50 Pako, 147/3/2679, l.190b.; Smirnov et al., *Ocherki*, appendix 2, 706. This gives us a total of 3,363 jobs as being part of the obkom nomenklatura; in the spring of 1944, still 3,813 positions fell under the nomenklatura of the oblast' leadership, which undoubtedly was a consequence of the larger size of the oblast at the time (cf. table 16). "Nomenklatura" refers to the responsible positions in party and government for which appointments needed to be ratified by the Central Committee or lower party committees, such as the obkoms. In practice, the Central Committee appointed people to these positions without paying much heed to local preferences. Similarly, the lower party committees distributed nomenklaturnye positions to which they appointed carefully selected individuals.

51 Pako, 147/3/2679, ll.18–180b.

52 Ibid., l.19.

53 Ibid., ll.180b.–19.

54 Ibid., l.190b.

55 Pako, 147/3/2679, l.210b.; Moscow, 17/43/741, ll.103, 110–1100b. and 1140b. Cf. the first and third sections of chapter 2.

56 Moscow, 147/44/546, l.19. The first section of chapter 4 gives some examples of these reports.

57 Pako, 147/3/2679, l.210b.

58 Pako, 147/3/2679, l.22–220b.

59 Pako, 147/3/2679, ll.23–230b.

60 Zhukov, "Bor'ba za vlast'," 32. Cf., as well, Aksenov, "Apogei stalinizma: poslevoennaia piramida vlasti."

61 Moscow, 117/116/381 (microfilm), l.1.

62 Moscow, 117/116/381 (microfilm), ll.10–17.

63 Ibid.

64 Ibid. In 1949 seven-year schooling would be declared compulsory, which must have put an additional strain on the rather limited educational budget of the different levels of the government hierarchy. Cf. *Bloknot Agitatora*, 1949, 9, 30; Lel'chuk, "Industrializatsiia", 346; Inkeles and Bauer, *The Soviet Citizen*, 156.

65 Moscow, 117/116/381 (microfilm), ll.10–17.

66 Ibid.; cf. Kaplan, *The Party*, 146–7. A reading of the oblast' newspaper *Proletarskaia Pravda* during this period gives an impression of the importance attributed to flax. In January, November, and December of 1945, there was hardly one issue of the paper that did not mention the (lack of) progress with flax procurements and treatment.

67 Pako, 147/4/1126, l.146. The resolution of 9 October 1948 was titled "On Measures to Aid the Collective Farms of Kalinin Oblast' with the Increase of Flax Cultivation and the Revival of Agriculture in the Districts That Have Suffered from German Occupation."

68 Pako, 147/1/527, l.200–1.

69 Pako, 147/4/1512, l.20b.–3; on the Leningrad affair, see Zubkova, *Obshchestva*, 79; Kutuzov, "Tak nazyvaemoe 'leningradskoe delo'"; "O tak nazyvaemom 'leningradskom dele'."

70 See, as well, Pikhoia, "O vnutripoliticheskoi bor'be," 5–6.

71 Cf. Kuleshov et al., *Nashe Otechestvo*, 438–9; Sudoplatov, *Special Tasks*, 296, 315–16, 325–7.

72 Pako, 147/4/1511, l.10b.; Pako, 147/4/1512, l.4.

73 Pako, 147/4/1512, l.20b.; l.5. This section was newly organized in the second half of 1948 (cf. Hahn, *Postwar Soviet Politics*, 108, n51).

74 Pako, 147/5/10, l.35; Pako, 147/4/1512, l.19; Schulz and Taylor, *Who's Who*, 377, 918, 920.

75 The resolution was called "On Shortcomings in the Work of the Kalinin Obkom of the VKP(b)" and was dated 20 June 1951; see, e.g., the title page of Pako, 147/5/10. According to these documents, Vorontsov had been released from his duties in November 1949 "for mistakes in the leadership of the oblast' party organization"(Pako, 147/5/10, l.5).

76 Central Committee resolution of 1 August 1950, called "On Shortcomings in the Work of the Kalinin, Kaluga, and Kirov Obkoms of the Party with Respect to the Amalgamation of the Collective Farms" (Pako, 147/5/7, l.3a). Konovalov, in his apology before the obkom plenum of July 1951, also referred to a confidential letter of 2 April 1951, in which additional resolutions on the errors of the Kalinin obkom had been enumerated (Pako, 147/5/10, l.124).

77 Pako, 147/5/10, ll.5–31. In all, 109 members and candidates of the obkom participated at the plenum, 29 of whom actually addressed the meeting (Pako, 147/5/35, l.1).

78 Pako, 147/5/10, l.27.

79 Pako, 147/5/10, ll.28–30.

80 Pako, 147/5/10, l.30.

81 Pako, 147/5/10, ll.30, 181. Konovalov admitted that he tried to work with a different style than his predecessor Vorontsov, who "was extremely rude, did not have any qualms about using foul language to a leading worker, about beating his fist on the table" (Pako, 147/5/10, l.127).

82 Kiselev (1907–?) was a native of the Saratov province; perhaps he was a protégé of Suslov, who was born in the same province, which would make the above explanation impossible, and would lead to the conclusion that Kiselev was merely transferred to another, similar job (Pako, 147/5/2, l.218).

83 Pako, 147/3/2679, l.15. When referring to "Communists" in the records of the party's archive, the sources always mean full members and candidates combined. The number given for 1 January 1945 by an official Soviet source is 28,667 (see table 14).

84 Pako, 147/3/2702, l.530b.

85 Pako, 147/3/2679, l.150b. Cf. chapter 4, particularly for the representation of women in the party.

86 Anokhina and Shmeleva, Kul'tura i byt', 280, 285. Cf. section 3 of chapter 6, as well.

87 Cf. Kaplan, The Party, 91–2.

88 Pako, 147/4/1551, ll.105, 110; 147/4/1495, ll.230b., 26. The resolution concerning the indiscriminate acceptance was titled "On the Growth of the Party and Measures for Strengthening the Party-Organizational and Party-Political Work with New Entrants into the Ranks of the VKP(b)." (Pako, 147/4/18, l.3). The Central Committee resolution was issued on 26 July 1946 (Zelenin, Obshchestvenno, 14–15). Of the 5,749 members and candidates who had been excluded, 1,576 had been involved in the embezzlement of kolkhoz property, 1,184 had become alienated (otryv) from the party, 398 had lived on occupied territory, while 84 had been involved in religious rites and the like (Pako, 147/4/1551, ll.67–8). In 1949 and 1950 an additional 2,681 would be excluded (see table 15).

89 Pako, 147/5/283, l.132.

90 Besides the relentless scrutiny to which they were exposed, the workload for professional party workers was extraordinarily heavy (testimony of N.G. Timofeeva in the survey).

91 Pako, 147/5/328, l.124. A.F. Antonov said in the survey that he was asked by the head of the organizational otdel of the Udoml'ia raikom to become a member. He was told that if he wanted to get anywhere in life, and not remain a kolkhoz brigadier forever, he should join the party. Antonov declined.

92 That is, if one uses for the calculation an estimate of 55,500 for the full

party membership; if the military members are added (which would give a total membership 61,282) the ratio is higher (38.30). Cf. Fainsod, *How Russia is Ruled*, 234, table 9; cf. table 14.

93 Fainsod, *How Russia is Ruled*, 192, 204; Kaplan, *The Party*, 145–7. As Fainsod eloquently put it: "In the Soviet Book of Acts, much is forgiven success, but nothing is forgiven failure" (*How Russia is Ruled*, 353). The obkom's composition corresponds exactly to Fainsod's description of the standard provincial party buro, except for the fact that it seems that the NKGB/MGB chief was the usual representative of the security organs, instead of the head of the local branch of the MVD (191–2). At times, however, both were members of the buro. For a more exhaustive treatise on the organization and role of the government, party, Komsomol, and MVD/MGB, the reader should consult Fainsod's magnificent work: his description of the way the oblasts in Russia were organized is confirmed in the records for Kalinin province. For this reason the description of the governmental system has been kept comparatively brief here.

94 Pako, 147/3/2701, ll.1–269. This record, for example, shows the plethora of issues that the obkomburo discussed in the course of three months in 1945.

95 Cf. Kuleshov et al., *Nashe Otechestvo*, 321, 414; Kaplan, *The Party*, 145, 147. Thus the obkomburo (although the record says obkom, the few plenums certainly did not discuss more than ten issues during entire war) looked into 305 issues that were related to agriculture in 1944 (Pako, 147/3/2679, l.81). It is, of course, wrong to assume that the obkomburo itself was free from supervision and control. Both the Central Committee and the MVD/MGB tried to keep a close watch on its activities. Many of the buro's decisions concerned the implementation of measures and decrees that came from above.

96 Indicative of this reliance on Sadovnikov was the allegation by Cherkasov in July 1951 of Konovalov being too friendly to the oblispolkom head and Sadovnikov's deputies Shcheplikov and Gorokhov (Pako, 147/5/10, l.35).

97 Pako, 147/5/10, ll.118–20. Central Committee representative Storozhev briefly discussed Sadovnikov's position at the end of the July 1951 plenum, but for no apparent reason asked the obkom members to give him another chance and give him more support in the future (Pako, 147/5/10, l.185).

98 Pako, 147/5/10, l.120.

99 This conclusion was indicated by a comparison of the records of Pako, 147/5/1, l.28; 147/5/283, ll.347–50.

100 Fainsod, *How Russia is Ruled*, 189; testimony of D.A. Dikushin in the survey; Pako, 147/5/283, ll.350–3. Obkom member Dubinin stated in

1952 that he felt Shatalin to be incompetent. I.I. Tiaglov clashed with
him in 1952, although he did not explain the cause (testimony of I.I.
Tiaglov in the survey). S.N. Shatalin is the father of the economist
Stanislav Shatalin who knew a brief moment in the limelight during the
last years of the existence of the USSR (see Roxburgh, *The Second
Russian Revolution*, 194, 198; Fairbanks, "The Nature of the Beast,"
52).

101 Pako, 147/5/283, l.356; N.N. Shatalin was a client of Malenkov, as we
have seen.

102 Cf. Pako, 147/5/764, ll.54–8; Fainsod, *How Russia is Ruled*, 173, 192.
According to Fainsod, there was no school department at the oblast'
level in 1939, when the reorganization took place upon which the organization discussed here was based (Fainsod, *How Russia is Ruled*, 173).
However, in the sources for Kalinin oblast' for 1945, evidence could not
be found that the school department had been replaced by a department
for military affairs. In fact, in 1947–48, evidence of the existence of an
obkom (and gorkom and raion) army department *together* with a
school department has been found in the records, at least within the
obkom secretariat (Pako, 147/4/1125, ll.71–71ob.). The obkom department for military matters supervised in 1947 the Osoaviakhim (the
paramilitary organization for civilians, again comparable to Britain's
Home Guard in World War II), the committee for physical exercise and
sport, and the Red Cross. It aided local army administration organs,
organized physical and military training for school children, helped the
war invalids find work, aided the families of soldiers, and was responsible for communication with units of the Soviet Army stationed in
Kalinin oblast'. The raion and town party committees had a similar
department. Apart from the military department in 1945, there was a
military commissar, who probably was subordinate to the Red Army
command and was presumably more or less independent from the
obkom leadership: 1945 was still a war year, and military representatives at lower levels of the party were under the direct command of the
General Staff (Stavka).

103 An enormous amount of the dela (for this term, see the appendix) in the
former party's archives were records that had been collected or created
by the "Special Sector" of the obkom after the war; for Poskrebyshev's
role, see, e.g., Zhuravlev, *XX s'ezd*, 217.

104 Samsonov, *A Short History of the USSR*, 264. Obkom secretaries
Vakhmistrov and Shatalin criticized the inordinate amount of paperpushing involved in obkom work (Pako, 147/5/10, ll.60, 112–13).

105 Pako, 147/5/10, l.182. Cf. Fainsod, *How Russia is Ruled*, 174–5, chart
5. In Kalinin, the Central Committee Foreign Otdel and the Main Political Administration of the Armed Forces were replaced by the obkom

financial and economic sector (which mainly dealt with the financial
state of the party organization itself) and the obkom machine-building
sector, the successor to the otdel of defense. Its name reminds one of the
Ministry of Medium Machine Building, in which, after Stalin's death,
the Soviet nuclear defense program was further developed (see
Sakharov, *Memoirs*, 104). The former schoolteacher and school director
Azarov headed the newly created education department in 1951; in
1953 the obkom otdels of industry, machine-building, light industry,
and transport were combined into one otdel of industry and transport
(Pako, 147/5/661, ll.127–8). The administrative otdel and that of planning, finance, and trade were also combined into one.

106   Laqueur, *The Dream*, 57.

107   Pako, 147/4/1125, ll.91.; cf. Fainsod, *How Russia is Ruled*, 193–5.

108   Pako, 147/3/2679, l.47.

109   Pako, 147/3/2679, ll.16–17.

110   Pako, 147/5/202, ll.28–9, 42, 46; on Belorussia, see Fainsod, *How
Russia is Ruled*, 195.

111   Pako, 147/4/18, l.7; cf. Fainsod, *How Russia is Ruled*, 196–200;
Laqueur, *The Dream*, 91.

112   It was similarly impossible for the Central Comittee to control every
action of the obkom; see Fainsod, *How Russia is Ruled*, 327–8.

113   Ivan V. Karasev agrees in his description of the room for manoeuvring
of the postwar kolkhoz chair in Pskov oblast' ("The Reconstruction of
Agriculture in Pskov Oblast'," 306–7).

114   Pako, 147/4/57, l.560b. It was of course certainly not true at lower
levels that all people in nomenklaturnye positions were party members
and vice versa. On 1 January 1952, when the party was probably larger
than in 1946 in this raion, Sonkovo raion had 887 Communists. Cf.
tables 16 and 18 for the comparatively low level of education of those
at the higher levels of the provincial party.

115   Baranov was born in 1912 in Tver' and had studied at a Leningrad
technical-industrial institute; in 1941 he became party member. In 1949
he became the party secretary of the railroad-car factory, after working
for a while as the head of one of its workshops. He apparently was promoted during the purge at the factory, as he already was party secretary
of the works in February 1949 at the seventh party conference, which
took place immediately after the "discovery" of the case (for this case,
see the first section of chapter 6; Pako, 147/4/1495, l.100). Perhaps he
had even been (one of) the person(s), who drew the attention of the
MGB and the party to the case in the first place. At the end of the July
1951 Plenum, he was appointed head of the obkom department of
machine-building on the recommendation of Kiselev (Pako, 147/5/10,
l.184).

116 Pako, 147/5/10, l.77. Cf. Fainsod's remarks on criticism (Fainsod, *How Russia is Ruled*, 182–3). A.S. Efremov became a party member in 1952. When he was interviewed, he described this reprobation as "criticism, measured out in doses [dozirovannaia kritika] ... *this* you may criticize, *that* is not permitted [to be critical about]." N.N. Panova described in the interviews the orchestration of this kind of criticism: "Even our 'stars,' our best weavers, could criticize in the best of cases something from the tribune [only] for the sake of appearances, and then their speeches were written for them, and corrected in the party committee [of the factory]."

117 Pako, 147/5/10, ll. 77–8. In fact, in March 1951, at the eighth oblast' party conference, Konovalov himself lashed out at people who suppressed criticism from below, a number of whom had been dismissed after Vorontsov's ouster (Pako, 147/5/2, l.19).

118 Cf. Fainsod, *How Russia is Ruled*, 337–9. "[The Communist Party] was not, and never had been, a political party in the true sense of the word but a mechanism for controlling the state" (Pipes, "1917," 79).

119 The term skhod remained in use for the village meeting, but the authority of the skhod was much reduced after collectivization. It seems that after Stalin's death an effort was undertaken to revive the skhod (Zelenin, *Obshchestvenno*, 141–2). It had, however, lost most of its power of decision in local matters. Instead, even after 1953 it functioned as another "transmission belt," with the task of organizing the execution of decisions made by higher authorities. The meetings of the skhod were called by the ispolkoms of the rural soviets.

120 Pako, 147/5/283, l.121. In February 1946 the USSR Supreme Soviet delegates elected for Kalinin oblast' were I.P. Boitsov, A.V. Simonov, A.M. Vasil'ev, E.I. Rybakova, M.P. Volkova, M.M. Gromov, A.D. Krutikov, and M.M. Pereslegin; V.P. Potemkin was elected to the Soviet of Nationalities. Some of these delegates were token workers or kolkhozniks, the rest party leaders (PP 7959, 15 February 1945, 1). See also Fainsod, *How Russia is Ruled*, 324–6. Not only the obkom, but also the MVD/MGB, the procuracy, Gosplan, the Ministry of State Control, and other ministries supervised the activities of the oblispolkom (see Fainsod, *How Russia is Ruled*, 329, 338–9). As Djilas remarked about the role of the party in governmental affairs: "The Communist Party, including the professional party bureaucracy, stands above the regulations and behind every single one of the state's acts" (Djilas, *The New Class*, 35).

121 Pako, 147/5/283, l.124.

122 Pako, 147/3/2679, l.89. N.A. Zabelin said during the interviews that he was told by an MVD officer in 1951 that he had been appointed director of secondary school No. 19, located in the "closed" airforce suburb of Kalinin, Migalovo.

123 Testimony of M.A. Smirnov in the survey.
124 Cf. Pako, 147/4/66, l.197; Pavlov's biography was written because he was up for promotion.
125 Pako, 147/4/1125, l.79.
126 "(Za)verbovat'" is the infinitive of the verb used for this practice (testimony of A.S. Efremov, who was an army signaller during the war). The organs did check the mail that Efremov handled, which is no surprise to us, because of the arrest of Solzhenitsyn. He also saw an officer who was beaten by the Chekists, until he bled, in the "special branch" (osobyi otdel) of the NKVD. Before the war his neighbour was arrested as a result of a denunciation that was sent to the raion authorities (testimony of A.S. Efremov in the survey). S.S. Sergeev testified in the survey that he was denounced by his own brother to the NKVD after the war; he was accused of having served in the German Polizei. Apparently the brother wanted to have the parental home all for himself. Sergeev was soon released by the NKVD, which apparently did not take sanctions against the brother either. Cf. the information network in Moscow ("Moskva voennaia," 101). The testimony of three interviewees, who were honest enough to admit their (forced) involvement with the security organs, proves the point of Valentin Turchin: "A society was created in which information was closed, and its flourishing, its take-off took place in the last years of Stalin's life. Hundreds of thousands of informers followed every word of its citizens" (*Inertsiia Strakha*, 21). Cf. also Solzhenitsyn, *The Gulag*, 3–4, 636.
127 Cf. chapter 5.
128 Pako, 147/4/519, ll.155–60.
129 See Fainsod, *How Russia is Ruled*, 410–13.
130 Pako, 147/4/1125, l.770b.
131 Kirichek, "Vozrozhdenie," 90; Moscow, 17/44/546, ll.1610b/162. This plenum was staged *before* – in July 1944 – the separation of the parts of the Velikie Luki oblast' in August 1944. The statement of Kirichek, that an obkom plenum took decisions on the Komsomol in 1942 or 1943 could not be verified in the archive ("Vozrozhdenie," 89). However, the plenum of July 1944 did deal with the "improvement of Komsomol and party work among the youth" of the oblast' (see Moscow, 17/44/546, ll.113–169). VLKSM: Vsesoiuznyi Leninskii Kommunisticheskii Soiuz Molodezhi, All-Union Leninist Communist Youth League, more often abbreviated as Komsomol.
132 Pako, 147/3/2679, l.14. In the countryside, 188 Komsomols worked as chairs and 469 as secretaries of rural soviets, 241 as kolkhoz directors, and 191 as heads of livestock sectors of collective farms; and 515 managed village reading rooms.
133 Pako, 147/3/2679, l.140b., ll.14ff.
134 Pako, 147/3/2679, l.140b. In other words, hardly any kolkhoz in this

raion had a Komsomol cell, because on 1 July 1946, 230 collective farms would be counted here (Pako, 147/3/1966, ll.39–390b.).

135   Cf. Kirichek, "Vozrozhdenie," 93n; Eremin, "O vklade," 97.

136   Pako, 147/4/18, l.10; Zelenin, *Obshchestvenno*, 149, 154; Pako, 147/4/1391, l.5.

137   Fainsod, *How Russia is Ruled*, 241; Smirnov et al., *Ocherki*, 553. According to provincial Komsomol secretary Smirnov, it had 72,000 members in early 1948, 77,000 in early 1949, and, according to his successor Beliakova, 108,000 in July 1951 (Pako, 147/4/1095, l.21; 147/4/1495, l.770b.; 147/5/10, l.71). Also, *Zare navstrechu*, 295.

138   Fainsod, *How Russia is Ruled*, 249. On 1 January 1951, a total of 101,530 Komsomols was counted in the oblast, of whom 56,401 had been accepted as new members of the youth organization in 1949 and 1950; at the same time the actual growth was 24,647, which shows the high level of attrition among the membership (Pako, 147/5/173, l.5).

139   Fainsod, *How Russia is Ruled*, 248.

140   Pako, 147/5/10, l.71; halfway through 1948, of a total of 7,382 kolkhozy, only 2,974 had Komsomol organizations (Pako, 147/4/1096, l.6).

141   Pako, 147/5/659, l.118; 147/5/10, l.72; 147/4/1495, l.770b.

142   This was the complaint of Konovalov in March 1951 (Pako, 147/5/2, l.22).

143   Pako, 147/4/1126, l.5.

144   Pako, 147/4/1095, l.21. In 1948 obkom secretary Parfenov maintained that up to 40 percent of the Komsomol membership did not pay its fees on a regular basis (Pako, 147/4/1095, l.210b.). Churchill's speech in Fulton, Missouri, in which he described the Iron Curtain that divided Europe, was published in *Proletarskaia Pravda* (PP 7976, 12 March 1946, 4).

145   Pako, 147/5/660, ll.93/94.

146   Pako, 147/5/659, ll.144, 147, 148, 201. During 1952, 1,830 people younger than twenty-six had been convicted by the oblast' courts. More than 80 percent of these accused were between eighteen and twenty-six years old. Hooliganism and theft each made up more than 40 percent of the crimes committed by the youth. Twenty-eight had been convicted of premeditated murder. Almost 15 percent of the 1,830 were Komsomol members.

CHAPTER FOUR

1   Bradbury, *Doctor Criminale*, 329.

2   This was evident in the testimonies of several people, in the survey, some of whom had joined the Communist Party at some point in time,

while others had not. Djilas gave a perceptive explanation for the inherent need of the Communist state for "enemies": "Founded by force and violence, in constant conflict with its people, the Communist state, even if there are no external reasons, must be militaristic. The cult of force, especially military force, is nowhere so prevalent as in Communist countries. Militarism is the internal basic need of the new class; it is one of the forces which make possible the new class's existence, strength, and privileges" (*The New Class*, 95). Zubkova comments: "the character of the war itself – patriotic, liberating, justified – supposed a unity of society (the narod and the authorities) for the solution of the general national problem: the resistance against the enemy" (Zubkova, "Obshchestvennaia," 7). According to R. Stites: "Nationalism, homeland, Russian history, lore, legend, and classical culture underlay the whole experience – in film and all the popular arts. The war so deeply popularized and legitimized these that they survived the renewed onslaught of Marxist ideology in the postwar period" (*Russian Popular Culture*, 115).

3 This was evident in the testimonies of twenty participants in the survey, sixteen of whom (or their spouses), were at one time or other members of the Communist Party.

4 See the second section of chapter 5. The spouses of eight of the survey respondents who felt there was no crime under Stalin, or they themselves, were Communists at some time; four never were candidates or full members of the Party.

5 "The history of all countries shows that the working class, exclusively by its own effort, is able to develop only trade-union consciousness, i.e., the conviction that it is necessary to combine in unions, fight the employers, and strive to compel the government to pass necessary labour legislation, etc." (Lenin, "What is to be Done?," 375). Cf., as well, Malia, "A Fatal Logic," 88.

6 Pako, 147/3/2679, l.210b.

7 Pako, 147/3/2679, l.210b.–23. More will be said in this section about the Short Course. Were these lectures always given? The case of Tsvetkov described below indicates that the interest in the lectures on the part of lecturers and their intended audiences was quite limited at times.

8 Pako 147/4/18, l.100b. The records of the discussion in the plenum are to be found in Pako, 147/4/18. For a recent discussion of Zhdanov's ideological offensive, see Babichenko, *Pisateli i tsenzory*, 111-47. Zhdanov's speech on the journals *Zvezda* and *Leningrad* was published in *Proletarskaia Pravda* (PP 8114, 22 September 1946, 2–3).

9 Pako, 147/4/528, l.1.

10 Pako 147/4/18, l.100b. And this problem was all the more urgent because half the secretaries of party cells had joined the party after 1944, according to the head of the orginstruktor otdel of the obkom (Pako,

147/4/18, l.25). The instructors with the raikoms, who were supposed to supervise ideological education, were often engaged full-time in economic work as plenipotentiaries. Within the raikoms the ideological work was supposed to be supervised by the second secretary, who often was not up to the task either (Pako, 147/4/18, ll.250b, 260b.).

11 Pako, 147/4/18, l.11. From the evidence in the archives of the Kalinin party organization, I tend to agree with Fainsod's idea about the function of the elections for the different level of soviets as a form of national mobilization (*How Russia is Ruled*, 323). Cf. the third section of chapter 3.

12 Pako, 147/4/63, ll.269–71.

13 Pako, 147/4/1095, l.100b.; Pako, 147/4/1126, ll.55–6.

14 Pako, 147/4/63, l.271. The question about grain was caused by the dire circumstances of the winter of 1946–47 (cf. Volkov, "Zasukha," 16). Similar questions were fielded when Central Committee plenipotentiaries visited other provinces of the Union around 1947 (see Zubkova, "Obshchestvennaia," 83).

15 Cf. Zubkova, "Obshchestvennaia," 10–11 and 13–14.

16 Pako, 147/4/63, l.271.

17 Cf. Fainsod, *How Russia is Ruled*, 324.

18 Pako, 147/4/1126, l.1080b. This kind of question was asked not only about foodstuffs in general but also about specific products such as bread and about the prices of other consumer goods such as shoes, cloth, and clothes. Abramov paints a picture of how the lectures given on the kolkhozy could be disrupted by the smarter kolkhozniks (*The New Life*, 60–2).

19 Pako, 147/4/1703, l.34.

20 Pako, 147/5/34, l.3; the Central Committee letter was titled "On the Task of Collective-Farm Construction in Connection with Strengthening Small Collective Farms," the letter of party and government combined "On the Antigovernment Deeds of the Former Leadership of the Ministry of Agricultural-Machine Building of the USSR," indicating that a purge had been or was being conducted within the Ministry of Agricultural-Machine Building.

21 Pako, 147/5/34, l.3.

22 See Heller and Nekrich, *Utopia in Power*, 474. Mark Frankland, e.g., describes the controversy that had arisen as a result of Khrushchev's proposals (*Khrushchev*, 84–5).

23 Pako, 147/5/328, l.58. The report is to N. Pegov, the head of the Central Committee Department for Party, Trade Union, and Komsomol organs (see Pako, 147/5/328, l.55). The Fifth Five Year Plan, meanwhile, had already started more than a year and a half earlier, on 1 January 1951.

24 Pako, 147/5/328, ll.89, 92.

25 Arbatov, The System, 22.

26 This paragraph is based on the testimonies of several participants in the survey.

27 Pako, 147/5/36, ll.14–15, 21. The report on the election preparations is once more addressed to S.D. Ignat'ev, who had become, by January 1951, the head of the Central Committee Department of Party, Trade Union, and Komsomol Organs.

28 PP 7960, 17 February 1946.

29 Pako, 147/5/36, ll.17–18.

30 A.M. Afanas'ev, a former professional party worker, remembered in the survey that the elections were accompanied by great parties in Udoml'ia, on a par with the religious holidays that continued to be observed. This practice shows how some of the more agreeable aspects of the "New Life" blended into more traditional habits. When obkom secretary Zimin wrote a report a few months later to the Central Committee on the RSFSR Supreme Soviet elections that had taken place, he did refer to certain less happy events (Pako, 147/5/36, ll.70–1): in Lukovnikovo raion, e.g., a group of drunken soldiers of an army detachment started a fight in which nine villagers were wounded with knives, one of whom subsequently died of his injuries.

31 Several Russians in Tver' confirmed this practice to me in personal conversations in the summer of 1992. The phenomenon is also described by Abramov (The New Life, 41–3).

32 Bloknot Agitatora, 1949, 5, 44.

33 Bloknot Agitatora, 1949, 6, 31. At the November 1949 obkom plenum, Ul'ianov, head of the oblast' committee for "radiofication" said, "This is an indicator of the very low cultural level of the oblast'" (Pako, 147/4/1512, l.26). In February 1949, 464 out of 7,500 kolkhozy were said to have radios, and only 250 had electricity (Pako, 147/4/1495, l.91). This also shows the very slow progress of the electrification of the countryside, because in March 1946, 69 kolkhozy (1 percent of the total) had electricity (PP 7978, 15 March 1946, 2). In three years only around 180 more had either been connected to the provincial electricity network or had started to operate their own hydro-powered generators.

34 Gako (the State Archive of the Tver' oblast'), 2913/1/28, ll.33, 36. In the agricultural tekhnikum (vocational institute) of Krasnyi Kholm students listened to the "Voice of America." This practice was still alive in 1953, when even in the town of Kalinin at the Gastronom office employees collectively listened to the "anti-soviet broadcasts of the American and English radio" (Pako, 147/5/662, l.78).

35 Pako, 147/5/2, l.29. Particularly during and in the first years after the war not enough copies of these papers were printed; consequently, newspaper windows were used to display them (Pako, 147/3/2679, l.51ob.).

In 1948 *Proletarskaia Pravda* appeared in Kalinin about four to five times a week, five other urban papers in the other towns three times, and all the other papers only once or twice a week (Pako, 147/4/1126, ll.48–490b.). Since August 1951 a Komsomol paper had appeared in the oblast', called *Stalinskaia Molodezh'* (Pako, 147/5/659, l.136; see the third section of chapter 3, above). In 1952 *Proletarskaia Pravda* started to appear six times a week, twenty-seven of the raion newspapers began to appear twice instead of once a week, and six raion papers appeared four times a week (Pako, 147/5/283, l.139). In January 1945, one oblast', five urban, and forty-one raion newspapers were published, with a total circulation of 226,000 copies per week (*PP* 7677, 14 January 1945, 3; see the first section of chapter 3, above). In January 1945, 48,500 copies per edition were printed of *Proletarskaia Pravda* (*PP* 7686, 28 January 1945, 2, for example).

36 Based on Pako, 147/4/57, ll.115–24. First obkom secretary Boitsov went along with the plan (Pako, 147/4/157, ll.126–7).

37 Pako, 147/4/57, ll.115–24.

38 Pako, 147/4/1934, l.70. Certain exceptional circumstances were allowed to upstage the preconceived plan of reporting. For example, when beloved native M.I. Kalinin died in June 1946, two issues of *Proletarskaia Pravda* were almost exclusively dedicated to the life and works of the deceased Soviet president (*PP* 8036, 5 June 1946; *PP* 8037, 6 June 1946).

39 Pako, 147/5/659, l.98. In February 1952 *Proletarskaia Pravda* was renamed *Kalininskaia Pravda* (*Bol'shaia Sovetskaia entsiklopediia*, 19:434).

40 *PP* 8082, 9 August 1946, 4; Pako, 147/5/663, l.161; Pako, 147/5/7, ll.105–7. The province had 9,972 settlements and probably approximately 1,000 rural soviets in 1953 (Pako, 147/5/663, l.161; *Narodnoe Khoziaistvo*, 7). For every thirty villages or hamlets, consequently, there was one library. In 1951, 93 stationary and 288 mobile film projectors operated in Kalinin oblast' (Pako, 147/5/7, l.95).

41 Pako, 147/5/7, ll.109, 119.

42 Chapter 4 of the book is supposed to have been written by Stalin (*Short Course*, 105–31).

43 Pako, 147/5/659, ll.45, 69, for example. For more on religion, see the second section of chapter 4.

44 For the increased repression, cf. Zubkova, *Obshchestvo*, 63–9, 77–90.

45 Pako, 147/4/1095, ll.11, 37. Cf. Heller and Nekrich, *Utopia in Power*, 488–92; the plenum's discussions are to be found in Pako, 147/4/1095.

46 Parfenov, "Shire razvernut'," 4–5.

47 Ibid., 6.

48 Pako, 147/4/1095, l.37.

49 Pako, 147/4/1095, l.60b. In the USSR as a whole the party experienced a profound transformation of its membership (Carrère d'Encausse, *Stalin*, 2:165–6). The number was slightly less according to Petrov, head of the obkom orgotdel, who said at the same meeting that 47,000 out of a total of 61,000 had become Communist during or after the war (Pako, 147/4/1095, l.29).

50 Pako, 147/4/18, ll.7–8.

51 Pako, 147/4/18, l.80b.

52 Pako, 147/4/1095, l.80b. Around June 1946, about 60,000 copies of the *Short Course* were made available for unrestricted sale in the province (PP 8073, 27 July 1946, 3).

53 As Zubkova rightfully notes as well (*Obshchestvo*, 63–9, 77–90).

54 As reported by Vakhmistrov to M.A. Suslov in July 1951 (Pako, 147/5/35, ll.11–12). Political schools were small affairs with a two-year curriculum of the study of Marxism-Leninism. In 1950–51, 655 operated under the auspices of primary party cells at collective farms (Pako, 147/5/35, l.15) The evening schools were for leading Party, soviet, and Komsomol aktiv, and secretaries of primary Party cells (Pako, 147/5/35, l.19); they offered a ten-month program in 1946, in which the students had a four-hour class once a week – in theory, although practice often led to neglect of the curriculum in the raions, because the students were too busy with other, mainly agricultural, matters (Pako, 147/4/18, l.9). The evening universities – which had opened in 1943 (Pako, 147/4/18, l.9) – were located in Kalinin, Vyshnii Volochek, and Kimry, and had about a thousand students, 80 percent of whom were Communists (Pako, 147/5/35, l.19). Among the students, hardly any genuine workers or peasants were to be found, as about half of them were leading party, soviet, Komsomol, and trade union workers, and the rest mainly engineers, technicians, teachers, and doctors (Pako, 147/5/35, ll.19–20).

55 Pako, 147/5/35, l.23. Thirty-one percent of the lectures were on the history of the Communist Party, 10 percent on philosophy, 13 percent on political economy, 8.5 percent on questions of Communist upbringing and Soviet patriotism, and 36 percent on the international situation and the current moment (Pako, 147/5/35, l.23).

56 Pako, 147/5/283, l.134, and Pako, 147/5/659, l.72, confirm the frequently encountered limited understanding of the ideological canon by both agitators and audience, even in 1952 and 1953.

57 In Soviet times, the term meshchanin means roughly "petit bourgeois" in a pejorative sense, even though, paradoxically, the taste in music, art, interior decoration, or literature of most Russians was that of the meshchanin (see Dunham, *In Stalin's Time*, 19–23).

58 For Stalin's death, cf. the next section of this chapter.

59 For example, in the first three months of 1947, the militsiia, on orders of

the obkomburo, carried out operations to combat fraud with ration cards, for which 290 people were arrested, even though criminal proceedings were instituted against only fifty-one of them (Pako, 147/4/984, l.36). "The simplicity of this mechanism originates from the fact that one party alone, the Communist Party, is the backbone of the entire political, economic and ideological activity. The entire public life is at a standstill or moves ahead, falls behind or turns around according to what happens in the party forums" (Djilas, *The New Class*, 71; cf., too, Fainsod, *How Russia is Ruled*, 351).

60 Djilas, *The New Class*, 87.

61 *PP* 7966, 26 February 1946, 3. Pako, 147/4/18, l.60b. This was not unique in this year (Volkov, "Zasukha," 8).

62 On the abyss between the narod and vlast', see Zubkova, "Obshchestvennaia," 79. Sheila Fitzpatrick has recently analysed the situation in the countryside during the early 1930s: her description of the imperfect operation of the command system may be applied to both town and countryside for the postwar period (*Stalin's Peasants*, 70–1). I do take issue with her implication that the government could not apply too much coercion, since it was attempting to make "informed decisions." How much more coercion was feasible than that applied by the authorities under Stalin?

63 Pako, 147/5/11, l.65. For industry, see the first section of chapter 6.

64 Her testimony is corroborated by V.G. Gavrilov, who remembered that, at the end of the war, a raikom worker and an NKVD plenipotentiary appeared in their village (both Kurganova and Gavrilov lived in Kotlovan in Udoml'ia raion) to make people subscribe to the state loan. They kept all the locals an entire night in an office, while playing with their pistols. They searched the houses and made an inventory of the possessions of those who refused to subscribe and threatened them.

65 A good example of this attitude is the article by A.N. Sakharov in *Kommunist* in 1991 ("Revolutsionnyi"). Nevertheless, this article provides an extremely interesting theoretical interpretation of the historical development of the Soviet Union and deserves attention. Sakharov's analysis of the wholehearted participation of the semiliterate masses in the butchery can be read as an addition to Hannah Arendt's analysis of the psychological mechanism that made people kill their fellow human beings in an unprecedented way during the twentieth century (*The Origins of Totalitarianism*, 337). Contrasting with Sakharov's ideas is the opinion of N.P. Poletika, which seems to me somewhat closer to the truth (*Vidennoe i perezhitoe*, 406–7). Poletika suggests that about 80 percent of the population, composed of all social strata, lived by fear (for the loss of their private cow, for a new purge of the party ranks, for an accusation of sabotage, etc.). The other 20 percent participated wholeheartedly in the system, because of the opportunities for upward social mobility that it

offered them. They became morally degenerate or even lost their minds as a result. His idea of the role of fear is echoed to a certain extent by Robert Tucker: "State terror is triadic. One element of the triad is a political leadership determined to use terror for its purposes. The second is a minority chosen for victimization in so frightful a form that a third element, a far larger body of people, seeing what can happen to the victims, will be motivated to fulfill the leadership's purpose, which may be to render it quiescent or, alternatively, to induce it to take actions that it otherwise would not be disposed to take" (Tucker, *Stalin in Power*, 174). Cf., for some evidence of Bolshevik and socialist suspicion towards peasants, e.g., Lewin, *Lenin's Last Struggle*, 22–9 or 111–12, and Gor'kii, *Nesvoevremennye mysli*, 86, 88–9.

66 This enthusiasm is, for instance, described by Volkogonov; it remained largely restricted to the urban population (*Triumf i tragediia*, 1:2, 70, 179–83; 2:2, 20). Obviously, less scrupulous people tried to use the system for their personal advancement and supported the politics of the regime for that reason. It is impossible, in my opinion, to assign these kinds of people to some layer of society, as Iu. Igritskii tried to do when he proposed that the collaborators and careerists came from the "lumpen-erized" (liumpenizorovannye) strata of society ("Snova o totalitarizme," 15).

67 Grossman, *Forever Flowing*, 31.

68 Cf. Lorenz, *Sozialgeschichte*, 291.

69 Pako, 147/3/2701, ll.67–670b. The full report of the discussion is to be found in Pako, 147/3/2701, ll.660b.–68. "Special contingent" was a term used for a group of prisoners (Kopelev, *Ease My Sorrows*, 133).

70 Pako, 147/3/2701, ll.670b.–68.

71 Ibid.

72 Ibid.

73 Pako, 147/4/1560, l.31. The five districts comprised Kashin, Lesnoe, Molokovo, Sandovo, and Bezhetsk raions.

74 See also the third section of chapter 4.

75 Pako, 147/4/57, l.560b. Cf. table 15 as well: it shows that many Communists were not above common human weaknesses.

76 This is, moreover, one of Stalin's important postwar speeches: the (in)famous pre-election speech on the occasion of the elections for the Supreme Soviet in 1946, in which Stalin explains the victory in the war as the consequence of his (or the party's) far-sighted policies in the 1930s (see Daniels, *A Documentary History of Communism*, 2:142–51).

77 Pako, 147/4/1097, ll.140b.–15; plenum discussions concerning this matter are to be found in Pako, 147/4/1096, l.2, 147/4/1097, ll.4, 140b.–15.

78 Volkov, *Sovetskaia derevnia*, 195.

79   Ibid., 199; Volkov (ibid., 196) mentions that from 1946 to 1950 3 percent of the kolkhozniks were excluded annually from the collectives for this reason.

80   Cf. Volkov, "Kolkhozy sssr," 61.

81   See the first section of chapter 8. The desperate efforts of chairman Anany Yegorovich Mysovsky to find assistance for the haying on the New Life kolkhoz illustrate the difficulties in trying to make people participate in kolkhoz work (see Abramov, *The New Life*).

82   Pako, 147/4/1703, l.24; Pako, 147/3/1966, ll.39–390b. The term "khutor" is rather vague: in some documents, it appears to mean only peasant houses not located in the kolkhoz village, whose occupants could still have participated in kolkhoz labour. Some might have been edinolichniki, individual farmers. How many of the latter belonged to the few who had persisted in their resistance to being collectivized and how many had been excluded from the kolkhoz at some point after collectivization is not clear. Between July 1946 and early 1949 the rural population and the number of kolkhozy was in general on the rise (see table 6).

83   Individual farmers, together with kolkhozniks, were warned to have a valid permit to trade on the kolkhoz markets of Kalinin in September 1946 in *Proletarskaia Pravda* (PP 8109, 15 September 1946, 4).

84   See the first section of chapter 8.

85   Cf. Verbitskaia, *Rossiiskoe krest'ianstvo*, 85–8.

86   Pako, 147/4/1132, l.3.

87   Volkov, *Sovetskaia derevnia*, 306–9, and Smirnov et al., *Ocherki*, 539 for the resolution. This resolution of the Central Committee was called "On the Amalgamation of Small Collective Farms and the Tasks of the Party Organizations in this Matter."

88   Pako 147/5/36, ll.1–11.

89   Out of a total of 1,905 collective farms on 1 May 1953, 77 percent of had a primary party organization; on 1 June 1950, right before the amalgamation, out of a total of slightly more than 7,000 kolkhozy, there were only 916 primary party organizations (Pako, 147/5/769, ll.94–5). Cf. Korytkov, *Kalininskoe selo*, 45.

90   Amalgamation was continued during the winter of 1951: by March 1951, out of a total of 1,956 kolkhozy in the province, 1,810 were composed of more than one kolkhoz that had existed before the summer of 1950 (Pako, 147/5/36, l.91). By that time, there were 73 female chairs. Already, 348 of the 1956 chairs (17.8 percent) were dismissed by the general annual meeting of the kolkhozy in the late winter of 1951. In October 1951, 70.5 percent of chairs were Communist (1,344 out of 1,906), with only 79 women working as chairs (Pako, 147/5/35, l.118–19). A report on the situation on 1 January 1952 notices that instead of only 12.3 percent (924) of the total of collective farms having

a party organization, as was the case two years earlier (on 1 January 1950), there were 1,486 (77 percent) with primary party organizations (Pako, 147/5/199, l.2)

91 Pako, 147/5/7, l.4.

92 Pako, 147/5/7, l.18. The kolkhozy were, until 1950, based on the villages that existed before collectivization (Volkov, *Sovetskaia derevnia*, 303). Cf. the following remark by Karasev on the results of the amalgamation of the kolkhozy in Pskov oblast': "However, the enlargement of kolkhozy alienated the kolkhoznik from the land because now it no longer coincided with the land of the former community (obshchina). The peasantry's response to amalgamation was increased flight from the village" ("Agriculture in Pskov Oblast'," 305). Karasev is thus of the opinion that the amalgamation, which was intended to make agriculture more efficient, failed to do so. In the light of the agricultural results in Kalinin oblast' during the early 1950s, one would agree with Karasev. This opinion was further corroborated in the interviews by that of the kolkhoz bookkeeper N.F. Alekseev and of L.S. Solov'eva-Ratataeva. Anokhina and Shmeleva indicate that, even after two rounds of amalgamation, the enlarged kolkhozy still consisted of a conglomerate of small villages in the early 1960s (*Kul'tura i byt'*, 80).

93 Pako, 147/4/2055, l.28; Volkov, *Sovetskaia derevnia*, 309. In the survey N.F. Alekseev said that "This [amalgamation] destroyed a strongly cohesive economic unit, in which people lived close to each other and knew each other well and therefore worked better. During the amalgamation matters got so far, that village rose against village – the village of Soroki against that of Bor'kovo." Z.M. Vinogradova, who was the chair of a kolkhoz before amalgamation, and then was relegated to lead a sector of an amalgamated kolkhoz, recalled in the survey that a chair in the village of Bakhmar was arrested in 1950 for opposing the merger of his kolkhoz with other kolkhozy. She did not know what happened to him.

94 Fainsod indicates an increase of direct party control over the kolkhozy during this period (*How Russia is Ruled*, 235); he seems to have been right to stress the importance of this aspect for amalgamation (cf. Pako, 147/4/2055, l.38). The average size of the collective farms increased from 35 hearths and 49 able-bodied workers to 130 hearths with 190 farm hands. The area of land in each kolkhoz swelled from 213 to 818 hectares, on average (Pako, 147/5/2, l.49). Although this was a significant increase in the size of the collective farms in Kalinin oblast', they remained smaller than in the Soviet Union as a whole, in which in 1949 the average kolkhoz had 80 households and, after amalgamation, 165 (Volkov, *Sovetskaia derevnia*, 112; Verbitskaia, *Rossiiskoe krest'ianstvo*, 93–5). In addition, the average kolkhoz household (around 3.0 persons in 1947–52) in Kalinin oblast' was smaller than in the USSR in general

(3.5 in 1950) (Volkov, *Sovetskaia derevnia*, 112, table 6). Another reason for the amalgamation was probably a desire to cut costs by having fewer administrative and executive personnel on the payrolls of the collective farms. In Udoml'ia raion the administrative staff of the kolkhozy fell from 1,093 in early 1950 to 702 in the second half of 1950 (Pako, 147/4/2055, l.26). This translated into a decrease of tru-dodni paid to kolkhoz staff: in Udoml'ia raion staff trudodni dropped from 24,500 to 17,600. Thus, in theory, it seemed that a very cheap way had been found to free more trudodni for the pay of the kolkhozniks, who, as a result, would be incited to work harder.

95 Pako, 147/5/104, ll.12–15, 14, 16–18, 27, 29. For a positive Soviet appreciation of the amalgamation, see Samsonov, *A Short History*, 257. Volkov, *Sovetskaia derevnia*, 141, 311–13, too, seems to imply that the amalgamation was an improvement, but only in the longer term.

96 Pako, 147/5/283, l.224; Volkov, *Sovetskaia derevnia*, 141.

97 Pako, 147/5/36, ll.8–10; Pako, 147/5/11, l.46. In a report to Malenkov, Konovalov complained already in January 1951 about the too-frequent replacement of chairs in certain areas (Pako, 147/5/36, l.10). After Konovalov's ouster, his successor Kiselev still reported in October 1951 to Malenkov that drunkenness, theft, and squandering of public (kolkhoz or state) property continued among them, despite more than 70 percent of the chairs being Communist (Pako, 147/5/35, ll.118–24).

98 Pako, 147/5/10, l.81.

99 Pako, 147/5/10, l.167.

100 Ibid. On a later occasion in the same year, Gerasimenko stated that 2.4 percent (380) of kolkhoz chairs – his calculations are somewhat flawed as he seems to have used the total of pre-amalgamation kolkhozy (about 7,500) to establish this percentage – had been convicted of wrongdoings by the courts, and 3.3 percent (200 of the total of roughly 2,000) in the first eight or nine months of 1951 (Pako, 147/5/11, l.151).

101 See chapter 7, as well.

102 Pako, 147/5/11, l.52.

103 Pako, 147/3/2679, l.22.

104 Pako, 147/4/1125, l.1270b.; Pako, 147/5/10, l.107. Before 1944, offi-cially fifty-eight churches functioned in the province (Pako, 147/4/1125, ll.126–1280b.). The highest density of churches in 1947 was in Kashin raion, where there were ten churches. Churches were found predomi-nantly east of the October Railroad, in the area that had not been occu-pied by the Germans and was – even traditionally – more densely popu-lated.

105 Pako, 147/5/2, l.144; 147/5/283, ll.259, 331. The MGB chief, Dekushenko, thought that the Baptists were an entirely new phenome-non, but they were already present in 1929, albeit in small numbers

(*Tverskoi tsentr*, 11). Dekushenko hoped that this sect would be prohibited and that their building could be taken away from them. The
plenipotentiary for religious affairs of the oblispolkom, Deguzov, had
been too lenient in the eyes of the MGB head. He had even allowed a
mass christening in the river T'maka in Kalinin, in which Baptists from
other oblasts had joined as well. In January 1950, mass baptisms of
youth were reported in Ves'egonsk raion, and a group of sixty Baptists
had acquired influence in Ostashkov (Pako, 147/4/1934, l.13).

106 Pako, 147/5/283, l.261.
107 For the tenacity of this organization (and of the True Orthodox Chris-
tians, a similar group) see, for example, Fletcher, *The Russian Orthodox Church Underground*, 180–229.
108 Pako, 147/5/10, l.106. More than a year later a similar complaint was
expressed by Kiselev and a rather appalled metal worker, Ivanov, in
front of the ninth oblast' party conference (Pako, 147/5/283, ll.139,
220). Ivanov spent a few days in August 1952 in the countryside near
Kalinin (in Mednoe raion) and witnessed the celebration of the Feast of
the Assumption of the Virgin: flax and wheat were scorching in the sun
while the villagers distilled samogon. The celebration started two days
before the actual feast day, and the villagers then fêted for four consecutive days. In the survey, professional party worker A.M. Afanas'ev
remembered with relish the great parties on religious holidays.
109 Pako, 147/5/659, l.158; as was the case in Emel'ianovo raion in 1952.
110 Cf. the second section of chapter 2. V.P. Krylov testified in the survey
that he and his wife partook of the celebration of religious holidays, but
neither he nor his wife thought about God. At Easter he did not go to
work at the brick factory in which he was employed between 1947 and
1951.
111 Pako, 147/5/183, ll.235–6. The factory managers apparently drove by
car into the countryside; at the conference, the kolkhoz director threatened to file a complaint about this misbehaviour with the Central Committee.
112 Pako, 147/5/183, ll.235–6; Pako, 147/5/659, l.158.
113 Pako, 147/5/764, ll.119–128.
114 Pako, 147/5/764, l.124. In Russian it waxes much more jolly, as
follows: "22 fevralia, golosuiu za tebia, za liubimogo tvortsa, druga
Stalina otsa. Druga Stalina otsa, pervogo za mir bortsa, kommunizma
rulevogo, vsemu miru dorogogo. Vsemu miru dorogogo, schast'ia net u
nas drugogo, STALIN v nashem gorsovete, schast'ia bol'she net na svete!
Schast'ia bol'she net na svete, poiut o Staline i deti, pesn' poiut na vsei
zemle, Stalin slyshit vsekh v Kremle. Stalin slyshit vsekh v Kremle,
khodit on po vsei zemle, narod Stalinskim trudom, stroit kommunizma
dom. Stroit kommunizma dom, vsemu miru viden on, za liubimogo

vozhdia, nash narod idet vsegda! V den' voskrenyi-fevralia, vse pridet na vybora, eto budet v svetlyi den', i za Stalina rodnogo my opustim biulleten'." Doggerel such as this may have inspired Aleksandr Zinoviev (cf. *The Yawning Heights*, 525, for example, or *Gomo sovetikus*, 101–2).

115 Pako, 147/5/764, ll.121–8.

116 Pako, 147/5/764, l.127. For the "Doctors' Plot," see, e.g., Rapoport, *The Doctors' Plot of 1953*.

117 For a not altogether convincing explanation of this odd phenomenon, see Poliakov, "Pokhorony Stalina," 195–207. Several participants in the survey – both those who were party members themselves or whose spouses were members and those who were not – testified to the grief about the demise of Stalin. A.A. Kondrashov was still an unrepentant party man in the summer of 1992: in different places he criticized both Perestroika and Khrushchev and, to a lesser extent, Brezhnev, who used to hunt with his entourage in Zavidovo raion. Instead of the Communist Party, which had been put on trial for its role in the coup of August 1991 and for other accusations, he wanted to see Gorbachev put on trial. Not surprisingly, I.I. Tiaglov, too, had little appreciation for some of Khrushchev's policies, in particular the sowing of corn, ordained in the later 1950s. A.I. Ryzhakova was in Moscow at the time of Stalin's burial and was almost crushed in the mêlée of mourners who tried to attend. L.P. Felkova went to Moscow when she heard that Stalin was gravely ill; however, she did not manage to see him lying in state.

118 Volkogonov, *Triumf i Tragediia*, 2:2, 21–2, 35.

119 Portelli, *The Death*, 114.

120 Smirnova recalled that after Khrushchev's ouster in 1964 she realized that her hopes had been in vain. In 1972 the renewed repression of opposing voices under Brezhnev was brought home clearly to her: she was joined in the workplace, a printing press for children's literature, by two dissidents who had been exiled to Kalinin, Petr Iakir and Viktor Krasin.

121 This is Malysheva's ditty in Russian: "Spasibo, Stalinu, Sdelal iz menia baryniu, Ia-i loshad', ia-i byk, Ia-i baba, i-muzhik."

122 Cf. Zubkova, *Obshchestvo*, 38.

CHAPTER FIVE

1 Pako, 147/5/283, ll.38–9.

2 Pako, 147/3/2479, ll.316–17.

3 G.V. Lubov observed that before the war arrests took place in Konakovo, but after his return from the army in 1948 no worker at his factory was arrested.

4 Fainsod, *How Russia is Ruled*, 378. As Conquest notes, "In the years which remained of Stalin's rule after the Purges, the all-out mass terror was no longer necessary" (*The Great Terror*, 447).

5 Pako, 147/5/2, ll.142–6.

6 Pako, 147/4/519, ll.113–14.

7 Pako, 147/4/519, ll.9–10; 147/5/214a, l.30; 147/4/519, l.271.

8 Pako, 147/5/214a, l.30. According to the oblast' MVD head, Grebchenko, in 1953 one Akhmetov, born on the Crimean peninsula (and thus a member of one of the peoples deported by the regime at the end of the war) and an active collaborator with the German army, was discovered at the railroad-car factory (Pako, 147/5/662, l.78). He had supposedly been recruited in Germany in June 1945 by the Americans and had been sent into the Soviet Union to commit subversive acts.

9 Pako, 147/5/283, l.135.

10 Pako, 147/5/341, l.66: one of the teenagers was even a Komsomol member.

11 Pako, 147/5/214a, l.30; 147/4/519, l.27.

12 Cf. Zubkova, *Obshchestvo*, 63–90; Naumov, "K istorii," 153; Sudoplatov, Special Tasks, 325–6; Heller and Nekrich, *Utopia in Power*, 487–92, 498–9. One of the survey respondents mentioned other arrests that took place in 1949. M.S. Kul'menina worked in the trade union committee of the oblast' directorate of trade. She testified that the heads of the cadre departments of her directorate and of the oblast' organization of consumers' cooperations (oblpotrebsoiuz) were apparently arrested almost simultaneously, and no one knew what happened to them or for what reason they had been arrested. Perhaps these arrests and those at the railroad-car factory indicate indeed a tightening of the reins in general (see below).

13 Pako, 147/4/1817, ll.6–7.

14 The speech of the MGB chief at the seventh party conference of 1949 was not entered in the type-written version of the stenogramma of this meeting in the party's archives (see the two copies of this stenogramma: Pako, 147/4/1495; 147/4/1496). According to V.A. Feoktistov, the current director of the archival centre in Tver', where the archive of the former Communist Party is kept, the MGB had, also at this level, the authority to forbid the Party to have speeches of its representatives entered in the records. From a later speech at the conference in 1949 by the raion secretary of Likhoslavl' raion, Leonov, it became clear that one Levina had been dismissed at the railroad-car works, because she had been exiled from Moscow by a decision of a special troika in 1937 (Pako, 147/4/1495, l.99). Levina's name had apparently been mentioned by MGB head Kovalev in his speech, to which Leonov referred. After her dismissal, according to Leonov, one Sergeev, of the oblast' directorate of

agriculture, had recommended Levina as an agronomist to the head of an MTS in Likhoslavl' raion, although Levina had no agricultural education whatsoever. The situation at the railroad-car factory had therefore apparently been part of Kovalev's speech.

15 Pako, 147/4/1817, ll.8–15.

16 Pako, 147/4/1817, ll.8–15.

17 This and the following paragraph are based on Pako, 147/4/1817, ll.8–15.

18 Pako, 147/4/1512, l.7. The official dismissal of both director Rumiantsev and the head bookkeeper of the railroad-car works, at least formally, was done by a collegium of the Ministry of Transport Machine Building on 14 February 1949 (Pako, 147/4/1495, l.101–1010b.). Rumiantsev was listed in April 1949 in the account of the nomenklaturnye workers in the oblast' as having been dismissed for the "dulling of political vigilance" (za prituplenie politicheskoi bditel'nosti) (Pako, 147/4/1887, l.89).

19 Pako, 147/4/1817, l.7. Rumiantsev was not immediately arrested, but his further fate remains in doubt (Pako, 147/4/1887, l.89). Subsequently Ionov first would be assigned work at a lower level, but he was excluded from the party on the orders of Vorontsov and Zimin during 1949 (Pako, 147/4/1512, l.7). According to one of the speakers at the obkom plenum that officially dismissed Vorontsov at the end of 1949, this exclusion was unjustified.

20 See the third section of chapter 5 for a further description of the people's awareness of the camp system.

21 Pako, 147/3/2748, ll.260, 262–4. The veteran militsiia man I.M. Solov'ev, who joined the force after his demobilization from the army in early 1946, remembered that in the postwar years criminals of all kinds were active in Kalinin (Badeev, "Istoki truda i podviga," 19). In the first postwar years "organized crime" resulted in great material loss in the province (ibid., 23). Solov'ev's account was confirmed by another militsioner in the same book (Popova, "Ekspertiza pokazala," 105).

22 Pako, 147/3/2749, ll.86–7.

23 Pako, 147/4/66, ll.15–16.

24 Pako, 147/3/2749, ll.278–85.

25 Pako, 147/3/2479, ll.301–6.

26 Pako, 147/4/1002, l.14; 147/4/1132, ll.85–6; 147/4/1133, ll.14–15. These numbers are much lower than the numbers of 1949 and early 1950, because the MVD reports of 1946 did not register all cases examined by the courts. It may be that they made a distinction between criminal deeds registered by the public and (planned) criminal activities discovered by their own investigations.

27 Pako, 147/4/1097, l.210b.

28 Pako, 147/3/2679, l.720b.; 147/4/63, ll.2440b., 2460b. The famine of

1946 in other parts of the USSR may have made the authorities more anxious about wasting rations on ineligible people.

29 Pako, 147/4/1097, l.21.

30 Pako, 147/4/66, l.187.

31 Pako, 147/4/66, l.193.

32 See, e.g., Zubkova, *Obshchestvo*, 54. The decree is called "On Criminal Responsibility for the Theft of State and Public Property," and dated 4 June 1947 (see also Volkov, "Zasukha," 16). It does not seem that the new decrees of 1947 led to the same avalanche of arrests that had plagued the 1930s (see Boitsov's account at the third Party conference of the enormous wave of arrests in 1935–37, discussed in the fifth section of chapter 1, and his account of the arrests during collectivization discussed in the fourth section; Rittersporn, *Stalinist Simplifications*, 274–77). Before the proclamation of this law, sometimes sentences were meted out after the war according to the equally harsh criteria of the law of 7 August 1932. In 1946, on the basis of this law, a factory worker received the death penalty, while his three collaborators were sentenced to ten years of imprisonment for the theft of goods from shops in Kalinin with a total value of 31,800 rubles (*PP* 8062, 12 July 1946, 4; this incident confirms Rittersporn's impression of the continued application of this law after the war (Rittersporn, *Stalinist Simplifications*, 274). It is noteworthy that the trial against the four apparently took place in the workers' club of the factory where the main culprit was employed. In this instance as well, the educative value of the show trial was appreciated by the authorities.

33 Pako, 147/4/2297, ll.9, 52–3. The basis for the prosecution of those avoiding assisting work in agriculture was a decree of 15 April 1942. The basis for the prosecution of those violating labour discipline was the infamous decree of 26 June 1940 (cf. also Heller and Nekrich, *Utopia in Power*, 321).

34 Pako, 147/5/35, ll.88–90; 147/5/328, l.2; Chapman, *Real Wages*, 179. The resolution of the Supreme Soviet on the establishment of these courts was of 14 July 1951. For the labour laws of June 1940, see, e.g., Chapman, *Real Wages*, 178–9. Chapman maintained that absenteeism was less severely treated by the "comrades' courts" (ibid., 179). In some places the new courts did function properly: at the "Vagzhanov" textile factory after twenty-five days of January 1952 119 violations were already registered, while for the first half year of 1951, 362 cases in total had been registered. This means that at least the detection of violations temporarily improved. The comrades' courts probably did not help to improve of the atmosphere on the factory floors. Only in 1956 were the laws of June 1940 fully abolished.

35 In 1949, in all, 21,388 people were convicted by these courts; the popula-

tion of the oblast' was around 1.6 million (see the fifth section of chapter 2).

36 Pako, 147/5/2, l.145.

37 Pako, 147/5/659, ll.147–50.

38 Pako, 147/5/341, l.72. Cf. Conquest: "The old criminal underworld of Tsarist Russia, which since the Time of Troubles had developed as an extraordinary milieu with its own dialect and its own law, had been greatly reinforced, and its character much modified, by the tumults of the Civil War and the famine of the early 1920s. Already then, the bezprizornye, the homeless orphan children assembling in gangs and living by their wits, had become a problem. Collectivization and other social experiments disrupted millions more families and provided large reinforcements to these now maturing criminals" (*The Great Terror*, 313). The war seems to have increased the besprizornye further. Beznadzornyi: "a youth largely unsupervised by parents or other adult guardians"(Ball, "The Roots of Bezprizornost'," 265).

39 Pako, 147/4/57, l.630; 147/4/57, ll.606, 612; the brawl erupted during a typical occasion of "strolling" (gulian'e), a custom still thriving in the Tver' of today: in 1992 fights occasionally occurred as well during gul'ian'e.

40 Cf. Volkogonov, *Triumf i tragediia*, 2:2, 60. It is doubtful that the law of 4 June 1947 brought considerably more uniformity in the sentencing; in Brusovo raion in 1948, two employees of a milk factory who had sold off milk and dairy products on the side to the value of 5,645 rubles received three years, while at the same factory two others earned ten and seven years for the same crime, but for the higher profit of 24,391 rubles (Gako, 2321/6/69, l.7; for the penalties introduced by the decree of 4 June 1947, see Fainsod, *How Russia is Ruled*, 346). In Bologoe raion, two people were given twenty years for the theft of butter at a value of 7,116.40 rubles (Gako, 2321/6/69, l.16). Sentences were in general severe, even before the 4 June 1947 decree. In February 1947, one Emel'ianov was sentenced to one year for misbehaviour in the tram (vandalism, smoking, interrupting the service) (*PP* 8209, 5 February 1947, 4). Two gang leaders were sentenced to be executed for the robberies and murder perpetrated by their bands (*PP* 8208, 4 February 1947, 4). After the decree of June 1947 some received extremely long sentences: five people each received from ten to fifteen years of corrective labour camp for the theft of thirty-three kilograms of onions from a kolkhoz (*PP* 8348, 20 August 1947, 4). The incidence of crime does not seem to have gone down after the decree, judging from the criminal statistics for 1949. The decree of 4 June 1947 and that of 9 June 1947 seem to have functioned as a kind of warning to the population and to the bureaucracy that crimes against public and private property would be treated in the same

way as before the war (for the decree of 9 June 1947, see Fainsod, *How Russia is Ruled*, 346).

41 In only a few months of 1946, about one hundred Communists were excluded for such offences (Pako, 147/4/57, ll.475–679).

42 Pako, 147/4/63, ll.119–23.

43 Pako, 147/4/735, ll.129–43.

44 Pako, 147/4/2055, l.4. Cf. Altrichter's description of the behaviour of the militsiia during the 1920s (Altrichter, *Die Bauern*, 103–9).

45 Pako, 147/4/1001, l.108. On the organization of the procuracy, see Fainsod, *How Russia is Ruled*, 317.

46 Pako, 147/5/35, ll.91–5; see Fainsod, *How Russia is Ruled*, 317, on the organization of the judicial system.

47 Pako, 147/5/7, l.68.

48 Tsvetkov went on to chair the oblast' court from 1956 to 1965 and was state prosecutor of the oblast' from 1965–83. Cf. Fainsod, *How Russia is Ruled*, 345, on the relationship between procuracy and MVD-MGB. "No law prescribes that the judiciary and prosecutors should be controlled by the secret police and the party committee, but they are" (Djilas, *The New Class*, 71).

49 Tsvetkov's memory is not fully accurate, because the Special Boards fell under the authority of the MGB after the war (see, e.g., Adamova-Sliozberg, "Put'," 122). Grebchenko, however, was indeed the head of the oblast' MVD around 1952–53.

50 E.g., Pako, 147/4/1002, ll.13–14.

51 Cf. Zubkova, *Obshchestvo*, 63–102. It could very well be that the number of convictions rose in 1949: the MVD figures on crime for 1948 appear to bear witness to a lower level of arrest, indicating a renewed offensive reminding one of the Ezhovshchina.

52 Cf. Fainsod, *How Russia is Ruled*, 378; Sudoplatov, *Special Tasks*, xxiii, 184; Iakovlev, *Kontsentratsionnye lageri SSSR*, 22. The competence of both the NKVD-MVD and NKGB-MGB seems to have sometimes overlapped and is difficult to assess (which is exemplified by the fact that the activities of both for a long while after 1943 were the responsibility of Beria in the Politburo); the fact that the MGB chief was always a full member of the obkomburo after the war leads one to think that it was more authoritative than the MVD. The MVD was involved with administrative and economic matters, including the administration of the POW camps and corrective labour colonies, and with crimes of a nonpolitical nature, often handled by the militsiia (the "normal" police), which was subordinate to it. The MGB, on the other hand, was engaged in the control over the political orthodoxy of the party and government, in recording the political mood of the population at large, and in foreign espionage.

53 Iakovlev, *Kontsentratsionnye lageri*, 125–6, 156–7; this seems to be the

camp to which David Holloway refers (e.g., *Stalin and the Bomb*, 246).

54 GULag: Glavnoe Upravlenie ispravitel'no-trudovykh Lagerei (Main Directorate of Corrective Labour Camps).

55 That is, in the Tverskoi kraevedcheskii muzei (which can be translated as Tver' Museum of Local Lore), on the (former?) Ploshchad' Revoliutsiia in the town of Tver'.

56 Pako, 147/4/1131, ll.2, 13, 140b.; 147/4/1002, l.46; 147/4/1001, l.92; 147/5/341, l.115; 147/4/67, l.93. The numbers of the colonies given here are the ones they carried around March 1948, as given in Pako, 147/4/1131, l.140b. That list was not complete, since there were eleven corrective labour camps and four camp points on 1 March 1948. The location of some of these fifteen was not indicated in the report. The Lykoshino camp still functioned in June 1952.

57 Pako, 147/4/735, l.131, 147/4/1001, l.131. One hundred and thirty-five of the 1,299 were officers, 311 administrators-technicians, and 853 guards. In June 1949, the number of employees of the MGB (which was *not* engaged with overseeing camps, etc., but more with the investigation of politically suspicious people and of certain economic crimes, that is, enforcing the political conformity of the party and the population) was 603 (Pako, 147/4/1574, l.22). The organization of camps within the MVD GULag was as follows: in a district it was headed by the directorate of camps (camp group)(upravlenie lagerem), made up of camp sectors/departments (otdeleniia lageria), which were divided into camp points (lagernye punkty); finally, they, in turn, were divided into camp parts (lagernye uchastki) (Iakovlev, *Kontsentratsionnye lageri*, 54).

58 Pako, 147/4/1126, l.34.

59 Iakovlev, *Kontsentratsionnye lageri*, 60; cf. Kopelev, *Khranit' vechno*, 589, 611. A chapter is named after the settlement where the camps were located: Bol'shaia Volga. The village was transferred from Kalinin oblast' to Moscow oblast' in 1956. Bol'shaia Volga is near the town of Dubna in Moscow province.

60 See Kopelev, *Khranit' vechno*, 585–613. According to the museum exhibition in Tver', in the 1955–87 period 1,980 people were politically rehabilitated, and in the 1988–89 period, 15,244. This number does not include all political convicts: the process was far from completed by the time the Soviet Union collapsed, while many people's names were never cleared because no relatives pressed for a rehabilitation (Gevorkian, "Vstrechnye plany," 19). The number of 1,980 rehabilitations is astonishingly small. According to one Soviet historian, 600,000 people in the whole of the USSR were rehabilitated in the 1953–57 period (Borisov, "Politicheskaia," 296). Apparently in 1948 the infamous "special regime camps" were created for political prisoners, according to Volkogonov

(*Triumf i tragediia*, 2:2, 39). None of these could be discovered by the present author on the territory of Kalinin oblast'. Conquest believes that criminal convicts in the camps were a small minority: "The percentage of 'criminals' was around 10 to 15 percent, but the majority of these were the petty embezzler type, rather than urkas proper, who were seldom more than 5 percent of a camp total" (*The Great Terror*, 313).

61 In Kalinin province, apart from Germans – who formed the great majority of the POWs, judging by the number of Germans who were convicted by the Military Tribunal in 1947 (78 out of 92) – at least Hungarians (8) and Rumanians (6) pined away in these camps as well (Pako, 147/4/1404, l.14).

62 Pako, 147/3/2748, ll.220–1; 147/3/2749, l.10; 147/4/92, ll.1–2, l.9–90b. In early 1945, camp No. 41 was one of the two camps holding prisoners of war, the other one being No. 216 near Vyshnii Volochek. Provincial NKVD head Pavlov reported to Boitsov that the two camps' combined population of 11,102 POWs of early 1945 had grown to 18,242 on 1 July 1945. Around May 1945, the NKVD notified the obkom that the province would receive an additional number of POWs who would augment the total to almost 50,000. The provincial NKVD began to organize six new camp directorates to accommodate these newcomers. The central NKVD, however, did not keep its promise: by 1 October 1945, 22,719 POWs had arrived, after which the shipment to Kalinin oblast' was discontinued for the remainder of the year.

63 See, e.g., Pako, 147/4/1404, ll.9–15. One individual was sentenced to death, another to twenty-five years, forty to sentences ranging from ten to twenty-five years, eleven to sentences from five to ten years, and thirty-seven to sentences from one to five years.

64 Pako, 147/3/2749, ll.92–920b. It should be stressed again that it is fully unclear how many of the inmates were convicted of political crimes and how many of other crimes. According to the testimony of V.E. Tsvetkov in the survey, those who were convicted of political crime by the oblast' courts were send to Vladimir and the North. This does not necessarily indicate that all inmates of the labour camps in Kalinin province were "criminals," as Kopelev's case proves and as N.A. Zabelin noticed in 1951 (testimony of N.A. Zabelin in the survey; see below). Political convicts could have been transported from other areas to Kalinin oblast'.

65 Pako, 147/4/66, ll.105–6. Fedosenko demonstrated remarkable staying power for the times in which he was living: in May 1952, he still was the head of the MVD camp system in the province (Pako, 147/5/341, l.91).

66 Pako, 147/4/66, l.106

67 Pako, 147/4/1131, ll.14–15.

68 A long list of camp points and colonies was given in 1948, including those of prisoners of war (Pako, 147/4/1133, ll.2–20b.). At this time,

Soviet convicts and POWs were taken off their work on the construction of industrial projects, after which many of them were transferred outside the oblast'. The camp near Konakovo, which had helped to reconstruct the porcelain factory, was closed in July 1948; camp No. 15 near Rzhev was dismantled as well in the same month. The POW camp of the cotton fibre kombinat of Vyshnyi Volochek was dissolved in April 1948, and so on. Towards the end of 1948, the camp population had greatly diminished in those that remained in operation.

69 Pako, 147/5/38, ll. 1–2.

70 Pako, 147/5/341, l.38.

71 Pako, 147/5/341, l.166.

72 Pako, 147/3/2679, l.590b.

73 Pako, 147/3/2702, ll.980b.–101. In 1949, there were sixty-eight orphanages in the oblast', with about 6,000 orphans; in addition to those, 3,500 children were living with foster families (Pako, 147/4/1495, l.73). The total number of orphans in the provincial orphanages was 4,182 on 1 January 1952 (Pako, 147/5/341, l.57).

74 Pako, 147/4/57, l.505.

75 Pako, 147/5/659, l.149. The title of the decree, issued on 8 April 1952, was "On Measures toward the Elimination of Children's Homelessness in the RSFSR".

76 Cf. the discussion of the Ezhovshchina in chapter 1.

77 Kruglova herself wrote the term "enemies of the people" in brackets; she was one of the few who filled out the survey herself.

78 PP 7801, 10 July 1945, 2; OITK: Oblastnye Ispravitel'nie Trudovye Kolonii, or provincial corrective labour colonies. Of course, the inhabitants could be under the impression that only criminals were held in these camps. These kind of camps for criminal convicts still exist in Russia today. Still, it seems worthwhile to quote Solzhenitsyn in this respect: "The permanent lie becomes the only safe form of existence, in the same way as betrayal. Every wag of the tongue can be overheard by someone, every facial expression observed by someone. Therefore every word, if it does not have to be a direct lie, is nonetheless obliged not to contradict the general, common lie. There exists a collection of ready-made phrases, of labels, a selection of ready-made lies" (*The Gulag Archipelago*, vols. 3–4, 646). It seems that the survival of this particular trait might have played a role in the denial by many respondents of having had knowledge of the system of corrective labour camps. Cf. also Turchin's appreciation: "Definitely, many did not know, of course, because they did not want to, they were afraid to know. There existed something of a not-agreed-upon-agreement between government and citizens: the powers that be created an informational barrier, and the citizens were happy, that they could not but be unable 'to know'" (*Inertsiia Strakha*, 21).

79 Zabelin also witnessed the school of which he had been appointed director in 1951 being built by convicts in the "closed" suburb of Migalovo.
He added that there were inmates among those zeks who had been convicted on the basis of the "political" articles of the RSFSR criminal code.

CHAPTER SIX

1 Laqueur, *The Dream That Failed*, 16.
2 Kennan, *Memoirs*, appendix A, 510–11. Cf. as well Malia's observation:
"For the Party-state of communism was not a static affair, nor did it ever
succeed in realizing fully its aspiration to total control over, or displace-
ment of, society. Since such total control is impossible, the Leninist
regime was constantly at war with the recalcitrant reality of Russian
society" ("A Fatal Logic," 89).
3 *Tsentralnyi Raion*, 143.
4 Ibid., 533–4; concentrations of this industry were found particularly in
and around Rzhev and Bezhetsk.
5 *Tsentral'nyi Raion*, 529, 531, 540.
6 Thus, obkom secretary Zimin stated in March 1951 that a request to the
Central Committee for funding the construction of public utilities for the
factory Parizhskaia Kommuna had been rejected by the Council of Ministers of the USSR (Pako, 147/5/8, l.4). During the war, because of the high
demand for armaments, the state had concentrated its investments in
heavy industry to the detriment of light industry (see Chadaev,
Ekonomika SSSR, 66-9, 197). This strategy led to a higher production
level of heavy industry in the years from 1941 to 1945 in comparison
with 1940 and, at the same time, to a lower output of light industry in
the USSR, which stood at only 59 percent of its prewar level in 1945. A
Soviet publication of 1978 noted that, in 1946, 24 percent of the USSR
budget was spent on defence; in 1947, 18.3 percent; and in 1950, 20
percent (Volokov, *Sovetskaia derevnia*, 26). N.A. Voznesensky states that,
in 1940, the USSR spent 32.5 percent of its budget on defence; in 1944,
52 percent; and in 1946 still 23.9 percent (*Voennaia ekonomika*, 179). In
actual fact, the share of the defense industries in the state's investments
may have been even higher. See, as well, Fainsod's remark on the extraordinarily difficult situation of the directors of light and consumer goods
industries (*How Russia is Ruled*, 436; see also Voznesenskii, *Voennaia
ekonomika*, 179, 181–2). Voznesensky stated that the first priority for
the recovery of the USSR's economy was the resurrection of heavy industry and transport (ibid.). Volkogonov maintains that Stalin, in his last
conversation with Voznesensky, sometime in early 1949, stressed once
more that the priority of the state's investments would be heavy industry
(*Triumf i tragediia*, 2:2, 56).

7 See *Bloknot Agitatora*, 1948, no.3, 43, which entreats industry "to use
every kopeck with intelligence, to economize on every minute." Also, in
Pako, 147/4/1501, ll.14–15, much stress is laid on accumulation of
means by economizing on costs within the enterprise.

8 Pako, 147/4/79, ll.1–9; as Molotov said: "After the war we took reparations, but it was small fry. For those reparations were old equipment, the
equipment itself had become obsolete. But we had no choice. This rather
small relief we had to use as well" (*Sto sorok besed*, 87).

9 Calculation based on Pako, 147/3/2759, ll.1–2 . The other quarter of
output value was produced by smaller factories, e.g., those involved in
flax processing, alcohol manufacturing, or energy production. Percentages are approximate, for the identity of some factories in this document
could not be established, while other factories' output seems to go
unlisted, probably for reasons of secrecy. There is, e.g., evidence elsewhere for the existence of an aircraft factory ("Factory No. 1 of the Ministry of Aircraft Industry"): in October 1946, Boitsov confirmed F.P. Voznesenskii as its head engineer (Pako, 147/4/57, ll.182–3, 191–2). This
kind of factory of the defense industry is hardly ever mentioned in any
record, probably because they operated – most likely under MVD or MGB
authority – fully outside the competence of the oblast' party organization.
Boitsov's confirmation was only a formality. How far this factory might
be equated with the project at Lake Seliger that Iakovlev refers to is
unclear (see *Kontsentratsionnye lageri*, 157).

10 Pako, 147/3/2702, ll.246–7.

11 Pako, 147/4/528, l.420b.

12 Nevertheless, the output of the war invalids' cooperatives was said in
1949 to have consistently failed to meet the plan from 1945 to 1949
(Pako, 147/4/1501, l.10).

13 Pako, 147/4/1501, ll.6–7. The industrial output in both state and cooperative industries grew steadily in those years. By 1950, the textile industry
in the oblast' still produced less than before the war; only 50 percent of
the plan of the cotton-fibre works was fulfilled (Luk'ianova,
"Vosstanovlenie," 292, 294).

14 The industries of the industrial People's Commissariats together produced
the following (in rubles of their 1926–27 value): under Union authority:
8,586,000; under RSFSR authority, 5,444,000; under oblast' authority:
6,416,000; and under raion authority, 2,991,000. The total was therefore
23,437,000 rubles (see Pako, 147/3/2759, ll.1–2). The output of the nonindustrial enterprises of the People's Commissariats was worth 333,000
rubles, and that of cooperative industry was worth 6,252,000 rubles.
Thus the total production of oblast' industry for January 1946 was
worth 30,022,000 rubles. Cf. Fainsod, *How Russia is Ruled*, 195, on the
issue of the "all-union significance" of certain factories. On the organiza-

tion of Soviet factories, see ibid., 425–9, and, for example, Eroshkin et al., "Biurokratizm-tormoz perestroiki," 441–3.

15 Pako, 147/3/2759, ll.1–2

16 See Fainsod, *How Russia is Ruled*, 437.

17 Pako, 147/4/1495, l.16. It is likely that this number included the workers of Velikie Luki for 1940. In 1944, 104,000 blue-collar workers were employed in industry.

18 Pako, 147/5/283, l.39; see the second section of chapter 4.

19   Cf. Danilov et al., "NEP," 187–8; see table 23.

20 In early 1949, the railroad-car construction works had 847 Communists and formed the largest party organization at a factory in the oblast'. The textile factory Proletarka in Kalinin had 582 Communists, and the cotton-fibre kombinat in Vyshnii Volochek had 560 (Pako, 147/4/1495, l.58).

21 Pako, 147/5/36, ll.115–18; in the USSR as a whole, the production of cotton textiles and leather footwear was still lower in 1950 than in 1940 (see Gordon and Klopov, *Chto eto bylo?*, table 1, 62).

22 Pako, 147/5/36, ll.116, 118. On 1 January 1951 the capacity of the textile enterprises of the town of Kalinin in spinning was only 45 percent of the prewar level, and in weaving 22 percent.

23 Cf. the first section of chapter 5.

24 As happened in Kamen raion in 1949 (Pako, 147/4/1495, ll. 50–500b.); Pako, 147/5/283, ll.41–2. Vorontsov had complained about the widespread failure of the lumberjacks to fulfill their daily norms in early 1949. Clear-cutting of forests at this time was recognized as a problem (Pako, 147/4/1495, ll.180b.–19). Peat and lumber industries started to give satisfactory production results only after Stalin's death, when large parts of the production process were mechanized (Smirnov et al., *Ocherki*, 554–7).

25 Pako, 147/5/10, ll.18–20.

26 Pako, 147/5/283, ll.173–6. The peat, wood-processing, and cheese industries performed poorly, as did the industrial cooperatives. The bread factories, which were under the auspices of the RSFSR government, were again not effectuating their plans.

27   Pako, 147/4/79, ll.4, 10 for example. Fainsod has summed up some of the manifold problems encountered by the different levels of management in the Soviet factories (*How Russia is Ruled*, 428).

28 Mertsalov, "Stalinizm," 402. Also, compare this statement to the remarks by Rittersporn about the production of defective goods in the 1930s (*Stalinist Simplifications*, 33). Complaints about inferior quality and the inability to produce the planned assortment of goods in light industry were uttered in a report on the performance of this industrial branch in early 1949 (Pako, 147/4/1501, ll.17–18).

29 Pako, 147/5/2, l.156.

30 Pako, 147/5/10, ll.18–20.

31 Pako, 147/4/519, ll.212–16.

32 Pako, 147/4/1814, ll.53–5.

33 Pako, 147/5/283, l.181. See Heller and Nekrich, *Utopia in Power*, 321, for the description of the laws that prohibited the free movement of workers.

34 Pako, 147/5/10, l.135. The provincial unions had a total of 295,000 members; 4,500 trade union organizations existed in March 1951 (Pako, 147/5/2, ll.22, 155). There were about 40,000 members of the railroad trade union in 1951, which, despite its size, was completely ignored by the higher authorities in the oblast' as well (Pako, 147/5/2, l.152). Cf. Fainsod, *How Russia is Ruled*, 350, 432–6 and Conquest, *The Great Terror*, 21.

35 Pako, 147/4/1512, l.13. The same complaint about grossly delayed payment of wages could be heard in Tver' in the summer of 1992.

36 Chapman, *Real Wages*, 122.

37 Ibid., 127.

38 Ibid., 114.

39 Pako, 147/5/662, ll.12, 31.

40 Gordon and Klopov, *Chto eto bylo?*, 65–6.

41 Pako, 147/5/36, l.119. The estimate of 12.3 percent is reached by comparing the square footage of housing space for 1939 to the estimate for 1956 and the population in 1959. At an obkom plenum in February 1953 the population in the town was given as 220,000 (Pako, 147/5/659, l.15), slightly more than in 1939. See also table 22.

42 For a fine discussion of what it meant to live in the crammed communal housing (kommunalki) cf. Boym, *Common Places*, 121–67.

43 Pako, 147/5/35, l.135. According to Chapman, the average urban dwelling space per person in the USSR was 4.0 square meters in 1944, 5.2 square meters in 1948, 4.9 square meters in 1952, and 5.0 meters in 1954 (*Real Wages*, 26). The drop between 1948 and 1952 was probably the result of an influx of rural inhabitants into the towns. See Gordon and Klopov, *Chto eto bylo?* 110–11, for the abominable housing circumstances in urban areas.

44 Pako, 147/4/1495, l.200b.; 147/5/659, l.158; cf. the second section of chapter 4. A.M. Afanas'ev, who lived all his life in Udoml'ia, commented in the survey that the ancestral wooden house in which he lived in 1992 had its disadvantages and demanded a lot of maintenance, but he still believed that his house was preferable to an urban apartment. The present author cannot but agree after having lived in several Soviet-built apartments in Moscow and Tver'.

45 Other participants in the survey described similar conditions.

46 Smolenskaia, "Uluchshenie fizicheskogo razvitiia detei," 263, 265, table

2, 267. Moscow was, until recently, always better provided with goods in comparison to other cities in the former USSR, which may partially explain the discrepancy between the two groups at the time.

47 Pako, 147/5/36, l.119; 147/4/1495, l.44; 147/5/2, l.76; cf. table 22. It might be, however, that in the semirural, recently urbanized settlements such as Konakovo the situation was better than in older towns such as Rzhev, Torzhok, or Bologoe. G.V. Lubov said in the survey that he lived with his parents in Konakovo until his marriage at the age of twenty-six, after which he and his wife were able to move into a house of their own, which was bequeathed to them. Perhaps the overpopulation in these smaller settlements was less severe than in the larger towns, and the accessibility to locally found raw materials necessary for the construction of houses – especially wood – was better in settlements the size of Konakovo (which probably had about 10,000 inhabitants during this period). Lubov's case is, on the other hand, not typical, since most town dwellers were relative newcomers and did not have relatives from whom they might inherit a house or apartment (cf. the above accounts of the survey concerning urban housing).

48 Pako, 147/5/283, l.25.

49 Pako, 147/4/1549, ll. 62–3.

50 Ibid., ll.71–179.

51 Pako, 147/5/36, l.120; see the second section of chapter 2.

52 Pako, 147/5/36, l.119; 147/4/1501, l.21. The figure includes the heating of cultural and social institutes as well as offices and homes.

53 Pako, 147/5/35, ll.137–41. In November 1951 Malenkov was told that: "The demands of the populace are not being met in respect to the waterworks and sewage, the provision of services and utilities, while the repairs of housing, and so on, make scant progress" (Pako, 147/5/35, l.135).

54 Pako, 147/5/283, ll.39, 240. A.A. Kondrashov stated in the survey that when he started to work in the obkom in 1959 under first secretary N.G. Korytkov, none of the smaller towns boasted asphalt roads, which Korytkov later organized during his long tenure during the 1960s. Neither were there radios in the countryside in 1959, according to Kondrashov; again Korytkov was responsible for their diffusion. Korytkov, too, succeeded in building many more bridges in Kalinin, through which three different rivers flow (the Tvertsa, the T'maka, and the Volga). Unwittingly, Kondrashov shows us the primitive state of affairs in some areas of infrastructure in the oblast' before 1959. In contrast to Kondrashov, the kolkhoz bookkeeper and sometime chairman D.A. Dikushin could not appreciate Korytkov very much. Dikushin was of the opinion that Korytkov was a bit of a fool and that he ruled by "administrative methods."

55 Pako, 147/5/36, ll.120–1.

56 Pako, 147/5/433, l.34.
57 Gordon and Klopov, *Chto eto bylo?*, 99–100; Pako, 147/5/328, ll.15–17. On 1 April 1952, the fifth or sixth postwar lowering of prices occurred. Chapman has pointed out that this probably did not mean much of an increase in real wages, certainly not in the 1940s, and perhaps only slightly so in the early 1950s (*Real Wages*, 165–75; see, as well, on the price reductions, ibid., 50). G.V. Lubov, very much of a supporter of the regime, said in the survey that he and his family complained about the slow pace of the price reductions.
58 Pako, 147/3/2679, l.120b.; cf. the final section of chapter 1.
59 Pako, 147/3/2679, l.120b.; Pako, 147/4/390, l.4.
60 Volkov, "Zasukha," 11.
61 Smirnov et al., *Ocherki*, 541–2. The Fourth Five Year Plan, accepted on 12 March 1946 by the Supreme Soviet, had deemed it feasible to have the ration coupons abolished by the end of 1946 (Volokov, *Sovetskaia derevnia*, 61–2). Particularly the famine of 1946–47 forced the postponement of this decision for another year. Ration cards were given only to urban dwellers and employees in the countryside, not to the kolkhozniks.
62 Pako, 147/5/36, l.121; 147/5/283, l.246; the phrase used in the record for poor customer service is, in Russian, "Nizkaia kul'tura v obsluzhivanii pokupatelei" (the low level of civilized behaviour in the service of customers). Apparently criminal proceedings were instuted against none of the cheating salespersons. In 1952 a similar complaint about shortages was repeated by provincial trade union leader Zubov (Pako, 147/5/283, l.246). He noticed that in every town regular shortages of essential products occurred. Many industrial workers were able to receive food products in special stalls on the premises of their factories. Railroad workers, for example, were able to buy additional sugar, sausages, and bread there (testimony of A.N. Nikolaev in the survey). Nevertheless, the diet of Soviet citizens in 1940 or 1950 had not improved over that of the inhabitants of Imperial Russia in 1913 (Gordon and Klopov, *Chto eto bylo?*, 105).
63 Pako, 147/5/10, l.67.
64 Pako, 147/6/8, l.123.
65 Pako, 147/5/36, ll.139–40.
66 Pako, 147/5/663, ll.167–8. Moreover, in 1951 blue- and white-collar workers had 1,909 cows for private use, the number of which also fell to 1,252 in 1953.
67 Pako, 147/5/342, l.23; Chapman, *Real Wages*, table 13, 109; Zima, "Golod v Rossii," 49; Zima has translated the wages into the value of the new ruble that was introduced under Khrushchev, worth 10 percent of the old ruble in use during the 1940s and 1950s.
68 Pako, 147/4/1501, ll.13–14.

69 The carpenter P.A. Kashinov, who was a member of a construction cooperative, worked with his brigade in his spare time, building privately
commissioned wooden houses. Korobova and Zabelin translated their
wages, which was common among survey participants, into the rubles as
they were valued after 1961.

70 Chapman, *Real Wages*, 177, table 21, 144, table 22, 145, 147–8 for the
interpretation of the numbers in the tables; Gordon and Klopov, *Chto eto
bylo?*, 104. On average, real wages were still very low in 1948. It should
be noted, too, that these calculations are somewhat suspect, as Chapman
indicates herself: "The widely divergent measures of the extent of the
decline in real wages since 1928 and the conflicting answers as to the
level of real wages in 1954 in comparison with 1928 emphasize the difficulties of comparing standards of living in very different periods or
places" (*Real Wages*, 150). However, she is quite convinced of the accuracy of the comparison between 1937 and later years; the evidence indicates indeed that in the towns of Kalinin oblast' the real wages of
workers and employees hardly increased between 1937 and 1953
(150–2).

71 Chapman, *Real Wages*, 178; for DOSAAF, see the glossary. Only army
officers, who received a package with foodstuffs every month, could
sometimes afford to live on one income with their families, as V.Ia. Semiachko and Kh.I. Leibovich testified in the survey. Similar packages were
distributed among all military and party leaders (*Sto sorok besed*, 517).
Their contents probably depended on the importance of the receiver, but
the highest leaders received large sums of money. In retirement, Molotov
noted that the leadership knew for a fact that the miserly wages of 60-
odd rubles – i.e., 600 rubles per month at the time – were not enough
(*Sto sorok besed*, 264). In the eyes of the Politburo, no possibilities
existed to increase them, for all means had to be dedicated to the defence
against the imperialist threat.

72 Pako, 147/5/105, l.85.

73 See also Fainsod, *How Russia is Ruled*, 318.

74 In the survey it was found that T.A. Novikova of Udoml'ia raion was an
avid participant in religious feasts; V.G. Gavrilov, a party member since
1947, stated that the days off in the summer were only those on which
the religious holidays were celebrated on the kolkhoz. M.A. Sysoeva,
A.K. Sumugina-Shepeleva, Z.M. Vinogradova, and A.E. Vakhmistrov
confirmed that one had more opportunity to relax during the winter in
the countryside. M.M. Kozenkova added that one still had work in the
winter, in the treatment and transport of flax to the factory and in the
wood procurements. Before collectivization, flax was not cultivated by all
peasants, although cultivation rose during the 1920s (Altrichter, *Die
Bauern*, 77–8). After collectivization, almost every kolkhoz was forced to

cultivate the crop. The sown area of flax grew from 12 percent of the total sown area in Tver' guberniia in 1927–28 to 17 percent in 1937 in Kalinin oblast', and it was between 14 and 15 percent in the years 1946 in 1927–52 (Altrichter, *Die Bauern*, 78; *Narodnoe Khoziaistvo*, 32–3).

75 It should be noticed here that in the 1940s the peasantry sometimes did have different pastimes – at least, if they had the time – than their ancestors, one of which was reading as V.P. Pimenova testified in the survey. After all, by 1945 the great majority had profited from some sort of education, while twenty years earlier still more than half of the adult population had been illiterate (Altrichter, *Die Bauern*, 47).

76 G.V. Lubov, conscious of "cultured" ways of spending one's time, combined new and old pastimes during his spare time: he said in the survey that he, too, liked the zastol'e type of gathering.

77 Testimony of various participants in the survey. Again, the satisfaction of G.V. Lubov, which was revealed in the survey, might be considered typical of the satisfaction of some zealots with life under Stalin. Nevertheless, professional party workers had to work extremely hard, from early in the morning until late at night. Those higher up on the ladder were entitled to an annual trip to a spa, as Kondrashov was (testimony of A.M. Afanas'ev and A.A. Kondrashov).

78 Gordon and Klopov, *Chto eto bylo?*, 114.

79 "This is not to say that the new party and the new class are identical. The party, however, is the core of that class, and its base. It is very difficult, perhaps impossible, to define the limits of the new class and to identify its members. The new class may be said to be made up of those who have special privileges and economic preference because of the administrative monopoly they hold" (Djilas, *The New Class*, 39); M.S. Voslensky, *Nomenklatura*; cf. also Laqueur, *The Dream That Failed*, 17. The appearance of the works of, e.g., Fainsod and Djilas in the 1950s is perhaps an indication of the stabilization of the Soviet system after 1945, because of which a definitive elite within society became perceptible. This culminated under Brezhnev, when it became exceedingly difficult for upstarts to join the elite. It is hardly conceivable that similar works could have been written directly after the 1930s, when membership in the ruling stratum was for most very temporary, as a result of the continuous purges (cf. Djilas, *The New Class*; Fainsod, *How Russia is Ruled*).

80 See tables 16, 18, and 23. Soviet intelligentsiia: "The stratum of society, professionally occupied with intellectual work" (Ivanova, *Sovetskaia Intelligentsiia*, 50). "In a socialist society an intelligentsiia of a new type is formed. Its specifics are entirely defined by the nature of socialist society" (50–1). In 1947, 9.8 percent of party members had higher or incomplete higher education (52). On the whole, people with higher, incomplete higher, and specialized secondary schooling are considered to

be part of the intelligentsiia: i.e., engineers, tekhniki (technicians), agronomists, cattle specialists, veterinarians, economists, planners, statisticians,
lawyers, commodity experts, doctors and intermediate medical personnel,
university graduates, teachers, librarians, artists, army officers and cultural workers (26, 113, 196–8, 215). The intelligentsia also included the
vydvizhentsy: practicians (practical workers) who had been promoted to
a responsible position at a factory, for example, without having the
required education for this position (36–7). The proportion of this group
became gradually smaller among specialists and managers in the course
of Soviet history, particularly after Stalin's death (37). Fitzpatrick has
noticed that the term "intelligentsiia" regained a positive connotation in
Stalin's speech to the extraordinary Eighth All-Union Congress of Soviets
in November 1936. "Intelligent" had been a pejorative word in Soviet
discourse, in particular, in the early 1930s: "In the first place, Stalin identified the intelligentsia as one of the three basic corporate entities of
Soviet society, the others being the working class and the peasantry.
Although he spoke of the three groups as having equal rights, it was not
long before Soviet public and popular usage arranged them in the natural
hierarchical order [a vague term, KB], with the intelligentsia at the top. In
the second place, 'the intelligentsia' as it was now defined was a much
broader group than it had been earlier, including not only the old intelligentsia and the newly risen vydvizhentsy but also, remarkably, the entire
corpus of Communist administrative and managerial cadres ... The word
'intelligentsia' had unmistakenly become a Soviet synonym for 'elite'"
(Fitzpatrick, The Cultural Front, 15). This last conclusion, however, is
unmistakenly wrong: the elite consisted of the higher professional party
workers and the Communist administrative and managerial cadres exclusively. Vera Dunham calls this elite the "middle class" (In Stalin's Time,
1314). She seems to imply that only Communist stalwarts, reared by the
trials of war, collectivization, terror, and industrialization, properly
belonged to it, although this is not spelled out entirely clearly. If this is
the case, then Dunham's "middle class" may be synonymous with "elite"
here.
81 Pako, 147/5/214a, l.5.
82 Pako, 147/5/214a, l.1.
83 Pako, 147/5/214a, l.31. I.e., if one includes the category "scientific
   workers" of table 23 as part of the group of teachers; see Pako,
   147/5/214a, l.1.
84 See the third section of chapter 3. The benefits that the elite derived from
   their position and their outlook on life are described by Tucker: "And as
   higher or up-and-coming party-state functionaries, why should they
   doubt that this system was indeed the socialist one that Stalin had proclaimed it to be, that socialism was a form of society in which a bureau-

cratic centralized state took charge of everything, and that those in authority, themselves included, had every right to the special shops, special dining rooms, special clinics, and special rest homes that served them and their families? Since most were of peasant or worker origin, it was natural for them to think of the late-1930s Russia as the worker-peasant state that it officially claimed to be, although they themselves were no longer members of either of these classes" (*Stalin in Power*, 547).

85 See Pako, 147/4/1887, ll.67–263.

86 For the legal changes in the status of women see: Engel, "Engendering Russia's History," 317.

87 In the USSR in 1950, 56 percent of the total population was female (see Ryan, *Social Trends*, table 1.7, 13).

88 Pako, 147/4/1814, l.23.

89 Pako, 147/4/1814, ll.39–41. See Smirnov et al., *Ocherki*, 554–7. It seems that, at least in the peat industry, some women may have had some respite from the heavy work through the import of seasonal workers from the Mordvi and Bashkir Autonomous Soveit Socialist Republics, and from some other oblasts.

90 Pako, 147/4/1814, l.51.

91 Cf., for example, Smirnov et al., *Ocherki*, 568, 571, 600–1, and the photo on 600, in which Gaganova shakes the hand of Soviet president Voroshilov in 1959. She was a delegate at the Twenty-Second Party Congress of 1961 (605).

92 This and following paragraphs are based on the testimony of Valentina Gaganova in the survey.

93 Pako, 147/3/2679, l.15; Smirnov et al., *Ocherki*, appendix 1, 694.

94 The number was 11,161 in 1940 and 12,650 in 1944; in 1947 the number was 15,781 (ibid.).

95 In 1950 in the whole of the Soviet Union, more than 56 percent of the population was female (see Ryan, *Social Trends*, table 1.7, 13). In the Soviet Union in 1939, 52 percent of the agricultural labour force was female; this proportion rose to 71 percent in 1943, while 80 percent of the adult labour force in agriculture by 1945 was composed of women (Chadaev, *Ekonomika SSSR*, 111; Volkov, *Sovetskaia derevnia*, 36). After the war, women formed the large majority of the work force in both agriculture and industry in Kalinin oblast' (see tables 18 and 24). In the USSR as a whole by the 1950s, as many men as women were part of the labour force (Gordon and Klopov, *Chto eto bylo?*, 85).

96 Pako, 147/1/554, l.9; 147/5/283, ll.347–50; 147/5/10, l.82; Fainsod, *How Russia is Ruled*, 235–6.

97 Pako, 147/4/1512, l.27.

98 An expression of their preferences can be found in the substantial popu-

larity today of organizations in Russia that try to find Western, and in particular American, husbands for Russian women. These women seem to think that they will be quite happy by "just" being a housewife (see, e.g., Du Plessix Gray, *Soviet Women*, 7–8).

99 Pako, 147/5/663, l.115. The unpopularity of work in the countryside among agricultural specialists is understandable when one considers the living circumstances of some of them. Already in 1950, Khrushchev had complained about the unwillingness of many of the graduates of the Timiriazev Agricultural Academy to work in their profession (Fainsod, *How Russia is Ruled*, 474).

100 Altrichter, *Die Bauern*, 64. Since divorce had become extraordinarily difficult, it seemed somewhat redundant when, in March 1951, MGB head Dekushenko rejoiced over the fact that the number of divorces had fallen by 2.5 times in 1950 in comparison with 1940 (Pako, 147/5/2, l.146). The number of registered weddings in 1950 was 1.5 times as high as in 1940.

101 Pako, 147/4/195, ll.420b.–43. Astashina was appointed third secretary – that is, "secretary for cadres" – of the Oktiabr' raion of Kalinin when it was formed at the end of the war (PP 7671, 3 January 1945, 2).

102 "In the family the roles of men and women changed only very slowly. The problem of the double burden arose, which laid the family on the shoulders of the women. A situation was created, surviving until today, in which the woman works in the economy as much as the man of the family; moreover she has to do the fundamental part of domestic work, hardly facilitated by time-saving household devices" (Gordon and Klopov, *Chto eto bylo?*, 85). Gordon and Klopov are wrong to conclude that the basis has been laid for women's full emancipation in society when, in Soviet times, millions of women were liberated from the old constraints that had limited them to an existence in the kitchen (ibid.). In pre-Soviet times, the great majority of the population lived in the countryside: women were often as much involved in farming as men. Even in the towns women worked in the factories before 1917. Furthermore, if the basis was laid for women's equality as a result of their participation in the production process in the USSR, why was this equality never in fact realized, in the same way that it was realized not before the October Revolution? Evidently, more is necessary than mere changes in economic position, to achieve social equality.

103 Pako, 147/4/195, ll.420b.–43. At plenums and conferences, speakers had to announce beforehand if they wanted to make a speech; due to time constraints, in the end there were always far more people on the list than appeared before the delegates; often those who were deemed to be less important were not allowed to speak as a result.

104 Pako, 147/4/195, l.430b.

105 Pako, 147/4/1814, ll.1–6.
106 Pako, 147/4/1814, l.3. Commenting on the feminine nature of household tasks, Nadezhda A. Smirnova, a former veterinarian, noticed in the survey that, besides her extremely demanding job, she also had to look after her animals, private plot, and household. She estimated that women worked about twice as much as men. The "benefits" for women of the economic transformation under Stalin are underlined in the following statement of Barbara Alpern Engel: "Since the 1930s, women have shouldered the burden of full-time, waged labor while continuing to do almost all housework without labor-saving devices" ("Engendering Russia's History," 319).
107 Pako, 147/4/1814, ll.4–6. Bobrova agreed that men were promoted solely because of their army rank, notwithstanding the fact that they often worked extremely poorly (Pako, 147/4/1814, l.6). See Heitlinger, *Women and State Socialism*, 57–63, 109, for a discussion of the creation and dissolution of the Zhenotdel. It had been abolished in 1930 (Clements, "The Utopianism of the Zhenotdel," 495).
108 Pako, 147/4/1814, ll.6, 56.
109 Heitlinger, *Women and State Socialism*, 108, 114; Pako, 147/4/1814, ll.24, 26. In each of 17 rural raions, there was at most one day-care facility in 1949. Neither were there many day cares in the towns of the USSR as a whole, when less than 10 percent of all children of the age group attended day cares (Gordon and Klopov, *Chto eto bylo?*, 88). The head of production and subsequent director of the porcelain factory of Konakovo, V.P. Sazhko, said in the survey that he was able to have a housekeeper look after his two children in the period; the household of A.A. Morozova was in a similar position. The rank-and-file, such as V.P. Pimenova, were helped by mothers or mothers-in-law. The testimony of the regular kolkhoznitsa M.V. Chesnokova, who gave birth to eight children between 1931 and 1951, indicates, however, that at times in the countryside large families also had a nanny.
110 Pako, 147/4/1814, ll.26–7. At the end of 1948 in Kalinin, Vyshnii Volochek, Rzhev, Bologoe, Bezhetsk, Kimry, and Torzhok the occupancy rate of available places in day-care centres was 74.5 percent. A grandmother looked after the children of E.N. Ratnikova and her husband, who worked respectively as a nurse and officer in the army, and of the schoolteacher N.N. Golubeva and her husband, according to testimony of Ratnikova and Golubeva in the survey.
111 M.M. Kozenkova-Pavlova said that she had no one to help her look after the children, and thus took them with her when she worked in the fields.
112 Pako, 147/4/1814, l.62.

113 Pako, 147/4/1977, ll.6–8; the resolution was called "On the Situation and Measures to Improve the Work among Women".

114 Ibid., ll.9–10.

115 Ibid., ll.18–34.

116 Moscow, 17/43/742, l.10; 17/44/546, l.730b. The relative share of women among the kolkhoz chairs was, at the same time, higher than in the USSR as a whole, where at the end of 1944, 11.8 percent of all chairs were occupied by women, the proportion of whom was already decreasing to 8.1 percent by late 1945 (Volkov, *Sovetskaia derevnia*, 42 and 47). A similar decrease was noticeable in other responsible positions in the collective farms, such as that of brigadier, bookkeeper, and head of the livestock sector.

117 Pako, 147/5/11, l.118. In the whole of the USSR the proportion of women tractor drivers plummeted from 55 percent in 1943, to 17.4 percent in 1946, and to 5 percent on 1 January 1949 (Volkov, *Sovetskaia derevnia*, 120).

118 Cf., for example, Popovskii, *Tretii lishnii*.

119 Pako, 147/4/1703, ll.103–1040b. Male homosexuality was outlawed in 1934 in the Soviet Union, while lesbianism was never officially made illegal (Heitlinger, *Women and State Socialism*, 21; also Mamonova, *Women and Russia*, 135). Men who were convicted for homosexuality got jail terms, while women were sent to psychiatric hospitals, according to Mamonova (*Russian Women's Studies*, 131; *Women and Russia*, 135). Mamonova's claim about the occurrence of lesbianism after the war is highly plausible, as this example perhaps shows (130).

120 On 14 August 1930, four years of primary education was made obligatory (Kerblay, *Du mir aux agrovilles*, 353).

121 Natal'ia A. Smirnova, born in 1913, said in the survey that she had never enjoyed any education and remained illiterate. So did M.K. Chesnokova, born in 1912. A.G. Murtsovkina and F.K. Romashova said they had had two years of likbez (likvidatsiia bezgramotnisti, i.e., education for illiterate adults), although they had wanted to have more education. Gordon and Klopov indicate that in the countryside, at least in this respect, collectivization might have had a beneficial effect (*Chto eto bylo?*, 91). It was much easier to control school attendance through the kolkhozy than before. The peasantry, much less interested after collectivization in optimal production from socialized lands and cattle, may have seen less necessity for their offspring to aid in agricultural work (ibid., 92). Nevertheless, the level of education was low: in 1939, 90 percent of the population, and in 1959, 64 percent of the population had enjoyed merely primary education (ibid., 97).

122 Iu. Borisov indicated that just before the war still 20 percent of the total

population of the USSR was illiterate (Borisov, "Stalin," 487). This number seems high, but let us remember that in a supposedly advanced country such as France the education of more than 60 percent of the population born before 1947 consisted of no more than primary education (Zeldin, *The French*, 380). Cf. tables 16, 18, and 22.

123 Cf. the education level on 1 January 1952 of the 1,467 leading workers (table 16). Pako, 147/4/1495, l.720b., gives evidence of the introduction of the seven-year curriculum for the school year 1949–50. G. Pomerants saw the key to the unrivalled cruelty of Stalinist times in this "semi-education" of the masses, who were no longer restrained by the norms and values of traditional society when their existence was uprooted after the revolutions of 1917. The masses had not yet been socialized adequately – through sufficient education – into cultured citizens of modern industrial society ("O roli oblika lichnosti," 137–40). Pomerants maintains that Soviet society under Stalin was the result of this "lack of culture" and older traditions of boorishness and lackeying, which found their roots in the time of the Tatar yoke. Although Pomerants exaggerates, the hysterical gatherings that called for the death of the accused at the show trials, or the enthusiastic cruelty of the party activists during collectivization seem to confirm the unsophisticated receptiveness of many Soviet citizens toward the manipulative propaganda from above. In the same way, A.N. Sakharov saw the essence of the events in Stalin's lifetime in the revenge exacted on the rich or educated by the "half-cultured, philistine, poor, and even lowest people" for centuries of oppression ("Revoliutsionnyi totalitarizm," 63–4). The experience of Nazi Germany, however, proves that "[one] can be educated and totally immoral" (Kerblay, *Du mir aux agrovilles*, 370).

124 Pako, 147/4/1391, ll.3–5, 11. Eighty-six had attended only one grade, 293 two grades, and 715 three grades. Thus 6.9 percent of young males born in 1929 had avoided the basic four-year curriculum of obligatory primary education.

125 Around 1970 a sociological survey was conducted in the countryside of Kalinin oblast' under the auspices of Iu.V. Arutiunian (*La structure sociale*, 206–7). It appeared that in small and medium-sized villages, most members of the agricultural labour force had received between four and five years of education. In the larger villages the picture was slightly better, for most of the inhabitants had profited from more than six years of schooling, even though the average was still less than seven years. This adds further support to the argument concerning the rather minimal education of many who had grown up during the time of Stalin, for many respondents were born during the 1920s or early 1930s (the average age of the labour force of Arutiunian's respondents was, in all villages, between forty and forty-seven). Obviously, a signifi-

cant number of the better educated had migrated to towns, but rural dwellers schooled in the 1930s and 1940s who stayed behind had benefited from four to six and a half years of education, on average. Other Soviet research confirms the low level of education in the countryside (Pankratova, *Sel'skaia zhenshchina v SSSR*, 40). Towards 1940 the majority of the rural population had about three to four years of elementary school at most, according to Pankratova.

126   "No aspect of Soviet society received more warm and spontaneous support than did the system of Soviet education ... Only the system of free medical care came close to it in popularity" (Inkeles and Bauer, *The Soviet Citizen*, 132); cf. Altrichter's description of the inimical attitude towards the schools of many of the peasants in the 1920s (*Die Bauern*, 171). In the interviews conducted in Tver' in 1992, A.F. Antonov testified that he had only two years of general education, somewhat enhanced by a few courses in land surveying. He lamented his lack of education, as did many other participants in the survey.

127   Pako, 147/4/1126, l.1; 147/5/2, l.32. Kiselev remarked in his closing speech before an obkom plenum in October 1953 that education in the towns was much better than in the countryside, a reason for many agricultural specialists to seek employment in the towns and have their children educated there (Pako, 147/5/663, l.196).

128   Pako, 147/5/36, l.120.

129   Pako, 147/4/1126, l.30b. Examples of the themes for essays of this kind are: "What is happiness?" "Does one have to dream?" "My most beloved hero" and "A memorable day in my life."

130   Pako, 147/4/1126, l.11; testimony of V.P. Krylov in the survey.

131   Kerblay, *Du mir aux agrovilles*, 355; Todorskii and Arbatov, "Bol'shoe v malom," 58.

132   Pako, 147/5/10, ll.52–3; one of the most common post-primary or secondary schools was the tekhnikum, some of which were independent, while others were closely connected with a local factory (the railroad-car factory of Kalinin, for example; see *Narodnoe khoziaistvo*, 91–4). There were also several musical institutes and medical schools, while Kalinin had a secondary party school. Then there were a few secondary pedagogical institutes, a library school, and some schools teaching aspects of the mechanization of agriculture, finance, planning and bookkeeping, veterinarian studies, and the lumber industry. The two institutes of higher learning in 1955 were the Pedagogical Institute M.I. Kalinin, today the State University of Tver', and the State Medical Institute of Kalinin.

133   Pako, 147/5/341, l.67. In 1940, jail sentences were introduced for students of trade schools, railroad colleges, and factory schools (FZOs) for violations of school discipline and the unauthorized departure from the

school (Gordon and Klopov, *Chto eto bylo?*, fn. 2, 127). FZOs and vocational schools (remeslennye uchilishcha or tekhnikumy) were geared toward teaching industrial skills.

134 Cf. Kennan, *Memoirs: 1925–1950*, appendix A, 508.

CHAPTER SEVEN

1 Todorskii and Arbatov, "Bol'shoe v malom," 57.

2 *PP* 7802, 11 July 1945, 2. The kolkhoz Krasnoe Trosukhino was located in the Kalinin rural raion.

3 Ibid.

4 Pako, 147/3/2701, ll.224–5.

5 See the second section of chapter 4. In Soviet jargon, this behaviour was dubbed "anti-Soviet." At the same time, similar phenomena were noticed in Ostashkov raion, for instance (Pako, 147/3/2701, ll.132–1330b.). In August 1945 grain was distributed among the kolkhozniks of Novokarel' raion instead of being delivered to the state (Pako, 147/3/2702, l.30). A few weeks later the same practice was condemned in Novokarel', Kaliazin, Nerl', Likhoslavl', Goritskii, and Esenovichi raions (Pako, 147/3/2702, l.550b.).

6 See chapter 9.

7 See *Kalininskaia oblast' za 50 let*, 59, where it is claimed that all land and all peasants' households were collectivized in 1945. See the second section of chapter 4 for a qualification of that level of collectivization.

8 See the second section of chapter 4.

9 Pako, 147/3/2702, l.23.

10 *PP* 8407, 12 November 1947, 3. Cf. Altrichter, *Die Bauern*, 61: newly weds lived traditionally for some years in their parents' house in the countryside.

11 Anokhina and Shmeleva, *Kul'tura i byt'*, 54, 57; Pako, 147/5/663, l.115. In 1951 raikom secretary Mozhaev of Goritsy raion complained about the unauthorized departure of many rural artisans of his raion, some of whom even joined construction brigades in the town of Kalinin (Pako, 147/5/11, ll.73–4). Cf., as well, Ivanov, "V rodnykh," 180.

12 Despite the obvious significance of these subsidiary farms, they were not always in the best condition. In July 1945 the situation of the sovkhoz Brednevo in Turginovo raion had become intolerable in the eyes of a vice-secretary of the obkom, Zakharov, who oversaw the retail-trade and public-catering organizations. He reported to Vorontsov and Boitsov that the food canteen and the housing barracks of the farm were infested with cockroaches and other insects and that ten families lived in one communal room. They had no bedding and few pillows or mattresses. He went on to say that "[i]n the obshchezhitie there were no chairs, stools, buckets, no laundry tub, and those who took home a

lunch from the food canteen, ate sitting on their bunks, holding their bowl on their knees. The clothes of these families were rags in fact, and a number of them did not have any footwear." Recently, matters there and in other subsidiary farms had improved, through disinfection, the construction of separate rooms, and the distribution of furniture and shoes (Pako, 147/3/2759, ll.77–8).

13 Pako, 147/4/63, l.215. Patolichev, Khrushchev, and Kaganovich were supervising the grain deliveries in the Ukraine in the autumn of 1946 (Volkov, "Zasukha," 7). In the end, the mobilization of the population to aid with the grain procurements proved successful and the oblast' exceeded the plan – it delivered 104.7 percent (Volkov, *Sovetskaia derevnia*, 273–4; Volkov, "Zasukha," 8–9). However, part of the deliveries consisted of seeds required for spring sowing (Volkov, "Zasukha," 8).

14 Pako, 147/5/10, l.66; 147/4/1097, l.8. In 1945 fifty thousand blue- and white-collar workers had pitched in with harvesting (Smirnov et al., *Ocherki*, 532). Matveev's criticism about the overambitious dispatch of the inhabitants of Vyshnii Volochek in 1950 was echoed by Baranov at the same plenum (Pako, 147/5/10, l.81); a few months earlier, another urban raion secretary had claimed that on certain days in October 1950 Kalinin had sent up to twenty thousand workers and employees into the countryside to aid with harvesting (Pako, 147/5/2, l.160). In November 1949 Zubov, head of the oblast' trade union council, spoke in the same vein (Pako, 147/4/1512, ll.20–200b.). Shortages of work hands at harvest time were not unique to Soviet times; cf. G.T. Robinson discussing pre-1917 farming in Russia: "It is in the very nature of the highly specialized grain-production of Russia, that for brief periods it demanded whole armies of extra plowmen and especially of harvesters" (*Rural Russia*, 105).

15 Pako, 147/5/10, ll.115–17. One raion secretary maintained, in March 1951, that it made the kolkhozniks complacent and lazy, since they were assured of the assistance of the urban population (Pako, 147/5/2, l.160).

16 Pako, 147/5/663, l.166. In the discussion of collectivization in chapter 1 it was noted how inhabitants of the town of Kimry aided harvesting already in 1931. G.V. Lubov noticed that he and his fellow workers helped with all kinds of work in the surrounding collective farms: hay, grain, and potato harvesting.

17 See, e.g., Volkov, "Kolkhozy SSSR," 52, 59–61, 64; or Samsonov, *A Short History*, 256–7 or Volkov, *Sovetskaia derevnia*. Iu.V. Arutiunian admitted in 1961 that the agricultural production of the territory of the USSR of the pre-1939 borders did not reach the level of agricultural production of the years 1926–29 until 1953 ("Osobennosti i znachenie," 404). The average grain yield per hectare in 1925–26 was 8.5 tsenter, and in 1949–53 7.7 tsenter (Arutiunian, "Osobennosti i znachenie," 406).

18 Pako, 147/3/2702, l.88. The eastern raions of Molokovo (with 1,505

head) Bezhetsk (with 1,169), Kashin (with 1,153), Brusovo (653), Maksatikha (589), and Vyshnii Volochek (259) were named as the main culprits.

19 Pako, 147/3/2702, l.186. Here the raions of Rzhev, in which the number of draught oxen decreased by 120 in July 1945, Lukovnikovo (101), Kalinin (47), Konakovo (45), and Bologoe (42) were mentioned.

20 Pako, 147/4/63, ll.52–3. Thirteen percent of milkmaids, 6 percent of cow breeders, and 2 percent of horse breeders received additional income. See also table 13 for livestock numbers. The number of poultry in the oblast' was 220,625 on 1 January 1946, and one year later, 190,436 (Pako, 147/4/528, l.60b.). The greatest loss among cattle herds was sustained in more remote areas (Pako, 147/4/528, ll.60b.–7). One cause was the "squandering" of the socialized cattle, that is, selling cattle on the side or unauthorized slaughtering for personal consumption. However, the Party often exaggerated the extent of this practice.

21 The absolute number of personal cattle of the kolkhozniks declined only a little between 1941 and 1946 in the USSR (Volkov, *Sovetskaia derevnia*, 52). In the Union as a whole in 1945, 80 percent of cows and 58 percent of pigs were privately owned by the kolkhozniks (ibid., 53). This livestock provided 82 percent of all milk and 61 percent of all meat produced in the USSR. In 1953, the personal livestock of the kolkhozniks in the USSR produced 65 percent of the milk, 82 percent of the eggs, 55 percent of the meat, and the private plots of the kolkhozniks 40 percent of the total kolkhoz production of potatoes and vegetables – that is, 40 percent of the production of the socialized and private sector combined – in the country (Arutiunian, "Osobennosti i znachenie," table 9, 419). Grain and fodder crops, as well as wool, were mainly produced by the socialized sector of the kolkhozy.

22 Pako, 147/4/63, l.223.

23 See Volkov, *Sovetskaia derevnia*, 68. Apart from this measure, two decrees were issued by the same authorities in the autumn of 1946 that sought to protect the grain deliveries to the state (Volkov, "Zasukha," 10). As in industry, many authorities on different levels in the state and party hierarchies could potentially interfere with agriculture. The most important measures were naturally taken by the Central Committee and its Sekretariat, sometimes in combination with the Council of Ministers. Apart from that, some decrees were issued by the Supreme Soviet. The measures of these higher organs were complemented and adapted for the local circumstances by measures of the obkom (buro) or its secretariat, which also issued their own decrees. Measures specific to a raion could be issued by the raikoms. Administratively, the lowest level of authority was the executive of the kolkhoz itself (or its general meeting); and – by way of the raion department (otdel) of agriculture of the raiispolkom, the

oblast' department of agriculture of the oblispolkom, and the RSFSR Ministry of Agriculture – the highest level was the USSR Ministry of Agriculture (Volkov, *Sovetskaia derevnia*, 144–7). Together with this ministry, other All-Union and RSFSR ministries (of the sovkhozy, of the procurements of agricultural production, and, temporarily between 1945 and 1947, of technical crops and of animal husbandry) and Gosplan top-functionaries were part of a Council of Ministers' buro for agriculture after the war. All could separately take measures that concerned agriculture. The Ministry of Agriculture was organized in many different branches. From October 1946, the Council for Kolkhoz Affairs under the USSR Council of Ministers began to function and drafted new laws and made recommendations to the Council of Ministers, had the power to issue directives and instructions about the operation of the kolkhozy, and investigated requests and suggestions that emanated from the kolkhozy. In this council some token grass-roots kolkhoz workers had a seat, but the show was run by Politburo member Andreev, Central Committee secretary Patolichev, and Orgburo member V.M. Andrianov (Volkov, *Sovetskaia derevnia*, 149), until of course, Andreev's disappearance in the early 1950s from the highest party level (Fainsod, *How Russia is Ruled*, 454). Even a Soviet publication has to admit that all these different levels of decision making and the frequent reorganization of these organs led to duplication and did little to improve agriculture during these years (Volkov, *Sovetskaia derevnia*, 146 and 151).

24 Fainsod gives perhaps the best translation of the word trudoden' with "workday credit" (Fainsod, *How Russia is Ruled*, 461). For more on the trudoden', see chapter 9, n18.

25 Pako, 147/3/2759, ll.311–312. Examples of these practices in Kalinin oblast' can be found in Pako, 147/3/1966, ll.2630b. In December 1946, S.A. Veselov reported to an obkom plenum that in 47 percent of all the collective farms of the province, examples of the improper use of kolkhoz land had been registered in the fall of 1946 (Pako, 147/4/18, l.34).

26 Pako, 147/3/2759, ll.311–12. For the kolkhoz Ustav, see the fourth section of chapter 3.

27 Pako, 147/3/2759, l.3110b.

28 Pako, 147/3/2759, l.312. Similar acrimonious discussions at party meetings took place in several other raions (Pako, 147/3/2759, ll.311–12).

29 See Pako, 147/1/527, l.198. Iamshchikov's career came to an end in 1950, when he was officially dismissed for allowing some of the kolkhozy in his raion to distribute grain among themselves before fulfilling the plan of the state procurements (Pako, 147/5/10, l.146; also 147/5/2, l.16). Severov shared the common opinion among party members that kolkhozniks deliberately sabotaged the grain deliveries and that as a consequence they had caused more than a thousand tons of

grain to rot in Lukovnikovo raion. This mistrustful attitude we saw expressed before in the statements of Baranov and Gerasimenko in July 1951 (see the second section of chapter 4).

30 Pako, 147/4/63, l.2350b.

31 Pako, 147/4/528, l.10. The personal plots had been illegally increased by 5,737 hectares in total through these abuses. Not all collective farms had undergone inspection, as the total number of them was approximately 7,060 at this time. The savings in trudodni seem impressive; however, the number constitutes only around 1 percent of the total amount of trudodni that the oblast' generated every year.

32 Pako, 147/4/528, l.110b.; Volkov, "Zasukha," 12. These numbers were repeated by obkom secretary Shatalin in early 1949 (Pako, 147/4/1495, l.930b.). Shatalin added that on the whole in 1947, 2,356 chairs were changed (32.5 percent) and 1,365 (18 percent) in 1948. The number, however, rose again in 1949, when in the first two months already about 1,000 were replaced.

33 Pako, 147/5/283, ll.159–60. The inspection was probably the result of a Central Committee resolution of 22 March 1952, titled "On Measures to Introduce the Directions of Party and Government Regarding the Struggle against the Squandering of Public Property on the Collective Farms".

34 See the second section of chapter 5.

35 The procuracy seems to have caught a few embezzlers in almost every raion (Gako, 2321/6/69, ll.1–58); not all were punished as harshly as the Stepanovs, but some received even longer sentences (as in Bologoe, where two people were put on trial for the theft of butter and were sentenced to twenty years of corrective labour camp).

36 Marx himself noted about peasants that "Nay more; they are reactionary, for they try to roll back the wheel of history" (Marx and Engels, *The Communist Manifesto*, 91).

37 Pako, 147/4/526, title page; the Central Committee Plenum resolutions were titled "On Measures for the Improvement of Agriculture in the Postwar Period". The obkom plenum took place on 14 and 15 March 1947. The convocation of the plenum was likely connected with the development of the famine (see Heller and Nekrich, *Utopia in Power*, 468–9, who indicate that the height of the famine was reached during the winter and early spring of 1947). Vorontsov said in March 1947: "You know from the decisions [of the February 1947 Plenum] of the Central Committee of the VKP(b), that in 1946 a severe drought occurred in a significant area of the European part of the USSR, which has had a strong impact on the agriculture of our country, and the total yield of the grain harvest in the country was substantially less than in 1945" (Pako, 147/4/528, l.13). For the plenary session, see Samsonov, *A Short History*, 256–7, or Kuleshov et al., *Nashe otechestvo*, 436. There were, however,

some "organizational matters" with which the Central Committee Plenum dealt: Donskii lost his membership for "not being able to fulfill the duties of a Central Committee member," Shakhurin had been convicted by the Military Tribunal of the USSR Supreme Court and lost his membership; in addition, Central Committee candidates Zhukov, Maiskii, Dubrovskii, Kachalin, and Cherevichenko lost their membership, for they had been unable to discharge their responsibilities as candidate members in a satisfactory way. Stalin was released from his duties as Minister of Defense and succeeded by Bulganin; Voznesensky became full Politburo member (Pako, 147/4/528, l.2).

38 Pako, 147/4/1495, l.150b.

39 Pako, 147/4/528, l.14.

40 On 2 June 1948, a Supreme Soviet decree was issued, titled "On the Exile to Remote Regions of the USSR of Persons Maliciously Shirking from Labour in Agriculture and Leading an Antisocial, Parasitic Way of Life," which was further explained by a confidential letter of the next day written by the Central Committee and Council of Ministers combined (Pako, 147/4/1125, l.157). It was obviously aimed at people who had more or less turned their backs on the work in the socialized sector of agriculture, although not being either able or willing or allowed to leave the collective farms and thus formally remaining members. In 1952, the Central Committee reiterated its warnings about the squandering of kolkhoz property in the resolution of 22 March, mentioned in note 33, above. As Fainsod remarked, "The history of Soviet agricultural policy in the post-World War II period is essentially a record of tightening control over all kolkhoz activities" (*How Russia is Ruled*, 453). In the light of the measures of 1946 and 1947, both in the field of ideology and in that of agriculture, it seems mistaken to suggest that "1948 brought an end to the postwar hesitations of the leadership about the choice of a soft or harsh course" (Zubkova, "Obshchestvennaia (1948–1952)," 79). The leadership does not seem to have doubted that it would follow a harsh line at any time after the war: a clear break for 1948 cannot be distinguished.

41 Pako, 147/4/1125, ll.1580b.–159; 147/4/1413, ll.2, 13. By August 1948, apparently thirty people had been exiled and three dependents chose to join them (Bugai, "20-40-e gody," 46). In July 1953, the raion secretary of Staritsa, Kutuzov, admitted that the decree had been ignored soon after its issue (Pako, 147/5/662, l.52).

42 See, e.g., Pako, 147/3/2702, ll.62–620b.

43 Pako, 147/5/10, ll.20–210b.

44 Pako, 147/5/10, l.65.

45 Pako, 147/3/2702, l.1860b. The sel'khozsnabzhenie was a provincial office responsible for the distribution of goods among the collective

farms, with local departments in the raions. The sel'po was the village general store. The same problem was once more the subject of discussions in the obkomburo somewhat later, in September 1945 (Pako, 147/3/2702, ll.1850b.–1870b.). At this time the supply was deficient in at least the raions of Molokovo, Rameshki, Kesova Gora, and Lesnoe, all in the east and northeast of the oblast'. Flax deliveries were not being encouraged due to insufficient delivery of goods in return, according to information in September 1945 (Pako, 147/3/2702, ll.1870b.–8).

46 Pako, 147/5/10, ll.20–210b.

47 Pako, 147/5/433, l.121. Cf. Kerblay, *Du mir aux agrovilles*, 257, 289–308. The grain, flax, and livestock raw material offices of the raion had no motorized means of transport. The poor state of the roads was a problem that continued to afflict agriculture in the early 1960s (Ivanov, "V rodnykh," 198–9).

48 Pako, 147/4/1095, l.570b.

49 For sheep the numbers were in 1916, 985,000; in 1928, 1,737,000; on 1 January 1948, 712,000. For hogs the numbers were in 1916, 146,000; in 1928, 233,000; on 1 January 1948, 111,000 (Pako, 147/4/1095, l.570b.). Altrichter's numbers for 1916 and 1928 are higher for bovines, but smaller for goats and pigs, yet the downward trend is confirmed by his work (Altrichter, *Die Bauern*, table 10, 209). Zhuravlev seems to have been relegated in the autumn at the reorganization of the obkom, when he was not selected to head an otdel; he was, however, re-elected in 1949 to the obkom.

50 Pako, 147/4/1495, ll.8–80b., 110b. Unfortunately for the kolkhozniks, the norms for one trudoden' were increased in April 1948 (Volkov, *Sovetskaia derevnia*, 169). It is therefore likely that the income they derived from the trudodni did not increase very much (they did receive more per trudoden' in 1948, but were awarded a smaller number of trudodni). The yield of potatoes was particularly high in these years: in the USSR the annual average yield in the Fourth Five Year Plan was reached again only in the Eighth Five Year Plan in the second half of the 1960s (Volkov, *Sovetskaia derevnia*, 240). Only a quarter of the total potato harvest in 1950 was grown in the socialized sector of agriculture, while one-third had been grown there in 1940. The private plots of the kolkhozniks, workers, and employees produced most of the crop. The kolkhoz Moriak was one of those in which the kolkhozniks performed extremely well, as A.K. Sumugina-Shepeleva testified in the survey. However, in many of the smaller kolkhozy of the oblast' – 90 percent of those who could field only one brigade for crop cultivation – trudodni were subtracted one year later for failing to meet the increased labour norms for harvesting in 1949 (Volkov, *Sovetskaia derevnia*, 173). In comparison with other flax-growing areas in the USSR (e.g., Belorussia and Smolensk oblast') Kalinin

oblast' did relatively well between 1947 and 1950; compared to the Central Region in these years, where the yield was on average 160 kilogrammes per hectare, Kalinin oblast' boasted a yield of an average of 200 kilograms per hectare (ibid., 237–8). See also table 24: 1948 and 1949 stand out as exceptionally good years for flax cultivation. Despite the disappointing results of livestock breeding, the number of farm animals on 1 January 1950 – that is after the good years of 1948 and 1949 – was probably the highest for the entire 1945–53 period (see table 11). Table 24 shows that the average production of wool, eggs, and milk was by comparison much higher in 1948 and 1949 than in other years.

51 Pako, 147/4/1495, l.14. Often used, this term "backward" (otstaiushchie) is rather vague. It signifies kolkhozy whose agricultural production consistently failed to meet the required norms (or, to be more precise, the obligatory state deliveries for different products), as laid down by the annual plans. The plans could and would vary from kolkhoz to kolkhoz and from year to year. The cause for this "backwardness" was invariably seen in a lack of labour discipline, the violation of the 1935 Kolkhoz Statute, poorly organized labour (particularly poor organization by the kolkhoz chair), or a too frequent change of kolkhoz chairs.

52 *Bloknot Agitatora*, 1949, 1, 22–3; the edition of the monthly (later published every fortnight) was 7,500 in 1948 (see, e.g., *Bloknot Agitatora*, 1948, 1); by January 1951 the journal came out in an edition of 16,000 (see, e.g., *Bloknot Agitatora*, 1951, 1). For Lysenko, cf., for example, Sudoplatov, *Special Tasks*, 317–18.

53 Pako, 147/5/36, l.6, 147/5/663, l.76; Volkov, *Sovetskaia derevnia*, 252. The representative of the Council for Kolkhoz Affairs of the USSR government, Tarasov, stated bluntly in 1951 that 1949 was a much more successful agricultural year for the province than 1950 (Pako, 147/5/2, l.147). This is confirmed by the statement of Kiselev in October 1953 that the livestock herd in the postwar period was most numerous on 1 January 1950 (Pako, 147/5/663, l.17).

54 Pako, 147/5/7, ll.3a–4. Private and kolkhoz livestock are combined here. The average size of the kolkhozy of Kalinin oblast' was much smaller than that of the Soviet Union in general, which was around eighty homesteads per kolkhoz in 1949 (Volkov, *Sovetskaia derevnia*, 112). The three-year development plan for livestock of April 1949 called for the smaller kolkhozy (with less than 500 hectares of land) of the Central Region to have, by 1953, in the *socialized* part of the farm, 80 head of strong-horned cattle, 55 to 75 sheep and goats, 65 to 120 pigs, and 750 to 900 poultry. Most of the cattle mentioned here by Konovalov were personally owned by individual kolkhozniks.

55 See the second section of chapter 4. The amalgamation was officially begun after a Central Committee resolution of 30 May 1950 (see Sam-

sonov, *A Short History*, 408). It was all the more a failure because, up to
1949, Kalinin province had been "advanced" (peredovaia) with respect
to the grain deliveries to the state, as the head of the oblast' Office of
Grain Procurements (Zagotzerno) said in November 1949 (Pako,
147/4/1512, l.19). By 1953 amalgamation resulted in the unification of
the total of 9,772 villages and hamlets within 1,909 kolkhozy and some
40-odd sovkhozy in Kalinin province (Pako, 147/5/663, l.161). The idea
of amalgamation, however, was certainly not just a whim of the Central
Committee: already in 1946 a raikom secretary of Kalinin oblast' suggested the unification of several kolkhozy into one in his sparsely populated, formerly occupied territory (Pako, 147/4/18, l.41).

56 Pako, 147/5/2, l.147. The amalgamation drive was particularly badly
scheduled, for it was in full force during the summer, as obkom secretary
Konovalov admitted in between the lines in January 1951 (Pako,
147/5/7, ll.6–7).

57 Pako, 147/5/10, ll.11.

58 Pako, 147/5/36, l.11.

59 There are indications that the brigades themselves were to increase in size
from twenty or thirty kolkhozniks to fifty or sixty (Pako, 147/5/7, l.16;
see Volkov, *Sovetskaia derevnia*, 170). The general replacement of the
zveno system was the beginning of the demise of Politburo member
Andreev, who had been its principal patron (see Fainsod, *How Russia is
Ruled*, 456). Fainsod indicates a possible political connection between the
attack on the preponderance of the zven'ia and the amalgamation (ibid.,
456–7). Both the small link and the small kolkhoz were seen as impediments to a more efficient and mechanized agriculture, while both hindered a firmer control over the countryside.

60 Pako, 147/5/10, ll.14.

61 Pako, 147/5/10, l.46.

62 For more on the trudoden', see chapter 8, n18.

63 Pako, 147/5/283, ll.162–5.

64 Ibid., ll.162–5, 167.

65 Pako, 147/5/283, l.162.

66 Pako, 147/5/660, l.99; Pako, 147/5/429, l.250; the resolution of Novem-
ber 1952, issued by the Council of Ministers of the USSR, was titled "On
Grave Violations of the Rural Artel' Statute in the Collective Farms of
Kalinin Oblast'."

67 Pako, 147/5/10, ll.10–17, 110. Kolkhoz monetary income in 1950 was
derived predominantly from the sale of flax (46 percent) and of livestock
products (28 percent) to the state; for 1953 these numbers were respectively 42 percent and 39 percent. Ninety-three percent of planed deliveries of flax to the state, 75 percent of planned grain deliveries, 88.7
percent of planned meat deliveries, 90.6 percent of planned milk deliver-

ies, and 86.5 percent of planned wool deliveries had been procured in 1950 (Pako, 147/5/36, l.108). In certain areas much of the harvest was lost through inadequate storage (Pako, 147/5/662, l.68). The evidence in the party archives for the postwar results repudiates the opinion of Leont'eva that meat and milk deliveries on the whole were met by the collective farms in the postwar period (see "Dokumenty po istorii," 31). Even a Soviet publication of 1965 admits that the three-year plan was a "dismal failure" (see Samsonov, *A Short History*, 264; see also Volkov, *Sovetskaia derevnia*, 257ff.: the plan was announced in a joint USSR Council of Ministers and Central Committee decree on 18 April 1949). By 1953 livestock had decreased significantly, except for horses (see table 11). The head of the party, trade union, and Komsomol otdel of the obkom, Fokin, stated in July 1951 that 1949 had been a poor year in crop tillage, 1950 had been worse, and spring sowing in 1951 had gone extremely badly (Pako, 147/5/10, l.140). Flax was often not treated quickly enough, and much of the harvest went to waste because of a lack of work hands for the processing procedure. Mechanization could have been a remedy for this problem, but was hardly expanding in the field of flax production between 1945 and 1953 (Volkov, *Sovetskaia derevnia*, 237).

68 Pako, 147/5/10, ll.10–170, 58. Anokhina and Shmeleva, *Kul'tura i byt'*, 45. In July 1953 some of the animals were still kept in shelters made of branches and straw (Pako, 147/5/662, l.68).

69 Pako, 147/5/36, ll.123–4.

70 Pako, 147/5/10, l.43; Pako, 147/5/36, l.107. The numbers for 1946 are calculated on the basis of table 13. Table 11 shows the tremendous drop in the number of cattle between 1950 and 1953. Already a few months earlier, Tarasov had spoken of a "catastrophical" decline in the number of cattle in many of the kolkhozy (Pako, 147/5/2, l.147). In early 1948 the main cause – apart from the oblique reference to "squandering" – for the disappointing growth of the cattle herd had been found in the absence of improvement of meadows and pastures, which had often become swampy or wooded (Pako, 147/4/1095, l.570b.).

71 Pako, 147/5/36, ll.123 often4.

72 Pako, 147/5/11, ll.54–5, 72; 147/5/283, ll.232–3.

73 As noticed in other places, the kolkhozniks were in general less than eager about the tasks that the state had in mind for them (cf. also Rittersporn's remarks, *Stalinist Simplifications*, 55, or Abramov's description of the attitude of the collective farmers in in his telling novel *The New Life*).

74 Pako, 147/5/37, ll.47–9.

75 Pako, 147/5/11, l.51.

76 Pako, 147/5/36, ll.123–124.

77 The resolution was dated 3 September 1951, and called: "On Measures

toward Rectification of Shortcomings in the Counting of Livestock and the Safeguarding of Animal Husbandry on the Collective Farms" (Pako, 147/5/11, l.15). The provincial state prosecutor, Gerasimenko, described several of these cases at the obkom plenum of September 1951 (Pako, 147/5/11, ll.42–4). He gave the example of three chairs who were given long sentences of corrective labour for failing to supply the cattle of their farms with fodder, as well as for theft, embezzlement, etc. It should be pointed out that the expenditure of animals annually was extremely high among the socialized herds; in 1946 almost half of all strong-horned cattle, 75 percent of the hogs, and 45 percent of the sheep of these herds were sold, slaughtered, or died. This enormous expense sometimes interfered with the buildup of a stable, permanent supply of livestock. In 1946, most strong-horned cattle were either slaughtered and consumed on the kolkhoz or procured by the state; most of the hogs were sold to consumers' cooperatives or on the markets; and most of the mutton and lamb was eaten by the kolkhozniks, although more sheep and lambs perished than were consumed. The term "enemies" is used in this respect by Sadovnikov at an obkom plenum of September 1951, for example (Pako, 147/5/11, l.15).

78 Pako, 147/5/283, l.153. See table 11 for a confirmation of Kiselev's words.

79 Bol'shakov, *Sovetskaia Derevnia*, 7.

80 Pako, 147/5/10, ll.57, 137. A factory for agricultural machinery and equipment was built in Bezhetsk in 1946 to mechanize flax cultivation (*Tsentral'nyi Raion*, 563; Pako, 147/5/663, l.184). It was to produce necessary machines, but, in the first few years after it went into operation, it did not seem to have increased flax production in any meaningful way.

81 Pako, 147/5/906, ll.1–18.

82 See chapter 8 for more about the report.

83 *Tsentral'nyi Raion*, 537. Still 50.0 percent of the sown area was for grain crops in 1950, 13.8 percent for flax, 10.3 percent for potatoes, and 25.9 percent for fodder crops (*Narodnoe Khoziaistvo*, 28–9). The cultivation of grain crops during the whole period from 1945 to 1953 was done on roughly the same area of land in the oblast' (between a minimum of 637,300 hectares, reached in 1947, and a maximum of 687,900 hectares, reached in 1948; *Narodnoe Khoziaistvo*, 26–7). Until the spring of 1953, the area sown with flax was on the increase yearly: in 1945, 153,600 hectares was sown and 184,100 hectares in 1952. In 1953, the area sown decreased to 169,400 hectares. Potatoes and vegetables were grown on between 135,000 and 150,000 hectares, approximately, during the whole period. By 1950 the area sown with fodder crops had surpassed the level of 1937 and was 341,500 hectares.

84 Anokhina and Shmeleva, *Kul'tura i byt'*, 84–5; Pako, 147/5/283, l.116.
85 Pako, 147/5/2, l.81.
86 Pako, 147/5/10, ll.92–4. The neglect of the specialists (agronomists, live-stock specialists) was all the more harmful, because there were so few. One agronomist in the Central Region, which included Kalinin province, was responsible for an average of twelve kolkhozy around 1950 (Volkov, *Sovetskaia derevnia*, 139).
87 Pako, 147/3/2679, l.190b.; 147/5/906, l.15.
88 Pako, 147/41934, l.89. Again, many MTS operators were seasonally employed kolkhozniks (Volkov, *Sovetskaia derevnia*, 127–8).
89 Pako, 147/5/10, l.103.
90 More than half the kolkhozy of the USSR had a smithery in 1945 because of extensive use of work horses and reliance on many simple tools in the production process: the MTS machinery was unable to help with most agricultural tasks (Volkov, *Sovetskaia derevnia*, 89). "Rural mechanization did not have so much an all-encompassing, but more a chiselled character; it only occurred in separate operations, and an overwhelming part of the kolkhozniks worked as before by hand" (Gordon and Klopov, *Chto eto bylo?*, 70).
91 Pako, 147/4/1125, l.30b. This problem was also noticed in a Soviet publication of 1978 (Volkov, *Sovetskaia derevnia*, 36–8). Furthermore, even the tractors turned out by the factories at the time were too standardized and consequently could not be adapted to various kinds of terrain and various kinds of production (ibid., 39). Apart from that, they used much more petrol than foreign tractors (ibid., 78–9). Much of the new agricultural machinery turned out to be defective (ibid., 80).
92 *Narodnoe Khoziaistvo*, 57. Compared to 1940, machine-driven spring ploughing had increased by 26 percent and machine-driven autumn ploughing by 43 percent of the total acreage cultivated. When more machinery began to become available in Khrushchev's time, it proved to be a mixed blessing. In Udoml'ia raion, for example, sowing by tractor-driven ploughs was impossible, because the terrain had too many hillocks and the soil was riddled with stones (Ivanov, "V rodnykh," 176). Harvest combines were not of much use here either, because of stones and the irregular elevation of the soil (ibid., 177). Nonmechanized ploughing did not reach further than a depth of fifteen centimeters, approximately, but tractor ploughing, which went much deeper, encountered many more stones and consequently had to be frequently interrupted (ibid., 178). In the early 1960s, manual labour was deployed to clear the soil of these stones (ibid., 179). See also Ivanov, "Snova," 209.
93 Pako, 147/5/663, ll.49–50
94 I.e., in Vysoko, Zubtsov, Lukovnikovo, Molodoi Tud, Olenino, and Rzhev raions.

95 Pako, 147/5/36, l.109.

96 Pako, 147/5/36, l.110; 147/5/10, l.95. The director of the All-Union Flax Institute in Torzhok underlined this fact at the July 1951 obkom plenum: "It is no secret for all of us, that the kolkhozy in Kalinin oblast' harvest grain crops frequently by hand: with scythes and sickles" (Pako, 147/5/10, l.137). By 1950 in the area of Torzhok, one of the local machine tractor stations was still not as well equipped as before the war (Pako, 147/5/2, l.164). In all, according to oblispolkom chairman Sadovnikov, there were 5 percent more tractors in early 1951 than before the war in the entire province (Pako, 147/5/2, l.171). In early 1947, the oblast' had had only 2,238 tractors, compared to 3,360 before the war (Pako, 147/4/528, l.30b.). Similarly, in neighbouring Iaroslavl' province, the prewar level of technology had yet to be reached by 1950 (Volkov, *Sovetskaia derevnia*, 83). The number of 30 percent given to the Central Committee more or less confirms the above numbers for 1950; therefore it is even more remarkable – and doubtful – that the mechanization of agricultural production had increased substantially by 1953.

97 Pako, 147/5/663, ll.51, 54, 194. MTS workers were often welcomed because of their skills in operating machinery (Volkov, *Sovetskaia derevnia*, 130–1).

98 Pako, 147/5/663, l.56; Zelenin, *Obshchestvenno*, 226; Zhuravlev, *XX s'ezd KPSS*, 125–6: the machine tractor stations were finally abolished in 1958.

99 See, e.g., Pako, 147/5/2, l.172; Zelenin, *Obshchestvenno*, 42; Fainsod, *How Russia is Ruled*, 454. The function was abolished by the September Plenum of the Central Committee in 1953 (Zelenin, *Obshchestvenno*, 58). According to R.F. Miller, the MTS politotdel returned only between 1949 and 1952 (Miller, "The *Politotdel*," 477).

100 Notice also the predictions about this in the 1920s among Soviet rural scholars: "On the basis of their examination, in 1925 the Organization-Production scholars declared that the unique properties of the family farm to which they had earlier drawn attention would permit the small-scale farm to withstand the process of rural capitalization; indeed, they asserted, over time there would take place a marked transfer of lands from capitalist to family farming. The implications of this position were clear: the Soviet rural sector would not evolve to capitalism, but would for the foreseeable future remain dependent upon the small commodity producer" (Solomon, "Rural Scholars and Cultural Revolution," 139).

101 Mehnert, *The Anatomy*, 267.

102 *Tsentralnyi Raion*, 535, 558–60; Ivanov, "V rodnykh," 176–7.

103 In the 1960s it began to dawn upon the authorities that perhaps agriculture would benefit from specialization. Kolkhoz director E.A. Petrov

is quoted as stating that only dairy farming and flax cultivation could really be profitable under the natural conditions of northern Kalinin province (L. Ivanov, "Snova," 189).

104 Beznin, "Krest'ianskaia bazarnaia torgovlia," 69.

105 Kerblay, *Du mir aux agrovilles*, 333, table 1, 334, 337–8, 340. Moreover, urban workers purchased on the kolkhoz markets in the early 1950s more than 50 percent of the foodstuffs that were eaten by their families. In Rzhev in 1953, 84 percent of the food sold on the kolkhoz markets was produced on the private plots of the kolkhozniks, and only 16 percent products on the socialized farms (Beznin, "Krest'ianskaia bazarnaia torgovlia," 72).

106 Cf. Lorenz, *Sozialgeschichte*, 208. Most of the taxation of the private plot had been by way of obligatory delivery to the state of part of the private produce (meat, milk, eggs – as was reported by M.M. Kozenkova-Pavlova in the survey). On the taxation of the plot and animals, see Fainsod, *How Russia is Ruled*, 454–5. The utter failure of socialized agriculture after almost twenty-five years of collective farming was at least partially admitted in the Central Committee resolution of 22 March 1952. During the war, the share of the private plots in grain production in the Soviet Union as a whole ranged from 12 percent to 19 percent; in potatoes their share rose from 65 percent to 75 percent (Volkov, *Sovetskaia derevnia*, 51). "The increase of production, so characteristic for industry, failed to happen in the agrarian economy both in the 1930s and in the 1940s–1950s" (Gordon and Klopov, *Chto eto bylo?*, 69). "[Collectivization] needs to be recognized as an economic and social catastrophy" (ibid., 77; also cf. 73–4, table 5, 75.

107 Altrichter describes how the households of larger families in the countryside in the 1920s were indeed often somewhat better off than the smaller households (Altrichter, *Die Bauern*, 83–4; see also Kerblay, *Du mir aux agrovilles*, 43–4).

108 Cf. Lel'chuk, "Industrializatsiia," 354. "The transition of Soviet society to a modern urban and industrial culture did not occur in the years of the first Five Year Plans, [but] it took place two to three decades later." (Gordon and Klopov, *Chto eto bylo?*, 97)

109 *Tsentral'nyi Raion*, 531, 535–6.

110 Ibid., 535, 537. A later source does not fully agree with these numbers and places them at a slightly higher level for certain operations around this time (*Kalininskaia oblast' za 50 let*, 63).

111 Kerblay, *Du mir aux agrovilles*, 371: "As much as this fragile border will remain inviolate [between the authorities and the family], we may hope that goodness, compassion, tolerance, those values which give society genuine humane traits, will not be extinguished."

112 Cf. Fitzpatrick, *Stalin's Peasants*, 254–6.

113   Cf. Jackson's definition ("Peasant Political Movements," 273; see also the discussion of collectivization in chapter 1).

114   Pako, 147/5/663, ll.117, 128. See also Abramov's description of the kolkhozniks' difficulty in providing for their private cows (*The New Life*, 99–100).

115   Korytkov, *Kommunist. Khoziaistvo. Reforma*, 65; although this work was based on a sociological survey of the 1960s, the kolkhozniks' division of labour cannot have changed fundamentally in the intermediate period. Women almost exclusively performed all household tasks (except perhaps that of chopping firewood).

116   Gordon and Klopov, *Chto eto bylo?*, 86.

117   Pako, 147/5/10, l.62. A varied arsenal of propagandistic means was used, but the "moral" stimuli did not result in noticeable improvements (Volkov, *Sovetskaia derevnia*, 178–92, describes the socialist emulation movements that were launched to stimulate agricultural production). As the report on the exodus from the countryside shows – see chapter 8 – only in late 1952 were the authorities finally prepared to capitulate to the idea that production would increase only if more material stimuli were offered.

118   It might be true that all kolkhozy possessed radios by the early 1960s, but, considering that several small villages composed one kolkhoz, some people were able to listen to the radio only if they visited the kolkhoz centre. It is probably correct that all kolkhozy had the use of telephones by this time; it should be remembered, nevertheless, that this does not mean that every village had a telephone line, and very few kolkhozniks owned a private telephone (cf. Anokhina and Shmeleva, *Kul'tura i byt'*, 319–20; *Tsentral'nyi Raion*, 526).

CHAPTER EIGHT

1   Mann, *The History of Germany*, 52.

2   Pako, 147/5/906, l.1.

3   Pako, 147/4/63, l.132. The full letter is to be found in Pako, 147/4/63, ll.132–5. Apart from the households that were to be transferred to Sakhalin in 1946, already in 1945, 150 kolkhoz households had been moved to Karelia, another recently acquired territory of the Soviet Union (Pako, 147/3/2701, l.202-3). These kinds of moves were made attractive by offering larger private plots of land (in Karelia from 0.6 to 1 hectare per household), payments in cash, and freedom from taxation (in Karelia freedom from taxation for the years 1946–48 was offered). In 1948, 600,000 kolkhozniks in the USSR were recruited for work in industry, 1 million worked in various seasonal occupations (logging, peatwinning) and an additional million were recruited into the State

Labour Reserves (Volkov, *Sovetskaia derevnia*, 109; on the State Labour Reserves, see Heller and Nekrich, *Utopia in Power*, 321; Fainsod, *How Russia is Ruled*, 348–9).

4 Pako, 147/5/906, l.1. See table 6. One document (Pako, 147/3/1966, ll.39–390b.) reported a mere 1,300 kolkhoz households more in July 1946 than on 1 January 1949, even though between 1946 and 1949 the population in the kolkhozy grew with the return of demobilized soldiers. They returned most of the time to already existing households and did not set up one on their own. Perhaps an exodus had occurred in the difficult period of the fall, winter, and spring of 1946–47 (on 1 July 1946, there seem to have been 5,000 households more in the collective farms than half a year later, on 1 January 1947: cf. Volkov, "Zasukha," 15; Zima, "Golod v Rossii 1946–1947 godov," 43). However, the most likely explanation is a mistake in the arithmetic here. Cf. also Karasev, "Agriculture in Pskov Oblast'," 307: 162,000 able-bodied kolkhozniks lived in Pskov oblast' in 1947; there were only 99,000 left at the end of 1953. The postwar exodus was an "All-Union" phenomenon, according to a Soviet publication on agriculture in the immediate postwar period (Volkov, *Sovetskaia derevnia*, 47, 108–9).

5 Pako, 147/5/906, l.2; 147/5/283, l.271. See also the remarks on the town of Kashin in the second section of chapter 4. A significant number of people engaged in all kinds of work outside the official economy. They were described as "people of the, so to say, free professions, hanging about without any business at the market or around the market" (Pako, 147/5/283, l.272). This opinion was shared by several party chiefs (Pako, 147/5/283, l.295).

6 Pako, 147/5/283, ll.289, 296.

7 Anokhina and Shmeleva, *Kul'tura i byt'*, 66. They probably went to Moscow province, too, if they had the chance.

8 Pako, 147/5/906, l.3. The report is to be found in Pako, 147/5/906, ll.1–18.

9 147/5/906, l.4. In Likhoslavl' raion the number grew from 442 (total kolkhoz population 16,829; adults able to work 6,202 – thus the 442 formed around 7 percent of the adult work force) in January 1950, to 869 in November 1952 (total kolkhov population, 12,186; adults able to work, 4,299: about 20 percent!), and in Kirov raion from 354 (total kolkhov population, 25,920; adults able to work, 10,658: around 3 percent) to 736 (total kolkhov population, 18,090; adults able to work, 7,531: almost 10 percent). Likhoslavl' raion had thirty-two kolkhozy in 1952, twenty-seven of which had party organizations, with a total of 271 Communists; apart from that, still four territorial party organizations existed, with a combined total of forty-four members and candidates (Pako, 147/5/426, l.102).

10 Pako, 147/5/906, ll.5–6. Many women went apparently, via the labour selection (orgnabor), to work in the peat enterprises in the summer months in order to earn money for a dowry, a habit which proved to be tenaciously observed and had survived against all odds (see Anokhina and Shmeleva, *Kul'tura i byt'*, 67). In general, both the lumber and peat industries worked with a large contingent of seasonal workers: in the winter of 1948 the lumber industry of Maksatikha raion had 859 permanent workers and 3,200 seasonal workers, most of whom were kolkhozniks (Pako, 147/4/1125, l.129).

11 Illegal hiring was criticized, for example, at the eighth oblast' party conference (Pako, 147/5/2, l.125). Cf. Buckley, "The Myth of Managed Migration," 905, 908.

12 Pako, 147/5/906, l.6.

13 Pako, 147/5/906, l.7. N.A. Kotov said in the survey that in 1951, after his three years of army service, he did not return to his native village in the raion of Novotorzhok, where he had worked before on the kolkhoz. He began to work as a metal worker on the cotton-fibre kombinat Proletarka.

14 Pako, 147/5/906, l.7.

15 Pako, 147/5/906, l.5. According to these statistics, very few people in both raions in those nearly three years had been arrested: in Likhoslavl' raion, 80 had been arrested, in Kirov raion, 103, that is, compared to the total able-bodied population (above 12 years old) of respectively 7,240 and 12,911 on 1 January 1950, respectively 1.1 percent and 0.8 percent had been arrested. If these numbers are correct, and there is not much reason to doubt them, then the arrests in the early 1950s in the countryside, as a percentage of the able-bodied population, were considerably fewer than in, for example, 1935–37. In Likhoslavl' raion, in the thirty-four months from January 1950 to November 1952, of 3,076 able-bodied people over the age of twelve, 963, or 31 percent, left samovol'no (without authorization); in Kirov raion these numbers were respectively 4,079 and 1,440, or 35 percent.

16 Fainsod explains in detail the manner in which trudodni were awarded (*How Russia is Ruled*, 461–2). Apparently, the apparat of the People's Commissariat of Agriculture hoped in 1946 that at the end of the Fourth Five Year Plan (1946–1950), the average kolkhoznik would be able to receive five kilograms of grain, at least, per trudoden' (Volkov, *Sovetskaia derevnia*, 61). Even a Brezhnevite account had to admit that these estimates were completely out of touch with the real situation of Soviet agriculture (ibid.). The procurement prices of grain, potatoes, and other products that had to be delivered to the state as part of the obligatory deliveries were far below the cost of production of these crops (ibid., 268–9).

17 In February 1946 N. Gur'ianov, the head of the kolkhoz organizational department of the agricultural department of the oblispolkom, described in *Proletarskaia Pravda* how the income of a kolkhoz was supposed to be distributed – according to the 1935 Ustav (*PP* 7962, 20 February 1946, 2; for a comprehensive overview of legislation affecting Soviet agriculture during the 1930s, see Fitzpatrick, *Stalin's Peasants*, xvii–xx; cf. the discussion of collectivization in chapter 1). On the size of the obligatory deliveries to the state and the payment of the MTS by the kolkhozy, see Volkov, *Sovetskaia derevnia*, 263–83.

18 The annual average amount of trudodni earned by each household in certain years is known: e.g., in 1950 this amount was 504, and in 1953 only 473 (Pako, 147/5/906, ll.2, 7–8). In 1951, on average per trudoden' a kolkhoznik received 85 kopecks, 765 grams of cereals harvested on his or her own kolkhoz, 704 grams of potatoes and vegetables, and 777 grams of hay and straw and, in addition, the kolkhozniks were allotted 225 grams of wheat, received for delivered flax. If a household worked on average 500 trudodni per year, which is a reasonable assumption provided the above numbers for 1950 and 1953 are correct, it thus received, in 1951, 425 rubles, 382.5 kilograms of grain, 352 kilograms of potatoes and vegetables, 388.5 kilograms of hay and straw, and 112.5 kilograms of wheat. The average household in 1951 consisted of three people. Cf. Volkov, *Sovetskaia derevnia*, 457, table 68, which shows that, in 1950 in the entire Central Region outside the Black Earth area the cash income of the trudoden' was even less on average (38 kopecks). Part of this income was withheld for the wheat; see Pako, 147/5/906, l.9; see also table 6. In 1949, the average amount of trudodni for each able-bodied peasant was 301, and in 1950, 325 (Pako, 147/5/36, l.112). In the USSR as a whole the average amount of trudodni earned by each kolkhoznik was 250 in 1945, 239 in 1946 (although in areas where the drought did not hit as hard, such as Kalinin oblast', the amount actually rose), and 243 in 1947 (Volkov, *Sovetskaia derevnia*, 193–4). According to a report from Konovalov to Malenkov, in 1950 at the advanced kolkhoz Komintern of Kalinin raion, for each trudoden' were paid one ruble, 2,000 grams of grain, 6,000 grams of potatoes, 1,600 grams of vegetables, and 1,000 grams of fodder, i.e., double the amount of grain, ten times the amount of potatoes and vegetables, but little more money or fodder than the average of 1951 (Pako, 147/5/36, l.6). The small amount of fodder was probably a reflection of the generally difficult situation with fodder crops in the province. Although on average kolkhozniks in 1949 made less trudodni than in 1950 (respectively 301 and 325, see above), they received much more payment in kind per trudoden' (Pako, 147/5/36, l.113). In 1948 the overall picture seems to have been better, but then 1948 was the best agricultural year after the war, according to most indicators (see

table 25). Even though 1948 was a good year, many still lived in miserable circumstances as a result of the low remuneration of the trudoden', and First Party Secretary Vorontsov felt thus obliged to say in early 1949: "The task of the party organization consists of liquidating the violations of the rural artel' Statute, increasing the harvest yields, attaining a sharp increase of the value of the trudoden', and in this way improving the material welfare of the kolkhozniks, all on the basis of the strengthening of the socialist farming of the kolkhozy, in the fastest amount of time" (Pako, 147/4/1495, l.15).

19   E.g., Adamova-Sliozberg, "Put'," 64, 82. Cf., too, the official rations in the Kolyma camps in the 1940s as given by Conquest: for 100 percent fulfillment of the norm convicts received 800 grams of bread per day, or perhaps 930 grams (*The Great Terror*, 327, 333–4). For less than 70 percent fulfillment they were allotted no more than 500 grams. Conquest says about this last rate, "This was just above starvation level; any further reduction to 300 grams (as a punitive measure) meant certain death" (ibid., 327). The bread ration was complemented by some soup, 100 grams of salt fish, and 60 grams of groats (ibid., 333–4). In December 1941, in besieged Leningrad, the starvation level of rationing for workers was maximally 350 grams of bread per day.

20   Pako, 147/5/906, l.9.

21   Pako, 147/5/906, l.8.; in 1950, hay was given in only 34 percent of the total amount of kolkhozy; in 1951, in 70 percent; for straw the corresponding percentages were 29 percent and 16 percent.

22   Adverse weather and the amalgamation led to a perhaps lower-than-usual production during the early 1950s (cf. Medvedev, *Soviet Agriculture*, 143–4, 154). Problems for the individual kolkhoznik were exacerbated by the especially middling potato harvest in 1951.

23   Anokhina and Shmeleva, *Kul'tura i byt'*, 45; Medvevdev, *Soviet Agriculture*, 155–6; Volkov, *Sovetskaia derevnia*, 294–5. In 1940, the socialized sector of kolkhozy and sovkhozy in the USSR produced only 28 percent of the meat, 23 percent of the milk, and 61 percent of the wool in the Union; in 1948, 17 percent of the milk, 25 percent of the meat, and 7 percent of the eggs; in 1950, 33 percent of the meat, 25 percent of the milk, and 79 percent of the wool; and in 1951, 29 percent of the milk and 39 percent of the meat (Volkov, *Sovetskaia derevnia*, 246, 259–60). Private plots, meanwhile, provided the Soviet population in general with foodstuffs, particularly livestock products and potatoes (Kerblay, *Du mir aux agrovilles*, 182). In the five-year period 1981–85 the average share of the production of personal plots in the total agricultural production was still 24.2 percent for the RSFSR and 26.0 percent for the USSR, according to Soviet sources; the personal cattle in this period on average yielded 30 percent of the total production of meat in the RSFSR and 32 percent of

that of the USSR; for milk the respective figures were 26 percent for the RSFSR, and 29 percent for the USSR; for eggs, respectively 24 percent and 30 percent; and for wool 20 percent and 24 percent (see *Soiuznye respubliki*, 161, 172).

24 See the last section of chapter 4.

25 Pako, 147/5/906, l.11. In 1949, 163,600 tons of fodder had been distributed among the kolkhozniks as remuneration for the trudodni; in 1950, 79,500 tons; and in 1951, 91,500 tons. Before 1950, the number of personal cattle per household had never been large. Vorontsov noticed in March 1947 that, on average, for every 100 kolkhoz households the kolkhozniks had 178 head of livestock: that is, not even two cows, pigs, sheep, or goats combined per household; this was, of course, an exceptionally lean year (Pako, 147/4/528, l.60b.). Altrichter remarks that in the late 1950s the kolkhoz household still derived more than 90 percent of most of its basic foodstuffs from the private plot and cattle: this was the case with vegetables, potatoes, fruit, milk, eggs, and meat (*Die Bauern*, 196). Even the February 1947 Plenum could not ignore the importance of the "private sector" for Soviet agriculture and took measures to help kolkhozniks who had difficulty resurrecting or maintaining their personal plot and cattle (Volkov, *Sovetskaia derevnia*, 253–4). Later that year, in August, credits were announced by the Council of Ministers for those individual kolkhozniks who were without a cow and wanted to buy one. However, these measures seem to have remained without much effect.

26 Pako, 147/5/906, l.11. In October 1953 Kiselev mentioned the decrease in personal cattle as a main cause for the exodus from the countryside. A mere 46.6 percent had a personal cow in January 1953 (Pako, 147/5/663, l.11).

27 Pako, 147/5/906, l.12.

28 Ibid. This explanation was confirmed by Anokhina and Shmeleva, *Kul'tura i byt'*, 66.

29 Pako, 147/5/906, l.12.

30 Pako, 147/5/906, ll.12–13.

31 Pako, 147/5/906, l.13.

32 Ibid.

33 Pako, 147/5/906, ll.1, 18.

34 Pako, 147/5/906, ll.14–18.

35 Ibid.

36 Ibid.

37 A blunt solution to this problem was perhaps found by Khrushchev when he prohibited nonagricultural workers from owning either plots of land or cattle.

38 Pako, 147/5/906, ll.14–18; see table 26.

39 Cf. Malenkov's analysis of the problems in agriculture at the Central Committee Plenum of July 1953 (Stickle, *The Beria Affair*, 177).

40 Cf. Kaplan, *The Party*, 145, chapter 3.

41 Cf. Karasev, "Agriculture in Pskov Oblast'," 307.

42 Volkogonov, *Stalin: Triumph and Tragedy*, 529, 570–1. Molotov denied that there was anything wrong with Stalin's health just before his death, but he was no longer part of Stalin's inner circle in the last months of Stalin's life (*Sto sorok besed*, 327; cf. the final section of chapter 8).

43 Pako, 147/6/8, l.80. Torzhok raion was mentioned as a positive example, performing better than most raions (Pako, 147/6/8, l.128).

44 In the RSFSR the proportion of urban dwellers rose from 33 percent in 1939 to 74 percent in 1989 (Kozlov, "Dinamika," 6). In absolute terms, the number of rural dwellers in the RSFSR was more than halved between 1926 and 1989 (ibid., table 2, 7). During the 1980s in the Soviet Union millions of peasants still moved to the cities (Laqueur, *The Dream*, 55–6).

45 The anthropologists Anokhina and Shmeleva noticed, though, that the incidence of departure did vary. They suggested that the likelihood of migration depended on the level of material well-being of the kolkhoz and the distance to an urban centre (Anokhina and Shmeleva, *Kul'tura i byt'*, 65). According to a statement of 1951 of the raikom secretary of Kirov raion, Pontiakov, even Communists had been leaving on their own initiative (Pako, 147/5/105, l.38). One custom particular to Kalinin province facilitated the idea of departure for the kolkhozniks: the tradition of seasonal work away from the farm (otkhodnichestvo). In October 1953, Kiselev complained about the lack of action of local authorities towards those who left their kolkhozy to work somewhere in a nonagricultural occupation (Pako, 147/5/663, l.195).

46 Pako, 147/5/10, l.33; in this case it was Kalinin gorkom secretary Cherkasov who was out for the kill. "One may therefore conclude that the [adverse] natural surroundings insufficiently explain the mediocre results of Soviet agriculture" (Kerblay, *Du mir aux agrovilles*, 233).

47 Heller and Nekrich, *Utopia in Power*, 260; Medvedev, *Soviet Agriculture*, 95; Borisov, "Stalin", 478.

48 Anokhina and Shmeleva, *Kul'tura i byt'*, 345. This was one of the promises that were supposed to materialize in a socialist society (cf. Marx and Engels, *The Communist Manifesto*, 105; see Kerblay, *Du mir aux agrovilles*, 231, 273–4). Djilas remarked about it in 1957: "It was believed that the differences between cities and villages, between intellectual and physical labor, would slowly disappear; instead these differences have increased" (Djilas, *The New Class*, 37). Although the life of the peasantry had definitely acquired some urban traits, urban life had "ruralized" too, owing to the enormous influx of peasants into the towns (see Gordon and Klopov, *Chto eto bylo?*, 133). The attraction of the

towns led to the desertion of many of the villages in Kalinin oblast *after 1960* (Kerblay, *Du mir aux agrovilles*, 249). In Brezhnev's time, 25 percent of peasant households consisted of one person.

49 Arutjunjan, *La Structure*, table 75, 320–1, 345.

50 Pako, 147/5/659, l.4.

51 Pako, 147/5/659, l.7.

52 For events in Moscow, cf., for example, Nekrasov, "Final," 381–415.

53 Pako, 147/5/660, ll.10–11, 93.

54 Pako, 147/5/673, l.47.

55 The full transcript is to be found in Pako, 147/5/662, ll.5–96. Apart from the obkom membership, the candidates and members of the gorkom of Kalinin were present, and 746 other party aktiv.

56 Pako, 147/5/662, l.21.

57 Pako, 147/5/662, ll.6–8. In the speech of the head of the Pedagogical Institute, Polianskii, the first criticism of the inflated role of individuals was uttered (Pako, 147/5/662, ll.33–4).

58 Pako, 147/5/662, ll.9–11. However, as Matveev, the gorkom secretary of Vyshnii Volochek, remarked, the obkomburo itself appointed and dismissed the local leaders of raion and town departments of the MVD without involving or explaining to the raikoms and gorkoms the reasons for these actions (Pako, 147/5/662, l.29).

59 One example is the speech of the new MVD chief (Pako, 147/5/662, ll.78–80); another, the remarks of factory director Alekhin (Pako, 147/5/662, l.86). In this way, they foreshadowed the Brezhnevite silence about Stalin's crimes. Baranov (Pako, 147/5/662, l.21) and Polianskii (Pako, 147/5/662, l.32) equated Beria with Zinoviev, Bukharin, or Trotsky.

60 Cf., for example. Heller and Nekrich, *Utopia in Power*, 514–515.

61 Pako, 147/5/663, ll.9–11. The investment by the state in agriculture rose by 41 percent in 1954, compared to the previous year (Arutiunian, "Osobennosti," 396). In the years 1951–53 capital investments in agriculture were around one-fifth of capital investments in industry, while in the period 1954–58 they amounted to around one-third of those in industry.

62 Pako, 147/5/663, l.11.

63 Pako, 147/5/663, l.13; also cf. Zhuravlev, *XX S'ezd*, 109.

64 Pako, 147/5/663, ll.18–19. See tables 11 and 25. In 1949 one cow produced, on average, 1,139 litres of milk annually; one sheep, 1,640 grams of wool; and one chicken, 46 eggs. In 1952 these numbers were respectively 890 litres of milk; 1,300 grams of wool; and 28 eggs. More cows died in the first eight months of 1953 than in the same period of 1952 (Pako, 147/5/663, l.20).

65 Pako, 147/5/663, ll.20–2. More than 20 percent of the total amount of

livestock (excluding horses or fowl) was "consumed" by the collective farmers in 1952 (Pako, 147/5/663, l.20).

66 Pako, 147/5/663, l.29; *Narodnoe Khoziaistvo*, 54. State farms have been almost invisible in the previous account, and for good reason: there were merely forty-four sovkhozy by 1953 in the province. They owned about 14 percent of all pigs, 2 percent of bovines, 1.7 percent of cows, 1.7 percent of horses, and none of the sheep in the province. Stalinist hypocrisy reaches unprecedented heights in a book published in 1952 on one of the local state farms, the "Molotov" sovkhoz of Torzhok raion, supposedly a phenomenal success (Trudoliubov, *Sovkhoz imeni Molotova*).

67 Pako, 147/5/663, l.30. In 1949, and again on 12 April 1952, state prices for flax deliveries had increased. The latter increase was by way of a res-olution of the USSR Council of Ministers, titled "On measures to lift flax cultivation" (Volkov, *Sovetskaia derevnia*, 270; Pako, 147/5/283, l.249). If they were to be paid as little for it as for grain, the authorities appar-ently realized that the kolkhozniks would try to avoid flax cultivation as much as possible. Because it was not edible, the crop as such had less appeal than grain. Part of the latter could at least be used for personal consumption, legal or not. The yield per hectare of flax fibre was, on average, between 235 and 237 kilogrammes in 1948 and 1949, and in 1952, only 219 kilograms, while the yield of flax seed had decreased three times in 1952 in comparison with 1948 (cf. table 25; the averages for 1948 and 1949 in the table are slightly higher, which probably has to do with the fact that the crop was measured "standing in the field").

68 Pako, 147/5/663, l.33–4; *Tsentralnyi Raion*, 219; for a description of the problems of flax cultivation, see also Ivanov, "V rodnykh," 196.

69 Pako, 147/5/663, ll.40–1. In 1952, a slightly better year for potato growing than the previous two years, the total potato harvest of the oblast' amounted to 59.2 percent of the result in 1940. In the four raions of Kalinin, Vyshnii Volochek, Bezhetsk, and Rzhev the vegetable harvest was between 13.8 percent (Rzhev raion) and 54.8 percent (Kalinin raion) of the 1940 level. These raions had a large share in the cultivation of potatoes and vegetables, due to their proximity to towns, which had a high demand for such crops.

70 Pako, 147/5/663, ll.42–3, 45–6. In 1940, 21.5 percent of the oblast' potato harvest was delivered to the state; in 1950, 23 percent; in 1951, 26 percent; and in 1952, 22 percent. For vegetables the proportion for 1940 is unknown, because the total vegetable harvest in 1940 seems to be unknown, but the deliveries to the state in 1940 had been less than in 1950 and 1951. In 1950, 49 percent of the total vegetable harvest was procured by the state, in 1951, 79 percent and in 1952, 96 percent!.

71 Pako, 147/5/663, l.118. See also Zhuravlev, *XX s'ezd*, 110. The reforms

undoubtedly improved the material well-being of the kolkhozy, as Abramov describes (*The New Life*, 67–9). In 1958 the kolkhozes' income came, as before, mainly from sales of flax (49 percent of the total), and strong-horned cattle – particularly dairy farming – (31 percent) (*Tsentral'nyi Raion*, 534). However, in 1955, after the increase of procurement prices after Stalin's death, the total income of all of the kolkhozy of the province was 3.4 times as high as in 1950, while the number of kolkhoz households had decreased in these five years by 33,900! Although the value of the trudoden' was much higher in 1954 and 1955, the yield per hectare of grain, the milk production per cow (1,305 litres in 1955), and the production of meat in Torzhok raion were far below the targets (Pako, 147/6/8, l.80).

72 Pako, 147/6/8, ll.88, 122. In 1956, the elderly and single-person households were entitled to no more than 0.25 hectares, rural employees and blue-collar workers to a plot of 0.10 to 0.15 hectares, and teachers to 0.25 hectares.

73 Pako, 147/6/8, ll.123–4. Goriachev stated that Tver' guberniia had 1,700,000 sheep in 1916 and Kalinin oblast' had 1,900,000 in 1937, while on 1 January 1951, 545,000 sheep were counted on the collective farms of the province; in 1953, 500,000, and on 1 January 1956, 280,000 (Pako, 147/6/8, l.123). In 1962, Leonid Ivanov noticed that many collective farms still experienced shortages of fodder for their livestock (Ivanov, "V rodnykh," 186).

74 Pako, 147/6/8, ll.124–7. By 1962, kolkhoz directors continued to complain about the oppressive regulations for their production plans by higher authorities (Ivanov, "V rodnykh," 189). The regime persisted in looking at personal initiative with suspicion.

75 E.g., Djilas: "Feeling itself sufficiently strong to destroy the cult of its creator, or the creator of the system – Stalin – it simultaneously gave the death blow to its own ideal basis" (*The New Class*, 161); Malia: "partial recognition of the truth only undermined the system" ("A Fatal Logic," 90); Odom: "According to totalitarianism's internal logic, the dictator has to sustain a bloody domestic struggle to keep power highly centralized – *or to risk letting the system decay and eventually collapse*" ("The Pluralist Image," 102; Odom's italics). The lead up to this speech and its rather half-baked contents are discussed in Zhuravlev, *XX s'ezd*, in particular 37–46, and in Naumov, "K istorii sekretnogo doklada."

76 Pako, 147/5/662, l.3.

77 Pako, 147/6/50, ll.1–3. The town of Bologoe had about 22,000 inhabitants at the time.

78 Pako, 147/6/50, ll.6, 8, 36.

79 Ibid., ll.1–3, 6, 8, 18–19. The question on the continued presence of Malenkov among the party leaders indicates that perhaps Khrushchev's

success in the political struggle with the other Stalinist leaders was aided by the speech, which was a possible motive for its delivery. The question about the documents on Eikhe, Kedrov, and other "comrades" could still be posed today by researchers.

80 Pako, 147/6/50, ll.19, 39.

81 Army officer V.Ia. Semiachko echoed the feelings of Samarova when he quoted his grandfather K.N. Semiachko on the difference between Imperial Russia and the USSR: "Rascals and drunks were neither strong men under the tsar, nor under the Bolsheviks. No one will be equal nor can be so." Another person who could make comparisons was A.G. Murtsovkina (born in 1903), who felt that in 1917 serfdom had been reintroduced. She worked as a "girl Friday," doing odd jobs, much of which was loading and unloading of heavy cargoes, brought by the boats along the Volga, for instance. She was of the opinion that everything had been better under the Tsar.

82 Khrushchev attempted to turn things around, in particular with his promises (at the Twenty-First Party Congress in 1959 and in the new Party Program of the CPSU in 1961) of the imminent arrival of Communism (e.g., Zhuravlev, *XX s'ezd*, 220–1, 229–38).

CONCLUSION

1 For this term, see Malia, "A Fatal Logic," 89: "the First Five-Year Plan – which created a permanent, institutionalized War Communism."

2 Cf. the more specific effect on Soviet society of the existence of the Gulag Archipelago in the opinion of Solzhenitsyn (*The Gulag*, vols. 3–4, 632–53).

3 In Kalinin oblast' the war was responsible for casualties whose number might have surpassed that of the whole of Great Britain (260,000) in World War II (see Laqueur, *Europe since Hitler*, 15).

4 It would seem, however, that these dismissals were more the result of political infighting in Moscow (certainly in the case of Vorontsov) than of poor economic management.

5 Since August 1991 Western researchers have had more opportunities to investigate the fate of the factory workers. It can be hoped that an avalanche of publications on the subject of the postwar industrial labour force will appear in the coming years similar to those that in recent years have appeared on factory workers between 1917 and 1941 (Ward, *Russia's Cotton Workers*, is only one example). Similarly, the destruction of the environment has been little explored in this work. Environmental problems were not recognized as such under Stalin. As a consequence, one can find only sparse information on the condition of nature in the records. Perhaps the malaria plague resulting from the opening of the

Moskovskoe More can be approached as an environmental problem
created by human beings. The prohibition on the unrestricted felling of
trees was a measure aimed at protecting nature. But it was not so much
the environment in Kalinin oblast' that suffered under Stalin: there were
hardly any polluting cars, there were few extremely contaminating factories, few chemical fertilizers, and so on. The human beings who lived in
the province were sacrificed instead.

6 "History, especially of its own – the Communist – period, does not exist"
   (Djilas, *The New Class*, 136).

7 Recently, Iu. Igritskii remarked rightfully that the regime might indeed
   have aimed for total control over society, but that this was unattainable
   in practice ("Snova," 11). Small pockets of life remained outside the
   control of the authorities, such as the family, certain habits and traditions, crime, and the innermost thoughts of the people.

8 See Zubkova, "Obshchestvennaia," 4.

9 For Khrushchev's criticism of Malenkov, see Zhuravlev, *XX s'ezd*, 25–7.

10 Cf., for example, the impact of the process in two different areas, one in
   Italy (Terni) and the other in the United States (Harlan), described by
   Portelli as follows: "In both places, a thriving traditional, rural culture
   was suddenly brought face-to-face with full-blown industrial development; there was hardly any gradual process of adaptation, or time for
   change and growth from within. So one theme of this book is the inter-
   play of traditional cultures and industrialization – the uses of traditional
   culture by working people as they struggled with and tried to make themselves at home in a world which they built but, to a large extent, they did
   not choose to make" (*The Death*, xiii).

11 Marx and Engels, *Communist Manifesto*, 105.

12 Cf. the opinion of Iu. Borisov: "The generation of the people, that had
   endured and won the war had a number of new traits in comparison
   with the prewar one. It was in the field of social relations both more
   independent, and, as a rule, more literate ... The people emerged from the
   war with a different psychology and different ideas than that with which
   they had entered it. And although after the war the former processes
   resumed once more, life definitely demanded changes, but the clear recognition of this took place significantly later" (Borisov, "Stalin," 482). In
   other words, the leadership displayed a startling absence of imagination
   to cash in on this changed attitude and the expectations among the population that resulted from it.

13 Cf. Mehnert's observation: "the concrete desires of the Soviet people are
   concerned not with a distant past or a distant future, but with the reali-
   ties and experience of the present" (*The Anatomy*, 265). Of course, that
   only proves that Russians, Ukrainians, etc., are in no way different from
   other human beings.

14 Conquest argues that the Ezhovshchina was stopped for strictly demographic reasons (*The Great Terror*, 433–5).

15 See Dunham, *In Stalin's Time*, 3–23.

16 Cf. Zubkova, "Obshchestvennaia," 63–102, esp. 79.

17 Lenin – when he had already decided that the Bolsheviks should take power – wrote in late September or early October 1917: "Yet we are told that the 240,000 members of the Bolshevik Party will not be able to govern Russia, govern her in the interests of the poor and against the rich" ("Can the Bolsheviks Retain State Power?" 111).

18 Certainly, the human capacity to overlook, ignore, or forget certain unpleasant phenomena is immense (see Turchin, *Inertsiia Strakha*, 21). Some Russians might not have noticed (or might not have wanted to notice or remember) the omnipresent activities of the NKVD. It is not impossible that in the countryside after collectivization some did not experience any acts of oppression by the authorities, except for prosecution for what would be considered crimes even in the contemporary Western world. And the Great Purge, owing to the highly biased and sparse information about its proceedings, may have been interpreted, as official propaganda proclaimed, as a just retaliation against culpable troublemakers.

APPENDIX

1 *Gosudarstvennyi arkhiv kalininskoi oblasti*, 7; *Tverskoi tsentr*, 6.

2 *Gosudarstvennyi arkhiv kalininskoi oblasti*, 11–12.

3 Its importance is described by the local archivist Leont'eva ("Dokumenty po istorii," 137). It seems possible that the State Archive of Tver' has more evidence on events before World War II, particularly on collectivization, as is indicated in an article written by the head of the archive, M.A. Il'in ("Raskrytie," 11–15). Much of the political repression from the second half of the 1930s and after remains hidden in the documents that can be found here. In the materials preserved by the State Archive, indications of the real state of affairs are buried among an enormous amount of bureaucratic trivia. In a sense it proves Volkogonov's point that "[i]n fact the course that Stalin took after the war was a course of *total bureaucracy*." (*Triumf i tragediia*, 2:2, 21).

4 Fainsod, *Smolensk under Soviet Rule*, 93.

5 Fainsod, *How Russia is Ruled*, 184–6; *Smolensk under Soviet Rule*, 90: "The transcendent position of the obkom bureau vis-à-vis the oblast congress of soviets and the oblispolkom is unmistakable. The obkom bureau laid down the policies and drafted the directives which guided their actions; it initiated the key appointments which were subsequently ratified and approved by the oblast congress of soviets and the oblispolkom.

The secretariat of the obkom paralleled the governmental departments; it intervened constantly to direct, scold, and prod the administrative organs subject to its supervision."

6 Rybakov, *Tridtsat' piatyi*, 262–3.

7 See, e.g., Stickle, *The Beria Affair*, 5–6.

8 Personal interview with V.A. Feoktistov, Tver', summer of 1992.

9 Pako, 147/4/1495, l.74. A part of the oblast prokuror's speech made at this meeting, involving a quote of Malenkov about the state organs, was also left out in the record (Pako, 147/4/1495, l.79).

10 Grimsted, *Handbook for Archival Research*, 84–101.

Glossary of Russian Terms

For terms in italics used in the definitions below, look for entries elsewhere in the glossary.

administrirovat'. To rule by administrative methods, in a bureaucratic or arrogant manner.

agitfurgony. Agitation carts used by Young Communists to visit villages to drum up enthusiasm for elections of *soviets*.

agitprop. Agitation and propaganda, the two means by which Communists show those outside the Communist Party the fundamental truth of Marxism (-Leninism) and the march of history toward the communist paradise. A special department dealt with this activity within the *Central Committee*, and at lower levels party secretaries (often the third secretaries) of *obkoms*, *gorkoms*, and *raikoms* were called upon to deal almost exclusively with this enforcement of the ideology.

aktiv. Literally, "active": those active as Communist Party members or as sympathizers of the Communist cause in enlightening, organizing, or mobilizing those outside the party behind the banner of Communism and the Soviet Fatherland/Motherland.

akusherka. A midwife.

apparatchik. A party functionary of the Central Committee or provincial or district committee apparatus; usually pejorative.

artel'. A collective or cooperative: commonly used for agricultural cooperatives or handicraft cooperatives.

batrak. A landless peasant.

bazar. A market.

bedniak (pl. sometimes *bednota*). A "poor peasant" in a pre-collectivization village, labelled according to the Communist idea of class relations in the village.

besprizornye. "Homeless" children: orphans wandering around the Soviet Union during and after the Civil War, collectivization, the Great Purge, and World War II.

beznadzornye. "Neglected" children: children wandering around Soviet

Union during and after the Civil War, collectivization, the Great Purge, and World War II.

Bukharinite. A follower of the party leader of the 1920s, N.I. Bukharin, who supported a policy of continued good relations between the party and the peasantry and who opposed stepped-up collectivization. After having been forced out of the *Politburo* in 1929 and losing his positions in the government and *Comintern*, Bukharin recanted his views, but this did not save him from appearing as one of the accused at the Third Moscow Trial in 1938. He was sentenced to death and executed after the trial. See also *Right Opposition*.

Bürgermeister. German-appointed mayor in German-occupied territory of the Soviet Union during World War II.

CPSU (KPSS). Communist Party of the Soviet Union. Official title since the Nineteenth Party Congress of 1952.

Central Committee of the Communist Party. Originally the highest decision-making body of the Russian Social-Democratic Workers' Party and of its Bolshevik branch; elected by the Party Congress. After the death of Lenin in 1924 it took the backseat more and more to the *Sekretariat, Politburo,* and *Orgburo* and was, in fact, pre-selected by the *Politburo* or Stalin himself.

Central Committee Sekretariat. Established in 1919 to handle most paperwork going in and out of the *Central Committee, Politburo,* and *Orgburo*; often – particularly under Stalin, who practically led it as general secretary from 1922 to 1953 – made decisions without referring to those bodies.

Central Executive Committee. Executive Committee of the *Supreme Soviet* since 1937. Its chairman was the official head of state of the Soviet Union.

Cheka (or Vecheka). (All-Russian) Extraordinary Commission to Combat Counterrevolution, Sabotage, and Speculation: the first Soviet secret police, founded in late 1917. It would change its name, but not its agenda, in 1922; eventually, by 1934, it would be called the NKVD. See also *OGPU, NKGB, MVD, MGB.*

Cominform. Communist Information Bureau. This organization was intended to strengthen ideological unity and streamline international and domestic policy of leading European Communist Parties (of the Soviet Union, Poland, Romania, Bulgaria, Czechoslovakia, Hungary, France, and Italy – and until 1948, of Yugoslavia). Founded in 1947, it became defunct by 1955.

Comintern. Communist International, or Third International of workers' parties, founded in 1919 in Moscow and dissolved in 1943.

DOSAAF. All-Union Voluntary Society for the Assistance of the Army, Airforce, and Navy.

dom. A house: in towns and cities usually a large house split up into apartments or offices, or an apartment building.

domokhoziaika. A homemaker, housewife.

edinolichnik. Particularly during and after collectivization, a single farmer, i.e., someone who was not a member of a *kolkhoz*.

edinonachal'e. One-person management, reintroduced in factories especially in 1929 because collective management was deemed ineffective.

ekonomika. "Economization": the effort to cut costs by taking care of machinery and equipment.

Ezhovshchina. Literally, "The Ezhov Thing" (the ending "-shchina" is not translatable into English but conveys something pejorative in Russian): the name given to the height of the Great Purge from 1936 to 1938, when N.I. Ezhov was People's Commissar of Internal Affairs.

FZO. A factory school.

feld'sher. A medical attendant.

filtratsiia. A screening process used by the NKVD in search of alleged traitors or collaborators among Soviet prisoners of war and forced labourers upon their return to the Soviet Union after World War II.

Glavlit. Chief Administration for Literary Affairs, responsible for censorship.

gorispolkom. Executive committee of the town *soviet.*

gorkom. Town committee of the Communist Party.

Gosplan. State Planning Committee.

gruppovshchina. The process of forming a group or clique.

guberniia. Until 1929, a province.

gubkom. Provincial committee of the Communist Party (until 1929).

GULag. Main administration of labour camps under the NKVD/MVD; often used for the entire concentration-camp complex under Stalin.

izba. Peasant hut or cottage.

izba-chital'nia. Village reading-room.

khuliganstvo. "Hooliganism," i.e., vandalism, brawling, intoxication, petty crime.

khutor. In the text, mostly used for homesteads that were not located in (*kolkhoz*) villages.

khutorianin. Inhabitant of a *khutor.*

kolkhoz (pl. *kolkhozy*). Collective farm (kollektivnoe khoziaistvo); officially owned by an agricultural collective (*artel'*).

kolkhoznik. A male collective-farm worker.

kolkhoznitsa. A female collective-farm worker.

kombinat. An industrial complex: a factory in which different stages of the production process of a certain manufactured good are combined (e.g., the spinning and weaving of cotton).

Komsomol. See VLKSM. Often used to indicate a member of this organization.

kraeved. A specialist in local history and geography.

krai. An administrative division of the USSR, usually of greater size than an *oblast'.*

kraikom. Party committee of a *krai.*

krasnyi ugolok. Literally, "red (or beautiful) corner": a reading corner.

kulak: Literally, "fist": a pejorative term meaning "rich peasant," or "capitalist peasant" in a pre-collectivization village; labelled according to the Communist idea of class relations in the village. The label was often given to anyone opposed to collectivization.

kult'tovary. "Cultural supplies": semi-luxury goods such as bicycles, radios, gramophones.

MGB. From 1946 until 1953, the Ministry of State Security.

MTM. Machine-Tractor Repair Station.

MTS. Machine Tractor Station.

MVD. From 1946, Ministry of Internal Affairs.

malaia rodina. "Little motherland": A sentimental reference to one's native region or district (somewhat like the German "Heimat").

Memorial. The society organized to commemorate the victims of Stalinism (and, subsequently, of all Soviet regimes).

meshchanin. Petty bourgeois, used before 1929 of the urban lower middle class, often pejorative and thus: Philistine.

militsiia. Regular police, part of the NKVD/MVD.

NEP. The New Economic Policy, introduced in 1921 at the Tenth Party Congress. It allowed a measure of private domestic trade and ownership and permitted the peasantry to work and sell their products for personal profit. The NEP came to an end in 1929 with the *Velikii Perelom*.

NKIu. People's Commissariat of Justice.

NKGB. In the 1940s, until 1946, the People's Commissariat of State Security.

NKVD. People's Commissariat of Internal Affairs, until 1946.

narod. The people, as in German *Volk*.

narodnye zasedateli. People's assessors in regular courts.

narsledovately. "People's investigators," assistants to the state prosecutors.

narsud. Judge in regular court.

nomenklatura. The system of appointments by which the Central Committee and lower party committees appoint people to responsible posts in the party, government, unions, secret police, Komsomol, industry, agriculture, etc.

OGPU. Unified State Political Administration, the name of the secret police between 1923 and 1934.

OSO *(Osobye soveshchanie)*. Special Board: the NKVD/MVD court dealing with cases of counterrevolutionary activities, sabotage, and treason.

obezlichka. Absence of taking personal responsibility.

obkom. Provincial committee of the Communist Party, officially elected by the provincial party congress, but in practice selected by the *Central Committee Sekretariat*.

obkomburo. The highest policy-making body of the provincial party, officially elected from the membership of the *obkom*, but practically selected by the *Central Committee Sekretariat*.

oblast'. Province, sometimes translated in English as "region."

oblispolkom. Provincial executive committee of a provincial *soviet*, i.e., the official provincial government.

oblvoenkom. Provincial military commissar.

oblzo. Provincial agricultural department, a sort of provincial ministry of agriculture.

obshchezhitie. Communal housing, in which tenants share common areas, e.g., bathroom facilities and kitchen.

OITK. Oblast' office of corrective labour camps.

okrug. A region.

okruzhkom. A Communist Party committee of an *okrug*.

opolchenie. Paramilitary troops organized against Germans during World War II, somewhat like the British Home Guard.

Orgburo. Organizational bureau of the Central Committee, formed in 1919, possible only second in importance to the Politburo (and Stalin or his successors as general or first secretary of the CPSU).

otdel. Department: in the text the word is mostly used for the departments of different decision-making bodies of the Communist Party, such as the *Central Committee, obkom*, and *raikom*.

partkom. Communist Party committee, usually in factories or institutions in which there were a significant number of party members

Pioneers. A Communist- and Komsomol-led organization for children younger than fifteen, somewhat reminiscent of Boy and Girl Scouts, but, of course, more politicized.

Politburo. From 1919 to 1952, the highest policy-making body of the Communist Party. The membership was officially elected by the Central Committee. Renamed the Presidium in 1952, it was called the Politburo again in 1966.

Polizei. German "regular" police organized in German-occupied Soviet territory during World War II.

praktik. A practical worker who was promoted on the basis of his/her experience on the job, having little formal education.

Presidium. The name of the (former) Politburo from 1952 to 1966.

prokuror. A state prosecutor.

RSFSR. Russian Socialist Federative Soviet Republic.

rabfak. A workers' faculty/school.

rabkor. A worker correspondent.

rabochii poselok. "Workers' settlement": a relatively small settlement (no more than a few thousand inhabitants) in which primarily factory workers reside.

raiispolkom. Executive committee of a district *soviet*, i.e., the official government of a *raion*.

raikom. District committee of the Communist Party. Apart from the members of the *raikomburo*, most of its membership, in practice, was selected by the *obkom sekretariat*.

raikomburo. The highest policy-making body of a district (*raion*), officially elected from the membership of the *raikom*, but practically selected by the *Central Committee Sekretariat*.

raion. A district.

raivoenkom. A district military commissar.

Right Opposition. Those who agreed with *Politburo* members Bukharin, Rykov, and Tomsky that the party was mistaken in unleashing all-out collectivization of agriculture in 1929. Although they actually continued to support the policy followed by the Communist leadership between 1921 and 1929, while the supporters of the "General," or Stalinist line rejected these policies, their adherence to a policy of gradual transformation of agriculture and a slower pace of industrialization earned them the damning label of Right Oppositionists.

roddom. A maternity home.

rotozeistvo. Heedlessness, lack of care, irresponsible behaviour.

SD. Sicherheitsdienst: German secret or political police.

SR. Socialist-Revolutionary: the Socialist-Revolutionary Party was a non-Marxist socialist party, mainly (but not exclusively) defending the rights of the peasantry. It was the most popular party in the elections for the Constituent Assembly in November 1917, but after some members had briefly served in the government, the SRs were outlawed during the Civil War.

samogon. Home-distilled vodka.

samogonshchik. Someone who distills vodka at home.

sekretariat. The secretariat in an oblast' or raion party committee. It handled most paperwork going in and out of the *obkom* and *raikom*. See also *Central Committee Sekretariat*.

sel'khoz snabzhenie. A state rural supply agency.

sel'po. A village general store.

semeistvennost'. "Familyness," forming a clique.

seredniak. A "middle peasant" in a pre-collectivization village, labelled according to the Communist idea of class relations in the village.

shabashnik. An illegal itinerant artisan or handyman, often with a legal occupation to cover his tracks.

shefstvo. Exemplary leadership and altruitstic aid offered by factory workers, predominantly to collective farmers.

shturmovshchina. The rush to fulfill and overfulfill plan targets at end of the month.

skhod. A village meeting: until 1929, a gathering in which villagers made most essential decisions regarding village life and agricultural work. Its task was more or less taken over by the *kolkhoz* meeting after collectivization.

soviet. A council: at all kinds of levels, the official representative body of the Soviet population. Since 1936 it has been universally elected by the entire population.

sovkhoz. A state farm (sovetskoe khoziaistvo). It was much less prevalent than the *kolkhoz* before Stalin's death.

Sovmin. Since 1946, the Council of Ministers, the official government of the Soviet Union, appointed by the USSR Supreme Soviet.

Sovnarkom. From 1917 to 1946, the Council of People's Commissars, the official government of the Soviet Union, appointed by the Congress of Soviets or Supreme Soviet.

Stakhanovite. An exemplary worker who has regularly overfulfilled the targets that he or she was supposed to meet according to the plan. The Stakhanovite movement was most popular during the second half of the 1930s. It began with the highly publicized (and padded) overfulfillment of planning targets by the Donbass miner Aleksei Stakhanov in 1935.

starosta. An elder, particularly a village elder before collectivization and during World War II.

stolovaia. A food canteen in factories and institutions; often warm meals are served here.

Supreme Soviet. The highest council (*soviet*), the official parliament of the Soviet Union.

tekhnikum. A technical college, attended by teenagers after completion of primary education according to a general curriculum.

thick journal. A journal that mainly publishes longer articles of a serious nature, literary criticism, and works of literature, usually published monthly.

tolkach. A "fixer": particularly in Soviet industry a middleman who tries in semilegal fashion to overcome supply shortages.

tovarnaia ferma. A subsidiary farm of a collective farm, e.g., the livestock section of a *kolkhoz*.

tovaricheskie sudy. Comrades' Courts: they judged violations of factory laws and rules. Workers were judged by their colleagues in these courts.

troika. A special judicial board composed of three members. It was one of the main instruments that executed the Great Purge.

Trotskyites. (Alleged) followers of L.D. Trotsky, one of the Party leaders during the early days of the Bolshevik regime. Trotsky was outmanoeuvred by Stalin during the 1920s and forced into exile in 1929. After this, many Soviet people were persecuted as Trotskyites during the repressions of the 1930s, when a supposed countrywide Trotskyite conspiracy was blamed for undermining the Soviet economy and security.

trudoden' (pl. *trudodni*). "Workday credit" on a collective farm.

tsentner. One hundred kilograms.

tufta. Work done only for show, purposely false inflated indicators in an official report. From TFT, or tiazhelyi fizicheskii trud (hard physical labour), later mockingly used as an abbreviation of Tekhnika Ucheta Fiktivnogo Truda (the technique of counting fictive labour).

USSR. Union of Socialist Soviet Republics.

uezd. A pre-1929 district.

Ustav. A statute: in the text, exclusively used for the Kolkhoz Statute of 1935, which laid down the rules according to which collective farms were to be organized in the Soviet Union.

VKP(b). All-Union Communist Party (bolsheviks): the official name of the Communist Party of the Soviet Union from 1918 to 1952.

VLKSM. All-Union Leninist Communist Youth League, more often called *Komsomol*. The age of entry varied during Soviet history, but the minimum age was usually around fifteen.

Velikii Perelom. The "Great Turn": used to indicate the radical transformation of the Soviet economy introduced on the instigation of Stalin in 1929.

vlast'. Authorities, power.

volost'. The name of a pre-1929 administrative district, a subdivision of a *guberniia*.

Wehrmacht. The regular German army in World War II.

workers' settlement. See *rabochii poselok*.

Zagotskot. State Procurement Office for cattle.

zakliuchennye. Camp or prison inmates: often abbreviated to *zeki* or *zeks*.

Zastoi. Period of Stagnation, largely equivalent to the tenure of Leonid Brezhnev as leader of the CPSU (1964–82).

zastol'e. Sitting around the table with friends and family, drinking and eating and making merry.

zek. See zakliuchennye.

zemleustroitel'. A crop specialist.

zemlianka. A dug-out.

zemstvo. A pre-revolutionary administrative body concerned with local affairs, such as building bridges, roads, canals, as well as fire fighting, health care, and education.

Zhdanovschina. "The Zhdanov Thing": the name given to the ideological offensive of 1946 to 1948, when, particularly, politburo member A.A. Zhdanov engaged in a public attack on those in the arts (and sometimes in other professions) who had supposedly shown too little Communist spirit in their works.

Zhenotdel. Women's department of the *VKP(b)*, dissolved in 1930.

Zinovievite Opposition. The name given to followers of the Leningrad Party boss, Politburo member, and *Comintern* leader G. Zinoviev, who clashed with Stalin in the mid-1920s. Zinoviev was ousted from the leadership and became one of the main accused at the first Moscow Trial of 1936.

zveno (pl. *zven'ia*). A team or link of collective farmers engaged in the same agricultural task.

Bibliography

Abarinov, Vladimir. *Katynskii labirint*. Moscow: Novosti, 1991.

– "More Troubled Waters in KGB Files." *Nezavisimaya Gazeta/Independent Newspaper* 3 (October 1992): 12–13.

Abramov, Fyodor. *The New Life: A Day on a Collective Farm*. New York: Grove Press, 1963.

Adamova-Sliozberg, Ol'ga. "Put'." In *Dodnes' tiagoteet: Zapiski vashei sovremenintsy*. Vol. I. Moscow: Sovetskii pisatel', 1989: 6–123.

Afanas'ev, V.G. "'Smolenskoe delo' 1928 g.: Podgotovka 'velikogo pereloma'." *Vestnik Moskovskogo universiteta*. Series 8 (Istoriia) 3 (1991): 56–73.

Akademiia Nauk SSSR, Institut Geografii. *Tsentral'nyi Raion: Ekonomiko-geograficheskaia kharakteristika*. Moscow: Gosudarstvennoe Izdatel'stvo Geograficheskoi Literatury, 1962.

Aksenov, Iu.S. "Apogei stalinizma: poslevoennaia piramida vlasti." *Voprosy Istorii KPSS* 11 (1990): 90–104.

Alampiev, P. "Promyshlennost' Kalininskoi oblasti (vvodnyi ocherk)." In *Uchenye zapiski MGU 37: Geografiia. Promyshlennost' Kalininskoi oblasti*. Bk. 2, pt. 2. Moscow, 1939: 4–22. [From here, MGU 37]

Alekseeva, L.V., and V.D. Chernyshov, eds. *Kalininskaia Oblastnaia Organizatsiia KPSS v dokumentakh i fotografiiakh*. Moscow: Moskovskii rabochii, 1989.

Altrichter, Helmut. *Die Bauern von Tver: Vom Leben auf dem russischen Dorfe zwischen Revolution und Kollektivierung*. Munich: R. Oldenbourg Verlag, 1984.

Anokhina, L.A., and M.N. Shmeleva. *Kul'tura i byt' kolkhoznikov kalininskoi oblasti*. Moscow: Nauka, 1964.

Anuchin, V.A. "Novozavidovskii raion." In *Uchenye zapiski Moskovskogo Gosudarstvennogo Universiteta; Trudy Kalininskoi ekspeditsii nauchno-issledovatel'skogo instituta geografii: Zony, goroda i raiony Kalininskoi oblasti*. Geografiia: no. 38, bk. 3, pt. 2. Moscow, 1940: 44–51. [From here: *MGU 38*.]

Aptekar', P.A. "Opravdanu li zhertvu? (O poteriakh v sovetsko-finliandskoi voine)." *Voenno-istoricheskii zhurnal* 3 (1992): 43–5.

Arbatov, Georgi. *The System: An Insider's Life in Soviet Politics*. New York: Times Books, 1993.

Arendt, Hannah. *The Origins of Totalitarianism*. New Edition. New York: Harcourt, Brace and World, 1966.

Arutiunian, Iu. V. "Osobennosti i znachenie novogo etapa razvitiia sel'skogo khoziaistva SSSR." In *Istoriia krest'ianstva i kolkhoznogo stroitel'stva v SSSR: Materialy nauchnoi sessii, sostoiavsheisia 18–21 aprelia 1961 g. v Moskve*, Moscow: Akademii Nauk SSSR, 1963: 392–426.

Arutjunjan, Iu.V. *La structure sociale de la population rurale de l'URSS*. 1971. Trans. Yves Perret-Gentil. Cahiers ISMEA Économies et Sociétés 13 Paris: ISMEA, 1979.

Asinkritov, Gennadi. "Raskulachennyi." *Glasnost' (Udomel'skaia obshchestvenno-politicheskaia gazeta Tverskoi oblasti)*. Vol. 2, no. 9 (July 1992): 4–5.

Babichenko, D.L. *Pisateli i tsenzory*. Moscow: Rossiia molodaia, 1994.

Badeev, B. "Istoki truda i podviga." In *Kazhdyi mig nacheku: Ocherki o militsii*. Moscow: Moskovskii rabochii, 1987: 16–27.

– "Neozhidannyi povorot." In *Poklialis' my v vernosti otchizne; Dokumental'nye ocherki, vospominaniia i stat'i o Kalininskikh chekistakh*. Moscow: Moskovskii rabochii, Kalininskoe otdelenie, 1983: 37–49.

Ball, Alan. "The Roots of Bezprizornost' in Soviet Russia's First Decade." *Slavic Review* 2 (1992): 247–70.

Barber, J.D., and R.W. Davies. "Employment and Industrial Labour." In *The Economic Transformation of the Soviet Union, 1913–1945*. Eds. R.W. Davies et al. Cambridge: Cambridge University Press, 1994: 81–105.

Beznin, M.A. "Krest'ianskaia bazarnaia torgovlia v nechernozem'e v 50-e-pervoi polovine 60-x godov." *Istoriia SSSR* 1 (1991): 69–85.

Bilenko, S.V., S.V. Borodin, and V.P. Maslov. "Vozrozhdenie i dal'neishee ukreplenie sotsialisticheskogo pravoporiadka v osvobozhdennikh raionakh." In *Vozrozhdenie prifrontovikh i osvobozhdennykh raionov SSSR v gody Velikoi Otechestvennoi voiny, 1941–1945*. Ed. Iu.A. Poliakov. Moscow: Nauka, 1986: 107–17. [From here: *Vozrozhdenie*.]

Biographic Directory of the USSR. New York: Scarecrow Press, 1958.

Bloknot Agitatora. Kalinin: Proletarskaia Pravda, 1947–1953. [Until 1952 a monthly journal, afterwards appearing every two weeks.]

Bol'shakov, A.M. *Sovetskaia Derevnia (1917–1924 gg.): Ekonomika i byt*. Leningrad: Priboi, 1924.

Borisov, Iu. "Stalin: Chelovek i Simvol. Fakty istorii i istoriia kul'ta." In *Perepiska na istoricheskie temy: Dialog vedet chitatel'*. Ed. V.A. Ivanov. Moscow: Politicheskoi literatury, 1989: 435–92.

Borisov, Iu., V.M. Kuritsyn, and Iu.S. Khvan. "Politicheskaia sistema kontsa 20–30kh godov: O Staline i stalinizme." In *Istoriki sporiat: Trinadtsat' besed*. Ed. V.S. Lel'chuk. Moscow: Politizdat, 1988: 228–303.

Boshniak, Iu.M., D.D. Slezkin, and N.A. Iakimanskii. "Kalininskoe operatsionnoe napravlenie v Bitve pod Moskvoi." *Na pravom flange Moskovskoi bitve: K 50-letiiu osvobozhdeniia g. Kalinina v Velikoi Otechestvennoi voine*. Moscow: Moskovskii rabochii, 1991: 7–61. [From here, *Na pravom flange*.]

Boterbloem, C.N. "Communists and the Russians: The Kalinin Province under Stalin." PHD diss. Montreal: McGill University, 1994.

Boym, Svetlana. *Common Places: Mythologies of Everyday Life in Russia*. Cambridge, MA: Harvard University Press, 1994.

Bradbury, Malcolm. *Doctor Criminale*. London: Penguin, 1993.

Braude, A. "Mashinostroitel'naia i metalloobrabatyvaiushchaia promyshlennost'." *MGU 37*: 38–47.

Buckley, Cynthia. "The Myth of Managed Migration." *Slavic Review* 4 (1995): 896–916.

Bugai, N.F. "20-40-e gody: Deportatsiia naseleniia s territorii evropeiskoi Rossii." *Otechestvennaia istoriia* 4 (1992): 37–49.

Bullock, Alan. *Hitler and Stalin: Parallel Lives*. Toronto: McClelland and Stewart, 1993 (1991).

Butenko, A.P. "O sotsial'no-klassovoi prirode stalinskoi vlasti." *Voprosy Filosofii* 3 (1989): 65–78.

Carrère d'Encausse, Hélène. *Stalin: Order through Terror*. Vol. 2 of *A History of the Soviet Union 1917–1953*. London and New York: Longman, 1981.

"The Case of the Russian Archives: An Interview with Iurii N. Afanas'ev." *Slavic Review* 2 (1993): 338–52.

Chadaev, Ia. E. *Ekonomika SSSR v period velikoi otechestvennoi voiny (1941–1945 gg.)*. Moscow: Mysl', 1965.

Chapman, Janet G. *Real Wages in Soviet Russia since 1928*. Cambridge, MA: Harvard University Press, 1963

Chernishov, V.D. "Rabochii klass i promyshlennost' Tveri v 1917–1918 gg." In *Tverskaia guberniia v pervye gody sovetskoi vlasti (1917–1920 gg.): Sbornik statei i dokumentov*. Kalinin: Kalininskoe knizhnoe izdatel'stvo, 1958: 42–66.

Chislennost', estestvennoe dvizhenie i migratsiia naseleniia v 1990g. Statisticheskii biulleten'. Moscow: Informatsionno izdatel'skii tsentr Goskomstata SSSR, 1991.

Chislennost' naseleniia soiuznikh respublik po gorodskim poseleniiam i raionam na 1 ianvaria 1991 g. Statisticheskii sbornik. Moscow: Informatsionno-izdatel'skii tsentr Goskomstata SSSR, 1991.

Clements, Barbara Evans. "The Utopianism of the Zhenotdel." *Slavic Review* 3 (1992): 485–96.

Conquest, Robert. "Academe and the Soviet Myth." *The National Interest* 31 (spring 1993): 91–8.

– *The Great Terror: A Reassessment.* Edmonton, AB: University of Alberta ress., 1990.
– *The Harvest of Sorrow: Soviet Collectivization and the Terror-Famine.* Edmonton, AB: University of Alberta Press., 1986.
– *Power and Policy in the USSR: The Struggle for Stalin's Succession 1945–1960.* New York, NY: Harper & Row, 1967.
– "Red for Go. How Western Pundits Got the Wrong Signals about the USSR." *Times Literary Supplement,* 9 July 1993, 3–5.
Daniels, Robert V., ed. *A Documentary History of Communism.* Vol. 2. New York: Vintage Books, 1960.
Danilov, V.P. "Kollektivizatsiia" In *Perepiska na istoricheskie temy: Dialog vedet chitatel'.* Ed. V.A. Ivanov. Moscow: Politicheskoi literatury, 1989: 355–400.
Danilov, V.P., V.P. Dmitrenko, and V.S. Lel'chuk. "NEPi ego sud'ba." In *Istoriki sporiat: Trinadtstat' besed.* Ed. V.S. Lel'chuk Moscow: Politizdat, 1988: 122–90.
Depretto, Jean-Paul. "Construction Workers in the 1930s." In *Stalinism: Its Nature and Aftermath. Essays in Honour of Moshe Lewin,* Eds. N. Lampert and G.T. Rittersporn. London: Macmillan, 1992: 184–210.
Djilas, Milovan. *The New Class: An Analysis of the Communist System.* New York: Praeger, 1957.
Drobizhev, V.Z., and Iu. A. Poliakov. "Istoricheskaia demografiia-vazhnoe napravlenie nauchnykh issledovanii." In *Istoriki sporiat: Trinadtsat' besed.* Ed. V.S. Lel'chuk. Moscow: Politizdat, 1988: 461–80.
Du Plessix Gray, Francine. *Soviet Women: Walking the Tightrope.* New York: Doubleday, 1989.
Dunham, Vera S. *In Stalin's Time: Middleclass Values in Soviet Fiction.* Durham and London: Duke University Press, 1990.
Dyadkin, Iosif G. *Unnatural Deaths in the USSR, 1928–1954.* New Brunswick, NJ: Transaction Books, 1983.
Eliseev, V.T., and S.N. Mikhailov. "Tak skol'ko zhe liudei my poteriali v voine." *Voenno-istoricheskii zhurnal* 6–7 (1992): 31–4.
Engel, Barbara Alpern. "Engendering Russia's History: Women in Post-Emancipation Russia and the Soviet Union." *Slavic Review* 2 (1992): 309–21.
Eremin, V.G. "O vklade molodezhi v likvidatsiiu ushcherba, nanesennogo fashistskoi okkupatsiei." In *Vozrozhdenie:* 96–107.
Eroshkin N.P., L.M. Ovrutskii, and A.M. Podshchekoldin. "Biurokratizm-tormoz perestroiki." In *Istoriki sporiat: Trinadtsat' besed.* Ed. V.S. Lel'chuk. Moscow: Politizdat, 1988: 432–60.
Fainsod, Merle. How Russia is Ruled. Cambridge, MA: Harvard University Press, 1955.
– *Smolensk under Soviet Rule.* Cambridge, MA: Harvard University Press, 1958.

Fairbanks, Charles H., Jr. "The Nature of the Beast." *The National Interest* 31 (spring 1993): 46–56.

Fedoseev, A. *Zapadnia: Chelovek i sotsializm*. Frankfurt am Main: Possev-Verlag, 1976.

Fitzpatrick, Sheila. *The Cultural Front: Power and Culture in Revolutionary Russia*. Ithaca, NY, and London: Cornell University Press, 1992.

– "Cultural Revolution as Class War." In *Cultural Revolution in Russia, 1928–1931*. Ed. Sheila Fitzpatrick. Bloomington, IN, and London: Indiana University Press, 1978: 8–40.

– *Stalin's Peasants: Resistance and Survival in the Russian Village after Collectivization*. New York: Oxford University Press, 1994.

Fletcher, W.C. *The Russian Orthodox Church Underground, 1917–1970*. London: Oxford University Press, 1971.

Frankland, Mark. *Khrushchev*. 1966. New York: Stein and Day, 1967.

Garmonov, O.A. "Bor'ba partiinykh organizatsii Kalininskoi oblasti za ukreplenie trudovoi distsipliny na promyshlennykh predpriiatiiakh (1937-iiun' 1941 gg.)." In *Iz istorii Kalininskoi Partiinoi organizatsii: Sbornik statei*. Kalinin, 1972: 62–74.

Gevorkian, Nataliia. "Vstrechnye plany po unichtozheniiu sobstvennogo naroda." *Moskovskie Novosti* 25 (21 June 1992 g.): 18–19.

Gordon, L.A., and E.V. Klopov. *Chto eto bylo? Razmyshleniia o predposylkakh i itogakh togo, chto sluchilos' s nami v 30-40-e gody*. Moscow: Politizdat, 1989.

Gor'kii, Maksim. *Nesvoevremennye mysli; rasskazy*. Moscow: Sovremennik, 1991.

Gosudarstvennyi arkhiv kalininskoi oblasti. Kalinin, 1986.

Gosudarstvennyi arkhiv kalininskoi oblasti; putevoditel'. Pt. 2, Kalinin, 1977.

Grimsted, P.K. *A Handbook for Archival Research in the USSR*. N.p.: The International Research and Exchanges Board, The Kennan Institute for Advanced Russian Studies, 1989.

Gross Solomon, Susan. "Rural Scholars and Cultural Revolution." In *Cultural Revolution in Russia, 1928–1931*. Ed. Sheila Fitzpatrick. Bloomington, IN, and London: Indiana University Press, 1978: 129–53.

Grossman, Vasily. *Forever Flowing*. London: Collins Harvill, 1986.

Hahn, W.G. *Postwar Soviet Politics: The Fall of Zhdanov and the Defeat of Moderation, 1946–1953*. Ithaca, NY: Cornell UP, 1982.

Heitlinger, Alena. *Women and State Socialism: Sex Inequality in the Soviet Union and Czechoslovakia*. Montreal: McGill-Queen's University Press, 1979.

Heller M., and A. Nekrich. *Utopia in Power: The History of the Soviet Union from 1917 to the Present*. New York: Summit Books, 1986.

History of the Communist Party of the Soviet Union (Bolsheviks): Short Course. Toronto: Francis White, 1939.

Hochschild, Adam. *The Unquiet Ghost: Russians Remember Stalin*. New York: Viking Penguin, 1994.

Holloway, David. *Stalin and the Bomb: The Soviet Union and Atomic Energy, 1939–1956*. New Haven, CT: Yale University, 1994.

Hoopes, James. *Oral History: An Introduction for Students*. Chapel Hill, NC: University of North Carolina Press, 1979.

Iakovlev, B., with the collaboration of A. Burtsova. *Kontsentratsionnye lageri SSSR*. Munich: Institut po izucheniiu istorii i kul'tury SSSR, 1955.

Igritskii, Iu.I. "Snova o totalitarizme." *Otechestvennaia istoriia* 1 (1993): 3–17.

Il'in, M.A. "Raskrytie arkhivov-vazhnoe uslovie vosstanovleniia istoricheskoi pravdy." *Sovetskie Arkhivy* 4 (1989): 11–15.

Il'ina, T.A. "Ustanovlenie sovetskoi vlasti v Tverskoi gubernii." In *Tverskaia guberniia v pervye gody sovetskoi vlasti (1917–1920 gg.): Sbornik statei i dokumentov*. Kalinin: Kalininskoe knizhnoe, 1958: 5–41.

Inkeles, A., and R.A. Bauer. *The Soviet Citizen: Daily Life in a Totalitarian Society*. Cambridge, MA: Harvard University Press, 1961.

Ivanov, Leonid. "Litsom k derevne." *Novyi Mir* 5 (1966): 201–21.

– "Snova o rodnykh mestakh." *Novyi Mir* 2 (1965): 181–212.

– "V rodnykh mestakh." *Novyi Mir* 3 (1963): 174–200.

Ivanova, L.V., ed. *Sovetskaia Intelligentsiia: slovar'-spravochnik*. Moscow: Politicheskoi literatury, 1987.

Jackson, George D. Jr. "Peasant Political Movements in Eastern Europe." *Rural Protest: Peasant Movements and Social Change*. Ed. Henry Landsberger. London and New York: Macmillan, 1974: 259–315.

Jamestown Monitor, Vol. 1, no .25 [electronic newsletter] (June 5, 1995). Available at <Jamestown-L@Peach.Ease.LSoft. com>.

Kalininskaia oblast' v gody Velikoi Otechestvennoi Voiny (V ekspozitsiiakh Kalininskogo gosudarstvennogo ob'edinennogo istoriko-arkhitekturnogo i literaturnogo muzeia). Kalinin, 1985.

Kalininskaia oblast' za 50 let v tsifrakh: statisticheskii sbornik. Moscow: Izdatel'stvo Statistika, 1967.

Kaplan, Cynthia S. *The Party and Agricultural Crisis Management in the USSR*. Ithaca, NY, and London: Cornell UP, 1987.

Kapus'cin'ski, Ryszard. *Imperium*. Toronto: Alfred A. Knopf, 1994.

Karasev, Ivan V. "The Reconstruction of Agriculture in Pskov Oblast', 1945–1953." *Soviet Studies* 43, no.2 (1991): 301–9.

Karpenko, Z. *Pod fashistskim igom*. Kalinin: Proletarskaia Pravda, 1945.

Keep, John L.H. *The Russian Revolution: A Study in Mass Mobilization*. New York: W.W. Norton, 1976.

Kennan, George F. *Memoirs: 1925–1950*. Boston, Toronto: Little, Brown, 1967.

Kerblay, Basile. *Du mir aux agrovilles*. Paris: Institut d'études slaves, 1985.

Khlevniuk, O.V. *1937-i: Stalin, NKVD i sovetskoe obshchestvo*. Moscow: Respublika, 1992.

– "Prinuditel'nyi trud v ekonomike SSSR. 1929–1941 gody." *Svobodnaia Mysl'* 13 (1992): 73–84.

– "30-e gody. Krizisy, reformy, nasilie." *Svobodnaia Mysl'* 17 (1991): 75–87.

Khlevniuk, O.V., et al. *Stalinskoe Politbiuro v 30e gody: Sbornik dokumentov*. Moscow: Airo-XX, 1995.

Kirichek, R.I. "Vozrozhdenie i organizatsionno-polticheskoe ukreplenie komsomol'skikh organizatsii v osvobozhdennikh raionakh." In *Vozrozhdenie*: 77–95.

Klatt, W. Review of *Die Mechanisierung landwirtschaftlicher Arbeiten in der Sowjetunion*, by Eberhard Schinke. *Slavic Review* 4 (1968): 675–6.

Kolakowski, Leszek. "Totalitarianism and the Virtue of the Lie." In *1984 Revisited: Totalitarianism in Our Century*. Ed. Irving Howe. New York: Harper and Row, 1983: 122–35.

Kondakova, N.I. "Partiia – organizator ideino-politicheskoi raboty v osvobozhdennikh i prifrontovykh raionakh." In *Vozrozhdenie*: 20–37.

Konev, I.S. "Vospominaniia." In *Na pravom flange*: 62–5.

Kopelev, Lev. *Ease My Sorrows: A Memoir*. New York, Toronto: Random House, 1983.

– *Khranit' vechno*. Ann Arbor, MI: Ardis, 1975.

Korytkov, N.G. *Kalininskoe selo: proshloe, nastoiashchee, budushchee*. Moscow: Kolos, 1978.

– *Kommunist. Khoziaistvo. Reforma*. Moscow: Moskovskii rabochii, 1969.

Korzhenevskaia, A.P., A.A. Lebedeva, and N.P. Nikiforov, "Likvidatsiia zabolevaemosti malariei v Kalininskoi oblasti." In *Zdravookhranenie Kalininskoi oblasti za 50 let*. Moscow: Moskovskii rabochii, 1967: 113–17.

Korzhikhina, T.P., and A.D. Stepanskii. In "Iz istorii obshchestvennykh organizatsii." *Istoriki sporiat: Trinadtsat' besed*. Ed. V.S. Lel'chuk. Moscow: Politizdat, 1988: 406–31.

Korzun, I.D. "Kalininskie vagonostroiteli i pervye mesiatsy velikoi otechestvennoi voiny (iiun'-dekabria 1941 goda)." In *Iz proshlogo i nastoiashchego Kalininskoi oblasti (istoriko-kraevedcheskii sbornik)*. Vol. 1, no. 1. Moscow: Moskovskii rabochii, 1965: 275–86.

– *Pervye shagi sotsialisticheskoi industrializatsii (Iz istorii bor'by tverskikh kommunistov za sotsialisticheskuiu industrializatsiiu v period mezhdu XIV i XVI s'ezdami partii)*. Kalinin: n., 1960.

Kotkin, Stephen. *Magnetic Mountain: Stalinism as a Civilization*. Berkeley and Los Angeles: University of California Press, 1995.

Kotliarskaia, L.A., and M.M. Freidenberg. *Iz istorii Tverskoi Kul'tury: Anatolii Nikolaevich Vershinskii (1888–1944)*. Tver': Uchebnoe posobie, 1990.

Kozlov, V.I. "Dinamika naseleniia sssr (Obshchii i etnodemograficheskii obzor)." *Istoriia SSSR* 5 (1991): 3–17.

Kozlov, V.P. "Ob ispol'zovanii dokumentov rossiiskikh arkhivov." *Novaia i noveishaia istoriia* 6 (1992): 77–82.

Krivosheev G.F, ed. *Grif sekretnosti sniat: Poteri vooruzhennikh sil SSSR v voinakh, boevykh deistviiakh i voennikh konfliktakh; statisticheskoe issledovanie.* Moscow: Voennoe, 1993.

Kuleshov, S.V., O.V. Volobuev, et al. *Nashe Otechestvo: Opyt politicheskoi istorii.* Part 2. Moscow: Terra, 1991.

Kurganoff, I.A. *Women in the USSR.* London, ON: SBONR Publishing House, 1971.

Kutuzov, V.A. "Tak nazyvaemoe 'leningradskoe delo'." *Voprosy Istorii KPSS* 3 (1989): 53–67.

Lagutiaeva, A.I. "Razvitie rodovspomozheniia v Kalininskoi oblasti." *Zdravookhranenie:* 66–72.

Lampert, N., and G.T. Rittersporn, eds. *Stalinism: Its Nature and Aftermath.* Essays in Honour of Moshe Lewin. London: Macmillan, 1992.

Laqueur, W. *Europe since Hitler: The Rebirth of Europe.* 3d. ed., rev. Harmondsworth, England: Penguin Books, 1984.

– *The Dream That Failed: Reflections on the Soviet Union.* New York and Oxford: Oxford University Press, 1994.

– *Stalin: The Glasnost Revelations.* London: Unwin Hyman, 1990.

Ledovskikh, S.I. "Kalininskii raion." In *MGU 38*: 38–43.

Lel'chuk, V.S. "Industrializatsiia" In *Perepiska na istoricheskie temy: dialog vedet chitatel'.* Ed. V.A. Ivanov. Moscow: Politicheskoi literatury, 1989: 329–54.

Lenin, V.I. "Can the Bolsheviks Retain State Power?" In *Collected Works.* Vol. 26 (September 1917–February 1918). Moscow: Progress, 1972: 87–136.

– "Malen'kaia kartinka dlia vyiasneniia bol'shikh voprosov." *Polnoe sobranie sochinenii (izdanie piatoe).* Vol. 37 (July 1918–March 1919). Moscow: Gosudarstvennoe izdatel'stvo politicheskoi literatury, 1963.

– "What is to be Done?" *In Collected Works.* Vol. 5 (May 1901–February 1902). Moscow: Progress, 1973: 347–528.

Leont'eva, O.G. "Dokumenty po istorii razvitiia Kalininskoi derevni v kontse 1940-nachale 1950-kh godov." *In Istoriia v cheloveke: Materialy (Seminara rabotnikov gosudarstvennykh arkhivov Kalininskoi oblasti po povysheniiu professional'nogo urovnia(1989g.).* Tver', 1990. [Rotaprint].

Leshchinskii, A.G. "Gorod Kalinin." In *MGU 38*: 26–37.

Lewin, Moshe. *Lenin's Last Struggle.* 1968. Trans. A.M. Sheridan-Smith. London: Pluto Press, 1975.

– "Society, State and Ideology." In *Cultural Revolution in Russia, 1928–1931.* Ed. Sheila Fitzpatrick. Bloomington, IN, and London: Indiana University Press, 1978: 41–77.

Literaturnaia Gazeta. 22 (5192) (1 June 1988): 12. [Mikhailov's interrogation and trial.]

Lorenz, R. *Sozialgeschichte der Sowjetunion I, 1917–1945*. Frankfurt am Main: Suhrkamp Verlag, 1976.

Lubov, G.V. *Material vstupitel'noi stat'i "Knigi Pamiati" Konakovskogo raiona*. Konakovo: n.p., sentiabr'-noiabr 1991. [Carbon copy.]

Luk'ianova, A.P. "Vosstanovlenie i razvitie khlopchatobumazhnoi promyshlennosti Kalininskoi oblasti v poslevoennyi period (1945–1955gg.)." In *Iz proshlogo i nastoiashchego Kalininskoi oblasti (istoriko-kraevedcheskii sbornik)*. Vol. 1. Moscow: Moskovskii rabochii, 1965: 287–304.

Malia, Martin. "A Fatal Logic." *The National Interest* 31 (spring 1993): 80–90.

Mamonova, Tatyana. *Russian Women's Studies: Essays on Sexism in Soviet Culture*. London: Pergamon Press, 1989.

– ed. *Women and Russia*. Boston: Beacon Press, 1984.

Mann, Golo. *The History of Germany since 1789*. London: Chatto and Windus, 1968.

Marx, Karl, and Friedrich Engels. *The Communist Manifesto*. Harmondsworth, England: Penguin, 1967.

"Materialy fevral'skogo-martovskogo plenuma TsK VKP(b) 1937 goda." *Voprosy Istorii* 3 (1995): 3–15. [Indicated as (I) in text.]

"Materialy fevral'skogo-martovskogo plenuma TsK VKP(b) 1937 goda." *Voprosy Istorii* 8 (1995): 3–25. [Indicated as (II) in text.]

Medvedev, Roy. *Let History Judge: The Origins and Consequences of Stalinism*. Revised and expanded Edition. Ed. and trans. George Shriver. New York: Columbia University Press, 1989.

Medvedev, Zhores A. *Soviet Agriculture*. New York and London: W.W. Norton, 1987.

Mehnert, Klaus. *The Anatomy of Soviet Man*. London: Weidenfeld and Nicholson, 1961.

Mertsalov, A.N. "Stalinizm i osvechenie proshlogo." In *Istoriia i stalinizm*. Ed. A.N. Mertsalov. Moscow: Politizdat, 1991: 382–447.

Miller, Robert F. "The *Politotdel* : A Lesson from the Past." *Slavic Review* 3 (1966): 475–96.

Miner, S.M. "Revelations, Secrets, Gossip and Lies: Sifting Warily through the Soviet Archives." *New York Times Book Review*, 14 May 1995, 19–21.

Miniuk, A.I. "Sovremennaia arkhivnaia politika: Ozhidaniia i zaprety." In *Istoricheskie issledovaniia v Rossii: Tendentsii poslednikh let*. Ed. G.A. Bordiugov. Moscow: AIRO-XX (1996): 11–21.

Minuskin, M.S. "Kalininskaia zona." In *MGU 38*: 10–25.

Moore, Barrington, Jr. *Social Origins of Dictatorship and Democracy: Lord and Peasant in the Making of the Modern World*. Boston, MA: Beacon Press, 1966.

Morozov, N.V. "L'naia promyshlennost'." In *MGU* 37: 65–72.

– "Osnovye proizvodstva silikatno-keramicheskoi promyshlennosti." In *MGU* 37: 80–93.

– "Pishchevaia promyshlennost'." In *MGU* 37: 94–106.

"Moskva voennaia: 1941 god ... (Novye istochniki iz sekretnykh arkhivnykh fondov)." *Istoriia SSSR* 6 (1991): 101–22.

Müller, N. "Überblick über die Okkupationspolitik in den vom faschistischen Deutschland besetzten Gebieten der UdSSR." In Müller et al., *Die faschistische Okkupationspolitik*: 28–99.

Müller N., et al. *Die faschistische Okkupationspolitik in den zeitweilig besetzten Gebieten der Sowjetunion (1941–1944)*. Berlin: Deutscher Verlag der Wissenschaften, 1991. [From here, *Die faschistische Okkupationspolitik*.]

My byli u Stalina: rasskazy ordenostsev sovkhozov i kolkhozov Oporetskogo raiona Kalininskoi oblasti. N.p.: Kolkhoznaia stroia, 1936.

Na pravom flange Moskovskoi bitvy: K 50-letiiu osvobozhdeniia g. Kalinina v Velikoi Otechestvennoi voine. Moscow: Moskovskii rabochii, 1991.

Naumov, V.P. "K istorii sekretnogo doklada N.S. Khrushcheva na XX s'ezde KPSS." *Novaia i noveishaia istoriia* 4 (1996): 147–68.

Narodnoe Khoziaistvo Kalininskoi Oblasti: Statisticheskii Sbornik. Kalinin: Kalininskoe Knizhnoe, 1957.

Ne zabudem! Ne prostim: Zlodeianiia nemetsko-fashistskikh zakhvatchikov v raionakh Kalininskoi oblasti. Kalinin: Izdanie Kalininskogo obkoma VKP(b), Kalinin, 1942.

Nekrasov, V.F. "Final (Po materialam sudebnogo protsessa)." In *Beria: Konets kar'ery*. Moscow: Politizdat, 1991: 381–415.

"O tak nazyvaemom 'leningradskom dele'." *Izvestiia TsK KPSS* 2 (1989): 126–137.

Odom, William. "The Pluralist Image." *The National Interest* 31 (spring 1993): 99–108.

Osipov, V.G., and A.N. Kosarev. *Obelisk pobedy (pamiati pavshikh bud'te dostoiny)*. Kalinin: Ordena Trudovogo Znameni Kalininskii poligraficheskii kombinat Glavpoligrafproma Komiteta po pechati pri Sovete Ministrov SSSR, 1971.

"Osnovy zakonodatel'stva Rossiiskoi Federatsii ob Arkhivnoi fonde Rossiiskoi Federatsii I arkhivakh." *Novaia i Noveishaia Istoriia* 6 (1993): 3–12.

Pankratova, M.G. *Sel'skaia zhenshchina v SSSR*. Moskva: Mysl', 1990.

Panov, Iu. "Etapy bol'shogo puti." In *Kazhdyi mig nacheku: Ocherki o militsii*. Moskva: Moskovskii rabochii, 1987: 5–16.

Parfenov, A. "Shire razvernut' literaturnoe dvizhenie." *Rodnoi krai: Literatur'nyi al'manakh* 2, (1948): 3–8.

Pashkevich, V.I. "Khlopchatobumazhnaia promyshlennost'." In *MGU* 37: 48–58.

– "Trikotazhnaia promyshlennost'." In *MGU* 37: 59–64.

Pervozvanskii, A.V. "Kozhevenno-Obuvnaia promyshlennost'." In MGU 37: 72–80.

Petrov, Iu. P. *Stroitel'stvo politorganov, partiinykh i komsomol'skikh organizatsii armii i flota (1918–1968)*. Moscow: Voennoe izdatelstvo Ministra Oborony SSSR, 1968.

Petrov, M. "Kul'tura v provintsii." *Novyi Mir* 8 (1989): 257–68.

Pigulevskii, A.G., and M.I. Novik. "Lesnoe khoziaistvo i lesnaia promyshlennost'." In MGU 37: 107–17.

Pikhoia, R.G. "O vnutripoliticheskoi bor'be v sovetskom rukovodstve. 1945–1958 gg." *Novaia i noveishchaia istoriia* 1 (1995): 3–14.

Pipes, Richard. "1917 and the Revisionists." *The National Interest* 31 (spring 1993): 68–79.

– *Russia under the Bolshevik Regime*, New York: Knopf, 1993.

– *Russia under the Old Regime*. New York: Charles Scribner's Sons, 1974.

"Podslushali i rasstreliali." *Izvestiia*, 17 July 1992, 7.

Poletika, N.P. *Vidennoe i perezhitoe (Iz vospominanii)*. Israel: Biblioteka-Aliia, 1982.

Poliakov, Iu. A. "Pokhorony Stalina. Vzgliad Istorika-Ochevidtsa." *Novaia i noveishchaia istoriia* 4–5 (1995): 195–207.

– ed. *Vozrozhdenie prifrontovikh i osvobozhdennykh raionov SSSR v gody Velikoi Otechestvennoi voiny; 1941–1945*. Moscow: Nauka, 1986.

Poliakov, Iu.A., V.B. Zhiromskaia, and I.N. Kiselev. "Polveka molchaniia (Vsesoiuznaia perepis' naseleniia 1937 g.)." *Sotsiologicheskie Isledovaniia* 6 (1990): 3–25. [*Polveka*, I.]

– "Polveka molchaniia (Vsesoiuznaia perepis' naseleniia 1937 g.)." *Sotsiologicheskie Isledovaniia* 8 (1990): 30–52. [*Polveka*, II.]

Pomerants, G. "O roli oblika lichnosti v zhizni istoricheskogo kollektiva. Diskussionnoe vystuplenie v institute filosofii." *Grani* 67 (1968): 134–43.

Popova, L. "Ekspertiza pokazala ..." *Kazhdyi mig nacheku: Ocherki o militsii*. Moscow: Moskovskii rabochii, 1987: 102–13.

Popovskii, M. *Tretii lishnii: on, ona i Sovetskii rezhim*. London: Overseas Publications Interchange, 1985.

Portelli, Alessandro. *The Death of Luigi Trastulli and Other Stories: Form and Meaning in Oral History*. Albany, NY: SUNY Press, 1990.

Rapoport, Ya. *The Doctors' Plot of 1953*. Cambridge, MA: Harvard University Press, 1991.

Reddaway, Peter. "The Role of Popular Discontent." *The National Interest* 31 (spring 1993): 57–63.

Remnick, David. *Lenin's Tomb: The Last Days of the Soviet Empire*. New York: Vintage, 1994.

Rittersporn, G.T. *Stalinist Simplifications and Soviet Complications: Social Tensions and Political Conflicts in the USSR, 1933–1953*. Chur, Swizterland: Harwood Academic Publishers, 1991.

Robinson, G.T. *Rural Russia under the Old Regime: A History of the Landlord-Peasant World and a Prologue to the Peasant Revolution of 1917.* Berkeley and Los Angeles: University of California Press, 1960.

Rossi, J. *The Gulag Handbook: An Encyclopedic Dictionary of Soviet Penitentiary Institutions and Terms Related to the Forced Labor Camps.* New York: Paragon House, 1989.

Roxburgh, Angus. *The Second Russian Revolution: The Struggle for Power in the Kremlin.* London: BBC Books, 1991.

Rutland, Peter. "Sovietology: Notes for a Post-Mortem." *The National Interest* 31 (spring 1993): 109–22.

Ryan, M., and R.C. Prentice. *Social Trends in the Soviet Union from 1950.* London: Macmillan Press, 1987.

Rybakov, Anatolii. *Fear.* Boston: Little, Brown, 1992.

– *Tridtsat' piatyi i drugie gody: Roman.* Bk. 1. Moscow: Sovetskii pisatel', 1989.

Sakharov, Andrei. *Memoirs.* New York: Vintage Books, 1990.

Sakharov, A.N. "Demokratiia i volia v nashem otechestve. " *Svobodnaia Mysl'* 17 (1991): 42–53.

–. "Revolutsionnyi totalitarizm v nashei istorii." *Kommunist* 5 (1991): 60–71.

Samsonov, A.M. *Znat' i pomnit': Dialog istorika s chitatelem.* Moscow: Politicheskoi literatury, 1989.

Samsonov, A.M. et al., eds. *A Short History of the USSR: Part 2.* Moscow: Progress, 1965.

Schast'e s nami. Kalinin: Kalininskoe knizhnoe, 1960.

Schulz, H.E., and S.S. Taylor, eds. *Who's Who in the USSR, 1961/1962.* Montreal: Intercontinental, 1962.

Semiriaga, M.I. "Sud'by sovetskikh voennoplennikh." *Voprosy Istorii* 4 (1995): 19–33.

Sergeev, G.S. "Sel'skoe khoziaistvo tsentral'no-promyshlennogo raiona v 1921–1929 gg." *Iz proshlogo i nastoiashchego Kalininskoi oblasti (istoriko-kraevedcheskii sbornik).* Vol. 1. Moscow: Moskovskii rabochii, 1965: 239–74.

Seton-Watson, H. *The Decline of Imperial Russia.* New York: Frederick A. Praeger, 1961.

Smirnov V.I., et al., eds. *Ocherki istorii kalininskoi organizatsii KPSS.* Moscow: Moskovskii Rabochii, 1971.

Smirnov, V.S. "Bor'ba s infektsiiami v Kalininskoi oblasti." In *Zdravookhranenie*: 35–40.

Smolenskaia, V.V. "Uluchshenie fizicheskogo razvitiia detei g. Kalinina i Kalininskoi oblasti za gody Sovetskoi vlasti." In *Zdravookhranenie*: 262–7.

Soiuznye respubliki: Osnovnye ekonomicheskie i sotsial'nye pokazateli. Moscow: Informatsionno-izdatel'skii tsentr Goskomstata SSSR, 1991.

Sokolov, B. "Tsena poter'-tsena sistemy. " *Nezavisimaia Gazeta,* 22 June 1993, 5.

Solzhenitsyn, A.I. *The Gulag Archipelago, 1918–1956: An Experiment in Literary Investigation.* Parts 1–2. New York: Harper & Row, 1973.

– *The Gulag Archipelago, 1918–1956: An Experiment in Literary Investigation.* Parts 3–4. New York: Harper & Row, 1974.

Specter, Michael. "In 'Real' Russia, the Modern World Finally Intrudes." *International Herald Tribune,* 15 August 1995, 1, 7.

Stalin, J.V. "Dizzy with Success. Concerning Questions of the Collective-Farm Movement." *Works.* Vol. 12 (April 1929–June 1930). Moscow: Foreign Languages, 1955: 197–205.

– *Works.* Vol. 13 (July 1930–January 1934). Moscow: Foreign Languages, 1955.

Stickle, D.M. ed., *The Beria Affair: The Secret Transcripts of the Meetings Signalling the End of Stalinism.* New York: Nova Science, 1992.

Stites, R. *Russian Popular Culture: Entertainment and Society since 1900.* Cambridge: Cambridge University Press, 1992.

Sto sorok besed s Molotovym: Iz dnevnika F. Chueva. Moscow: Terra, 1991.

Stone, Norman. *Europe Transformed 1878–1919.* N.p.: Fontana, 1983.

Stone, Norman, and Michael Glenny. *The Other Russia.* London and Boston: Faber and Faber, 1990.

Strizhkov, Iu.K. "Deiatel'nost' SNK SSSR po organizatsii vosstanovleniia narodnogo khoziaistva na osvobozhdennoi territorii v pervyi period velikoi otechestvennoi voiny (1941–1942 gg.)." In *Vozrozhdenie*: 38–64.

Sudoplatov, P.A., et al. *Special Tasks: The Memoirs of an Unwanted Witness–A Soviet Spymaster.* Boston: Little, Brown, 1994.

Suslov, A., and A. Fomin. *Torzhok i ego okresnosti.* Moscow: Moskovskii rabochii, 1983.

Svet oktiabria: Kalininskaia oblast' za 70 let. Sobytiia. Fakty. Dokumenty. Moscow: Moskovskii rabochii, 1987.

Sysoev, N.G. "'Praktik marksizma.'" *Voenno-istoricheskii zhurnal* 2 (1993): 84–7.

Thurston, R.W. *Life and Terror in Stalin's Russia, 1934–1941.* New Haven, CT: Yale University Press, 1996.

Todorskii, A. *God-s vintovkoi i plugom.* Ves'egonsk: Izdanie Ves'egonskogo Uezdnogo Ispolnitel'nogo Komiteta, 1918.

Todorskii, A., and Iu. Arbatov. "Bol'shoe v malom." *Kommunist* 5 (1960): 45–59.

Trudoliubov, B.A. *Sovkhoz imeni Molotova.* Moscow, 1952.

TSSU. RSFSR, Statisticheskoe Upravlenie Kalininskoi oblasti. *Kalininskaia oblast' za piat'desiat let v tsifrakh: Statisticheskii sbornik.* Moscow: Statistika, 1967.

Tsaplin, V.V. "Arkhivnye materialy o chisle zakliuchennykh v kontse 30-kh godov." *Voprosy istorii* 4–5 (1991): 157–63.

Tucker, R.C. *Stalin in Power: The Revolution from Above, 1928–1941.* New York: W.W. Norton, 1990.

Tumarkin, Nina. *The Living & The Dead: The Rise and Fall of the Cult of World War II in Russia*. New York: Basic Books, 1994.

Turchin, Valentin. *Inertsiia Strakha*. New York: Khronika, 1977.

Tverskoi memorial. Vol. 3 (July–August 1990).

Tverskoi tsentr dokumentatsii noveishei istorii: Reklamnyi spravochnik. Tver', 1992.

Vakser, A.Z. "Personal'nye dela chlenov KPSS kak istoricheskii istochnik." *Otechestvennaia istoriia* 5 (1992): 91–104.

Venturi, Franco. *Roots of Revolution: A History of Populist and Socialist Movements in Nineteenth-Century Russia*. New York: Knopf, 1960.

Verbitskaia, O.M. *Rossiiskoe krest'ianstvo: ot Stalina k Krushchevu. Seredina 40-kh-nachalo 60-kh godov*. Moscow: Nauka, 1992.

Vershinskii, A., ed. *Kraevedcheskii atlas Tverskoi gubernii*. Tver': Izdanie Tverskogo Gubono i komiteta assotsiatsii po izucheniiu proizvod. sil. gub., 1928.

Vershinskii, A., and D. Zolotarev. *Naselenie Tverskogo kraia*. Tver', 1929.

Vershinskii, A.N. *Boi za gorod Kalinin*. Kalinin: Proletarskaia Pravda, 1945.

– *Goroda kalininskoi oblasti. (Istoricheskie ocherki)*. Kalinin: Kalininskoe Oblastnoe Literaturnoe, 1939.

Vinogradov, V. *Karel'skoe "delo"*. Tver', 1991.

Volkogonov, D.A. *Lenin: Politicheskii portret*. Bk. 2. Moscow: Novosti, 1994.

– *Stalin: Triumph and Tragedy*. Ed. and trans. Harold Shukman. London: Weidenfeld and Nicholson, 1991.

– *Triumf i tragediia: Politicheskii portret I.V. Stalina*. Bk. 1, pt. 1–2; bk. 2, pt. 1–2. Moscow: Agentstva pechati Novosti, 1989.

Volkov, I.M. "Kolkhozy SSSR v gody chetvertoi piatiletki (1946–1950 gg.)." In *Razvitie sel'skogo khoziaistva SSSR v poslevoennye gody (1946–1970 gg.)*. Moscow: Nauka, 1972: 41–71.

– "Zasukha, golod 1946–1947 godov." *Istoriia SSSR* 4 (1991): 3–19.

Volkov, I.M. et al., eds. *Sovetskaia derevnia v pervye poslevoennye gody, 1946–1950*. Moscow: Nauka, 1978.

Volobuev, P.V. "Posleslovie." In *Obshchestvo i reformy 1945–1964*, by Elena Zubkova. Moscow: Rossiia Molodaia, 1993: 189–98.

Voslensky, M.S. *Nomenklatura: The Soviet Ruling Class*. Garden City, NY.: Doubleday, 1984.

Voznesenskii, N. *Voennaia ekonomika SSSR v period otechestvennoi voiny*. N.p.: OGIZ. Gosudarstvennoe izdatel'stvo politicheskoi literatury, 1948.

Vvedenskii, B.A., ed. *Bol'shaia Sovetskaia entsiklopediia*. 2d. ed. Vol. 19 (Istorizm-Kandi). Moscow, 1953 (2).

Walzer, Michael. "On 'Failed Totalitarianism'." In *1984 Revisited: Totalitarianism in Our Century*. Ed. Irving Howe. New York: Harper and Row, 1983: 103–21.

Ward, Chris. *Russia's Cotton-Workers and the New Economic Policy: Shop-*

Floor Culture and State Policy, 1921–1929. New York: Cambridge University Press, 1990.

Wheatcroft, S.G., and R.W. Davies. "Population." In *The Economic Transformation of the Soviet Union: 1913–1945*. Ed. R.W. Davies, M. Harrison, and S.G. Wheatcroft. New York: Cambridge University Press, 1994: 57–80.

Zare navstrechu; ocherki istorii Kalininskoi oblastnoi organizatsii VLKSM. Moscow: Moskovskii rabochii, 1968.

Zavorina, V.A. "Brat postradal za brata." In *Znat' i pomnit': Dialog istorika s chitatelem*. Ed. A.M. Samsonov. Moscow: Politicheskoi literatury, 1989: 215–17.

Zeldin, Theodore. *The French*. London: Collins, 1983.

Zelenin, I.E. *Obshchestvenno-politicheskaia zhizn' sovetskoi derevni, 1946–1958 gg*. Moscow: Nauka, 1978.

– Review of *Ural'skaia derevniia v period velikoi otechestvennoi voiny (1941–1945 gg.)*, by G.E. Kornilov, and of *Kolkhozy Urala v gody Velikoi Otechestvennoi Voiny* by V.P. Motrevich. *Istoriia* SSSR 6 (1991): 168–72.

– "Krest'ianstvo i vlast' v SSSR posle 'revoliutsii sverkhy'." *Voprosy Istorii* 7 (1996): 14–31.

Zhukov, Iu.N. "Bor'ba za vlast' v rukovodstve SSSR v 1945–1952 godakh." *Voprosy Istorii* 1 (1995): 23–39.

Zhuravlev V.V., ed. *XX s'ezd* KPSS *i ego istoricheskie real'nosti*. Moscow: Politicheskoi literatury, 1991.

Zhuravleva, N.S. "Konfiskatsiia pomeshchich'ikh imenii v tverskoi gubernii v 1917–1918 gg." *Istoricheskie Zapiski* 29 (1949): 48–64.

Zima, V.F. "Golod v Rossii 1946–1947 godov." *Otechestvennaia istoriia* 1 (1993): 35–52.

Zinoviev, Aleksandr. *Gomo sovetikus. Moi dom-moia chuzhbina*. Moscow: KORINF, 1991.

– *The Yawning Heights*. Trans. Gordon Clough. London: Bodley Head, 1979.

Zoria, Iu. "Rezhisser katyn'skoi tragedii." *Beria: Konets kar'ery*. Moscow: Politizdat, 1991.

Zubkova, Elena. "Obshchestvennaia atmosfera posle voiny (1945–1946)." *Svobodnaia Mysl'* 6 (1992): 4–14.

– "Obshchestvennaia atmosfera posle voiny (1948–1952)." *Svobodnaia Mysl'* 9 (1992): 79–88.

– *Obshchestvo i reformy 1945–1964*. Moscow: Rossiia Molodaia, 1993.

Zubok, V., and C. Pleshakov. *Inside the Kremlin's Cold War: From Stalin to Khrushchev*. Cambridge, MA: Harvard University Press, 1996.

Index

abolition of serfdom, xxiii, 255

abortion. *See* health care

Afanas'ev, A.M., survey interviewee, 26, 134, 153

Afanas'ev, Iu., xix

Afanas'ev, V.F., 28

Afanas'eva, 125

agitation. *See* agitprop

agitfurgony, 21

agitprop: attempts at improvement, 124; attendance at activists' lectures, 128; in Civil War, 7; criticized by Orgburo in 1948, 96; and economic results, 94; ignorance of activists, 125, 133; and lecturers, 124, 126, 133; and local soviet elections, 128; and Lysenkoism, 217–18; number of activists, 128; obkom department of, 124–5; postwar reactions to, 122, 259; and provincial secretariat, 107; and RSFSR elections, 125; in World War Two, 93–4. *See also* Bloknot Agitatora

agriculture: around 1970, 246; alternatives to collective farming, 227, 232; and amalgamation, 218–19, 260; apiaries, 220; and cattle specialists, 93, 224; and crop specialists, 93, 224; and drought of 1946–47, 73; and fallow, 6; geographic parameters of, 172, 228, 245, 255; grain harvest, 4, 85, 210–11, 218, 223; grain procurements, 90, 95, 210–12, 216–17, 225, 238, 249–51, 261; grain requisitions, 7, 13, 255–6; grain seeds, 237; geographic variation of results of, 86; under German occupation, 57–8; greenhouses, 4; harrow, 6; haying, 4, 220–1; horticulture, 220, 249–51; incurs Stalin's wrath, 221; and inflated statistics, 85–6, 115; livestock in 1920s, 222; and Lysenkoism, 217–8; Malenkov's assessment in 1952, 234; and meadows, 4, 220–1; mechanization of, 4, 22, 86, 109, 224–6, 230, 243, 260; planning for, 135–6;

ploughing, 4; post–amalgamation results, 142–3; post-liberation recovery of, 85; post–Stalin reforms, 231–2, 236, 243–4, 248–51, 263; postwar flaws of, 122, 214, 227–8, 260; and postwar private farming, 207–8, 219–20, 228, 260–1; postwar situation of, 211, 214, 216–17; potatoes, 6, 85–6, 90, 95, 210, 223, 225, 238, 249–51; pre-1917 economic role, 6, 256; and provincial first secretary, 108; and rainfall, 4, 218; results of 1947, 215; results of 1947–51, 223; results of 1948, 217; results of 1949, 217–18; results criticized by Orgburo, 95; results in early 1950s, 98–9, 218, 258–9; rhythm of labour in, 4; and security organs, 160; significance for Soviet Union of, 96, 229–30; soil improvement, 4, 226–7; sowing, 4, 94; and specializa-